The

Neglected

War

The
Neglected
War

The German South Pacific
and the Influence of
World War I

HERMANN JOSEPH HIERY

University of Hawai'i Press
Honolulu

00 99 98 97 96 95 5 4 3 2 1

Library of Congress Cataloging-in-Publication Data
Hiery, Hermann.
    The neglected war : the German South Pacific and the
influence of World War I / Hermann Joseph Hiery.
        p. cm.
    Includes bibliographical references and index.
    ISBN 0-8248-1668-4 (alk. paper)
        1. World War, 1914–1918—Oceania.   2. Germans—
Oceania—History.   3. Oceania—History.   4. Germany—
Colonies—Administration.   5. Australians—Oceania—
History.   6. Australia—Colonies—Administration.
    I. Title.
    D577.H48   1995
    995—dc20   95–13075
                                                CIP

Designed by Paula Newcomb

au nahumu emu raona'au Toto

Contents

Figures, Maps, and Tables

FIGURES

MAPS

TABLES

Preface

"Do not bring Aids into Samoa!" read the poster clearly visible to all who had landed at Faleolo Airport and were about to enter Samoa i Sisifo early in 1989. The reaction of a group of Europeans, who were transformed into Papalagi upon leaving the plane, was to giggle. They partly suppressed their hilarity, less out of shame than because they were anxious not to provoke the Samoan customs officer standing nearby. As is so often the case, arrogance was combined with ignorance, and the result was derisive smiles at what was considered to be excessive South Pacific naïveté.

I am sure that none of those who displayed such (typically European?) broad and lofty grins had ever heard of the *faama'i*, the Samoan influenza epidemic of 1918. If they had, they would probably have been quiet. But such things do not feature in travel literature, guides, or handbooks. Strangely enough, many history books are little better.[1] For the Samoans, however, the influenza of 1918 and the end of the First World War in the Pacific remain deeply engraved on their minds right to the present. The epidemic has been regarded as a distinctive historical watershed. This view was so universally held among Samoans that their age was expressed in terms of whether they were born before or after the *faama'i*.

The Samoan influenza epidemic of 1918 is just one episode, but an important one, of the 1914–1918 European war in the Pacific. Here I argue that this war, its implications, and its consequences, have been largely neglected by historians in the past. But this book is not a new military history. The military campaigns in the Pacific can indeed be summarized in a few sentences. My interest centers around the impact the war had on the indigenous societies of the former German island territories in the Pacific: the northeastern half of New Guinea, the Bismarck Archipelago, and the Northern Solomons, Micronesia, and Western Samoa. What changes occurred as a result of the war, and how did Pacific Islanders perceive them? What actions did they initiate in response to these changes, and how did they react?

The current consensus among historians is that there was no real change at all. The shift from one colonial power to another as a result of Germany's defeat and the loss of its Pacific empire is seen as only nominal. As one of the most ardent supporters of this orthodoxy has put it: "the fundamental institutions of colonial society in New Guinea, all of German origin, were kept intact by the Australians. . . . The Australians . . . established contact with villagers more peacefully than the Germans but in many other respects they were simply running the same colonial business under new management."[2] Similar views have been expressed about the New Zealanders who took over from the Germans in Samoa.[3]

These judgments can at best be described as superficial, but such assessments have probably contributed to the fact that more thorough research has not been carried out in this field. Even a brief glance at what actually happened after 1914 reveals a different story. It does not reflect well upon economic historians that an anthropologist was the only one to point out that after the Australians took over in New Guinea the local wages were statutorily fixed at a level lower than it had been in 1895. Nevertheless, the number of indentured laborers rose sharply during the war. "The result was predictable: a series of regulations ensuring the planters' absolute control over workers and trade, against which German officials had so far resisted."[4]

One would have thought that Salisbury's observations, made from data available even to nonhistorians, might have initiated an interesting debate among historians. Was the Australian occupation changing New Guinea into a colony in which the plantocracy became the decisive political element at last? There was other evidence which seemed to support such an interpretation. The ratio of copra gathered by independent local producers to that harvested by the European plantations rose sharply in favor of the latter after 1914. New Guineans were increasingly regarded as a source of labor rather than as direct producers (who would compete with the Europeans) for the export market. Government control over education—never the planters' favorite cause—was given up almost immediately after the Australian occupation. But no historical debate ensued, and no further research was undertaken in this field. Instead, almost a decade after Salisbury's work appeared, a textbook by three eminent Pacific historians, widely considered to be the authorities on the history of Papua New Guinea, stated categorically: "The old German priorities were maintained by the Australians: business first, and all else afterwards."[5]

As no questions were asked, it comes as no surprise that some historical myths extending back to World War I propaganda have survived even among historians.[6] What really happened with the advent of the First World War in the Pacific? This book sets out to show that to tell this story, hitherto shunned, provides a worthwhile enterprise for a historian. After all, this "neglected war" can in many respects be considered a real turning point in the history of the Pacific Islanders. I confine my study to the area of the former German colonies, but it seems clear to me that the war was a historical divide in other areas of the Pacific as well. Much has been written about the indigenous revolt of 1917 in

New Caledonia, which was a direct result of France's policy of drafting Melanesians. But little is known about local unrest in the New Hebrides in the second half of 1916. There were also serious "native troubles" close to the end of the European war in the southern Gilberts and in Fiji. In all these cases, cruisers were considered necessary to quell the "disturbances." In March 1919 the Polynesian soldiers who had been returned to the Cook Islands rioted; and February 1920 marked the beginning of a series of strikes by Indians in Fiji. Even in quiet Tonga, there was an attempt by a number of nobles to reduce British influence by appealing directly to the United States.[7] In my opinion, all of these events need to be seen in context. From the outside, it looks as if the European war stirred up a hornets' nest. Surely much more research is necessary to fill a gap that has been left wide open by historians in the past.

This is a revisionist book, and it is revisionist in many ways. I consider it also to be an original book. And it might be controversial as well. Behind its Pacific story line lies the more general issue of differences in colonial policy and their impact on the colonized. How important are differences in the nature of particular colonial regimes? And what effect do these differences have on indigenous peoples? Do indigenous people differentiate at all among colonial regimes? And if so, where do they see differences, how do they evaluate them, and what conclusions do they draw?

In the past, historians have insisted that there were indeed differences in colonial rule and in their effects on the ruled. A decade ago Lewis Gann, one of the leading historians of colonial Africa, claimed that "no reasonable man in any part of the world" would have preferred Japanese, German, Russian, or Chinese colonial rule to that of the British.[8] Gann's statement summarizes the gist of current historical opinion. If there *were* any differences in the impact of colonial rule, then surely British rule stands out from the rest. Yet at this point I should like to stress that I am not interested in a debate on which colonial rule was the best. I wholly subscribe to Ranke's famous words that *jede Epoche ist unmittelbar zu Gott,* that each century is equally close to (and, I would add, equally distant from) God. And Ranke, just as much a child of *his* time, had national histories and national epochs in mind. What I am saying is that New Zealanders of today, for example, cannot be blamed for what their great-grandfathers did in Samoa (if they were there at all). As a German, I would be the last to argue that there is anything like a historical fall from grace. To align the behavior of modern New Zealanders with the possible faults of some of their forebears would be reminiscent of the kind of racism which claims that once a cannibal, always a cannibal. On the other hand, the danger that someone might misinterpret my book is no reason to avoid criticizing attitudes *of the past* if they deserve criticism.

It is also important to stress that any assessment of colonial policy would be incomplete if it did not take into account the changes that occurred within that colonial power's administration. I would not go so far as to describe overall Australian rule in New Guinea as "an outstanding illustration of those philanthropic contributions which have marked the best and finest stage of colonialism,"[9] or New Zealand's record in Samoa as having been guided by "humanitarian imperial ideology."[10] But there can be no doubt that Australia's policy in New Guinea and New Zealand's policy in Samoa after 1945 were in many respects quite different from the policies they had pursued before the Pacific War. This represents another, and indisputably even greater, watershed in relations between the Pacific Islanders and their European colonizers.

Yet I believe that it is of immense historical interest to study and analyze the differences in colonial rule in, for example, the Pacific. This will bring us closer to the cardinal question: how did Pacific Islanders act toward nonindigenous people in their environment? And why did Pacific Islanders act as they did? What motives did they have in mind, and what schemes did they invent to influence their contacts with Europeans? Why did they develop different or similar strategies? Why were some more and others less successful in achieving their aims? Tracing the heterogeneity among European approaches could help us achieve a better understanding of Pacific Islanders' attitudes, actions, and behavior, which were enormously diversified and changed dramatically as time passed.

Acknowledgments

Rarely does an idea drop from the sky or appear overnight. Usually it grows, takes shape, and is eventually born. That the idea for this book finally saw the light of day is due to the help, support, and advice of many people. It originated around 1985, when I was lecturing at the Divine Word Institute in Madang, Papua New Guinea. The place and its people somehow provided the stimulus. I am therefore most grateful to the people who took me there: Frans Kangoi Saiwan, who first proposed the idea, and the Society of the Divine Word and the AGEH, Cologne, who made my stay possible. In Madang itself, I could not have done without Father John Tschauder's lifelong experience and understanding. Brother Walter Fuchs' friendship became a continuous source of encouragement of the sort one could live off for the rest of one's life. And, of course, there were the students who gave me insights that I still count as invaluable. A special word of thanks therefore goes to them: Anna Kaluwin, Bare Duin, Barbara Tomi, Buni Dorea, Carolyn Werror, Clara Toure, Hendy Payani, Herman Kose, Korah Ape, Kwin Kei, Margarete Yasangi, Michael Kanako, Stephen Damien, Veronica Bizei, Willie Yangi, Wilson Tima, and many others whose names I may have forgotten but whose faces are still with me as if it were yesterday: *tenkyutru*.

In the middle of 1985 I met Dirk Anthony Ballendorf for the first time. It proved to be a crucial experience. His advice and support have been vital for my research, though the responsibility for what I have written, of course, lies with myself alone. And a hearty *dankeschön* to his wife, Francesca Remengesau, who introduced me to the Belauan side of the story and arranged interviews with men and women who were witnesses of the times and events I describe. Most of them are now dead; apart from their knowledge, it was their wisdom and detached attitude which left the deepest impression. Above all, the tales of Masiofo Noue Tamasese, Henriette Godinet-Taylor, and Berta Anspach née Hahl, created an atmosphere that brought to life for me spells of a time which had long been dead.

In Samoa I would have been lost without the help provided by the honorary consul of the Federal Republic of Germany, William Keil. The late Père Joseph Allais opened the church archives for me and brought me into contact with Samoans outside Apia. Tupua Tamasese Efi shared his broad knowledge of Samoan affairs. And I am particularly grateful to the prime minister of Samoa i Sisifo, Tofilau Eti Alesana, who gave me permission to use the German files still kept in government offices and libraries. Without his official orders, I am sure I would never have been able to see the documents housed at the Nelson Memorial Library. The librarian facilitated my work by kindly allowing me to sit directly on the boxes in which the records are kept. Thus I did not have to carry the documents to a table.

Many archives and libraries provided source material for this book. I am grateful for the assistance and help I received from the staff of the National Archives of New Zealand and the Alexander Turnbull Library in Wellington, the National Archives of the United States in Washington, D.C., and the Australian National Archives in Canberra and Melbourne. I also thank the staff of the Australian National Library and of the Australian War Memorial in Canberra, and of the Mitchell Library in Sydney. In Germany I was given access to the records of the Bundesarchiv in Potsdam and Koblenz, and to numerous mission archives. The latter in particular, which have few staff and less money, were especially helpful.

My research was supported by the Deutsche Forschungsgemeinschaft, Bonn. Of the many people who encouraged and supported my research, I can name but a few: Wolfram Breuser (Berlin), Eddie Cabrera (Saipan), John and Elizabeth Crawford (Wellington), Hank Driessen (Wellington), Jena Gaines (Kalamazoo), Gerlinde Grahn (Potsdam), John Koava and family (Port Moresby), John and Jo Lambert (Wellington), Joe Naguwean (Port Moresby), Ken and Kristina Scadden (Wellington), Brother Fridolin Schlierenzauer (Port Moresby), Petra Steimle (Stuttgart), and Pamela Swadling (Port Moresby). Margrit Davies of the Research School of Social Sciences at the Australian National University gave generously of her time to provide me with copies of the *Rabaul Gazette*. I should also like to mention the Papua New Guinea High Commission in Wellington, which saved my books when I had to move on, and the hospitality of Fritz Schelb's family in Hackett, A.C.T.

Ruth Froese and Angela Davies of the German Historical Institute in London helped me put the manuscript into its final form; without Angela, it probably would not have appeared at all. I am grateful to the University of Hawai'i Press for its willingness to publish my manuscript, and to Pamela Kelley in particular, for her guidance and ideas. Special thanks go to Hans Fenske, Adolf M. Birke, and Gerd Hardach. The first, my academic supervisor of old, taught me the *essentialia historiae*. The second, my academic foster-father in London, was always prepared to give support and advice, and provided many new insights. The third, a colleague and good friend, is one of the few scholars in Germany who shares my enthusiasm for Pacific history; he stimulated my research by discussing his own work with me. My final thanks go to Robert J. Ross III. We stumbled over him when lost in the aftermath of a tropical typhoon in Samoa i Sisifo. He showed us that American generosity and helpfulness is indeed proverbial.

The

Neglected

War

Introduction

THE GERMAN LEGACY

In the European summer of 1914, Germany's Pacific colonies seemed to be a quiet backwater of its empire. German colonial policy in the Pacific and Africa had gone in different directions since at least the turn of the century. After the financial and political disaster left by the Neuguinea-Kompanie, Germany's share of New Guinea had been placed under the direct control of the Reich. At about the same time, Berlin had acquired its last colonies: most of Micronesia, and, a little later, the western half of Samoa.[1] There is evidence enough that Germany was prepared to learn from its previous mistakes in Africa.

What set German New Guinea, the Micronesian Islands, and German Samoa so much apart from German Africa? First of all there was the geographical factor. The Pacific colonies were at the periphery, in every sense of the word. The fact that they were so far away from Europe—much farther than Africa—had a variety of consequences. The German public, like German politicians, were much less concerned about developments in the Pacific than in Africa. Germany's Pacific possessions were certainly regarded as conclusive evidence that Germany had finally attained the status of a world power. But there was little strategic value in extending the Reich to the Pacific. Indeed, as the world war was to show, it brought Germany more disadvantages than advantages. As early as December 1898, the German Naval High Command had advised against the acquisition of Micronesia, pointing out that the islands were too remote from Germany to be of any military use.[2]

Nonetheless, pride in having acquired a real "place in the sun" at last, harbored by the future German chancellor, Bülow, the Kaiser, and many other Germans, gave the Pacific colonies something like collectors' value. They represented an ideal that allowed Germany to show off, enhancing the prestige of a country still striving to be acknowledged as an equal by the old, traditionally accepted world powers. If Germany had not been able to gain economically or strategically important territories in the South Pacific, it had at least "acquired" the "best" people, inspiring the envy of the other European powers. Germany's Pacific empire was like "beautiful jewellery, which is of value only to its collec-

tor and does not yield a profit, but which gave us pleasure."[3] Or, as the governor of German New Guinea put it in the German Reichstag, defending the
acquisition of Micronesia: "Admittedly, Germany is unlikely to gain much economic advantage from this island territory. But I still think that we can pursue a
highly idealistic purpose there. This is to preserve the Polynesian. . . . [Polyne-
sians] are a proud, but peace-loving and beautiful people, and Germany should
take pride in preserving and gradually civilizing them. Germany should hold
tight to the idea that this purpose alone is enough to justify keeping and administering these islands." At the end of this speech, German parliamentarians
from all sides joined in with "lively cheers of 'bravo!'." A little later, Solf, the
governor of Samoa, added: "I can assure you that Samoa is indeed the pearl of
the South Seas. And I should like to express my gratitude, in my own name and
in that of my brown protégés, if this House does not stint in providing gold for
the setting of this pearl." Again, the response was unanimous: "Cheering and
lively applause from all sides." Seconds later, the colonial budget for the Pacific
had been passed.[4]

A direct result of this attitude was that colonial administrations in the
Pacific were given much more time and latitude to develop, pursue, and implement their policies than in Africa. Berlin's marked tolerance toward the Pacific
meant that administrators there were under less pressure to show immediate
results. The rush to produce results that was so characteristic of some, if not
all, parts of German Africa was largely absent from the Pacific, where a
much more relaxed, balanced, and flexible attitude prevailed.[5] As it was not a
place where laurels could be gained, the Pacific was also spared the political
careerists and military adventurers who had such a disastrous impact on Germany's African colonies.

Indeed, the administrators who went there provide one of the most striking contrasts between the German Pacific and German Africa. In German
Africa public officials, especially those who filled the top positions, were largely
drawn from the aristocracy,[6] and many of them translated their idea of a class
society into a race society. The Pacific, by contrast, was the domain of the German middle classes. They arrived on the scene usually with a university degree
and administrative training behind them. Compared with German Africa, there
was also much more continuity in the Pacific; the majority of German officials
there regarded the Pacific not merely as a place to work but one that offered an
opportunity to combine work with their interests. For many, it was a hobby to
study and write down the local history of the people and the areas in which
they lived, note local customs, and try to preserve them. Some even emulated
them. An enormous amount of ethnographic data was collected by German
officials.[7] But because of the language barrier (exacerbated by the German
script), many anthropologists today cannot make use of this material. After
their initial tours of duty, normally three years, were over, most officials in the
Pacific extended their contracts. Others really took root, becoming part of their
environment and adopting Pacific ideas and patterns of behavior. Far from

their puritanical backgrounds, most Germans enjoyed the liberties that many Pacific cultures offered.[8] The story of those German colonial officials who not only lived with local women but actually married them has yet to be written. This was far more common among the Germans than among the officials of other European colonial regimes; and as a result these Germans gained considerably greater insights into indigenous affairs and patterns of behavior.

At least one month away from communication with Berlin, German governors in the Pacific enjoyed great influence. Policy-making fell to them, de facto if not de jure. Albert Hahl and Wilhelm Solf were exceptional men, in any sense of the word.[9] Hahl was a doctor of law. Solf, a law graduate and a doctor of philosophy, was also an expert in Eastern languages and culture. Both men were multilingual and determined to learn as much as possible from the mistakes of colonial policy in German Africa, as well as from the examples set by the British, Dutch, and French in the Pacific. Both shaped conditions in the colonies over which they presided to a far greater extent than any German governor in Africa or any other European governor in the Pacific at the same time. Hahl stayed in the Pacific for eighteen years, of which more than eleven were spent as governor of German New Guinea. Solf worked in Samoa for eleven years, ten as governor.

What was typical of German colonial policy in the Pacific and of internal developments in Germany's Pacific colonies? Germany's colonial activities in the Pacific have not been well documented in the past. Peter Hempenstall's standard work is still the best study available. Concentrating on indigenous resistance movements, Hempenstall found "that, for the German Pacific empire, violence was not automatic nor always the prerogative of the Islander, and that resistance to Germans and their policies, when it did occur, was a great deal more subtle and limited than contemporary German colonists, and indeed a long line of later historians, were prepared to accept."[10] Stewart Firth's account of German New Guinea is a good study of economic and social relations, but his interpretation of the overall picture of German–Melanesian relations raises doubts.[11] It is highly questionable whether economic motives were always paramount, as has so often been suggested in the past.[12] To be sure, although German policies in the Pacific were very different from those in its African empire, Germany was not an extended arm of the Salvation Army. If economic goals seemed realizable, they played an important part in shaping the administration's policies; but they were never pursued without taking into consideration the other motives that the colonial government, or governor, might have had.

In German New Guinea, for instance, Hahl was determined to prevent the European settlers from realizing their dream, which was to transform New Guinea into a plantation colony run in the interests of the white minority. He was also quite able to do this. He repeatedly dismissed demands for the introduction of forced labor regulations.[13] Instead, year by year, he pushed through more stringent laws reducing the capitalist latitude that European employers had enjoyed as one of the fatal legacies of Neuguinea-Kompanie (New Guinea Company) rule. But though Hahl's government clearly supported the indigenous economy by protecting native land as far as possible from European greed and encouraging the cultivation of copra,[14] Hahl nonetheless regarded the European plantations as the other basic, even indispensable, pillar of his colony's economy. And whereas the indigenous side was able to take advantage of growing economic prosperity,[15] officially upholding the colony's hybrid character made it increasingly difficult for the administration to maintain the balance. Neither wanting to give in to the demands of the European settlers always to be given priority and to enforce compulsory labor, nor prepared (or able) to appease indigenous interests alone, Hahl decided to shift the problem by favoring the introduction of foreign labor. But he was only too aware that this policy had had tremendously negative consequences for the people involved, and had also turned out to be economically disastrous when it had been tried by the Neuguinea-Kompanie before the turn of the century. The war saved the German administration from being forced to sort out their perplexities.

A look at village level, at what the German administration called the "free" Melanesians (in contrast to the "unfree" Melanesians who were bound by contract as laborers), may give us further insight into the rather complex German attitude, and into the Germans' relationship with their indigenous contacts. From the start, it was made clear that Germany's overlordship could never be questioned. Melanesians, like other Pacific Islanders, had to recognize Germany as the sole authority for the overall political destiny of the Islands. Indigenous resistance to this fundamental principle of German rule was never tolerated. In theory, this was not much different from the behavior of other colonial powers, but the German approach was possibly more determined and coherent. When it came to the internal workings of the system, however, it was a different story. Here a great deal of local input was possible and, indeed, invited by the colonial administration.

In New Guinea, Hahl "hardly made a decision without having listened to the advice of trustworthy and experienced natives."[16] The system of *luluai* and *tultul*, much misunderstood by historians in the past, which Hahl introduced, guaranteed the indigenous side an area of autonomy in which the colonial administration did not interfere as long as peace was maintained. Most conflicts that occurred in Melanesian societies could be solved internally. Thus two of the basic pillars of Melanesian society, the system of internal conciliation and compensation as the basis for all forms of reconciliation, were not only officially acknowledged by the German administration but were integrated into its colonial policy, thus becoming a substantive part of it. There is a great deal of evidence that the Germans supported their indigenous administration in applying the Melanesian principle of compensation to atone for violations of the local code of behavior or to give satisfaction to those who had been offended. In such cases, the *luluai* was permitted to set the balance straight by imposing fines in traditional shell money right up to the end of the German colonial period.[17]

The fact that the Germans incorporated Melanesian principles into their administrative system helped to smooth German–Melanesian relations to a degree that has been overlooked in the past. It also exerted a dynamic force that attracted more and more unpacified Melanesians, who came forward and asked to be included in the German administrative area. Increasingly, the Pax Germanica developed an impetus of its own, as the indigenous population aspired to join the German colonial organization. Hahl's attempts to pacify the country were supported in particular by the women, who obviously preferred the Pax Germanica to the Perpetuum Bellum Melanesicum pursued by their menfolk.[18]

Admittedly, Germany's attempt to pacify and unite the fragmented Melanesian cultures under its tutelage was based on the conviction that the use of force was necessary. The application of universal laws and the pacification of the country were achieved by superior strength. Yet superior strength alone would not have been enough, even if it had always been available to the colonial government: Germany's Pacific colonies, unlike its African colonies, had no *Schutztruppe* (colonial force). The gunboats stationed in Tsingtao only paid flying visits, which came to be regarded as days of celebration, and did not offer the kind of military security that was readily available to the governor and upon which he could really rely. Hahl's Pax Germanica therefore was anchored in a combination of German and Melanesian patterns of behavior.

Little attention has so far been paid to the special nature of Germany's attempt to establish, and systematically to expand, a Pax Germanica on the basis of Melanesian principles. During Hahl's period of office, Germany usurped supremacy over many indigenous societies in New Guinea. It established an unprecedented monopoly of power in all the islands of the Bismarck Archipelago, the Northern Solomons, Manus, and the northeast coast of Kaiser-Wilhelmsland. The German administration put an end to tribal warfare by fighting (and thus damaging) belligerent tribes until they gave up. Violence was part of Germany's colonial administration, but it was a means to an end. It was but one element in the long-term goal of imposing internal peace. It is important to stress that there was a system behind this use of violence, and possibly even more important to point out that the Germans were able to communicate this idea to the local side. German consistency and steadfastness played an important role in achieving the Pax Germanica. For the indigenous peoples, strength and especially steadfastness were the most striking features of German behavior.

But the real key to the German approach gradually coming to be accepted among the indigenous societies was the official adoption of traditional, indigenous patterns of behavior. In order to put an end to "eternal" blood feuds and tribal warfare, the colonial power also resorted to traditional Melanesian measures such as taking hostages and making whole kin-groups responsible for the actions of their members. When actual or potential damage reached a certain level, Melanesian village communities were prepared to give up their weapons and conclude the strife in peace, or to hand over the accused member to face German justice. Peace was established in the same traditional way in which "war" had been waged. There was an official ceremony, an exchange of goods, and weapons were destroyed under the eyes of all concerned. The Germans demonstrated their goodwill by destroying some of their weapons as well.[19] German and Melanesian traditions mingled. As the Germans were increasingly accepted as arbiters between feuding tribes, a simple declaration of peace by the administrative officer alone was sometimes enough to stop the fighting. His authority rested solely upon the fact that he was known by the offenders and familiar with them and their customs, and on his reputation for impartiality: "The following amicable agreement is concluded. The two parties are reconciled again and shake hands."[20]

One of the most striking features of German colonial rule in the Pacific, and one that, again, has hitherto largely escaped the attention of historians, was its marked tolerance toward indigenous ideas of behavior. In the legal system of German New Guinea, traditional behavior was considered a mitigating circumstance. Although groups that resisted the Pax Germanica were dealt with firmly, individual cases were treated with remarkable leniency. Headhunters, cannibals, and those pursuing blood feuds were, as a rule, banished for an average of three years. Longer periods of imprisonment were practically unknown. In any case, the maximum period of punishment was five years. Death sentences were extremely rare, by comparison not only with Germany's African colonies but also with other European colonies in the Pacific. In Fiji, for example, the British *executed* thirty-eight people between 1903 and 1910 alone, whereas in German New Guinea only thirty-seven death *sentences* were imposed in the entire period from 1899 to 1913, almost half of them in connection with an alleged indigenous "revolt." Moreover, the Germans replaced hanging by shooting as the preferred method of execution; and by the end the German administration had abolished public executions.[21]

If a culprit came from an area where the colonial administration had not yet been established, this was considered a special mitigating circumstance. In such cases, even murderers were not punished, but only reprimanded, or at most removed from the scene for a while in order to calm the area. As late as 1912 a "murderer" from Karkar was remitted because he came from an area that had not yet been integrated into the German colonial administration.[22] Local views could even be given absolute precedence over German-European legal concepts. At the beginning, German officials obstinately refused to deal with cases of local sorcery, which they regarded as mere superstition. However, they increasingly came to acknowledge that indigenous people had good cause to complain about the effects of what Melanesians called witchcraft. As the German legal system (which was officially valid in the colonies) provided no basis on which to punish "sorcerers," Hahl ordered his officials to use their power to quell the disturbances caused by such "sorcerers" by deporting them or punishing them on the pretext that they had committed acts of "public nuisance." (In this way, a European-German legal term was made to seem applicable, at least superficially.) "Further, sorcerers are as a matter of course liable to pay compensation for the damage which they have caused."[23]

To be sure, there were conflicts right up to the end of the German colonial period. But in retrospect it must be said that the Germans achieved pacification relatively quickly, and without encountering much resistance. To compare the German approach and the Melanesian response to the well-known colonial wars fought in German South West and East Africa, in which thousands of people were killed, is absurd.[24] Similarly, it is at the very least unsatisfactory to argue that the lack of stronger Melanesian resistance and/or German violence was due only to the fragmentation of Melanesian village society.[25] Just a brief glance at the colonial wars in New Caledonia and Fiji suggests that this was not the case. It is also an exclusively Eurocentric view of history to criticize the colonizing power for not having introduced Melanesian villagers to Western notions of jurisprudence but having adopted Melanesian customs of warfare and retribution.[26] On the contrary, it was probably the fact that Germany did adopt indigenous patterns of behavior which made the 'German system' seem much less disturbing to indigenous eyes than could have been expected.[27]

When Hahl left New Guinea early in 1914, his acting successor was an engineer. At first glance it looks as if Eduard Haber was sent in only to put economic above indigenous interests at last and to expedite the exploitation of the colony's mineral resources, which Hahl had deliberately shelved until pacification of the area was completed. But, in fact, Haber's first concern was the indigenous population. On his return from a tour of inspection to the Micronesian islands, Haber reported to his superiors in Berlin that "we must convince the Islanders that they fare better under German rule than under any other foreign flag. . . . The colonial administration must be more concerned to ensure that the natives are content with German rule than with higher or lower profits for the leasing companies." And, he continued, its experience in Ponape should make the administration "cautious about modernizing the customs and views of the natives." Like Hahl, Haber supported the creation of an indigenous administrative elite as, in his view, the people of the Marshall and Caroline islands were not only "intelligent," but also keen for education and "hard-working."[28]

A beginning had already been made. The first graduates of the government school in Rabaul-Namanula had been employed by the colonial government as administrative assistants since October 1913. A similar step had been taken earlier in Micronesia, where graduates of the government school in Saipan had started to fill positions in the local administration. Micronesia was the only area in the German Pacific where the majority of the young generation spoke German. The colonial administration had intended to expand the system of secondary education provided by government schools to cover all of New Guinea and the Island Territories (Micronesia) from 1915 on.[29]

Samoa also had its government school. Solf had early decreed that Samoan was to be the exclusive language of instruction in all schools for Samoans. The children of the European and mixed population who had their own government school were officially asked to attend the Samoan government school from time to time in order to learn Samoan.[30] This was in line with the official policy of respecting and preserving the Samoan character of the islands, of preventing European immigration, and opposing the Germanization of Germany's part of Polynesia. It reflects far more than a linguistic peculiarity that all non-Samoans, including the Germans, were officially termed "strangers" by the government.[31]

The principles of Solf's policy in Samoa are well known. As in New Guinea, and indeed in all the other German colonies, Germany's claim to hegemony and the right to formulate the overall rules for the colony had to be accepted. Opposition was not tolerated, whether it came from Samoans or German settlers. On the other hand, both sides enjoyed some sort of political participation. For the Europeans, there was the government council, in which non-Germans were also represented. Indeed, for a long time English was the language of the council (and of other offices), and Germans who had no knowledge of English had to have their speeches translated.[32] For the Samoans, there was at first Mata'afa Iosefo as *ali'i sili* ("the highest chief"), a title clearly beneath that given to the Kaiser (*tupu sili*, or "highest ruler"). But in status, it came right after the emperor who, after all, was not present in Samoa.[33] Certainly Solf, who preferred to be called *tama* ("father"), tried to limit the significance of the concessions Germany made to Samoan traditional authority. On the other hand, there is some indication that, at the beginning at least, Mata'afa had much more influence than has been assumed. He was definitely not the naïve figurehead as which he is sometimes portrayed.[34]

After the death of Mata'afa and the abolition of the title of *ali'i sili*, the *fautua* ("adviser") became the highest Samoan official in the German colonial system. Because of Samoa's past and its complex hierarchical structure, Solf chose to have two *fautua*, one representing the Malietoa line, and the other the Tamasese line. Since 1905 there had been the *fono a faipule*, a council of chiefs, which met once or twice annually to discuss the possible Samoan input into the general political future of the islands. In the way it worked and was consulted by the administration, it closely resembled its European equivalent, the government council.

But the sphere of actual Samoan autonomy lay elsewhere. Outside the capital Apia, which was increasingly receiving a German-European overlay and where Samoan influence was limited, the Samoans continued to be the real masters of their environment. As long as peace was maintained and the German claim to overall hegemony was at least tolerated, the German administration was little concerned with what happened in the villages. There Samoan views and traditions remained unchallenged, and their predominance was guarded by an autonomous Samoan administration that had officially been acknowledged by the Germans at the beginning of German rule.[35] The inner circle of Samoan life was untouched by Europeans. Its sacrosanct character was underlined by a number of decisions by the colonial government in which it made clear that the Samoan sphere was taboo for Europeans. Any European infringement of this taboo was liable to be punished by the government. Thus the daily life of the Samoans remained relatively unchanged under the German regime.

One of the cornerstones of this policy was Solf's decision to exempt Samoans from working for Europeans. Samoa was the only German colony in which the indigenous people were not "persuaded" to work in one way or another. But as not even Solf was prepared to sacrifice at least the appearance of running an economically profitable colony, the consequence of his decision was the importation of foreign labor from China. If we examine the brutal treatment the Chinese received, the contrast with the German approach toward the Samoans becomes even more apparent. The Chinese, like the "black boys" employed by the Deutsche Handels- und Plantagengesellschaft, the biggest German company and the one that had a monopoly on importing foreign labor from the Bismarck Archipelago and the German and British Solomons, were subjected to disciplinary corporal punishment. The fact that this punishment was frequently carried out by Samoans, who themselves were free from this form of castigation, strengthened the Samoan belief that they were a special people. After all, this notion appeared to be acknowledged by the leading European power in the country.[36] The second cornerstone of Solf's system, the setting up of a Land and Titles Commission in order to avoid the recurrence of civil war, has been well studied.[37]

Solf's successor as governor, Erich Schultz (-Ewerth), was less resolute. But as a former chairman of the Land and Titles Commission, he was fully familiar with Samoan customs and therefore seemed to be the perfect man to carry on the principles of German rule laid down by Solf. The aim was still "to provide the means for the inevitable process of individualization to take place without damaging consequences, so that the Samoan is not forced to run before he can walk."[38] There can be no doubt that one major result of German rule in Samoa up to 1914 was the strengthening of a special identity and traditionalism that were becoming increasingly rare in the changing Pacific landscape around Samoa. By the end of German rule, the old Samoan elite had come to terms with the German administrative elite, and vice versa. But the success of this policy, which was to a large extent propped up by the personality of the governor, should not obscure the fact that a strong current was already building which might have undermined the whole structure. Just as more and more young German officials tended to question the old, largely unwritten, and tacit agreement with Samoa's traditional elite, so a young Samoan elite, itself the product of Germany's education policies, was ready to challenge German hegemony and demand more rights for Samoans in the shaping of Samoa's political future.[39]

Although it differed in many respects from that in New Guinea, the German administration in Samoa was also trying to maintain a balance that was becoming more and more difficult to achieve. It had to tread a narrow line between appeasing economic and indigenous interests. For the government, pursuing commercial aims while not really subscribing to the views of the European settlers, on the one hand, and trying to introduce a German form of the European concept of modernism without endangering the local traditions, on the other, became an increasingly impossible task. The fact that the German system did not collapse under the sheer weight of all its contradictions was due to the war, which came as a complete surprise. It was to play a special part in saving the image of a German rule that had, in fact, come to the end of its rationale.

The First World War as a Turning Point

THE PACIFIC IN GERMAN WAR PLANS

Until 1914 the German protectorates in the Pacific were undefended. No marine stations had been established, and the crews of warships from Tsingtao regarded their more or less regular visits to the Pacific as welcome recreational breaks. There were no military laurels to gather there; nor were they sought. Even in the worst case East Asia was of only secondary significance to the German fleet. The warships were intended, if necessary, to make Britain's Far Eastern and Australian trading routes unsafe. Their main objective was to prevent wool being shipped from Australia to Britain.[1] The German navy had made no contingency plans to defend Germany's Pacific colonies.

Provision had not even been made for the fleet to have adequate access to coaling stations in the case of a conflict. Most of the coal depots in the German sphere of influence in the Pacific were under the control of private companies, the most important of which were the Norddeutsche Lloyd and the Neu-guinea-Kompanie. The navy had only a contractual right to use these depots. Unprepared for a war at sea, the Germans had given equally little thought to the defense of their colonies by land. The only fortifications, those in Kolonia on Ponape, had been razed after having been taken over from the Spanish. What cannons there were in the German Pacific were useless for defensive purposes because they had always been used exclusively for firing salutes, and no live ammunition had been ordered.[2]

No colonial troops were stationed in Germany's Pacific colonies. The Germans had not introduced obligatory military training for the colonial population. Nor had any attempt been made to organize a civil defense or military reserve for the contingency of an invasion. A large number of German planters had evaded military service at home. In Samoa, not even the governor had served. The native police was all that existed in the way of military support. In Samoa, this had been disbanded in January 1914 after four of its members had run amok.[3] German New Guinea alone possessed a larger number of "police soldiers." Badly equipped with old Mauser rifles, they had been employed only to pacify Melanesia and to maintain order in Micronesia. There had been no military training for the eventuality of countering a European or Asian invasion. The only thing that had been started before 1914 was a planned network of Pacific radio links.

War was not on the agenda of the German colonies in the Pacific. Their failure to take defensive measures could be interpreted as the result of a rather naive belief in a general consensus among Europeans to leave the colonies out of any military conflicts in Europe. The Congo Act, although it did not apply to the Pacific, may have nourished such ideas. Moreover, there was a historical precedent. During the Franco-Prussian War, the naval commanders of the French and Prussian fleets in the Far East had come to a private agreement not to attack each other.[4] Whether colonists in Rabaul and Apia were aware of this precedent, however, is another matter. It is more likely that the German colonial government in the Pacific was hostile to any move that would have given the military greater influence over local administration. The Pacific under German administration was at the periphery, a world of its own where exceptions were possible and local solutions could be found. Those who benefited from this situation had no wish to be dictated to by military constraints and pressures from outside. The fact that Berlin did not initiate any moves to put its Pacific colonies in a position at least to defend themselves against attack indicates how little political value was placed on them. On closer inspection, all talk of the Islands' economic and strategic value proves to have been empty. These were merely "show colonies" to boost Germany's prestige as a world power. But until 1914 the German Reich was not in a position to back up its claim to be a world power, with all this entailed. The Pacific colonies reveal as a sham a self-professed world power that suffered from "imperial overstretch" even before it became a real world power.

This also meant that Germany did not want to know about developments that would have required an urgent change of policy. During the Agadir crisis of 1911, the British warship *Challenger,* under the command of Captain (later Admiral) Gaunt, entered the harbor of Apia at night and unannounced. The circumstances surrounding this event—all the ships' lights had been put out, and the regulation that a German pilot was to be taken on board had been ignored—suggest that there was more than a grain of truth in the rumor soon circulating that the *Challenger* had received orders to occupy Samoa on the outbreak of war in Europe. As the ship arrived, the British settlers in Samoa gathered at the harbor to welcome it, while the Germans fled into the bush in panic.[5] Even after this, the German administration saw no reason to revise its naive idea that its paradise of Anglo-German harmony was not under threat.

In Australia, the German consul-general in Sydney constantly pointed out the dangers posed by a militant, subcolonial Australian imperialism directed against the German presence in New Guinea.[6] No observer could be in any doubt about Australian hostility to German activities in the Pacific. In order to meet Australian demands, Germany pursued a type of appeasement policy in Berlin as well as in the Pacific. There were no preferential tariffs in Germany's Pacific colonies. But when the Australian company Burns Philp complained vociferously that the Jaluitgesellschaft (Jaluit Company) exercised a monopoly of trade in a German colony, Germany paid considerable financial compensation.[7] Burns Philp went so far as to put political pressure on Germany via London. In 1913, ignoring the guidelines regulating the acquisition of land in New Guinea by Europeans that he himself had introduced, the governor allowed a dummy company acting for Burns Philp to acquire a total of 10,000 hectares in the German Solomons. This was one of the largest tracts of land Germany permitted to pass into European ownership after taking over the administration from the Neuguinea-Kompanie.[8] And when, in preparation for opening up the interior of New Guinea, the government considered expanding the Melanesian police force, the German colonial office expressly asked it to take Australian fears of German expansionism in the Pacific into account. The government in Rabaul was to make it clear that its measures applied only to a local police force, and that it had no intention of establishing a colonial force.[9]

THE ENTENTE

In the course of the nineteenth century the British population of Australia and New Zealand had developed a hypersensitivity toward all non-British colonial ventures in the Pacific. The list of potential enemies and invaders was long. In addition to Russia, which was believed to be capable of launching a seaborne attack on Australia from Vladivostok, it included France, Germany, and even the United States. During the Boer War, Australian fears escalated into a phobia. In August 1901 MPs speaking in the Federal Parliament conjured up the spectre of a combined German-French-Russian naval attack on Australia.[10] The Australian dislike of the French, Britain's traditional rivals in the Pacific, was especially well developed; in 1891 the military governor of Victoria saw France as Australia's main enemy in a future war. One year later, the *Melbourne Argus,* one of Victoria's most influential papers, insisted stridently that France was threatening Australia. France had just brought Saint-Paul and Amsterdam, two small and insignificant isles in the Indian Ocean, under its control.[11] Forty years earlier, New Zealand had already drawn up concrete plans for a war against the French in the Pacific. In 1852 Governor George Grey intended to occupy Tahiti with one thousand European and three to four thousand Maori soldiers, who were to be used as fifth columnists in French Polynesia.[12]

New Caledonia, which was a French colony, and the New Hebrides were a constant bone of contention. In 1902 the British MP Charles Dilke suggested to the British commander of the Australian Commonwealth's military forces that they should invade New Caledonia and the New Hebrides.[13] The Anglo-French rapprochement of 1903 had little effect on their mutual aversion in the

Pacific. In the debate on the Naval Agreement Bill in July 1903, the Australian prime minister, Edmund Barton, publicly called France a threat to Australia.[14] While the Australians objected to the French presence as such, and wanted to see the French possession of colonies in the Pacific brought to an end as quickly as possible, the French in the Pacific feared Australian influence. These fears were not unfounded, for Australian secret agents, or Australian spies working for the British government, were active in New Caledonia and the New Hebrides. As late as April 1914, G. Galitzenstein of the Comité de l'Oceanie française wrote: "The Entente Cordiale does not apply in Australasia. Great Britain may be our friend, but her colonies certainly are not."[15]

The spectre of a Japanese attack on Australia existed from 1895 at least, when the Japanese occupation of Formosa sent shock waves as far as Sydney. In annual maneuvers, white Australians practised driving Japanese warships out of Sydney harbor.[16] Existing fears flared up overnight when the outcome of the Battle of Tsushima completely changed the strategic situation in the Pacific. Although complaints about French and German activities in the Pacific continued, Japan suddenly became the main threat. Leaders of public opinion believed that a military conflict was only a matter of time. In New Zealand, too, the attitudes of politicians changed from one minute to the next. In 1897 Prime Minister Seddon had proposed that London undertake a joint campaign with Japan in order to stop their "potential enemies," the Americans, in Hawaii. Six years later, speaking in Parliament, Seddon called Russia the only real threat to the security of New Zealand.[17] Now concern about the "Yellow Peril" suddenly emanated from both sides of the Tasman Sea. In Australia and New Zealand these fears fell on fruitful soil because each country was pursuing its own racist immigration policy. The White Australia Policy and the White New Zealand Policy designated Asians in general as an inferior race and excluded them from migrating to Australia and New Zealand, respectively.[18] Yet, it was generally believed, the vast open spaces of New Zealand and Australia must act as a magnet for the overpopulated countries of Asia. Barely two months after Tsushima, New Zealand's supreme judge, Robert Stout, published a pamphlet entitled *Yellow Races,* in which he presented an imminent Asian invasion of northern Australia as a foregone conclusion. The only thing that was debatable was the timing. In Australia the minister for defense, Thomas Ewing, a Liberal, had already developed similar fantasies in his book *Yellow Peril,* predicting a racial war of extermination within a generation.[19]

Neither of the Pacific dominions greeted the Anglo-Japanese alliance, which was renewed and extended in 1905, with much pleasure. As far as they were concerned, it was "a pact with the devil."[20] At the London Colonial Conference in 1907 the prime minister of New Zealand, Ward, voiced the fears of Australians and New Zealanders about the millions in the East. At the Imperial Conference two years later, Ward expressed the opinion that any attempt by Britain to enlist New Zealand support for Japan if the alliance were activated, would be rejected unseen and would precipitate New Zealand's separation from the British Empire. Australians and New Zealanders were especially concerned because immediately after the Russo-Japanese War Britain had begun to recall its Pacific fleet to Europe: on the day after Tsushima, five British battleships had been withdrawn.[21]

The decision by Britain to concentrate its fleet in the North Sea profoundly affected Australia and New Zealand. They soon began to cooperate more closely on political and military matters. It began with Rear Admiral Fanshawe, commander of the Australian Station, warning Wellington about a war with Japan—"Real and Only Danger from an Enemy"—one month after Tsushima.[22] In both countries the process of detaching themselves from the mother country's political apron strings began, as did the search for new, common allies against the "Yellow Peril." The Australian prime minister, Deakin, invited the American fleet without informing the Colonial Office. The prime minister of New Zealand joined in the initiative. When the American 16th Fleet, significantly known as the Great White Fleet, arrived in New Zealand in August 1908 before going on to Australia, popular emotions overflowed. Thousands of people turned out to welcome the American sailors. In Sydney and Melbourne between four to six hundred thousand people turned up.[23] It was almost as if the white Australians and New Zealanders were applauding their future "liberators." In all speeches, the Yellow Peril was more or less openly castigated. The commander of the fleet, American Admiral Charles Sperry, did not restrain himself. The coarsest invective, however, came from the host country. In New Zealand, MP Hornsby said: "I am thankful that Uncle Sam has come into the Pacific to keep the yellow and brown men busy if there is to be any trouble. . . . I would rather live in the most abject manner under Uncle Sam's flag than I would tolerate the monkey-brand any time."[24]

In Australia, the arrival of the Americans coincided with the publication of a new thriller. Previous stories of this type, strongly influenced by Britain, had cast Germany as the aggressor. This one, however, centered on a Japanese invasion of Australia. Its scenario had Japanese soldiers attacking Australia in 1912–1913, Britain standing aloof and refusing to help, and the Aborigines acting disloyally while white Australians of British origin fought alone against the Asiatic hordes, defending "Aryan ideals" in a war that lasted until 1940. The story, initially serialized in newspapers, was such a success that it was also published as a book.[25]

When Japan annexed Korea in August 1910, the Australian public's fear of an imminent Japanese invasion escalated into hysteria. Australian journalists quite openly asked the new Japanese consul-general, on his arrival in Sydney in October, about the likelihood of a Japanese attack.[26] Early in 1911, one of the largest New Zealand dailies, the *New Zealand Herald,* sent a special correspondent to New Caledonia, where Japanese workers were employed in the French nickel mines. The general view was that the Japanese on the site were using this as a cover for spying, and that they were turning the area into a base from which to realize their political and military ambitions in the region.[27]

Australia's and New Zealand's fear of Japan and misgivings about Britain's withdrawal from the Pacific set in motion an armament and military policy that, within a relatively short time, made Australia militarily the strongest of the British dominions. In 1909 military training was made compulsory for all white male Australians from the age of fourteen. Men aged between fourteen and twenty had to perform sixteen days of military exercises every year. In addition, on the insistence of the Labor Party, whose leader, Hughes, "at once the greatest labor man, the greatest Imperialist, the greatest nationalist and the greatest militarist in the country,"[28] had long advocated the introduction of military service, men between twenty and twenty-six had to do seven days of military exercises annually. In the parliamentary debate the minister of defense, Joseph Cook, justified the bill on the grounds of white Australia's geopolitical position: "We are surrounded by nations hungry for room and breathing space." The only nation mentioned in the debate, where it recurred frequently, was Japan.[29] Armaments and munitions factories sprang up quickly, and an Australian navy, which was only indirectly dependent on Britain, was created. By 1914 the "Australian naval unit" was practically ready. The Australian fleet comprised three destroyers, two light cruisers, the supermodern battleship *Australia,* and two submarines. An Australian military academy was founded to train Australian and New Zealand officer cadets. Australia was the only one of the dominions to experiment with military aircraft before the First World War.

Between 1902–1903 and 1913–1914 Australian defense spending increased more than sixfold, from £ 750,353 to over £ 4.7 million. In the last national budget before the war, defense spending accounted for almost 31 percent of total expenditure. This was a higher percentage than in any other dominion, and more in both absolute and per capita terms than was spent by comparable European countries such as the Netherlands, for example.[30] New Zealand relied more strongly than Australia on direct support from the British navy. Its isolated position gave it a strategic advantage over Australia. New Zealand's defense strategy of June 1913 assumed that, in the event of a war between Germany and Britain, it was unlikely that German warships would attack New Zealand. It was regarded as much more likely that Germany would attack trading ships in the Pacific. In fact, a surprise attack on New Zealand "of any form" was regarded as "beyond all reasonable probabilities."[31] Nevertheless, New Zealand doubled its defense spending in just under a decade, from £ 257,562 in 1902–1903, to £ 512,307 in 1911–1912. On 15 July 1914 New Zealand also acquired its own cruiser.[32] Most importantly, however, New Zealand, like Australia, had introduced compulsory military service in 1909. Applying to males between the ages of twelve and thirty, it was even more comprehensive than in Australia. Kitchener's assessment, during a visit of inspection, was: "splendid material for creating a first-class fighting machine."[33]

The widely held view that there could be no peace before the whole of the southern Pacific was in the hands of people of British origin was the basis on which a specifically Australian and New Zealand imperialism flourished. Although both countries were themselves still in relationships of colonial dependence, a subcolonial imperialism emerged in Australia and New Zealand. Since the 1870s, Melbourne, Sydney, and Wellington had sent a constant stream of annexation requests to the Colonial Office. There was hardly an island in the southwest Pacific, and no colonial power in the area, that was not the object of Australian and New Zealand greed.[34] From as early as 1870, the idea of a British Monroe Doctrine for the Pacific, proposed by various Australians and New Zealanders, was in the air. In 1894 the government of the Australian state of Victoria supported New Zealand's demand that Britain should annex Samoa, referring tersely to the "manifest destiny of Australasia to be the controlling power in the Southern Pacific."[35]

Under these circumstances, Germany's expansion into the Pacific stirred up a hornets' nest of Australian and New Zealand ambitions. Both countries wanted to defy Germany by confronting it with a fait accompli. On 4 April 1883, Queensland annexed New Guinea; and on 9 February 1885, under the influence of New Zealand MP Lundon, the Malietoa government declared Samoa to be part of New Zealand.[36] When London, going over the heads of Queensland and New Zealand, canceled both initiatives and Germany dug itself ever more deeply into its Pacific positions, the tension grew. Britain's withdrawal from Samoa and the division of the islands between Germany and the United States was the last straw. An indignant New Zealand prime minister demanded, as "compensation" for the loss of Samoa, the extension of New Zealand's borders to include the Cook Islands, Tonga, Fiji, and the French Society Islands. When the German flag was hoisted in Apia, Seddon was on a tour of the Pacific, looking for further places to annex. Without previous announcement, the prime minister put a bill for the annexation of the Cook Islands before a half-empty Parliament, at 2:30 A.M. on 28 September 1900. It was rushed through in one sitting like an emergency decree. Toward the end of April, the Cook Islands chiefs had unsuccessfully tried to prevent the threatened annexation by New Zealand.[37]

In 1901 the Australian states had come together in a federation, the Commonwealth of Australia. One reason for seeking political union was to create a joint administration for the British part of New Guinea. In March 1902 Australia took over the southwestern part of New Guinea from Britain, renaming it Papua in 1906. Thus New Zealand and Australia, without themselves having attained political independence, had become imperial powers. Their main interest, however, was simply to eliminate foreign influence in the Pacific. They had little concern for the people of the territories under their control; neither schools nor hospitals were set up. The amount allocated annually for the administration of Papua was exactly twice as much as the governor-general of Australia's salary.[38] Yet Australia was the richest country in the British Empire. Its gold reserves were so high that one of the current invasion scenarios, contributing to the hysteria, was that a few cruisers might one day appear off the coasts of Sydney and Melbourne and hold the towns for ransom until the gold had been carried off into the ships.[39]

Nor did domestic policy prevent greater investment in Papua. Australia's development was confined to the coastal regions. Australia's and New Zealand's imperial interests were based on strategic objectives. And if the territories acquired could be made to yield a profit, so much the better. In Papua, Australia demonstrated how to maximize yields with minimum investment. Since 1888, four years after the Union Jack was raised there, gold had been mined in Papua and exported to Australia. When Australia took over the administration of the colony on its own, gold accounted for almost three-quarters of Papua's exports. Between 1900 and 1914, gold to the value of to £721,343 had been exported. In the same period, only a little over ten miles of road were built. Australia's behavior in Papua is a classic example of colonial exploitation.[40]

The takeover of Papua and the Cook Islands was only the beginning of increased efforts to gain more Pacific territories. Mostly, geostrategic reasons were cited as "forcing" expansion.[41] In principle, Britain was prepared to support Australia's and New Zealand's annexation demands. However, Australia's attempt to take over the New Hebrides and the British Solomons and New Zealand's attempt to take Tonga failed. Possible reasons were mutual rivalries, Australia's categorical refusal to accept the financial responsibilities arising from annexation, or antipodean administrative incompetence.[42]

This failure, however, did not discourage the two smallest British dominions: in 1912 Australia's population was just under 4.8 million; New Zealand's, just over 1 million.[43] On the contrary, they redoubled their efforts to change the status quo in the Pacific by extending their own spheres of influence there. New Zealand concentrated mainly on Tonga and Rapa, a small French Polynesian island; the opening of the Panama Canal, it was claimed, had given it special strategic significance. Australia kept mulling over plans to acquire the Portuguese part of Timor, the Dutch possessions in New Guinea, or even the whole of the Dutch East Indies. Both Australia and New Zealand were interested in the New Hebrides.[44]

What role did Germany and its Pacific colonies play in Australia's and New Zealand's ideas? Both had regarded Germany's penetration of the Pacific as interference in their internal affairs. They had tried everything to prevent Germany from acquiring New Guinea and Samoa. Australia and New Zealand never recognized Germany as a Pacific power and never gave up their claims to Germany's Pacific possessions. Although in Europe, whether by chance or design, Germany was undermining the status quo and fomenting political unrest, the opposite was the case in the Pacific. Here Germany made desperate efforts to preserve the situation of 1900, while Australia and New Zealand tried with all their might to change the status quo. No attempt was made to conceal opinions. Press campaigns directed against the German presence in the Pacific and in favor of an Australian or New Zealand annexation of German possessions were a regular feature of public life before 1914. The highest political circles took part in them.[45] At times, the tone of these campaigns was extremely aggressive. It was even publicly claimed that a European war was necessary so that Australia and New Zealand could realize their political ambitions in the Pacific.[46]

One man, James Burns, stood behind almost all of these campaigns. A colonel with a dubious past in the Boer War, he owned Burns Philp, the largest Australian company trading in the Pacific. Burns' personal connections with the leading Australian politicians and regular government subsidies guaranteed his company a unique place in the Pacific region. The way in which Burns Philp conducted itself in certain Pacific islands must have increased the impression that its private interests were identical with Australia's Pacific policy.[47]

Before 1914, however, public opinion in Australia and New Zealand had more or less come to the conclusion that it was not so much Germany as Britain's ally, Japan, that posed the greatest military threat to their security.[48] The ministers of defense in Britain's two Pacific colonies, Pearce and Allen, both members of the Labor Party, were extreme hawks, militant advocates of their own subimperialism and fanatical supporters of the Yellow Peril theory.[49] Yet, on sober reflection, it was only the German colonies in the South Pacific that were threatened by the aggressive subimperialism of Australia and New Zealand. Japan had no Pacific colonies. And whatever was felt about France, military action against French possessions seemed to be out of the question as long as Britain depended on France as an ally against their common rival, Germany. And there was no chance at all of persuading France to withdraw from the Pacific voluntarily.

The hardening of the Anglo-German antagonism in Europe made the possibility of Australia and New Zealand taking military action against the German colonies in the Pacific seem ever more likely. A memorandum drafted early in October 1912 by the New Zealand military commander, Major General Godley, presented Germany as the most likely enemy in a future war. The plan for mobilizing New Zealand's troops completely ignored the possibility of using them to defend New Zealand, instead concentrating from the start on potential lines of attack. It specifically included the seizure of Samoa and New Guinea. Godley quite realistically pointed out that the geographical proximity and unarmed state of the German colonies meant that they could be taken with relatively few soldiers, in a subsidiary campaign. This would not affect the sending of New Zealand troops to Europe and Egypt. The minister of defense, Allen, approved the plan and authorized Godley to start building up a New Zealand expeditionary force for the war.

Only one month later, Godley discussed the plan with his Australian colleague, Brigadier General Gordon, at a joint conference in Melbourne. It was firmly agreed that in the event of war between Germany and Britain, New Zealand would occupy German's Pacific colonies east of 170° longitude; Australia, those lying to the west. Thus New Guinea would fall to Australia, Samoa to New Zealand. This coincided exactly with the long-term subimperialist ambi-

tions of the two colonies. Armed with this plan, Allen went to London and collected the official approval of generals Henry Wilson, John French, and
L. E. Kiggell in the War Office.[50]

This indirect blessing given to New Zealand's long-held desire to annex
Samoa did not stop Allen from returning to old themes and making further territorial demands. In talks with Colonial Secretary Harcourt, Allen called for the
annexation of Tonga. Harcourt agreed that the end of Tongan self-rule was only
a matter of time. But it would be wise to wait, he suggested, until the king of
Tonga "did something which could be taken exception to." When this happened, Britain would remember New Zealand's wishes.[51] In the Admiralty,
Allen demanded the annexation of Rapa. Churchill agreed with Allen that a
German attack on New Zealand was "almost unthinkable." The German Reich
and, possibly, the Netherlands, on the other hand, he pointed out, were "the
only probable European enemies of Great Britain in the near future." New
Zealand, he said, would have to accept this. Thus peace was all that stood in the
way of Australia's and New Zealand's plans to invade Germany's Pacific colonies
in the event of a deterioration in relations between Britain and Germany.
Churchill tried to calm Allen's fear of a Japanese attack by sketching the likely
scenario that all the European powers in the Pacific, including the United
States, would undertake a joint action against Japan.[52]

Japan's imperialist ambitions were concentrated on the mainland of East
Asia, Korea, Manchuria, and China. It is true that toward the end of the 1880s
there was a wave of enthusiasm in Japan for expansion into the Pacific. In 1884
the Japanese flag briefly flew over a small atoll in the Marshall Islands. This
"South Seas fever" was a temporary phenomenon, but "Nan'yo" was always
there as an alternative to expansion northward.[53] With the financial support of
the Japanese government, Japanese samurai had been trading in western
Micronesia since 1890. The biggest Japanese enterprise in the islands, Nan'yo
Boeki, had been expelled from the German protectorate in 1901 because of
arms trading with the Truk islanders. But since 1907 it had been licensed again
in Palau and Ponape. At the beginning of 1913 there were seventy-three Japanese in the Western Carolines, the Mariana, and Palau islands. In absolute
terms this was a very small number. But in comparison with the Germans (105
on 1 January 1913), the Japanese could certainly hold their own. Most importantly, however, the smallness of their number bore no relation to their influence on trade in western Micronesia. On some islands, the Japanese practically
had a monopoly.[54]

THE WAR AMONG THE EUROPEANS

The outbreak of war in Europe came as a great shock to Germany's totally
unprepared possessions in the Pacific. Unlike in Germany, the main reaction
there was consternation. The fact that no instructions had been received for

what to do in the event of belligerent action in the Pacific increased the perceptible uncertainty of the administration and the German colonists. In Samoa, where news of the deterioration in the European situation arrived relatively early because of the new radio station, the governor complained about a lack of information. The famous Solf telegram, which had given the colonies the all clear, was quickly overtaken by events, but no new instructions were issued.[55] The island of Angaur in Micronesia received a number of telegrams in cipher from Berlin, but no one had a key with which to decode them.[56] The large distance separating them from home and the impossibility of offering military resistance made any efforts to defend the colonies seem practically hopeless from the start. Even if the German East Asia squadron were to stay in the Pacific for the rest of the war, the colonies could not hold out for long, because both the European population and the plantation laborers were totally dependent on food supplies from Australia, New Zealand, and Eastern Asia.

It is therefore not surprising that on 5 August 1914 an expanded governing council decided, with only one dissenting vote, to accept the expected military occupation of Samoa without offering resistance.[57] The islands' colonial population of British background were allowed, after giving their word of honor, to continue their normal daily lives in freedom. The *Amtmann* (district officer) of Savai'i, a British citizen, naturally had to give up his position, but he was not subject to any restrictions on his movements either. The Germans in Samoa quite clearly believed that the good relations between the different nations which had existed so far could continue in the future, even under changed circumstances.[58] In any case, there was no alternative to this course of action.

When the war broke out, the acting governor of New Guinea was on a tour

Trying to defend the empire: German settlers hastily mustered for military service, Apia, August 1914. (Bundesarchiv Koblenz, Samoa Bildarchiv. Sammlung Demandt)

of inspection in the southeast of the mainland, several days' journey from the capital Rabaul. Eduard Haber, like the governor of Samoa, had not done military service. On his return, the call-up of German men began. Anybody who was more or less capable of marching was put into some sort of uniform and hastily given basic military training. It soon became apparent, however, that the colonialists, who were unaccustomed to this sort of activity, had no stamina, and that in the event of a military confrontation they would do more harm than good. All hopes were now pinned on a few officers of the reserve in the administration and the Melanesian police-soldiers. The majority of these, however, had been deployed in the interior of New Guinea as an escort for those surveying the border between German New Guinea and Australian Papua, and they could not be ordered back quickly enough. Of those left in Rabaul, there were hardly fifty men who had served more than six months. None of them had ever faced an enemy with firearms. Their ranks were hastily filled with plantation workers. The only weapons available were 280 extended '98 carbines. As in Apia, the cannons were only for firing salutes, and there was no live ammunition. There were no machine guns or other automatic weapons. It was clear that in New Guinea, too, resistance could only delay the occupation of the colony, not prevent it.

In order to allow the German defenses to be organized more effectively, the administration of the colony was moved from Rabaul, which was completely exposed to attack from the sea, a few kilometers inland to Toma. Plans for the government to withdraw even farther into impenetrable country, for example the Baining Hills or the Sepik District, were given up as impractical.[59]

According to their arrangement, New Zealand occupied Samoa, and Aus-

Samoa's youth meets the occupying force. Apia, 29 August 1914. (Ross Collection, Alexander Turnbull Library)

tralia took over New Guinea. On 29 August, New Zealand troops marched into Apia without meeting any resistance. Samoa was the first German territory to be occupied in the First World War. Thus a dream that New Zealand had harbored for decades came true, and Britain's threat, made after the agreement of 1899, that it would get Samoa back, was fulfilled.[60] New Zealand's move had been preceded by a British order to put the radio station on Apia out of commission. An official request of this sort had long been a fixed part of British wartime planning. The New Zealand government thus knew what was expected of it on the outbreak of war.[61]

The same applied to Australia. The Australians were annoyed that New Zealand had beaten their troops in the race to occupy German territory. Despite the breakneck speed of Australian armament over the past few years, the planned invasion of New Guinea posed a number of difficulties. The expeditionary force was badly equipped, and what equipment it did have was totally inadequate for fighting in the tropics. The troops did not receive light tropical clothing until after they landed, when they obtained it from German stores. A chest of replacement parts for their machine guns was stolen from the expeditionary ship during the journey.[62] The force itself contained many completely unsuitable men. A large number of those who had volunteered in the hope of adventure were young greenhorns who had obviously never held a gun before in their lives. There were also men with highly dubious pasts, and many former convicts.[63] The Queenslanders were the worst behaved. Five hundred of them had hurried ahead to Port Moresby in order to await the arrival of the Australian fleet and to join the expeditionary force. As the Australian flagship *Australia* was first required in Samoa, however, the departure of the troops from Sydney was delayed. In the capital of Australian Papua the tension grew unbearable. A German invasion was feared daily. On his arrival, Holmes, the leader of the expeditionary force, found a panic-stricken and hysterical European population. The five hundred men from Queensland were totally undisciplined. When the stokers on their troopship, *Kanowna,* heard that they were to enter the German combat area, a mutiny broke out. The leader of the expedition immediately sent the Queenslanders home.[64]

Nor did the occupation of New Guinea turn out to be as simple as expected. The last meeting with Admiral Patey had concluded that no resistance was to be expected from the German side.[65] Yet Australia put together a mini armada: the battleship *Australia;* the cruisers *Melbourne, Sydney,* and *Encounter;* three destroyers; two submarines (the only two that Australia possessed); the 11,000-ton troopship *Berrima,* which had been converted into an auxiliary cruiser; and several coal and supply ships. The expeditionary force consisted of many more than the originally planned fifteen hundred men.[66] The entire Australian fleet was sent out to occupy the German colonies. This course of action, which left Australia's coasts totally exposed to any enemy attack, shows how little a German attack on Australia was expected. All Australia's efforts were channeled into an expedition of conquest.

PUBLIC NOTICE

1. Residents of Port Moresby and Konedobu are informed---

    (i.) that it is not intended to surrender the Wireless Station even under threat of bombardment of the town ;

    (ii.) that the A.C. cannot even attempt to protect the town against bombardment.

2. The presence of non-combatants will not only not assist, but may seriously embarrass the efforts of the A.C.

3. Non-combatants are warned that there is a real danger that food supplies may run out.

4. Non-combatants are therefore requested to proceed South by the "Matunga." The fares of those who are in necessitous circumstances will be paid by the Government.

J. H. P. MURRAY,

Lieutenant-Governor, O.C.A.C.

Government House,
    Port Moresby,
        16th August, 1914.

War scare in Port Moresby. Public notice, Port Moresby, 16 August 1914. (Australian Archives Canberra)

The Australian unit lulled itself into a false sense of security. The where-abouts of the German Pacific fleet was unknown, but all reports agreed that the German squadron was somewhere north of New Guinea. An Australian advance guard, led by the cruiser *Sydney,* which landed in Herbertshöhe on 12 August, encountered no resistance and saw no German defenses. After they had destroyed the telephone wires, they left again.[67] When Australian troops landed in Blanche Bay on 11 September 1914, there were no German naval formations waiting for them in the harbor. On land, however, they met a small but determined troop of German and Melanesian soldiers. Although badly trained, it engaged the Australian soldiers in a tough bush fight and held them at bay. A short but fierce battle for the radio station at Bitapaka cost the lives of six Australians (including two officers), about thirty Melanesians, and one German NCO. Four Australians, ten Melanesians, and one German were injured, some seriously.[68]

This unexpected German resistance, the mobilization of indigenous auxil-iary troops whose aim may not have been very accurate but whose activities certainly troubled the Australians,[69] and the difficulties the Australians had with the unfamiliar climate and country were the main reasons for the signing of a treaty of surrender on 17 September. Its terms were highly favorable to the Germans in New Guinea. Haber, a shrewd negotiator,[70] managed to put through the provision that German civilian officials who wished to leave were to be repatriated to Germany at the Australian government's expense, and without having to declare themselves neutral. Those who wished to remain had the choice, after swearing an oath of neutrality, to remain in their jobs "in an advisory capacity." They were to continue receiving their salaries, and were to work under Australian supervision. The property of German settlers and plant-ers was guaranteed, and the Australians promised that local laws and regula-tions would remain in force.[71] The capitulation of the German "troops," with military honors, on 21 September, was the end of the war in New Guinea. Only the leader of the German border surveying expedition, Captain Detzner, con-tinued to play cat-and-mouse with the Australians, who never found him, in the hinterland of Morobe, until the armistice in Europe in November 1918. It is astonishing that he had such good relations with the local tribes, and that his hideout, which was known to the indigenous people, was not betrayed until the end of the war. But without the help of the Neuendettelsauer Mission, which built him a house in the forest and kept him supplied with food, books, and English newspapers, Detzner could not have survived. The stories he spread after the war about his heroic deeds, his attempts to breakthrough against the Australians, and his journeys across New Guinea were all manifestly untrue.[72]

The treaty of capitulation referred explicitly to the whole of German New Guinea, and to all the districts that were administered from Rabaul. This included Micronesia. On 12 August, the British battle cruiser *Hampshire,* one of two that had remained at Britain's China station, had shot at the radio station on Yap and severed deep-sea international cables, without occupying the

The Australian Occupation of German New Guinea

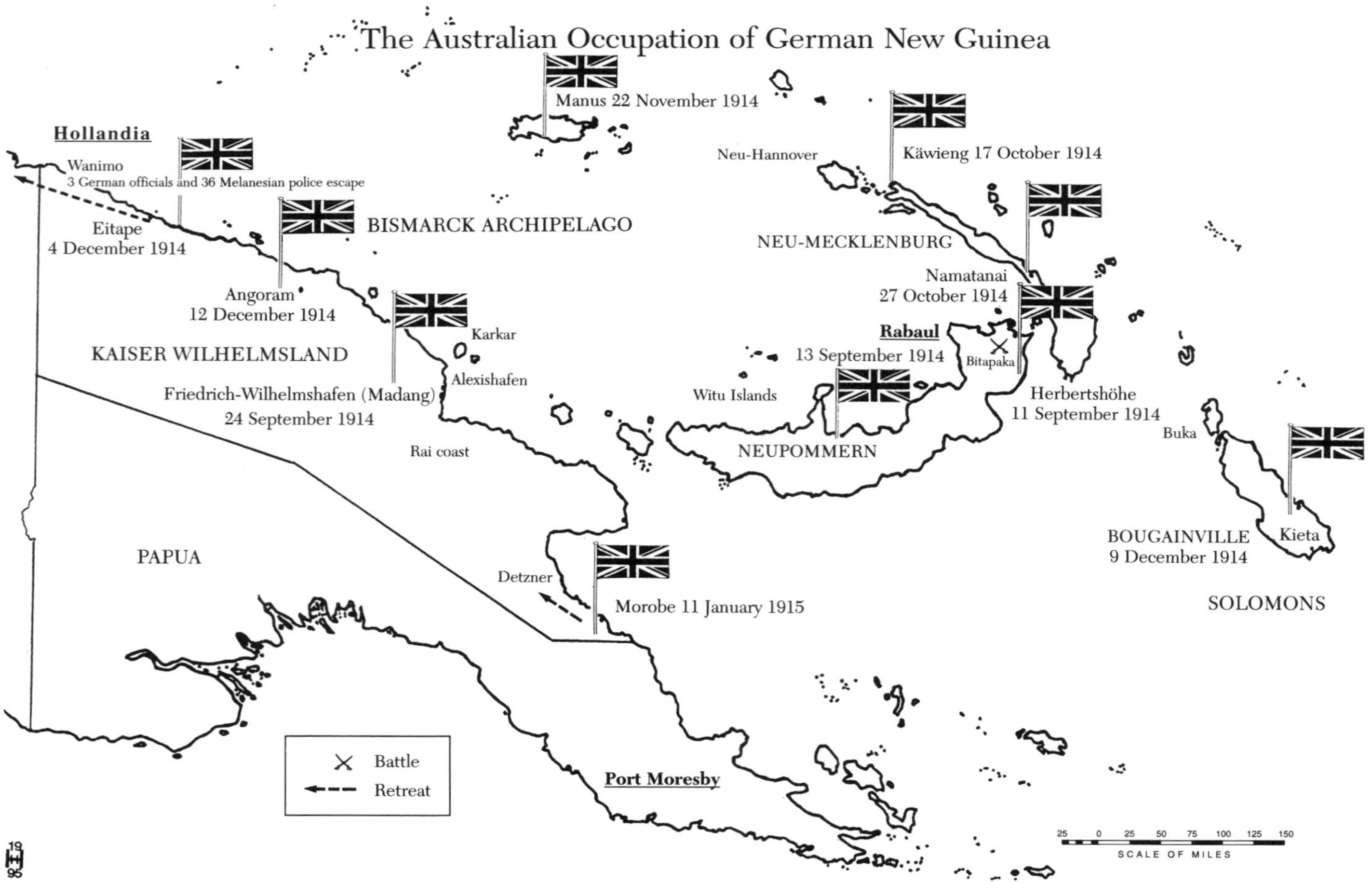

SOLOMONS

BOUGAINVILLE
9 December 1914

Kieta

Buka

Herbertshöhe
11 September 1914

Namatanai
27 October 1914

Käwieng 17 October 1914

Rabaul
13 September 1914

NEUPOMMERN

Neu-Hannover

NEU-MECKLENBURG

Witu Islands

Manus 22 November 1914

BISMARCK ARCHIPELAGO

Bitapaka

Morobe 11 January 1915

Detzner

Port Moresby

3 German officials and 36 Melanesian police escape

Karkar

Alexishafen

Rai coast

Angoram
12 December 1914

KAISER WILHELMSLAND

Friedrich-Wilhelmshafen (Madang)
24 September 1914

PAPUA

Hollandia

Wanimo

Eitape
4 December 1914

	Battle
✕	
	Retreat

SCALE OF MILES

25 0 25 50 75 100 125 150

island. The same happened in Nauru, where the Australian cruiser *Melbourne* bombarded the radio station on 9 September. Instructions from London had specified that Nauru and Angaur, the two phosphate islands in the German-controlled area, were to be occupied as quickly as possible. Commercial lobbies in London and Sydney were impatient to be presented with a fait accompli.[73] But Australia made no progress in this respect. The German Pacific fleet continued to sail the Pacific unmolested. On 14 September, Count Spee lay off Apia with the *Scharnhorst* and the *Gneisenau,* but left the island on the same day, his business unfinished. In the absence of enemy ships, the expected battle did not take place. Spee, however, had insufficient troops and ammunition to take Samoa. The option of bombarding the harbor was rejected because of the damage it might have caused to German property and the danger it might have posed to the Samoan civilian population, which was highly esteemed by German naval commanders. Instead, he bombarded Tahiti eight days later.[74]

In this situation, Japanese intervention could no longer be prevented. Up to this time Britain had done all it could to stop the Japanese government from intervening in Micronesia and to encourage it to limit its activities to Tsingtao. Under the pretext of hunting down the German squadron, the Japanese fleet occupied all the islands of German Micronesia between 29 September and 21 October 1914. On the small islands of Micronesia, German resistance was even less likely than on Samoa and in New Guinea. Except for the *Bezirksassessor* of Ponape, who withdrew inland for a few days and marched around in the bush until he saw the hopelessness of his position, all the German officials surrendered immediately and without resistance. An offer made by the last Spanish governor of the Caroline Islands, Eugenio Blanco, to make available five thousand trained Filipino volunteers, without pay and with responsibility for their own rations, was refused by the German Foreign Office and the German naval staff. It is hardly conceivable that Blanco's offer was made without the knowledge of the American officials in the Philippines. It is well known that the Americans were highly concerned about the imminent Japanese actions in the Pacific.[75] We cannot exclude the possibility, therefore, that the Americans were looking for an opportunity to stop the Japanese advance without being directly involved themselves. Blanco seems to have been exactly the right man for this purpose. He was a curious eccentric, whose escapades and brutality were well known. (These would make it easy for the United States to distance itself from him at any time.) On the other hand, he was a tough old veteran, a daredevil who did not lack courage.[76] But the German Foreign Office got cold feet precisely because the Philippines were under American administration. It was feared that accepting this offer of help could place Germany in opposition to the neutral United States, and Blanco's proposal was therefore rejected.[77]

In Micronesia the Japanese successfully combined careful tactics with rapid and decisive action when the opportunity arose. Their campaign was a model of its kind. They first occupied Jaluit, the Micronesian island most distant from Japan and where Australian influence was strongest. Rota, closest to

The Japanese Occupation of German Micronesia

MARSHALL ISLANDS

Jaluit
3 October 1914 **Y**

Kusaie

First Japanese landing 29 September 1914

EASTERN CAROLINE ISLANDS DISTRICT

Nauru 6 November 1914
Official proclamation 7 November 1914
Wireless destroyed by HMAS *Melbourne* 9 September 1914
Germans deported 8 November 1914

Ponape 7 October 1914 **Y**

Truk 12 October 1914 **Y**

MARIANAS

Saipan 14 October 1914 **M**

Tinian

GUAM (U.S.A.)

Rota 21 October 1914 **M**

148°
EASTERN LONGITUDE

Yap 7 October 1914 **M**
Wireless destroyed by HMS *Hampshire* 12 August 1914

PALAU
ISLANDS

Koror 8 October 1914 **M**
Angaur 9 October 1914 **M**
Landing HMAS *Sydney* 26 September 1914
Germans deported 16 November 1914

WESTERN CAROLINE ISLANDS DISTRICT

Y: Occupied by the First South Seas Squadron (Vice Admiral Yamaya Tanin)
M: Occupied by the Second South Seas Squadron (Rear Admiral Matsumura Tatsuo)
Yap/Ponape: German *Bezirksamt* for the Western/Eastern Caroline Islands District

Japan, was taken last. The occupation took place in a number of steps. On Jaluit, the head of the German station was at first informed that Japan had decided to put Jaluit under Japanese administration for as long as the German fleet was in the Far East. A few days later, the Japanese landed again and explained to the puzzled official "that the Japanese government had changed its mind." Only at this stage was the Japanese flag raised and possession officially taken of the island.[78]

Tokyo was quite clearly pushing forward to a certain point from which it could withdraw without losing too much face while keeping all its options open. When Britain, whose reaction was probably being awaited, signaled its acquiescence by remaining silent, Japan went ahead. For more than a week after the occupation of Jaluit, Japan took no further action. Then it occupied Ponape and Yap. Thereafter everything happened quickly. But even now the Japanese proceeded with great caution. On Yap, their behavior was the most curious. As the center of an international cable, this island was of special importance. Moreover, a British cruiser had already taken up position there briefly in mid-August. Here the Japanese raised a Union Jack along with the Japanese flag. Later, the British flag was taken down, and thereafter only the Japanese Rising Sun fluttered over Yap.[79]

The Australians arrived too late. By the time another expeditionary force, this time for Micronesia, had been put together in Sydney, most of German Micronesia was already firmly under Japanese control. All that remained for the embittered Australian commander, Pethebridge, was Nauru, which was occupied on 6 November.[80]

Relations between the Australians and New Zealanders and their unloved allies in the Pacific remained strained until the end of the war. Their fears were not exactly calmed by Japanese behavior. In mid-December 1914, two Japanese cruisers were sighted off Nauru. On 28 December a Japanese convoy consisting of two cruisers and two destroyers under the command of Captain Sakamoto arrived in Rabaul. It did not receive a hearty welcome. In February 1915 the Japanese 7,820-ton cruiser *Nisshin* visited Samoa. A total of 560 Japanese troops patroled Apia. Their officers ordered meat from the German butcher and secretly passed him a letter with questionnaires printed in German. They contained "enormous numbers of questions, going into the smallest detail." These asked for information about factions or parties among the Samoans, the size of plantations, and Samoa's revenues. Other German tradesmen received similar questionnaires, and the Japanese offered to pay large sums of money to those who filled them in.[81] On its way back at the beginning of April 1915, the *Nisshin* also called in at Rabaul and Madang. For their part, the Australians sent a lieutenant from Nauru on a holiday aboard a Pacific Phosphate Company recruiting ship. On the orders of the head of Australian Naval Intelligence, Captain Thring, Lieutenant Sawyer went on the *Pukaki* to the Japanese-controlled Caroline Islands, where the British Phosphate Company had recruited some of its workers before the outbreak of war. Under the suspicious gaze of the Japanese officials, those laborers who had served their contracts were disembarked, and new workers were even taken on board. In the meantime, the "holiday-maker" Lieutenant Sawyer kept his eyes as wide open as possible.[82] Melbourne and Wellington were well aware of the secret agreement London and Tokyo had arrived at early in 1917, recognizing the Equator as the line dividing their respective spheres of interest. They were not happy about this arrangement, but it helped to calm the mutual distrust between Australia and New Zealand, and Japan.[83]

THE INVOLVEMENT AND BEHAVIOR OF THE INDIGENOUS PEOPLE

Except for New Guinea, Germany's colonies in the Pacific followed a policy of offering no resistance to the threat of invasion. This protected the indigenous people from involvement in military action. Only in the coastal areas around the capital of German New Guinea were indigenous civilians among the victims of the bombardment by the Australian cruiser *Encounter*.[84] The outbreak of war in Europe, which the authorities generally announced to the indigenous population through their chiefs or headmen, revealed at a stroke the weaknesses of the colonial system. Similarly, it showed where the Germans had succeeded in gaining the cooperation of the indigenous people. The dependence of the Germans on the local population was made clear overnight, for suddenly an alternative existed that made it possible to question existing patterns of behavior. To this extent, the European war considerably increased the room for maneuver of the "German" Polynesians, Micronesians, and Melanesians. They could now exploit the obvious conflict of interests among the Europeans and use them to achieve their own aims even more than before. Early in September, a rumor was circulating in northern Friedrich-Wilhelmshafen that the people of Ragetta (on Kranket Island) who, after a two-year exile in the Baining Hills had been led back to the village of Megiar, about 40 kilometers north of their old home, were waiting for the arrival of the British in order to kill the Germans in Madang (Friedrich-Wilhelmshafen) with their help, and return to their old homelands.[85] It is possible that the Ragetta people, embittered because of the treatment they had received, saw a glimmer of hope in the outbreak of the European war. They certainly knew that the Australians had briefly been in Herbertshöhe in mid-August and had destroyed the post office. However, there were indigenous interests other than those of the Ragetta people. The source of the rumor that the Ragetta wanted to ally themselves with the British against the Germans was the *luluai* of Sarang. He had complained several times, so far without success, about the presence of the banished Ragetta in his district. This time his denunciation was successful. On 14 September 1914, the Ragetta man Malai and his father, Lawetat, were sentenced to five years' imprisonment with hard labor for "treasonable conspiracy." Perhaps the

Ragetta people did want to play the British off against the Germans. But it is quite certain that on hearing news of the war between the Germans and the British, the Sarang people developed a successful strategy for getting rid of strangers who, on government orders and against their will, lived in their midst at their expense, made advances to their women, and, moreover, as rain sorcerers, seemed to be responsible for the extreme drought.[86]

The war between the Europeans acted like a magnifying glass: the attitude of the indigenous people toward the German colonial administration suddenly stood out much more clearly than before. Local people were most willing to help the Germans where German officials had laid the foundations for the development of a relationship that went beyond pure coexistence and had produced a symbiosis between new forms of behavior that were profitable to both sides. The heart of this mutually advantageous relationship was always German acceptance that local measures and traditions would take priority over the European demand for innovation and change, and, on the other hand, the tacit agreement by the local people not, in principle, to question German-European moral or intellectual leadership. The result was as unbalanced as the relationship between partners in a marriage. What was important was not a general leveling out and constant balance, but that the pendulum of influence and drive did not swing too far, or too often, in one direction. Where this was achieved, the legacy of German colonialism was not disharmony but something like mutual respect for the Other. Thus it is no coincidence that some of the local population were prepared to take up arms, unasked, to defend the German administration on the Mariana Islands, where the long-serving district administrator, Fritz, had developed an exemplary relationship with the local people, and on Samoa, where relations between the Germans and the local people were proverbially good. In both cases reactions to the rejection of these offers were highly emotional.[87]

Conversely, when the compulsion to work was removed in a number of parts of New Guinea, it became apparent that the obligation to work, which the Germans had not decreed by law but had tried to encourage by their regulations, had not been internalized as a new, positive achievement of culture contact. Workers on the big plantations on the Bismarck Archipelago initially ran away in droves. "Mi no laik" (I'm fed up) was the response of Melanesians when they were told by Australian soldiers that much higher rates were paid in Australian-controlled Papua than in German New Guinea.[88]

In a number of areas, plantations burned down either because there were no workers to put out the regularly occurring bush fires, or because the workers themselves deliberately lit them. A drought such as had not been known for many years made the situation worse. On top of this, the Melanesian plantation workers now faced starvation. Almost all of them came from far distant parts of the colony and had no means of getting home. Strangers in their own land, they roamed through country unknown to them, and with a potentially hostile population, in the search for food. Some were armed. Their daily ration of rice, tinned meat, and tinned fish had stopped when the plantation economy came to an abrupt end and merchant shipping collapsed as a result of the war. The Australian commander-in-chief therefore quite correctly described the disturbances caused by runaway plantation laborers in parts of Neupommern (New Britain) as bread riots.[89]

The situation was similar when the Australians arrived in Friedrich-Wilhelmshafen. Workers ran away from European plantations by the hundreds and, leaving a trail of blood behind, forced their way through unfriendly villages to reach their homes in the Sepik district. They were joined by Melanesian police-soldiers who came from the same area and whose leadership structure and raison d'être had collapsed with the colonial order. [90]

The Melanesian policemen who had been employed in the Micronesian islands faced exactly the same problem. With the coming of the Japanese, all their previous ties and hierarchies had become irrelevant. The whole system on which their work was founded had broken down, and it seemed unlikely to be continued under a different leadership. Most of them were taken back to Rabaul during the war. On the Marshall Islands, fourteen police-soldiers refused a Japanese offer of continued employment.[91]

The behavior of the Melanesian police-soldiers in the battle for the German radio station deserves special mention. It is quite astonishing that at Bitapaka a hastily assembled indigenous troop of former plantation laborers and

Melanesian soldiers who fought for the Germans as prisoners on board the Australian battleship *Sydney*, 12 September 1914. (Australian War Memorial P 0316/03/02)

half-trained policemen, numbering just under forty, together with five Germans, could hold four hundred Australians armed with machine guns at bay for five hours. In the clash between German and Australian interests, Melanesians paid the highest toll in lives.[92] Finally, however, they were no longer prepared to die for others. Even the threat of execution could not persuade them to leave the protection of the trenches to shoot. After the first defeat of a German-Melanesian "unit," Melanesians in other formations mutinied. "They said it was a fight between the whites, and was nothing to do with them," noted the German officer in charge.[93] In any case, it was the deployment of Melanesian police-soldiers which allowed the Germans in New Guinea to gain favorable terms for the treaty of surrender. Without the support of the indigenous police, the Germans would not have been able to offer any resistance. The high Australian losses had convinced the Australian commander that they could not win a protracted bush war.[94]

The indigenous police were undoubtedly under the greatest pressure in the colonial system. As a rule, they alleviated this pressure by means of a pecking order which ensured that those who were beaten could in turn beat others. At the moment when the tip of this hierarchy broke off, the long and carefully repressed hatred erupted. When the arrival of the Australians in Friedrich-Wilhelmshafen changed the situation, a Melanesian NCO spat in front of his German police chief.[95] Such cases were, however, isolated. The announcement that a war had broken out among the Europeans led to a certain amount of short-term unrest in some areas. But with the exception of Melanesian plantation laborers, who had been temporarily displaced from their homes by the colonial economy, the population in general remained calm.[96] In contrast to German Africa, where the outbreak of war intensified regional tensions between the local population and the Germans,[97] nowhere in the "German" Pacific did the news of war among the Europeans cause a revolt against German rule. This cannot be emphasized enough, given that the Germans in the Pacific were totally undefended, and that there were so few of them that their survival depended entirely on the toleration of the local population. Indeed, it was often the indigenous people who first warned the Germans of an impending attack by Germany's enemies in the European war. Outstanding taxes were even paid.[98]

However, regional outbreaks of hatred against people of other ethnicities and nationalities were not unknown. After the outbreak of war between Germany and Japan, the people in the Palau islands vented their anger against the Japanese traders, who had completely dominated trade with the Palauans. In all seriousness, a number of Palauan men asked the head of the station for official permission to throw the Japanese living in Palau into the sea.[99]

The non-German colonies in the Pacific seemed, at first, to be less affected by the outbreak of war than the German colonies. But here, too, the European war opened valves which had previously seemed to be firmly closed. An apocalyptic mood spread. And just as after the Second World War cargo cults began to blossom, so now indigenous prophets appeared, preaching the imminent end of European norms. In Fiji and New Zealand, prophecies centered on a German victory over the British. In Fiji, Ratu Sailose stirred up the indigenous population when he claimed that his familiar spirit had revealed to him that Britain had surrendered unconditionally to Germany. The British governor had been removed from office, he announced, and the people of Fiji no longer needed to pay taxes.[100] In New Zealand the prophet Rua Kenana was even suspected of arming his tribe, the Tuhoe, in order to enter the war on Germany's side. Such anxieties were probably grounded in the war hysteria that was especially rife in Australia and New Zealand. Doubts about the loyalty of the Maori had been fostered in particular by the behavior of the Waikato tribe, which obstinately refused to comply with the call-up. It is unlikely that Rua ever really planned to enter the European war, but it seems certain that he was in favor of a German victory, believing that it would lead to the "emancipation" of the Maori from British rule in New Zealand. After a skirmish between the New Zealand police and Rua's supporters, Rua was arrested. Convicted of rioting, he was sent to prison. Maori who refused to do military service still openly supported the Germans because they hoped that after a German victory they would get back their land, which had been expropriated by the British settlers.[101]

It was not only the Maori who were caught up in the military conflicts of the European war. In New Caledonia, France enlisted Melanesians for service on European battlefields. The local response was a rebellion.[102] The governor of the Australian part of New Guinea also sent a division of Papuans to the European war.[103] The people in the now occupied German colonies were unlikely to be called up for active service in Europe, but not completely immune. When the military administrator appointed by New Zealand, Colonel Logan, took his first home leave at Christmas 1915, he brought a dozen "volunteers" from Samoa with him. They had enlisted for active service in the war— "the idea being to show that Samoa was loyal."[104] This was a hastily assembled and racially mixed group consisting of Samoans, Anglo-Samoans, Anglo-Fijians, and Tongans. Together with other Polynesians, most from the Cook Islands under New Zealand administration, the Samoans were allocated to the Maori units. A subsequent review of the troops revealed a naturalized American and an underage youth. Two more Samoans could not tolerate the climate in New Zealand and were sent home. Early in May 1916, finally, just eight "Samoans" left Wellington for Europe with the Fourth Maori contingent.

Their time in Europe turned into a nightmare. In training camp, a Samoan had written:

> *When munitions run out, our boys will not scruple*
> *If stones and sticks are handy, they are experts at the game*
> *Their war cries will resound like the bellow of a fierce bull.*[105]

However, it quickly became apparent that sticks and stones were not much use on the Somme. Two Samoans died in the inferno at Flers, and the rest soon had to be evacuated from the front. Even more than the barrage of the shells, the thundering cannons and whine of projectiles, it was the clammy fog and the jarring cold in the trenches that smothered the war cries of a handful of Samoans. Heavy colds, bronchitis, and tuberculosis repeatedly put them in the military hospital. Finally, they were sent to Egypt, where they were employed in munitions depots with the Rarotongans, doing extremely dangerous work. The unfamiliar routine of night shifts, malaria (which was unknown in Samoa), and sandfly fever took their toll. One Samoan died there. The five survivors returned to Samoa as invalids. Within a few years, two more had succumbed to the mental and physical aftereffects of the European war.[106]

At least the Samoans were volunteers. The Melanesian crew of the *Cormoran*, by contrast, was trapped by the outbreak of war. In mid-December 1914 the German gun boat *Cormoran*, with 33 officers and a crew of 340, took shelter in the neutral harbor of Guam, the American part of the Mariana Islands, now controlled by Japan. There the ship and crew were detained. After the United States entered the war—the scuttling of the *Cormoran* on 7 April 1917 was the first hostile act between Germany and the United States—the Germans were taken to POW camps on the American mainland. The four Chinese ships' laundrymen from Shantung were distributed, on the spot, among the "upper class" of Agaña as domestic servants.[107]

The twenty-eight Melanesian crewmen were also detained on Guam, officially classified as POWs on the basis of a legal expert's report.[108] They were the only Pacific Islanders who were confined in this way for being part of the German Empire. The difference between their treatment and that of white POWs, however, soon became apparent. On the instructions of the secretary of state for the navy, the usual monthly benefit of three dollars was cut in their case.[109] In addition, their rations were cut, "because it was more than they were accustomed to. They went to sleep after meals and could scarcely be aroused for work. They do better on smaller ration."[110]

On the small island of Guam, the Melanesian POWs from German New Guinea caused a sensation. Horror stories of their treatment on board the *Cormoran* circulated, as did rumors that they were all cannibals and that one of them had eaten his own grandmother. Their quarters were nicknamed Cannibal Town. One died on Guam. On 2 January 1919 the survivors were put on board a Japanese schooner and sent back to Rabaul, where they arrived nine days later. Their war, too, was now over.[111]

THE "PACIFIC GERMANS" DURING THE WAR

Under the terms of the treaty of surrender of 17 September 1914, the Germans in New Guinea started from a relatively favorable position. Most of the measures for the protection of the civilian population were adopted from the Hague Convention. On paper, they did not look like special concessions on the part of the Australian military government. In the everyday reality of war, however, they proved to be extremely important, especially when what happened in New Guinea is compared with events in the other German protectorates in the Pacific. When the conditions of the surrender were made public in Australia, they caused an outcry. Colonel Holmes, who had negotiated the treaty, was blamed for not having held out for an unconditional surrender.[112] Criticism of Holmes eventually reached such a pitch that his career was seriously threatened. At this moment, a scandal broke. Innocuous in itself, a more prudent man with a greater natural sensitivity would have been able to deal with it quickly and decisively. Under the pressure of Australian public opinion, however, Holmes decided on a course that was justified neither by the behavior of the Germans in New Guinea nor by the military situation. It made a mockery of any legal process.

The essence of the Cox Affair, as it became known, was bad relations between European planters and the Australian Wesleyan Methodist Mission in New Guinea. The Germans accused the Australian missionaries of being largely responsible for the fact that so many of their plantation laborers had run away, claiming that they had turned them against the Germans. The northern Bismarck Archipelago, the area in which most of the "desertions" took place, was in fact the territory of the Wesleyan missionaries. But it would be wrong to assume that after the arrival of the Australians, the behavior of the Melanesian plantation laborers could be explained by the actions of the Wesleyans alone. We need look only at the parallel case of Friedrich-Wilhelmshafen, where exclusively German missions were active. On the other hand, it is quite clear that the Australian Methodists did try to set their indigenous clientele against the Germans. As in Samoa, the invading troops used indigenous adherents of the Australian mission as guides and spies.[113] The head of the mission, the Reverend William Henry Cox, a Briton, had taken the oath of neutrality before the German administration and had thus been allowed to go free. This did not prevent him from making himself available to the Australians immediately after their arrival and revealing German military secrets.[114] The Germans were unaware of the precise details, but the rumors going around were enough to provoke the plantation owners, who were already angry with the mission. One evening a group of drunk planters lay in wait for Cox and beat him up.

On receiving news of this incident, Holmes thought he should make an example of the case. The accused planters were given short shrift. They were not granted a trial, not to mention a defense council. Not even a court martial took place. Instead, given "that the German laws in force here do not provide adequate punishment for the offence,"[115] Holmes ordered a public whipping, which was administered to four offenders on 30 November 1914. On the express orders of the Administrator, all German men in Rabaul had to attend. The missionaries, too, were invited to view the proceedings.[116] All the Australian occupation troops were present. Each man was given ten shots, bayonets were fixed, and arms presented. The Union Jack was run up, the national anthem was sung, and three cheers were given for the king. Then the punish-

Public caning of Germans, Rabaul, 30 November 1914. (Australian War Memorial P 0095/03/03)

ment was administered. One after the other, the accused, secured by manacles and leg irons and unable to move, received twenty-five or thirty lashes of the whip. Two further alleged accomplices were whipped on 5 December. Ironically, one of these was a Belgian citizen. This, however, did not spare him the Administrator's revenge; nor did the attempted suicide of the other save him from public humiliation.[117]

The legality of the Australian Administrator's action was questionable. The *Manual of Military Law* that he cited explicitly forbade corporal punishment.[118] Cox himself had been able to identify only one of the accused.[119] Nonetheless, the Australian public registered the incident with deep satisfaction. The governor general had doubts but ran up against a brick wall when he tried to express them. He communicated them to the minister of defense, who dismissed him with the brusque comment that he himself had sent Holmes his personal congratulations that morning.[120] The Cox Affair was one of those rare moments in the history of a people when emotions are deliberately given free rein and quickly and recklessly break down all the barriers raised by reason. Yet such moments reveal a great deal about the soul of a people. Holmes' action, the Australian reaction, and the obstinate defiance that international, and especially British, criticism of the incident evoked,[121] all need to be explained in psychological terms. Many factors were involved. The most important seems to be the experience Australians themselves had had of corporal punishment, which had been one of the main instruments of colonial justice in the convict colony. An Australian administering corporal punishment to members of a nation that itself used beatings to assert its colonial interests lifted a little of the trauma that cast its shadow over British Australians. The fact that it was Germans who suffered under this was convenient, for without the war this form of Australian emancipation would not have been possible. The common aversion of Britons and Australians to Germans provided a shield under which autonomous interests and objectives could shelter. Decades of pent-up rage against non-British imperialism on Australia's doorstep—in its own "duck pond," as the governor general was aptly to describe the Australian attitude[122]—was part of it, as was a rejection of British tutelage. The call to occupy New Guinea came from Britain, although it had been expected and hoped for in Australia. The Australian colonel's idea of making a demonstration of military and political power in Rabaul while parading the national symbols of empire, by contrast, was a purely Australian decision. As it turned out, the whole country supported it. When Holmes returned to Sydney in January 1915, there were already postcards in circulation depicting the whipping of the Germans. This was one of the first autonomous foreign-policy decisions made by the Australian Commonwealth; it was not going to let anyone, especially not from London, interfere.[123]

The Cox Affair had immediate repercussions on relations between the Germans in New Guinea and the Australian occupiers. One day after the incident, all the German officials who had remained in Australia's service resigned. Without their voluntary resignation, it would have been difficult, in the long term, to fulfill in more than name only the provisions of the surrender (and Article 43 of the Hague Convention) concerning the continued employment of German officials. As early as 15 October, the German language was forbidden for official use. Given the state of war, however, Germans in New Guinea continued to live relatively unmolested even after the Cox Affair. They were generally left in peace by the occupying Australians and could pursue their own affairs unhindered. After the majority of laborers had returned, the European plantations functioned "normally" again, and little changed in the operations of the missions. The most important factor in this was certainly that their property rights remained untouched. Except for minimal military requisitions and plundering by Australian soldiers, property belonging to Germans remained untouched until 1918. There were no sequestrations. The German market, which had been important for New Guinea, had of course disappeared overnight, but businesses in Sydney and Brisbane were only too glad to fill the gap. The problem of how the Germans would have survived in an unoccupied New Guinea in which practically no supplies could have been imported from outside was quickly solved by the occupation. On occasion, the Australian military government even helped them out with loans.[124] Colonel Samuel Pethebridge, Holmes' successor who was responsible for this policy, had farsightedly recognized that the economic value of New Guinea as a future Australian colony depended on the German plantations continuing production with as few interruptions as possible. He did not allow himself to be deterred by an aggressive propaganda campaign of hatred directed against the Germans in Australia.[125]

The Germans could move around New Guinea relatively freely, but post was censored in the colony. At first, all contact with Germany stopped completely. From 16 September 1915 communication with the German Reich was possible via neutral third countries and subject to censorship. Compared with their compatriots in other colonies, the Germans in New Guinea could not complain of harsh treatment by the occupying power. In cases involving Euro-

"Reprisals," by Norman Lindsay. The cartoon is typical of the racism prevalent and excessive anti-German mood that swept Australia during the war. The text states: "Reprisals in kind are urged in return for repeated German raids on England." "Reprisals? Don't worry! Germany has supplied civilisation with an eternal one." (*The Bulletin,* 19 July 1917)

peans that came to court, sincere efforts were made to comply with international law, which stated that in colonies under military occupation the law of the colonial power continued to be valid. No attempt was made to conceal the official symbols indicating that New Guinea was a German colony, although now under Australian military occupation. The military government stamp showed the German imperial eagle with the imperial crown, surrounded by the words "British Military Occupation."

Although relations between the German colonists and the Australian military authorities in New Guinea cannot be described as good between early 1915 and 1918, they were tolerable. In Pethebridge's absence, however, a serious incident took place. It was of brief duration, but this time almost all Germans were affected. The peace and quiet of the country aroused the Acting Administrator's suspicions that the indigenous people were preparing a dangerous conspiracy under German leadership. Lieutenant Colonel Fred Toll does not seem to have been able to cope with the tropical heat. Nightly practice alerts were intended to whip the Australian soldiers, who had been bored since the sinking of the German Pacific fleet, back into shape. All applications for leave were temporarily stopped. Each man received one hundred extra rounds of ammunition, and two machine guns were installed above the building housing the government. Sandbags were heaped up in front of the treasury so that it could be protected against a full-scale attack. All private telephone calls were to be tapped and reports written about them. A search of the houses of the Germans turned up German flags, a broken Mauser, binoculars, "6 dry cells (exhausted)" and a "large magic lantern." Toll regarded the dispatch of a war ship as essential.[126]

On his return, the Administrator, to his surprise, found the colony a hive of activity. Martial law had been declared, and the Germans of Rabaul and Herbertshöhe, including women, had been interned behind barbed wire. Even the French bishop of Rabaul had been taken from his house at 2 A.M. Germans from the neighboring islands were to be taken to the "concentration camps" of Rabaul and Herbertshöhe as soon as possible.[127] Pethebridge immediately canceled the warlike measures introduced by his overzealous deputy, but did deport a number of Germans to Australia. On the whole, the number of Germans deported to Australia as POWs during the war was not large. Apart from a few spectacular cases, only Germans who had refused to take the oath of neutrality were deported.[128]

Nauru, which was occupied by Australian troops in November 1914, was part of German New Guinea. The administration of the island was therefore subject to the conditions of surrender negotiated by Haber and Holmes. In the case of Nauru, however, Australia did not observe these conditions. The forty-five Germans on Nauru were deported in three stages, and Australian officials completely ruled out the possibility of their return during the war. Behind this was the Pacific Phosphate Company, which wanted to continue trading with the people of Nauru and mining phosphate without being observed by the Germans. Thus the British colonial secretary ordered the expulsion of the last remaining Germans, a Catholic priest, and four nuns, on 1 November 1915, "at the expressed desire of the Company."[129] It early became apparent that private business interests, with the help of high politics in London and Melbourne, were to be given free rein in Nauru.

All the German employees of the Pacific Phosphate Company had already had to leave Nauru on 8 November 1914. It seems more than a coincidence that exactly one week later, the Germans on the second "German" phosphate island in Micronesia, Angaur, received orders to pack their belongings and leave the island within twenty-four hours.[130] Angaur was now under Japanese control, and the Japanese were obviously waiting to see what the Australians did in Nauru before they implemented their own measures against the Germans. On various islands, the Japanese commanders had previously issued decrees which, like the German–Australian treaty of surrender, in principle gave the Germans the right to remain and guaranteed their private property. On all the larger islands, the Japanese had also asked the German officials to continue working in Japanese employment.[131] In Angaur, this policy was reversed. After the Germans were deported from Angaur, it was "suggested" to the Germans on the other islands that they, too, might like to return to Germany via Japan. The reaction to this "offer" was so muted that from the beginning of January the Japanese issued expulsion orders. They came into effect at different times because of the difficulty of transport. The last German settlers, among them the last officials, were dispatched from the Marshall Islands in June 1915.[132]

In general, the Japanese were courteous to the Germans. Officers and men conveyed the impression that it was only the Anglo-Japanese mutual assistance pact that had forced them "to take action against Germany in this way."[133] In Japan, the Germans were asked to sign an oath swearing that they would not take part in any enemy actions against Japan during the war. No mention was made of Japan's allies.[134] Thereafter the Germans were set free and were able to return to Germany unhindered, with the help of the American consul, via the United States. The government doctor in Yap, Ludwig Kohl-Larsen, even managed to save most of the Yap station funds, about 20,000 marks.[135]

Köhler from Ponape, who had held up the whole Japanese squadron for two days by marching around in the interior of the island, received rather rougher treatment. The Catholic missionaries in the Palau islands were treated worst of all. The fathers were kicked and beaten; the nuns were molested by Japanese soldiers. After a show trial, they were taken away from Palau at the end of November 1915, under the threat of violence. The reason for this behavior by the Japanese was that the official government funds had been hidden in the mission. As the money had been walled in behind the altar in the church, the Japanese could not find it despite much searching and vented their anger on the mission staff. In March 1916 the Capuchins of Saipan were also deported, and at the same time the number of Protestant and Catholic missionaries on Truk was considerably reduced. Truk became the Japanese general headquarters, and the Japanese presence was especially strong in Saipan. The Japanese there quite clearly did not want any uninvited German onlookers.[136]

Until the end of the war, German missionaries stayed on Ponape and Yap, and on some of the smaller islands. Contact and any communication among individual islands was strictly forbidden. It was almost impossible to have any contact with home by letter. Occasionally mail did arrive in Germany from Micronesia, having gone by some strange route. But hardly anything ever got through in the other direction. With special permission, Protestants and Catholics were able to get the funds they urgently needed to continue their work via America; the apostolic curate of Ponape even received permission to travel to America for this purpose.[137]

The Germans in Samoa had the worst time of all. The fact that the island had been occupied so quickly did nothing for relations between Germans and New Zealanders. In the absence of an official treaty of surrender, the guidelines for the military administration of an occupied territory laid down in the Hague Convention applied to relations between the German civilian population and the occupying troops. The New Zealand Administrator, Colonel Logan, interpreted these guidelines in a highly unconventional way. Their basic idea was continually diluted, until all that remained of the German law theoretically still in force was marriage law. For the rest, the colonel ruled by means of proclamations, military decrees, and courts martial.

From the destruction of the German Pacific fleet at the latest, Samoa was a complete backwater as far as the European war was concerned. Relations between the German and the British colonists had been affected by the war, but in general good personal relations stood up to its strains. The Samoans gave no cause for concern. Nonetheless, Colonel Logan ruled the islands with extraordinarily coercive measures that were otherwise used only in direct war zones. All Germans, including those who lived in the remote parts of the island, had to report once a week, and they had to observe a complete blackout between 9 P.M. and 6 A.M. A general curfew was in force from 6 P.M. The post to and from Germany came to a complete halt from 6 November 1914. Even censored letters were no longer carried, and the last consignment of German mail that reached Samoa was burnt in sight of the Germans.[138]

Higher German officials, including the governor, were sent to New Zealand as POWs immediately after the occupation of Samoa. They were interned on the island of Motuihi off Auckland. The wooden barracks in which they were housed were dirty, not weatherproof, and unheated. Almost all the Germans therefore suffered from skin diseases and rheumatism. Complaints were punished by confinement in the dark and not being allowed to wash. The German governor, accustomed to special treatment, suffered especially. There had already been tension between him and his deputy, who came from German South West Africa; under these conditions it simply exploded. After the United States entered the war, the situation was made even worse by the fact that the Swiss consul in Auckland was an Englishman who did not pass on any complaints made by the civilian POWs.[139]

Gradually, the remaining German officials on Samoa were also sent to New Zealand as POWs. They were taken to Somes Island in Wellington Bay, where the suspect New Zealand Germans were also interned. More and more German civilians from Samoa joined them there. They had fallen victim, for various reasons, to the rapid mood-swings of the unpredictable colonel. Conditions on Somes Island were even worse than on Motuihi. A public investigation undertaken on the request of Count Luckner, who was widely admired in New Zealand and himself detained on Motuihi, revealed extremely harsh conditions. The Samoa Germans, accustomed to the tropical heat of Samoa, were forced to sleep on muddy floors in clammy rooms, which were freezing cold in winter. Little straw was provided. Just under three hundred prisoners[140] were exposed to constant harassment by the warders. Their speciality was ordering the prisoners to do "physical exercises." This included the prisoners bending over backwards to pass under sticks that the warders held at a higher or lower level, depending on their view of the prisoner, leapfrogging, and running around in a circle. They were kicked, shoved, and slapped—"to make them move at the proper speed." The judge who was reporting on this found nothing strange.

Count Luckner (*waving to German prisoners-of-war*) escapes Motuihi internment camp on board the prison-commandant's launch. Luckner, later recaptured, was instrumental in improving the conditions in the camps. (Sammlung Karl Brenner)

"None of the exercises described seem to me to be unreasonable; they would not be unreasonable if applied to schoolboys."[141]

Nor did the Germans who remained in Samoa have an easy time. Their businesses were sequestered in 1915. If anyone complained about the extreme application of martial law in Samoa, Colonel Logan replied that compared with what the Germans were doing in Belgium it was nothing. He pointed out that he could personally shoot every German with his own revolver.[142] Legal proceedings against Germans accused of crimes were a farce. There were cases where the Administrator set the maximum penalty by proclamation only after a trial. Among the most unfairly treated were three employees of the German Handels- und Plantagengesellschaft (trading and plantation company) who were stopped by a military patrol on their way home and subsequently sentenced to six months of prison with hard labor for breaking the curfew. In Auckland Prison they spent their time breaking stones with ordinary criminals. Thereafter they were taken into captivity as POWs. During their trial, in which they were denied a defense counsel, the presiding military judge refused their application to call witnesses for the defense. When they insisted, they were threatened with an additional punishment for "contempt of court."[143]

So many POWs were sent from Samoa to New Zealand that the government eventually refused to accept any more. A special prison camp was therefore set up in Samoa. Men who had hung German flags from their windows or had been caught singing "Heil Dir im Siegerkranz," "Die Wacht am Rhein," or

"Deutschland über Alles" were sent there. Toward the end of the war, the situation in Samoa escalated. An unsuccessful attempt by German POWs to escape from Sogi, the internment camp, gave Logan occasion to issue a special decree placing all Germans, including children, under house arrest. He wanted to execute the POWs by court martial. When Wellington telegraphed that according to international law an attempt by POWs to escape was not a statutory offense, Logan reacted by deciding to intern all Germans in Samoa, including Samoans of German descent.[144] Before Samoa could be transformed into a giant POW camp, however, the armistice was signed in Europe.

The German South Pacific under the Shadow of War

AUSTRALIA AND NEW GUINEA

(1914–1921)

Despite the geographical proximity of New Guinea to Australia, Australians had little interest in the island and its population. The number of Australian explorers before 1914 can be counted on the fingers of two hands, and there were certainly no large-scale expeditions. This striking lack of interest did not change after Australia took over the British part of New Guinea. Although news from Papua was reported regularly in the Australian press, it dealt almost exclusively with internal squabbles between the few settlers and the administration, which were of little general concern. Only occasional reports about the discovery of gold caught the attention of the Australian public. A sporadic enthusiasm for the unknown country up north broke out at regular intervals but generally subsided as soon as it appeared. The average member of the German public was certainly far better informed about the country's far-distant colony than were Australians of British origin.

It was only when the Australian armada arrived in Rabaul that a wider Australian public became aware of New Guinea. Hundreds of reports about an idyllic South Pacific paradise were sent to Melbourne, Sydney, and the other Australian towns, pointing a sharp contrast with conditions in Australia's own colony of Papua. Favorable comparisons with Papua now became a fixed part of Australia's image of New Guinea, which, until the outbreak of the Pacific War (1941), was increasingly equated with the former German part because Australians were ashamed of the "under-development" of their own colony of Papua and preferred to ignore it.[1]

THE MILITARY

The majority of Australians who went to New Guinea between 1914 and 1921 were soldiers—men of widely varying origins and family background. A conquering mentality was common to most of them. It expressed itself mainly in looting and plundering, and in an almost anarchic frenzy of destruction. No doubt this sort of thing happens in all wars at all times, but the behavior of the Australians deserves special mention because, especially during the first six months of the occupation of German New Guinea, it was not the exception but the norm. Drunken hordes of looting Australian soldiers, reminiscent of today's hooligans, regularly created an uproar and stole everything that was not nailed down. Their officers, themselves not above plundering (even the provost marshal was involved),[2] could not hold the troops in check. Drunkenness and brawls "were the orders of the day—men punching each other and blacks and chows [Chinese] generally. When so many get on it, we cannot deal with them properly as there's nowhere to lock them up and if we attempted to put the lot in the guard room it would mean a shooting match. . . . I've never struck such a crowd before. They take all sorts of spirits and drink them neat—get as much down as they've got and then seem to go half-mad."[3]

Especially notorious were the militias, which had already acquired a reputation as "farm burners" during the Boer War.[4] At first, courts martial were an almost daily occurrence. But even this did not stem the tide of violence, for there were too many upon whom they made no impression. The looting did not stop until early June 1915, when there was simply nothing left to loot.[5] At first, the Australians concentrated on the belongings of the German settlers, but then they turned more and more to the property of non-Europeans. Pigs and chickens were stolen and gardens wantonly destroyed. Several armed raids were made on the Chinese quarter of Rabaul. In one case, on the pretext of looking for opium, military police broke open a strongbox and stole 5,200 marks.[6] After the first troops returned to Australia early in 1915, the behavior of the Australian soldiers in New Guinea was the subject of a heated debate in Parliament. It centered on the charge, made publicly, that whereas ordinary soldiers were being prosecuted for their deeds, officers had been let off scot-free. As no agreement could be reached about taking proceedings against the officers—even the highest-ranking officers such as Colonel Paton and Commander Bracegirdle were implicated—the soldiers who had already been sentenced were let off and all prison sentences for troops were canceled. The governor-general had to report "a good deal of whitewashing" to the king.[7]

The Australian soldiers who followed the "champion looters"[8] were not much better,[9] but open refusal to obey orders was less common.[10] However, a destructive, exploitative mentality continued to be the norm, and it did the administration and the country itself a great deal of harm. The heads of the post offices in Rabaul and Herbertshöhe misused their positions to withdraw from public circulation the highly prized German colonial stamps, overprinted with the military government stamp, and sell them for huge private profits.[11] Nor was embezzlement of government money and the abuse of official positions and official symbols for personal gain uncommon in other areas as well.[12] Much more serious for New Guinea was the attitude of many Australian soldiers, who wanted to take as much as possible out of the country, without regard for the law and ignoring any moral scruples. The *Rabaul Record*, a monthly newspaper established and edited by the military government's press officer, initiated and supported this sort of attitude. It described in detail exactly how Australians in New Guinea could make their fortunes. It was no coincidence that the *Rabaul Record* focused on gold mining. This obsession with gold was not the result of wishful thinking but rested on solid facts. For years, gold had been the main export from Australian Papua to Australia. Shortly before the outbreak of the European war, Acting Governor Haber, a trained mining engineer, had undertaken scientific investigations that verified rumors of enormous gold deposits in German New Guinea. Such rumors had been circulating for years.[13]

An "insider," who was obviously aware of what was going on in Papua, published articles in the *Rabaul Record* telling Australian soldiers exactly how to go about things in order to be successful. "It is usually necessary to fight," he wrote, "and it is as well to be prepared." As a rule, he suggested, the local people would not tolerate penetration of their settlements, but this had to be brushed aside. "You must be . . . inevitably tactless with a rifle . . . teacup tact and the small amenities of civilization are usually quite out of place when prospecting in hostile country." It was advisable to attack villages strategically, and "to do some strafing. . . . Having strafed the hillmen into acquiescence, the next thing is to find the gold." It should be remembered that the stakes were high. After all, since 1888, £2.5 millions-worth of gold had been taken out of Papua.[14]

The inaccessibility of the region and the attitude of the military officer who had been given responsibility for it prevented the potential goldfields from being overrun by soldiers under the very eyes of the Australian Military Government. The district officer of Morobe allowed only a small number of selected prospectors to enter his territory. Under his care and protection, they found out which were the most profitable mining areas. When military government was replaced by a civil administration and legal claims could be made to these fields, the district officer posted the first claims in his own name and then resigned from office. As a private citizen he became one of the most successful miners in the gold rush that quickly developed around the Waria and its tributaries.[15]

The bird of paradise was the "gold" of the ordinary Australian soldier in New Guinea. At the end of 1914 the unsuccessful Australian Expeditionary Force, whose original objective had been Micronesia, was rerouted to the Sepik district. The admiralty suspected that German warships were hiding out there. The grain of truth at the heart of this wild rumor turned out to be a camp and canoe belonging to the Austrian anthropologist Richard Thurnwald. In his absence, part of his equipment was destroyed and the rest taken away, along with the results of his research.[16] Whether out of disappointment over their military failure or for other reasons, the members of the expedition transformed their venture into the Sepik district into a hunt for native birds that degenerated into a mass slaughter. Every day, the soldiers led by Lieutenant Commander Hill

Hunting birds in New Guinea. A member of the Royal Australian Navy with three slaughtered crown pigeons, c. 1915. (Australian War Memorial J 03341)

went to the bush to hunt birds—birds of paradise, crowned pigeons, and white herons. They were fully aware that these species were protected according to German law.[17] When the first expeditionary troops returned to Australia, thousands of bird skins with the feathers attached were smuggled out of New Guinea and into Sydney, circumventing customs regulations, which prohibited the import of birds. These transactions yielded 200 to 300 percent profit. The Australian soldiers thus laid the foundation for a new women's fashion in Sydney.[18]

On 15 May 1915 the German regulations, which were valid only for a limited period, expired. Thereafter the Australian Military Government permitted the indiscriminate shooting of birds. If they were not already aware of the opportunities, soldiers could read all about them in the first issue of the *Rabaul Record*.[19] In theory, German settlers could also now hunt, but limited amounts of ammunition were given out, and the use of guns was subject to wartime regulations. By mid-September 1915, twenty to twenty-five thousand skins lay in Madang alone, waiting to be exported.[20] As import into Australia continued to be prohibited, most of the birds were taken across the border illegally via Dutch New Guinea. Early in 1916, the Administrator estimated that about thirty thousand were waiting in the colony to be exported. He had no moral

TABLE 1.   Number of Birds of Paradise Killed
in New Guinea under the German
Colonial Administration

YEAR	NUMBER OF BIRDS OF PARADISE KILLED
1908	[1,000?][a]
1909	3,268
1910	5,706
1911	8,779
1912	9,837
1913	16,691
TOTAL	44,281

[a]The fashion began in 1908, and birds of paradise were first
killed in large numbers in this year. The figure given is a very
rough estimate, representing a maximum. It is impossible to
be more precise, because the birds were not listed separately
in the statistics but were included under the column
"Miscellaneous."

Source: *Jahresberichte über die Entwicklung der deutschen
Schutzgebiete. Statistischer Teil.*

scruples: "The question is one of sentiment as it affects *bird* life, and while war continues to be waged against *human* life, its importance seems rather obscure."[21]

At the end of the European war, Melbourne insisted on stopping the bird hunting in New Guinea. A ban that was to come into force on 2 March 1921 was canceled by the military government, which was still in office. Instead, it raised the export duty from one to two pounds per bird.[22] In mid-November 1921, export duty was surprisingly dropped to 10 shillings per bird in order to allow the last officers of the military government to export the birds they had killed as cheaply as possible on their departure. Although there was a national law prohibiting the import to and transit through Australia of birds of paradise, the birds were shipped via Sydney to France and South America, where they could be sold legally.[23] On 31 December 1921 the export ban came into force. Nonetheless, another 1,279 birds were exported in the new year.[24] According to a conservative estimate, 80,000 birds of paradise were shot under the auspices of the Australian Military Government in New Guinea between the end of 1914 and the beginning of 1922; a more likely figure is 100,000. This was twice as many birds as were killed in the German bird of paradise boom, before they were protected in 1914.

In theory, birds of paradise and crowned pigeons were protected by the civil administration from January 1923. In reality, however, hunting continued near the border with Dutch New Guinea, with officials playing a leading part.

TABLE 2.   Number of Birds of Paradise Killed
in New Guinea under the Australian
Military Administration

YEAR	NUMBER OF BIRDS OF PARADISE KILLED
1914–1915	c. 3–5,000[a]
1915–1916	c. 30–40,000[b]
1916–1917	125[c]
1917–1918	not known
1918–1919	100[c]
1919–1920	34,704[c]
1920–1921	5,811[c]
1921–1922	6,000[d]
TOTAL	c. 80–92,000

[a]Estimate; includes white herons and crowned pigeons.
[b]Estimate; see Chap. 2, nn. 21 and 22.
[c]Figures based on export duty duly paid (£1 = 1 bird);
    Memorandum Officer in charge of Trade and Customs, E.
    Featherstone Phibbs, Rabaul, 17 July 1920; AAC: A 1–23/
    18422. For 1916–1917 and 1918–1919 these figures certainly
    show only a tiny fraction of the actual number of birds killed.
[d]Administrator Wisdom, Rabaul, 18 November 1921, to the
    Office of the Prime Minister; AAC: A 518/1–A 846/1/77.
    According to official statistics (AAC: A 1–23/18422) export
    duty was paid on only 2,354 birds.

As the birds were being shot anyway, argued the Australian Administrator in 1926, it would be better to lift the protection ordinance; the colony was losing valuable customs duties on them.[25] Neither in theory nor in reality, however, did the status quo change. Hunting birds of paradise in New Guinea was prohibited until 1941 but nobody took any notice of the ban.

THE ADMINISTRATION

The exploitative mentality of a number of soldiers occupying New Guinea could be given such free rein because the new administration was recruited exclusively from military personnel. The resignation of all the German officials in the wake of the Cox Affair saved the military governor the embarrassment of having to dishonor one of the provisions of the surrender treaty. On 22 November the Australian Ministry of Defence had telegraphed orders to the Administrator that on no account were German officials to be kept on.[26] Hence officers were employed as administrative officials. At the head of the military administration was the Administrator of the occupied German colony. By the time a civil administration was introduced on 9 May 1921, a total of five high-ranking Australian officers had held this post. Colonel Holmes was succeeded by Brigadier General Pethebridge, who was transferred straight from his position as secretary in the ministry of defense to Rabaul, then by Johnston and Griffiths, also brigadier generals, and finally, Major General Wisdom. Wisdom symbolized the seamless transition from the military administration to the mandate period. He was both the last military Administrator of German New Guinea and the first governor of the civil administration of the Australian-mandated territory of New Guinea.[27]

Much more than in the German period, administrative measures depended on the personal whim of individual officials. The idea that Rabaul could exercise any control over local administrations seemed a utopian dream for a number of reasons. Officials lacked administrative experience, the military had no interest in developing certain parts of the country so long as law and order were not threatened, and the state of war meant that circumstances were exceptional. Added to this was the fact that officials received relatively little guidance concerning their behavior on the site. Only general political decisions on basic principles were known and binding. Apart from this, individual military officials in the colony had a relatively free hand. This could make the exceptional circumstances of war more tolerable because ad hoc decisions were possible, and their effectiveness was not blocked by paper regulations. On the other hand, military officials had a large amount of responsibility, and this encouraged them to abuse their authority. It also favored the exploitative mentality mentioned above. A number of other factors also increased the room for maneuver of individual officials. There was a high degree of turnover in the staff of the military administration because of the war, and it was practically impossible to hold individuals accountable for their administrative work after the event. In extreme cases, a district officer, the new designation for *Stationsleiter* (head of station), could, on taking office, completely ignore what his predecessor had done and completely reverse policy without encountering any serious resistance. There was no opportunity for civilians to appeal against the decisions of a military official. The consequences of complaining about officials were potentially more serious than suffering in silence, because the official to whom the complaint was addressed was almost always the subject of the complaint. In theory, the district officer's power was limited in that he could impose prison sentences only up to six months' duration and fines only up to fifteen pounds in value. Anything beyond this had to be confirmed from Rabaul. In practice, however, the district officer could do whatever he pleased, at least outside the law, as the center hardly bothered about what was going on in the outlying stations. In Madang, the district officer threatened his critics by telling them that he could convict someone "if only he personally was convinced of their guilt, even if all the evidence pointed in the other direction."[28] A characteristic of the military administration was a high degree of uncertainty regarding the law. Together with the irregularity and instability of administrative decisions, this resulted in a growing uncertainty among the population. As we shall see, this had lasting consequences for the attitude of Melanesians toward Europeans.

One of the main directives for the Australian-occupied colony was that the status quo was to be preserved in the area of property ownership. The ownership of land remained untouched, and attempts by Australian private citizens to change the legal status of 1914 were unsuccessful.[29] With one important exception I shall return to, all applications by Europeans to buy land were deferred until the end of the war. Until 30 June 1916 the German mark remained the official currency. Its replacement by the pound was a direct consequence of the fact that the Commonwealth Bank opened a branch in Rabaul on 14 April 1916 —the first bank ever in New Guinea. Thereafter, however, German silver coin was still in circulation. Only from 31 July 1919 were German coins no longer accepted as legal tender.[30]

British attempts to influence Australia's economic policy in New Guinea were rejected. The military administration and the Australian federal government refused to comply with two requests from London to liquidate German firms, as had happened in Samoa. The official explanation was that there was no military justification for such drastic intervention in existing circumstances.[31] The real reason had already been given by Holmes, the first Administrator. The value of New Guinea lay in its coconut plantations. But as most of them were still young, it was necessary to protect this "embryo wealth" from any harmful influence. At the end of the war, they would have "bright and valuable possessions." Things had to be kept going until then.[32]

Holmes' successors continued this policy. The longest-serving Administrator, Pethebridge, justified this action in the face of growing criticism in Australia. It would be unwise, he argued, for Australia to damage the colonial economy growing under Australian military protection: after all, it was pretty certain that at the end of the war all the profits would end up in Australian hands. The Germans presently working to produce these anticipated profits on their plantations, unmolested by the military government, would not, of course, be able to share in them: "Before that hope can be realised every acre in the Colony must cease to belong to Germans, and every enemy subject must be required to leave the country."[33]

During the war, the military government was already able to achieve large balance-of-trade surpluses. The German export duty on copra—10 marks per ton—was raised to the equivalent of 10 shillings; then in stages to 15, 20, and finally to 25 shillings per ton. New Guinea's revenues from duties had been £18,300 in 1913 and £19,950 in 1914. Rising almost continuously, they amounted by 30 June 1920 to £108,682.[34] This meant that Australia's objective of making the occupied colony financially independent of outside sources was soon achieved.[35]

The fact that Australia's long-term goals were most likely to be achieved by minimal administration and a laissez-faire attitude was a result of the wartime

TABLE 3. Copra Exports from German New Guinea ("Old Protectorate," without Micronesia), 1915–1920

CALENDAR YEAR	QUANTITY IN IMPERIAL TONS	VALUE IN POUNDS	COPRA AS A PERCENTAGE OF TOTAL EXPORTS	TOTAL VALUE OF EXPORTS IN POUNDS	TOTAL VALUE OF IMPORTS IN POUNDS	BALANCE OF TRADE SURPLUS
1915	14,574	155,135	92.7	167,427	152,848	14,579
1916	11,253	284,850	91.8	310,437	139,684	170,753
1917	19,104	409,850	92.8	441,616	231,599	210,017
1918	21,179	480,292	93.4	514,150	333,520	180,630
1919	18,710[a]	442,763	93.1	475,489	396,289	79,200
1920	23,101					

[a] The total harvest was considerably larger, amounting to 26,101 tons. However, lack of shipping because of a strike in Australia meant that no more copra could be exported.

Source: Statistical tables in: AAC: A 1–23/18422 and AAM: B 197: 2021/1/260.

TABLE 4.   Public Revenue from Occupied German New Guinea, 1914–1921

DATE	PUBLIC REVENUE IN POUNDS
From occupation to 30 June 1915	55,542
1 July 1915–30 June 1916	88,449
1 July 1916–30 June 1917	115,559
1 July 1917–30 June 1918	139,921
1 July 1918–30 June 1919	143,636
1 July 1919–30 June 1920	202,158
1 July 1920–30 June 1921	193,957
TOTAL	939,222

Source: Memorandum Piesse, 23 September 1921: "Notes for a ministerial statement of policy"; AAC: A 2219 vol. 19. Memorandum, Administrator Johnston, 10 March 1920; AWM: 33–57/2. Data on public expenditure over the same period is incomplete.

situation. Above all, the administrative costs of the occupation could be kept to a minimum. But the longer the war lasted, the more clearly the negative aspects of this policy emerged. The lack of continuity in administration that had begun as a temporary response to an exceptional situation began to establish itself as the rule in the Australian administration. Similarly, it became more and more apparent how much the Australian administration was living off its capital. What is accepted in wartime as politically expedient—investing as little as possible in a country under military occupation—increasingly jeopardized the potential benefits which, it was hoped, the colony would bring Australia after the conclusion of peace. In the humid tropical climate, roads and public buildings suffered first.[36] Vandalism and a mentality of exploitation were the final blows.[37]

Australia abdicated responsibility for many areas that had previously been regulated by government. This was most drastic in relations with "free" indigenous people, who were not employed by Europeans. At the end of February 1915, the government station of Angoram was given up after having been manned for three months. Thereafter the people living in the catchment area of New Guinea's biggest river, the Sepik, were abandoned to the laws of the jungle. This did not mean, however, that contact with the outside world came to an end. On the contrary, the encroachment of outsiders on the basis of the local people's existence increased during the war. Precisely because the Sepik district now lacked a well-ordered colonial administration, it became an El Dorado for unscrupulous bird of paradise hunters and European, Asian, or nonlocal Melanesian recruiters of labor. Four years later, when a patrol from the administration visited the region again, the whole area was like an angry wasps' nest. Even where tribal warfare had stopped during the German period, it had revived. The people living near the old government station of Angoram were in a permanent state of war: several villages had been razed; evidence of terrible massacres was discovered.[38] Superficially, the action taken by the patrol resembled the German measures dating from before 1914. Acting on the administration's instructions to impose law and order, the patrol set fire to the huts of the most warlike villages and destroyed their gardens. But as the administration's measures ended there for the time being, it is more than likely that local unrest increased rather than decreased. The confusion in the interregnum between the end of the war and the appointment of the civilian authorities (1919 to 1921) did, in fact, further aggravate relations among the local people, the Europeans, and the administration.

As well as Angoram the "flying" station, Burgberg in the Markham valley, which was just being developed in 1914, was also shut down. Similar complaints about anarchic conditions caused by the withdrawal of the administration came from all other parts of the colony. The few cases in which the administration tried to assert its claim to sovereignty ended in military conflicts with the local people, who pointed out that there was no government any more and that they could do what they liked.[39]

The Australian Military Administration's influence on the local population can best be gauged by looking at the head-taxes collected. By the end of 1915 the tax was being raised only from Melanesians in the direct environs of Rabaul. Thereafter, too, tax gathering was clearly concentrated in the northern Bismarck Archipelago. Except in 1920, its population continuously provided more than 80 percent of all revenues from taxation. Little was raised in taxes from the mainland; sometimes nothing at all. The influence of the military administration seems to have been minimal here.

The strange fluctuations in the tax revenues raised in individual regions are striking. In Kieta, for example, the yield from taxes decreased steadily from £1,883 in 1916, to £1,087 in 1917 and £827 in 1918. The method of collecting taxes by the district officer or his often ad hoc agent left the door wide open to abuses. It is therefore hardly surprising that after the end of the war, but before the civilian administration was installed, the government auditor accepted as a fact that those who were responsible for tax collecting were guilty of embezzlement on a massive scale. All the officials involved, however, were in reserved occupations in Australia and could no longer be called to account.[40] The fact that Australian officers had accepted a certain responsibility as officials of the military administration does not seem to have deterred a number of them from enriching themselves at the expense of the occupied country and its people. The unusually long duration of the military administration helped to maintain and conceal irregular practices. As late as mid-1920, the officer who had been appointed to supervise the native hospital in Rabaul found nothing wrong with withholding their rations and secretly selling them to a Japanese merchant.[41]

It is not only when we consider the military administration's retreat to the centers of German administration that the amounts of taxes paid by the

TABLE 5.   The Australian Military Administration and the Indigenous Head-Tax in New Guinea

PERIOD	9/1914–31/8/1915	1/9/1915–31/12/1915	1916	1917	1918	1919	1920	1–6/1921	1921/22 (CIVIL ADMINISTRATION)
Total head-tax collected (in pounds sterling):	2,837	1,318	15,433	10,897	12,102	15,735	14,108	8,222	20,546
Total head-tax revenues collected, in percentages*, from:									
Rabaul/Kokopo	100.0	100.0	32.9	32.5	31.1	24.5	17.8	38.0	16.1
South and West New Britain	0	0	0	0	0	1.4	2.8	9.7	7.3
New Britain as a whole	100.0	100.0	32.9	32.5	31.1	25.9	20.6	47.7	23.4
Käwieng			28.1	34.5	29.4	23.2	14.9	22.8	19.2
Namatanai			12.0	15.5	14.1	13.0	14.5	1.6	15.3
New Ireland as a whole			40.1	50.0	43.5	36.2	29.4	24.4	34.5
Kieta (Solomons)			12.2	10.0	6.8	18.3	16.4	13.2	18.4
Bismarck Archipelago	100.0	100.0	85.2	92.5	81.4	80.4	66.4	85.3	76.3
Manus			10.9	3.7	8.4	8.3	10.5	6.8	8.9
Madang			3.5	3.7	10.2	5.1	13.1	5.8	4.5
Morobe			0	0.1	0	1.7	1.7	0	3.1
Eitape			0.3	0	0	4.4	8.3	2.0	7.3
Former Kaiser-Wilhelmsland			3.8	3.8	10.2	11.2	23.1	7.8	14.9

* Full hundreds are achieved by rounding up or down.

Source: Data and calculations from the table "Head-Tax" in AAC: A 1/23–18422.
Different figures are given in the report by the Officer in charge of Native Affairs, T.J. McAdam, Rabaul, 10 October 1919, to Atlee Hunt. According to these figures, the total income from head-tax in 1916 was only £11,530; for 1917, only £9,143; and for 1918, only £10,409; AAC: CP 661/15/1.

Melanesian population between 1914 and 1921 seem rather strange. Between September 1914 and June 1921, a period that corresponds pretty exactly to the military administration of New Guinea, indigenous people paid a total of £80,652 sterling in tax. At contemporary exchange rates (£1 = 20 marks), this was the equivalent of 1,613,040 marks. Compared with tax revenues before 1914, this is an incredible sum. It can be explained only by assuming that taxes were raised, that plantation workers who had been exempt from taxation under German administration were now being taxed, and/or that some people were taxed twice.[42] Even if we also assume that in certain regions the administration did nothing but collect taxes, we cannot avoid concluding that local people had amassed a considerable amount of wealth. We can only speculate about to what extent this can be attributed to Governor Hahl's policy of compulsory planting.

Collecting the head-tax was only a continuation of established German administrative practice (although it was probably implemented in a completely new way). It thus fits into Australia's general policy of maintaining the status quo ante in occupied New Guinea. Australia's policy of continuity concentrated on areas in which German decisions had laid the foundations for the successful economic development of New Guinea in the future. In other fields, Australia was rather more reticent in interpreting the provisions of the surrender treaty and of international law. Least notice was taken of German regulations in the whole area of general living conditions. Here the aim seems to have been to bring in Australian practices, even if this meant that previous principles were turned upside down. One of the military administration's first measures was to introduce driving on the left.[43] The decimal and metric systems were increasingly replaced by British weights and measures.

The Australian attempt to shape even the natural environment into familiar Australian patterns on the British model was in complete opposition to German policy. When introducing new species into the colony, the Germans had always had long-term economic benefit in mind. The Australians, in contrast, were trying to transfer Australia to New Guinea by importing nonendemic species. Australian birds (kookaburras, peewits, and magpies) were released in the Botanic Gardens in Rabaul. The military administrator had them imported especially, in order that "the presence of such birds will tend to Australianise the Colony in a way that will appeal to Australians."[44] Though native birds could be killed with the permission of the director of the Botanic Gardens, Australian birds were protected by strict regulations. The penalty for merely injuring an Australian bird was one month in prison.[45]

The attempt to Australianize the colony amounted, in part, to a blatant destruction of the environment. The well-known Australian dislike of tropical trees was especially marked.[46] In Rabaul as well as Madang, the military government ordered the felling of large numbers of trees. Shortly before the end of the military administration, Rabaul's famous tropical avenues, which had contributed largely to its reputation as a jewel in the Pacific, were systematically cut down. Since September 1914, the Botanic Garden had been used by the garrison as a firewood reserve. Every month, between sixteen and twenty tons of wood were cut there. By September 1919, 110 acres of what had originally been 200 acres of cultivated ground had been totally cleared.[47]

The decision to permit fishing with dynamite, which had been prohibited by the German administration, led to further despoliation of the environment. The German administration was initially responsible, having suspended its ban on the outbreak of war, presumably to alleviate the food supply situation, which threatened to deteriorate when relations with the outside world were broken off.[48] What was intended as a temporary measure became a permanent state of affairs under the Australian Military Administration, with all this implied for humans and animals, long after food was regularly being imported again.[49]

THE INFLUENCE OF TRADE AND INDUSTRY: THE "BURNS PHILP COLONY"

On 17 October 1914, exactly one month after Germany and Australia had signed the treaty of surrender in New Guinea, the *Moresby* steamed into the bay of Rabaul. This ship belonged to the Australian South Pacific trading company, Burns Philp, and on board was its islands manager, Lucas. The company had expanded during the Pacific labor trade period, when it was involved in the dubious business of recruiting Melanesian workers for Queensland's sugarcane plantations.[50] When the Australian Commonwealth was founded, and government and opposition unanimously announced that their main objective was a white Australia, Burns Philp secured for itself a contract with the federal government that gave it the exclusive right to deport Pacific workers. Burns Philp earned a fortune from the forced repatriation of Melanesians. The ministry official who prepared the ground for this campaign in the ministry and supervised its implementation was Atlee Hunt. A close connection developed between him and Burns Philp. Their relations went far beyond what was usual between a private company and a government official. In order to keep Hunt in a good mood, Lucas and Burns regularly gave him contributions from the company's current business ventures: valuable pearls from Torres Strait were especially acceptable.[51] Hunt reciprocated by using all his influence to ensure that the cabinet regularly awarded Australian government contracts for postal services with the Pacific Islands exclusively to Burns Philp.[52]

Colonel James Burns, director and owner of the company, was associated with the highest political circles in Australia. His connections with the governor-general of Australia proved to be of the most practical value. Whenever the governor-general was in Sydney, he stayed at Burns' home in Paramatta. For the crafty businessman Burns, the letters of recommendation that opened the doors of the most important London offices to him were more important than the honors and title for which the governor-general successfully nominated his personal friend. Before Burns, Foreign Secretary Grey had never entertained an Australian with a personal letter of recommendation from the governor-general.[53] During the war, the company's influence spread far beyond the Pacific Islands under Australian influence. It was easy for its manager, Lucas, to place his own people as officials in the Western Pacific High Commission. The selection of staff was entrusted to him.[54]

Australia's conquest of Rabaul gave Burns Philp & Co. an opportunity to start trading with a colony that they had had to leave in 1906. The company had been unable to compete with the Norddeutsche Lloyd, which was subsidized by the German government, and had been forced to give up its shipping routes between Australia and German New Guinea as unprofitable. However, when Lucas arrived in Rabaul on the *Moresby*, he found that traders there were not prepared to pay the inflated prices which he demanded. The company had miscalculated, expecting such severe shortages as a result of the war that the white colonists would simply accept the prices it asked without question. But before the end of the German administration, the manager of the Neuguinea-Kompanie, Georg Täufert, had gone to Dutch New Guinea and brought the colony urgently needed food and supplies.

Burns Philp's attempt to gain a foothold in New Guinea looked as if it was going to fail until it was rescued by the Australian Administrator. Colonel William Holmes requisitioned all the rice and food the Neuguinea-Kompanie had brought over from the Dutch part of the island and pressurized the Ger-

Burns Philp's *Matunga* in Alexishafen, close to Madang, October 1914. The *Matunga* was the first ship to arrive after the Australian occupation of Madang. She was later captured and sunk by the German raider *Wolf*. (Australian War Memorial J 03109)

man traders into buying the goods offered by Burns Philp at fixed prices. In order to be quite sure, he had the general manager of the Neuguinea-Kompanie—"a disturbing factor in this place"—put aboard the departing *Moresby* and taken to Australia as an "undesirable." Täufert was the first German civilian to be deported to Australia from occupied New Guinea. The obviously satisfied Administrator noted that this measure "has had a very decided effect, as practically the whole of the cargo brought here by the 'Moresby' has been disposed of."[55]

Above decks, on board the ships that had been requisitioned by the occupying power, traveled Australian soldiers on their way to occupy other centers of the colony besides Rabaul. Below decks was stored Burns Philp cargo. It was taken ashore, along with the Union Jack, in Friedrich-Wilhelmshafen, Käwieng, Manus, and Bougainville. Thus the military expedition was, at the same time, always "a business trip" which, "in addition to achieving its object of Military occupation," resulted "in a sound profit as a commercial venture." According to the Administrator, the net profits amounted to over £865.[56] Rates for the transport of Australian troops from New Guinea to Australia on Burns Philp's ships were personally negotiated with the manager of the company by the Administrator, although he had not been authorized to do this by the relevant authorities. Afterward the Administrator informed his superiors that he had taken this step "in order to facilitate the passing of Burns, Philp & Coy.'s account when presented in Australia."[57]

How did it come about that the military governor could adopt as his own the aims of an Australian private trading company, and even boast about this at home? To the present day, little is known about the personal career of William Holmes before his appointment, seemingly out of nowhere, as leader of the Australian expedition and first Administrator of the occupied colony. Holmes seems to have held no prominent position in military or civilian life. At the beginning of the expedition he appears to have been given a remarkable degree of freedom. He received no detailed instructions on how to proceed once the colony was occupied—this was left to his discretion. The most important officers were all related to him. His personal adjutant was his son, Basil Holmes, who directed the occupation of Käwieng and Kieta; and the head of military intelligence was his son-in-law, Captain R. J. ("Jack") Travers. Finally, the military secretary and supervisor of government stores, Keith Heritage, a man who had been promoted very quickly from lieutenant to captain to major, was Holmes' nephew. Allegedly, in civilian life all were employees of Burns Philp. William Holmes himself was said to be an authorized signatory of the company; according to other accounts, he was the son-in-law of a partner who had a controlling interest in the company.[58] The occupation troops called those who arrived first in New Guinea simply "the Wallingfords—Burns Philp," after Frederick Wallin, the manager of the company's Island Department.[59]

On the face of it, it is almost unbelievable that all these interests—military, political, and commercial—should be combined in the hands of the most important individual in occupied New Guinea. Surprisingly, however, Holmes' activities obviously had the protection of his superiors. Burns Philp, however, did not stop there. On arrival in Rabaul, Manager Lucas claimed that the Australian authorities had agreed to grant Burns Philp a monopoly on supplying goods to the military administration in Rabaul from Australia. Burns Philp had been given the green light, he claimed, to mark up Sydney prices by 10 percent. On the other hand, the company gave no concession for government freight for the troops and in Rabaul could decide independently whether it would accept cargo for Australia or not. Although Lucas had no official letter, it turned out that his claims were true.[60] During the entire Australian Military Administration, that is, from 1914 to 1921, Burns Philp had a monopoly on transport, and practically also on trade, with occupied New Guinea, under conditions that benefited the company but not Australia, and certainly not New Guinea.

Burns Philp succeeded in pulling off another surprise coup early in 1916, which turned it into the largest Pacific trading company at a stroke. Until this date, the transit trade in goods from German New Guinea had been handled by Lohmann & Co. and Justus Scharff Ltd. In 1915 Lucas had tried, unsuccessfully, to persuade German merchants in New Guinea to use Burns Philp not only to transport their products to Australia but also to market their goods. Lohmann and Scharff seemed to some extent to be protected against the consequences of the war because they had acquired British citizenship. In order to achieve his aims Burns exploited his behind-the-scenes connections with cabinet and the Australian press, which had been stirred up against the Germans to an extraordinary degree. At the end of 1915 Lohmann, Scharff, and the other German-Australian owners of businesses and their employees were interned. As early as 14 January 1916 Lucas appeared in Rabaul and showed a surprised Administrator Pethebridge a letter from the Australian prime minister, Hughes, addressed to Burns Philp, dated 6 January, which more or less amounted to a blank check for the company: "You may take what steps you think proper to secure the trade which was until recently in the hands of Lohmann & Coy. and Justus Scharff Ltd." Behind this was an attempt to prevent other agents, especially British ones, from securing for themselves the transit trade between New Guinea and world markets. With astonishing openness, it was admitted that, in this case, "the objects of the internments will be largely defeated."[61] The Administrator was far from pleased about this development, which gave Burns Philp a practical monopoly on trade in addition to their monopoly on transport. As an old officer, Pethebridge was above suspicion of being involved in shady deals. His aim was undoubtedly to hand over a flourishing colony to Australia at the end of the war, and he was obviously well aware that the preferential treatment given to one private trading company seriously jeopardized this objective. Its monopoly on trade and transport gave Burns Philp so much control over New Guinea's economic power that the prices at which German New Guinea's products were purchased were dictated by Burns Philp, not the world market. In order to escape this stranglehold, Pethebridge worked out a plan by which the occupied colony's most important export crop, copra, was to be bought by the Administration at a price it had fixed. It was then to be transported by government steamer direct to Japanese and British harbors. This scheme, however, got stuck somewhere in the bureaucratic machinery of an Australian government department.[62] Thus the colonel had no option but to give in to Burns Philp's invisible accomplices and come to terms with the all-powerful company. The transport agreement dating from Holmes' period of office was recognized, but with the proviso that Burns Philp would give the administration special rates to compensate for the monopoly now officially acknowledged.[63] As Burns Philp consistently refused to accept German tax regulations, which were still in force and applied to all other businesses, and the authorities in Australia could not be persuaded to put pressure on the company to observe existing laws, the Administrator concluded an agreement with the company that exempted it from income tax. Instead, a special arrangement was made. Regardless of the company's turnover or profits, it was to pay the administration the paltry sum of £300 "business tax" annually.[64]

Burns Philp knew how to exploit any loopholes in the existing law in its own favor. Whenever the company clearly overstepped the limits, it always found helpful protectors who shielded it. There seemed to be no question about Burns Philp, during the war, using German trading ships that had been detained in Australia.[65] The military administration in New Guinea strictly observed the rule of not permitting any land to be sold until the position was clarified under international law—with one exception. It concerned Burns Philp. Governor Hahl, ignoring his own guidelines, had already granted the company 10,000 hectares on Bougainville. In June 1918 the Australian Military Administration allowed the Solomon Islands Development Company—whose sole owner was Burns Philp, Sydney—to acquire 12,500 acres of freehold land on the island of Buka. Burns Philp had claimed that all the necessary formalities to do with buying land had already been completed, in principle, during the German period. Although there was no entry in the land register, and no documents could be found about the alleged sale of land, the military administration allowed itself to be persuaded to ratify and complete the sale.[66] Martial law did not prevent the company from supplying large quantities of weapons and munitions to civilians—here, too, the hands of the military administration were bound.[67] One of Burns Philp's specialities was supplying alcohol to Pacific Islanders, which had been the basis of the company's growth during the Pacific labor trade at the end of the nineteenth century. The practice of selling large quantities of alcohol to local people in exchange for cheap copra and other products had been made impossible by the administration in the German-controlled areas of the Pacific. But outside the German area, the trade with cheap spirits flourished. To a certain extent, the war facilitated the continuation of these practices because it extended existing gray areas. In mid-1917 Britain suggested that, given the negative effects of the sale of alcohol on the Pacific

Islanders, the Australian Commonwealth should pass a law against it. The Australian governor-general responded without mincing his words: "I think it extremely doubtful that the Commonwealth Government would take up this matter in any way, seeing that it would to some extent provide for prolonging the lives of the coloured races."[68] At stake were not only the profits of Australian trading companies—above all, Burns Philp; to white Australians, Pacific Islanders were also unwanted competitors for work and seemed to threaten their own social achievements.

By the end of 1920, when the military still set the tone in the occupied German colony and martial law was still in force, the preferential treatment of Burns Philp & Co. had become so ingrained that attempts by the then Administrator even to inquire about the conditions governing Burns Philp's postal contract, again due for renewal, and the offers they had submitted, were in vain. (In the event, the contract was once again extended without opposition.) Two telegrams from the Administrator to the Prime Minister's Department, asking for information about the freight and passenger rates proposed by Burns Philp, remained unanswered.[69] The responsible official in the Prime Minister's Department was Atlee Hunt. There are few other historical cases in which the connections between politics, or individual politicians, and the commercial interests of a private company are so clearly documented. Late in 1914 a German ship's captain who had fled to Dutch New Guinea sent a report home, mentioning the strange coincidence between the Australian military occupation of the colony and Burns Philp's seemingly unchallenged supremacy, which began immediately afterward: "The whole Australian campaign against New Guinea seems to be a business trick by the firm Burns Philp & Co."[70] There was probably little reaction to his report in Germany. Germany had other concerns, and reports from its distant, now occupied colonies in the South Pacific were of interest to few. In the German Colonial Office the receipt of this, as of every piece of information, was carefully recorded. The report was placed in a file and stored in the archives, but its contents were ignored and finally forgotten. Such information was too inconsistent with the official view of the primacy of politics and military concerns—if not always in times of peace, then certainly during wartime. In addition, the report has the feel of having been written by an unsuccessful business rival. Surely the activities of Burns Philp alone cannot explain Australia's moving against German New Guinea and its behavior there from 1914 to 1921. But although the statement quoted above sums up events very briefly, there is more than a grain of truth in it.

An account of Burns Philp's activities in Australian-occupied New Guinea, and its influence there, would be incomplete without some mention of the enormous profits the company made out of the war. The company's monopoly meant that it could set practically any price for the goods it brought to the colony. The prices it demanded were exorbitant. For example, an imperial pound of powdered arsenic cost 49 shillings in Madang; in Sydney, 50 (*sic!*) pounds of the same medicine cost only 40 shillings.[71] Truly fantastic profits, however,

TABLE 6.   Burns Philp Net Profits between 1910 and 1920

YEAR (ENDING 31 MARCH)	NET PROFIT (AFTER DEDUCTING ALL TAXES, LEVIES, AND SALARIES) IN POUNDS
1910	78,137
1911	86,141
1912	113,542
1913	120,228
1914	131,281
1915	83,655
1916	125,594
1917	157,725
1918	195,295
1919	215,013
1920	249,886
TOTAL WARTIME PROFITS	1,027,168

Source: Private and confidential reports nos. 20–30; Burns Philp Archives Sydney, Box 21.

Note: See also Table 8 in Buckley and Klugman 1983, 74, in which lower profits are given (but see the explanatory remarks ibid., 73).

were made on selling copra from New Guinea. After the company managed to break into the transit trade, its profits escalated. From 1916, the company's profits increased in every financial year in which New Guinea continued to be under martial law. At the turn of 1918, yields skyrocketed. Until this time, a net profit of £1,000 per shipment from buying, transporting, and selling copra was the norm. Now it increased more than sixfold. In January 1918 a single consignment of copra weighing 1,450 tons yielded a net profit of £11,015 on the sale alone.[72] On 31 March 1914, Burns Philp's total turnover was £4,628,019; in 1917 it was £5,884,972; and in 1918 £7,197,527. This was the highest turnover in the company's history so far. It was a direct result of the occupation of Germany's colonies in the South Pacific, as the company's partners were confidentially informed.[73]

Profits rose strongly with turnover. At Burns Philp's thirty-seventh annual meeting in May 1919, shareholders were informed that in addition to a new record turnover (£8,085,550) the company had made a gross profit of over £625,664. After deduction of taxes and salaries, officially more than £215,013 net profit remained. The true figure was much higher, but the exact amount of profit was kept secret even from shareholders.[74] Once again, the company had proved to have a good nose for business, access to reliable information, and an extraordinary feel for economic necessities. Six months before the conclusion of the armistice, Burns Philp's head office in Brisbane instructed all its branches in the Pacific to sell whatever could be sold. It correctly anticipated that after the armistice the transport situation would improve, and that prices would temporarily drop.[75] In 1920, with the end of the military administration in New Guinea, Burns Philp could see that the special conditions which they had enjoyed in the area would also come to an end. The most profitable branches of the business were separated from the parent company and a new company was founded—Burns Philp South Sea Co. Ltd.—with a capital stock of two million pounds. The company headquarters were in Fiji. This decision allowed Burns Philp to kill two birds with one stone. At the center of the Pacific island world, they were close to potential trading areas. Most importantly, however, they could also circumvent Australian regulations that forbade the employment of nonwhite ships' crews. In public, Colonel James Burns had always been one of the most vociferous supporters of the White Australia Policy, which had contributed to the company's expansion. But when it came to maximizing profits, it was of course cheaper to employ nonwhites because the company could not be compelled to offer them the same social conditions of employment.[76]

THE AUSTRALIAN VIEW OF MELANESIANS

When white Australians occupied New Guinea in 1914, they had had contact with the indigenous black people of their own country, the Aborigines, for just under 125 years. It is well known that this relationship was characterized more by conflict than by cooperation. The encounter between two extremely different worlds showed that the sphere of the Aborigines was incompatible with the scientific and technological thinking and individualistic concepts of the British settlers, and vice versa. Of all the Pacific peoples, the Aborigines were the least prepared to make concessions to the invaders in order to share in any possible innovations through exchange. Similarly, of all the Europeans in the Pacific, the British in Australia proved to be the least tolerant of indigenous traditional ways of life. The Aborigines were not regarded as human, but as animals to be hunted and killed without penalty. In Queensland, "game licences" were issued for this purpose. The legal basis for this was a clause in the Australian constitution specifying that Aborigines were not considered human.[77]

This record promised little for relations between white Australians and Melanesians. The treatment of Pacific Islanders during the period of the Pacific labor trade and under the White Australia Policy was an aggravating circumstance. Superficially, what happened in Papua under the direct supervision of the Australian government seemed more humanitarian. Nonetheless, it was teeming with racist decrees and punishments.[78]

At first, however, white Australians expressed a completely different, and more positive, aspect of their character in occupied German New Guinea. No strong class differences had yet developed in Australian colonial society. Social safeguards and gratifications strengthened the fundamentally egalitarian nature of Australian society. Trade unions had a strong place within the social system, and they contributed to the fact that the image of the open-hearted Australian, always ready to help, did in fact define certain areas of Australian life. This type of Australian was certainly also in evidence on arrival in New Guinea, giving the local people tinned meat, biscuits, cigarettes, and shillings, or exchanging these things for local food and souvenirs.[79] The leaders of the expedition had perhaps encouraged the troops to behave in a friendly fashion toward the local people. On their first stop in Port Moresby, where they encountered Melanesians for the first time, the troops were instructed: "do not bully but bribe with tobacco."[80] In Rabaul, however, cooperation between Australian soldiers and the local people soon wandered from the prescribed paths and took its own forms. While they were looting, Australians sometimes sent local Melanesians into the houses of Germans to fetch out for them the objects they wanted. In one case, when two Germans caught the putative Melanesian rogues and started to beat them up, some of the soldiers intervened and taught the Germans that beating was by no means a race-specific punishment.[81] But such solidarity did not last for long.

"Bloody Niggers!"—Racism as a Constituent Part of
Australian Indigenous Policy

The military surrender of German New Guinea on 21 September 1914 in Herbertshöhe was accompanied by the rituals with which Europeans assure each other of mutual respect, even if one side has been defeated by the other: in spite of everything that separates them, they are united by something fundamental that is common to both. The Melanesian police-soldiers, by contrast, who had been wounded in the fighting, risking their lives so that the Germans did not lose the respect of other Europeans, had been left to their fate, while the local policemen who were fit for work were passed on from one European master to the next under the terms of the surrender. They quite clearly belonged to the inventory that was unhesitatingly handed over to the new rulers, because if circumstances had been reversed, the Germans would have expected the British to behave in exactly the same way. The Melanesians themselves were not consulted. Some regarded their duties as having come to an end with German rule and went home. They were shot by the Australians—"a useful and much needed lesson," as the new European leader in New Guinea put it.[82] Australian soldiers were quick on the draw, and their guns went off easily, even if they merely suspected that the Melanesians did not have the necessary respect for their European masters. A large number of local men fell victim to attempts by the Australians to show the locals that the end of the rule of these white men did not mean the end of rule by white men in general. Most died in a hail of bullets, without even knowing why they were being shot at. The cynical banality with which Australians recorded these events and passed

on to the day's business—"We shot a few niggers," soldier O'Hare noted on 11
September 1914—indicates that Australians in New Guinea were beginning to
revert to the patterns of behavior that were notorious at home in Australia.[83]

The stereotype of the dangerous black man who could never be trusted
because the wild animal in him could break out at any time was the leitmotiv of
the Australian Military Government from the start. It influenced the administration's attitude toward the occupied colony. Fear of Melanesian unpredictability was closely linked with anxiety that the local people might rise up in
support of the Germans. This was one of the reasons why more German colonists were not deported to Australia; the Australians feared that if this happened, the bomb might go off.[84]

As the Australians stayed in New Guinea longer and the exceptional circumstances of military rule became permanent, they perceived greater differences between themselves and the local Melanesians. They separated themselves more and more, condemning Melanesian customs and ridiculing and
mocking the people. The negative side of Australian egalitarianism now
became apparent. To everyone, from privates to the highest officers, the
Administrator, senators, and the governor-general, all Melanesians were indiscriminately "niggers."[85]

The Australian military administration's descent to the depths of linguis-
tic-racist rhetoric marks a clear stage in relations between Europeans and
Melanesians. To be sure, the same basically racist principle was accepted during both the German and the Australian administrative periods—namely, that
the Europeans' technological superiority justified the whites adopting an attitude of moral superiority most visibly expressed in the master–servant relationship. (The everyday colonial reality of German New Guinea, where black house
servants came running at every call, was quickly adopted by the Australian soldiers.) Nonetheless, the difference between the German and the Australian
interpretation of this principle was not merely a matter of form.

The German system rested upon an established framework of reference,
known to all. It defined duties and responsibilities under the umbrella of Germany's supreme authority. This framework was prescribed by the German colonial administration, and any attempt by the local people to place it in question
was regularly suppressed. Within these constraints, however, the local people
enjoyed certain freedoms—prerogatives that normally could not be touched by
whites. The administration ensured that these "taboos" were respected and
recognized the legal right of indigenous people to appeal against European
encroachment upon their areas. For all the Germans' clear feelings of superiority, they had something like respect for the otherness of the Melanesians, recognizing that despite their primitiveness, they, as humans, had a right to it. And
there was a subliminal feeling that any attempt to change this otherness by
force could not be morally justified. This attitude was most clearly expressed in
the discreet, judicious German treatment of Melanesians engaged in traditional feuding, in the cautious expansion of the limits of European-German

priorities, and above all in the fact that the Melanesians' right of domicile was never disputed, at least after 1900.[86]

Australian-occupied New Guinea lacked both this fixed framework of duties and prerogatives, and a vigilant authority to ensure that they were observed. Officially, German law was still valid and continued to apply to the Melanesians. But the few who could read German regulations were even less aware of how the colonial order was in fact implemented before September 1914. For the Germans who remained in New Guinea—planters and missionaries—the indigenous people represented either direct competition or purely a target group. The interests of both planters and missionaries had turned them into the fiercest opponents of German local administrations. If they had been asked, they would have expressed no interest at all in prolonging the German rule of New Guinea, provided that their own "rights" were guaranteed. The exceptional circumstances of war favored quick, ad hoc decisions. But the rapid turnover among officials meant that many ad hoc decisions had a strictly limited life span. Often they were overturned and replaced by others without apparent reference to any clear guidelines. Contradictory regulations and directives were common. This left the indigenous population in a deeply insecure state: they could no longer discern any rules governing behavior. To Australians, the word *nigger* may suggest a kind of presumptuous, racist familiarity,[87] but in any case it lowered the threshold of resistance to brutality. The limits of the German system had been deliberately and clearly signaled to all. The lack of such limits under the Australians, who behaved much more arbitrarily than the Germans anyway, increased the tendency to react in an extreme manner.

This predisposition was reinforced by another typically Australian feature. The Germans and the Australians both accepted that the "otherness" of the Melanesians was an obstacle to their assimilation to European-dominated modernity. But whereas the German colonial administration assumed (and worked toward this goal) that, with patience, Melanesians could gradually be led toward modernization without having to give up the characteristic features of their own culture that were not inconsistent with the Christian humanitarian tradition, the Australians equated the otherness of the Melanesians with a serious congenital defect. They believed that, if it could be eliminated at all, it would be only with the greatest difficulty. The otherness of the Melanesians, like that of the Australian Aborigines, was regarded not as having any intrinsic value but merely as a stain. Thus the Australian view of Melanesians oscillated between absolute condemnation of them as nonhuman (and thus unreformable) and the belief that they must be quickly and rigorously assimiliated—if necessary, by force: "the natives of these Islands are unprogressive and lazy. Still there must be either progress or perish, there is no third alternative. . . . they must advance—progress in spite of themselves."[88] This system did not allow for Melanesian characteristics to be preserved but, rather, to be regarded with contempt and disgust or ridiculed. A good measure of cynicism and malice was usually involved, together with a feeling of gratitude for not being like the Melanesians. A great deal of evidence can be cited for these attitudes.[89]

One of the features specific to New Guinea is its lingua franca. The structure and vocabulary of Tok Pisin provided the raw material for jokes—always the same ones—among generations of "enlightened Europeans." The Germans had at first strongly disapproved of Tok Pisin, but becoming accustomed to its irresistible advance, they had eventually come to appreciate the advantages it offered for the administration of the colony. From the start the Australians considered it bastardized English that should be eradicated. Their contempt for the people and the language they used reached a peak in the names Australians gave to newborn babies and under which they entered them in village rolls— "pek pek" (excrement), "pis pis" (urine), and "push push" (Tok Pisin paraphrase for sexual intercourse).[90] Young workers were universally called "monkey,"[91] a word that entered Tok Pisin as "mangi." Today the word is used simply for indigenous young men, and the majority of the population is unaware of its racist origins. The Australians also bragged that the vocabulary of the local people had been increased by Australia's most important swear words.[92]

Contempt for the Melanesians was so general that it is astonishing the Australians differentiated among them at all. But they perceived degrees of primitiveness. "If he is more than usually stupid and clumsy we take it for granted that he belongs to the New Britain inland tribes known as Baininges," explained Press Officer Lyng.[93] It was often denied that Melanesians were human beings at all. Comparisons were drawn with animals, or words were used that by definition were reserved for animals.[94] When defending corporal punishment for Melanesians, Administrator Johnston went so far as to say:

> It must be remembered that
>   1. The native is a primitive being, with no well developed sense of duty or responsibility. . . . With a native as with an animal—correction must be of a deterrent nature. Would a man imprison his horse for offering to bite him?[95]

Attempts were also made to provide scientific proofs for the assertion that Melanesians were more like animals than human beings. Australian military doctors insisted that Kanakas felt less pain than Europeans, because "the central nervous system of the Kanaka is comparatively poorly developed, and accordingly one would expect that the peripheral nerves are in a like state, the result being that pain which in a European would be acute, would be less marked in the Kanaka, owing to the slower and less active transmission of sensation." Their conclusion was that "there is no possible doubt that the Kanaka makes an excellent patient."[96]

Melanesians who put themselves at the mercy of the doctors in the hospitals for local people in Rabaul and Kokopo had to be patient indeed. Often, they were treated simply as guinea pigs. During the influenza epidemic toward the end of the war, an American doctor, with the permission of the Australian authorities, used Melanesian "patients" in the hospital in Rabaul to try out various remedies against hookworm. The Melanesians survived this torture, but it weakened their immune systems to such an extent that they were unable to cope with another wave of influenza. The person responsible for the experiments justified himself by pointing out that they would have died anyway. They had been condemned to hang as cannibals, he said—at least he had saved them from a death by hanging.[97]

Most of those who had come to the hospital for locals during the German period had been outpatients, seeking plaster and bandages from the government doctor. At the end of 1920, while New Guinea was still under military administration but it was clear that it would become an Australian mandate, the way in which the local people preferred to seek medical advice and help was made practically impossible. Sick people were given a form and told that they could not be treated until all the details had been filled in. As few could read (and even fewer could read English), this prerequisite served the purpose it was probably designed to fulfill, and outpatients could no longer be treated in the hospital.[98] This measure was almost certainly prompted by the right of military doctors to run their own private practices. Though local people received free treatment at the hospital, or were asked to make a nominal contribution, the government doctor could demand high fees in his capacity as a private practitioner.[99]

During the German period, government doctors were expected to undertake tours of inspection into remote jungle areas. The Australians gave up this practice. The system of *Heiltultuls* was on the point of collapse because the local assistants to the white doctors no longer received supplies of medicines. The German regulation that all Melanesian workers had to be immunized before starting work had not been adopted by July 1919, despite the fact that the number of indigenous workers had grown significantly since 1914.[100] A confidential report prepared in 1922 by order of the prime minister was scathingly critical of the health system in what was now officially Australian New Guinea. In 1914 the Germans, "in regular German fashion," had handed over hospitals with inventories, instruments, and medicines to the Australians, all in excellent condition. By the beginning of the Australian civil administration, they were in a condition that defies description. Some of the furniture, apparatus, and instruments had disappeared. The buildings themselves were in a state of collapse, as nothing had been repaired during the military administration. The hospital for locals in Kokopo had been closed during the war, and had not reopened since. That in Madang was unusable. The hospitals for Europeans in Kaewieng and Madang were closed at the beginning of the civilian administration, "considered to be then beyond repair." In Madang a patient had fallen one and a half meters through a rotten floor in the building; here, too, the hospital had to be closed down. The best-preserved hospital for local people, that in Rabaul, was shifted on the ground that it was "a danger to the white community"; in addition, the land on which it stood was a valuable commercial building site. The report also criticized the Australian staff of the hospitals. Not a single Australian doctor in New Guinea had been trained in tropical medicine. Drug and alcohol dependency was common among the doctors. Without the mission hospitals, which were rated as exemplary, the local people would have had practically no access to medical care.[101]

The fact that the Australian military administration cared little about the physical well-being of the local people, primarily for racist reasons, also became evident in areas that lay beyond the direct control of the health authorities. Reference has already been made to the practice of fishing with dynamite. The dangers associated with it were well known. The indigenous people were left to take all the risks. The following statement by Officer Lyng betrays an unbelievable cynicism: "Now and again a would-be fisherman is blown to pieces, for which reason the throwing of the dynamite is entrusted to natives."[102] Thus it is hardly surprising that the sale of alcohol to the local population by the troops was tolerated.[103]

In education for the local people, as well as in health, a specifically Australian form of racism made itself felt. The Australians had closed the German government school for Melanesians soon after the military occupation. Any potentially elitist feelings harbored by its ex-pupils were driven out of them by putting them on street-sweeping duties.[104] It is not reasonable to expect education to be a high priority for a temporary military administration. But when things had settled down and it was clear that New Guinea would remain Australian, it became obvious that the Australians' rejection of education was the result not of a temporary organizational problem but of a more fundamental attitude. Captain Tennent, the Australian official with responsibility for native affairs, actually said that teaching Melanesians to read and write was "a waste of time."[105] The general Australian view was that the only point of educating Melanesians was to provide "cheap skilled labour."[106] To be sure, the aim of the school set up by the German colonial administration had also been to create a relatively cheap supply of local government employees. But precisely this was now regarded as undesirable. Atlee Hunt, the secretary for Home and Territories, the ministry responsible for New Guinea, categorically refused any suggestion that Australia should again set up a government school in New Guinea to educate local children to become government employees. Melanesian government employees were not wanted; nor was education for Melanesians going beyond the elementary level: "We should not teach too much of that class of learning which trains a man to be a mere clerk. We do not want to develop a race of Pacific Island Babus. It is far more important that a native should know how to drive a nail straight or use an axe or an adze than to work a sum in practice or solve a quadratic equation."[107]

All that was left was primary teaching by the missions, which the German colonial administration had regarded as completely inadequate. Its plan to expand the existing school (*Regierungsschule*) in Rabaul from 1915, and to integrate it into an education system spanning the whole country with a *Regierungsschule* in each district, remained no more than a piece of paper. Not even the status quo of 1914 was maintained. In July 1921 all teaching was done by the missions. By 1921 the education of Melanesians had regressed to pre-1909 levels. In addition, the missions were no longer to teach in the vernacular, which had so far been preferred. An order issued toward the end of the military administration and adopted without change by the civil administration prescribed English as the only language of education. Here, too, methods of assimilation displaced the more associationist approach that had been practised by the Germans before September 1914.[108]

MELANESIAN WOMEN AS TARGETS OF RACISM
AND OBJECTS OF DESIRE

The attitude of the Australians toward Melanesian women deserves separate investigation. Through the filter of gender-specific perceptions, racist preconceptions of Melanesian men were exaggerated when applied to local women. Opinions were even stronger and more negative, and behavior expressed even less respect for the "other." Racism was combined with a fundamental hatred of women, and the result was a mixture of extreme misanthropy, misogyny, and machismo.

Melanesian women were "about the most miserable bits of humanity you could run across . . . indeed the source of all evil in these islands," Warrant Officer Lance Balfour Penman confided to his diary.[109] District Officer Major Balfour Ogilvy, by contrast, did not think it necessary to conceal his contempt from the other soldiers, and wrote in the *Rabaul Record:* "I have seen far more fascinating pigs than most of the ladies, and I'm certain I'd sooner kiss a pig than a native woman, because the pig would not understand."[110] Australian officers most frequently came into contact with local women in their capacity as magistrates. In this function, Major Ogilvy vented his full hatred of Melanesian women. Two young women whom he had convicted of "immoral acts" were ordered to undress and parade naked before the local police for several hours.[111] In Kokopo, the Australian district officer did not condemn the local practice of paying a bride-price as such; but he did introduce a completely new criterion for assessing the amount. Traditionally, the level of bride money varied according to the region from which the woman came, but was also influenced by her individual skills, knowledge, and capacity for work. As her family would have to do without these qualities in future, the bride-price was intended to be some form of compensation. It is doubtful whether the Australian official understood this system at all. If he did, he placed no special value on it. For him, the only crucial factors were appearance and price, which seemed to him exorbitantly high. On closer inspection, he was convinced that the woman was not the equivalent of the two pigs demanded; at most, he concluded, she was worth one.[112]

Sexual attacks and the raping of local women by Australian soldiers began almost on the very day on which they marched into Rabaul. The first victims were girls at mission schools, women patients in hospitals, and women prison-ers—women who could hardly run away.[113] In remote areas, above all, Austra-lian patrol officers used the local police to procure women for them from villages in the bush. Punitive expeditions against "insubordinate" Melanesians were often transformed into raids for tracking down indigenous women. There is clear evidence of this happening in the westernmost part of the colony (Sepik), the east (Bougainville), the south (Morobe), and the north (Manus), and there are indications from almost all other regions. On Manus, the district officer abducted and raped a local woman during a punitive expedition, after driving away her husband. A number of women and children were taken to the government station in Lorengau as hostages. "Lieutenant Singleton, who was in charge there, selected the best-looking of the women, and divided them amongst the white soldiers who were willing to sleep with them."[114] The offic-ers responsible did not deny the accusations but did not feel they had "done anything very wrong in violating the women held by us as hostages." In order to avoid a scandal, they were encouraged to retire, and both were sent back to Australia. They were never directly punished for their behavior. The Australian soldiers who had committed the rapes could not be brought to account at all because no replacements for them were available.[115]

An almost analogous case took place under District Officer Lieutenant Hunter in Kieta early in 1917. A woman was raped in the village of Ungano during a "visit" by the district officer. Two other women, whom he had taken away to his official residence on the coast as hostages, escaped under cover of night.[116] In Morobe, the district officers used the jail as a convenient place to get rid of indigenous rivals or relatives who had tried to protect their women. In Wanimo, Police Master Pole used the native police under his command to round up local women for him from villages in the bush and take them to his station. As the Sepik people would not tolerate this sort of behavior toward their women, bloody clashes took place, and there was a massacre of the local population in April and May 1921.[117] Here, too, there was a parallel. The first Australian police master in the southwest of New Britain had used the native police to hunt down Melanesian women. His successor found a completely ter-rified population. Where they had already had contact with Europeans, local women ran screaming into the jungle whenever they caught sight of a white man.[118] In none of the cases mentioned were the guilty punished. Officials were either quietly sent back to Australia or found their own way to more southerly climes where no questions were asked.

THE MILITARY ADMINISTRATION AND MELANESIAN LABOR

The Australian military administration in New Guinea had to deal with local people who could be divided into three categories based on their actual and legal relationship with the Europeans: Melanesian workers who were employed by Europeans; "free" indigenous people who had been absorbed into the colonial administration and "pacified" (and were thus subject to European jurisdiction); and free indigenous people who were not yet part of this system.

The first Melanesians from German New Guinea with whom the Australian soldiers came into contact were plantation workers, domestic servants, and the native police. The reactions of Australian troops ranged from abhorrence at the obvious exploitation of the Melanesians to admiration for a system which, although it disregarded elementary human rights, seemed to function smoothly, thus stirring a neurotic desire to project an image and awakening instinctive longings to dominate and give orders. For most Australians it was a completely new experience for blacks to accept orders from their white "masters" and generally to set about fulfilling them without any obvious protest. Australian Aborigines behaved very differently in this respect. They could be punished, pursued, even killed—nothing had proved effective in persuading them to enter into a settled relationship of employment for any length of time in one place: Australian Aborigines continued in their primarily nomadic way of life.

During the whole period of the Australian military administration, the pendulum swung wildly between rejection of and admiration for the German system. At first, the social conscience mentioned above, especially strongly developed among Australians, predominated. In a number of cases, they intervened against harsh treatment of Melanesians, responding at a purely emotional level. In Madang, the district officer dismissed the Malay foreman for being too brutal, explaining to the plantation owner that, for him, humanitarian concerns outweighed economic considerations: "it is better your plantations are rotten than your boys are ill treated."[119]

On 15 July 1915 Australian intervention was placed on a firm legal footing. The new labor ordinance issued on that day was typical of the attitude of the early military administration under Pethebridge. The first attempt by the Australian administration to take an active part in the affairs of the colony, typically, affected social welfare legislation. On the other hand, it did not violate the principle, based on international law and recognized in the treaty of surrender, that German law continued to be valid. In fact the Australian military government put into force the last German labor regulations, which had been drafted shortly before war broke out. They had been submitted by Governor Hahl to the Gouvernementsrat (governing council) on 5 March 1914 and forwarded to the German Colonial Office at the same time. They were meant to come into effect on 1 January 1915.[120] Hahl's intended reforms had aimed to eliminate at last some of the serious weaknesses in the labor regulations of 4 March 1909, and in the regulations of 31 July 1901, which had formed part of the later legislation. Among the new measures that were long overdue were the introduction of compulsory cash wages, the prohibition of payment in goods, a ban on the common practice of deducting the cost of tobacco and loin cloths from wages and retaining another part of the wages until the expiry of the labor contract, limiting working hours to nine (instead of ten) hours per day, and various regulations designed to protect workers against the many excesses perpetrated by recruiters. The recruitment of Melanesians for work outside the colony was to be banned altogether, and an end was to be put to the privileges of the German trading and plantation company in Samoa.[121]

With the Australian ordinance of 15 July 1915, most of these regulations came into force. For a short time New Guinea experienced the conditions, at least in theory, which Governor Hahl had long wanted to introduce. It is questionable whether this could have been achieved had the German colonial administration continued in office undisturbed.[122] But it soon became clear that the Australian military administration was either no longer willing, or simply not able, to enforce the improvements for local workers. The regulations were first diluted as early as October 1915; in August 1917 the regulations passed in July 1915 were completely replaced by a new ruling, which was much more open to interpretation.[123] The old provisions were progressively watered down until conditions were worse than they had been in September 1914. There were a number of reasons for this. First, there was the pressure of actual events. The labor regulations were generally disregarded, and almost all European employers in the colony (including the missions) boycotted them. The military administration possessed neither the staff nor the means to enforce the progressive aspects of the ordinance. It lacked the essential experience of how a colonial administration could realize its objectives in agreement with the colonists, although these objectives were diametrically opposed to the colonists' primary interests. The institution that had previously given the colonial government most support in such undertakings, the Governing Council of German New Guinea, had been dissolved by the Australians after the occupation. Second, racism was breaking through and exerting more and more influence over the decisions of the military administration. The desire to gain profits in German New Guinea was also an important factor. If the colony was to be profitable, as all the Administrators hoped, for the benefit of Australia after the conclusion of peace, then not much notice could be taken of alleged or real abuses in relations between European employers and Melanesian workers, especially if any change might reduce profits.

Sooner or later, every Australian soldier had an indigenous servant, and the methods of treating them that had been used by the Germans—bawling out and shouting—were soon adopted by the Australians. By 1919, when another new labor ordinance had been issued,[124] payment in goods and deferred pay—that is, retaining most of a worker's wages until the end of his contract—had long since been legal again. And if a worker ran away and was caught, the cost of this procedure was deducted from his pay and the length of any prison sentence he received was added to his work contract—just as it had been before the Australian intervention. In fact, the position of Melanesian workers was worse by comparison with September 1914. At that time, the monthly *average* pay of plantation workers had been five marks. In 1919, the sum of 5 shillings (1 shilling was equal to 1 mark) was established as the *maximum* legal pay. And after the expiry of his second work contract of three years, a worker was no longer automatically sent home but was permitted to conclude a third contract, which bound him to his employer for life.[125]

The recruitment of workers suffered most. The German administration had not been able to put an end to the excesses of the so-called labor recruiters by 1914. Now the situation escalated, assuming almost chaotic proportions. This development was fostered by a number of factors: the confusions of the war, the military administration's shortage of officials on the site, their lack of experience, the quick turnover in district officers, and probably also the willingness of quite a few military officials to turn a blind eye in return for a "consideration." The only constants in this situation were the use of armed force and the ruthlessness of the recruiters, competing with the ability of the Melanesians to take to their heels in time. The recruitment of Melanesian labor had become completely divorced from legal guidelines and taken on a life of its own that was no longer controlled; in fact, it had probably become uncontrollable, at least with existing means. The view that the Melanesians must be forced to provide labor for the European plantations—a view the German governor had successfully rejected to the last—now had influential advocates within the Australian military administration.[126] The German administration had banned the recruitment of unmarried women because of the obvious abuses to which they were subjected. Now they could be recruited with as little trouble as underage children.[127]

The recruitment of Melanesian labor is reminiscent of slaving expeditions in Africa or of serious organized crime. A plantation company that needed a new supply of labor would turn to a "recruiter," usually a planter, who passed on the order to an agent of his selection, generally a Chinese or Malay. The agent would take a troop of indigenous bearers and thugs into the jungle, and "recruit." The delegation of responsibility from top to bottom made it possible for companies and planters to pretend to be unaware of the conditions under which their workers had been recruited. At the same time, the procedure faithfully reflected the racist pecking order in the colony. At the end of 1919 the company paid the planter it had commissioned to supply laborers six pounds per worker delivered. Of this, he passed on three pounds per "head" to the Chinese recruiter, who gave his indigenous troop 5 shillings for every Melanesian "caught." The system was well known to the authorities, who did nothing to put an end to the inhuman practices.[128]

There was a sort of inner compulsion which increasingly drove the recruiters into hitherto unknown regions in order to complete their missions successfully. Melanesians who had witnessed the behavior of the recruiters and their men, and experienced the methods they used, took good care not to come into contact with them again. They fled from their villages when the guard set up for the purpose reported the arrival of the recruiters. Thus the labor recruiters penetrated ever more deeply into remote areas that had not yet come into contact with Europeans. Violence was the automatic consequence. Local men were killed, women raped, and children abducted from their parents—the whole scenario of ancient and modern slave hunting seemed to have been revived. Complete areas were in turmoil. Under Pethebridge, the excesses were to some extent restrained.[129] But in the period of transition after his death, and especially under his successor, Johnston, the last restraints were cast off. Everybody, it seemed, wanted to have a share in the business of recruiting. After hunting birds of paradise, capturing black workers now became the most profitable business in the occupied colony. In some areas, the two activities could be combined. Suddenly the European war no longer loomed large in relations between Germans and Australians. The worst German and Australian characters came to an understanding that allowed them to vent their aggression on the backs of the Melanesian population. Without hesitation, German planters cooperated with Australians and vice versa. Patrol and district officers requisitioned *luluai* to supply more local workers, and soldiers demanded their severance pay in order to increase their income by recruiting. Everywhere in New Guinea, but especially in Kaiser-Wilhelmsland, "a vast unexploited labour reserve,"[130] a gold-rush atmosphere, prevailed. The Administrator himself boasted that during his period of office, recruiting had penetrated much farther inland than ever before. He claimed that the recruiters not only brought work but were also bearers of civilization.[131]

There are reports from all parts of occupied German Melanesia about the unrest that gripped the local population as a consequence of the unrestrained behavior of the recruiters. Early in 1918 the Japanese trader Komine reported that all the places on the south coast of Neupommern (New Britain) which he had visited had been deserted for a distance of 160 miles. Fearing the recruiters, the local population had sought refuge in the interior. A little later, a Swede had a similar experience—"always the same story"—when unsuccessfully trying to find workers in twenty-two places in the same area.[132] Local eyewitnesses gave him an account of the "working methods" of the men accompanying the recruiter Patterson: "Shot some native pigs. . . . Creeping cautiously into the village, they met a native who on sighting them ran for his life. The boat's crew gave chase, and catching up with the man, struck him in the back with a tomahawk—the man fell and was left bleeding on the ground."[133]

Most of these incidents are not known to posterity because what happened deep in the jungle rarely came to the attention of the white public. Only when Europeans—traders, other recruiters, or missionaries—were shocked by the negative consequences of these events was some light thrown onto what had taken place in the bush. Sometimes the Melanesians who were affected also turned directly to Europeans and asked for help. Typically, in the cases of which we know, the Melanesians turned to the missions and not to the military administration. The Azera from the southeast of Kaiser-Wilhelmsland informed the Neuendettelsauer Mission that, in the hinterland of Morobe, the recruiters had mounted proper campaigns to abduct people. At least fourteen bush people had been shot, and many women and girls had been raped. Villages had been burnt, and huts and gardens plundered. During the whole operation and the forced abduction of the captured Melanesians, the Chinese and Malay recruiters, with their Melanesian troops, had secured the assistance of the neighboring enemies of their victims.[134]

A few months later, the responsible district officer personally visited some of the destroyed villages and met the intimidated population of his district.[135] Reports about the recruiters' excesses were coming in from everywhere.[136] Nonetheless, the first reaction was to sweep the matter under the carpet. The minister of defense personally ordered that the censors were to be instructed that no news about this or similar incidents was to reach the international public: "These reports would be calculated to seriously endanger our position at the Peace Conference and should not be permitted circulation or publication."[137]

During and after the peace conference, the excesses of recruiting went on in New Guinea, which continued to be under military administration. One reason was that the Australian district officers, if they themselves were not directly or indirectly involved in the business side of recruiting, did not regularly patrol the districts under their care (as had been the case under the Germans), and thus left the field open to criminals. The first large patrol undertaken under the auspices of the Australian military administration, in July 1920, discovered profoundly disturbed and frightened people deep in the bush in the south of New Britain. They complained bitterly about the recruiters and their behavior. The recruiters had brought measles and influenza with them, and the patrol saw evidence of the many fatalities which these had caused.[138] The new Administrator, Brigadier Thomas Griffiths, acting in response to reports by his district officers, at last decided offically to close at least two areas for recruiting because of the "present unsettled state of affairs."[139]

The extent to which the people of former German New Guinea were pressed to enter European service as workers under the Australian military administration can be statistically illustrated. On 1 January 1913, 17,930 Melanesians were employed by Europeans in the "old protectorate" (New Guinea excluding Micronesia); 14,990 of these (83.6 percent) were plantation laborers.[140] On 1 January 1914, there were 17,529 plantation laborers out of a total of about 20,000 Melanesian workers.[141] There is no data for the total number of Melanesian workers under the Australian military administration, but the statistics for plantation workers demonstrate the large increase in their number during the final years of the military administration. By 1919 the number of Melanesian plantation workers of both sexes had risen to 22,622, an increase of 29 percent as compared with 1914. Between 1913 and 1919 the number of workers and police employed by the government increased from 1,040 to 2,819—that is, by 171 percent![142] On the last day of the military administration, 9 May 1921, 27,428 Melanesian men and women were employed by European planters—almost 10,000 more than in 1914.[143] The overwhelming majority of these workers were men. Given that a census in 1920 counted a total male indigenous population of only 70,581 (including children and old people), in 1921 about 35 percent of the total male population of the area of New Guinea that had been opened up was in permanent European employment. Of an estimated total population of 167,000 under the influence of the administration, about 16.5 percent were in European employment. Toward the end of the effective German administration, this figure had been between about 10 and 12 percent.[144]

In a number of regions, more than alarming figures were reached. In the colony's Mecca, Rabaul, the figure for workers employed was 25 percent higher than the original male population of the area. Thirty percent of all New Guinea's workers were concentrated in the area of Rabaul/Kokopo. At most, 10 percent of men lived with their wives; the rest increasingly developed homosexual tendencies.[145] In Talasea, in the southwest of New Britain, 84 percent of the male population was in European employment; in Madang the figure was 67.2, and in Manus, 66 percent.[146]

Hahl had intended to regulate the recruitment of workers more strongly and to abolish abuses because he was convinced that there was a connection between the excessive employment of Melanesians by Europeans and the noticable decline of the population in many areas of the protectorate.[147] After Pethebridge's unsuccessful attempt to implement Hahl's plans, the business of labor recruitment in New Guinea had cast off all regulation and had gotten completely out of control. The German planters and settlers who had been restrained, with difficulty, by the colonial administration under Hahl, suddenly saw a chance to realize their dreams, which had never been crushed, of New Guinea as a colony that was there exclusively for their personal use, and of the Melanesians as objects freely available to them for use in achieving their aims. In real terms, New Guinea became a different colony between 1917 and 1921. It was a colony in which the high priority given to economic success swept away almost all the barriers that had been erected between 1900 and 1914 to protect the indigenous population. The procedure, typical of the German colonial administration, of systematically but carefully expanding the areas in which European ideas took precedence, was submerged in the onslaught of the unleashed labor recruiters. For many segments of the Melanesian population who had hitherto been unaware of the European presence, this sort of cultural contact was a considerable shock. The Australian prime minister's special commissioner for New Guinea, comparing the census results of 1914 and 1920/1921, believed that they demostrated precisely what Hahl had suspected in 1913: the decline in the Melanesian population in some parts of the country was attributable to excessive labor recruitment. From the statistics available to him, he calculated that the population had fallen by 1.9 percent annually between 1914 and 1921. The ratio of adult women to adult men, which had been calculated as 100:123 in 1914, had declined to 100:164 by 1920.[148] The change was particularly dramatic in Neu Mecklenburg/New Ireland, where 12,000 fewer people (or one quarter less) were counted in 1920 than in 1914.[149]

PUNISHMENTS

The history of Australia as a British penal colony, where flogging was an everyday occurrence, had made the white population highly aware of this type of punishment. A central plank of the German plantation economy, however, had been the right of employers to administer disciplinary corporal punishment to their Melanesian workers, with the permission of the authorities. The fact that many plantation laborers ran away after German rule effectively stopped seemed to ring in the end of the plantation economy. On the instructions of the first Administrator, Holmes, workers were forced to return to their employers. The officers involved indulged in downright orgies of beating.[150] After the return of the workers, everything on the plantations at first continued to run as it had before the occupation. The only difference was that planters received authorization to flog their workers from the military administration instead of from the German local authorities. The labor ordinance of July 1915 limited the number of strokes to ten, but did not, in principle, change the old procedure.[151] When the new ordinance was made known in Australia, the minister of defense in the Labor government, Pearce, instructed the Administrator, by telegraph, to abolish corporal punishment immediately. On 15 August 1915 Pethebridge abolished flogging as a disciplinary punishment administered by employers, but reintroduced it immediately as part of the repertoire of criminal justice. The minister indicated that he accepted this solution, on the condition that flogging was the penalty only for the same offenses as in Australia. Thereupon, in September 1915, the Administrator issued a proclamation that permitted the flogging of indigenous people to be authorized by district officers, the officer in charge of native affairs, and the judge in Rabaul only for the most serious crimes, such as murder and rape. Such cases were to be preceded by a detailed investigation, and twenty strokes could now be administered.[152]

Since the New Guinea Company had introduced a criminal code for indigenous people in German New Guinea, the sanctions it prescribed had not changed: fines; prison sentences, with and without compulsory labor, of up to five years; and the death sentence. In theory, the same punishments could have been imposed on Europeans, with the exceptions that there was no time limit on prison sentences for them and that sentencing a white person to death in the colony was simply impossible. Pethebridge's decision officially made flogging an instrument of criminal justice specifically for the indigenous population for the first time in the German Pacific. A racist criminal law, which did not exist before, was introduced. It represented a considerable deterioration in the legal position of the "free" indigenous people, in particular. Although they had theoretically been under a European code of laws before, they had not been exposed to the whip as had the Melanesian laborers. The situation was similar to that in neighboring Australian-administered Papua and approached that prevailing in Germany's African colonies.

In theory, the position of the Melanesian contract laborers, however, fundamentally improved overnight. If the abolition of flogging as a disciplinary punishment for Melanesian workers had been permanent, and the whole enterprise had not been exposed as a fraud, the Australian Labor government and the military administration in Rabaul would rightly have gone down in history as dragon-slayers, eradicating the degrading labor conditions in German New Guinea. But it soon became apparent that the regulations existed only on paper, because officials in the outer stations interpreted them as meaning that flogging could continue but could only be administered by them, or with their express approval.[153] In addition, the same factor that had already frustrated attempts by the early military administration to remedy abuses in the recruitment of labor came into play. If the colony was to be economically productive, then mechanisms to suppress the indigenous workers were indispensable; and corporal punishment was the alpha and omega of the functioning European colony of New Guinea.

The large German plantation companies, missionaries, and the Australian officer in charge of native affairs, Ogilvy, argued for the reintroduction of flogging for labor offenses.[154] Early in December 1915 the Administrator submitted an official request for this. As well as the oft-cited reason that more and more Melanesians were refusing to obey orders, Pethebridge pointed to the practice of corporal punishment on the British Gilbert Islands and also mentioned the allegedly growing danger of white women being molested by indigenous men. The minister of defense, Pearce, officially sanctioned the procedure suggested by Pethebridge. Under its terms the military administration and the district officers could, from January 1916, administer "corporal punishment of a more merciful kind" in cases of theft, desertion from work, offenses against women, "gross insubordination," arson, or assault.[155] Nominally, all that had happened was that the offenses punishable by flogging had been extended. But they had not merely been multiplied; qualitatively different offenses were now liable to corporal punishment, compared with September 1915. For example, running away from work, previously a disciplinary matter, had now become a criminal offense. The catch-all phrase "gross insubordination" revealed the real intention behind the measure. Gross insubordination covered everything for which a worker had been flogged in German times. The prohibition on corporal punishment as a disciplinary measure for offenses at work lasted less than five months, even in its theoretical form. The situation thereafter was worse even than that of July 1915, against which the minister of defense had intervened in the first place. At that time a maximum of ten stokes could be administered. Now it was twenty again, just as in German times.

Overshadowed by the war and protected by press censorship, occupied German New Guinea increasingly developed into a colony in which the interests of the planters and the colonial companies were given the priority they had always demanded but had never yet fully achieved. In March 1918 the list of offenses punishable by flogging was extended to include adultery and lying to an official authority.[156] The war was already over when the new labor ordinance of 1 January 1919 again extended the list of offenses subject to corporal punishment. It could now be imposed in a total of eighteen cases, which can be divided roughly into one-third sexual offenses, one-third labor offenses, and one-third serious criminal offenses. Employers had the additional right to put their workers under confinement in chains.[157] The end of the war had turned Australia's attention more than before toward the mysterious tropical north, where a German colony seemed about to be transferred into Australian hands. On 27 February 1919 the *Sydney Bulletin* published a cartoon of a German planter beating a Melanesian victim while an Australian soldier stood guard. The artist was the most famous Australian caricaturist of his day, Norman Lindsay. There was an outcry among the Australian public. Pressure on the government became so strong that on 10 March 1919 the Australian cabinet ordered the abolition of flogging in New Guinea, which was still under military administration.[158]

Thereupon the Administrator in Rabaul almost outdid himself in defending corporal punishment—"the best possible and most effective means of enforcing discipline, obedience, and drilling into the minds of our natives who are not ill treated nor illused by such canings any more than a horse which requires a certain amount of corrective control with a whip"—and demanded drastic alternative punishments, for the "calaboose" (*Kalabus:* Tok Pisin for prison) "is the native's paradise."[159] Three hundred pairs of handcuffs and 100 leg irons were to be sent to New Guinea immediately by the next ship. Experimental models of a type of pillory had already been produced in Rabaul.

"Staining the Australian flag," by Norman Lindsay. (*The Bulletin,* 27 February 1919)

Melanesian prisoners sentenced to labor were to work in chains and be forced to break stones; their working hours were to be considerably increased; and in order to make their status more clearly visible, in the future their hair was to be close-cropped and they were to wear a brightly colored lavalava.[160] The equipment of a medieval chamber of horrors was to offer a substitute for the corporal punishment that had been abolished.

Johnston introduced the pillory as the favored replacement for flogging. He had two models to choose from. In one, the offender with legs stretched apart was strapped onto a seat; in the other, he had to stand on a public platform where his hands and head were tied. The Administrator decided in favor of the public platform. This type of punishment seems to have been used from as early as mid-March 1919, but did not become legal until the issuing of Administration Order No. 636 on 3 December 1919.[161] It became known as Field Punishment No. 1 for Natives. In New Guinea, however, this punishment, as it was applied in practice, did not comply, in one detail, with the British military penal code on which it was based. The Melanesian fastened to an iron bar with outstretched arms did not have full foot contact with the ground. In a complete perversion of an already perverted punishment, offenders were attached to the bar in such a way that their full body weight was taken by the

Field Punishment No. 1 in its mild form. The date given (1915) is probably too early, as this form of punishment seems to have been introduced after Administrator Johnston was in charge of the colony. (Marie von Hein Collection, Mitchell Library, State Library of New South Wales)

wrists. A special procedure was used to ensure that only the tips of their toes could touch the ground. In this way, unfortunate Melanesians were exposed to the tropical heat for up to three days at a time. Because of their loud cries, the victims were called "birds" by their tormentors.[162]

A Methodist pastor hurrying past on 1 December 1919 saw four Melanesians strung up in this manner. Four more lay on the ground, waiting to be tied to the bar. He went to fetch Administrator Johnston, who had introduced this procedure, although he was not personally responsible for the perversion of the perversion. Johnston called what he saw "really a species of torture, which was revolting."[163]

Captain Tennent, the officer in command responsible for native affairs, was dismissed and sent back to Australia. Field Punishment No. 1 for Natives, however, was not at first abolished. In Geneva, the Australian representative on the mandate commission claimed that this sort of punishment was "confined to military discipline."[164] A German planter who used Field Punishment No. 1 on his own plantation later justified himself by pointing out that he had only done what the administration had been doing for a long time. His argument must have been convincing, for although the worker he had punished in this way did not survive the consequences of the ordeal, the planter left the central court in Rabaul a free man after paying a fine of £100. "Field punishment" does not seem to have been abolished in New Guinea until 1922.[165]

Corporal punishment itself was removed from the indigenous labor ordinance by an amendment of 23 May 1919. The political change of direction, however, took place only on paper. Those who continued to flog were, if a charge was brought against them, declared to have contravened the labor ordinance; but they were rarely fined.[166] Even these "show trials," however, soon stopped. After a short period of reflection, the whipping of indigenous workers gradually began again. At first individual district officers beat workers themselves or authorized floggings.[167] Bit by bit, planters too went back to using the old method in full. In 1921, during the transition from military to civil administration, an Australian eyewitness in New Guinea did not come across a single planter or district officer who had not used physical violence against a Melanesian at some time. Officially, locals could complain to the district officer, but in practice they did not.[168] Nor did the civil administration, which abolished the other types of punishment the employers could use,[169] do anything to put an end to this situation. A great deal of evidence exists that flogging, as the punishment that whites preferred to administer to their Melanesian dependents, continued to exist in Australian New Guinea.[170] Even after 1914/1921, New Guinea remained a colony in which the whip dominated relations between Europeans and the local population. The only difference between the German and the Australian method was that, under the Germans floggings were officially permitted, and the historian can find documented statistics about officially authorized and approved brutality. As corporal punishment officially no longer existed from 1919, there are, of course, no statistics for the Australian period. The German mania for bureaucratizing brutality was replaced by Australian hypocrisy, intent on maintaining a facade of humanity but tolerating brutality on the spot. Its degree and frequency were now, in practice, left up to district officers in each case. As an integral part of the Australian code of native criminal justice, flogging in New Guinea continued from its introduction in September 1915 until after the Second World War.[171]

THE MILITARY ADMINISTRATION AND THE RIGHTS OF "FREE" MELANESIANS IN PACIFIED NEW GUINEA

Those Melanesians who lived in their villages and had become part of the system governed by the German colonial administration fell outside the scope of the special labor regulations. Cooperation between them and the administration was based on the system of indirect rule through *luluai* and *tultul* introduced by Hahl. The point of this system was less to transmit official orders via local agents of the colonial goverment than to relieve the German colonial judiciary. Most intra-Melanesian disputes could be settled by the *luluai* on the basis of the Melanesian principle of compensation, without European intervention and without court proceedings.

At first, even after the Australian occupation, little seems to have changed in this procedure for that part of the local population of New Guinea which the Germans, interestingly enough, called "free" (in contrast, presumably, to the "unfree" Melanesian workers). The Australians registered surprised disapproval at the existence of the indigenous institutions of *luluai* and *tultul*, which Governor Murray had firmly rejected for neighboring Papua and which the Australian Aborigines did not possess. Pethebridge mockingly called them "loo loo eyes" and "tool tools."[172] As long as the district officers limited their activities to the immediate surroundings of the government stations, as was generally the case during the European war, there was little encroachment on the space the Germans had granted the Melanesian model of conflict resolution. But with the end of the war the situation changed. Although the military administration was to stay in office for a further two and a half years, greater efforts were now made to bring the affairs of the indigenous free people more firmly under Australian control. At the end of 1920 the positions of *luluai* and *tultul* were officially recognized by the new colonial masters. Their functions, however, were reduced to administrative tasks. The *luluai* became the first assistant to the colonial administration in village society; the *tultul*, as his Pisin-speaking translator, the deputy assistant. In principle, the *luluai* retained the role, which the German colonial administration had given to him, of arbitrator in everyday Melanesian disputes, but his judicial authority was considerably reduced. In particular, he lost the right to treat any resistance to his position as contempt of the existing order and to punish it accordingly. This undermined the *luluai*'s authority, and the system of internal arbitration began to collapse. The position of the district officer had been strengthened at the expense of the *luluai*. The *luluai* now also had to pass on to the district officer the shell money which he had imposed in fines, and which, under the Germans, he had been permitted to keep as remuneration for his work. Only one year later, a special native administration ordinance revoked all the *luluai*'s remaining legal prerogatives. The only semilegal task left to him was to act as the police bailiff, whose job it was to ensure that an indigenous defendant appeared before the European court.[173]

It is not clear whether the Australian administration was fully aware of the significant differences between the system in force at the time of the German colonial administration and the situation under their rule. At any rate, this fact has so far escaped Australian historians.[174] Yet the end of official toleration of an autonomous area of Melanesian legal authority was one of the crucial turning points separating the Australian from the German colonial administration. To be sure, this change in everyday reality was probably not so acute and abrupt as it seems if we merely look at the regulations. In many areas, the Australian aspiration to deal with all intra-Melanesian conflicts at first lay far beyond the administration's actual means. In fact, the Melanesian model of conflict resolution by internal arbitration and compensation continued, even in the already pacified regions, without the *luluai* who prescribed the compensation payments immediately getting into trouble. However, the fact that his behavior now, unlike before 1914, was officially no longer permitted, made the functioning of Melanesian legal autonomy highly dependent on internal acceptance and on simply being far enough away from the centers of administration. The closer a village was to a center of European administration, the less likely it was that the *luluai* could continue to exercise his old legal functions. In time, the Australian administration penetrated ever more deeply into the hinterland of the pacified zone, and thus the areas of Melanesian legal autonomy constantly decreased. In these terms 1920/1921, not 1914, was a turning point in Melanesian–European relations.

Compared with this crucial difference between the German and the Australian approach to "native questions," all other interventions by the Australian military administration in local affairs were of secondary significance. The noticeably more assimilationist Australian approach toward the Melanesian population was also in evidence here. But in this context, another point must be emphasized. The complete transfer of intra-Melanesian disputes to European colonial justice increased the tendency toward bureaucratization. Previously, the compensation payments prescribed by the Melanesian "judge," equipped with the full authority of the German colonial administration, had restabilized the system of social interaction. One advantage of this procedure for the administration had been that public order had been reestablished without great expense. The other cases had been decided relatively quickly by the *Bezirksamtmann*, at little cost and involving few staff. All in all, it was an extremely cost-efficient system, which was free for the local population. During the military administration, cases that could not be settled by the district officer (the highest fine he could impose was £15), went before the officer in charge of native affairs in Rabaul. The local people had to contribute one pound per person to court costs. After the abolition of corporal punishment, the Administrator introduced an additional translation fee of two shillings and sixpence for each local person who needed the services of an English translator.[175] This was, quite obviously, an attempt to keep to a minimum actions for mistreatment brought by local people against Europeans: the right to justice was dependent on the income of the plaintiff. This was, indeed, a completely new experience for the people of New Guinea.

THE AUSTRALIAN MILITARY ADMINISTRATION AND THE LIMITS OF "CIVILIZATION"

The military administration at first had very limited contact with Melanesians outside the areas subject to the administration. The German administrative region shrank; the stations at Angoram and Burgberg were given up. Typically, the military administration made its first contact with Melanesians who were not, or no longer, subject to the administration in connection with its efforts to put the plantation economy back on to its feet. In December 1914 native policemen in Manus who had been sent into the bush to recapture runaway plantation workers killed a villager and took a number of hostages. Two of the hostages were shot while trying to escape. In May 1915, three indigenous people lost their lives while being pursued as deserters from the Forsayth plantation in northern Neupommern (New Britain).[176] From early 1915, there was permanent unrest in the south and west of Neupommern because of the activities of the recruiter Samuel McKay and his Melanesian troops. When McKay and his companions were murdered, the unrest got as far as the offices in Rabaul. Two punitive expeditions in May killed five Melanesians, took women and children hostage, burned houses, destroyed gardens, and gave the pigs belonging to the inhabitants to the local police as booty.[177] This did nothing to calm the local population. The officer in charge of native affairs, Captain H. Balfour Ogilvy, now thought he should take matters in hand himself. Again villages were burned and gardens destroyed. He had instructed the police boys to continue shooting into the villages until they heard his whistle. Moreover, he had offered five shillings per head for every male Melanesian caught. When Ogilvy finally blew his whistle and the police were supposed to capture the Melanesians, the police preferred to make short work of it. At least sixteen Melanesians were killed. As a further deterrent, Ogilvy had the body of a dead Melanesian strung up in a main street. With the retrospective agreement of the Administrator, two other bodies were decapitated and the heads put on display where the recruiter had allegedly been murdered.[178] This procedure is reminiscent of German New Guinea's earlier colonial past, when it was still administered by the Neuguinea-Kompanie and the administrator of this company, Curt von Hagen, was murdered in 1897; his murderers, the native policemen Ranga and Opia, were decapitated and their heads put on public display.[179] However, the colonial administration that had been taken over by the German government in 1899 had always avoided such excesses.

In November 1915 Ogilvy repeated the whole process on Bougainville. At the request of the manager of the Soraken Plantation, which belonged to Burns Philp, neighboring tribes into whose villages plantation workers had escaped, and who had not sent them back after having been ordered to do so, were "taught a lesson." Again the native policemen continued to shoot into the villages until the white officer blew his whistle; four Melanesians were killed. One of them was shot dead on the police officer's orders while he was lying defenseless on the ground. Pethebridge had given the instruction beforehand to carry out the death sentence on the spot. Another man, accused of cannibalism, had his head cut off for identification.[180] The manager of the Burns Philp plantation summed up his opinion of the Australian punitive expedition's actions thus: "I have seen some smart police patrol work in various parts of the world but nothing smarter than that of Capt. Ogilvy and his merry men."[181] In 1916 and 1917, District Officers McGregor and Hunter undertook further punitive expeditions against the indigenous people in the south of Bougainville. Locals were ill treated and shot, apparently at random. Hundreds were intimidated and fled to the neighboring British Shortland Islands. On the mainland of New Guinea, Ogilvy's brother, Captain W. M. B. Ogilvy, as district officer of Madang, led a number of punitive expeditions against the people of the district in August and September 1915. There were also deaths in Madang, but the bodies seem not to have been mutilated.[182]

Under Johnston, conflicts between the local people and the military administration escalated as a result of unsupervised recruitment. The Administrator had direct responsibility for this policy, which practically gave the recruiters a free hand, making abuses the rule, not the exception. Most punitive expeditions were revenge campaigns by the administration for the murders of recruiters. It was almost always Germans whose unrestrained methods provoked resistance among the local population, thus giving cause for punitive expeditions by the government. In May and June 1918, two German recruiters were killed in the Sepik district when, despite a warning, they had assaulted a local woman. Captain Hunter led two punitive expeditions to discipline the local population, but the people did not calm down, because the unrestrained recruiting continued. In another punitive action, at least twelve Melanesians were killed in November 1918.[183]

The largest punitive expedition mounted by the Australian Military Administration was again to the Sepik district. And again, the cause was a German recruiter, who complained to the Administrator in Madang that his troops had been attacked while recruiting. Although Johnston was aware that the behavior of the recruiter had caused the disturbance—he did not deny that he had shot between twenty-five and thirty Melanesians—the Administrator simply accepted that it was only the Melanesians who had to be brought to see reason. A steamer equipped with a cannon, two machine guns, fifteen Australians, and seventy-five Melanesian police soldiers steamed up and down the Sepik, bombarded villages, destroyed a *tambaran* (mens'/ancestors') house, collected the human heads displayed there for an Australian museum, and took hostages. This expedition apparently cost only a few human lives.[184]

Retrospectively to excuse Administrator Johnston, who was primarily responsible for the uncontrolled explosion of recruiting because he had given orders to the expedition as far as possible to avoid spilling blood,[185] is both unjustified and historically untenable.[186] Either Johnston was extremely naive, or he simply did not want to know what was constantly happening in the colony under his control. In either case, he was a most unsuitable person to fill the post of Administrator. During his period in office, the central administration lost the last vestiges of the authority it had still retained under Pethebridge. Anarchy and chaos were the result. Under the arbitrary rule of individual district officers and the unrestrained behavior of recruiters, the indigenous population suffered as it had not done since the days of the Neuguinea-Kompanie. In fact, much that happened in the Johnston era is reminiscent of the New Guinea Company's period of administration: the intemperate, uncontrolled behavior of the whites toward the Melanesians, the frenzy of exploitation, and the taking of justice into one's own hands.

How did German and Australian punitive expeditions against the local people differ? At first glance, they seem similar in many respects: the idea that conflicts could be resolved by the superior arms technology of the Europeans; the way in which expeditions were mounted, rather like organized campaigns against an enemy power; the taking of hostages; and the destruction of life and property. The difference between the German colonial and the Australian military administrations lies elsewhere. Under Hahl, the Germans developed a purposeful policy of pacifying New Guinea. Working from its bases in Herbertshöhe/Rabaul in the Bismarck Archipelago and Friedrich-Wilhelmshafen on the mainland, the German administrative organization aimed gradually to extend its borders. Any resistance to European rule was to be met with force. It is pretty certain that, at the beginning, German punitive expeditions were more extensive and cost more human lives than those mounted by the Australian Military Administration. But the excessive brutality that was not uncharacteristic of the period 1914/1921 was practically unknown during German rule after 1900. In addition, as time went by, German punitive measures increasingly lost their original character as campaigns of revenge. The traditional form of German punitive expedition as retaliation for the murder of Europeans was replaced more and more by action to put an end to purely intra-Melanesian tribal warfare and blood feuds. This frequently began to happen in response to Melanesian requests, and it increasingly replaced the old warlike behavior. The area subject to German administration, which had largely been expanded by punitive expeditions, was secured by the establishment of government stations. Local station leaders had a great deal of freedom in building up relations with the indigenous population, but the basis of this policy was decided by the governor in Herbertshöhe/Rabaul, not by individual local officials. By 1914 the Pax Germanica had developed an impetus of its own, which carried it out into areas not yet under its control, almost without the government itself having to do anything.

No system is recognizable in the Australian campaigns undertaken between 1914 and 1921. The military administration did not develop a policy to pacify the Melanesian population. If the administration had really limited itself to maintaining the status quo, it would presumably have got by with pure administration. But from Administrator Johnston's period in office, if not before, individual Europeans were constantly overstepping the official limits set, without the administration doing anything about it. Conflicts with the local people were an inevitable consequence. The situation was not made any easier for the administration by the fact that the European intruders were motivated by private interests, not by any interest in pacifying hitherto unopened regions. The position was now exactly the opposite of what it had been in the period before the outbreak of the European war. During the German period, the administration was pushing ahead, securing its organization by appointing *tultul* and *luluai*, and building up government stations. Only at this stage were recruiters allowed in. Now the order was reversed: the recruiters came first, followed by the administration. The latter limited itself to purely punitive measures. The Sepik was a typical case. The German station at Angoram was closed, and constant reprisals seemed necessary. This was a regression to conditions in the period before and shortly after the turn of the century, when punitive expeditions had been acts of revenge by Europeans. Almost all Australian punitive expeditions were a reaction to the murder of Europeans, who had overstepped official limits and invaded by force hitherto unpacified regions. The Australians hardly began to arbitrate in intra-Melanesian community disputes as the German colonial administration had done.[187]

Punitive expeditions were not dictated by any policy toward the actions that undermined the limits set by the administration. They were more an outlet for day-to-day political problems and the result of ad hoc decisions than the outcome of long-term political planning.[188] For the indigenous people, the center of European power was no longer Rabaul but the local district officer. He had almost unlimited authority to make decisions, as there was practically no control from Rabaul. Power was often abused, as this account has tried to show. Thus the impression was established that Australian rule was arbitrary rule, because it depended on the mood of a few individuals. The high-handedness of the officers was, at times, shocking. Self-criticism hardly existed. The only people who occasionally dared to criticize the officers were the missionaries. In Manus, a Catholic priest complained to the district officer that after the killing of a planter, two punitive expeditions against the Drukul had only produced

even greater unrest. Thirteen villages had been reduced to ashes, thirteen people had been killed, and the district officer had abducted eighty-two young
people. For a fee, he had given them to the big planter Hernsheim for three
months. "That you should aspire to criticise the action taken by the District
Officer . . . is really outrageous. . . . I am not used to disobedience to my orders.
. . . It would perhaps be as well to say right here, Father, that I am the
appointed custodian of the natives of this District."[189] Soon thereafter the district officer started another punitive expedition against the Drukul. In this
action, the white men on the expedition raped the women taken as hostages.[190]

The German administration had been remarkably restrained in applying
European legal norms to Melanesian blood feuders, cannibals, headhunters,
and poisoners. Exile with forced labor had become established as the usual
punishment; the length of the sentence rarely exceeded three years, and never
five. Death sentences were extremely rare, and were most likely to be imposed
and executed in "political" cases. The Australian soldiers streaming into the
country were well aware of this "soft" German approach, which was noted as a
feature characteristic of the German colony.[191]

Australian practice toward the Aborigines was completely different. In the
Northern Territory, one of the last refuges of the original inhabitants of the
continent, executions were certainly nothing unusual.[192] We do not know for
sure when the first Melanesian was executed by the Australian Military Administration; but we can be sure that it happened on an outlying station, where
officers did not hesitate to take decisions concerning life and death on their
own authority. The administration found out that this was so merely by chance.
A police master who had been brought to Rabaul for drunkenness while on
duty and fighting with another soldier admitted that on the orders of his superior he had had a local man, Kaipath, shot in Namatanai. No trial had taken
place. Even less had the regulations of the German law still in force been
observed. These prescribed the presence of two assessors *(Beisitzer)* in the
case of a death sentence being passed against an indigenous defendant, and the
governor's consent had to be obtained before the sentence was carried out. The
clause concerning the presence of two assessors was ignored until mid-August
1918, although the Australians were aware of its existence.[193] Not even the
Administrator had been informed in the case mentioned above. The only evidence available was a confession by Kaipath, transcribed by a priest, that he
had practised cannibalism. Kaipath had been lured to his execution by the
promise of a new hat, stick (he was evidently *luluai*), and lavalava.[194]

The Administrator immediately issued instructions that, in future, death
sentences were to be carried only with his explicit written permission. Thereupon reports began to come in from all over New Guinea about death sentences that had recently been imposed and carried out. The official responsible
for Neu Mecklenburg (New Ireland) even had two Melanesians shot after the
Administrator issued his instructions. He justified himself by claiming that he
had received the instructions too late. The deed of which the two Melanesians

were accused was a classic example of traditional Melanesian pay-back. But only one of them had committed the crime; the other had not even been present. Two more Melanesians were unlucky enough to have been seen in the company of the culprit. Although there was no evidence of their complicity, they were sentenced to six years' imprisonment for aiding and abetting.[195]

The cases we know about are certainly only the tip of the iceberg. They provide one more illustration of high-handed rule by the Australian officers in all areas outside Rabaul. This behavior also demonstrates a completely different attitude toward Melanesian actions from that expressed during the German period. Traditional behavior was no longer regarded as a mitigating circumstance in cases of violent death, which were now condemned as straightforward murder and punished by execution. Under Administrator Johnston, at the latest, the death sentence became a general tool of native policy in the Australian Military Administration. Strikingly, Johnston had the first execution during his period of office carried out only after the abolition of corporal punishment. It took place at the scene of the alleged crime, before 430 onlookers, including 300 women and children. This guaranteed, according to the Administrator, that it was "most impressive." The reason for the execution was almost certainly the result of a Melanesian blood feud.[196]

After Johnston, Griffiths, and Wisdom, the common models of Australian criminal justice for the indigenous people included public executions—which, by the end, the German administration had given up—and execution at the scene of the crime, a procedure the German administration had prohibited before the turn of the century because it feared that it would only perpetuate the cycle of blood feuding.[197] The method of execution preferred by the Australians was hanging. Because of bad experiences with this method, the German administration had replaced hanging with shooting.[198] It was not uncommon for the Australian Administrator to grant reprieves, but even here the German criminal law that was still in force was not always observed, and the longest sentence that could be given to Melanesians was increased from five to ten years.[199]

In a little over a year, between 1 January 1920 and 8 May 1921 (the end of the military administration) alone, the Australian Military Administration pronounced almost as many death sentences as the German administration of New Guinea had throughout its whole period in office from the turn of the century. In any case, the number of death sentences given by the Australians between September 1914 and February 1921 in New Guinea exceeds the total of all death sentences imposed in the whole of Germany's Pacific sphere of influence (New Guinea, Micronesia, and Samoa) between 1900 and 1914. Between July 1918 and February 1921 at least as many Melanesians in New Guinea were executed as between 1900 and 1914.

If we also take into account that by far the majority of the German death sentences and executions were "politically" motivated—such as the emergency regulations directed against the alleged fomenters of the Friedrich-Wilhelms-

Public hanging of a Chinese by the Australian Military Administration in Rabaul. (Thomas J. Denham, *New Guinea Notebook*, Mitchell Library, State Library of New South Wales)

TABLE 7.   The Death Sentence in the Criminal Justice
Administered to the Indigenous Population of
New Guinea by the German Colonial Govern-
ment ("Old Protectorate," excluding Micronesia)

YEARS	NUMBER OF DEATH SENTENCES IMPOSED	NUMBER OF THESE PARDONED
1899–1900	1	
1900–1901	0	
1901–1902	0	
1902–1903	0	
1903–1904	1[a]	1
1904–1905	23[b]	5
1905–1906	2	
1906–1907	0	
1907–1908	0	
1908–1909	1	
1909–1910	0	
1910–1911	0[c]	
1911–1912	1	
1912–1913	6	3[d]
TOTALS	35	9

[a]Plus one Chinese (pardoned; Hahl, 23 October 1903, to the Colonial
Department; BAP: RKolA no. 4949).
[b]Fifteen death sentences imposed by courts-martial in connection with the
Friedrich-Wilhelmshafen "revolt."
[c]No indigenous people, but one Chinese.
[d]*Stationsleiter* Arbinger, Eitape, 20 January 1913, to the Bezirksamt Friedrich-
Wilhelmshafen; AAC: AA 1963/83 Bun 64.

Source: *Jahresberichte über die Entwicklung der deutschen Schutzgebiete.
Statistischer Teil.*

hafen conspiracy and the murderers involved in the Baining massacre—then
the huge difference between German practice and that of the Australian military administration becomes even clearer. As far as we know, in none of the
Australian judgments were Melanesians accused of murdering Europeans. In
the majority of cases, the offenses were typical Melanesian pay-backs, for
which the accused would have received three years' exile with hard labor from
the German administration. In twenty months the Australian military executed
more than eight times as many people for intra-Melanesian acts of violence as
the German colonial administration had done in the fourteen years during
which it had been in office.

On 31 March 1921 the new Administrator, Major General Wisdom, the
last military and the first civil governor, celebrated his appointment by giving a
party for officers in the Baining district, where he attended the public hanging

TABLE 8.   The Death Sentence in the Criminal Justice
Administered to the Indigenous Population
of New Guinea by the Australian Military
Government (September 1914–8 May 1921)

YEAR	NUMBER OF DEATH SENTENCES IMPOSED	NUMBER OF THESE PARDONED
1914	?	
1915	5[a]	
1916	1	1
1917	?	
1918	9	9(?)
1919	13	8
1920	28	16
1921 (to 8 May)	5	
TOTALS	61	34(?)

[a]Plus a Chinese; *Namanula Times,* no. 2, 1 January 1916, 4 (mockery of an obituary).

Sources: Pethebridge, Report nos. A 4 and A 15; AWM: 33/12–10. District Officer Charles Cork, Kaewieng, 17 April 1916 to the Administrator; AAC: AA 1963/83, Bun 245: 259/16. Intelligence Reports Administrator Johnston, Griffiths, and Wisdom, nos. 4A, 6, 9, 15, 18, 20, 23, 24, 25, 26, 28, 30, 31, and 32; AAC: CP 103/11—NG Reports 2/15. Central Court, Rabaul. Criminal Cases (Gerichtsbuch 1919/1920); AAC: AA 1963/83, Bun 239. Native Affairs Correspondence 1915–1918; AAC: AA 1963/83, Bun 240. *Government Gazette Rabaul,* 5 (1918)–8 (1921). Cf. Nelson 1978.

Note: This data represents minimum figures. Lack of standardized material and gaps in the statistics mean that no complete overview can be given.

of two Suvlitt people. Two weeks later two more Suvlitt people were executed in their home district, in front of two hundred people. One of the two tried to escape, but was recaptured by the police. However, a number of attempts had to be made before the Suvlitts were hanged. Heavy rain made the ropes slippery, turning the hanging into a long-drawn-out and difficult matter.[200] It was the worst start imaginable for the new man in Rabaul. The background to the executions carried out with such difficulty is remarkable in every respect, because it casts light into the shadows surrounding the way in which the military administration treated the Melanesians who lived outside its administrative organization.

Ruthless recruiting had deeply unsettled the people in the Baining district, as everywhere in New Guinea. The beneficiaries of the uncontrolled recruitment tolerated by the Johnston Administration included the Catholic Sacred Heart Mission, which needed labor for its plantations and mission grounds. It had already come into conflict with the Melanesians during the German period

because of its practice of removing children and young people from the influence of their parents and relations to bring them up as Christians on the
mission station.[201] The Catholic mission exploited the military administration's
inactivity in order to continue their old policy by tougher means. Led by
Garuki, the Malay overseer of the mission plantation in Mandras, a group of
ten Melanesians forced their way into a Suvlitt village at the end of 1917 to
coerce young villagers into going with them to the mission as workers. In a
bloody clash, five of the attackers were killed, but twenty-four young Suvlitt
people were abducted, including a number of children. Two children each of
the Melanesians Kaining (Kaning) and the Bikman Aluaite (Aluet) were
abducted.[202]

For the abducted children and young people, the Catholic Sacred Heart
mission station was not only an alien world but a prison. Within a short time fifteen of them had died. When the news reached the Baining district, the Bikman Aluaite urged Kaining to take revenge. Both had lost a child in the
mission. Local custom dictated that Kaining had to obey his Bikman. Even if
Kaining had refrained from blood vengeance despite the loss of his own child,
it would have been impossible for him to ignore the order he had been given.
Such an action would probably have led to his own death. In September 1919
Kaining killed the Baining man Sanganieki, who was paid by the mission to
provide Melanesian recruits. Sanganieki had obviously also been involved in
the raid led by the Malay in 1917, for before Kaining struck the fatal blow with
his axe, he called out to his victim: "You have abducted my two children and
given them to the Mission. I am very angry with you. You have abducted other
peoples' children also; I am going to kill you."[203] Soon after, the Suvlitt man
Kaminarvet killed Sanganieki's wife. Kaminarvet, who had also lost his children
to the mission, had similarly been ordered to do this by Aluaite. The Melanesian verdict of "guilty"—because she was the wife of the man who was responsible for the abduction of the children—was again called out to her before
Kaminarvet struck her down.[204]

When the Catholic mission heard of the death of its informer, it notified
the military administration of "unrest" among the Baining. A punitive expedition, led by Lieutenant Hanlin and consisting of two police masters and fifty
Melanesian police soldiers, rushed to the Baining district. Although Hanlin
soon discovered that the real reason for the unrest was the illegal acts by the
mission and its Malay and Melanesian recruiters, he did not see any reason to
cancel the expedition. On the orders of the Australian officer, the police
stormed a Baining village with fixed bayonets and shot off 120 rounds of
ammunition. A German Catholic priest continually spurred them on. The
unholy alliance between German missionaries and Australian soldiers cost the
lives of six people. "The Natives have been taught a good lesson," reported the
lieutenant.[205]

It is unlikely that the expedition actually identified the village from which
Aluaite, Kaining, and Kaminarvet came. In March 1920 Aluaite and his son

Malbrinkkapokman were brought to court in Rabaul and sentenced to death for the violent resistance offered to the Melanesian and Malay hunters of men who had penetrated their village in 1917. Administrator Johnston reprieved them both. One received five years in prison, the other a three-year sentence. The rationale behind this decision was not so much the exceptional circumstances of the case, but the political consideration that the natives needed to be shown that the administration, not the mission, had the authority to pronounce judgments, and to repeal them.[206] Neither the court nor the Administrator ever considered that the two Baining might have acted in self-defense. The murders of Sanganieki and his wife were not mentioned.

This was precisely why Kaining was brought to court late in 1920, and Kaminarvet early in 1921. The whole case was reopened. Two German assessors argued "that it is a dangerous thing to interfere with the native customs and particularly to recruit the young children,"[207] and ensured that their misgivings were placed before the Administrator. Nonetheless, the judge and Administrator agreed unanimously that the Melanesians should be sentenced to death. It is true that both judge and Administrator were critical of the mission, and Administrator Griffiths immediately issued a regulation that was intended to prevent missions from acting in this way in the future.[208] But the ease with which he and others brushed aside serious doubts when passing judgment and sentencing people to death was indicative of the self-righteousness and racism that the civil administration had inherited unchanged from the military administration.

THE MELANESIAN VIEW OF AUSTRALIANS

Ethnological studies of New Guinea now number in the hundreds, and a historian, in particular, can hardly keep up with them. What is still lacking, however, is a study of how Melanesian New Guineans perceived Europeans. The appropriation of the term *racism* by political interest groups and its undifferentiated use as a term of abuse for assorted political (and academic?) opponents has perhaps prevented anthropologists from taking a closer look at something that is of vital importance in explaining Melanesian reactions to Europeans. Despite a general reluctance to grasp this nettle, it is quite clear that present-day Melanesians differentiate both between European and Melanesian, and among different types of European behavior.[209] For Melanesians, cultural contact with Europeans was no reason to change their traditional, dualistic worldview, characterized by sharply contrasting categories.[210] Europeans as such were initially and frequently identified as bearers of technological progress.[211] Probably the most universal Melanesian interpretation of the basic difference in behavior between themselves and Europeans refers to their different attitudes toward time and its use—although no scholarly verification for this statement yet exists. In any case, conversations with the people of Papua New Guinea repeatedly reveal their astonishment at Europeans' apparent ability to separate social relations and responsibilities from, or even to subordinate them to, their personal work (or, conversely, their inability to recognize the significance of "social time" as opposed to "economic time").

It is unlikely that Melanesians differentiated among Europeans on the basis of real or alleged national characteristics before 1914, because the Germans dominated the administration, the economy, and the missions almost completely. In the systematization[212] that is the usual response to personal experience of the "other," however, Europeans were placed into three contrasting groups: planters, missionaries, and administrative officials. The arrival of the Australians in 1914 added a fourth category that was different from the other three and deliberately set itself off from them. "No more 'um Kaiser, God Save 'Um King," read the Australian proclamation explaining what was new to the local people. More than the words of the national anthem had changed.[213] Nonetheless, its impact on a people highly aware of symbols should not be underestimated. For the first time they had a chance to attach national characteristics to another type of European behavior. The first time most Melanesians came into direct contact with Australians—excluding for the moment the special experience of some of the native police—they encountered the willingness of Australian soldiers to share their tinned meat and biscuits or to swap food for local products such as wood carvings. "Planti Inglis man gutpela, planti kaikai i giv" (Many Englishmen are good, because they give us a lot of food). Such comments are typical of the first phase of contact between Australians and Melanesians.[214] The suspension of communications with the outside world that began with the war affected the Melanesian population, particularly plantation workers, much more than it did the European population of the colony. The impact of the end of food deliveries was exacerbated by the unusual drought. Some Germans had made the Melanesians additionally insecure by spreading dreadful apocalyptic visions of the Japanese coming to New Guinea and burning everything down.[215] For many Melanesians the presence of Australian soldiers was a truly liberating experience. Not only was their behavior very different from what the Germans, with their artificially inflated fears of the end of German rule, had led the Melanesians to expect, but the Australians also relieved them of real concern for their usual daily ration of rice and tinned fish.

The positive assessment of the Australians in New Guinea and, based on this, of Australians in general went hand in hand with a negative view of German behavior. In this case, criticism was also generalized to Germans as such: "German—no good—push face—kick man back—English no do."[216] The fact that the Europeans were not all the same—that many of the Germans kicked and beat the Melanesians whereas the Australians did not (yet) do so—left a big impression. However, careful observers such as the missionaries (this was part of their job), noted that "free" Melanesians reacted differently from those who were in European employment. The latter were friendly with the Australian soldiers, calling them "Kanaka bilong Sydney," which can be interpreted as a gesture of fraternization.[217]

In the remote stations, particularly where German officials had built up a special relationship with the local people, reactions could be quite different. When the Australians occupied Bougainville and it was announced that all the Germans had to leave the island on 8 December 1914, the Solomon Islanders wanted to get rid of all Europeans at one stroke. But when they noticed that the Germans in Kieta were only to be replaced by armed Australians, some shouted: "We want the Germans back. We want Döllinger. . . . He was our father, he was good to us."[218] Döllinger, head of the German station, was a colonial official who had married a woman from the Pacific. Although his wife was not a Melanesian but was descended from the Samoan clan of "Queen Emma," through her he had much greater insight into (and much better emotional access to) local patterns of behavior than most of his colleagues. Personal ties and loyalties that had developed between "the German" and his former Melanesian subjects survived, on the Melanesian side, all the tensions and vicissitudes of the war, as Germans who visited the area many years after the end of the war discovered.[219]

The head of the German station in Morobe was married to a local woman, and the German influence remained stronger there than elsewhere. Captain Detzner was roaming the jungle, but the strongest factor was the presence of the Neuendettelsauer mission. Here the local people were soon critical of the Australian occupation. On a patrol late in 1915, the Australian district officer was told in many villages "that the English were no good and that they could easily kill the kiap [district officer]."[220] As late as mid-August 1915, a different Australian patrol found a village south of Madang still flying a number of German flags over its huts. They were attached to high poles, and the *luluai* assured the Australians that they had been fluttering there for several months. It seems unlikely that this was a political demonstration by the villagers against Australian rule; but this cannot be totally ruled out if we remember that although the village was relatively far away from the nearest administrative center, it could be reached from there without great difficulty. We can be sure that the villagers were aware of the Australian occupation of Madang, and they certainly knew of the high value Europeans placed on coats of arms, emblems, and other national symbols. Nonetheless, the more likely explanation is that the *luluai* did not remove the flags for fear of punishment by returning Germans.[221]

It was not only the German residents who repeatedly warned the local people that the German colonial government would come back soon and punish them if they cooperated too closely with the Australians. The losers of the war in the colony also included Asians, who were the object of especially racist prejudice on the part of the Australians. Malays who came from what is now Indonesia were not very happy about the loss of their former privileges as foremen, plantation overseers, and government employees. Quite a number of them wanted the Germans to return. At the end of May 1916, Rabaul wit-

nessed a confrontation between Malays and Melanesians, when Melanesians in
a boisterous mood mocked some Malays they met and the annoyed Malays
threatened them with the return of the Germans in two or three months. The
Malays suggested that the Germans would soon wipe the grins off the Melanesians' faces.[222]

Although the first phase of Australian rule had a "liberating" effect on
Melanesian workers in the European centers, in time this exclusively positive
image of the Australians acquired more and more cracks. It is not surprising
that the plantation workers were the most enthusiastic about this political
change. By the same token, the free Melanesians were the first to experience
its disadvantages. The Melanesians who had been included in the German
administrative organization and had come to appreciate the benefits of the Pax
Germanica, openly criticized the Australian military administration for giving
up the practice of regular patrols, thus tolerating incursions into the pacified
zone both by locals and Europeans.[223] In the region between Madang and
Morobe, local functionaries who had been appointed by the former German
colonial administration took advantage of the legal vacuum left behind by the
military administration. On their own authority, they put an end to the anarchic
conditions by usurping rights that had belonged to the European administration. *Luluai* and *tultul* punished local men and women by administering whippings, after having established their "guilt" in a brief trial. In some villages,
twenty to twenty-five whippings per day were not unusual. They threatened to
flog a German planter as well, if he dared to recruit workers in their district
again. The acting Australian district officer in Morobe was totally ignored, and
all indigenous disputes were resolved internally. The neighboring (Neuendettelsauer) mission supported this procedure, which the district officer of
Madang, W. M. B. Ogilvy had approved because he was unable to deal with the
area himself. His colleague in Morobe now launched a crusade against the
behavior that seemed to have established itself.[224]

The constant turnover in district officers, their frequently contradictory
policies, and in general, the lack of clear and lasting guidelines for action
caused a deep insecurity among those members of the local population who
had welcomed pacification. This feeling was exacerbated by the behavior of a
number of Australian police and station officials, whose arbitrary rule over the
local population under their control could almost be called a reign of terror.
There was no lack of local strategies to cope with the worst excesses, but they
were rarely successful in these cases. In order to prevent the women of his village from being sexually intimidated, the *tultul* Karkilami of Marklow ordered
them to hide from the Australian officers who were carrying out a census. During a census, it was normal practice to line up all the inhabitants of a village in
front of the district officer. This made it easier for the official to register all men
who were liable for taxation (and facilitated recruitment). Obviously, it also
made it easier to take note of the best-looking women. The district officer punished the *tultul* for his behavior by officially sentencing him to a whipping,

which was administered on the spot, although corporal punishment had already been abolished.[225]

Other Melanesians who regarded submitting to German rule as a loss of traditional freedoms endeavored to make the most of these developments by attempting to restore their lost hegemony over tribes that had previously been subject to them. In Potsdamhafen, north of Madang, and on the Sepik, near the old government station in Angoram, tribal fighting broke out. In both cases, those who benefited from the breakdown of state order let it be known that there was no longer a government, and that they could now do as they liked. On the island of Karkar the old tactic revived of attaching oneself to government forces as an armed local escort in order to attack traditional enemies in a European-legal way.[226]

In general, it is clear that many of the Melanesian strategies for coping with Europeans which had already proved themselves during the German period were now applied to the Australians. Once again, the Melanesians' primary aim was to manipulate the Europeans to their own advantage or to adopt European ways in order to manipulate other Melanesians. A Melanesian dressed up as a police boy collected the head tax, allegedly in the service of the Australians.[227] In a number of cases, the Australian military administration clearly scored points over the German administration. In Manus, the district officer was officially asked to use his weapons to shoot dead evil spirits. And when Melanesians had disputes with German settlers, appealing to British authority certainly did them no harm.[228] Under the German administration the missionaries had had to be treated with kid gloves out of a constant fear of Erzberger's public criticism of colonial affairs in the German parliament, the Reichstag. Even the missionaries' power could now be shaken by playing the card of their problematic nationality. Wood carvings with exaggerated sexual organs had, from the start, been a source of conflict between Melanesians and missionaries. In the area around the Sepik River the Catholic missionaries of the Divine Word regularly raided the "Tambaran" or spirit houses where statues and masks of this sort were generally kept. When one of the priests once again wanted to remove an "obscene" figure on the ground that the German official had tolerated this sort of behavior before, the *tultul* argued that "Maski, German Kiap he go finish" (I don't mind; it's all up with the German district officer). The missionary soon received the necessary support from the Australian "kiap."[229] Melanesians also occasionally appealed to a common background in order to achieve a favorable judgment, like the *luluai* who told the Australian magistrate that, after all, he was a really a Queenslander too, as he had worked on the plantations there for years.[230]

Certain trends from the German period continued, or were strengthened, under the Australians. One was the tendency of the Melanesian population to decrease in a number of areas. Up to twenty different methods or herbs were used as contraceptives. Sick children were frequently killed. "He sick—he no good—I made him die quick," replied a woman on one of the northern islands of the St. Matthias group when a European came across her stoning her child.[231] We have already referred to a probable link between European employment and a decline in the Melanesian population. Evidence is mounting that Melanesian women deliberately chose not to give birth, in order to prevent their children from being forced to work for Europeans. An Australian official was convinced that women refused to have children out of fear that they would bear sons who would be taken away from them to work for the Europeans. "Mary no like" (The woman does not want to), a Melanesian Bikman replied when a district officer asked him why they had only one child.[232] Another Australian heard a Melanesian say: "What for me make him picanninie for white man—he no more can live all same father belong him" (Why should I father a child, just for the whites? He would no longer be able to live like his father did.)[233]

We should not seek to devalue these statements by pointing out (correctly) that they fit in exactly with the thinking in categories practised by the social Darwinist theoreticians of earlier times (who believed that Pacific Islanders were inferior to Europeans, and would, as a "lower race," inevitably have the worst of the clash between cultures and die out). Similarly, they fit equally well into the arguments put forward by modern critics of colonialism, who see the indigenous population as pure sacrificial lambs, the Europeans as the incarnation of evil, and backward-looking traditionalism as a panacea for the salvation of non-European cultures. To be sure, the conflict between European and Melanesian priorities also revealed a fatalistic attitude of resignation—*maski* in Tok Pisin, meaning "I don't mind." (This, incidentally, suggests that another view often indiscriminately applied to the Third World—namely, that populations increase in an uncontrolled fashion as a consequence of cultural contact—needs considerable qualification in terms of period and region.) Fatalistic resignation, however, was not the only or even the usual or majority attitude of Melanesians to the consequences of forced contact with Europeans. If this had been the case, there would no longer be an indigenous population in Papua New Guinea. On the whole, the people of New Guinea, with regional variations, came to terms astonishingly well[234] with the changes in their world wrought by the German and then the Australian colonial administration. This is less a retrospective justification for the behavior of the Europeans than an admission of the superior adaptability of the Melanesians.

GOLD MINE AND STRATEGIC SHIELD:
NEW GUINEA IN THE EYES OF AUSTRALIAN POLITICIANS

On the question of the future of Australian-occupied New Guinea, most Australian politicians had no doubt about the essential point. They agreed that after the war New Guinea should be transferred into Australian possession under international law. Almost exactly one month after German New Guinea's

military surrender, Atlee Hunt, acting on the instructions of the prime minister
and the foreign minister, Hugh Mahon (Labor), asked the foremost Australian
authority on Melanesia, Murray, the governor of Papua, to present his ideas on
the future of New Guinea to cabinet. Hunt enclosed with his letter a summary
of his own reflections, in which he made four main points. New Guinea, Papua,
and the Solomons, which Britain was to cede to Australia, were to form a single
Australian colony. The islands were to be administered by one governor. He
was to be based, not on the islands, but in northern Australia (Townsville). A
royal commission was to develop detailed suggestions for future policy. As
members of the commission, Hunt named himself, Murray, and his own bosom
friend, Lucas, general manager of Burns Philp. Hunt tried to dispel any possible reservations Murray might have about such obviously favorable treatment
for one company: "Of course his firm is financially interested but that is no real
drawback. . . . Moreover I do not think we could find anyone of real knowledge
who is not in some way or other financially interested." And finally, the Australian government had already agreed that, unlike Germany, it would not subsi-
dize the administration of New Guinea: the colony would have to be financially
self-supporting. In order to achieve this, the system of head-taxes would have
to be expanded (and if possible extended to Papua and the Solomons). Government control would have to increase, to allow better access to local labor.[235]
Thereupon, in mid-December 1914, Murray developed his ideas on the amal-
gamation of New Guinea and Papua, still working on the assumption that he

Administrator Pethebridge and staff, Rabaul 1917 (*from left:* Colonel C. L. Strangman,
P.M.O.; Lady Pethebridge; Administrator Pethebridge; and Lieutenant Colonel Mackenzie, the judge). (Photograph by Thomas J. McMahon. Australian Archives Canberra)

would be governor of the united Melanesian territories. He did not believe in the incorporation of the British Solomons but assumed that what was left of the German possessions in the Solomons, the islands of Buka and Bougainville, would be given to Britain.[236]

The first Australian to develop ideas for the future of the colony on the basis of his own experience in the military administration of New Guinea was Pethebridge. For the Administrator, the cornerstone of an Australian takeover of the colony was the expulsion of the Germans after the conclusion of peace and the expropriation of their property in New Guinea. In a detailed memorandum dated late in 1915, the former secretary of defense was one of the first to justify imperialist ambitions in terms of strategic considerations. He pointed out that Australia and New Zealand were the only British dominions vulnerable to attack only from the sea, and that they both had almost purely British populations. The main consideration in the acquisition of Papua had already been that it would form a buffer zone between Australia and "the millions of the East."[237]

Pethebridge's reasoning is one more example of the fear, universal in Australia and New Zealand, of the "yellow peril." On the fifth continent, this fear amounted to more than the grandiloquent statements, effectively staged for the media, made in Europe on the same subject. In Australia and New Zealand the near-hysteria seemed less artificial. It was not that fear of the Yellow Peril there was based on historical experience reaching back, as in Europe, into the obscurity of their own past. Rather, it was the immediate past and, strangely enough, their own actions, not those of Asians or others, which had given Australians and New Zealanders such a shock that almost the only explanation is psychological. The ease with which the Britons had taken Australia from the Aborigines and brought the Aboriginal population to the brink of extinction was the fundamental historical experience of white Australians. Since then, they had lived in constant fear that one day they might suffer the same fate. Their own racist policies that excluded Asians only fueled these fears, because they implied that the Asian "hordes" would one day take bitter revenge for the discrimination they had suffered.

If New Guinea was joined to Papua, there would be an effective buffer between Australia and Asia. In addition, at least part of the toll of lives to be paid in a military confrontation with China—or, as seemed likelier, with Japan—in which the only thing that still seemed uncertain was the timing, could be paid by a non-British population. As early as December 1914 the Australian navy had already advised the Ministry of Defence to develop Rabaul into a naval base after the war.[238] And Pethebridge himself described the main task of a future Australian colonial administration as being "to preserve the racial stamina of the mountain tribes for military resources most of all. Their courage and physique make them splendid raw material."[239] Thus the belligerent qualities of the Melanesian hill tribes were to be preserved in order to deploy them against the Japanese in case of war. The coastal tribes, by contrast, were to be forced to work. In Pethebridge's view, "forced labour . . . is the most beneficial kind of taxation." Cheap labor and large plantations were the two most important prerequisites for the desired economic success: "To work the gold and petroleum deposits also, no less than to cultivate the copra, rubber, sisal hemps and other products, the native must be exploited." Australia had the advantage, he pointed out, that Germany had not so far attempted to extract quick profits from New Guinea. As only one-third of the cultivated plants in the plantation were mature, a great economic future lay ahead of Australian New Guinea. Therefore, he suggested, all the land that was still in the possession of the indigenous people should be confiscated as Crown land.[240]

Of all the Australian concepts of New Guinea, the most widespread was the notion of the colony as a natural strategic shield for Australia that could, in addition, generate fabulous profits without large investment. Not least, Prime Minister Hughes furiously defended both positions and Australia's claim to New Guinea in several fiery speeches during the war. The best known of these were his lectures in the Savoy Hotel, New York, and at the Pilgrim Club in London. In these lectures, given at the end of May and in mid-July 1918, respectively, he summed up the old Australian dream of a Pacific Monroe Doctrine in the slogan Hands Off the Australian Pacific.[241]

A secret memorandum, produced by the Australian chief of the general staff, Brigadier General Hubert Foster, in May 1917 at the request of the minister of defense, Pearce, confirmed the strategic significance of Rabaul for Australia in a future war with Japan. Micronesia, by contrast, was strategically unimportant and too far away from Australia to represent a real danger. According to the report, there were no military reasons to object to the equator as the de facto border between Japan and Australia.[242] At that time not even Foster knew that at a meeting with Grey in London as long ago as April 1916, Prime Minister Hughes had already designated the equator as the postwar demarcation line. Pearce had advised Hughes before this meeting that except for Nauru, which was of economic value, the Micronesian islands were economically and strategically unimportant for Australia. Exactly the opposite applied to the islands south of the equator. New Guinea, "a shield to the Northern portions of our continent," and Melanesian soldiers—these were Pethebridge's precise thoughts in the mouth of the minister of defense.[243]

In the whole of Australia, only one person of any public standing expressed doubts about a New Guinea under Australian rule. Behind the scenes, and without the cabinet discovering what he was doing, the governor-general, Ronald Munro Ferguson, worked against Australia acquiring any new colonies. Instead, he advocated that the Pacific islands under British control should be united under two high commissioners answerable directly to the Crown. One commissioner, to be based in Auckland, should take charge of New Zealand's sphere of influence in Fiji and Samoa; the other should reside in Sydney and administer the rest of Melanesia plus Tonga, as well as New Caledonia and the New Hebrides, which were to be acquired from France. In

Munro Ferguson's opinion, the simplest solution would be for the existing governor-general of Australia to assume the functions of this high commissioner as well.[244]

In the governor-general's view, there were many reasons why responsibility for the British-controlled Pacific Islands should not be given directly to the Australian federal government. The most important factors in his view were: first, Australian lack of sympathy for black people, as demonstrated in the "blackbirding" scandal of the Australian-dominated Pacific Labour Trade, in the Queensland government's infamous practice of issuing white settlers licences to hunt—in fact to kill—Aborigines, and in the White Australia Policy, implemented in response to pressure from the trades unions; second, the lack of trained officials; and finally, Australia's obvious inability to develop tropical regions like its own Northern Territory.[245] In the crucial hours of the Versailles negotiations, the Australian governor-general wrote to the British colonial secretary, Milner, saying that for these reasons Australia should be denied the mandate for New Guinea.[246] Almost at the same time, he wrote down his own ideas of the policy for the indigenous population, which would be implemented in the Pacific Islands under his leadership. In this document, the English nobleman revealed that his indignation toward Australian ambitions was prompted less by a principled humanitarianism than by royalist and imperialist convictions. The guidelines governing Munro Ferguson's "native policy" can be summed up in one sentence: "it is essential that the native should be made to respect and fear his white master." In order to realize this categorical imperative of colonial policy, Ferguson believed it was absolutely necessary to adopt the German system of corporal punishment unchanged. And in order to underline the difference between the white masters and the natives, natives would not be permitted to wear European clothing but would be compelled to go naked.[247] In the governor-general's view, the pressure to conform to European patterns of behavior should be replaced by a prohibition on adopting European models. Perhaps this is an appropriate place to point out that racism and antiracism are defined, not in terms of refusing or approving of tradition, but of rejecting or accepting the indigenous decision, whatever it may be.

Munro Ferguson's colleagues, the British high commissioner for the Western Pacific, Bickham Escott, and the governor-general of New Zealand, Liverpool, put forward similar notions. All their ideas were based on the assumption that Britain would directly administer Germany's Pacific colonies, which it had occupied during the First World War.[248] Although these men had good connections with the highest circles in Britain, their proposals never had the faintest chance of being adopted. In London, too, the times when policy was made in order to satisfy a few lords were past. Too much was involved. Nothing less than the future membership of Australia and New Zealand in the empire was at stake. And what these two Dominions were worth to the mother country had just been demonstrated by the war.

Despite the private policy being pursued by Britain's highest representatives in Australia, expectations of the commercial value of New Guinea as a future Australian colony grew among the Australian people and their politicians. Hopes were focused on the coconut palms the German settlers had planted and continued to cultivate, in spite of the war. Reports about an economic wonderland that could supply Australia with practically everything it needed filled the space left in the Australian newspapers by bad news from the war.[249] Early in 1916 a commission was founded on the instigation of the Australian minister for trade and customs. The commission's main aim was to secure Australian–British control over the copra trade in the South Pacific. In addition, it was instructed to investigate the economic potential of other tropical plants. In principle, this was simply a government contract to investigate the agricultural and economic prospects held out by a political takeover of the German colonies in the South Pacific.

Speculation about New Guinea's fabulous mineral wealth, however, generated far more enthusiasm among Australian politicians and people alike than did all its agricultural produce taken together. Rumors about secret German discoveries of gold and oil did the rounds of Australia's pubs, their credibility and the deposits of mineral wealth constantly growing. On the express wish of Prime Minister Hughes, a scientific expedition left Australia for New Guinea late in 1920 "to take stock of what the country possesses."[250] It was led by Dr. Campbell Brown, a mineralogist who had already explored osmiridium deposits in Papua. Brown, however, got no farther than the river Ramu, where he found photographs of "undiscovered" tribes more interesting than the mineral wealth upon which the Australian government had pinned its hopes. Finally, he ran out of funds. Thereupon an incensed Hughes had everything relating to the case, including Brown's pocket-watch, seized.[251] The one-sided orientation of Australia's trade toward Britain during the war and the transfer of capital to the motherland had destroyed Australia's flourishing economy. The country and its politicians were desperately seeking a financial solution. The minister for the navy, Joseph Cook, speaking to Australia's student elite early in 1920, pointed out that if oil were to be discovered in New Guinea, "it would be a source of infinite financial gain for Australia."[252] At the beginning of January 1921, when the League of Nations was just in the process of confirming the mandate but the military administration was still in office in Rabaul, the Anglo-Persian Oil Company, which had already unsuccessfully drilled for oil in Papua, began to prospect for the mysterious German oil finds in the area around Eitape. Once again, Prime Minister Hughes was the driving force behind the venture.[253] Hughes, who had practically tied his political career to Australia's takeover of New Guinea, had to satisfy an expectant Australian people. At first, however, only promises could be made, and an increasingly anxious population had to be kept going with propaganda. New Guinea was "a land fertile and rich in all products . . . a land of abundance," the prime minister claimed in mid-September 1922 at the showing of an advertising film for the new Australian colony

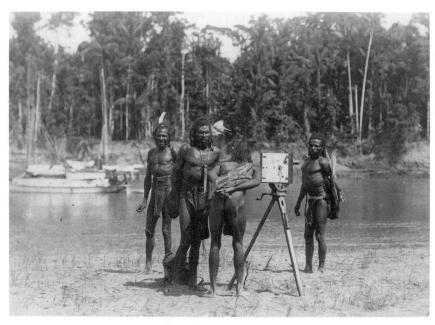

Timid Melanesians halfway up the river Ramu. The Campbell Brown expedition, 1920. (Photograph by William J. Jackson. Australian Archives Canberra)

made from what had been salvaged from Campbell Brown's disastrous expedition.[254] Those for whom these words were not merely comforting mood music were already preparing to gather in their wealth.

THE INFLUENCE OF TRADE AND INDUSTRY

During the war, nobody was more active and persistent in agitating for Australian control of German New Guinea than James Burns. From November 1914, Australian and British politicians were inundated by a constant flood of memoranda from Burns Philp, attempting to influence the political future of the Pacific Islands in the company's favor. All of Burns Philp's demands were based on three basic assumptions: (1) German New Guinea must remain Australian and the Germans should not be allowed back; (2) the Germans remaining in the colony were to be expelled, their property expropriated, and its value set against the compensation that Germany would have to pay to Britain after the war, "leaving it to the German Proprietors to recover the value from their own German Government"; and (3) only Australian ships were to carry on trade with New Guinea.[255] The flag of Australian imperialism barely disguised the company's real goal, which was to secure and retain the monopoly on trade and transport it had gained during the war: the Australian nationalism that Burns

Philp promoted with enthusiasm was nothing but a means to an end. The company rejected the idea of a British administration for the Pacific Islands because they feared that British colonial officials might place the welfare of the local people above that of the company. For exactly the same reason, they wanted Australian rule after the war to cover not only former German New Guinea but also the British islands of the western Pacific, the Solomons, and the Gilbert and Ellice Islands. The company operated in all of these islands.[256]

Burns spent August and September 1915 in London in order to win over to his cause the really influential people, those who held the reins of power in the empire. He had prepared his mission thoroughly. The governor-general of Australia had always been well disposed toward him. Burns had apparently gained his favor by supporting a central island administration based in Sydney, while playing down the obvious discrepancy between Munro Ferguson's idea of a purely British and his own of an Australian hegemony. The Colonial Office was already aware of Burns' memorandum on the future of the Pacific, as the governor-general had passed it on to Harcourt early in 1915. All the officials in the Colonial Office and all British MPs had received a copy of the pamphlet "British Mismanagement in the Pacific Islands," originally written by Burns in 1907. This polemic had first been serialized anonymously in the *Sydney Morning Herald,* Australia's highest circulation newspaper, where it had successfully mobilized Australian public opinion against the German presence in the South Pacific.[257] Now an expanded version appealed to the mother country's bad conscience. Britain, the pamphlet's author pointed out, had "betrayed" its colonies in the Pacific for the sake of an agreement with Germany and France. This argument did not fail to make an impression at a time when the mother country urgently needed the help of its colonies.

Without the knowledge of the Australian foreign secretary, Mahon, but equipped with personal recommendations from the governor-general, Burns found all doors open to him in London. He had detailed talks with Bonar Law, Harcourt, and John Anderson, in which he vigorously pushed his political and economic ideas, and presented a complete "Australian" shopping list. In addition to German New Guinea, he said, the Solomons, the Gilbert and Ellice Islands, and Tonga should be entirely administered by Australia. Australia and Britain should come to an agreement on the phosphate islands of Nauru and Ocean Island. The New Hebrides should be divided between Australia and France. The Dutch part of New Guinea should at least be under British control. New Zealand, which was to come off badly in large areas of the Pacific, should be compensated by getting Samoa and the French part of Polynesia (nothing was said about compensation for France). Above all, however, the Germans should be removed from New Guinea at the end of the war, and Australian companies should take over the German plantation companies.[258]

In general, James Burns was well received by the people to whom he spoke, and in one matter his listeners were more than sympathetic. They noted the hegemonial ambitions of a greater Australia but passed over them without discussion because they were aware that, even with British support, most of them were totally unrealistic.[259] But things were different when it came to the Scottish-Australian's economic and political fantasies concerning Germany's Pacific colonies. While Burns was packing his suitcases in Munro Ferguson's private residence in Scotland, which the governor-general had put at his disposal, Bonar Law was already writing to Australia with instructions to set up a new Australian company to take over German property in New Guinea and Samoa, "so as to get rid of the German element together."[260] This suggestion was Burns' contribution to the general shadow-boxing during the war. Such ideas came and went. What remained was Burns Philp.

The most important result of Burns' visit to Britain was the assurance that German New Guinea would become Australian after the war. Any objections that settlers or officials could raise would, in the final analysis, have little effect.[261] In the meantime, it was hoped that Britain would fight hard to make the desired goals possible. After all, the present struggle was nothing less than a "battle for commercial supremacy," as Walter Lucas, the company's manager, put it late in 1915.[262] With British support, Burns Philp could concentrate on the next steps. One of these was to prevent New Guinea from being administered jointly with Papua. Burns Philp argued that New Guinea would be better off under an independent, autocratically led Australian administration. Otherwise the labor potential of New Guinea would be at risk, as workers for Papua could be recruited from New Guinea, thus damaging the commercial interests of the plantations in New Guinea. The same argument now suddenly made it seem less favorable for the British Solomons to join Australian New Guinea. In this case, too, an outflow of Melanesian labor from New Guinea was feared.[263]

Exactly ten days after the armistice came into effect in Europe, James Burns went to see the acting Australian prime minister, Watt. In order to ensure that the future control of New Guinea would really benefit Australia, Burns insisted, the Australian government would have to pass a formal resolution to expel the Germans from New Guinea immediately after the conclusion of peace and to transfer their property to an Australian company to be set up for the purpose. The cabinet resisted making an official commitment so quickly, but Watt told Burns that, in principle, his suggestions had been positively received. In Britain, the London director of the company, Lord Inchcape, bombarded the colonial secretary with the same demands. The colonial secretary informed Lord Inchcape that he was "very sympathetic" to the model proposed by Burns Philp.[264] By the end of December 1918, a majority of the Australian cabinet had come down on the side of Burns Philp.[265]

Even Burns Philp could not allow itself to drop its mask entirely. The suggestion of founding a new Australian company to take over German property was the necessary sheep's clothing for the wolf hiding underneath. In January 1919 James Burns warned the company's London representatives that "it would be unwise to have the appearance of limiting the scheme to one or two capitalists—Doing so would invite criticism all round. . . . It would be the old story of the War having been fought in capitalistic interests etc. etc. We want the control, in the interests of all concerned. . . . We have the whole thing well in hand."[266] The main thing was to get rid of the Germans first, and then to buy up all the German property before the other interested parties got to it—"then we hold the key to the whole position."[267] At the same time, he suggested, any attempt by the Australian government to take the economic development of New Guinea into its own hands must be blocked. Officers on duty there now should be forbidden to start up businesses of their own.[268]

In P. B. O'Connor the company gained a successful lobbyist, who considerably stepped up the pressure behind the scenes. O'Connor was Burns' neighbor in Paramatta, a lawyer, and vice president of the New South Wales parliament. He tirelessly lobbied ministers, and above all, Acting Prime Minister Watt. Journalists who were prepared to write articles supporting Burns Philp received a free tour of the islands.[269] As early as 22 January, Watt promised O'Connor that he was "entirely" behind Burns Philp's plans.[270] In London, it would be necessary to be rather more careful, "so as not to appear to put forward our requests as it were for the aggrandizement and interests of our company, but to put them forward more in the interests of the Empire's and Australia's trade."[271] At the end of May 1919 the London branch of Burns Philp could report a decisive breakthrough. On 23 May its director had met with the Australian prime minister, Hughes, who had just returned from Paris. It was a highly sensitive meeting, held at a secret location and with all the precautions dictated by Hughes' fear that the matter could become public—"the quieter this matter was handled, the better." Burns Philp had summed up its main demands again in a memorandum: the elimination of all foreign influence, the takeover of German property, and all shipping connections with New Guinea to be exclusively Australian. Burns Philp was aiming for a monopoly on the transport of Australian manufactured products and food to New Guinea and on shipping copra from New Guinea to Australia. It wanted the government to use its influence to keep potential competitors out of the country—especially the Japanese, who were waiting for their chance and were prepared to pay higher prices for copra than the firm from Sydney. After all, the colony could be economically developed for Australia's benefit only "if sufficient cheap labour is obtainable."[272]

To the prime minister, it almost seemed as if what the company put before him summed up his own thoughts. Hughes gave Burns Philp's London representative detailed information about the decision taken at Versailles to expropriate enemy property and set its value against the reparations owed by Germany. The German government would have to compensate its citizens itself. He advised Burns Philp that the most practical course of action for it to take would be to set up a new private company in which the Australian government would have a small interest. Although he had no intention of the state exercising greater economic influence, the prime minister explained: "the reason for the Commonwealth desiring some interest is to be able to give the lie to any statement which might be made that the Government had given a monopoly of this trading over to such a Company as B. P. & Co., by stating that the Government had an interest in the Company. . . . You know I am a Socialist and have been all my life and believe in Socialistic trading, but I am not foolish and unless Socialistic trading makes for profits it must be cut out."[273]

Burns congratulated his London representative on his tactics—"the more quietly we work the better, and all things considered we seem now to be fairly safe."[274] The company now really needed the influence of the prime minister, as with the end of the war, competition had revived. On 30 May 1919 the Administrator in Rabaul had permitted a Japanese ship to load copra for the Australian company W. R. Carpenter and transport it to Sydney. Thereupon all the larger German firms canceled their contracts with Burns Philp because they no longer wanted to pay its high freight rates. In a hastily convened meeting on 31 May, the Australian cabinet approved Shepherd's (the secretary to the prime minister) request that only British ships be permitted to transport freight from New Guinea. The Administrator was immediately informed of this decision by telegraph, and the Japanese ship had to leave Rabaul empty.[275]

Not quite three weeks later, on 18 July 1919, the Australian cabinet appointed Lucas, the general manager of Burns Philp, to a royal commission that was to work out proposals for future arrangements in New Guinea. After all, as Shepherd argued, it was important "that lines should be laid down to ensure that the Commonwealth will reap to the fullest extent possible some real benefit from the acquisition of the Territory," and nobody was better equipped to do this than Walter Henry Lucas.[276] The commission was chaired by the governor of Papua, Murray, and the Australian government was represented by the secretary for home and territories, Atlee Hunt. Everything was developing just as Hunt had predicted at the beginning of the war. Even before his nomination, Lucas had provided a slogan for the commission: Hobble the Hun.[277]

With the nomination of Lucas and the presence of Burns Philp's old family friend, Atlee Hunt, the company was halfway to achieving its goal. "There seems to be a good chance of German New Guinea being treated somewhat in the manner we previously suggested," rejoiced the company's founder.[278] In New Guinea, in the meantime, a division of labor emerged within the commission. While his colleagues were interesting themselves more in administrative questions and the missions, Lucas was left undisturbed to collect detailed data about German property in the colony. Working for the firm, he concentrated on finding out how much the property owned by the Germans had originally cost in marks. Armed with this information, the company intended to make its offer for the property in marks at the moment when the German currency was at its lowest value.[279] Officially, Lucas had left the company when he was called to serve on the commission. As a member of the commission he was not permitted to pass on information, but he nevertheless kept Burns Philp well informed about the state of the commission and every confidential discussion.[280]

In their closing report the majority of commissioners, Lucas, and Hunt, recommended to the Australian government a plan that was practically identical with Burns Philp's war aims. All Germans, including missionaries, were to be deported from New Guinea. German plantations should be sold to private individuals; German businesses and companies liquidated and replaced by Australian firms. New Guinea should continue to be administered separately from Papua (commercial reasons were given, whereas considerations of international law were considered unimportant); Australian subsidies would not be necessary, as the colony would pay its own way. All shipping should continue to operate exclusively via Sydney, as had been the case during the war. The Australian Navigation Act, which discriminated against all non-British ships, was not enough. Preferential tariffs that advantaged Australian ships above British ships also had to be introduced.[281]

The commission's chairman, Papua's Governor Murray, saw himself pushed to the wall, with all his suggestions. He had developed alternative models on almost all points: the unification of Papua and New Guinea under one administration and the nationalization of the four big German plantation companies and larger plantations over 400 hectares, while keeping as many German colonists in the colony as possible. As in South West Africa, they were to be granted full citizenship, including the right to elect a government council, which was to be reintroduced. Finally, he suggested founding a government shipping company so that the colony would not be dependent on a private shipping line (naturally, this referred to Burns Philp). Moreover, Australian subsidies for the colony of New Guinea would be unavoidable.[282] Military Administrator Johnston supported Murray on many points. Although Johnston rejected the idea of combining Papua with New Guinea—"New Guinea is in every way much more advanced than Papua"—he, like Murray, supported the idea of a continuing German presence. And he was more critical than the governor of Papua of the planned auction of the large plantations, which he saw as something that would benefit only capitalists and syndicates. He argued that the right to buy should be dependent on an obligation to settle in the colony; in that way, interested parties could come to New Guinea from all over the world. Johnston was most critical of the colony's lack of access to world markets. The regulation that all of the colony's trade had to go through Sydney, he argued, would benefit only a few businessmen in Sydney, while the colony as such would suffer and its development be checked.[283]

Murray and Johnston had good reason to fight so vigorously against Burns Philp's monopoly on transport. Since the beginning of the war Dutch steamers from neighboring Dutch New Guinea had no longer been able to put in at Papuan ports. With the conquest of New Guinea, the interest of Australian traders had shifted, and even Burns Philp's government-subsidized ships called at Port Moresby ever more rarely.[284] In New Guinea the disadvantages of a lack of competition and dependence on Burns Philp steamers had long since become clear. When dockworkers in Australia went on strike from late 1919 to early

1920, the colony's trade collapsed completely. Between 20 December 1919 and 20 March 1920 only a single ship—a British one—went to New Guinea. Thousands of tons of finished copra simply rotted.[285]

Johnston found it difficult to make anyone listen to his opinion. All his subordinates were questioned by the commission; only he was passed over. Eventually he decided to put his views before the commission in writing. Later, Murray was convinced that the whole commission had only been a front to conceal the fact that decisions had already been made much earlier.[286]

While official representatives examined New Guinea from administrative and commercial points of view and ignored the local population (except as a cheap labor force), members of the missions drew up alternative scenarios for the indigenous people. Most of their suggestions, however, reveal the familiar condescending attitude. The Methodist leader, Pastor Cox, called for all land to which the Melanesians did not lay claim to be taken from them and declared Crown land. He also advocated raising the head-tax. The Catholic bishop, Couppé, demanded a ban on recruiting single women but endorsed the reintroduction of corporal punishment for local workers. Both Cox and Couppé wanted to drive the Chinese out of the country.[287]

The Australian government accepted the advice of the majority of the commission and sent Lucas to New Guinea again to implement its suggestions. As the prime minister's "technical adviser" for New Guinea and chairman of the Expropriation Board, he became the most powerful man in the colony, ranking above even the Administrator. Nothing could be done without him, and certainly not against him, as even Australians were to discover.[288] The expropriation of German firms and private individuals began on 1 September 1920. Australia had not yet officially received the mandate over New Guinea, and, strictly speaking, this procedure was against international law. But Germany was in no position to complain, and Lucas had pressed the Australian government, pointing out that the rise in copra prices on the world market made it imperative to expropriate the Germans as quickly as possible.[289] The liquidation was backdated to 10 January 1920, the day on which the Versailles treaty came into effect. During the war, it had been impossible to send profits out of the country or to invest outside New Guinea. Between 1914 and 1920, therefore, the Germans had put all their capital into expanding existing plantations and creating new ones. Between 1914 and the end of 1918, the area of New Guinea planted with coconut palms almost doubled, increasing from 76,847 to 133,960 acres.[290] On the day of their expropriation, the four large German plantation companies, Neuguinea-Kompanie, Hamburger Südsee Aktiengesellschaft, Hernsheim, and Wahlen, possessed a total of 2,366,532 coconut palms, of which only 780,812, or one-third, were fully mature. The rest had been planted as an investment in the future; 687,972 trees were between one and six years old. Thus more than 29 percent of their palm trees had only been planted during the Australian military administration. Between 1914 and 1918, the net profits of these four companies amounted to £365,451. Early in

1919 the military administration's chief surveyor assessed the total value of German property in New Guinea as at least £4,894,900. What Administrator Pethebridge had always predicted now came true: Australia collected the profits that German planning and Melanesian labor had produced.[291]

The backdating of the expropriation order to 10 January 1920 did not prevent the confiscation of German income earned after this date. The Expropriation Board ordered the German planters to continue working their old plantations for the board, under threat of punishment. All their personal property was confiscated. Many who were left destitute were looked after by Melanesian and Chinese friends. Those who could still afford it were permitted to buy back some of their personal possessions, such as wedding presents, at public auction of their property. In Sydney, where most of them began their journey back to Germany, they were permitted to keep fifty pounds in cash, but anything more in their possession was taken away.[292] Under Lucas' leadership, the Expropriation Board auctioned the German businesses between 18 May and 31 August 1922. Bidders had to be "natural born British subjects."[293] Here at last was the opportunity for which Burns Philp had waited so long, and toward which it had so purposefully worked.

3

Micronesia and the War

A SPECIAL CASE OF DIVIDE AND RULE

IN PURSUIT OF WHITE GOLD: NAURU, 1914–1922

Northeast of New Guinea, a few degrees south of the equator, lies the small island of Nauru (about one-third of the size of San Marino). The people who live on Nauru are Polynesian, but they have many Melanesian characteristics.[1] Germany declared the island a protectorate on 14 April 1888. Administratively, Nauru was part of the Marshall Islands and the protectorate of the Jaluit Society. On 1 April 1906 the Micronesian island group comprising Nauru and the Marshall Islands became part of German New Guinea, but Nauru remained under the district office of Jaluit. When this office was dissolved on 1 April 1911, the station of Nauru became subordinate to the headquarters of German Micronesia, the district office in Ponape.

Life on Nauru had continued relatively undisturbed by the colonial administration. All this changed with the discovery of phosphate deposits on the island. The Pacific Phosphate Company took over the organization and sole exploitation of the mines on the island. This unique situation, in which a British company exercised a monopoly in a German colony, was the result of an agreement with the Jaluit Society. With the permission of the German chancellor, the Jaluit Society had granted the Pacific Phosphate Company a monopoly on the guano in Nauru early in 1906. In exchange, the society held three of seven directorships on the board of the London company and received a share of the profits from the phosphate deposits on Ocean Island, a neighboring island belonging to the British protectorate of the Gilbert and Ellice Islands. On 1 January 1901, Britain had leased it to the Pacific Phosphate Company for ninety-nine years. For its concession, Germany received the relatively modest sum of 25,000 marks annual tax. The Pacific Phosphate Company paid an additional duty of 50 pfennigs for every tonne of phosphate over 50,000 exported, direct to the German Colonial Office. The Nauruans received the least of all. In principle, their rights of ownership were not questioned. The Pacific Phosphate Company had to pay the indigenous owners 5 pfennigs per tonne of phosphate exported as compensation for the destruction of their land, and they received a one-off payment of 20 marks for every copra palm that was felled.[2]

On Nauru the war began on 9 September 1914, when the battleship *Melbourne* destroyed the radio station. The island was not occupied because the Australian navy regarded Nauru as strategically useless. It also wanted to avoid the consequences of such a step under international law—namely, "the responsibility of feeding the inhabitants."[3] Immediately thereafter, the Pacific Phosphate Company began to negotiate with the British government and the Australian navy with the aim of resuming phosphate mining, interrupted on the outbreak of war, as soon as possible. At the instigation of the company, the colonial secretary instructed the Australian governor-general to remove the company's German employees from the island immediately. The company's representative in Australia managed to persuade the government to deport the German officials as well, on the ground that otherwise "the matter becomes more complicated."[4]

When the Australian expeditionary troops eventually occupied Nauru on 6 November 1914, their commander, Colonel Holmes, the Administrator of occupied German New Guinea, had written instructions to deport all Germans to Australia as POWs and to leave the administration of the island in the hands of a representative of the Pacific Phosphate Company. In future, the British high commissioner for the western Pacific in Fiji was in charge politically.[5] The

Australian soldiers in Nauru, 1917. (Photograph by Thomas J. McMahon. Mitchell Library, State Library of New South Wales)

Germans were removed from the island under heavy guard and in a closed column. In order to calm the Nauruans, Australian officers had let it be known, via the chiefs, that the Germans would return in three months.[6]

Holmes left behind a garrison with fifty-two men under Captain E. C. Norrie as an Australian occupying force. The arrival of the British high commissioner's representative, Charles Workman, on Christmas Day 1914 marked the beginning of what was, in fact, joint rule by Australia and Britain. The British high commissioner in Suva was responsible for the civil administration of the island; in military matters, however, the island was dependent on Rabaul.[7] The Australian government refused a request from London to withdraw the Australian garrison. The Administrator of Rabaul argued that behind the request lay a cold-blooded, calculated attempt to eliminate Australian influence, and that this must be prevented at all costs. After all, he pointed out, Nauru was worth several hundreds of millions of pounds. On the other hand, the military government in New Guinea gave in to British pressure and withdrew a proclamation about post and quarantine regulations in which they had included Nauru. Both sides were jealous of their respective rights.[8]

Workman distinguished himself by renaming the island Pleasant Island. He persisted in this, even after the Colonial Office informed him that under international law the name could not officially be changed until after the end of the war.[9] Otherwise, Workman gave the Pacific Phosphate Company a pretty free hand. When a company employee, Pope, was appointed administrative assistant, the company was even given access to the administration's confidential information, with the explicit consent of the colonial secretary.[10] The Pacific Phosphate Company tried several times to persuade the administration to give it permission to acquire land. Like Burns Philp in New Guinea, the company also claimed that it had already gained the verbal agreement of the German administration. At first, the request was rejected on the usual grounds that the applicants must wait until the end of the war.[11] However, while Workman was on holiday in January 1917, the Pacific Phosphate Company went on the offensive. The Administrator's deputy in his absence, S. F. Anderson, was the company's bookkeeper on Nauru. Now Pacific Phosphate could copy the German land registers undisturbed and establish the names of the indigenous owners of phosphate-bearing land. Under the aegis of Anderson, the company drew up a document stating that the land claimed by the company had been bought by it between 1907 and 1914, with the permission of the German government and the Nauruan owners. As supposed proof that Nauruans had given their approval, their "X" had been added. But anyone who knew the Nauruans was aware that they, like the Samoans, had long since become literate. The whole process was clearly a swindle, a fraudulent attempt on the part of the Pacific Phosphate Company to seize the phosphate-bearing land of the Nauruans. The British high commissioner was not informed.[12]

The company resumed work in the phosphate mines soon after the Australian occupation of the island and before the British high commissioner's repre-

TABLE 9. Phosphate Mining on Nauru during the Military
Administration, 1914–1921

CALENDAR YEAR	QUANTITY OF PHOSPHATE EXPORTED IN IMPERIAL TONS
1914	53,740
1915	85,808
1916	105,012
1917	101,267
1918	76,440
1919	69,336
1920 to 30 June 1921	364,424

Source: Annual Report Nauru 1916: ANL: G 21152. Report on the
Adminsitration of Nauru during the Military Occupation and until 17
December 1920; AAC: A 2219–22. 1920/21: AAC: A 6661–396.

sentative arrived. Instructions from London to await his arrival were ignored,
with Australian connivance.[13] German influence in the company had in fact
already come to an end. Late in July 1917 it was completely eliminated officially when all the shares that had been in German hands—four-ninths of the
company's capital—were publicly auctioned in London.[14] Phosphate mining,
however, continued uninterrupted throughout the war, although levels were
reduced by the difficulty of transport. The labor problem was solved when the
Japanese government, in response to a British request, permitted the continued recruitment of workers for Nauru from the Caroline Islands. During the
war, as well as immediately after it, the Pacific Phosphate Company hired its
workers from the Japanese-occupied Caroline Islands. Chinese coolies had
worked on Nauru since 1907, but no further reinforcements arrived until early
in 1920.[15]

The "Battle for Nauru," 1919–1922

At the end of the war, a battle for Nauru began between Britain and its allies in
the Pacific. It was far fiercer than the quarrels about the future of German
New Guinea, Samoa, or the rest of Micronesia. Behind the scenes, all manner
of wrangling took place, using all possible means to jostle for the best position.
The main actors in the struggle were the prime ministers of Australia and New
Zealand, Hughes and Massey, and the British colonial secretary, Milner. The
setting for this fraternal feud was the British Empire Delegation, which met
regularly in London and Paris. Here attempts were made to find a common
position that the representatives of the British Empire could all endorse in
order to ensure that, as far as possible, British demands were accepted at the
forthcoming peace conference.

Hughes registered the first claims. Almost as soon as he arrived in Europe, he began agitating vigorously for Nauru to be given to Australia. In mid-February 1919 Massey put New Zealand's argument on the table: phosphate from Nauru was indispensable for the New Zealand agriculture. Early in March, Milner also got involved. The British memorandum he presented to the Empire Delegation suggested that the mandate should go to Britain; the island was to be administered through the British high commissioner in Fiji. The colonial secretary did not conceal his opinion from Hughes: "Britain wanted it, as it was valuable." Five days later the Australian prime minister retaliated in kind. In a meeting of the Empire Delegation he openly demanded that Australia should be given the mandate for Nauru—"the other islands are a liability, this is an asset."[16]

As no decision could be arrived at, the matter was postponed. During this period, the Australian cabinet, at the suggestion of its prime minister, prepared a detailed statement outlining why Australia had to have Nauru. It is typical of the Australian obsession with the Yellow Peril that the issue of acquiring Nauru was imported into the chain of argument about Australia being defenselessly exposed to potential invaders. Nauru, argued the Australian cabinet, was vital to the people of Australia (meaning Australians of British origin), because without its phosphate the interior of Australia would remain empty and unpopulated while the majority of the population clustered around the coast, "where they will be a comparatively easy prey to any predatory power, . . . League or no League, we must always remember that more than half the people of the world look with hungry eyes across narrow seas at our great empty land."[17]

One day before the Council of Four met to announce how the mandates over the former German colonies had been distributed, the British side had still not come to an agreement about the political future of Nauru. Neither the United States, Japan, nor any other victorious power disputed the British claim to Nauru. At a meeting of the ministers of the British Dominions on 5 May, the established fronts hardly changed. Hughes again expressed Australia's claim to a mandate; Massey protested vigorously. From time to time, the Australian and the New Zealander let fly at each other. The old rivalry between the two Anglo-Saxon colonies in the Pacific broke out again, and there was a full-blown domestic argument. Hughes raged: "New Zealand has absolutely no claim or standing in the matter at all. Massey's opposition to us . . . is an intolerable insult to Australia. I am going to stand fast for our just rights. . . . to be robbed of Nauru that is for me the end. I will not sign Treaty. I will not accept the mandate for other islands."[18] One day later, the Supreme War Council announced its decision on the mandates. The mandate for Nauru was given to the British Empire. The British were to sort out for themselves what this meant on the ground.[19]

Intense negotiations went on for the whole of May and June. The Australian delegation's legal expert, Robert Garran, suggested how the deadlock could be broken. He explained to his prime minister that all Australia needed was to secure actual control of the island. Apart from that, they could share:

"There is plenty for all in Nauru."[20] Another moderating influence on the Australian prime minister was a resolution by his own cabinet formally instructing Hughes not to refuse to sign the peace treaty under any circumstances. "We are grabbing at valuable asset," Watt calmed the prime minister.[21]

By 4 June it was clear that the three governments would reach agreement. Access to the phosphate deposits on Nauru was to be divided among the three on a percentage basis, and each country was to nominate a commissioner to represent its interest. An Administrator, with no influence over the actions of the commissioners, was to have sole responsibility for the civil administration. He was to be appointed by Australia for the first five years, and then in turn by the other governments involved. Agreement was finally reached on Thomas Griffiths, a former Australian military governor of New Guinea. He assumed office on 10 June 1921. All that remained to be decided were the quotas. Massey finally accepted 16 percent as New Zealand's share, while Australia and Britain were to receive 42 percent each. On 28 June 1919, Hughes and Massey signed the agreement and passed it on to Milner for ratification by Lloyd George.[22]

In the meantime, Milner negotiated with the management of the Pacific Phosphate Company for rights to be transferred to the three governments. The company's management was personally closely connected with leading members of the English upper class and also with the Colonial Office. The founding managing director of the Pacific Phosphate Company, Baron Stanmore, had, as Arthur Gordon, been the first British high commissioner in the Western Pacific. He made use of his local knowledge and personal connections to have the annexation of Ocean Island, another phosphate island, accepted by the Colonial Office, and to advance the company's interests instead of those of the indigenous Banaban people. His successor was his nephew by marriage, a man who was believed to be an intimate friend of the king and who had great influence over Milner.[23] Within a short time, he had developed the company into one of Britain's most profitable enterprises. In the period from 1902, when phosphate mining began on Ocean Island, to the end of 1918, it had made enormous profits from its phosphate works on Ocean Island and Nauru. Average net profits were 13 shillings, 3 pence per ton of phosphate exported. This was 265 times the sum that the Nauruan landowners received. Total net proceeds amounted to £2,125,045.[24]

Around the middle of July 1919, Milner sent the text of the agreement, dated 2 July, to the governments involved. At Milner's request, the haggling among Britain, Australia, and New Zealand was to remain secret, "as it is undesirable that its existence should become known publicly before the whole question of Mandates has been finally settled."[25]

The situation was highly peculiar. The League of Nations had not yet laid down the conditions governing the mandates, but Britain, Australia, and New Zealand had already divided up the spoils on their own authority. The matter was to remain secret from the international public, but to be put into effect the treaty had to be ratified by three parliaments. New Zealand's most eminent legal scholar of the day, John William Salmond, summed up his view in two words, "exceedingly obscure."[26]

In September 1919, after many personal meetings, Milner negotiated the price for which the Pacific Phosphate Company would be prepared to transfer its right to exploit phosphate deposits on Nauru and Ocean Island to the three governments. The sum was £3,540,000—according to Milner, "a good bargain," for as a result of rising demand after the end of the war, profits had jumped to one pound per ton of phosphate exported.[27] The Australian prime minister's well-known temper—"the price named far too high . . . the copingstone of their impudence"[28]—brought the price down a little. On 1 July 1920 the privileges of the Pacific Phosphate Company on Ocean Island and Nauru were finally transferred to the governments of Great Britain, Australia, and New Zealand for a sum of £3,539,000, after the three governments had agreed among themselves to divide the purchase price in the same proportions as their respective phosphate quotas.[29]

In the House of Commons, the reading of the Nauru agreement in mid-June 1920 unleashed harsh criticism. But it was artificially whipped-up indignation that served only as a demonstration of hypocrisy, as it was clear from the start that the agreement would not come to grief. Nor was it the eloquent silence of the agreement on the rights and the future of the people of Nauru that was criticized. Only a few months before, the introduction of the mandate system had been justified by claiming that it protected the people from exploitation. Now this was ignored both by the representatives of the British people and by their government. No one even asked to what extent the mining of phosphate would impair the quality of life and limit the rights of the Nauruans, or whether the agreement violated their right to self-determination. Rather, opponents criticized the open disregard shown for the international agreements governing the League of Nations' prerogative in defining mandates. Most of all, they revealed their concern that the treaty would run counter to liberal trade policy. The bill was finally passed by 217 to 77 votes, that is, by a majority of almost two-thirds. The arguments put forward by Leslie Wilson, parliamentary secretary to the Ministry of Shipping, could hardly be contradicted: "there was never a more sound investment for this country and the Empire, not only from the financial point of view, but also from the point of view of securing for all time . . . an all-important raw material."[30]

Of all attempts to undermine the original principle of the so-called sacred trust over the former German colonies, the cattle trading over Nauru among the British, Australians, and New Zealanders was probably the most brutal violation of the mandate idea. The impotence of the League of Nations and the commissions responsible for mandates was clear even before they met. Their first meeting almost ended in a row when the Australian representative quashed any criticism of what had happened in Nauru by declaring that he would not put up with it. The final report to the Council of the League of Nations was a whitewash, and the hypocrisy continued in Geneva.[31]

The fact that, in the event, the League of Nations just ignored such a blatant infringement of the principles it had been entrusted at Versailles to uphold simply encouraged the three phosphate representatives to push ahead in a direction that was completely contrary to the spirit of the mandate. The Treaty of Versailles had confirmed Japanese rule over Micronesia. The Japanese policy of sealing Micronesia off from the outside world meant that laborers could no longer be recruited from the Caroline and Marshall Islands. British control over Hong Kong appeared to guarantee a source of Chinese labor for Nauru for the foreseeable future. But as the Australian phosphate commissioner Harold Pope, former chief accountant of the Pacific Phosphate Company on Nauru, pointed out, it was important to be able to fall back on Pacific Islanders for labor in addition to the Chinese. He stressed that conflict between the two different racial groups among the phosphate workers could only facilitate exploitation, for one could be played off against the other. This would be especially useful if the Chinese were to make trouble.[32]

In April 1921, on the suggestion of the Australian representative on the phosphate commission, the Australian prime minister instructed the Administrator of the Australian mandate in New Guinea to support fully the recruitment of two hundred Melanesians for Nauru. Apparently no consideration was given to the fact that this might violate the conditions of the mandate for New Guinea. On the Administrator's recommendation, the labor recruitment commando from Nauru was accompanied by "experienced" recruiters from the mandate, all former soldiers in the occupying force, plus a number of *luluai*, who had been instructed by the district officers to use their influence in favor of the recruiters. Government ships were used in order to impress the official nature of the expedition even more clearly upon the indigenous population. Nonetheless, by June 1921 only forty-one Melanesians had been persuaded to go to Nauru. In October, they were joined by a further sixty-nine young Melanesians from Morobe, Manus, and the Sepik district. When it became clear that nothing further could be achieved, the expedition left New Guinea directly for Nauru, ignoring all customs and recruiting regulations, and without putting in at Rabaul, as required.[33] One year later, the process was repeated. This time Pope asked for special police protection, as the coasts were deserted and it was necessary to penetrate farther into the interior in order to recruit. Again, labor regulations were blatantly violated. And again, the target was two hundred Melanesians; but in the end no more than seventy-one were recruited.[34]

The men from New Guinea, completely unused to regular work, were forced to work at the same rate as the Chinese. The daily quota of piecework was loading five one-ton trucks with phosphate. But on the special request of the Administrator of New Guinea, Wisdom, they were paid according to New Guinea regulations. Whereas the Chinese received 32 shillings per month,

New Guinea laborers working phosphate in Nauru, early 1921. (Mitchell Library, State Library of New South Wales)

Melanesians received only 5 shillings, which the labor regulations in Australian New Guinea specified as the maximum wage. The average wage of a Melanesian plantation worker in German New Guinea in 1914 set the piece-work rate for Melanesian phosphate workers in Nauru until 1924. And, as in New Guinea, the system of deferred payment applied. Of their already meager wages, 3 shillings per month were retained until the end of their three-year contracts.[35]

Removed from their familiar environment and deprived of the protection of their small-scale societies, the men from New Guinea had to perform extremely strenuous work that posed a high and immediate risk to their health. The food they were used to, *kaukau* (sweet potato), taro, yams, and sago did not grow on Nauru and was not imported. It is therefore not surprising that the Melanesians fell ill of tuberculosis in droves. Two-thirds were additionally weakened by a dysentery epidemic in March 1922. Of the total of 181 Melanesians recruited for work in Nauru, twenty-two were sent back early because they were unfit for further work. Most of them died on the way back, or shortly thereafter. This meant that the official mortality rates could be massaged. Nonetheless, by June 1924, when the contracts of the first batch of Melanesian workers expired and came up for extension, twenty-six phosphate workers from New Guinea had died on Nauru. This represented a mortality rate of over 16 percent. It is extremely doubtful whether their families ever received the "deferred pay" that was now due them. Given that a meeting of the Mandate Commission in Geneva was imminent, the Australian cabinet, in agreement with the Administrators of New Guinea and Nauru, decided to stop recruiting for Nauru from New Guinea and to remove all Melanesians from Nauru. On 25 July 1924 the survivors left the small Pacific island.[36]

The Role of the Nauruans

For the people of Nauru, the arrival of the Australians was not a liberation. However, shortly before the flag was hoisted on 7 November 1914, Colonel Holmes had promised their chiefs, who had been assembled with the support of the head of the German station, Wostrack, "that as long as they and their people did what was right the King of England would protect them." German rule had come to an end, he went on, and the British flag would never be taken down.[37] But the king of England was a long way away when, a little later, the Australian soldiers left behind by Holmes shot the Nauruans' dogs and pigs out of boredom.[38] Nor did the change in the ruling power do the local population much good in other respects. Nauruan landowners had received minimal compensation for the mining of phosphate on their land; this was reduced even further by the introduction of British currency and British weights and measures. Instead of 5 pfennigs per tonne of phosphate exported, the Nauruans now received a ha'penny, which at contemporary rates was a little more than 4 pfennigs. In addition, the metric tonne was replaced by the imperial ton overnight, without the Nauruans being aware or informed of this change. Because the imperial ton was more than 16 kilograms heavier than the metric tonne, the amount of compensation received by the landowners was reduced again. In April 1916 the British high commissioner for the Western Pacific decreased the value of the mark, which was still official currency on Nauru, to 6 pence, amounting to a devaluation of 50 percent. This increased the value of the compensation the Nauruans received. But because almost all they owned was in marks—in 1915 the Administrator estimated their holdings as 300,000 marks—the money in their hands was devalued by 50 percent from one day to the next. There was considerable anxiety among the Nauruans as a result of this, but they were unable to influence the decision in any way.[39] It seemed that the people of Nauru were among the losers of the war.

A new situation arose with the end of the war in Europe. The news of Germany's defeat and the definitive end of German rule in Nauru was followed by a long silence concerning the future of the island and its people. Throughout, the Pacific Phosphate Company continued to work as it had done before 1914. In mid-July 1919 the Nauruans sent a petition to the king of England referring to this peculiar situation. The Germans, they said, who had cheated them by paying only 5 pfennigs per tonne, had gone. But why was the same company that had worked in Nauru before the war, under the German administration, still there?

Ever since the wresting of the Island from the Germans this same Company is still carrying on and perpetuating the same iniquity by paying us a halfpenny per ton of phosphates. A great part of our island from which phosphates had been dug is now absolutely useless. Nothing remains except rocks and stones. It is so badly ruined that no tropical tree of any kind could grow on it. We never received a penny for these spoiled acres of land above mentioned. We have been robbed of our lands by the Germans and we now, as British subjects, are hoping that these lands will be restored to us.[40]

The people of Nauru used exactly the line of argument the British had adopted during the war. Germans were presented as the source of all injustice in the world, Britons as the standard-bearers of fairness. The people of Nauru had been promised the protection of the king when the British flag was hoisted in November 1914. Thus, for them, as British subjects, to appeal to this promise, and at the same time to point out that it was only a matter of removing the last relics of German injustice, was only just and fair. Local self-determination over the land that belonged to them was the Nauruans' primary demand. The demand for compensation for damage to the environment was secondary. Criticism of the environmental damage done by phosphate mining was closely connected with the hope that the actual power of disposition over the land would be given back to them. The only way to stop the environmental damage was to restore the Nauruans' right of usufruct. The demand for use of the land to revert to the local people implied a desire on the part of the Nauruans to put a halt to the environmental damage done by phosphate mining. It is likely that the people of Nauru, using a method of arguing characteristic of many Pacific cultures, were aiming for nothing less than to stop the phosphate mining altogether.

While the people of Nauru were appealing to the king's sense of justice in order to put right an injustice perpetrated in the past, or at least to put a stop to it, the king's colonial secretary was negotiating for the state to take over those privileges which the local people had clearly declared to be theft. The contract that enshrined official British disregard for the Nauruans' right of disposition and ensured the continuation of environmental destruction on Nauru had already been signed. When it became clear to the Nauruans that only the actors were to change, and that the situation they had criticized would nevertheless continue, they enquired of the Administrator whether they could at least be compensated for the damage and deceptions of the past, and in future receive higher rates.[41] This request was more comprehensible to the new phosphate hunters, implying, as it did, indigenous acceptance of the status quo.

In an agreement of 1 July 1921, Nauruans for the first time ceded land for phosphate mining. It was a leasing agreement that provided for a one-off payment of twenty pounds per acre of phosphate-bearing land to the indigenous owners of the land. In exchange, the British Phosphate Commission received the right to mine phosphate until 31 March 2000. It was free to do what it liked with the trees, bushes, and fruits growing on the leased land. As a consequence of this agreement, further serious environmental damage was done. In addition, it was inconsistent with the traditional Pacific legal understanding that separated rights over land from the right to use the plants growing on the land. The special compensation that had originally been offered for every coconut palm destroyed now lapsed. Compensation for every imperial ton of phosphate exported, however, was increased from a ha'penny to three pence. One-third of the amount paid was deposited with the Administrator, who used this fund to finance the introduction of compulsory schooling, which he had decreed. When the colonial secretary pointed out that the written consent of the chiefs was not adequate, efforts were made to obtain permission from all the individual owners of the land. Finally, 244 signatures were collected.[42]

There is no doubt that in real terms the "agreement" between the British Phosphate Commission, supported by the Colonial Office and the Administrator, and the local landowners improved the economic situation of the people of Nauru compared with their position before the war. In legal terms, however, their position was considerably worse. It was never disputed that they were the owners of the land, but this fact was simply ignored. The right of disposition was "temporarily" acquired by means of a compensatory payment. Now the indigenous owners had, for the first time, agreed to a leasing contract that legally sanctioned the exploitation of their land. For the moment, so long as the Nauruans had no chance to protest against the actions of the strangers, the difference between tolerating the violence that was actually happening and giving their formal consent may have seemed irrelevant. However, when the Nauruans were recognized as independent subjects under international law, the situation was different, because in a Europeanized world only legal formalities opened the door to historical reparations. Before 1921 the local population *in principio* contested the actions of the Europeans in Nauru. Thereafter, with the creation of a precedent, all that remained to be disputed were the details of an extension of the term of the contract, its expansion, and the level of remuneration.

This fact has no bearing whatsoever on the justified question of the ethically binding force of a formal agreement that was possibly legal but morally dubious—"the natives are simple-minded people, not versed in land values," wrote the Administrator later.[43] There is absolutely no doubt that without considerable pressure the Nauruans would not have consented to a change in their constitutional rights. Even without their formal agreement, their existing rights were being altered. Land that was not phosphate-bearing could now be leased to Europeans for the first time. Granting the opportunity to acquire cheaply land that had originally been declared nonphosphate-bearing was in the gift of the Administrator alone. In some cases, phosphate was later mined on this land after all. The Administrator possessed sole authority to classify land as phosphate-bearing or nonphosphate-bearing, and to make it available for lease. The owner's consent to the leasing agreement was not required.[44] The people of Nauru became increasingly dependent on an Administrator who ruled over them almost arbitrarily per administrative order.[45] The German administration had prohibited contact between foreign workers and the Nauruans. Now the tables were turned and the local population was forbidden to leave its strictly delimited areas between sunset and sunrise. The chiefs had the privilege of making sure that the Nauruans did not break these rules.[46] The colonial order on Nauru depended heavily on the cooperation of the chiefs. When the Chinese coolies went on strike because of the excessively high prices the shops in Nauru charged non-Europeans for food, the Administrator demanded that the chiefs of Nauru provide 250 men to risk their lives for the interests of the Pacific Phosphate Company (which, although it had transferred its phosphate rights to the three governments, had been permitted to keep its stores on Nauru). Together with the police and the Administrator, they marched to the Chinese settlement, where the Administrator delivered an ultimatum. Either the Chinese went back to work or his forces would open fire on them.[47] As for the Nauruans, the Administrator banned a cooperative venture they had planned in order to break their dependence on Australian and British traders.[48]

In September 1920 a serious influenza epidemic broke out on Nauru. It was probably brought into the country from China by the newly recruited coolies. Although alarming news was coming in from all over the world about the devastating effects of a flu epidemic, especially on non-European populations, the administration of Nauru proved to be incapable of preventing the illness from gaining a foothold. Given the island's isolation and the difficulty of landing on it at all, more stringent health policies could easily have prevented the illness from entering the country. Influenza again demonstrated its deadly nature. "Only" 301 inhabitants of the island (including two Chinese) died of the illness. But because the number of Pacific Islanders living on Nauru was not particularly large, this represented a considerable proportion of the population. The worst affected were the phosphate workers from the Caroline and Marshall Islands on Nauru. More than one-third (exactly 36 percent of the population counted in 1919) did not survive the illness. The indigenous population was reduced by 18 percent.[49] The spread of the disease was facilitated by a change in the behavior of Nauruans since 1914. During the war, they had given up their traditional clothes in favor of European textiles.[50] The habit, common to many Pacific Islanders, of wearing European clothes day and night, it has been shown, reduced their natural resistance to colds. In addition, the exceptional circumstances of the war had made it possible for Burns Philp to sell whisky illegally to the indigenous people.[51] New Zealand's phosphate commissioner blamed the Nauruans themselves for the tragic impact of influenza. He claimed that they were "extremely lazy," and that this was the greatest obstacle to living longer.[52]

As soon as the influenza became less virulent, the first Nauruans were afflicted with leprosy. Weakness caused by the flu epidemic had, it seemed, made them susceptible to leprosy, which was almost certainly also imported

Nauruan woman with leprosy at the Leper Station Nauru, September 1922. (Mitchell Library, State Library of New South Wales)

from China. In March 1922, up to 10.3 percent of the indigenous population in certain areas was affected by leprosy. The Administrator had tried to get medical assistance from Australia or London, but apparently the only thing of concern there was profit from phosphate. In the absence of any medical aid, the proportion of the population suffering from leprosy constantly grew. By October 1922, 12.5 percent of all Nauruans were afflicted; in one particularly badly hit area, the percentage was 20.3. This was the highest rate of leprosy in the world for a single administrative district. Only at this stage did medical aid reach Nauru.[53] The drastic reduction in the local population inspired the Administrator to take up an idea put forward by the British resident commissioner for the Gilbert and Ellice Islands. He had suggested deporting all the inhabitants of Ocean Island to Nauru, because phosphate mining on Ocean Island required more and more land. "There is certainly ample room in Nauru for the Ocean Island Natives," claimed Thomas Griffiths, supporting his colleague.[54] But the steady resistance of the Banaban people prevented their forced deportation from Ocean Island at this stage.

THE JAPANESE IN MICRONESIA

Japanese rule in occupied German Micronesia differed greatly in style from either British or Australian rule in New Guinea and Samoa. The only superficial similarity between them was that they were all administered by the military. The military administration of Micronesia was responsible to the Japanese naval ministry. Japanese administrative headquarters in Micronesia, under the control of a naval commander, were at first located in Truk (not in Ponape, where they had been before the war) and from July 1921 in Koror on Palau. In June 1918 a civil administration had been appointed under Rear Admiral Tezuka Toshiro, but this was a merely nominal change, because control remained with the naval ministry. Not until 1 April 1922—that is, a year later than in Nauru, New Guinea, and Samoa—were naval units withdrawn from the islands and a civil South Sea administration, Nan'yo-cho, set up. Its governor was responsible directly to the Japanese prime minister.[55]

On 8 October 1914, when the Japanese captured the administrative center of German Micronesia, the Japanese commander had reassured the Capuchin mission, in German, that nothing would change.[56] This statement was true, if at all, only of the first few months of the Japanese occupation, that is, until about the end of 1914, when it gradually became clear that the islands would not be handed over to British or Australian troops as the Japanese had feared. From 1915, however, the Japanese began to pursue an almost tempestuous occupation policy that had little in common with German practice, and next to nothing with that followed by the Australians and New Zealanders farther south.

What made Japanese practice so different was the extraordinary determination and sense of purpose apparent in every action. There is nothing to sug-

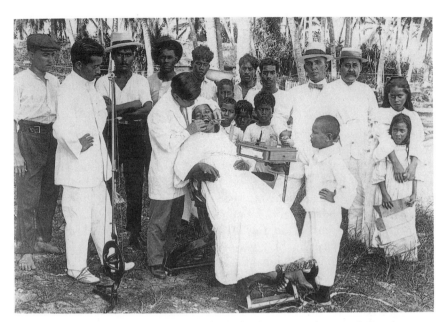

A Japanese dentist at work in the Marshall Islands, 1917. (Photograph by Thomas J. McMahon. Mitchell Library, State Library of New South Wales)

gest that the Japanese occupiers had any doubts about Micronesia remaining Japanese, but even if they did have such doubts, they spared no effort to ensure that Japan could present a fait accompli on the day peace was declared. Three chronological phases can be distinguished in the activities of the Japanese in occupied Micronesia: the assessment, the development, and the exploitation of resources. During the first period, which lasted from the end of 1914 to around the early autumn of 1915, the Japanese systematically investigated what the islands of Micronesia had to offer. Almost every ship brought more Japanese scientists, agricultural economists, and medical doctors. Scholars and experts in all sorts of specialized areas methodically set about surveying the potential of the islands. As a German eyewitness noted, "there was not a house or a tree that was not photographed."[57] Some of these Japanese researchers were so preoccupied by their task of mapping and surveying the country that they took no notice at all of the indigenous population and the few Europeans who had remained.[58]

By about the middle of 1915 the scientific survey of Micronesia was more or less complete. Yamamoto Miono, a young professor at the Imperial University of Tokyo, submitted the research group's final report to the Japanese government. It seems that the scientists had not been able to discover any exciting economic prospects, for several Japanese newspapers began a detailed debate about Micronesia's doubtful economic value to Japan and questioned whether it was worth keeping the islands at all. Suggestions were made that are familiar

from European colonial history, such as allowing a trading company to administer the islands.[59] As in the case of Australia's presence in New Guinea, however,
strategic considerations suddenly became more important than economic
interests. The most common argument, and one Yamamoto himself endorsed,
was that the islands were an important springboard for further Japanese expansion south.[60]

The second phase of Japanese military rule was marked by energetic
attempts to develop the little potential that did exist in Micronesia. For this
purpose, the infrastructure was developed to an extent unprecedented under
German rule. New harbor installations, wharfs, roads, and public and private
buildings were built. The setting up of radio stations on all the important
islands was primarily a military measure, but private communications also benefited from the establishment of a public telephone network (for example, on
Saipan toward the end of the war). All the sources document a highly aggressive and resolute push by the Japanese to make the Micronesian islands economically more profitable, and at the same time, more "Japanese." These two
goals were so closely intertwined that often they cannot be separated. This also
makes it relatively difficult to pass judgment on Japanese actions. The extraordinary energy of Japanese initiatives, the development that they achieved, and
their early economic successes undoubtedly inspire some respect. But the
force and speed with which the Japanese modernized the islands make us think
again. There is little to suggest that any account was taken of indigenous interests or traditions, and the whole exercise begins to look like a violent and brutal
rape by Japan of Micronesia's original character.[61]

The Japanese took up the economic development of Micronesia where the
Germans had left off. As early as 6 November 1914 representatives of the Japanese South Sea Company, Nan'yo Keiei Kumiai, landed on Angaur to investigate the chances of continuing phosphate mining under Japanese control. The
director of the company, Nishizawa Kichiji, had allegedly concluded an agreement at the end of September 1914 with Admiral Akiyama Saneyuki, director
of the bureau for military affairs in the Japanese naval ministry, giving the company exclusive phosphate mining rights on Angaur. When the Germans there
refused to cooperate in any way with the Japanese company, they were immediately expelled, and the Nan'yo Keiei Kumiai started work straightaway. In
mid-June 1915, about a year after the last German phosphate ship had left
Angaur, the first Japanese consignment of phosphate left the island. After the
company had transported about six shiploads of phosphate (roughly 35,000
tonnes) to Japan, however, a huge scandal broke out there because of the preferential treatment given to one company by certain high-ranking naval circles.
On 1 September 1915 the naval ministry revoked the company's exclusive
rights on Angaur. Thereafter the phosphate was mined under the supervision
of the ministry and, under the terms of a Japanese government resolution of 8
October, publicly auctioned in Japan. Public discussion of the preferential
treatment of a single company by certain high-ranking "patrons" in the navy,

and the cancellation of this arrangement by the Japanese government, separate this from such cases as Burns Philp, which was backed by Australian politicians, and the Pacific Phosphate Company, supported by the British. The phenomenon of Japanese speculators attempting to make quick profits by exploiting the new and sometimes confusing conditions in the wake of Japanese colonial expansion had long been known from Korea and Taiwan.[62]

Japanese innovations for the economic development of Micronesia were astonishingly imaginative and versatile. Although the Germans had maintained experimental gardens and plantations, they had been rather halfhearted ventures, as if to prove—against the German local administration's convictions—the old theory that colonies provide economic benefits for the mother country. The few Germans working in the experimental botanical station in Ponape were like amateur gardeners cultivating flowers—well aware that a thing well done cannot be done quickly, especially in the tropics. Japanese efforts, by contrast, displayed an internal drive and a need to succeed which can be explained only by assuming that they grew out of the feeling that things had to be set in motion in Micronesia as quickly as possible, in order to have concrete achievements to support Japan's territorial claims after the conclusion of peace. Factories and industrial plants appeared, seemingly overnight and out of nowhere. In Ponape experiments were made with rice; in Kusaie, with cotton. Almost every island supported its own small experimental program. The best known, because most successful, ventures were the sugarcane plantations on Saipan and Tinian. Under the Germans, Tinian had been completely uninhabited and was declared a reserve for wild cattle. From 1917 every male Chamorro on Saipan was compelled to plant at least one hectare with sugarcane, and every woman at least half a hectare.[63]

On the Mariana Islands sugar was a major factor in the relatively quick transition from development and investment to exploitation. Sugar production began shortly before the end of the European war and developed into a success story in the early 1920s. From 1921 the value of exports from Micronesia, excluding phosphate from Angaur, exceeded that of imports. In 1920 sugar accounted for 24 percent of the total value of all exports from Micronesia (excluding phosphate). In the first six months of production alone, 442 tonnes of sugar were exported from Saipan, while even Ponape managed eight. The long domination of copra monoculture was increasingly being broken down.[64] There is no doubt that the Micronesians also benefited from the economic development work done by the Japanese (and their laborers from Korea and Okinawa).[65]

Where their own methods held out no prospect of success the Japanese adopted German practices, but took them to extremes. The Japanese adaptation of the compulsory planting program introduced by the German colonial administration in the Marshall Islands is a typical example. The Marshall Islands had the most limited economic potential in Micronesia. For this reason the German administration had retained an exceptional tax in kind, payable in copra. The Japanese adopted the compulsory planting law introduced by the Germans but combined it with an ultimatum that made its observance practically a matter of life or death. In May 1918 the chiefs were instructed that any land that had not been planted with coconut palms within three years would immediately be declared government land.[66] The Japanese strategy of threatening the indigenous population with the loss of their land if they did not work to support Japanese economic goals was also applied elsewhere. In Ponape the managing director of the Japanese sugar factory, a former naval officer, had imposed a contract on the indigenous landowners that provided for automatic confiscation of their land if they did not keep it weeded. Finally, a Japanese decree of 1920 declared that any land in Micronesia which had not been cleared and planted by 1921 would pass into the ownership of the Japanese state.[67]

Compared with the German colonial administration, the Japanese system was more totalitarian. The Japanese administration's attempt to force development in a particular direction was more pressing, comprehensive, and direct. Japanese practice invites comparison with a steamroller, inexorably flattening everything in its path and compelling the front line of people fleeing before it to remove the rankest weeds. It may be that, to Micronesians, who had a strong sense of tradition, German methods also resembled the progress of a steamroller. But it was a different one; or, at least, its drivers were different. Its progress was slower, more careful, and less decisive. The driver took account of the changing landscape around him, often hesitating in his forward march, making a detour, or even changing direction. Occasional use of reverse gear was not unknown. From the start, the Germans lacked the Japanese determination to stick rigidly to a particular route. By the end, it is doubtful whether the German driver even knew where he was meant to be going. Above all, however, there were many fewer steamrollers during the German period than under Japanese rule. The impression left by a handful of German officials, dispersed throughout the whole of Micronesia, was certainly out of all proportion to their number. But compared with the impact of the hundreds of Japanese military officials who poured into Micronesia after 1914, it was marginal. One fact is undisputable: under Japanese rule there were many fewer niches for those who rejected the directions given by the traffic policeman, or who wanted to get out of his reach altogether.

This does not mean that the Japanese control extended to every corner of Micronesia. How the indigenous population came to terms with the Japanese will be discussed below. Europeans commonly regard Japanese-controlled Micronesia as a hermetically sealed, impenetrable, monolithic empire. This is a popular exaggeration of an important aspect of historical reality which, however, obscures the fact that between the end of 1914 and the beginning of 1922 there were a number of areas where Japanese influence was limited. It is true that communications with the non-Japanese outside world were almost completely broken from the end of 1914. This affected American missionaries in the Marshall Islands as much as the few Germans who had remained. The situation did not change until the secret agreement of 1917, under which the British, Russian, and Italian governments promised to support Japanese claims to Micronesia in a peace treaty. Thereafter, the mail between Micronesia and the United States officially resumed, and the Marshall Islanders who had been stranded in San Francisco since 1914 could at last return home.[68]

But even before 1917 there were two important exceptions to the embargo on contact with the outside world that the Japanese had declared in Micronesia. Both cases involved existing Australian–British trade in Micronesia, which was allowed to continue. The Pacific Phosphate Company in Nauru was permitted to continue returning its workers to the Caroline Islands in its own schooners after expiry of their contracts, and even to recruit new labor from there. And in mid-February 1915, Burns Philp, with the support of the British government, received official Japanese permission to continue trading in the Marshall Islands; it even managed to expand during this period. In 1915 its turnover in the Marshall Islands doubled by comparison with average figures for the five years before the war. Burns Philp benefited above all from the elimination of German competition when the Jaluit Company (Jaluitgesellschaft) was forced to cease trading on 31 March 1915. Early in 1917 the Australian

"There's Australia." Marshall Islands children discover Australia on a Burns Philp calendar, c. 1917. These calendars showed Micronesia as being "under British occupation" long after its conquest by Japan. (Photograph by Thomas J. McMahon. Mitchell Library, State Library of New South Wales)

Australian traders weighing and buying copra for Burns Philp. Marshall Islands, 1917. (Photograph by Thomas J. McMahon. Mitchell Library, State Library of New South Wales)

company was permitted to open an official branch office in Jaluit and ten trading stations in the Marshall Islands. Before the war it had only sent its ships to call regularly; now it had agents on the spot. In the shadow of the war, business boomed for Burns Philp, even in the remotest corners of Japanese Micronesia. From mid-1917 at the latest, agents of the American trading company Atkins Kroll & Co. were also permitted to travel through the islands of Micronesia from bases in Guam and San Francisco.[69] None of this detracts from the image of the Japanese steamroller in Micronesia; it merely adds a further dimension. Atkins Kroll, Burns Philp, and the Pacific Phosphate Company were officially sanctioned speed limits imposed on the steamroller drivers—all in all, more annoying than alarming. In any case, the general speed was not affected by them, and the Japanese were aware that these warning signs could be removed as quickly as they had been set up.

The Japanese evidently regarded Burns Philp as an official representative of the Australian government. Early in 1915 the Japanese consul-general visited James Burns and proposed that Japan and Australia conclude a separate treaty to delimit their mutual interests.[70] However, neither Burns nor the Australian government was prepared to consider this. Despite Japan's remarkable openness toward Australian economic interests, Australia maintained an anti-Japanese policy of exclusion. New Guinea was to remain "a closed colony" to the Japanese. Japanese concessions toward Burns Philp had to be compensated by the British, who permitted the Japanese trading company Nan'yo Boeki Kaisha to open a trading station on the Gilbert Islands.[71] Between the Australians and the Japanese, however, relations deteriorated visibly. Japanese secrecy in Micronesia increased the mutual distrust. Added to this was the White Australia Policy and Australia's phobia about the Yellow Peril, and on the Japanese side an excessive self-confidence that sometimes took aggressive forms. Each country harbored highly racist ideas about the other. Thus it is hardly surprising that rumors were soon circulating about secret Japanese military installations and the construction of defenses in Micronesia. Stobo, captain of the Pacific Phosphate Company's recruiting ship the *Pukaki,* and Handley, captain of a Burns Philp steamer in Micronesia, fanned the flames of this speculation. Handley was a covert informer for the British admiralty, whereas Stobo was a lieutenant in the Australian navy and a special agent. Their reports about secret Japanese military preparations in Micronesia must be viewed with skepticism, for their method of gathering information was to feed rumors rather than to find out whether there was any truth behind them, typically by asking leading questions and spreading anti-Japanese propaganda.[72]

The uneasiness felt by Micronesia's European neighbors was largely caused by the increasing "Japanization" of the islands. Anxiety was caused less by the permeation of Micronesia by aspects of Japanese culture, which will be described in the next chapter, than by the sudden increase in the size of the Japanese population in the area. One of the points made by the Japanese commission of inquiry in 1915 was that Micronesia's economic efficiency could be increased by settling Japanese in the colony. A steadily growing stream of Japanese settlers had gone to the colony during the early years of Japanese rule. In 1918 the Japanese government seems to have officially adopted a program of encouraging settlement in Micronesia. The state-funded Nishimura Colonization Co. took settlers to Saipan—mostly small farmers from Kiushu and Hachijojima, but also fishermen from Okinawa, and Korean laborers. Micronesia began to change demographically. In 1920 Japanese made up more than 6 percent of the total population of Micronesia. More than three thousand Japanese were highly visible in a population of not much more than fifty thousand people. In Saipan, 28 percent of the population was Japanese, and more than 5 percent Korean. Chamorros and Caroline Islanders made up just under two-thirds of the total population. This was a revolutionary change that went much deeper than any other Japanese colonial measures, however much they may have differed from comparable models in the same region. Micronesia was beginning to be a Japanese settler colony; and, in the British settler colonies of Australia and New Zealand, the only European colonists in the Pacific who had a similar experience behind them grew more and more agitated.[73]

Japanese Cultural Influence and Indigenous Responses

When European visitors went to Micronesia soon after the end of the First World War and before the introduction of the official mandate administration, they were astonished at how much the islands had changed. Garapan, the capi-

tal of Saipan, felt like a Japanese town.[74] Public and private buildings in the
Japanese style dominated the townscape in all the Micronesian administrative
centers, but especially in the Mariana and Palau Islands. The Micronesian way
of life had been remarkably transformed within a relatively short time. An Australian journalist who traveled through the Marshall Islands in September and
October 1918 on a Burns Philp steamer noted that Micronesians almost everywhere were wearing the kimono instead of the traditional loincloth (lavalava)
and that Micronesian women were pinning up their hair in the Japanese fashion. Japanese fans and umbrellas were "in." Japanese dishes and ways of eating
were popular among the islanders. In Palau new dances were influenced by
Japanese styles, and Japanese methods had been adopted by islanders in building their own homes.[75]

Under certain circumstances, however, Japanese innovations could also
revitalize Micronesian forms of behavior. Nowhere was this clearer than in
the introduction of the geisha system into Micronesia in the early autumn of
1915. The timing coincided so precisely with the beginning of the second
phase of Japanese rule in Micronesia that it is tempting to see this innovation
as a response to a suggestion made by the Japanese commission of inquiry. In
any case, the geisha system was such an important part of Japanese life that
the decision to make the islands more Japanese made its transferral to Micronesia inevitable. In mid-September 1915 two brothels were opened in Truk,
one for Japanese and one for indigenous men. As far as the people of Truk
were concerned, this was a Japanese variation on the traditional *im en lisau*.[76]
Because there were no geishas in Ponape, the Japanese commander, Ida,
asked a Japanese trader and two headmen to supply local girls. The chiefs
most likely saw this as an opportunity to establish closer social ties with the
military governor via the well-known practice of exchanging women. The
Ponapeans, too, regarded this as a reintroduction of the *im en li kirip*.[77] In the
late 1920s the governor of Saipan, Goto Juzo, openly led a life dominated by
Japanese prostitutes and alcohol abuse.[78] In Palau a whole street, Geisha
Road, was reserved for geishas. At its busiest time, toward the end of the
1930s, this street is said to have had about twenty establishments housing up
to three hundred women. Officially, only Japanese men were allowed to visit
these, but it was apparently not difficult for local men to bend the rules and
gain access.[79]

This illustrates another way in which Japanese rule was totally different
from that of the Germans. However determined and severe the Japanese could
be in implementing their economic and political objectives, there were certain
areas in which they tolerated local infringement of the rules in an amazingly
relaxed manner. When speaking of the difference between the Germans and
the Japanese, older Micronesians always come back to three things: alcohol,
fishing with dynamite, and the possession of firearms. All three were forbidden
by both the German and the Japanese administrations (the Japanese prohibition on alcohol was not introduced until the mandate), but the Germans seem

Adopting the Japanese fashion. King Jebrick and his Queen of Majuro Lagoon, 1917. (Photograph by Thomas J. McMahon. Mitchell Library, State Library of New South Wales)

A Marshall Islands woman dressed à la Japan, 1917. (Photograph by Thomas J. McMahon. Mitchell Library, State Library of New South Wales)

Saipanese boys imitate Japanese sumo wrestling; their Japanese teacher stands nearby, c. 1921. (Fritz Collection, Frankfurt a.M.)

to have been much stricter than the Japanese in enforcing the rules. Some of the islanders were under the impression that Japanese negligence in these areas was deliberate.[80] This is understandable if we remember that both alcohol and firearms were among the traditional staples of the Japanese trade with the South Sea islands, and that this trade was first prohibited by the German administration. The Japanese also used alcohol to control Micronesian forced laborers in the phosphate works on Angaur.[81] Firearms were sold under the counter by Japanese or Korean retailers. Fishing with dynamite was normal practice in Japan itself, and the Japanese did not seem to regard it as a particular offense.

However, the Japanese were not so tolerant when it came to respect for their values in the Pacific. To disseminate these values, the Japanese established schools for indigenous children all over Micronesia from late October 1915. The large-scale development of an educational system for the indigenous people is another feature typical of Japanese rule and was an innovation, at least in the western Pacific. The Germans had repeatedly planned to expand their only government school in Saipan, but action was always postponed for financial reasons. The Australians in New Guinea, as we have seen, actually took a backward step in this area. The Japanese, in contrast, spared no cost or effort to organize an educational system in Micronesia that was as comprehensive as possible. Compulsory schooling for Micronesians was never introduced as such, but the system of taking children from the smaller islands to school on the larger islands by government boat came close to it. Schools, including

Pupils at the Japanese school Jaluit, 1917. (Photograph by Thomas J. McMahon. Mitchell Library, State Library of New South Wales)

books and materials, were free for Micronesians. By the end of 1918 there were twelve schools in the Japanese part of Micronesia, and 1,370 indigenous students. Two years later the number of schools had risen to seventeen, and the number of students to about 2,000.[82]

The Japanese cultural mission was clear and strictly defined. The youth of Micronesia were to learn the Japanese language as quickly as possible and in addition were to adopt the Japanese life-style. As Kurita, the Japanese commander on Ponape, explained, the aim was "to be civilized, according to the Japanese style. Japan has her own soul which must assert itself over all requirements and she is capable of doing so."[83]

On Truk it was said that the purpose of the school was "to train the people to work."[84] Teaching was limited to the most elementary level, and schooling was normally completed in three years. As a rule, only the simplified *katakana* system of Japanese ideograms was taught. In some schools, children were not even taught multiplication and division. Great stress was placed on order and discipline, and corporal punishment was common. Very old Micronesians who can still remember both colonial regimes unanimously agree that the Japanese teacher beat the students even more than the German teacher. Girls were not exempt. In western Micronesia this was tolerated because traditional education specified a number of strict punishments to be administered in the case of disobedience.[85] For the central Caroline Islands, where traditionally children were never physically punished at all, we unfortunately have no records of interviews with the people.

The Japanese did not set up any secondary schools for Micronesians, not even after 1922. Graduates of the former German school in Saipan were favored for administrative jobs, while apprentices from Tsingtao were employed in technical positions. It is quite clear that the main task of the Japanese schools was to transmit Japanese ideology to the Micronesians and thus stabilize Japanese rule. Although this concept deserves harsh criticicism, it cannot be denied that it was the Japanese who first introduced Pacific Islanders to a more general education, even though the attempt was limited and ideologically motivated. Pacific Islanders had now begun to gain access to some of the mysteries associated with European (or Japanese) "progress." What use they would eventually make of this knowledge lay only partly in the hands of the Japanese. It should also be mentioned that there were exceptions to the rule. Individual Micronesians were permitted to attend the *shogakko* school for Japanese children, and it was not completely unknown for Micronesians to study at a Japanese university. Conversely, Tsukamoto, the Japanese governor *(secho)* of Saipan, chose to send his two children to the school for indigenous children *(kogakko)*.[86]

Of all the criticisms which can be leveled at Japanese cultural activities in Micronesia in retrospect, the gravest is that Japanese schools not only inculcated Japanese ideology but also tried to destroy the identity of the Micronesians. In school and outside it, young people were forbidden to use their mother tongue on pain of punishment.[87] Any rival ideology was eliminated. When the Japanese opened their schools, the German Catholic and Protestant missions were forbidden to continue teaching, with the exception of practical domestic science for girls. Religious instruction was subjected to ever more restrictions, until it was permitted only in conjunction with mass on Sundays. On Ponape the Japanese teacher, accompanied by soldiers, entered church after the service and dragged the children out. Finally, religious instruction was completely banned.[88] Catholic services could be held only on Sundays. When the Catholics of Ponape celebrated Assumption in 1916, the Japanese commander held discussions with the headmen. Thereupon the Catholics were informed that in future no more services were to be held at all, on pain of imprisonment. The messenger was Henry Nanpei, leader of the Protestant Ponapeans. At a stroke, the Japanese ruling seemed to have put an end to the long-standing conflict between the Catholics and the Protestants of Ponape. The Catholic mission, however, did not observe the ban and, strangely enough, registered more people attending mass than before.[89] The traditional Ponapean spirit of opposition to orders from outside had been aroused. In the face of such blatant nonobservance, the Japanese administration backed down. After the end of the war, in mid-June 1919, orders of expulsion went out to all Germans remaining in Micronesia. At this time the ban on religious services was reimposed. The Japanese obviously feared the consequences of a final German sermon and influence on the people of Ponape, for the Ponapeans were not even permitted to go to confession. The Germans were threatened with banishment to the Japanese-occupied parts of Siberia as punishment. Thereupon a large delegation of Ponapeans marched on Japanese headquarters and urged the Japanese to revoke the order. When the mission rejected a compromise suggested by the Japanese, according to which a Ponapean-speaking Japanese official would be present at mass and for the sacraments, the Japanese finally gave in.[90]

On Saipan, which had already been forced to give up its Catholic mission in 1916, the Chamorros also remonstrated with the Japanese authorities.[91] The Mariana Islands had, after all, been Catholic for centuries. But a similar thing happened even on Palau, where Catholic missionaries had been active for less than a generation. The priests, lay brethren, and nuns who had been expelled at the end of October 1915 had been particularly badly treated by Lieutenant Bandai and his men, who suspected, correctly as it turned out, that they had concealed German government funds. Despite open chicanery, physical maltreatment, and the strictest prohibitions, many Palauans continued to support the mission. When the missionaries were forced to leave, Japanese soldiers lined the road all the way to the harbor. Behind them stood Palauans, who cried and called out to the missionaries in German, "Komm wieder zurück!" (Come back again). Immediately after the deportation of the German missionaries, a delegation of Christian Palauan men, led by Ibedul Louch from Koror, one of the most important men in the indigenous hierarchy, appeared at the Japanese offices and demanded that the governor provide new Catholic priests.[92]

This behavior on the part of the Ponapeans and Palauans is striking. It becomes even more remarkable when we take into account that the repeated interventions on behalf of the missions are the only occasions we know of on which relatively large numbers of the indigenous population resisted any orders issued by the Japanese administration. To ignore the significance of these incidents would be absurd. The records of Ponape Mission demonstrate that the mission by no means interpreted the behavior of the local population too favorably. It was noted that the missionaries, as the only remaining Germans, were at first treated icily. The indigenous elites were a constant source of danger, immediately informing against every German who said anything against the Japanese. Nor did the popularity which the Germans had expected to gain among the nonaristocratic Ponapeans ever fully materialize.[93] It would not be improbable to see this as a reaction by the local people to the German suppression of the Sokeh uprising.[94] However, the mission records also document a change in the people's attitude toward the missionaries. Surprisingly, the more the Japanese tried to limit their influence, the more the public mood swung in the missionaries' favor. In any case, we have only indigenous sources for events on Palau.

How can we explain the behavior of the Ponapeans, Chamorros, and Palauans described above? Despite the relatively short time they had been active in the area (less than a generation in the case of Palau), the Catholic mis-

sionaries seem to have established personal and emotional links with large segments of the indigenous population. But there was more to it than this;
otherwise the local people would have demanded the return of familiar faces,
rather than immediately demanding new priests. Explanations from religious
psychology, both optimistic (a need for faith) and pessimistic (fear of punishment in the afterlife), suggest themselves. But a political motive is also possible. The mission was the only institution that could provide a counterweight to
the power of the Japanese administration. The very reason that made the Japanese close down the mission may have been enough to make the indigenous
population want to keep it.

The Japanese clearly treated Protestant missions better than Catholic
ones. On Truk, the Liebenzeller were allowed "to work more or less undisturbed, and even to hold baptisms" until 1918.[95] Like the Catholics, they were
deported in June 1919, but this had nothing to do with their missionary activity. Rather it was an attempt to eliminate German influence. A number of facts
suggest that the Japanese placed a high value on the work of the Protestant
missionaries. The first Protestant Japanese missionary arrived in Ponape at the
end of April 1917 in order to support the Liebenzell mission there. The Japanese commander sent out official invitations to his sermons. Shortly after the
end of the war, more Protestant Japanese missionaries from Nan' yo Dendo
Dan followed, and they began work in Truk and Ponape.[96] Catholic priests did
not return to Micronesia until 1921, after protracted negotiations between the
Japanese commander Yamamoto, a Catholic (a former student at the Marist
Brothers' school in Tokyo), and the former nuncio in Australia, Archbishop
Cerretti. As the indigenous Catholic population was becoming increasingly
restless over the delay, Japan was finally forced to telegraph for the departure
of the new missionaries to be brought forward. The Japanese government subsidized their journey from Europe to Japan, and from there to Micronesia they
traveled free. Tokyo and the Vatican had agreed on Spanish Jesuits. The return
of Germans and Austrians was deliberately excluded.[97] The German Liebenzeller, by contrast, were able to return to Micronesia from 1927. Even missionaries who had been expelled in 1919 were permitted to resume their work.
The suggestion that the Japanese regarded the German Protestant ethic as
useful for colonization because it inculcated in the Micronesian population a
duty to work is certainly not far wrong.[98] In the case of the Catholics, the Japanese seem to have feared that they would use the confessional, which was
beyond the control of the Japanese administration, in the service of nationalist
propaganda.

From 1919 a Buddhist missionary in Saipan, where a temple had been
built, supported the Japanese cultural mission. Buddhists and Shintoists among
the indigenous population were mainly in Palau. The headquarters of the Japanese South Sea administration and the proximity of the phosphate island,
Angaur, attracted so many Japanese to Palau that the indigenous population
gradually became a minority.[99] However, the missionary activities of Japanese

Buddhists and Shintoists should not be overrated. Their main target group was the steadily growing stream of Japanese; "converting" South Sea islanders was at most a secondary goal. The aim of the Japanese colonization was not to spread religion in the European way. The Micronesians were "Japanized" through school. Banzai, bowing daily in the direction of Japan, singing the "Kumiyaio," and reciting by rote, "I am a good citizen of Japan," were adequate substitutes for religion. Japan and the Japanese in Micronesia were not concerned about the fate of the Micronesians in an afterlife; nor were they interested in saving their souls. What counted was making them recognize, and submit to, the overlordship of the Japanese in the here and now.

In order to underline the lesson of Japanese cultural superiority, selected groups of Micronesians were regularly taken to Japan starting from July 1915. The first group to be targeted for this treatment was the indigenous elite—male and female chiefs from all over Micronesia. In Japan they were taken to architectural monuments, temples, sights of interest, museums, theaters and musical performances, Japanese cavalry maneuvers, and flyovers of warplanes. They traveled by train to Yokohama, Osaka, and Nikko, where the program included city tours. Visits were arranged to schools, fortifications, wharfs, and factories—at first, mostly sugar factories. Large numbers of gifts were distributed. These were public relations exercises which, given that they were intended to dazzle Micronesians with Japanese culture, could not have been bettered. Those who had been left behind were shown a film about the experiences of their chiefs in Japan. They had already been impressed by the accounts of the returned travelers, and this reinforced the impact of the trips. *Kanko dan* tours were repeated annually and became a fixed part of Japanese colonial policy in Micronesia. Gradually the target group was expanded, and the principle of a free advertising trip was given up in favor of participants bearing part of the cost themselves. These propaganda trips for Micronesians were supplemented by equally methodical exchange programs for Japanese: while Micronesian chiefs toured Japan, members of the Japanese upper house traveled through Micronesia. One month later they were followed by the first group of Japanese high-school students.[100]

There can be no doubt that the Micronesians who took part in these trips were highly impressed by the display put on by the Japanese. All those who went have positive memories of their travels. In most cases we can only guess to what extent they were inwardly changed by their experiences. In one case the Japanese "conversion" had a direct impact immediately after the end of the *kanko dan*. After his return from Japan, Chief Uong Ngirateuid from Ngiwal on Palau turned the local society that was subordinate to him inside out. On his orders the village was moved from inland to the coast, and straight streets were built. All the men had to cut their hair short, like the Japanese, and landowners were instructed to transfer part of their land into the possession of nonland-owning clan members.[101] The distribution of land was probably prompted less by the desire to introduce a democratic system per se than by the idea, put about by the Japanese, that it would make more effective economic management possible.

A number of factors facilitated the Japanization of Micronesia. By far the most important was Japan's determination to incorporate the islands into the Japanese Empire, with all the consequences this would entail for their inhabitants. Formal Japanization was achieved in two steps, after the military occupation and before the final decision was taken about the political future of the islands. In mid-1915, Japanese time and the Japanese imperial calendar were officially introduced in Micronesia; and from the beginning of 1918, the islands were systematically renamed. Toloas Island in the Truk Archipelago, for example, was renamed Natsushima (Summer Island), and Wela became Harushima (Spring Island). As the number of indigenous island people was small, it was argued, they would be unlikely to insist on their traditional names.[102]

As we have shown, the Japanese made a much greater effort to win over the Micronesians than any of the European colonial powers in the Pacific before 1918. At the start of the Japanese administration, the local people were treated astonishingly well. Japanese efforts amounted to much more than the Australian food handouts in New Guinea. Although the Japanese occupying troops also gave out crackers and biscuits on their arrival, the manner of giving reveals a different attitude. Whereas the Australian soldiers all behaved individually, apparently acting out of sympathy for the Melanesians, the Japanese food distributions took place at specified times and included the whole of the indigenous population,[103] suggesting that this was less a spontaneous expression of Japanese concern for the local people than a systematic attempt to gain the sympathy of the Micronesians. Applied to the Japanese strategy of "brotherly racial equality," which was soon introduced, this interpretation rests on pretty firm ground. Sources for the Marshall Islands, Ponape, Truk, and Palau all claim that, at the start, the Japanese tried to convince the Micronesians that they and the Japanese were of the same race, and therefore practically brothers.[104] Here we see the idea of equality being used as a political weapon in the arsenal of Japanese colonization. It is true that during the first phase of their rule the Japanese hardly interfered in the internal concerns of the local people. This began to change at the beginning of the second period of their military administration, the phase of development, when it soon became apparent that the Japanese by no means regarded the Micronesians as equals with the same rights as themselves.

The claim that the Japanese and Micronesians were of the same race was in fact an ideological preparation for the total and unconditional assimilation of the Micronesians. Being of the same race does not necessarily mean being at the same stage of development, and there was no doubt about who was at the top. The aim was for the Micronesians to develop into Japanese, not merely ideologically and culturally, but above all physically and racially. Every specifically Micronesian feature was an obstacle, and thus had to be eradicated. The right to become more Japanese therefore included the duty to relinquish one's Micronesian identity. The Japanese policy of theoretical equality thus resulted in a policy that was no less racist than the German-European policy of insisting on a fundamental difference among the races. Japanese policy turned out to be even more ruthless than German policy. Whereas the German colonial administrators debated about which features of Micronesian culture should be preserved in the face of European modernism, and which should be rejected as "unethical" or "inhumane," no such discussion took place among the Japanese. In their view, anything Micronesian that was un-Japanese was also unethical. The Japanese did not, like the Germans, regard Micronesian "underdevelopment" primarily as a cultural problem to be overcome by education, but as a racial problem. In the Japanese view, the Micronesians had gone their own way racially, but their separate existence was not worth preserving because it represented a primitive retrogression or lateral offshoot of Japanese development. The Japanese "civilizing" mission in Micronesia assumed that the physical identity of the Micronesians would come to an end. In fact, this was probably its goal.

Sexual relations between Micronesian women and Japanese men were encouraged, but relationships were legitimized only in the case of Japanese traders, farmers, and fishermen. Officials were permitted to have Micronesian mistresses, but not to marry Micronesian women. The custom, common on the Micronesian islands, of raising the social status of a group by means of a sexual connection between a woman from the clan and a higher-ranking man made sexual contacts easier, even if they remained extramarital. Girls were encouraged by their families to approach Japanese men.[105] The administration put pressure on Micronesian women to produce a mixed Japanese-Micronesian population. On Kusaie the Japanese naval secretary, called "governor" by the local people, assembled all the island women and told them that it was their duty, and the duty of the women of all the other islands, to do everything they could to produce "half-caste Japanese."[106]

At least as long as Micronesians and Japanese were still physically different, there was no question of the Micronesians' achieving the privileged position of the Japanese. Increasing immigration from the north produced a four-class society based on race, consisting of Japanese, Micronesians, Okinawans, and Koreans. It is not clear exactly what the pecking order was in Japanese eyes. Probably it varied from region to region. In western Micronesia, where the Japanese were numerically strongest and the Japanization of the indigenous population had advanced furthest, the majority of survivors agree that the Micronesians took second place before the Okinawans, while the Koreans came last. This may well be an accurate representation of everyday life. In any case, there is evidence of brutal Japanese exploitation of Korean workers.[107] Things were probably different on the more remote islands and in eastern Micronesia, where the local people were called *tomin* by the Japanese, a word—as ambiguous as the term *kanaka*—meaning both "South Sea islander" and "savage."[108]

The Japanese deliberately used violence to achieve their colonial aims.

During the second half of the Japanese military administration, reports from all over Micronesia document the fear the islanders had of physical punishment by the Japanese or their subordinates.[109] Japanese rule was not one of arbitrary terror, but the use of force was an integral part of their colonial policy, demonstrating Japanese determination not to let any doubts arise about their "path." The stick used to discourage anyone from straying from this path was the equivalent of the carrot of cultural propaganda tours through Japan. Fear of Japanese harshness encouraged a certain fatalism among some Pacific Islanders: "I always went along with what the Japanese said. It is not that deep in my heart I believed everything they said, but why go against their wishes? We would be punished if we did that."[110] Japanese orders had to be obeyed; the question "Why?" did not exist. Workers for the phosphate mines in Angaur were no longer recruited but simply "enlisted." A man from Palau who was told that he had to go to Angaur to work did not have the option of saying no.[111] The Japanese possibly made an exception of Ponape. Henry Nanpei informed foreign visitors that the Japanese had good reason to treat the Ponapeans better than the people of the other Caroline Islands; they knew that if they did not, "there would be more fighting than under the German and Spanish Regime."[112] Outside of Ponape the Pax Germanica had made such a deep impact that any revival of Micronesia's warlike past was out of the question. As the Micronesians had become accustomed to the positive side of the German presence, their old belligerence had gradually faded until to all intents and purposes it no longer existed. Germany's successful pacification of Micronesia had deprived the islanders of an effective weapon of defense. On the other hand, it made it easier for the Japanese to take over the islands, for which they later duly expressed their gratitude.[113]

Organized indigenous action against the Japanese was nonviolent, at least during the period of Japanese military government, and only the Palauans themselves can inform us about it. Of all the Micronesians, the Palauans were most affected by the change of regime. The Japanese transferred their headquarters to Palau, which then attracted large numbers of immigrants. The men of Palau were also ruthlessly exploited as phosphate workers on the neighboring island of Angaur. One year after the Japanese took over the administration, a nativistic movement arose that became increasingly anti-Japanese. Nevertheless, it would be wrong to label the Modekngei (literally: "being or coming together") as a group of Palauan traditionalists. It is unlikely that the Modekngei had any connection with the "sorcerers," a resistance group that had aimed to preserve their traditional privileges during the period of German rule. The founder of the Modekngei was a Palauan noble named Temedad. Employed as a policeman on Angaur during the German administration, he represented both the new and the old elites. After experiencing a vocation as a prophet and allegedly raising someone from the dead, Temedad gathered a growing number of disciples around him from 1915. At the heart of his sermons was a non-Christian monotheism based on the cult of the village god,

Ngirchomekuul of Chol, combined with apocalyptic visions of the future. Temedad preached that everyone was equal before God, and that a time was coming when the Palauans would be recognized as the equals of others. He also claimed that his influence could cause traditional Palau money to multiply, in other words, that faith in him could raise one's status within Palau society. This feature points forward to the post-1945 Melanesian cargo cults. Like them, the Modekngei also adopted various elements of Christianity.[114]

Temedad preached against a number of old Palauan customs, such as chewing betel nut, and against adultery. But his campaign against Palauan food taboos was the most successful. After all, he argued, God had made food for everyone to use. This suggestion obviously fulfilled a long-felt need, and the change was quickly adopted. Temedad also revived the old notion that the sick could be truly healed only if they regained a sense of inner and outer peace. Therefore they had to compensate anyone they had harmed by making payments of money.[115]

The movement founded by Temedad was thus by no means antimodern—it can be described as syncretistic with a holistic tendency—but it was certainly anti-Japanese. The Japanese presence and their cultural mission were not only a threat to the physical existence of the Palauans, but their work ethic was also diametrically opposed to Temedad's ideas. At a meeting with all of Palau's chiefs, Temedad asked them for their help against the Japanese. Temedad's openly anti-Japanese strategy was directed at the pillars of Japanese ideology: the school and Japanese–Palauan relationships. He wanted to destroy the school and to dissolve all marriages between Palauans and Japanese, as well as purely Palauan marriages in which one partner worked for the Japanese.[116] Before the Modekngei could become militant, the Japanese stepped in. They accused Temedad of what, in their eyes, was the Micronesian original sin: his teachings discouraged the Palauans from working. In addition, they claimed that his cures were totally unscientific and unhygienic. Temedad and two supporters were imprisoned for three years on the island of Angaur until Japan took over the mandate in 1922 and they were freed. After another period of imprisonment in 1924, Temedad died. Under his successor, Ongesii, the Modekngei finally turned into a covert resistance movement, becoming more and more reactionary and racist. At its height, about half of the people of Palau were members of the movement. Today it has a following of about eight hundred.[117]

In areas where the Japanese presence was relatively small, they began by trying to ignore the power of the chiefs. This led to passive resistance by the locals, whereupon the Japanese returned to the German method of indirect rule. German administrative methods were adopted almost unchanged. Chiefs continued to collect the head-tax as before, and the exemptions recognized by the Germans remained in force. After the German criminal justice system was abolished in October 1915, Japanese penal legislation was supplemented by local regulations and customs for the punishment of local offenders.[118] Were these the officially recognized "niches" in "Japanized" Micronesian society?

How did the Japanese treat areas where the Germans had left traditional Micronesian social structures more or less untouched?

In the Marshall Islands, the last stronghold of oligarchic feudalism, the Japanese government acknowledged the special position of the chiefs in a decree issued one year before the introduction of the civil administration. The Japanese presence in the Marshall Islands was the smallest, except for that on Yap. The economic potential of the islands was limited, and copra was the only export worth mentioning. The judicial functions of the chiefs and the indigenous judges (now called *dri-kien*) were preserved, and the penalties they could impose on their own responsibility were actually increased. The conduct that the chiefs now had to enforce was a mixture of traditional, Western, and Japanese ideas—any violations of Japanese etiquette, such as swearing or deliberately turning one's back, were punished by five to ten days' imprisonment. Marriage law is a good example of how these varied elements came together. Long-term cohabitation was recognized as legal marriage, but the Western notion of free choice was accepted as the basis for marriage. Thus there was no longer a role for the traditional matchmaker. The ruling that after marriage the woman belonged to her husband's island had the greatest impact on the traditional way of life; the Marshall Islands societies had previously been matrilineal. Now this form of organization was practically destroyed at a stroke. The intention was probably to create a more disciplined economy. In general, the aim of Japanese regulations was to increase copra production. They introduced a new law, based on an old island custom, that particular ceremonies and certain anniversaries were to be marked by the planting of coconut palms. The 1918 ultimatum according to which unplanted and unsettled land would be confiscated if it was not planted with coconuts within three years was extended for another year. The chiefs were to take away the land of anyone who still did not plant it at this stage and distribute it among those who were willing to work. Women were also encouraged to work: "The women are not to do washing only, they are also to help the men on work." The chiefs were not to sit around lazily, but were to make sure that the land was being worked. Instruction in health and hygiene was to keep the working population healthy.[119] The Japanese had continued the German health system, including monthly tours of inspection by government doctors, throughout Micronesia. In addition, they considerably increased the number of hospitals and the number of beds in them.[120]

Japanese control in the Marshall Islands was largely exercised by the commercial agents of the Nan'yo Boeki Kaisha (NBK). This South Sea trading company was founded in 1908 as the result of a merger between two Japanese companies that had long been active in western Micronesia. Before the war, NBK was the largest Japanese trading company in German Micronesia. It profited from the war in much the same way as Burns Philp did in New Guinea. A contract NBK concluded with the Japanese navy in 1915 gave it a monopoly on all government shipments between Japan and Micronesia. The closing down of the Jaluit Company and the expulsion of its general manager in the first six months of 1915 enabled NBK to expand from western into eastern Micronesia. On the Marshall Islands, NBK quickly assumed the semiofficial status the Jaluit Company had enjoyed: it continued to collect copra via the chiefs, some of it on behalf of the government as a substitute for the head-tax. In return, Japanese naval cruisers accompanied the company's employees on their trading expeditions, thus creating the impression that NBK *was* the Japanese administration of the Marshall Islands. The practice of selling Japanese goods at excessively high prices and buying copra at low ones soon made the local population financially dependent on the company, whose methods included extending credit. The Japanese military administration tolerated such practices because it also profited from them. As most of the chiefs were deeply in debt, the company could be used to put pressure on them.[121]

The Marshall Islands did not really slip through the net of Japanese control, because the NBK "governed" in place of a largely absent administration. The real "niches" were found on the small islands where neither Japanese government officials nor traders had settled—for example, the mini-atolls of the central Caroline Islands. At least until the beginning of 1922 the Japanese showed little interest in these areas. Thus, compared with the period of German rule, the islanders' "freedom" actually increased. On the other hand, time had not stood still there either. On Pingelap, for instance, the islanders did not feel badly treated by the Japanese but regarded themselves as neglected by them.[122] German colonial activity had created dependencies, and the people had expectations of a colonial government which the Japanese obviously did not fulfill. Japanese methods veered between two extremes: an attempt to make territories that seemed economically or strategically important as much like Japan as possible, and a clear lack of interest in the small islands that had no direct value but would have been expensive to administer.

The fact that the indigenous population felt neglected by the colonial government does not square with most current theories of imperialism, unless we assume from the start that this was the reaction, not of a truly autonomous society, but of a degenerate colonial one that had already been infiltrated by foreigners—which, of course, removes the need to explain anything that runs counter to one's own theory. This "feeling" registered by the indigenous island population, however, was based on concrete experience and very real anxieties and fears. Almost without exception, the Micronesian population of the smaller islands lived on atolls that barely stood out above the sea. Typhoons not only destroyed the islanders' huts and uprooted the few fruit trees growing on these islands but also regularly caused flooding, which washed away the thin layer of humus and could make it impossible for survivors to continue living there. Measures taken by the colonial administration had not been able to eliminate these hardships, but they had been able to alleviate them. Between the beginning of the crisis in Europe in the summer of 1914 and the end of the year, the Mariana Islands in northern Micronesia suffered four cyclones. The worst damage was done by two typhoons that swept over Rota and Saipan at the beginning of October and in mid-December 1914. Almost all the local houses were destroyed, and the sweet potato fields were spoiled by salt water.

Neither in Saipan nor in Rota did the Japanese administration take any interest in the plight of the islanders. As a Japanese administrative center, Saipan was in contact with the outside world and with Japanese traders, and conditions gradually stabilized. Rota, however, was one of the small islands which lacked economic or strategic value, and which the Japanese therefore "neglected." The island was completely cut off from the outside world, as on the orders of the military administration no independent interisland traffic was allowed and all communication was prohibited. No Japanese ships called there. At the beginning of July 1915, when famine was about to claim its first victims, the head of the local village and a German Capuchin monk who had stayed on Rota organized a boat to fetch help from American Guam. The expedition was successful, but it embarrassed the Japanese government.[123] Thereafter communication among individual islands was made easier, but there is no evidence that Japanese policy changed.

4

Samoa and the New Zealand Experience (1914–1921)

MILITARY GOVERNMENT UNDER COLONEL LOGAN: BUSINESS AS USUAL?

Tiny New Zealand had struck out with a vengeance, going down forever in the annals of the war. Samoa was the first territory under German sovereignty to be occupied during the First World War. German companies celebrated along with the occupiers. This represented "salvation from incalculable calamities arising out of the war situation," wrote the representative of the Deutsche Samoagesellschaft (German Samoa Company). Its founder and co-owner, Deeken, had given the colonial administration a great deal of trouble by spreading pan-German propaganda while the administration had been aiming for a peaceful settlement. If only Samoa would remain British, was the cry now. This would solve the tiresome labor problem, because the British would surely bring in Indian coolies, as they had done in neighboring Fiji. Other German firms shared the German Samoa Company's positive view of the occupation. To have remained with Germany would have been "disastrous," because they would certainly have been cut off from world trade, the firm Zuckschwerdt sighed in relief.[1]

The rejoicing did not last long. In mid-December 1914, German companies in Samoa were forbidden to import and export; Burns Philp declared itself the sole importer.[2] Thereafter, German commercial influence was cut out, step by step. From 26 April 1915, German currency was replaced by sterling. One day later, a branch of the Bank of New Zealand was opened in Apia. The German coins and banknotes withdrawn from circulation were exchanged for pounds on the London money market and the proceeds invested in New Zealand war loans. The coins alone had a face value of over 812,000 marks, and filled ninety-two cases for transport to New Zealand. The British notes and coins imported from New Zealand were charged to the Samoan national budget and repaid in full to New Zealand at the end of July 1917.[3] In September 1915 the largest German firm, the Deutsche Handels- und Plantagengesellschaft

"Der Conquerors." The Australian view of the New Zealand occupation of Samoa. (*The Bulletin*, 10 September 1914)

(German Trading and Plantation Company) was sequestered, and on 25 April 1916 the military government closed all German businesses in Samoa, began liquidating them, and auctioned off their stock. These steps had been preceded by an intense correspondence with London, and Britain had urged New Zealand to push ahead. The proceeds of these actions secured New Zealand the highest budget surplus in its history.[4] Once again, Burns Philp's hour seemed to have struck. It secured for itself the bulk of the goods and the right to use all of the German Trading and Plantation Company's buildings and trading stations, without having to pay a penny in rent until the end of the war.[5] Somehow, Burns Philp had managed to have the right men in the right spot in Samoa and New Zealand, as elsewhere. The liquidator of the German Trading and Plantation Company was an employee of Burns Philp. Consequently, everything ran like clockwork. Officially declared an auction, few people and even fewer bidders were present. Burns Philp was also able to buy the premises of the firm Grevsmühl in the most desirable location on the harbor, with their own wharf and railway siding, for the ridiculously low price of just under £2,000.[6]

The state did not, at first, intervene directly in the running of the German plantations. But almost at the same time as the German businesses were liquidated the military administration introduced an export tax designed to siphon off as much of the profits made by the plantations as possible.[7] Internally, the military governor advocated concentrating entirely on copra in the future, because the cacao and caoutchouc plants took too long to become profitable. The military governor was supported in this by all leading circles in New Zealand. A commission set up along the same lines as the Australian Royal Commission in New Guinea opposed any further planting of cacao, caoutchouc, and coffee, and recommended closing Samoa's only fruit-processing plant, a pineapple-canning factory. After visiting Samoa, the governor-general of New Zealand endorsed the view that in Samoa only copra held out the promise of quick profits, and that the cultivation of other agricultural products should cease.[8] In December 1917 the Samoa Kautschuk Compagnie (Caoutchouc Company) was compulsorily closed by the Administrator. Seven thousand imperial pounds (over three tons) of finished caoutchouc was left to rot because the New Zealand Administrator, Logan, prohibited its sale.[9] In 1914 Samoa had been well on the way to casting off the predominance of copra as a monoculture. Thus its economic progress was brought to a sudden halt. Logan believed that after the war the German owners would have to be paid compensation for New Zealand's probable takeover of their plantations. It was therefore necessary to accumulate profits as quickly as possible, while avoiding anything that could increase the value of the German plantations.[10]

In terms of economic policy, Australia and New Zealand pursued diametrically opposed goals in the areas under their occupation. Australia tolerated the expansion of the German plantation economy—indeed, even encouraged it by ruthless labor recruiting. New Zealand, in contrast, did what it could to damage the German plantations. In pursuit of his policy (and, as will become apparent, for racist reasons), Logan refused to replace the coolies who were repatriated to China on expiry of their contracts. The plantations became more and more overgrown. At the end of the war, the flourishing copra plantations fell like ripe fruit into Australia's lap. What New Zealand got was not exactly spoiled, but certainly included a number of rotten apples. The hasty expropriation and deportation of the Germans, which began four months earlier than in New Guinea, on 1 May 1920 (that is, after the peace treaty came into effect but before the handing over of the mandate), could change nothing.

During the war, however, New Zealand removed as much money as possible from Samoa. From the start it had been established that Samoa would have to repay New Zealand for the losses it had incurred as a result of exchanging German currency into pounds, plus interest.[11] In 1916 the Administrator advocated charging to Samoa all the costs of occupation and diverting this sum, plus interest incurred, from Samoa's national income to New Zealand over a period of fifteen to twenty years.[12] In that year, Samoa paid £50,000 to New Zealand; in 1917, as much as £78,000. This sum was the equivalent of about 2.5 million marks and came mainly from the liquidation of Samoa's German businesses.[13] From 1 April 1916, the military governor's salary was paid directly by the Samoan administration (and no longer by New Zealand's military authorities). In June 1917, the military governor, with the approval of the governor, also helped himself to £2,000 (40,000 marks), for personal use, from the private funds of the liquidated German Trading and Plantation Company.[14] From New Zealand, the governor recommended that a start should be made on clearing the island's forests as soon as it was established that New Zealand would keep Samoa. The Germans had not exported any wood from Samoa, he pointed out, and this was "a national advantage" for New Zealand.[15]

Colonel Robert Logan had been deliberately selected for the job of military governor of Samoa. A farmer who had migrated from Scotland to New Zealand, he had little military experience; as an internal memorandum pointed out, he was therefore debarred from an officer's career. But for Samoa, where no armed conflict was expected, his "good business ability" made him a suitable choice.[16] As soon as the German East Asian squadron was withdrawn from the Pacific, the war became something unreal. More than ever, Samoa was a peaceful refuge from the turbulence of the world war. However, it soon became too peaceful for the taste of the fourteen hundred plus soldiers stationed there. They were bored, and felt useless. On Christmas Eve of 1914, hundreds of soldiers rampaged through Apia, plundering the German stores and stealing anything that looked as though it might be drinkable. (In their haste, they even took bottles of vinegar.) Thereafter about forty drunk soldiers went to the government house in Vailima (formerly Robert Louis Stevenson's residence) and shouted to the Administrator that he should go home to New Zealand and look after his sheep. The commander of the military police could go too, they added. If he did not quickly go back to hunting rabbits again, they threatened, they would beat him up one day.[17]

At Stevenson's tomb. Colonel Robert Logan, the first New Zealand Administrator of Western Samoa, reading the service. At *right* are the two *fautua*, Tamasese and Malietoa, June 1915. (Private Collection, London)

When the main New Zealand force began to be withdrawn in stages from 10 March 1915, it became even more boring for the soldiers and officers left behind in Samoa. No real military tasks remained, and the daily work created by the mere presence of the soldiers was done by the plantation laborers commandeered for the troops. Melanesian "black boys" did the laundry and cleaned the latrines, and Chinese coolies did the cooking. Those who had not been driven out of Samoa by the heat and inactivity were there "to have a good time."[18] While their comrades bled to death at Gallipoli, they passed their time playing billiards and bowls. Cricket was given up when their local sparring partners began to beat their teachers.[19] The soldiers' favorite recreation, however, was drinking. Military communities of all types probably tend to consume large amounts of alcohol, but if the Guinness Book of Records had existed in 1918, the New Zealand soldiers on Samoa could have claimed the record for the smallest occupying force with the largest capacity for drink during the war. As the beer crates were regularly emptied before the arrival of the next steamer, it was decided early in February 1916 to draw supplies directly from one of the largest Pacific breweries in Australia:

> We must procure for the men absolutely the best quality beer that is on the market, at the lowest possible price. . . . In order to satisfy ourselves as to the best beer to provide for the men, we have tried almost every brand that is on the market here. Since July 13th we have purchased over £1000 worth of beer for the troops. . . .

The men are bound to talk beer to their friends. What better advertising proposition can you have in Samoa than this! The soldier if given the opportunity will lay a foundation for the name Resch in Samoa which will remain long after the war is over.[20]

The Administrator spent his time playing private war games, issuing one military regulation after another, and pestering the German settlers. When most of the German men had been deported to New Zealand, and in Samoa itself the military governor had successfully created the impression of a permanent state of siege, Logan turned to the "neutral" population on Samoa. His antipathy toward Americans grew with the commercial success of the U.S. traders on Samoa, who had also profited from the liquidation of German businesses and the sale of their stock. In addition, Samoa's exports were increasingly going to the United States. As most of New Zealand's ships were being used to transport troops, mutton, and butter to Great Britain, more and more Samoan copra ended up on U.S. schooners and in the harbors of America's West Coast. Although Logan obstructed the export of copra to the United States in 1916, and even temporarily banned it, more than half of Samoa's exports went there in 1916. There were simply no British ships available to fill the gap. Instead of copra being diverted to Auckland, Sydney, or London, it was left to rot in Samoa.[21] In 1918 and 1919, when New Zealand's troops were withdrawn from Europe, all Samoan copra went to the United States. Before the war, Samoa had been a German colony politically but commercially an Australian–New Zealand colony. During the war, New Zealand succeeded in turning commercial into political dominance, but it increasingly lost its commercial lead to the United States.

The Administrator vented his anger at the United States' economic success not only on the most prominent U.S. trader in Samoa, but also on the U.S. consul. Logan used the fact that the consul's job included representing German interests as an excuse to open the diplomatic mail and confiscate post at his discretion. The consul's tax privileges were abolished. Even after London issued direct instructions to Logan to stop this behavior, the military governor remained obstinate. In his view, the representative of U.S. interests in Samoa was "typical of the bullying American cowboy type, a type with which thirty years' residence on colonial goldfields has made me perfectly familiar." He was convinced that a "conspiracy" was being hatched against him.[22] Shortly thereafter, when the United States entered the war on the side of Great Britain and its allies, Logan's fury rose to fever pitch. He had an article printed in the *Samoa Times* accusing the United States of entering the war after Germany had been practically defeated purely out of selfish interest in a share of the booty.[23] But it was not only the Germans and the Americans who offended the Administrator: sooner or later, he came into conflict with almost every European in Samoa. The dictatorial powers he possessed and made full use of somehow went to his head. In addition, he was obviously affected mentally by the tropical climate.

TABLE 10. German Samoa's Trade under the New Zealand Military Administration

Financial Year	Total Imports[a] in £	Thereof From NZ	Aus	USA[b] in % of all Imports	Total Exports in £	Thereof To NZ	Aus	USA in % of all Imports	Total Value of Trade in £	% Share of Total Trade NZ	Aus	USA
1914	236,239	n.d.[c]			220,519	n.d.			456,758	n.d.		
1915	267,091	n.d.			262,389	n.d.			529,480	n.d.		
1916	180,340	36.0	36.2	20.7	235,415	11.8	24.8	51.9	415,755	22.3	29.7	38.4
1917	301,173	28.8	31.2	35.7	320,444	7.8	13.6	77.3	621,617	18.0	22.1	57.1
1918	309,396	23.4	34.9	36.4	306,640	5.5	11.7	82.8	616,036	14.5	23.4	59.5
1919	291,368	n.d.			532,500	n.d.			823,868	n.d.		
1920	561,153	n.d.			386,587	n.d.			947,740	n.d.		
1921	408,892	32.5	26.7	17.9	241,539	5.3	7.7	71.8	650,431	22.4	19.6	37.9

[a]Figures do not include imports of money and military supplies.

[b]NZ = New Zealand; Aus = Australia; USA = United States.

[c]n.d. = no data available.

Sources: Compiled and calculated from figures in *Trade between New Zealand and Fiji, Tonga, Western Samoa, and Cook Islands*, Vol. 1 of *New Zealand. Appendix to the Journals of the House of Representatives of New Zealand 1920* (Wellington, 1920), 30–46. *Mandated Territory of Western Samoa*. First Report, 1 May 1920–31 March 1921, 18. *New Zealand Official Year-Book 1923*, 657. Samoa Trade; AAC: A 2219 vol. 27.

TABLE 11. Main Products Produced for Export in Samoa under the New Zealand Military Administration

Financial Year	Main Products Exported	Export Value (in British pounds)	Percentage of Total Exports	Share of Importing Country in Total Exports (percent)		
				USA	Aus	NZ
1914	Copra	146,627	66.5		n.d.	
	Cacao	62,477	28.3			
	Caoutchouc	10,446	4.7			
1915	Copra	187,429	71.4		n.d.	
	Cacao	59,322	22.6			
	Caoutchouc	13,907	5.3			
1916	Copra	143,245	60.8	84.8	9.9	5.3
	Cacao	63,970	27.2	0.2	38.3	29.3
	Caoutchouc	20,228	8.6	0	93.2	6.8
	Pineapples	1,432	0.6	0	0.1	3.0
1917	Copra	230,971	72.1	95.9	0	4.1
	Cacao	69,549	21.7	33.1	44.3	18.7
	Caoutchouc	14,087	4.4	9.5	85.9	4.6
	Pineapples	1,777	0.6	0	0	100.0
1918	Copra	246,576	80.4	100.0	0	0
	Cacao	54,169	17.7	10.3	61.4	28.3
	Caoutchouc	2,850	0.9	0	75.5	21.2
1919	Copra	449,917	84.5	100.0	0	0
	Cacao	81,110	15.2	23.6	48.7	27.7
1920	Copra	296,356	76.7		n.d.	
	Cacao	90,222	23.3			
1921	Copra	190,520	78.9	90.9	0	0.5
	Cacao	36,363	15.1	0.2	31.3	31.4

Sources: See Table 10 and Trade and Commerce and Shipping of the British Military Occupied Territory of Samoa for the Calendar Year 1917; NZA: G 21/4.

"Bob Up!" New Zealand cartoon alluding to the furious side of the Administrator, Colonel Logan. (*The New Zealand Observer*, 24 October 1914. From the collection of the Alexander Turnbull Library)

The longer the war lasted, the more Samoa under military occupation began to resemble a madhouse. The islands possessed a profound natural tolerance and were able to cope with a great deal. Although not especially big, they were large enough to absorb the small number of foreigners living there, so long as they were restricted to the capital; it required a great deal of energy for them to have any impact beyond Apia. The real extent of the unrest that had emanated from Apia since mid-1914 can be demonstrated by looking at the true occupants, the Samoans themselves.

SAMOAN SELF-ADMINISTRATION UNDER
NEW ZEALAND MILITARY RULE

New Zealand had inherited the Samoan autonomous administration and a total of 434 indigenous officials from the German regime. All were paid out of the income generated by the Samoan head-tax. A number of Samoan officials received quite handsome salaries. The highest paid among them were the secretary of the Samoan native administration and the highest-ranking Samoan police officer, each receiving 2,160 marks annually.[24] Under Logan some of the practices put in place by the Germans changed considerably. The New Zealand military governor proved to rise to the hopes placed in him and implemented a strict policy of economizing. This had not only financial but also administrative implications. The office of *failantusi,* who had acted as the village secretary to the indigenous village official *(pulenuu),* was abolished. This undermined the position of the Samoan local representatives. An even bigger change took place on 1 April 1915, when the salaries of the remaining Samoan officials were slightly increased but the dog tax was abolished. The dog tax had been the de facto local rates and had financed the village administrations. Its abolition represented a significant change in the system of local self-sufficiency, as the dependence of the local officials on the colonial central administration increased while their ties with their local communities were weakened.[25] Logan suspected the Samoan officials of having manipulated the German system of paying wages. He therefore introduced a card system intended to prevent the double or multiple payment of salaries. For the Administrator, the financial aspect was the deciding factor.

Under the Germans, methods of paying salaries had been adapted to Samoan customs as a direct result of the policy of Samoan self-administration. When a Samoan regional official paid an occasional visit to the Samoan central administration, *mulinuu,* it was customary to pick up a quarter's salary. Income from the *lafoga,* the Samoan head-tax, had by definition been for the exclusive use of the Samoan administration. The colonial administration had prescribed the guidelines for distributing this revenue among the Samoan officials; the practical implementation of this policy was left to the Samoans themselves. Logan noted the existence of this system with some surprise—"It appears to

have been the expressed policy to expend for the benefit of the natives all revenue derived from native taxation"—but saw no reason to continue it. From
then on the proceeds of the Samoan taxation were no longer earmarked for the
Samoan administration alone but were used for all sorts of other purposes.
Annual figures showing how Samoan taxes were spent had previously been
published in the Samoan government information sheet, *Savali*. This practice
now ceased.[26] Logan's measures, which aimed to limit expenditure, placed a
question mark over the continued existence of the whole concept of Samoan
self-administration, because one of its main pillars, financial autonomy, had
been sawn through.

Many of the New Zealand military governor's decisions were clearly
prompted by his attempts to save money, or to increase revenue, even if such a
stringent finance policy had negative consequences for the Samoans. The only
German official left in office by Logan, Amtmann Osbahr from south Upolu,
was needed to collect the *lafoga*. By the end of September 1914, Samoan head-
tax had been collected to the value of 77,294 marks. One year later, Osbahr was
deported to New Zealand as a prisoner of war.[27] When New Zealand had taken
over from the German administration, there had been more than 279,000
marks in the public coffers. On Logan's instructions, the money earmarked for
outstanding government contracts—about 44,000 marks for public buildings
and public works—was not spent. A number of positions were eliminated, such
as the health inspector of the harbor police; it was argued that this job did not
keep him fully occupied. It is not clear exactly what happened to the money
thus saved. Some of it went into the governor's fund. It is suspected that the
rest was sent directly to New Zealand, to compensate the government for the
loss it took on selling German currency and to help pay for the introduction of
British coin and notes.[28]

A flood of new charges and fees was introduced, inflating the administrative work load and increasing the number of officials without making the
administration as such noticeably more efficient. On the contrary, the opposite
seems to have been the case. Early in 1914, the German colonial administration employed 46 white officials, and New Zealand had taken over 434 Samoan
officials. On 1 April 1915, the Samoan administration consisted of 59 European
and 452 Samoan officials and government employees; one year later it had
grown to 69 Europeans and 472 Samoans. In one year, between 1915 and 1916,
staff costs rose by more than £2,500, although New Zealand had one department fewer to administer than the Germans (Logan had abolished the Education Department as early as September 1914).[29] The new taxes included court
fees, which had not existed during German times, for the Samoan administration that led to an increase in the number of white officials; license and stamp
duties—fees for the "declaration of facts."[30] However, these only partly covered
the increased cost of the extra officials. In order to disguise the rise in staff
costs to some extent, resort was taken to a trick. The cost of medical personnel,
which the German administration had included among the civil administration,

was now transferred to the Health Department, which had previously registered only operating expenses. This made it look as though New Zealand spent far more on medical care for the people than the Germans had.[31] Logan's introduction of an export tax for Samoan agricultural produce on 1 April 1916 killed several birds with one stone. It allowed the administration both to siphon off the profits made by the German plantation owners and to exploit the spending power of the Samoans. It was clear to the Administrator from the start that the Samoans, as the main producers of copra, would have to foot the lion's share of the bill: the European traders simply passed on the tax to their Samoan copra producers and lowered the prices at which they bought.[32]

The Samoan reaction to lower copra prices and increased prices for European goods was to retreat into traditional patterns of behavior. They refused to work and imposed trade boycotts.[33] The economy of the foreigners suffered, but the Samoans themselves did not: though a life without European commodities, money, and food required a certain degree of sacrifice, the produce of their gardens and fields guaranteed survival. Samoan conservatism had been, if anything, strengthened by contact with the German colonial administration. The Samoan need for "cultural" possessions was limited. A Europeanized Samoan consumer society did not exist in 1916, and thus there was no dependence on the European economy. Of course, individual Samoans occasionally made use of the range of European goods available, but this could always be reversed. Samoan patterns of behavior had been established long before 1914 and remained constant. As long as copra prices were low, the Samoans produced no copra and bought no European goods. It made no difference to them whether the world market or regional factors were responsible. When prices rose again, Samoans harvested coconuts again, produced copra, and sold it to the Europeans. Thus the European traders were more dependent on the Samoans than vice versa. The Samoans deliberately applied and exploited the basic rules of a market economy.

This sort of independence had always been a thorn in the side of most foreigners in Samoa. But as long as Governors Solf and Schultz held the reins, there had been a guarantee that Europeans outside Apia would not interfere with Samoan conservatism. The New Zealand military administration, however, had completely different priorities. Its aim was to increase Samoa's economic efficiency. Although this aim had, of course, also existed during the German colonial period, it had not taken precedence over all other aspects of policy. There were things on Samoa that seemed more important than economic success. Appearances were more important than reality, and the desire for prestige in foreign policy dictated the need for a smoothly functioning administration and an absence of local disturbances that would have damaged Germany's reputation as a would-be world power.

Now, however, any traditional Samoan behavior that stood in the way of the colony's economic success was to be ruthlessly swept away. The New Zealand military administration's director of Samoan trade, Mulcahy, was convinced that the Samoans had to be systematically trained to be good consumers: "the first and most necessary aim—in direct opposition to the German idea—should be, to educate the Natives to adopt as far as is possible our own manner of living." If this were to succeed, they could sell the Samoans furniture, crockery, mattresses, and curtains, thus improving New Zealand's balance of trade. As most Samoans still went barefoot, he pointed out, there was a huge potential market for the New Zealand shoe industry. The use of articles of clothing and goods that the Samoans would be unlikely to understand, such as scarves and rugs, should be encouraged by sending clothing parcels and exhibiting New Zealand goods in Apia, where the prestige of the specially invited chiefs "would create the most favourable impression" upon the ordinary Samoan consumer. New Zealand had a right to make money out of Samoa in this way, he argued, because, after all, it had liberated the Samoans from German servitude.[34]

For the time being, such suggestions existed only on paper. New Zealand was unable to put them into practice for a number of reasons. Relatively unimportant among them was the continued validity, at least in theory, of German law. In other respects, too, the military administration under Logan ignored this regulation. Much more important factors were the lack of trained colonial officials and the difficulty of communication between the New Zealand government and the administration on Samoa. Because of the demands the war made on New Zealand's ships, the connection between Samoa and New Zealand depended on one old steamer belonging to the Union Steamship Company. At best, it chugged between Auckland and Apia every two weeks. At the administrative level, communication suffered because all correspondence between the Administrator and the New Zealand government had to go via the governor (later the governor-general) of New Zealand. Once again wanting to appear more "British" than its brother and rival across the sea, New Zealand's loyalty to London proved to be an obstacle to the development of its own colonial policy (but thus an advantage to the Samoans). Finally, after the successful occupation of the Polynesian islands, New Zealand's interest in Samoa decreased. Much as in Australian-occupied New Guinea, the colonial administration in Samoa under New Zealand occupation became less active during the war.

In New Guinea, this situation had largely negative consequences for the indigenous population because they were increasingly at the mercy of European entrepreneurs or their agents. The Samoans, by contrast, at first stood to benefit from it. Logan wanted at all costs to prevent any expansion of German plantations. New Zealand entrepreneurs, at most, had time to play commercial war games, but initially lacked the means to put them into practice. Thus, under the New Zealand military administration, Samoan self-administration probably had more scope for action in the villages than before. The farther one got away from Apia, the more likely traditional means of internal arbitration were used in settling Samoan quarrels and the less the Samoans depended on the military administration. Moreover, it seemed to the Samoans that it was easier to manipulate the New Zealanders than the Germans. Although the German administration had given the Samoans independence in a number of areas, there was absolute clarity on one point: the limits for the Samoans were as firmly fixed and as clearly marked as those for the European traders. In cases of doubt, the colonial administration sometimes decided in favor of the interests of the local population. In fact, it did so much more frequently than in any other German colony. However, it was under no obligation to do so, and whether it did so or not depended on the colonial administration alone (that is, mainly on the personality of the governor), and not at all on the Samoans. On a number of occasions the Samoans had been made to feel their subordination to German sovereignty.

But since August 1914 it had seemed as if the New Zealanders had not only acquiesced in the room for maneuver the Samoans had enjoyed under the Germans but had even accepted its expansion. The military administration's activity—and lack of it—gave many Samoans the impression that it was entirely up to them whether or not they uprooted the border posts and moved them forward. The return of Lauati's supporters who had been exiled to Micronesia by the Germans was the result of Samoan initiatives, although the military governor had approved and implemented them. The seemingly mutual interests of the Samoans and the New Zealanders, however, in fact had very different sides. The Administrator was mostly interested in popularizing New Zealand's policy, whereas many Samoans saw this incident as demonstrating New Zealand's acceptance of the Mau-a-Pule movement, which had been condemned by the Germans. The Mau-a-Pule, however, had aimed for nothing less than for Samoan interests to take absolute priority over European interests.[35]

There were also common interests held by most Samoans and the New Zealand military administration at other levels. One was Logan's religious puritanism, supported by the majority of Samoans, who were Protestant.[36] Many Samoans and New Zealanders were also brought together by their attitude toward the Chinese. Samoan young men were critical of cohabitation of Samoan women with Chinese men; Anglo-Saxon New Zealanders had a deeply rooted anti-Asian phobia and an ingrained racism concerning the so-called Chows. Immediately after the Samoan police had taken the oath to George V, their new masters set them on the Chinese who had marched from the plantations to Apia. The cause of the unrest was that at the beginning of the war German companies had reduced the rice ration without reducing the amount of work required. New Zealand soldiers and officers chased the Chinese through the streets of Apia with bayonets and sabers, while the Samoan police beat them with their truncheons. The Chinese had no chance against the united hatred of Samoans and New Zealanders (with their German employers as the third players in the game). A number were beaten up so badly that they had to be taken to hospital. Some were seriously injured, and one Chinese later died. "It was something worth seeing," noted one observer who had obviously enjoyed the spectacle.[37] In July and September 1915 there were more Chinese riots, in which troops were deployed. The Administrator made no secret of his dislike for the Chinese and did everything in his power to expel them from Samoa. In October 1914 there were 2,184 Chinese in Samoa; by the time of the armistice in Europe, their number had dropped to 876.[38] The repatriation of the Chinese was prompted by commercial as well as racist motives. More Chinese plantation laborers would have made the German plantations more productive, which would have increased their value—something that the Administrator wanted to prevent at all costs.

Shortly before their departure from Samoa, the coolies returning to China were forced to exchange their English silver money for German money. In a procedure reminiscent of the treatment of criminals or prisoners of war, their luggage was searched for gold or silver coin. This money, which they had legitimately earned on Samoa, was simply confiscated. In the New Zealander governor-general's opinion, the Chinese should not complain. After all, if New Zealand had not occupied the islands the Chinese would have starved.[39]

Logan's antipathy toward the Chinese population steadily increased, finally turning into a mania. At the end of 1915 he indirectly advocated prohibiting future relationships between Chinese men and Samoan women. In his view, Chinese men were intent only on depraving Samoan women. In August 1916 the military governor instructed the Samoan police not to allow Chinese men to enter Samoan huts. Five months later, this instruction was officially declared a proclamation of war.[40] On the Samoan side, the chief agitators against the Chinese were the local secretary of the Samoan administration, Afamasaga Maua, and his brother, Toleafoa Lagolago. In the *Savali,* Toleafoa wrote that from the moment when a Samoan woman started to live with a Chinese man, she altered physically—"her eyes change very quickly to those of her Chinese husband."[41] Afamasaga issued a decree from the Samoan central native administration ordering all Samoan women married to Chinese men to leave their Chinese husbands by 18 September 1917 and return to their Samoan relatives. Through the autonomous local system of justice, Samoan villages passed various regulations banning cohabitation of Samoan women and Chinese men.[42]

We can assume that the Samoan administration did not issue its regulations without the knowledge of the Administrator. A suspicion has even been voiced that the military governor contributed to the wording of the Samoan regulations. But it would be a mistake to see the New Zealand military governor as the sole driving force behind this anti-Chinese policy.[43] Under the German administration, Samoans had already attempted to prohibit sexual relations between Samoan women and Chinese men and, if possible, to drive the Chinese out of Samoa completely.[44] How many Samoans were anti-Chinese, and what social and generational groups they came from, is a matter of dispute. But there is no doubt that there was a vociferous group of Samoan men who, on their own initiative, regarded a policy of apartheid between Samoans and Chinese as desirable. It cannot be totally ruled out that this group skillfully exploited the military governor's racism in order to implement their own ideas and that they were behind his specific measures, especially proclamation No. 42. Finally, it is important to point out that it was German and not New Zealand colonial policy which was responsible for bringing the Chinese to Samoa. Solf had played the "Chinese card" because he wanted to grant the Samoans' request to be released from the obligation of working for the Europeans without completely alienating European employers. From the start, it had been clear that the Chinese were merely a means to an end.[45]

Samoan women who did not want to leave their Chinese husbands were forced to do so. Early in October 1917 four Samoan women were arrested because they steadfastly refused to leave their Chinese husbands. Sina, who had three children with her Chinese husband, the youngest of which was only a few weeks old, was brought before the Samoan central native court by Logan. The Administrator himself subjected her to embarrassing questioning, asking her: "If you don't like Samoans, why not marry a white man? If you like to marry Chinese, you have to go to jail."[46] When Sina resisted this peculiar racist logic, Logan had her put in prison, together with her baby, for one month. The police forcibly separated her from her eight-year-old daughter and her five-year-old son, and placed them in the care of their Samoan relatives. The Chinese husbands and fathers in mixed-race Samoan–Chinese marriages suffered from the forced separation of their families no less than their wives. One Chinese man committed suicide; another died under strange circumstances.[47]

The Administrator seemed to suffer no twinges of conscience over all this. The main thing, he wrote to the governor-general, was to keep the Samoan race pure. If anything, he stepped up the propaganda campaign against the Chinese: "The Wily Chinese and His Devious Devices" was the title of an article leaked by Logan to the *Samoa Times*.[48] The Administrator's despotic power, which he was in fact already exercising, was legally sanctioned from Wellington: a memorandum from the attorney general of New Zealand confirmed that the only legal basis existing in Samoa was the will of the military governor.[49] Australia advised its neighbor New Zealand to follow its successful example in expelling the Asians. As though it concerned an Australian and not a New Zealand colony, the governor-general of Australia, Munro Ferguson, suggested to his colleague that he implement the Papua Immigration Restriction Ordinance in Samoa. This would get rid of the Asians.[50] The hopes entertained by the German plantation owners that New Zealand would replace the Chinese with Indians proved to be illusory. (Employing Indians as cheap plantation labor was British policy in Fiji.) As far as New Zealanders with their Yellow Peril psychosis were concerned, Indians, as Asians, possessed the same negative qualities as the Chinese. They were regarded as "immoral, unreliable, and often lawless and dangerous" and considered to be full of "evil influences."[51]

In addition to the Chinese, there was another group of foreign workers on Samoa: the Melanesian laborers employed by the German Trading and Plantation Company. Their lot in Samoa was no more enviable than that of the Chinese. Regarded by their German employers merely as yet another means to an end, they could be physically punished, like their compatriots in New Guinea. Most Samoans treated them with arrogance and contempt.[52] During the war, the "black boys" and Samoans came to blows.[53] After the liquidation of the German Trading and Plantation Company, the New Zealand military administration took many of the Melanesians away from the plantations and set them to cleaning latrines and loading and unloading ships as government employees. Once again, the aim was to ensure that the value of the German plantations was not enhanced.[54] Logan forced the Melanesians, in contrast to the Chinese, to remain in Samoa. When the last labor contracts had expired in May 1917 and the Melanesians demanded to be sent back home, the Administrator compelled them, under threat of force, to continue working.[55] He needed them to do the dirty work that the New Zealand soldiers did not want to do. When New Zealand occupied Samoa, there were 877 Melanesian workers there. On only one occasion, just under two hundred of them were sent home. The rest were obliged to accept new labor contracts that contained little or no provision for pay increases. The New Zealanders flogged them just as the Germans had done. When his successor asked, Logan later admitted that alcohol had been used to keep them under control.[56] Nonetheless, there were a number of strikes and riots because the Melanesians kept demanding to be sent home. With equal regularity, they were bloodily suppressed. In New Guinea, the Melanesians' relatives began complaining and asking where their relations from Samoa were.[57] After the expropriation of the Germans, exactly four hundred Melanesians remained in Samoa. All of them wanted to go back home, but now New Zealand wanted to keep as many as possible in Samoa to work the plantations that had been taken over. After many discussions, half were persuaded to stay for another year in exchange for a small pay rise. These contracts were repeatedly extended. In May 1952, after a second European war, relatives from New Guinea again asked what had become of their "wantoks," whom they had not seen for more than forty years. At that time, eighteen Melanesians were still alive in Samoa. They either could not or no longer wanted to return to New Guinea. By this time, they had come to terms with their Samoan neighbors.[58]

Common ground between New Zealanders and Samoans, even if it consisted only of common antipathies, strengthened the feeling, widespread among Samoans, that they could get along better with New Zealanders than with Germans. Most Samoans did not notice that identical aims actually concealed different motives. Also, they interpreted the New Zealanders' inability during the war to change economic and political priorities and alter the accepted status quo ante as a type of powerlessness which they could get the better of more easily than of German behavior. The Samoan elite's categorical refusal to accept Polynesian Maoris from New Zealand as replacements for Anglo-Saxon soldiers was a clear victory for them.[59] The experience that Samoan interests could take priority in foreign-policy matters was quite new. No German governor would have given Samoans the right to share in foreign-policy decision making, let alone overturned his own decision. (It is more likely that Solf or Schultz would never have dreamed of bringing other South Sea islanders into Samoa as police or soldiers because they were aware of how much trouble such a move would cause. Samoa was the only German colony in the South Pacific in which no Melanesian police were stationed, despite the presence of Melanesian labor and problems with the Samoan police.) Logan, however, informed the Samoan chiefs in advance about the New Zealand cabinet's decision. When the local oligarchy protested, the Administrator gave in. Moreover, it looked as if, together with Logan, the government of New Zealand was bowing to Samoan dictates. The Samoans saw this as their first foreign-policy victory over a European power.

It seemed as if Logan was exactly the right man for Samoa. As a governor officially appointed by a European power, he could represent the views of the Samoans in a world dominated by Europe better than could any Samoan. (The fate of the indigenous monarchy on Hawai'i had not been forgotten.) On the other hand, his actions seemed to suggest that he was relatively easy to manipulate—at least, easier than the German governors had been. To be sure, the Samoans were aware of his pettiness in financial matters and his aversion to certain of the country's customs. But they were convinced, first, that transport would improve again after the end of the European war (and thus that copra prices would rise), and second, that if necessary Samoan ingenuity could easily get the better of the Administrator's Scottish hairsplitting. Logan rejected as too expensive the European traders' suggestions for checking the plague of rhinoceros beetle that damaged coconut palms. Instead, he offered the Samoans rewards for catching the beetles and their larvae. At first, his initiative seemed to have worked, for after a short time the Samoans delivered masses of beetles and larvae. Only when the flood of beetles brought in showed no signs of abating and the funds allocated to the project were running out was it discovered that the Samoans were breeding the beetles under rotting palm trees.[60] In another case, the military governor sent the Samoan police to hunt down the stray dogs belonging to Samoans, which he regarded as pests. Led by a local corporal, Samoan police were on the lookout for nights on end, but they concentrated on shooting dogs belonging to white settlers and officials, which their owners let out at night. The dogs shot included one belonging to the New Zealand collector of customs, who had set the whole initiative in motion by complaining to Logan. On the Samoan side, the dog of the *fautua* Malietoa Tanumafili was killed, shot personally by the Samoan corporal. Obviously, a private Samoan feud was being waged under cover of European approval. The New Zealand commissioner of police had given the Samoan police permission to cut off the ears of their victims. Thereafter, the military governor disbanded the police division.[61]

The Administrator's responsiveness to Samoan wishes was a result only of the exceptional circumstances governing New Zealand's presence in Samoa. This fact, however, was not recognized by the local population. New Zealand was fighting on two fronts. A military victory by Germany was not the only thing that could frustrate New Zealand's ambitions. The Samoans' potential friendliness toward the Germans was a real danger, and Anglo-Saxon experts on the island repeatedly issued warnings about it. Nothing would be more damaging for New Zealand's imperial dreams than to alienate the Samoans. It was therefore no accident that late in 1917 Logan suggested to his superiors in New Zealand that "it [is] politic to grant any reasonable request of the Samoans."[62] On the other hand, since the beginning of 1918 the local elite had agreed unanimously that in the future a British administration was preferable to a German one.[63] If a referendum had been held in Samoa at this time, and the people had been asked whether the Germans or the British should determine the fate of the islands in the future, the result would probably have diverged only slightly from the opinion of the chiefs. At the beginning of 1918 a majority of Samoans favored British rule because they believed it would lead to greater Samoan autonomy. A minority, including Catholics and families that had profited from German rule, noticed that existing privileges were being restricted, and were already against the New Zealanders by 1918. Nor was discontent with the New Zealand military administration unknown among the majority of Samoans. In the direct environs of Apia the excessive administrative apparatus was criticized; in the country, the exact opposite was a grievance—a lack of any administrative control that left the situation threatening to degenerate into anarchy.[64] This was, however, a matter of emphasis. So long as Samoan autonomy emerged stronger from its encounter with New Zealand, and any negative side effects could be explained away as the result of the war, the direction in which the Samoan pendulum would swing was clear. Even the flogging of a Samoan offender on the orders of the New Zealand commander of the military police was tolerated.[65] Like the New Zealanders, the Samoans also looked forward to the end of the war. Whereas the former hoped to have their occupation ratified under international law and then to shape Samoa according to their own priorities, the latter expected official confirmation of the greater autonomy they had achieved during the war. They also hoped for what they regarded as the negative side effects of the war to come to an end. When the armistice was at last announced in Europe, the dreams of the Samoans burst as quickly as soap bubbles.

THE REALITY AND UNREALITY OF A DREAM: SAMOAN AUTONOMY AND THE END OF THE WAR

With the end of the war, death came to Samoa. The horrors of the epidemic of Spanish influenza that spread throughout the world in the summer and autumn of 1918 reached Samoa with the regular ship from New Zealand, the *Talune*, on 7 November 1918. Why the ship was not quarantined will remain a mystery forever. When it called in at Fiji, it was already apparent that the bouts of fever from which a number of passengers were suffering were not a light flu but a serious illness. The shipping company asked the passengers joining the ship in

Fiji to pay a higher fare, because it was counting on being isolated in Apia and wanted compensation for the financial losses it would incur. When they landed in Samoa, many passengers could not walk and had to be helped off the ship. A New Zealand soldier had to be stretchered out of his cabin. Without examining the patients more closely, the government doctor responsible gave the ship permission to land. Rumors were soon rife that he wanted to spare from any unpleasantness the wife of his superior, the first medical officer in Samoa, who was traveling on the ship. The official New Zealand commission of inquiry assembled later, however, hushed up rather than got to the bottom of the obvious contradictions between the statements made by the government doctor and Samoan eyewitnesses.[66]

Once it was in the country, the epidemic spread with almost incredible speed. It is possible that Samoa's isolation from the rest of the world during the war had increased the people's susceptibility to infection. But the crucial factor in producing a mortality rate later estimated as having been between 20 and 25 percent of the total population was the administrative incompetence clearly demonstrated during the epidemic by the military administration, and at its head, the Administrator. No attempt was made to stop the epidemic from spreading by isolating the infected areas. Something of this kind might very well have been successful, as a cynical footnote to the catastrophe demonstrates. The only area to escape the horrors of the epidemic was the leprosy ward, situated a few kilometers outside Apia.[67] Medical help was given to Samoans only in the immediate surroundings of Apia. Inland, they were left to their fate. The only European doctor on the largest of the Samoan islands, Savai'i, took care only of the few Europeans; Samoans who sought his help were turned away. In the end, the government doctor locked himself away and refused to see anybody.[68] At least as many Samoans died of starvation and exhaustion as of the illness itself. As the epidemic struck down whole extended families and villages almost at the same time, there were not enough healthy people left to fetch food from the fields and gardens. By 19 November 1918 there were so many deaths in Apia that the military government could not keep up with the funerals, and Logan telegraphed the New Zealand government for help. His request was immediately turned down. New Zealand, he was told, could not send any doctors because they were needed in New Zealand itself.[69] Even the departure of the *Talune,* which was ready to set off for Samoa according to the timetable, was delayed. The ship was loaded with food and aid, but the crew refused to go to Samoa. Attempts to find a replacement crew were unsuccessful. In the whole of New Zealand, no ship's crew could be found that was prepared to set sail for Samoa. In the end, a New Zealand aid expedition went to help the influenza victims in Fiji instead of to Samoa.[70]

In neighboring American Samoa, the governor had imposed strict quarantine on receiving news of the epidemic raging in the western islands of the archipelago. This saved Eastern Samoa—it was one of the very few Pacific territories to escape infection. The American governor had offered Western

Samoa his assistance via the American consul in Apia. For hours, a fully equipped team of doctors and nurses carrying medical aid was ready in the harbor of Pago Pago, waiting for official news from Apia. Colonel Logan, however, who read the telegram offering American help first (in his function as censor), simply put it in his pocket. He did not reply when Consul Mitchell asked him what he was going to do now. Instead of informing Pago Pago, he instructed the head of the radio station to break off all radio communications with American Samoa immediately, and without prior warning. The head of the radio station later testified that Pago Pago had tried several times to contact Apia by radio, but that the military governor had forbidden him to respond. Logan's behavior becomes explicable only if we remember how much he despised Americans. The fact that it was the Americans who were offering to help him out of this fix was obviously too much for him. Rarely would anti-American prejudice have more disastrous consequences than in Samoa under New Zealand occupation. This seems to justify the view that the authoritarian powers that Logan enjoyed as a result of the war situation had somehow gone to his head, and that he was out of touch with reality. His successor in office called him "mad."[71] When medical help at last arrived in Samoa from Australia, the worst was already over. Dismayed survivors noted with bitterness that the food unloaded was intended not for them but for the white members of the aid expedition. They were told that they were healthy again and could collect fruit out of the gardens for themselves.[72]

We shall probably never know how many Samoans died in the influenza epidemic. The official New Zealand Epidemic Commission put the figure at eighty-five hundred dead.[73] But the real figure was certainly higher, and not only because mortality was disproportionately high in the first months of 1919. The New Zealand Statistical Office clearly wanted the first census after the epidemic to show as great an increase in population as possible and obviously published false figures.[74]

One special feature of this particular type of influenza had especially disastrous consequences for Samoan society. Surprisingly enough, its victims were not so much children and old people as men and women in the prime of life. It affected men even more than women. As Samoan society was structured as a hierarchical oligarchy, the consequences can hardly be overrated. The two *fautua* survived, but of thirty *faipule*, only six were still alive to attend the first council meeting after the catastrophe. The twenty-four dead were replaced by young, inexperienced men.[75] On Savai'i, every second *matai* (headman) died; out of a total of 1,486 *matai* before the epidemic, only 755 were alive at the beginning of 1919.[76] Similarly shocking were the losses among church leaders, who enjoyed the greatest authority after the chiefs. One hundred and three of the 220 Samoan pastors of the London Missionary Society, to which almost two-thirds of all Samoans belonged, had died. Only one member of the church's council of elders (*Au Toeaina*) survived.[77] At a stroke, a new generation moved into positions of responsibility. Most of them had not had a chance to gain the requisite qualifications. Many *matai* died so suddenly that they took the family secrets to the grave with them, without having initiated others into them. Carefully guarded and meticulously handed-down knowledge of genealogies, and of traditional claims and privileges, was lost in many families. The influenza epidemic not only inflicted a great deal of personal suffering, it also represented an irreversible break with the past for Samoan society. It was a turning point in Samoan history probably more profound than the beginning or the end of German colonial rule. For a central European, the most obvious comparison is with the impact of the Thirty Years' War.

Solf had created the Land and Titles Commission to deal with the most important intra-Samoan disputes. Instead of drafting new laws, this commission interpreted existing law on the basis of traditional Samoan principles and models. As most disputes were settled by internal arbitration anyway, the commission could concentrate on the really difficult cases requiring interpretation. After the influenza epidemic at the latest, the military government aimed to have as many Samoan quarrels as possible settled by the Land and Titles Commission. Many conflicts could no longer be resolved internally, because knowledge of the exact extent of established privileges and ancient precedents had been lost with the victims of the epidemic. The uncertainty created by the lack of knowledge, and the immaturity of the younger chiefs, turned many of them into enraged fighting cocks. They attacked each other for titles, privileges, and territorial borders, which were claimed or defended. The number of disputes that came before the commission simply exploded.[78] Because the interpretation of past cases had become controversial, factors other than historical correctness and the observance of parallel cases suddenly became more important in the decision-making process. The relationship between the plaintiff and the colonial power moved more and more into the foreground. Sympathy or antipathy toward New Zealand could replace missing historical evidence of claims, or make existing ones worthless. The former Land and Titles Commission continued to exist in name only. In reality it had changed from an institution created in order to settle Samoan disputes because the colonial administration feared a recurrence of the bloody civil wars of the nineteenth century into an instrument the European rulers used to play one Samoan party off against another for their own advantage. The influenza epidemic not only killed people; it also, for the first time, shook the firm foundation in tradition that had long supported the Samoans. Neither Christianization nor contact with European traders, the civil war, German colonial rule, or the New Zealand military administration had ever constituted a similarly serious threat.

The influenza weakened the Samoan population both mentally and physically. The military governor argued that the local people themselves were to blame for the extent of the catastrophe because they had behaved quite wrongly. They had to be shown that they had no right to complain. But the present situation, he suggested, provided a good opportunity to reform the Samoan government. The prerogatives of the Samoan native administration should be abolished. Logan proposed that in future the colonial administration should nominate the *faipule* directly, and that local influence should be totally eliminated in their selection. His recommendation that German law relating to land ownership be changed to make it easier for Europeans to acquire Samoan land went one step further. Logan wanted to confiscate thirty to forty thousand acres of "fairly good land" on the main island of Upolu from the Samoans as quickly as possible and make it available to European settlers. This was twice as much land as had been planted in the whole of Samoa so far. All Logan had to do was to take out of his drawer a report by the head of the land registry, N. H. Macdonald, who was also chair of the Land and Titles Commission.[79]

Was this the end of Samoan autonomy? If the Samoans had resigned themselves to their fate, the days of Samoan self-administration would indeed have been numbered. The shock of the epidemic unleashed the fatalistic features of the Samoan makeup. People blaming each other and self-accusations were not unknown. A number of Samoans were (and some still are) convinced that they had been punished by God. Members of the London Missionary Society and the Wesleyans encouraged this belief, thus distracting attention from their own mistakes. When asked why God should punish them in this way, Samoans reply that the families affected are well aware of their own sins, but that they naturally do not want to tell the whole world about them.[80] According to another version, this punishment was connected with their behavior toward the Germans during the war: the Samoans had been punished for leaving the Germans in the lurch. This view was reinforced by the deaths of the "Lauati conspirators." None of the chiefs who had returned from exile during the war with the help of the New Zealanders had survived the flu epidemic. It received further support from the fact that Iʻiga Pisa, who had steadfastly refused to make moves toward returning without the permission of the German government, survived. It seems likely that the Germans on Samoa encouraged this interpretation, but there is no direct evidence in support of this view.[81]

Not all Samoans reacted to the catastrophe by blaming themselves. It was lucky for Samoa that the horror which befell the people did not paralyze their energy for long. The surviving representatives of the Samoan oligarchy pulled themselves together with amazing rapidity. Traditional behavior was swept away by anger at what had happened. Whereas requests had generally been made indirectly, couched in a flood of typically Samoan formulae of politeness, people now reacted directly and decisively. On 4 January 1919, a deputation of the surviving *faipule* appeared before the governor, unannounced and without advance warning. They did not request, but demanded, an official inquiry into the causes of the epidemic and insisted that in the future ships were to be investigated more strictly on arrival. Logan rudely dismissed the Samoans,[82] which, however, embittered rather than silenced them. More important than anything else was the fact that the Samoans had demonstrated that they would not take this lying down. Given the military governor's ambitious aims, a confrontation with him seemed inevitable.

Logan's departure for home leave (from which he was not to return), cleared the air a little but did not calm down the angry Samoans. The new Administrator, Colonel Tate, was at first appointed only in an acting capacity. A delegation of Samoan chiefs presented him with their demands on 28 January 1919. They seemed to have chosen this date deliberately. The annual council meeting *(fono)* between the governor and the Samoan deputies, the *faipule,* had always taken place on 27 January, the Kaiser's birthday. In order to give the British claim to Samoa a symbolic dimension, Logan had rescheduled the *fono* meetings for the middle of June, the official birthday of the king. Now the Samoan elite called a *fono* on their own initiative, without having been summoned by the Administrator as was usual. It was attended by 128 chiefs (including the two *fautua*). The surviving Samoan oligarchy was represented almost without exception. The date and organization of the *fono* was a Samoan affront to New Zealand in every respect. It was less a matter of nostalgia than a clear indication that, under all circumstances, the Samoans wanted to retain the institution of Samoan self-administration in the form originally accepted by a European colonial power. New Zealand's new man in Samoa was presented with a long list of Samoan complaints and demands, all of which centered on the influenza epidemic, its causes and consequences. Paragraphs eight and nine contained the main demands of the petition. In them, the Samoans called for political union with the rest of Samoa in the east of the archipelago under American sovereignty. If the Great Powers were to refuse this request, the Samoans wanted an administration for Western Samoa under the direct supervision of the Colonial Office. Under no circumstances did they want New Zealand to have a share in the administration of Samoa.[83]

The Samoan oligarchy had moved from the defensive to the offensive. There is no doubt that the demand, voiced in public by the Samoan elite, for a change in the political situation reflected the mood of the overwhelming majority of the Samoan people. The dissemination of the petition calling for unification with American Samoa developed a momentum of its own that could not be stopped, even long after the original petition had been withdrawn. In Samoan style, new songs came into being, criticizing the New Zealand administration and praising the American administration. The words were sung to the tune of the American national anthem. Years later, any appearance of the U.S. flag in Apia's cinema, one of the favorite meeting places for Samoans of all generations and classes, was greeted with rapturous applause.[84]

There were two main reasons for the desire to be united with American Samoa. One, stated in the petition itself, was the wish for the whole of Samoa to be united under a single government again. It was not a matter of creating something new, but simply of reunifying with relatives in the east who had been subject to a different political regime since 1899–1900. The second motive was no less important than the first. Samoans agreed unanimously, it seems, that the colonial administration in Pago Pago had proved itself more capable of protecting the Samoan people from harm than the one in Apia.

When the Samoans in the American sphere of influence heard how their relatives in the west had voted, an indescribable rejoicing broke out.[85] It would be wrong, however, to conclude from the actions of the Samoan elite that Samoa would voluntarily submit to a European country and renounce its independence. The opposite was the case. At stake was the preservation of Samoan self-administration and the survival of the Samoan people in a world dominated by European institutions and values. The Samoans had learnt from historical experience that this was not the right moment to attempt to create a totally independent Samoan government. This recognition did not imply a renunciation of autonomous rights; rather, it was dictated by political good sense. To start with, it was a matter of working to obtain a colonial administration that would be most likely to fulfill Samoan objectives, and to prevent initiatives that ran counter to Samoan priorities.

It soon became apparent, however, that the common experience of profound suffering during the influenza epidemic was not enough to remove old and deep-seated conflicts of interests within the Samoan oligarchy. Even the greatest unity among the masses about a political future for Samoa without New Zealand could not obscure the fact that there were opposing positions within the leading oligarchy that could not be reconciled with this view. The majority of Samoans could not prevent Fautua Malietoa Tanumafili from quickly repudiating the whole petition and labeling the "Samoan" objectives as the ambitions of political rivals. Even while the petition was being presented, the clause about union with American Samoa was withdrawn. Two weeks later, both *fautua* distanced themselves from the rest of the demands without having sought the approval of the original signatories to the petition.[86] There is no doubt that by 1919 the traditional Samoan social system had become counterproductive because the political expectations of most Samoans were frustrated by the people at the top of their hierarchy. If Samoa had been democratically structured, it would have been easier to gain an international hearing for the majority of Samoans. As it was, however, New Zealand could always point out that the "voice" of Samoa was the voice of Malietoa, who repeatedly sided with the Anglo-Saxons. Why he did this largely lies beyond the reach of European explanations. In any case, it is too simplistic to assume that it was a purely selfish response.[87]

The main initiators of a consciously Samoan policy were Toelupe, who had been elected by the *faipule* as their spokesman and was a well-known *tulafale* (orator) from Malie and the Samoan with the longest experience of dealing with the European colonial administration, and Toleafoa Afamasaga Lagolago, brother of Afamasaga Maua, secretary of the Samoan self-administration, who had died during the influenza epidemic. It was Toelupe who greeted the new Administrator in the name of the Samoans, making it clear that the representatives of Samoa would not accept any blurring of responsibility for the outbreak of the influenza: "God alone will not send such an epidemic."[88] And it was Toleafoa who presented the petition. The fact that he was also prepared to give up the demand for unification with American Samoa makes the whole incident even more puzzling. Even the New Zealand Administrator, Tate, did not believe in such a sudden change of mind, suspecting an especially insidious Samoan intrigue.[89] In private, the Burns Philp representative in Samoa, Allom, bragged that he had made sure that the relevant passage had disappeared from the petition.[90]

At first glance, this story of the manipulation of the Samoan petition of 1919 seems so farfetched that one is tempted to see in it no more than the idle boast of a company employee who wanted to present himself and his abilities in the best light. It is indisputable, of course, that Burns Philp tried by all possible means to influence any political decisions that could be useful or harmful to its business interests. It is also understandable that the company would by far have preferred British to U.S. control of Western Samoa. But the question remains of how it could have influenced the Samoans. Even before 1914, Burns Philp had its own local agent in Samoa, who was obviously used for far more than simply to buy up the local copra.[91] But even this is not evidence. At best, it strengthens a suspicion that the Burns Philp representative may not merely have been boasting. The chain of evidence is incomplete.

The man who presented the petition and had played a prominent part in drafting it, Toleafoa Afamasaga Lagolago, was in every respect an exceptional case. His family was part of the Samoan oligarchy; the titles *afamasaga* and *toleafoa* were among the highest in the district of A'ana, although not among the four most important in Samoa. During the civil war, his father had supported the British, while his brother had built a career in the German administration, becoming the indigenous secretary and government interpreter under Governor Schultz, a position which gave him more real influence than that of the two *fautua*. Logan, who left him in this position, gave him a great deal of freedom over "purely" Samoan matters, which increased his power further. Toleafoa Lagolago himself had worked as a foreman in shipyards in New Zealand and American Samoa, and for a Samoan he had gained an outstanding insight into European ways. He spoke excellent English, and the Administrator, who could not stand him, in private called him "the most intelligent Samoan."[92] As director of the Toea'ina club, Toleafoa crucially influenced the basic features of Samoan policy opposing the military administration. Leading members of the Samoan oligarchy came together in the Toea'ina club. Under the guise of pursuing common social and commercial initiatives, this club worked purposefully toward realizing Samoan political independence. It can therefore be seen as the precursor of a Samoan independence party. A similar enterprise had already been nipped in the bud by Solf.[93] Logan, however, allowed the club to continue functioning during the war, which the Samoan side saw as yet more evidence of their increased freedom in the period before the outbreak of the influenza. For the new Administrator it was clear from the start that nothing was more dangerous to New Zealand's colonial ambitions in Samoa than this club, in which local plans were made and discussed. By August 1919 at the latest, it began to put about the idea of a completely independent Samoa.[94]

Tate eliminated this crystallization point of Samoan hopes for more political responsibility through a dirty tricks campaign. The Administrator persuaded the members of the club that Toleafoa was a gambler who had lost their money. The club more or less disintegrated under vehement mutual recriminations and accusations. Financially discredited, Toleafoa also lost his politically prominent position. The whole affair became such a scandal among the members of the Samoan oligarchy that it has left a nasty taste in people's mouths to the present day. In fact, Tate was fully aware that the club was not involved in financial irregularities as he had tried to make out. Toleafoa's allegedly loss-making expenditure was the result of putting money into investments that might have given the appearance of a short-term cash-flow problem but were sensible in the long term. The official auditor, instructed by the Administrator to examine the club's books, protested in vain when newspaper reports, originating with Tate, claimed that the club was bankrupt. He insisted that the books were well kept and the balances in order; Toleafoa had demonstrated a sound understanding of business principles.[95]

The breaking up of the Toea'ina club did not mean the end of Samoan attempts to gain more autonomy. After all, the Samoan administration, recognized by the government, still existed; and under the leadership of Toelupe, the Samoan opposition, consisting of the *faipule,* or councillors, organized itself. Tate's next objective was to bring this official representation of Samoan interests into line. In order to do this, he used a suggestion made by his predecessor, Logan. The existing system of "representative oligarchy"—the *matai* elected their village *pulenuu,* and the *pulenuu* elected the *faipule* for their district— was abolished. In future the *faipule* were to be directly nominated by the government.[96] The privileges of the members of the Samoan administration were to be cut back to a purely representative level. From November 1919 on, the Samoa Constitutional Order provided the guidelines to be followed by the New Zealand administration in Samoa. At a stroke, land hitherto owned by Samoans became New Zealand Crown land, and only the right of usufruct was left to them. In the future, whether the previously sovereign owners retained their land or not would depend on the goodwill of the colonial administration. No mention was made of Samoan self-administration or the *faipule.* The council of *faipule* with President Toelupe at its head protested against this procedure and asked to speak to the Administrator. Tate gave them the cold shoulder. Without even listening to the deputation, he left it to his subordinates to get rid of the Samoan delegates.[97]

There were certainly voices within the New Zealand government in favor of involving the Samoan oligarchy more strongly in the process of political decision making. The Maoris had the vote, were represented in parliament, and even had a number of ministers in the New Zealand cabinet. The New Zealand solicitor general had therefore recommended that the two *fautua* be included as unofficial members of the Governing Council of Samoa that was to be revived; but the Administrator's veto made this impossible. Tate's distrust was not limited to Samoans; he suspected the white settlers of permanently conspiring against the New Zealand colonial administration. They, too, were denied a role in decision-making within the Samoan administration. Therefore the Governing Council, officially reestablished on 1 May 1920, consisted only of Tate himself and his leading officials.[98]

What was left of the Samoan self-administration? During the European war, the illusion flourished that the old dream of Samoan autonomy could be realized with New Zealand's help. The end of the war seemed to bury all these hopes. The nightmare of the influenza epidemic drove a huge wedge into Samoa's traditional networks of relationships. The loss of social information and important members of Samoan society made it easier for the New Zealand administration to turn back the clock and place into question even those autonomous rights which already existed. The only cases in which Tate did not put obstacles in the path of the Samoan oligarchy were those in which he could turn their independent activities to his own personal advantage. Thus he allowed the two *fautua* to inform the New Zealand government directly, by telegram, that Logan's presence was no longer desired in Samoa.[99] And the Samoans' determination not to accept a foreign Polynesian as minister for Samoa matched the Administrator's aversion to taking orders from a Maori.[100]

Tate's almost desperate attempt to minimize Samoan participation in the administration should not, however, obscure the fact that the influence of the Samoans on Samoan politics was by no means marginal; it was possibly even larger than it had been under the Germans. Solf and Schultz had to some extent recognized the indigenous desire for autonomy. But the Germans' acceptance of local self-administration had directed Samoan claims into specific channels, and these were kept under control. In 1914 Samoa's traditional elite had come to terms with the status quo. With the outbreak of the war, the conditions previously governing the situation became increasingly obsolete. Everything was somehow in flux. Tate tried to eliminate the Samoans' influence in shaping the future of their country as much as possible, while Samoan demands for greater involvement in politics went far beyond the limits staked out before 1914. The history of Samoa after 1918 is a permanent tug-of-war between Samoan attempts to gain greater autonomy and New Zealand's efforts to limit Samoan demands. After the influenza epidemic, peace never returned to relations between the New Zealand administration and the Samoans.

Tate was able to counter the idea of Samoan autonomy, which was gaining a dynamic and force of its own, only by physical violence. On his insistence, the Samoa Constitutional Order specified more punishments that could be employed against the Samoans and increased maximum sentences. Although he had the foreign minister's approval, Tate was unable officially to introduce corporal punishment for Samoans. He could not get a majority in the New Zealand parliament to support this suggestion.[101] The ship that took the last New Zealand soldiers away from Samoa early in 1920 brought in a unit of military police. Later it was supplemented by its own secret service, which Gurr had urged the administration to set up urgently.[102] But none of these measures could guarantee that New Zealand rule put down roots. More and more Samoans were dissatisfied with New Zealand. Even among the Samoan political elite, the supporters of the New Zealand administration were never more than a minority. Sometimes it seemed as if both sides had tacitly agreed to accept some form of status quo. But these breathing spaces never lasted long, and they were generally followed by even more violent clashes. In Samoa much earlier than on other Pacific islands, the validity of a political truism was demonstrated: a government cannot rule against the will of the majority of the population; at best it can hope to administer. New Zealand failed completely in its attempt to break the will of the Samoan people. Nonetheless, the various attempts it made to achieve this goal caused a great deal of damage.

From what sources did the Samoans draw this determination, their will to reject New Zealand ambitions, and the strength to go on the offensive themselves? It seems paradoxical, but the Samoan independence movement was born out of the deadly influenza bacillus. New Zealand was aware of the strength of solidarity forged out of defeat—after all, Gallipoli was commemorated like a victory every year. But their racist arrogance prevented them from wanting to perceive the consequences. "Native unrest is my constant anxiety," Tate confided to his colleague in American Samoa early in 1921. The reason for the constant unrest among the Samoans, he said, was their idea that whites and blacks had the same rights. In his view, Samoan attempts to realize this idea were ludicrous, and pathetic in every case. They wanted to govern themselves, but the only form of rule they knew was that of the chiefs.[103]

On one crucial point the influenza epidemic even gave the Samoans a direct advantage. The New Zealand administration's plans to abolish the most important Samoan prerogative, their exemption from providing labor for the Europeans, and to force them to work on the plantations had to be abandoned because the Samoans were physically and numerically so weakened by the epidemic. Thus, once again, recourse was taken to the Chinese. An emissary from New Zealand's administration on Samoa traveled to China and organized fresh labor supplies. In August 1920 the first contingent of Chinese arrived from Hong Kong. The Hong Kong authorities had banned the export of coolies, but the New Zealand emissary got around this by putting them down as tourists to Samoa. Completed labor contracts were presented to them only on their arrival in Apia. In order to persuade them to sign, the prison sentence for refusing to work had recently been abolished. Six months later it was reintroduced.[104] Like the Germans, the New Zealanders regarded the Chinese coolies merely as a means to an end and subjected them to brutal exploitation. The specifically Anglo-Saxon form of racism in the Pacific gave rise to regulations that in no way lagged behind German discriminatory laws, and in some areas even outstripped them.[105] While the Samoans struggled to achieve a greater degree of autonomy and more equal rights, the Chinese had difficulty in being recognized as humans at all.

Indigenous Responses to
the First World War

How did the indigenous peoples in Germany's South Pacific colonies react to the events that, in effect, led to the end of the German administration? This chapter does not look at how individuals came to terms with their new rulers during the war—previous chapters have dealt with that problem. What concerns us here is the essence of the new arrangements and the attitudes of larger indigenous groups toward them. We shall be looking at local responses to crucial changes in the balance of power and local strategies for dealing with them. Above all, this chapter addresses the question of how Pacific societies tried to influence the changes that were occuring in colonial rule.

NEW GUINEA

The diversity of groups in New Guinea meant that there could be no unified response to the change of power. The splintering of society into a large number of small groups makes it extremely difficult to discern a majority attitude toward any changes in power structure. This does not mean, however, that such a majority attitude did not exist or that the Melanesians on the whole were indifferent. Despite their differences, the indigenous people often took a common attitude toward European prescriptions. This unanimity, achieved without prior consultation or organization (which were not possible), allowed them to be highly effective. This is not a paradox. Despite all their internal differences and diversity, Melanesian cultures were always closer to each other than they could ever have been to any of the European cultures. Because Melanesians perceived European behavior from approximately the same vantage point and often had similar experiences with Europeans, certain indigenous patterns of behavior emerged, as it were, overnight.

Once these experiences and patterns of behavior had been internalized, it required a great deal of evidence, both qualitative and quantitative, over a long period of time, to change the stereotypes that had developed. As this evidence was rarely forthcoming, Melanesian views and fundamental convictions have proved to be extremely long-lived, and their conservatism is often as stubborn as a dictionary definition of prejudice.[1] In contacts with Europeans, this Melanesian obstinacy was certainly no disadvantage. The only pan-Melanesian action against a change in the German system of which we know was based on the indigenous people's unshakeable attitude toward norms they had once accepted. Thus the Australian military administration found it impossible to make the Melanesian people acknowledge the devaluation of the mark that it had proclaimed. Since the days of the Neuguinea-Kompanie, the mark had been legal tender in the German colony. The Melanesians had gotten used to the fact that coins could have different faces (they did not accept notes), because the German mark had replaced the Neuguinea-Kompanie's mark. The shilling, therefore, was accepted without any problem as *niupela mak* (new mark) as long as its value was the same as that of the mark. However, when the military administration proclaimed that the mark was worth only eleven pence, the local reaction was incomprehension. The indigenous people also began to refuse to accept the shilling in trade. This response occurred at the same time at various places in the colony and reached such proportions that the military administration decided to introduce a special exchange rate for Melanesians. The old shilling–mark parity was reintroduced, but only for trade with Melanesians. The administration was to be partly compensated for the losses it thus incurred by paying its rent for Melanesian land solely in marks. On 31 July 1919, after the end of the war, German currency ceased to be legal tender. Again, an exception was made for the local population, who were able to exchange their mark coins at an official rate of one mark per shilling for one more year. But even at the beginning of the mandate, the Australian government still decided it was more sensible to continue to allow the local population to pay its taxes in marks, and simply to accept the losses it incurred as a result.[2]

How did the indigenous population of what was at that time German Melanesia assess the change in power as such? We have already pointed out that Melanesians hardly made distinctions among different European nationalities before 1914. At most, Europeans were categorized as "officials," "missionaries," or "planters." Personal relations between Melanesians and Europeans were the most important thing. National differences among Europeans were difficult to detect simply because there were few opportunities for comparison. More than 80 percent of all Europeans in the colony were German; not even every twentieth European was an Australian.[3] There was no opportunity to get to know what could be considered "typically" Australian or "specifically" German, and it was unimportant.

This changed with Australia's occupation of New Guinea. Both Australians and Germans wanted to demonstrate to the local people how they differed from each other. Differences in attitudes and behavior affected both plantation labor and the "free" Melanesians, but in conflicting ways. In assessing and classifying European behavior, the local people began to take alleged or real differences into account. But even now the national aspect was secondary to Melanesian interpretations. What was undoubtedly noted and compared was the difference between the "old" and the "new" administration. The contrast between Australian and German was not crucial so long as German settlers, planters, and missionaries remained in New Guinea alongside Australian soldiers. Early in January 1918, when Britain called on all the Dominions that had occupied German colonial territories to find out what the local people thought about the changeover in power, the Australian government rejected the idea of consulting the Melanesians about their political fate by holding a referendum, pointing out that, because the Germans were still in the country, the Melanesians had little understanding of the fact that the British were the new rulers. Melbourne suggested that a vote might be pro-German, "so long as the natives are treated by them [the Germans] fairly decently."[4]

In April, London tried again, making its real concerns more explicit this time. It wanted evidence of the brutal treatment of the local population by Germans to place before the Imperial Conference: (1) "Neglect of native Rights or feelings as well as injustice or cruelty"; (2) "Any evidence suggesting natives better under British than German control"; (3) "Information re mental capacity of natives to formulate ideas re own government or destiny."[5]

On the Administrator's instructions, the officers responsible for the native administration more closely investigated the German past and what the local people thought of it. In mid-June 1918 the Administrator was forced to admit that, despite all their efforts, nothing of significance had been found to hold against the German colonial administration. Newspaper reports about German atrocities had no foundation in fact; individual excesses that were brought to the attention of the former colonial government were dealt with swiftly and severely. And as for corporal punishment, any plantation that had the reputation of flogging too much would never have been able to recruit new labor. On the contrary, the local people had a certain esteem for the German officials: "I consider that the Germans generally respected native rights and customs, natives speaking very well indeed of many of the Officials especially Governor Hahl. . . . There is no doubt in my mind that it was chiefly due to Governor Hahl that the Administration of the natives under German rule was as good as it was. I am of opinion generally, that it was very good."[6]

The Administrator and his closest colleagues indirectly referred to the fact that there were two groups, with differing interests, among the Melanesian people. Possibly a large majority of plantation workers favored a continuation of Australian rule: "I do not, however think that this is of any value; . . . They prefer our rule because we are less exacting, our soldiers play with them, (and spoil them)."[7]

The Australian administration had given up regular tours of inspection among the "free" Melanesians, "and in these parts the British Administration is practically unknown." But all this was really of no importance, he suggested, because, after all, it was nonsense to consult the Melanesians about their political future: "The natives as a race are most indolent, and their ideas seldom extend beyond eating, sleeping, smoking, and an occasional 'sing-sing' dance."[8]

In Australia, Prime Minister Hughes had appointed staff officer Commander Banks to "obtain evidence as to German ill usage of natives or unjust dealing as to land or property or stirring up trouble among natives or selling liquor."[9] Banks' findings, based on statements by Australian planters and missionaries in New Guinea, tallied with the information sent by the Administrator. There was no evidence of German atrocities or neglect of native rights and customs. Again and again, the word *just* was used to describe relations between the German administration and the Melanesians.[10] In his own report to the Australian government, Lucas recommended that the Melanesians—"very little superior to the wild aboriginals of Australia"—should on no account be consulted in a referendum. The local population of New Guinea had been influenced by the Germans, "and the natives still stand in awe of them." Pethebridge, the long-serving Administrator, had expressed a similar opinion in his final letter to the Ministry of Defence.[11]

Because of these unanimous assessments of the German colonial administration in New Guinea, the British white paper on German colonial excesses ignored New Guinea.[12] More relevant than this footnote to intra-European diplomatic history is the question of to what extent the Australian commentators really conveyed the views of the local people. It is necessary to point out that the Australian officials, missionaries, and certainly planters, saw flogging as an appropriate punishment. By far the majority would have welcomed its official reintroduction. Approval of German methods of government contained an implied criticism of the Australian administration; this may have been deliberate. Even if all these circumstances are taken into account, however, the frequency with which the word *just* crops up is still striking. This is not the place for an explanation. I shall attempt one later, in the context of a larger overview of developments between 1914 and 1921–1922, when the various influences and factors at work can be better balanced against each other.

What is clear is that many Melanesians held individual German colonial officials—above all, the long-serving governor, Albert Hahl—in high regard, in marked contrast to their opinion of German planters and traders. There is a great deal of additional evidence for this, to which we shall return elsewhere. The Melanesian people who came into contact with German officials, however, did not judge them by national criteria. Hahl, Döllinger, or Berghausen were not regarded as good officials *because* they were Germans: judgments were based on personal contact with them. It has already been mentioned several times that personal relations between members of the colonial administration and the local people was of crucial importance. An association among "officials," "colonial administration," and "German" developed later, if at all, and was influenced decisively by contrast with the Australian colonial administration and Australian officials. One thing, however, is certain. Hahl's reputation for having gained the respect of the Melanesians was, if anything, enhanced during the war. In mid-1919 the governor-general of Australia reported the impression gained by his private secretary during a visit to New Guinea. Hahl, he said, "combined an earnest desire for developing the possession with a strong sense of justice towards the native population."[13]

In 1918–1919, the only evidence of local opinions of the German administration consisted of individual impressions and Melanesians' experiences with German officials. Melanesians did not identify their personal experience of individual officials in the colonial government with Germany or the Germans. It was more the Australians who did this. For Melanesians, nationality was not yet important. They judged Europeans by their behavior and function, not according to nationality. In 1918–1919, therefore, most Melanesians in the European colonial administration's sphere of influence had no reason to take much interest in the question of whether the change that had taken place in the European order in 1914 should be perpetuated or reversed. In 1919 the vast majority of the people of New Guinea lived beyond all European control and was in this sense "independent" anyway. Indigenous concepts and strategies for influencing European decisions are not recognizable and almost certainly did not exist. They would have required mechanisms for shaping public opinion and a higher-level local organization. New Guinea lacked both. The fact that this was so then did not mean, however, that it would remain so forever. To one of Australia's leading legal minds, however, the Melanesians' lack of activity in 1918 symbolized a natural state of everlasting infancy: "They are a kind of perpetual infants. Like Peter Pan, they will never grow up."[14]

NAURU

In Nauru the Micronesian population had left its new rulers in no doubt about its opinion of the continued phosphate mining. The administration had even sent the especially stubborn son of the chief, Detudamo, to prison for seditious behavior.[15] The small size of the Nauruan population was a handicap, as was the determination of their new rulers not to lose the phosphate business. Statements by the local people about the change in power were in great demand, because they could be used as evidence to support one's own case. The Nauruans were asked several times to express their opinions about the change in government. A visit by the Administrator of occupied New Guinea, Pethebridge, late in September 1915, provided the occasion for all the chiefs of Nauru to make the declaration they had been asked to prepare. However, it was not exactly what the British had been expecting: "As children they had always understood and hoped that at some time the British Flag would be hoisted on their Island, however the Germans came and for many years had treated them with kindness. For this reason they could not help feeling a certain affection for the late German Government, but they realized that what

they had expected had now come to pass, and already they could see the benefit of British rule."[16]

The ambiguity of this declaration will not escape anyone who is familiar
with Pacific patterns of argument. The polite submission to British expectations is closely associated with a view of the German past which, to European
eyes, seems almost melancholy. This positive view on the part of the Nauruans
of German activities on their island is unknown from the times of the German
administration, and it is doubtful whether such a statement would have been
made then. The Nauruans' main concern was the exploitation of the phosphate on their island. Under nominal German sovereignty, there had been
competition between the German administration and the phosphate company,
which was in the majority control of Britons. This had given the Nauruans a
certain amount of room for maneuver. The reference to the Germans, and the
opposition between "kindness" and "benefit of British rule" could also be seen
as a strongly stressed expectation that the new rulers had yet to fulfill. Nauruan hopes for British cooperation and British expectations of a renunciation
of sovereignty by the Nauruans were carefully balanced against each other.
The declaration was a typical example of Pacific diplomacy. Outwardly, one
behaved as was expected, but the last step was deliberately not taken and a
way out was left open; while the right hand was outstretched, the left kept
something back in reserve. What the Nauruans (and many other Pacific
Islanders in other places, at other times, and in relation to other Europeans)
did not take into account was the simple fact that most Europeans either did
not, or did not want to, understand the finer points and deeper meaning
of Pacific Islanders' negotiations. Independent Nauruan ideas were not
required. Rather, the Europeans impatiently expected the Nauruans to
acclaim European rule.

When this did not happen in 1915, new attempts were made. In May 1918
the Nauruan chiefs asked the British Administrator to pass on their wishes concerning phosphate mining on Nauru to the European decision makers. Thereupon the Administrator called the Nauruan people together on a number of
occasions, in order to explain to them the difference between British and German rule. On 29 October 1918 he sent a petition from the Nauruans to the
British high commissioner, in which the chiefs and the people of the island
asked to remain British after the war. An exact copy of this petition has survived. It lists 616 names, most signed with crosses instead of a signature. Strikingly, these crosses display no individual characteristics. Of the marks made by
the fifteen chiefs, three are recognizable as personal signatures, four are written in the same handwriting, and the rest consist of identical crosses.[17] The
whole thing was a put-up job, like the one the Pacific Phosphate Company had
already tried. Now it was the administration's turn. There were practically no
illiterates on Nauru.

In order to document more closely the unscrupulousness with which the
British colonial administration, too, pursued economic interests on the phos-

phate islands, it is necessary to look again at neighboring Ocean Island. Less than two weeks after the events on Nauru—that is, at precisely the time when he would have found out exactly what had happened there—the resident commissioner of the British colony of the Gilbert and Ellice Islands decided that it was time at last to sort things out. It was the duty of the administration, he felt, to produce some concrete proposals about how the Banaban people could be forcibly deported from their homes to Nauru within a period of eight to ten years. This was necessary, he suggested, "not only in the interests of the Company, but in order that this high grade phosphate may be available for the needs of the Empire at the cheapest cost of output."

Scruples were unnecessary, he wrote. After all, they had not had any so far: "Eighteen years ago the Government allowed the Company to make its own initial terms with a handful of ignorant and illiterate natives [Ocean Island, unlike Nauru, had no mission]. A child wrote down the names of the 'so called King' and Chiefs, who were equally ignorant of the purport of the document. This constituted the so called 'Agreement with the Banabans for 999 years' under date of 3rd May 1900. This agreement has never been queried by the Government." What was intended now was an "Imperial Measure of Necessity." For reasons of expediency, the Banabans should not be informed about what was planned, otherwise they would try to resist the forced relocations that were being contemplated.[18] This measure could not be implemented as quickly as had originally been planned, but the Second World War offered an opportunity to dust off the old plans and put them into practice. At the end of 1945 the Banabans were taken off Ocean Island, against their will. Instead of Nauru, which was too close to the Banaban homeland, they were taken to a small island in the far-distant Fiji archipelago, where the Banabans and their descendants still live today.[19]

JAPANESE MICRONESIA

The relative isolation of the Micronesian islands under Japanese occupation makes it difficult to say much about how the local people reacted to the change in rulers, or to what extent they attempted to influence their own political future. Five points, however, can be made about the regions from which we do have evidence: (1) from the start the Micronesians regarded the Japanese takeover as a fundamental turning point in their history; (2) from an early date they started to draw comparisons between German and Japanese rule; (3) the Micronesians had their own ideas about what they wanted, and especially what they did not want; (4) they were aware that the Micronesian question had not been settled; and (5) there is evidence that they tried to make an international public aware of their views.

We know least about the northern and western regions of Micronesia—those areas where Japanese influence was strongest. On Saipan, it is said, the

Chamorros and the Caroline Islanders were so frustrated by the changes which had taken place that by mid-1915 they wanted the Germans to return.[20] There were emotional scenes when the last Germans left Palau and Yap. On Yap, in particular, the relationship between the local people and the few Germans seems to have been extraordinarily good. The government doctor, who had only been on the island for seven months, was presented with a shell axe and a necklace, and was asked to return after the war. But on Yap something more than the usual familiar relations between Germans and locals had evolved: from these personal ties the people of Yap gained access to the abstract concepts "German" and "the Germans." Because the Europeans they knew, and whose presence and activities they had come to value, called themselves Germans, the people of Yap took an interest not only in the personal fate of these known Germans but also in the destiny of the group to which they belonged. This explains why some Yapese could be seen rejoicing at news of German military feats in Europe. Whereas the Germans enjoyed the real advantage of being familiar and known, no personal ties had yet been established with the Japanese. They were foreign in every respect, and their enmity toward the Germans made them suspect from the start. The local people's pro-German attitude was based on the activities of a few individual Germans on Yap. If these had been judged negatively, the arriving Japanese, too, would have been regarded in a different light. As it was, however, the people of Yap also said that "they had liked the Germans because they had been fair."[21] What exactly constituted the "fairness" that many Pacific Islanders attributed to the Germans they knew, however, still remains an open question.

In the Marshall Islands, the local people kept in touch with the Europeans even during the war. The American Board Mission had been established there for more than fifty years, and Burns Philp trading ships regularly called at the atolls of the Ratak and Ralik Group. American and Australian interests, therefore, were present from the start. It is likely that both Americans and Australians stoked local resentment of the Japanese and looked for local voices to justify an annexation of the Marshall Islands by the United States, or by Britain or Australia. On the other hand, the presence of the Americans and Australians did indeed offer the islanders an alternative to Japanese rule. In any case, it gave them a chance to make public their own ideas opposing Japanese authority.

As early as 1917 the Boston Mission was convinced that, in a vote, the overwhelming majority of Marshall Islanders would opt for an American administration for the islands.[22] One year earlier, the captain of a Burns Philp steamer reported that all the chiefs he had spoken to had asked him to pass on to the relevant authority their desire for a British government.[23] In one particular case, when a number of chiefs wanted his help in drawing up a petition to give their wishes formal expression, he refused: "in the absence of any direct evidence outside the Natives' words I fear nothing could be done." The racist arrogance of his view that without a European witness the word of a Pacific

Islander was worth nothing is the best evidence that the Marshall Islands chiefs expressed their wishes on their own initiative. The core of the petition the European had refused to accept was the desire "to be governed by a white race, whose ways they are familiar with and from whom they have always received fair treatment."[24] In January 1919 the master of another Burns Philp trading ship was handed an almost identical declaration, consisting of only two sentences: "We Chiefs, Petty-chiefs and people of Ratak and Ralik Group want that white-men European shall take charge of us and our islands. This is our wish." When the Australian asked them whether they wanted Britain, the chiefs gave an evasive reply.[25]

The oligarchy of eastern Micronesia, like that of Samoa, certainly had no intention of giving up its sovereignty. On the contrary, the chiefs' request was intended to halt the advance of Japanese culture. The objective was to restore a situation with which they had been familiar and to which they had adapted. Their aversion to the Japanese and their methods formed the nucleus of these attempts. At all costs, they wanted to prevent Japan from continuing to control the islands. There is a great deal of evidence, dating from throughout 1918, that the Marshall Islanders were desperately trying to find out how they could gain recognition for their views at the end of the war. European visitors to the islands were regularly bombarded with questions about whether the local people would be given a chance to participate in deciding their fate on the conclusion of peace. However, the Marshall Islanders were not prepared to say which country's rule they favored.[26]

At the end of December 1918 the Japanese military government ordered all the chiefs and many of the petty chiefs of the Ralik and Ratak Group to Jaluit and kept them there for three months. In meetings with government officials from Micronesia and Japan, as well as with higher officers, attempts were made to persuade members of the indigenous oligarchy to sign a document asking for the Marshall Islands to remain Japanese. The chiefs stepped up their efforts to establish contact with the outside world in order to make their true views known. Letters to personal friends among the sailors and officers of the *Cormoran* had been intercepted by the Japanese censor. In an unsupervised moment, the hastily written note mentioned above was passed to the Burns Philp captain. Most of the chiefs, however, eventually gave in to the Japanese request. Many were heavily in debt because of the unlimited credit extended by Japanese traders, and this was also used against them. Only the head chief Laborio steadfastly refused to sign to the end.[27]

The Japanese seem to have used similar methods on other islands at the turn of the year 1918–1919 in order to be able to present native "declarations" in favor of a continuation of Japanese rule at the forthcoming peace conference. At Christmas (*sic!*) 1918, the Catholic mission in Ponape received a proclamation from the Japanese commander, enclosing a copy of a letter from the supreme chiefs of the five Ponapean tribes. The whole tone of the document suggests that it was written by the Japanese themselves:

We remember earlier times, when the Germans ruled these islands—at that time we were not content because they did not look after us well. They were proud and arrogant and treated us badly. They thought we were like animals, and that is why we were always unhappy. . . .

In 1914, however, when the Japanese took over these islands, we began to become contented because you (our present) rulers treat us as though we are born Japanese. You send our children to school, so that they will soon become Japanese. . . . And we will always obey you. We therefore bow before you and ask that the Japanese will rule over us for ever.[28]

To the extent that the Sokeh uprising can be interpreted as a criticism of the German administration, this declaration may have reflected real local views, although it is diametrically opposed to the view expressed in Ponapean sources.[29] The rest of the document, in which the Ponapean elite of its own accord promises obedience and submission—strangely enough, in terms which are in line with Japanese rules of behavior—and expresses a wish to be under foreign rule for ever, is patently untrue. As recently as April of the same year, Nanpei had said that the Ponapeans could not stand the Japanese.[30]

SAMOA

Of all the Pacific societies whose authority structures changed at the beginning of the European war as a result of their "German" past, none tried to influence developments more than the Samoans. During the war, the Samoans made use of the room for maneuver that New Zealand rule left them compared with German rule. On only one point did they press the military administration to reinstate a German institution: the Samoans asked for the state education system, which had been abolished, to be restored. One of Logan's first actions had been to dissolve the Education Department and close the government schools. Although the school for Europeans was reopened in 1916, the military administration repeatedly postponed the reestablishment of a government school for Samoans. Logan believed that this sort of education was "useless."[31]

In the meantime, the Samoans turned to a former German teacher and persuaded him to give private lessons. Relatively soon this was banned, and the teacher was first arrested, then expelled.[32] As representatives of the Samoan oligarchy put more and more pressure on the Administrator to reopen the government school, Logan finally gave in and permitted a "technical" school to be established. There, according to the plans of the military governor, the young men of Samoa were to be trained to become agricultural producers and sheep breeders. The curriculum was to contain "subjects" such as taro and cocoa planting, and the systematic extermination of the rhinoceros beetle.[33] Logan's ideas were derived from his fundamental political conviction that, after the last Chinese had been deported, the Samoans would have to be forced to work on the European plantations. The economic commission set up by the New Zealand government came to the same conclusion: the whole education of Samoans should, in future, be directed toward agriculture "so that the child may grow up with a wider knowledge of what must, in the nature of things, be his future life's work."[34] But this was not what the Samoans expected from the government school. Their knowledge of the cultivation of taro, their staple food, far outstripped that of any New Zealander anyway. After a great deal of toing and froing, the government school opened its doors at the beginning of 1918, but the students stayed away. The influenza epidemic finally halted the experiment for good: there was nothing left to eat in the school that was intended to teach the Samoans to grow food.[35]

When the governor-general of New Zealand visited Samoa in mid-1919, the only schools for Samoans were mission schools, offering no more than an elementary education. Even here striking problems presented themselves. Under the Germans, Solf had issued a decree declaring Samoan the official language in all schools. At some time during the war, Logan had commanded that English was to be used as the sole language of education. The majority of mission teachers, however, were Samoans, who themselves had an imperfect grasp of English. In his report, therefore, the governor-general recommended that Samoan should be reintroduced as the language of teaching. The recommendations of New Zealand's highest representative were published, but only after the minister for external affairs had deleted his comments on the Samoan education system.[36]

By the time of the governor-general's visit, Samoan dissatisfaction with the New Zealand administration had gone way beyond the question of education. New Zealand's refusal to establish a government school such as had existed until 1914 was but one of the many Samoan grievances. The struggle for a government school was to go on for years, without either Samoans or New Zealanders budging from their opposing points of view. Whenever the Samoans believed that a change in government personnel provided a better chance to influence the administration's attitude, they gave voice to the local desire for better education. As soon as Logan's successor, Colonel Tate, went on home leave, they asked the Acting Administrator whether there was any chance of giving the Samoans access to more than elementary education.[37] New Zealand, however, remained obdurate. Education for Samoans was to remain "for some years to come, mainly if not entirely elementary," as the second report on the mandate of Samoa bluntly summed up New Zealand's position.[38]

The Samoans did not simply accept declarations such as this. They had recognized that there was a direct connection between their desire for self-administration and education. If they could not acquire the key to the world of the white man directly, then they had to approach it from a different angle. The *afakasi*, those inhabitants of Samoa whose fathers were European and mothers Samoan, were obvious mediators between Samoan culture and European knowledge; they had access both to Samoan culture and to the European world. The most important man in promoting Samoan interests and indigenous aspirations for autonomy was Olaf Frederick Nelson. The son of a Swedish trader, he became one of Samoa's most successful businessmen. His mother, Sina Tugaga Masoe, was a member of the Samoan elite. In Samoa, Nelson, who spoke Samoan, English, and German fluently, was known only as "Frederick the Great."[39] After Nelson visited Europe early in 1921, the *faipule* called a secret meeting at which they asked him to explain the European education system and discussed its possible application to Samoa.[40]

Contact with the outside world was essential in order to allow the most recent developments that could have some bearing on Samoa's destiny to be observed. It was also necessary to learning European strategies and passing on Samoan ideas. Those Samoans who knew enough English subscribed to New Zealand newspapers in order to keep abreast of political developments outside Samoa. Increasingly, they discovered the value of newspapers as a medium for expressing their own views, using letters to the editor in the *Samoa Times* to present their ideas to Europeans both in Samoa and beyond. The Administrator responded by prohibiting the publishing of letters to the editor from Samoans.[41] Samoan resistance to the New Zealand administration took place at a number of levels. Whatever the Samoans attempted, their opposition never took violent forms but made use of passive resistance and civil disobedience. The change in Samoan behavior, compared with the bloody civil wars of only one generation ago, and with Lauati's action against the Germans that never got off the ground, is striking. A number of factors may have played a part in this reorientation: historical experience, which showed the Samoans that violence against the Europeans achieved little; the withering away of military functions during the Pax Germanica; and finally, the death in the influenza epidemic of the last leaders with personal experience of war.[42]

What did the Samoans want? We can be sure that since the influenza catastrophe, the overwhelming majority of the Samoan population was against a New Zealand government. The petition in favor of joining American Samoa was, in fact, well-timed. A new, inexperienced Administrator had just arrived, and in Europe the Peace Conference was gathering to decide, among other things, the future of Samoa. Via relatives in American Samoa, copies of the petition reached the State Department and the major American dailies. But by the time the *New York Times,* the first really influential newspaper on the American East Coast, reported the Samoan desire for unification with American Samoa in mid-April 1919, the points had already been set in Paris.[43] Quite apart from the fact that Samoa's political elite itself, by back-pedaling, had already defused any potential political impact its petition might have had, the Americans were not prepared to support the Samoan wish. While Samoans in Tutuila celebrated on receiving the news from Apia, American officials hoped that nothing would come of it. An original version of the petition, which had been handed to the American secretary for native affairs in Pago Pago and to the governor, to be passed on to Washington and to the Peace Conference, disappeared under mysterious circumstances and was never found. When the American governor heard that the whole matter had petered out, he was visibly relieved.[44]

It is possible that the Americans were concerned about relations with their Anglo-Saxon neighbors in the Pacific. Perhaps they were the only ones who were sincere in declaring that they did not want to make any territorial gains of their own by entering the war. But the most likely explanation is that they had had enough trouble with the Samoans already under their rule. One year after the western part of Samoa expressed its desire to amalgamate with the eastern part under American rule, large-scale unrest broke out in Tutuila and the neighboring islands. It culminated in the suicide of the governor and the death of three chiefs who had been taken into custody.[45] In the west of the archipelago, this contributed to a cooling off—at first slowly, but then more and more rapidly—of feelings in favor of unification. Today, little remains of the once passionate mood in favor of a unified Samoa. The Samoans in the west admire the greater wealth of their cousins in the east, but they look down on them a little because, although the American Samoans escaped the ravages of the influenza epidemic, they have lost contact with their past even more than the Samoans in the west.

The Samoans' second choice was to be administered directly by the British Colonial Office. In June and July 1919 the Samoans had experienced the behavior of the governor-general of New Zealand as a representative of British interests in Samoa. It was known of him that he personally favored the model of a "British" Samoa. His racist escapades, however, had the effect of destroying Samoan illusions that an administration by the Colonial Office might bring advantages.[46]

It is striking that Germany seemed to play no role in any of the specific initiatives undertaken by the Samoans. There is some evidence that after the influenza epidemic the question of whether a protectorate under the United States or Germany was preferable was debated in Samoan villages.[47] In October 1919 a traveler from England noted that only one topic was discussed at typical Samoan *malagas* (social visits to neighboring villages): the end of New Zealand rule. While the cava bowls were passed around, people debated whether it would be better to aim for the establishment of an American administration, the status of a British Crown Colony, or the restoration of German rule. Others argued that Samoa should appeal directly to the League of Nations. In one hut, the British traveler listened in amazement to an animated discussion about the German Social Democratic movement, the end of the revolution in Germany, and their possible impact on Samoa.[48]

Many Samoans did, in fact, take a lively interest in the fate of the Germans in Europe. The more tarnished the image of the New Zealanders became, the brighter the island's German past seemed. An unfavorable comparison between the New Zealand administration and its German predecessor soon became a standard feature of the speeches of the Samoan *tulafale* (orators).[49]

However, during the period when the Samoans still hoped to be able to influence their political future because the League of Nations had not yet announced the mandate (that is, before the end of May 1921), no clear Samoan initiative to restore the pre-1914 political situation was undertaken.

The idea of renewed German supremacy was not a realistic alternative for Samoa in 1919–1920. The Samoans were well aware that Germany bore the stigma of the loser, and that it was diplomatically, politically, and economically isolated. A return to the old conditions was not a desirable objective for the Samoan oligarchy. If any such suggestion had ever been seriously discussed, Malietoa in particular would have resisted it strongly. But most of the rest of the Samoan political elite, too, would probably have regarded it as a step backward, almost as a personal defeat, and an admission of their own inability. The opposition to New Zealand rule had long gone beyond the aim of restoring old Samoan privileges introduced or recognized by the Germans. The increased room for maneuver the Samoans had enjoyed during the war had boosted their own political ambitions. Even before the war, the Samoans had had a certain respect for the German administration that had nothing to do with colonial subservience. After the war, this esteem increased with every mistake made by the New Zealanders. But however good relations had been between the German administration and the Samoans, there were always frictions and disagreements. Above all, the Samoans had not invited the Germans into their country. Ultimately, they had come to terms with their presence, had reached a fairly comfortable arrangement, and had put up with Samoa's loss of sovereignty. Inwardly, however, they had never accepted it. The relationship between the Samoans and the Germans before 1914 was at best a marriage of convenience, never a love match. Furthermore, many Samoans regarded it as a temporary marriage that could be dissolved unilaterally as soon as a suitable opportunity presented itself. In many marriages of convenience, something like sympathy eventually develops between the partners; and this is exactly the feeling that spread throughout Samoa after the marriage had been dissolved from outside.

Positive Samoan statements about the German past cannot, however, hide the fact that times had long moved beyond the constellation of 1914 not only in Europe and the West. Samoa was in the forefront of attempts by Pacific societies to press the demand for autonomy. The 1919 petition was only a start, but it was typical of the stage of development of Samoan political ideas. What was presented to the Administrator contained only the essential Samoan complaints about the influenza epidemic, along with the central demand for an end to New Zealand rule and the transition to American or direct British rule. But Samoan ideas for the future had already developed much further. The Samoan oligarchy, including Toleafoa, Tuatago, and, apparently, even Malietoa, had enlisted the support of an Australian who was to convey their political wishes, via the Australian government, to Britain, and via Britain to the Peace Conference. R. Broadhurst Hill had been a member of the Australian aid expedition during the influenza epidemic. He had been granted a Samoan title and thereby officially accepted into the Samoan community. The political objectives entrusted to this European agent were listed in order of urgency and importance, and comprised five points: no mandate, as this would mean that Samoa was subject to the mandatory power; as quick an end as possible to the New Zealand administration; their own legislative council or indigenous administration; a federation with other Pacific nations, each of which would have its own local administration, the federation to be responsible for the foreign policy of the islands; and official protection by Great Britain or the United States of America.[50]

Toleafoa was behind this initiative, as had already been the case with the petition; it was probably put forward under Malietoa's name only in order to give it greater weight. Toleafoa was well aware that a mandate was the most likely solution. But he had also realized that this would be detrimental to Samoa's attempts to gain autonomy, because it meant that the mandatory power could introduce its own laws into the mandated territory—a fear that was in fact later realized in the "C" mandate. However, his attempt to appeal directly to Woodrow Wilson through a European agent failed because the American president was unaware of Samoan voices. Perhaps he did not want to be aware of them. The Australian and British politicians approached had no interest in passing on suggestions from Samoa. Furthermore, the New Zealand military administration, which was still in office, censored communications between Toleafoa and his European intermediary after the latter had left Samoa, thus breaking contact between them completely.[51]

From now on, Samoa's indigenous leadership seized every opportunity to express its opinion in the outside world. Early in March 1920, before the mandate for Samoa had been declared, a group of New Zealand MPs, led by James Allen, the minister for defense, and accompanied by a number of journalists, visited Apia and the surrounding areas. One day after their arrival they met local representatives. The Samoan chiefs did not mince words. Retaining the customary Samoan politeness but speaking more and more directly and determinedly, in the European manner, they demanded Samoan judges and district officers, as was the practice in American Samoa, the resignation of Administrator Tate and the New Zealand official in charge of the native administration, Captain Cotton, as well as the withdrawal of the New Zealand military police who had been sent to Samoa. More or less bluntly, they called for the United States to take over the role of protecting power in future.[52] These demands went unheeded and unheard.

The nominal introduction of a civil administration on 1 May 1920 exacerbated the situation, and Samoan opposition assumed new forms. Without authorization from the League of Nations, New Zealand introduced the British legal code of 1840, which was binding on New Zealand, to Samoa, along with many New Zealand regulations. New points of controversy were added to the existing unresolved ones. The land belonging to German settlers, businessmen, and trading companies on Samoa was declared New Zealand Crown land. No distinction was made between land that German citizens had merely leased from its Samoan owners and actual German property. The profits from these Samoan Crown estates went directly into the New Zealand state coffers every year, without Samoa being financially compensated or having a chance to participate in any way. New Zealand's minister for external affairs later justified this measure by pointing out that New Zealand had feared that it would lose the mandate. It had wanted to create a fait accompli before the mandate was granted in order to have something in reserve if it lost the mandate. The precautionary measures taken ensured that even in the worst case the Samoan Crown estates would remain in New Zealand ownership.[53]

In order to protect its own trade and keep American competition as minimal as possible, New Zealand also introduced new customs regulations at the same time. Existing import duties of 12.5 percent on all goods were increased to 15 percent ad valorem for British imports, and to 22.5 percent for all other imports. Export duties were raised to one pound per ton of copra, and two pounds per ton of cacao. The intention was for Samoa to be able to finance its administration without being subsidized by New Zealand. Other financial cuts followed. In November, the privilege of free medical treatment for members of the Samoan administration and their families, dating from German times, was abolished, and fees were drastically increased.[54]

Enormous price increases had been one legacy of the war. The new customs regulations now set the inflationary spiral spinning again. Despite all European contact, the Samoans had maintained their own conservative lifestyle. European furniture, clothes, and shoes and socks were almost unknown. Although they occasionally enjoyed European food, Samoans had not become dependent on it as had some Melanesians. The only European commodities that had become widely established were lamps, sewing machines, and black cotton umbrellas. However, even the Samoans were dependent on two products from outside. The lavalavas they wore were made of imported cotton cloth, and their lamps needed kerosene or petrol.

The Samoan oligarchy reacted immediately to the price rises, demonstrating that it was quite capable of organizing resistance. It was decided to impose a *sa*, a boycott of all European goods. The chiefs instructed all Samoans to avoid European goods as far as possible in the future. Imported food only made them lazy and ill, the chiefs claimed, and they demanded that Samoans concentrate more on working their own gardens as they had done in former times. European goods could be bought only with the *sa* committee's express permission, in cases of emergency or illness. Lavalavas were no longer to be worn. Instead, Samoans were to go back to wearing *siapo* clothes, producing them from the *uʻa* plant as before. More *uʻa* plants were to be cultivated immediately. The chiefs set a good example, themselves wearing the old-fashioned *siapo* clothes. Samoan copra was to be sold only to the highest bidder. Anyone who broke these rules was ordered to appear before the chiefs, who issued a warning. Repeat offenders were fined.[55]

These directives issued by the chiefs proved to be highly effective. One of the factors responsible for their success was the Samoans' habit of living within their means—a legacy of the prohibition, once imposed by the German administration, on debt and the granting of credit to Samoans.[56] By the end of 1920, Samoa's imports had practically ground to a halt. Because the European traders could not sell anything to Samoans, they did not import anything. Revenues from tariffs and duties dried up almost completely. In Apia, chiefs patroled the streets of the harbor and European stores as pickets, thus ensuring that the *sa* was maintained. Unrest was endemic all over Samoa. The *sa* increasingly developed into a passive resistance movement by the Samoans against the New Zealand administration as such. New Zealand laws were openly ignored. After a decision by the Land and Titles Commission in the south of Upolu, something resembling a civil war broke out in September. One chief was murdered, and his relatives took the law into their own hands in seeking redress. The revival of the tradition of self-administration of justice came to an end only when blood revenge had successfully been exacted. In the overheated atmosphere, the wife of the New Zealand official in charge of the native administration shot a Samoan dead, turning the mood of the local population even more against New Zealand. Similar unrest occurred in American Samoa. There, suicide was the only way out for Governor Terhune.[57]

In December 1920, the Administrator at last decided to leave his European glass house in Apia and take a personal look at the country in turmoil. Everywhere he encountered signs of considerable Samoan ill-feeling. According to old Samoan custom, every *malaga* (tour), especially by the governor, was greeted with signs of respect. In this case, they were often omitted, being replaced by deliberate snubs. As Tate had no idea of Samoan customs, he noted only that the Samoans were not as polite as they usually were—and indeed, should have been. He was uneasy during a number of speeches because the speaker's intonation sounded somehow strange. But as he did not understand Samoan, and New Zealand officials who understood the language were few and far between, all he could do was have the Samoan speeches written down and take them home with him.

Once seated at his desk in the seclusion of his official rooms in Apia again, the Administrator could no longer deny the extent of Samoan discontent, for what he read was a general settling of accounts with New Zealand policy. In Faleapuna, the *tulafale* (orator), in his "welcoming" address, had accused him of all sorts of things: New Zealand should not imagine the Samoans were fools, even if nothing had come of the petition; the New Zealand administration was arrogant and overbearing, and compared badly with the German administration in almost all areas; New Zealand was to blame for the swollen European administration, the waste of money, the high duties and prices; it was bleeding the country dry; Samoan officials were earning less than they had under the Germans, and they were not consulted. The source of Samoan dissatisfaction, the influenza epidemic, was now presented as the result of a crime deliberately planned by New Zealand—"as you wish the Samoans to be all wiped out, and take the Islands for New Zealand." New Zealand doctors, it was claimed, were "exceedingly bad. . . . We want quickly clever doctors for Samoa. Let no doctors come to learn his profession with the Samoans." The Samoan critique of New Zealand activities climaxed in the pronouncement: "GOD witnesseth the dissatisfaction of the Samoan with you."[58]

An angry Administrator summoned the heads of the oligarchy to an extraordinary meeting and threatened to take them to court if the *sa* were not brought to a speedy end. He accused the chiefs of behaving undemocratically by denying the Samoan people the chance freely to choose European goods. The minister for external affairs was warned that the Samoan movement for self-administration was intensifying and could only be halted by drastic means. The *faipule* insisted on retaining influence over legislation. Malietoa, who still supported the government, was already being called a weakling. Special powers to deport Samoan troublemakers were required.[59]

On 7 January 1921, Tate issued two new proclamations. One declared that the chiefs' action in punishing individual Samoans on the basis of traditional local law for breaking the *sa* was a criminal offense. The other threatened that anyone who encouraged dissatisfaction against the administration "will be severely punished." On 10 and 11 January, the warships *Chatham* and *Veronica,* which Tate had summoned by telegraph, entered the harbor of Apia. The Samoans, however, did not allow themselves to be intimidated so easily. Two days later at a meeting with Tate, the chiefs presented him with a thick bundle of signatures testifying to the willingness of Samoans not to buy European goods. At the same time, they had begun to extend the *sa* to copra, in order to damage Samoa's exports as well as its imports.[60]

At the official spring *fono* early in February 1921, the *faipule* renewed their demand for the right to take part in legislating for Samoa and to have a say in nominating officials. Tate did not engage in any dialogue on this point, but he made a concession in another area: the law of August 1919 on vacant Samoan titles was abolished. This law had been one of the main sources of Samoan discontent, because the New Zealand administration had made recognition of a title dependent on the payment of a fee. Samoan preliminary proceedings were thus finally driven to absurdity. Claims escalated. The situation was exacerbated by the fact that eventually the decisions of the Land and Titles Commission, which had hitherto been final, could be challenged on payment of a simple fee and at the discretion of the European (but not the Samoan) members of the commission, allowing proceedings to begin again. Tate now promised that, in future, appointments would again be made according to old Samoan custom, and that New Zealand officials would not have the final say.[61]

In other respects, too, the Samoan mass boycott achieved some success. In December 1920 the New Zealand official responsible for native affairs, Captain Cotton, resigned from office and left Samoa. Soon after, another European who had aroused the anger of the Samoans threw in the towel. James Wilberforce Sibree had been a pastor in Samoa for the London Missionary Society since 1898. In an interview he gave on a visit to the United States late in 1920, he suggested that the reason for all the anger in both parts of Samoa was that the American government had mollycoddled the Samoans. But the Samoans were always well informed about events beyond their islands. On Sibree's return, they extended the *sa* to include the London Missionary Society and boycotted its sermons. In order not to damage his own mission, Sibree had no choice but to pack his bags and leave. From the end of January the actual *sa* lost a little of its impetus. It was not so much New Zealand's threat to apply force that took some of the wind out of the Samoan boycott's sails as its promise to set up an official commission to investigate the increased prices in Samoa.[62]

At the end of April 1921, New Zealand at last received the mandate over Samoa from the acting secretary-general of the League of Nations, Jean Monnet.[63] In the eyes of the world, this sealed the political future of Samoa. For the Samoans, the news from Geneva merely wound up the spring of opposition and once again set in motion the mechanism of resistance. Using different means and strategies, they made another attempt to rid themselves of the unwelcome New Zealand administration and thus to achieve Samoan independence at last.

6

Paris, the Versailles Treaty, and the Fate of Germany's South Pacific Colonies

When the points were set for the political future of Germany's colonies in the South Pacific, the indigenous people were not asked for their opinion. At the meeting of the victorious powers in Paris the only issues of principle to be decided were the conditions under which Australia, Japan, and New Zealand were to transform their military administrations into colonial administrations recognized under international law. On 24 January 1919, representatives of the main victorious powers met at the Quai d'Orsay to discuss the former German colonies for the first time. The British Empire, providing nine of the twenty-six delegates (five Americans, five French, four Italians, and three Japanese), represented more than one-third of those present. In his introductory speech, Lloyd George ruled out the possibility of returning the colonies to Germany. Germany, he said, had not only treated the indigenous people of Africa badly but had also organized native troops "and encouraged these troops to behave in a manner that would even disgrace the Bolsheviks."[1] The Pacific was not mentioned. Speaking after Lloyd George, Woodrow Wilson pointed out tersely that everyone agreed that restoring the colonies to Germany was out of the question. This was accepted without more discussion as the basis for further talks, with the proviso that the decision was not to be made public.[2]

All further "negotiations" now concentrated only on whether, or to what extent, the German colonies were to be administered under a mandate from the League of Nations. After the decision had been taken not to allow the colonies to go back to Germany, the talks on 24 January were dominated exclusively by the British, and discussion was not permitted. When Lloyd George advocated that Australia and New Zealand annex the German colonies in the Pacific directly, there was no stopping the Australian prime minister, Hughes. In his inimitable manner, he pushed his way forward, arguing and gesticulating in favor of New Guinea becoming an Australian colony. With the aid of a distorted map he had brought with him showing the Pacific Islands like floating fortresses grouped around Australia's shores, Hughes tried to bring to life for the other delegates the typically white Australian fear of foreign invasion. "Any

Almost the real thing. Australian Prime Minister William Morris ("Billy") Hughes examines the barrel of a disabled German gun, France, 1916. (Australian War Memorial P1212/01)

strong Power controlling New Guinea controlled Australia," he claimed, and did not shrink from referring directly to the Japanese sitting in the same room: "The policies of nations were liable to change, and history showed that friends in one war were not always friends in the next."

"The islands were as necessary to Australia as water to a city," he insisted, and any foreign mandatory that was to administer New Guinea under international control was "a potential enemy" of Australia.[3]

Massey of New Zealand did not want to be outdone by Hughes. Following his colleague's example, he too used a map to demonstrate the enormous strategic significance of Samoa—"the key to the Pacific"—for New Zealand. And the New Zealand prime minister also more or less openly accused Japan of being the next enemy of the Anglo-Saxons in the Pacific.[4]

Three days later Baron Makino presented Japan's claims to Micronesia. He reminded the delegates that Japan had occupied the islands to liberate the Pacific from the threat posed by German warships. But his further arguments in favor of a Japanese colony of Micronesia went in a completely different direction from the strategic considerations put forward by the Australians and New Zealanders. Japan called for possession of the islands "to protect the inhabitants and to endeavour to better their conditions." After all, Japan had shown a strong interest in the welfare of the island people immediately after the occupation. It had taken care to maintain their livelihoods and had set up schools to educate them. The local people felt comfortable under Japanese administration and were contented. Makino was the only representative of the three powers who had been on the winning side in the Pacific even to address the question of the right of local populations to self-determination: he pointed

"The True Controller." President Wilson and the idea to have a mandate system as seen through Australian eyes. (*Melbourne Punch*, 6 February 1919)

out that the local people were too primitive and their languages too diverse to allow self-administration.[5]

When Wilson outlined the central points of his proposed mandate system, it became clear that it was based on the notion that a mandatory could technically administer its mandated area as if it were an annexed territory. The only exception made by Wilson was that there were to be no tariffs discriminating against members of the League of Nations. For South West Africa, the U.S. president saw no alternative to an administration by South Africa. In the case of New Guinea, he did not yet want to commit himself, but he made it clear that, for geographical reasons, Australia was the only possible mandatory. Since Hughes' visit to the United States in 1916, relations between Wilson and the Australian prime minister had been strained. Wilson could therefore not resist making a direct dig at Australia's resurgent subimperialism. Australia, he said, reminded him of a greedy real-estate owner who "would never be satisfied so long as anyone owned any land adjoining his own."[6] The American president had hit the nail on the head; but in the process, he stirred up a hornets' nest. Hughes, angry and indignant, was allegedly hard of hearing. But, like many supposedly deaf people, he could suddenly hear very well when his interests were at stake. Australia had "a just claim," he burst out, honestly earned by its contribution to the war and the price paid by its soldiers in the war. Geographically and strategically, New Guinea was as important for Australia as Alsace-Lorraine was for France, and as far as the indigenous people were concerned, there was no doubt that "Australia knew what New Guinea wanted far better than any League of Nations."[7]

On the evening of 27 January, the British Empire delegates met in secret in order to agree upon their negotiating strategy for the next day. A preliminary decision on the future of the German colonies might be taken on 28 January. At the start, Colonial Office representatives emphasized that acquiring colonies made economic sense. All of Britain's African colonies, with the exception of Nigeria and Somaliland, were self-sufficient. The same was true of the West Indies. The only colonies that needed financial support were those which had been acquired for strategic reasons—Aden, Cyprus, and Somaliland. General Smuts and Robert Cecil were asked to prepare a memorandum as a "compromise suggestion" for the British side to put forward at the Peace Conference opposing Wilson's ideas for the mandate. It was to propose a three-tier mandate system based on Smuts' wartime suggestions. The claims of the British Dominions (South Africa, Australia, and New Zealand) were to be satisfied by the watered-down mandate obligations, so that if possible the German colonies could still be directly annexed. This is where the subsequent three-class mandate was born.[8]

The real question—which powers would be granted mandates—soon turned out to be purely rhetorical. On the morning of 28 January, before the real meeting on the fate of the German colonies began, Lloyd George took Wilson aside and tried to convince him that his idea that the mandatories should be selected by the future League of Nations was completely out of place. The British prime minister threatened that if this were to happen, not a single victorious European power would sign the peace treaty.[9]

If Wilson still entertained any hope that the choice of mandatories would be left to the League of Nations (which was yet to be founded), they soon proved to be illusory. When the official meeting of delegates from the main victorious powers plus representatives of China (the meeting was about Tsingtao) began at 11 A.M., one European after another came forward and laid on the table the secret agreements in which the European powers had given each other mutual assurances during the war that they would recognize each other's most important colonial war aims. The booty had long been divided; all that mattered now was to give the distribution the stamp of approval, and thus make it official. Clemenceau was the first. He linked French claims to German colonial territory in Africa with the wartime agreements between Britain and France concerning the former German colonies and called on Baron Makino to disclose the relevant secret agreements with Japan. When Baron Makino was trying to play them down, Balfour explained that, as early as 1917, Britain had come to an agreement with Japan concerning the political future of each country's sphere of influence in the Pacific. The last to speak was Orlando, who reported on Italian claims to German colonial territory under the terms of the treaty of London.[10]

After the Europeans, an Anglo-Saxon from the Pacific again stepped up to the rostrum. This time it was Massey, who obviously thought that New Zealand's prestige and its claim to Samoa were impaired by his Australian colleague's outbursts, which no debating rules could curb. The New Zealand prime minister again emphasized the strategic importance of Samoa for New Zealand. In addition, it could be seen as compensating New Zealand for its financial losses during the war; but compared with New Zealand's war debt of 100 million pounds, he said, Samoa was worth only "a mere trifle." New Zealand had already done more for the welfare of the indigenous population, he claimed, than any mandatory could do. And as for the Samoans themselves, he added, "if any change in control were to be made, the inhabitants of Samoa would be intensely dissatisfied."[11] Some of the wartime cavalry still seemed to be active at the Peace Conference. Lying like a trooper was nothing unusual there; the boldness of this statement by Massey would have been enough to destroy the faith of any God-fearing Samoan present. Naturally, the New Zealand prime minister was kept informed by telegraph about the tragic consequences of the influenza epidemic in Samoa. At almost exactly the same time as Massey was claiming Samoa as reparation for New Zealand, the representatives of Samoa were presenting Administrator Tate with their petition containing the "on no account . . . New Zealand" clause.[12] After Massey in Paris had received the news from Apia, he did nothing to bring the true opinion of the Samoans to the attention of the world. On the contrary, he regarded Samoan views as a kind of enemy barrage designed to destroy New Zealand ambitions, the potential consequences of which must be prevented.[13]

The Paris peace negotiations produced not clarification but obfuscation. The destiny of Samoa was discussed neither at the meeting on 28 January 1919 nor later, except when Wilson mumbled something about the United States also possessing rights in Samoa.[14] The situation in the former German colonies in the Pacific, and what had happened there before and during the war, was and remained terra incognita for the delegates to the Peace Conference who were to decide the political future of these areas. Of course, they had less information than the countries which had occupied the former German colonies, but it is surprising that no attempt was made to cast light on any of the claims and statements bandied about by the occupying powers. There was not a single initiative to find out more about what the indigenous population in the various territories felt and thought, and whether they wanted to participate in the decision-making process or not. No working group or committee of the Peace Conference concerned itself with this. The countries that had occupied the former German colonies had thrown their demands for diplomatic recognition of their conquests into the ring. Although specific details of the future relationship between colonial power and colony were in dispute, no realistic alternative mandatories were ever put forward.

Machinations and manipulation, disguise and deceit were common in Paris. Wild statements were made and facts misrepresented. Horse trading went on, and blackmail was tried and carried out. Dissimulation was the order of the day. As a peace conference, the whole thing was a farce. This was true in particular of the plenary sessions, which did not take decisions and for which only speakers who were certain to support the attitude of the council of victorious powers were called upon.[15] On only a single occasion, 14 February 1919, after Wilson had broadly outlined his mandate system before the plenary assembly, was anything like opposition voiced. The senior secretary of Emir Faisal (to become Faisal I, king of Iraq, in 1921), the only delegate representing an area that was to be placed under a mandate, criticized the mandate system for being too theoretical and vague. He put his finger on the secret treaties among the victors, which were incompatible with the right of self-determination to which Wilson repeatedly referred, and stood in the way of a practical implementation of the concept. This criticism by an Arab bird of paradise hit the bull's-eye, but the Big Four and the main victorious powers did not allow his comments to deter them.[16]

It could justifiably be pointed out that most high-level diplomatic meetings, especially when, as was the case at Versailles, a great deal is at stake, have nothing in common with a tea party at a girls' boarding school. Cunning and camouflage, bluffing and browbeating, double-dealing and distortion are all among the basic features of diplomacy. And even if the stigma of a nonorganic and quasi-illegitimate birth often adheres to a new status quo from the start, it often proves to be extremely tenacious, despite the fact that it has emerged from the collapse of the existing order and has only become established under the exceptional circumstances of war. Even "peace conferences" cannot get around this fact. Thus, in the light of previous experience, what eventually came out of Versailles was only to be expected—at least as far as the political fate of Germany's former Pacific colonies was concerned. The prestige of the victors of this war was theoretically on the agenda, but in reality it was never at stake. All that remained to be sorted out were the modalities—that is, how the world, especially, Woodrow Wilson's America, would cope with it.

Thus the moral club that had already been wielded during the war, first by the British and then by the American president, served in Paris and Versailles to justify the takeover of German colonial territory, adding a new dimension to the old tactics of imperial acquisition. Of course, there was a great deal of hypocrisy behind it. A frustrated Wilson early threw in the towel. At the meeting on the afternoon of 28 January 1919, the following note of resignation is recorded in the minutes: "the question of deciding the disposal of the German Colonies was not vital to the world in any respect."[17] The British saw their chance. During a break in the meeting on 29 January, they met behind locked doors in the rue Nitôt and consulted on how to proceed. The British prime minister thought it was an opportune moment to settle this question once and for all in Britain's favor. Once Wilson was back in the United States, he would be exposed to completely different influences—most of them anti-British. The mandate proposals that had been completed in the meantime were presented and thoroughly discussed. The only point at issue now was how the Japanese could be refused a mandate as generous as that to be given to New Zealand and Australia without contravening the principle of equality and the secret agreement of 1917. One proposal under discussion was to classify New Guinea as only a second-class mandate, not, like South West Africa and Samoa, a third-class mandate. Lloyd George had to promise the hotheaded Australian delegates, Joseph Ward and William Hughes, that under all circumstances Australia would retain the right to apply its Navigation Law and White Australia Policy in New Guinea: to non-British, and to the Japanese in particular, New Guinea was to remain a closed colony.[18]

On the morning of 30 January the British delegation put on the table its suggestion for a three-class mandate system. This provided for the Dominions of South Africa, Australia, and New Zealand outwardly to accept the mandate solution but allowed them to apply their laws in the German colonies they had occupied. As a minimal concession to the idea of a mandate, they would report annually to the League of Nations, promise to keep arms and slave trading out of the territories under their control, and not allow the indigenous people access to alcohol. Military training for the indigenous people and military development of the mandated territories were forbidden.[19]

During the afternoon session, Massey put Wilson on the spot by asking him to say whether or not he accepted the British proposal. Wilson, already infuriated by a press campaign in favor of direct annexation and against the mandate system, orchestrated by Hughes in sensational newspapers such as the *Daily Mail,* replied by asking heatedly whether Australia and New Zealand were giving him an ultimatum by asking this? Hughes, unmoved, snapped back that this precisely "was their attitude." The "concessions" to the mandate solution the British deputation had worked out were the maximum that Hughes was prepared to concede. Wilson did not dare to challenge Hughes further. Lloyd George tried to distract attention from the quarrel between the American and Australian leaders by abruptly turning the discussion to the "nigger armies" with which the mandates were to dispense. But this was no longer necessary. In the battle between the two fighting cocks, Wilson had secretly and quietly retracted his spurs. As though he still had everything under control, the president of the United States announced at the end of the meeting that a provisional agreement had been reached about the German territories outside Europe.[20]

In fact, nothing concrete had been discussed, and not a single point presented by the British had actually been debated. What had really happened, and what had put an end, so to speak, to any "discussion" of the future of the German colonies, was Woodrow Wilson's obvious failure to defend his concept in the face of a direct challenge by William Hughes. The illusory world of the American president had burst like a bubble in seconds. When it came to the crunch, he proved to be incapable of defending his ideas against the age-old maxim that might is right. The news of Wilson's apparent capitulation, and the ease with which this had been achieved, was soon doing the rounds. From then on, the label of weakling or braggart—at best, the accusation of having behaved unrealistically—adhered to the American president like chewing gum. If anything, the further course of the conference and Wilson's part in it helped to consolidate these ideas. For his adversary from the southern hemisphere, the success of 30 January 1919 was like David's victory over Goliath. He dined out on it for years. For the rest of his life, Hughes had only contempt for Wilson, whom he saw as a failure. He regarded the American president as a puffed-up cock who gave in when it came to a real fight.[21] Wilson's climb down opened the way for acceptance of British ideas on the political future of the German colonies. The proposed three-tier mandate went down in the minutes, without opposition, as "Resolutions in Reference to Mandatories."[22] The dice had long been thrown, but only now were the numbers on them revealed.

The only question remaining was how to keep the unloved Japanese at as great a distance as possible. The British suggestion for a third-class mandate represented only a superficial compromise by the Anglo-Saxons in the Pacific with Wilson's ideas, which went much further. In fact, great care had been taken to build the Australians' and New Zealanders' traumatic fear of the Japanese threat unobtrusively into the mandate package. This is why the development of an indigenous army and the use of mandated areas as military bases were prohibited for C class mandates. Similarly, it was hoped that the obligation to provide regular mandate reports would make it possible to have a better overview of what Japan was doing in its area. In this case, New Guinea could also be classified as a C class mandate. For, as Hughes and Ward argued at the meeting of empire delegates on 8 March 1919, it was less disadvantageous to

Australia to allow the Japanese to exclude other nationalities from their area north of the equator than to accept free trade in general, because it would also give Australia the right to keep the Japanese out of its own mandates. It was relatively simple for the British side to put its ideas into practice, and to hide the real reasons for the various clauses, because the working out and implementation of Wilson's suggestions concerning the League of Nations' mandate

"The Bing Boys Coming Home Again." New Zealand's leading politicians Massey and Ward arrive with their gifts from the Paris Peace Conference. (*The New Zealand Truth,* 2 August 1919)

for the former German colonies was in the hands of the British Empire delegation from start to finish. What finally went into Article 22 of the League of Nations Treaty was, therefore, an almost unadulterated British interpretation of the mandate system.[23] For the Dominions at least, it was only one step away from direct annexation. As Hughes put it, the difference between a colony and a C class mandate from the League of Nations was like that between freehold and a 999-year lease.[24]

On 7 May 1919 the mandates for the former German colonies were made public. The announcement was made, not by the newly created League of Nations, but by the main victorious powers of the war, the Supreme War Council. The League of Nations' only duty was to hand over the mandate certificates. In itself, this was purely a formal matter, but because of the United States' and Japan's second thoughts and objections, it dragged on for eighteen months. When the Versailles Peace Treaty officially came into force on 10 January 1920, the mandates for the former German colonies had still not been granted. The Japanese were infuriated by the humiliation they had suffered in Paris when Wilson and Hughes had succeeded in having the principle of racial equality rejected; officially, the Japanese resisted the granting of the mandates on the grounds that the application of Australia's Navigation Laws would keep Japanese trade out of New Guinea. In the United States, the public mood had swung around completely, and criticism of the provisions of the Versailles Treaty was on the rise. America now brought up the infringement of free trade by the mandatory powers Australia and New Zealand and called for equal trading rights in the mandated territories. Eventually, late in 1920, after considerable British pressure, Japan gave up its resistance in a "spirit of conciliation and co-operation." Thus the Council of the League of Nations was finally able to issue the mandates on 17 December 1920. However, Australia, Japan, and New Zealand did not receive their official copies of the mandates until late April 1921. This marked the formal end of the German colonial period in the Pacific.[25] From now on, according to the Australian prime minister, there was no further need for an Australian representative in Geneva, as the League of Nations was nothing but a "pompous debating society."[26]

American resistance to the implementation of the mandates in the Pacific continued even after the League of Nations had officially presented them. In January 1921, the American envoy in London handed the Foreign Office a note in which his government formally protested against the infringement of the Washington Samoa Agreement of 2 December 1899. Here, as in New Guinea, the United States demanded "most favored nation" status. But as the United States had withdrawn completely from the League of Nations, London simply ignored its complaint.[27] The Japanese, by contrast, preferred to come to a diplomatic agreement with their eastern Pacific neighbor after Washington had registered its claims to Yap in the Caroline Islands, the headquarters of an internationally important cable station. In connection with the Washington Pacific Conference, Japan granted the United States a number of special rights on Yap. Thereupon, early in February 1922, the United States officially recognized Japan's territorial possessions in the Pacific under international law.[28]

Were there any real alternatives to the Versailles policy of confirming the conquests of war? Was there any chance that the ideas of the Pacific Islanders could have played a part in the decisions taken at the Peace Conference? Did any groups or individuals in Australia, New Zealand, or Japan put forward counterproposals to official government policy? If so, how strong and how representative were they? And finally, what, if any, influence did Germany have on the political future of its colonies in the South Pacific?

One point can be established relatively briefly and simply. At no time were the Pacific Islanders consulted about their ideas for their own political future. Their possible interests played no part in the negotiations except as pretexts used to justify imperial greed. The manipulated declarations approving of the status quo, held in reserve, did not even have to be unpacked. No one, it seems, was bothered by the fact that no attempt had been made to find out the views of the indigenous people on the decisions that were about to be made. And none of the participants, including the Germans (who were excluded from the discussions), was ultimately prepared to be a spoilsport. Whatever the German delegation might claim, on one essential point it differed not one jot from its opponents in the negotiations. For all Europeans, the idea that the colonized peoples could be given any real influence in deciding their own political future was equally taboo.

Most German people had become disillusioned with the whole colonial idea after the quick military conquest of Germany's colonies, which had put up almost no resistance. Africa continued to exert a certain attraction, and discussions of the allegedly great economic and political value of Germany's African colonies, which were the subject of numerous memoranda, filled many column inches in the German press. The German east of the Black Continent still seemed to offer a platform for the gaining of prestige. The value of Germany's colonies in the South Pacific, by contrast, was subjected to increasingly frequent and vehement questioning by German public opinion. As early as the end of November 1914, Hahl had written to Solf in a tone of resignation that they had both probably sacrificed their lives to the Pacific in vain, as Germany would withdraw completely from Asia and the South Pacific in order "to facilitate the conclusion of peace, and to prevent future complications."[29] All that New Guinea, Micronesia, and Samoa had to offer, it seems, was their status as bargaining counters in a future peace. In 1916 the German foreign office had promised to cede Micronesia, as well as Tsingtao, to Japan, in order to achieve the separate peace with Tokyo that it wanted.[30] As early as 1899, the German government had been prepared to hand over the Mariana Islands to Japan.[31] Even former German colonial officials who had been responsible for Micronesia, such as the *Landeshauptmann* of the Marshall Islands, Georg Irmer, were now openly critical of the acquisition of Micronesia—"one of the more expensive ironies of world history"—and recommended that Germany should renounce its claim to the islands.[32] The only people and associations who advocated that Germany retain its colonies in the South Pacific were those who had direct interests there. This included the missionaries.[33] But the lead was taken by the Vereinigung deutscher Südseefirmen (Association of German Companies in the South Pacific), based in Hamburg. However, it did not have much political influence, and it achieved little beyond occasional promises by the German colonial office not to give up the Pacific colonies "from the start." But those who had real political influence were convinced that the Pacific was of little value to Germany and should be given up. Already in spring 1915 the vice president of the German Reichstag, Paasche, a member of the National Liberal Party, publicly said just that. Even at a point in the war when Germany's chances of victory seemed better than ever—the peace of Brest-Litovsk had just been concluded and the German spring offensive was overrunning the French trenches—Solf, the German colonial secretary, refused to speak in support of Germany's colonies in the South Pacific for fear that he might dupe the Japanese.[34] Solf himself, although he had made his career in the Pacific, was among those who advocated the colonial war aim of concentrating Germany's colonial possessions in Africa. In its recommendations, presented early in 1916, a commission he had set up to work out colonial war aims placed Melanesia (Papua, the Solomons, the New Hebrides, and New Caledonia, but not Fiji) at the bottom of the list of colonial territories that were to be claimed from Britain and France in the event of a "decisive victory." If it turned out to be only a "middling victory," New Caledonia was to be demanded from France (because of its chrome and nickel deposits) in the case that the attempt to gain French West Africa or Somaliland (Germany's first and second priorities, respectively) was unsuccessful. If Germany won a "moderate victory," it was prepared to renounce any expansion of its empire in the South Pacific. Indeed, the command of the colonial forces that was asked to assess colonial war aims "from a military point of view" went one step further. By the end of the same year it had come to the conclusion that, even if Germany won a resounding military victory, it should concentrate exclusively on Africa and give up its possessions in the Pacific—"in military and power political terms, colonies as scattered and distant as our possessions in the South Pacific . . . have no value."[35] Of the high-ranking officers, only a retired admiral, Grapow, strongly advocated the retention of Germany's Pacific colonies. He was one of those for whom the South Pacific had value as a "collector's item,"[36] because he could not forget his visits to Samoa and the show that had been put on for him there. It was owed to Germany's reputation and honor, he said, "to keep the German flag flying there, so that her *prestige* does not suffer!" But even Grapow believed it was necessary to cede at least the Marianas to Japan.[37]

In reality, these were nothing but sand-table exercises. The German colonial secretary was fully aware of this. In July 1916 he wrote to his wife: "I really do not know what will become of our colonies in future. But I consider it my duty to continue acting as if we were sure of getting them back. The Chancellor no longer believes this."[38] One year later the German colonial office began the process of dissolving its administration in regard to German New Guinea. Resistance within the administration, however, forced Solf to backtrack. On 14 December 1917, another governor for German New Guinea, Eduard Haber, was appointed, because "it is necessary to document in the eyes of the foreign, and especially the German, public, that we are certainly not prepared to give up the colony [German New Guinea]." This was the only case in which a governor was appointed to a German colony during the war. It had become formally necessary because Governor Albert Hahl was increasingly showing the strain of his long tour of duty in the tropics. In February 1915, Hahl, who had volunteered as an infantryman, suffered severe heart failure and was declared unfit for active service or garrison duty. Medical treatment in Kissingen, one of Germany's most renowned spas, provided only limited relief. On 28 April, therefore, Hahl was withdrawn from any further active colonial service overseas "for the foreseeable future." Haber and Hahl exchanged places. Hahl took over Haber's position as a *vortragender Rat* in the German colonial office while Haber was appointed governor of German New Guinea. Both kept their existing salaries.[39]

The Kaiser and Ludendorff both protested against Haber's formal appointment. They saw this step, taken "during the war and without being able to provide any assurances on the future of the colony," as rushing ahead inappropriately. In their opinion, it would unnecessarily prejudice Germany's bargaining position on colonial matters at the forthcoming Peace Conference. Quite clearly, both had long since written off a German presence in the South Pacific. Nor did it fit in with their image of a postwar Germany.[40]

Germany entered the peace negotiations pursuing defensive tactics on colonial policy. It was interested only in limiting the threatened loss of prestige. From the start, it was clear that Germany would have to cede colonies. Its first aim was to recover as many colonies as possible apart from Tsingtao, which had officially been relinquished. If the status quo ante on the question of colonies could not be achieved even partially, Germany was prepared to give the colonies to the victorious powers as a kind of pawn to be redeemed when it had fulfilled the peace terms imposed on it. In the worst case, Germany expected to receive at least a League of Nations mandate, though not necessarily for its former colonies; it would have been prepared to accept different territory simply to avoid German prestige suffering a knockout blow in the eyes of the world.[41] All the talk about access to raw materials was only a pretext, because German officials were aware of the influence of European colonial rhetoric on their wartime enemies. But just as the main point of Germany's colonial ambitions, at least since the 1890s, had been to increase its international standing, the real concern now was desperately to preserve its dented prestige. When even this proved impossible, all German efforts were concentrated on restoring its lost international reputation by revising the sentence of professional and moral incompetence that had been passed on German colonial policy and written down in the peace treaty for all the world to see. Thus, German revisionist ambitions for colonial policy were more a matter of political prestige than of obstructed economic interests. The real economic value Germany placed on its colonies is shown by the fact that colonial interests were represented by a single member of the peace delegation. He was a totally unknown *Geheimrat,* who had little experience in the subject. Only after the C class mandatories were made public in May 1919 was a second, more competent official, Eduard Haber, assigned to the colonial commission in the German peace delegation. Haber soon gave up when he noticed that no real interest in his advice was being taken.[42]

Germany's chances of regaining its colonies, or some of them, in the peace treaty were not increased, to say the least, by the behavior of its delegation to the Peace Conference. But the Allied secret treaties were the main factor working against a modification of the colonial situation achieved as a result of the war. Added to this was the British determination under no circumstances to agree to any weakening of the position on the German colonies it had achieved in wartime. During the war, London, with great diplomatic skill, had avoided making any clear statements on the future of the German colonies, while creating the impression that each case was open to negotiation after the war. Within Britain's decisive political circles, however, it was clear from the start that the conquered German colonies would be given back only if Britain had to admit complete defeat. If they had had their backs to the wall, the British would have been prepared at most to return Togo and Cameroon, which during the war were regarded as belonging more to the French than the British sphere of influence anyway. Under no circumstances, however, was Britain prepared to give up German East Africa or the German colonies occupied by the Dominions.[43]

Of all those who took part in the Peace Conference, the British delegation was by far the best prepared to push through its colonial war aims. Erzberger's damning statements on German colonial policy in Africa lay prepared in the drawer. Similarly, materials were ready for white papers discrediting the German colonial administration, presenting it as especially cruel and monstrous, and the finishing touches were feverishly being put to them in November 1918. It was well known within the British government that the German public's enthusiasm for the colonies had evaporated, that the supporters of the colonial movement had become a minority in Germany, and that Germany was almost unanimous about giving up its Pacific colonies.[44]

The British government, the Commonwealth of Australia, and the Dominion of New Zealand had set the points for a takeover of Germany's Pacific colonies, with as few conditions attached as possible, by the late autumn of 1918. The people of Australia and New Zealand certainly felt some pride in their military achievements in conquering the German colonies. War propaganda had stirred up extremely hostile feelings against Germans living in Australia and the Pacific Islands,[45] and the majority of the population approved of excluding the

Germans from the Pacific, although most had little interest in the political future of the islands in the north. The same was true of the press. It is no exaggeration to say that, despite the widespread aversion in Germany to further colonial experiments in the Pacific, at the time of the Paris negotiations the Germans were much better informed than the Australians and New Zealanders about the geography and people of New Guinea and Samoa. Opposition to official Australian and New Zealand policy on the German colonies was limited to marginal groups. The Australian Labor Party's attitude toward imperialism was long dominated by its leader, William Hughes, the prime minister who had begun his career as a trade unionist. Finally, in the course of his attempt to introduce universal conscription, Hughes was expelled from the Labor Party on 15 September 1916,[46] and the party became more anti-imperialist again. Nonetheless, its representatives were unable to express a joint opinion on the issue of the occupied German colonies. In August 1917, when the Senate and the House of Representatives debated the nonreturn of the German colonies, Ferricks, the Queensland MP, expressing a minority opinion, spoke against a continued Australian presence in New Guinea. Ferricks argued that Australia was not even capable of developing its own land. The Northern Territory was evidence enough of this. He suspected that the strategic arguments concealed commercial greed and a wish to exploit the black workers of the islands. Ferricks called for the people of these territories to be allowed to vote on their own future. His lone voice, however, went unheard and unheeded.[47] Occasionally, the *Australian Worker,* organ of the radical socialists, spoke out against the continuation of Australia's activities in New Guinea. At its interstate conference in June 1918, the Federal Labor Party resolved at least to keep the future of the occupied Pacific Islands open.[48]

The armistice in Europe put the future of Germany's Pacific colonies onto the agenda. As soon as the news became known in Australia, the premier of New South Wales, Holman, instructed New South Wales' agent-general in Britain—each of the Australian states had a representative in London—to inform the British colonial secretary, Long, of the views of the New South Wales government on the future of the neighboring Pacific Islands. The government of New South Wales, the most populous of the Australian states, regarded itself, together with Queensland, as most likely to be called upon to express an opinion on the future of the Pacific Islands, largely because of its geographical position. Premier Holman was a peculiar character. Like Hughes, he was a member of the Labor Party, and like Hughes, he had been expelled from the party because of his militaristic views. This did not affect his popularity. As the cofounder of the Nationalist Party, he was reelected to office with a majority of the vote. In the same way as Hughes, he had extremely imperialistic or subimperialist-nationalistic impulses; on a visit to Fiji in 1916 he had called for Australia to annex the British Crown Colony. Now, however, he showed a much more moderate side. Apparently overcome by the prospect of peace at last, he seemed to revert to socialist ideals: "Ministers' own view is war not fought for conquest or annexation. Important demonstrate this by not insisting unduly upon steps which, though justified as precautions, may be interpreted as aggressions," he cabled to Charles Wade, New South Wales' diplomatic representative in London.[49] Wade was instructed to inform Long that, in the view of the New South Wales government, Australia's only strategic interest was for the former German Pacific Islands to be neutralized under the supervision of an international commission, in order to guarantee that no bases from which Australia could be attacked be set up there in the future—a completely justifiable demand. Holman added: "If, however, Allied Governments are satisfied no fear of future hostilities with new German Government, probably Republican, Ministers' feeling is question of Pacific Islands can be left unreservedly to Peace Congress. Under such circumstances, Australia will have no interests."[50]

On the same day, Acting Prime Minister Watt introduced a resolution in the Senate and the House of Representatives that opposed returning the Pacific Islands to Germany. It also called on the Peace Conference to take Australia's interests into account when deliberating upon the disposition of the islands "essential to the future safety and welfare of Australia." There was little evidence of any dissenting views. After a short debate, the Senate passed the resolution unanimously—the Labor MPs also voting for it. In the House of Representatives, the Socialists voiced a certain amount of opposition, but here too the resolution was adopted by the chamber by a straight majority vote.[51] Hughes was already in Europe, and when Watt found out what Holman had done, he issued two severe reprimands and forbade state governments to express opinions to imperial authorities directly, bypassing the federal government.[52] Thus the only initiative suggesting an alternative to Australian control of New Guinea to come from men of political influence in Australia was killed before it had even seen the light of day. The Australian Labor Party held back from criticizing an Australian takeover of New Guinea. In its manifesto for the federal elections of 1919, it even attacked the government for having accepted the Japanese penetration of Micronesia too easily at the peace negotiations.[53]

After this initiative by the premier of New South Wales, there was no other serious attempt to question Anglo-Saxon control of New Guinea—apart from one marginal note. On 23 November 1921—just over six months after Australia had received the mandate so long desired by the federal government—Lynch, a West Australian, said in the Senate, more or less out of the blue, that the mandate for New Guinea should be given to the United States, as it placed too much of a burden on the Australian taxpayer. After some protest from his irritated colleagues, the previously unknown backbencher from the bush retracted his motion.[54]

What criticism there was of Australian subimperialism was concentrated among those supporters of mainstream imperialism who advocated the idea of an intact British Empire. Some, such as the governor-general, for example, were opponents of a national subimperialism because they saw it as posing a threat to the coherence of the empire. Others were deeply suspicious of the

Australian federal government's ultranationalist policy; but the only chance they saw of taking effective action against it was under the pretext of protecting the interests of the British Empire. The fact that the Australian government regularly bombarded the Colonial Office with petitions in an attempt to expand the country's political influence in the region has already been demonstrated above. There was hardly a Pacific island that had not been the object of Australian greed at some time or other. The war and the military occupation of New Guinea and Nauru were an added stimulus; Australia had sat down to its meal with a good appetite, but while eating, its stomach had expanded, and it wanted even more.

Early in 1915, in a conversation with the governor-general destined to be transmitted to higher circles in London, Prime Minister Fisher had referred to "the long-standing wish cherished in Australia to be possessed of New Caledonia and the New Hebrides." Still, it was the same story as in the case of British New Guinea in the late nineteenth century: Australia wanted it but did not want to spend any money on it. As both New Caledonia and the New Hebrides were governed more from Paris than from Whitehall, and France was Britain's principal ally in the war, the governor-general proposed instead an "administrative area from New Guinea to the Solomons, inclusive." This "would suit Australia well." Another target was Portuguese Timor. The local manager of an Australian firm apparently became impatient. Late in 1915, he made a quick decision and raised the Australian flag in the interior of East Timor, presenting himself to the indigenous people as their new commander. At the end of 1917 application was made for the phosphate-rich Christmas and Ocean Islands, which were under British control, to be transferred to Australian rule. The armistice in Europe was barely a month old, and the government was discussing, not the mandate for New Guinea, but the acquisition of Dutch New Guinea, Tonga, and even France's possessions in the Pacific.[55] According to the 1921 census, just over 4.5 million whites—the Aborigines were not counted—lived in Australia, in an area four-fifths the size of Europe, but the Australian government's land hunger was seemingly insatiable. When news of the Australian prime minister's political success in Paris reached Australia, the Protestant missions urged the government to finish the job properly and annex the New Hebrides as well.[56] After his return, Hughes himself persuaded the cabinet to expand the Australian territories of Papua and New Guinea to include the hitherto British Solomons. Speaking to Australian soldiers who had just disembarked, he explained, "I believe that at no distant future Australia will occupy a greater position than England."[57]

Australia regarded the Pacific as its very own private duck pond and would tolerate no rivals, the governor-general had written to his superiors in Britain,[58] hoping that at the appropriate time the British government would accept his proposal to set up a Pacific High Commission for all the islands under British control, and place him at the head of it. Sir Ronald Munro Ferguson watched the Japanese incursion into Micronesia with a certain degree of cynicism,

believing that it would give the Australian government a jolt and make it concentrate on developing its own continent: "This fool's paradise needs a rude
awakening, and if a Japanese naval base near the Line should act as a solvent
then it would be a blessing in disguise!"[59]

The Australian governor-general's hope that Britain could be persuaded to
intervene more actively in the fate of the former German Pacific colonies, and
thus to repress Australian subimperialism, was illusory from the start. The war
had brought home clearly to the motherland how much it depended on the
help and support of the Dominions. To refuse their wishes, or to offend their
governments, would have put the continued existence of the empire at risk,
after it had just got away again with a black eye.[60] Hughes gave these fears further substance when, during the conference, he openly threatened to break off
Australia's special relationship with Britain if it refused to accept what he
regarded as Australia's justified demands. The governor-general's plans had no
chance of success. The few people who developed similar models had even less
chance of seeing them adopted. Their activities were dismissed as the acts of
political muddleheads. At best, no notice was taken of their criticism of Australia's posturing as a great power; at worst, it was defamed as the prefabricated
slander of agents paid to spread German propaganda.[61]

The governor-general on the other side of the Tasman, too, believed that
the former German colonies should not be administered by New Zealand. In
his view, New Zealand had its own difficulties, which had not been lessened by
the war. It was more than likely that Samoa's problems would take a back seat.
New Zealand, he pointed out, could not afford to develop Samoa. And just as
the governor-general of Australia cited Australia's failures in the Northern Territory and Papua, so governor-general Liverpool emphasized New Zealand's
unsatisfactory policy in the Cook Islands, which had been under direct New
Zealand control since 1900. The only solution he could see was for Samoa to
become a British Crown Colony. He suggested that all the British islands in the
Pacific (plus the Cook Islands, which had so far belonged to New Zealand),
should come together under one high commissioner, who should be based in
Fiji, not in Australia.[62]

There was some support for the governor-general of New Zealand's views
among the white population of Samoa—as early as the end of 1915, the thirty-
seven leading non-German businessmen in Apia had petitioned the colonial
secretary to set up the same administration as under the Germans, "only under
the British Flag."[63] In addition, the longer the New Zealand military administration lasted, the more the general mood of the Europeans in Samoa swung
against rule by New Zealand. Nonetheless, the idea of Samoa becoming a British Crown Colony was illusory for the same reasons that the notion of New
Guinea becoming a Crown Colony or being ruled by Britain under a mandate
was illusory. In New Zealand public criticism of a takeover of Samoa was much
stronger than that in Australia, but the fact that the liberal-conservative-nation-
alist New Zealand government had shown itself far more loyal than Australia to

Britain during and after the war was enough to make it impossible for London to deal differently with the subimperialist dreams of Melbourne and Wellington. In addition, criticism in the press, like that expressed by the Labour opposition in New Zealand, concentrated on one main point: the dependence of the Samoan economy on Chinese labor instinctively gave many New Zealanders a bellyache. This was caused less by social and economic considerations, or sympathy for the exploited Chinese, than by the deep-seated Yellow Peril syndrome combined with the New Zealand variant of the White Australia Policy. "It is a remarkable feature that New Zealand is being asked to take over the control not only of a captured German colony but the loving care of a horde of cheap and nasty Chinese coolies," wrote the (Auckland) *Truth*, one of New Zealand's highest circulation dailies, in October 1919. It went on to admit to "the instinctive horror of the white at the thought that his country is to become the dumping ground of Asiatic hordes." Surely it would be better for the mandate for Samoa, with its "scum of Asia," to go to Britain, or for Samoa to become part of a western Pacific confederation under a British high commissioner, argued the paper.[64]

The MP James McCombs put forward the same views, for the same reasons, after returning from a visit to Samoa. McCombs was a member of the Social Democratic Party, which was to the left of the Labour Party.[65] In theory,

"The Principle of a White New Zealand Endangered." (*The New Zealand Truth*, 25 October 1919)

"A Mixed Marriage." (*The New Zealand Truth*, 10 April 1920)

the anti-Chinese front commanded a majority in the New Zealand government as well. But the problem was that, since the influenza epidemic, the old idea put forward by the military governor, Colonel Logan, of forcing the Samoans to work on European plantations and then repatriating the Chinese no longer seemed feasible. The weakened Samoans had trouble ensuring their own survival, and there was no question of forcing them to work for Europeans. In response to this quandary, the cabinet in Wellington decided on a compromise. Chinese workers were to continue to be imported into Samoa, but under parliamentary pressure from the Labour Party the government promised at least to do away with the coolie system; and Samoan women were to be protected from sexual advances by Chinese men. Of course, the government declaration that the system of using Chinese laborers as coolies in Samoa had been abolished was pure hogwash. But it kept criticism by the Labour Party at bay for the time being. Nonetheless, the excited debate in parliament prevented the government from sneaking a paragraph allowing corporal punishment exclusively for Samoans into the Samoa Constitution Order, as Administrator Tate had asked it to do.[66] The leader of the New Zealand Labour Party, Harry Holland, an Australian, was one of the strongest critics of New Zealand policy on Samoa. But even the Labour Party did not produce any concrete suggestions for an alternative to New Zealand rule there.

Voices against a continuation of their country's rule in the German Pacific territories occupied during the war were probably even rarer in Japan than in Australia or New Zealand. But they did exist.[67] Despite the considerable economic progress made during the military administration, a majority of public opinion agreed that Japan's acquisition of Micronesia had brought it few economic benefits. All the more, therefore, were the islands to be retained for reasons of prestige; Japan could not afford to lose face in front of Europeans and Pacific Islanders. Strategic reasons, too, were repeatedly cited for the retention of the islands. It was argued that they served as a forward defense against the American threat from the Philippines, and especially from Guam.[68] Just as Hughes had developed a South Pacific variation of the Monroe Doctrine, so the Japanese had a northern Pacific version, according to which the political future of the North Pacific area was to be decided by Japan alone.[69] Radical imperialist circles made no secret of the fact that they regarded Micronesia only as a springboard for the south or southeast. In the Marshall Islands, the captain of a Japanese warship is alleged to have told the local people that New Caledonia and Australia were next on the list. Greedy Japanese eyes were fixed mainly on Indonesia. But even India was regarded by some as the end of one stage of Japan's southern mission, which had started in Micronesia.[70] A position paper prepared by the Japanese navy for the Paris peace negotiations emphasized the value of the islands, with Palau (the Japanese headquarters) as the geographical center of a region that included the Philippines, Indonesia, New Guinea, and Polynesia.[71]

Germany being driven out of the Pacific area had seriously upset the balance of power. More than anything else, Japanese inroads caused nervousness and anxiety. Australia's agitation was at first considerable, although the Carolines were one of the few areas in the Pacific that had never figured in Australian dreams of great-power status—they were too far away and had no commercial value. It was therefore argued internally from an early stage that these islands could be left to Japan or the United States. The Marshall Islands, however, were to be attached to the Anglo-Australian sphere of influence because they were one of Burns Philp's main markets.[72] Informed by London of Britain's secret agreement with Tokyo, Melbourne and Sydney raised no objections, although they were not particularly happy about this whole development. On the eve of the peace negotiations, Hughes tried again to question the agreements that had been made, but Lloyd George was not to be moved. Eventually Hughes gave up, accepting that the British Empire would stick to its wartime agreements regarding Micronesia.[73] Thereafter, he endeavored to obtain as many guarantees as possible that Japanese influence of every sort would be eliminated and excluded from the territories occupied by Australia. Ultimately, his policy was successful.

Nobody was more aware that the military situation in the Pacific had nevertheless deteriorated considerably compared with the position before 1914 than responsible politicians and high-ranking officers in the United States. Contrary to all Anglo-Saxon, especially Australian, propaganda, the German presence in the Pacific had never posed a military threat to the other Pacific nations. It had been a weak point for Germany—as the war had demonstrated only too clearly. Germany had no great ambitions in the Pacific, which could not be said of the "successor states" of New Zealand, Australia, and Japan. The State Department and the United States Navy were more than worried when Japan entered the war, and their unease increased during the war. There was certainly no issue in Paris that touched on the United States' interests more closely than the Pacific question. In American eyes, Samoa's fate was clearly of secondary, or even tertiary, significance. After all, America had the only useful harbor in the island group, and neighboring New Zealand, a would-be great power, posed no military threat. New Guinea, by contrast, and especially Micronesia, were of high strategic value to the United States: Guam and the Philippines were right on its doorstep.

It has recently been suggested that Wilson's anger at the demands made by the Australian prime minister at the Peace Conference had less to do with Hughes' open contempt for Wilson's ideas on the mandate system than with the American president's fear that the Japanese, like the Australians, might annex the areas they had occupied and then use them as naval bases.[74] One could go a step further and argue that Wilson's mandate concept had little to do with idealistic motives, but was based on the United States' concrete political interests. The State Department in Washington had become aware of the secret agreement reached between the Allies and Japan during the war.[75] Primarily interested in blocking Japanese influence, the United States had to find a strategy of circumventing this agreement in such a way that neither openly questioned Britain's Allied commitments nor forced Japan into taking a special role. Only a mandate system supervised by the League of Nations offered any guarantee that Japan would not one day use Micronesia as a military takeoff point against America.[76] This not only explains why Wilson was so annoyed about Hughes' stubbornness on annexation, but also casts new light on the American president's apparent indifference toward the mandate question once it had been established that C class mandates (and thus Micronesia) could not be fortified and that annual reports would provide some information about what Japan was doing in its islands, which—thanks to Hughes' stubbornness— were so cut off from the rest of the world.

In any case, important voices in the State Department considered Micronesia in Japanese hands, or even in British ownership, as such a dangerous threat to America's position that they even regarded returning the islands to Germany as a better solution. In the latter case, it might be possible to acquire the territory from Germany at a later date in exchange for American reparations claims—an idea that was not so far removed from the German delegation's alternative scenario.[77] Leading American diplomats did not join in the sharp international criticism of Germany's colonial rule in Micronesia. From an early stage they defended the German colonial administration there against attack, even expressing something approaching modest praise for it.[78]

To calculate political probabilities in retrospect is always a risky business, because human behavior cannot be measured in any absolute way. If I nevertheless cannot resist the temptation, I shall initially go no further than to say that the indigenous peoples of the Pacific colonies never had any chance of influencing the future of their homelands. Similarly, it could be said that Germany's chances of getting back one of its former colonies on the basis of a return to the status quo ante were nonexistent. If it had conducted its negotiations more skillfully, if it had possessed better information about disagreements among the Allies, and if, especially, it had been more determined on the colonial question, we cannot totally exclude the possibility (although many question marks remain) that Germany might have been given a mandate, under strict conditions, for Micronesia (or parts of it)—that is, the area which, apart from Tsingtao, it was most prepared to relinquish. If history had taken this course, the consequences might have been significant. A minimal concession of this nature would have considerably reduced the heavy psychological burden the Treaty of Versailles placed upon the young German republic. Micronesia would have been spared Japanese pressure, at least for a while. Perhaps German democrats would have decided to put an ideal into practice and to grant independence earlier than others did elsewhere. Micronesia's political future was not fixed quite as firmly by the war situation as that of New Guinea, Nauru, and Samoa. This is shown not only by the variety of American plans for the region,[79] but also by Japan's readiness to accept some of the United States' demands for Yap. And whereas Nauru, New Guinea, and Samoa were more than Australia and New Zealand could digest anyway, a broad majority in Japan always considered Micronesia to be of secondary importance to the East Asian mainland, where Japan's political ambitions were focusing. Micronesia remained an offshoot of Japanese imperialism. But whatever might have happened if . . . , one thing is certain. The French, who also wanted their mother country to participate in the run on Germany's Pacific colonies,[80] never had the faintest chance of success.

"New" Colonial Policy and Indigenous Interpretations of Colonial Rule in the Light of the First World War

THE LASTING IMPACT OF THE MILITARY IN THE SOUTH PACIFIC MANDATES

Martial law and military administration ended in 1921–1922 (Japanese Micronesia) in Germany's former Pacific colonies. It soon became apparent, however, that the changes which had taken place during the European war, or had been set in motion by the new colonial rulers, did not dissolve into thin air overnight on the introduction of a civil administration. On the contrary, patterns of behavior that had emerged under the exceptional circumstances of military rule were consolidated, and were only now able to put down real roots. In other words, the Australian, Japanese, and New Zealand colonial administrations all grew out of, and were based upon, the respective military administrations that had preceded them. Without the military administrations, the civil administrations are unthinkable. The years 1921 and 1922 were by no means a "zero hour" in the Pacific. The break with the German past and its legacy, and the development of specifically Australian, Japanese, and New Zealand colonial administrations took place at different times in the various regions. In Japanese Micronesia it began as early as 1915, during the reconstruction phase in which Micronesia was "Japanized." In New Guinea the turning point was 1917–1918 at the latest, when it became clear that the administration was unable, and probably unwilling, to act against the excesses perpetrated by the recruiters. From that time, lack of a clear policy toward the local population, with a daily vacillation between the extremes of sympathy and the most brutal inhumanity, depending on the attitude of each individual Australian official, increasingly established itself as the main feature of the Australian presence in New Guinea. The end of the German administration etched itself more deeply into the memories of the local people in Samoa than elsewhere, because the transition from one foreign ruler to another was, in retrospect, firmly associated with a specific event—namely, the influenza epidemic. In the process, the fact that a majority of Samoans saw the arrival of the New Zealanders as a stroke of luck, because they believed (and this hope lasted for four years) that this would give them greater autonomy and a better chance for self-determination, is generally suppressed.

For Samoa i Sisifo and Papua New Guinea, both independent states today, and the Micronesian islands, 1914–1918 was a turning point, less because of the nominal switch of colonial masters than because of the fundamental changes in living conditions that took place during those years. The contrast with the period before 1914 is especially clear in one specific area. The territory that had once been the "German" South Pacific had become a zone of potential military conflict of the first rank, whose explosive nature was exposed, rather than concealed, by the provisions of the C class mandate. Before 1914, militarism in New Guinea, Micronesia (except for Guam), and Western Samoa had been expressed only in parades and the military marches given by the German imperial navy on its occasional visits. These festival-like events were popular among the local population, and also met the need of sailors and naval officers for rest and change after the monotony of life on board ship. Samoa had much to offer in this respect—an attractive landscape, cava ceremonies with a real Pacific chief, and the opportunity to flirt with the *taupou* (village virgin). The adventurous could undertake small expeditions into the swamps of New Guinea, where malaria-induced fevers transformed leeches into greedy monsters and the startled bush people into bloodthirsty cannibals.

But despite all military justifications for colonial rule, the Pacific was not a theater for German dreams of world domination. The aspiration to be a world power may have been a background factor when, at the turn of the century, Germany decided to become more politically active in the South Pacific and to accept "responsibility." But at least in military-strategic terms, this claim was never translated into reality in the Pacific. The hypocrisy on which the Wilhelmine Empire was built was clearly revealed in the South Pacific. Germany wanted to be a world power, but in putting this aim into practice, it became apparent that Germany's eyes were bigger than its stomach. There was not a single naval base in Germany's sphere of influence in the Pacific, and none was ever established. Plans do not even seem to have been drawn up—at least, they have yet to be found. But quite apart from the lack of naval bases, Germany did nothing to protect its colonies from external attack. Nowhere were weapons or ammunition stored for an emergency; settlers were not given any military training; there was no such thing as a colonial force. Unless we assume that the bombastic words spoken in Germany were nothing but rhetoric, the only conclusion we can draw is that imperial overstretch was a reality for the German empire long before the First World War.

At least in retrospect, it is clear that, contrary to Australia's passionate declarations, Germany's Pacific colonies had been a force for stability among the powers in the Pacific. Germany's military exclusion from the Pacific opened up a Pandora's box. Now the real potential for conflict that had been concealed by the alleged German threat became obvious. Instead of the Pacific becoming a zone of peace and security, as war propaganda proclaimed, the feeling of being under threat and in danger grew. The Australian prime minister's "success" at Versailles in obtaining the right to apply national laws in C class mandates, and in keeping other powers out of mandated areas, boomeranged. Micronesia, cut off from the rest of the world, became a constant source of suspicion and distrust. In addition, the seeming secrecy of the Japanese fed constant speculation in Australia, the United States, and New Zealand that, contrary to all League of Nations regulations, Japan was attempting to prepare some sort of aggressive act.

The Australian government's main motive in acquiring New Guinea had been strategic. Few recognized that it might have been in Australia's strategic interests to maintain New Guinea as a German colony.[1] Africans, Asians, and, to a lesser extent, Pacific Islanders, had been exploited as European cannon fodder during the war. But now, for the first time in the history of imperialism in the Pacific, whole territories were acquired primarily to be used by colonial powers as forward defenses in a future war. Micronesians and Melanesians were sitting on a powder keg that could be ignited by any quarrel between Tokyo and Washington, or Tokyo and Canberra. By the mid-1920s, Supreme Chief Joel of the small Micronesian island of Mokil was already convinced that the outbreak of a war between Japan and America was only a matter of time.[2] At the end of 1919 the Japanese press, agitated by the American president's refusal to recognize the principle of racial equality at Versailles, was full of threats of war against the United States. In August, Japanese shipyard workers vented their anger on a steamer of the Pacific Mail Line in Kobe, and two American ships' officers were temporarily detained. The second act of this drama took place one year later, when drunken Australian soldiers insulted the Japanese crew of the steamer *Madras Maru* and threatened to throw her captain, Ishikawa, overboard.[3] Public figures poured more oil on the fire. In London, the Speaker of the Australian Senate, Millen, said in an interview with *The Times:* "racial purity must be maintained to the very point of death."[4] In March 1919, the director of the Australian secret services, Major Piesse, predicted in a secret memorandum that a racial war between East and West would break out in the near future. A little later, on Hughes' express wish, Piesse was appointed director of the prime minister's special department for all matters relating to the administration of New Guinea under the mandate.[5]

The Washington Conference let off some of the steam that had built up in the Pacific since 1914. But there was little change in the basic antagonism between Japan on the one hand, and the Europeans and Americans on the other. Even after the "official" beginning of the civil administration, the military continued to dominate the routine and day-to-day business of most of the colonial mandates in the Pacific. Strangely enough, this was least evident in the Japanese mandate, where the tone was set by graduates of the imperial universities, especially law graduates from the University of Tokyo.[6] Nonetheless, the Japanese soldiers and officers who had been stationed at the radio communications station in Saipan, and who had left their position after the Washington

A six-inch gun mounted at Fort Raluana commanding the entrance to Blanche Bay, c. 1918. (Australian War Memorial H 01987)

Conference, all without exception returned on the next ship, but in civilian clothes. A number of Japanese small traders on the Micronesian atolls were former soldiers who had ended up in Micronesia at the beginning of the war.[7] A naval liaison office *(kaigun bukan-fu)*, led by an officer below staff rank, was maintained as part of the civil government in Koror on Palau.[8]

The military was a much stronger presence in the Australian-mandated territory of New Guinea and in New Zealand-mandated Samoa than in Japanese Micronesia. The Australian and New Zealand administrations were civil in name only. Although they fulfilled the C class mandate's prohibition on militarizing mandated areas,[9] essential areas of the administration could hardly have been more militarized. Before 1914 the military had had no influence on the policy of the colonial administration. In fact, two out of the five German governors of Germany's South Pacific territories had not even done military service (Schultz and Haber). Now the tone was set by generals throughout. Before the outbreak of the Second World War, all the Administrators of the Australian-mandated territory of New Guinea (Major General Wisdom, Brigadier General Griffiths, Brigadier General McNicoll) and all the Administrators of the New Zealand-mandated territory of Samoa (Colonel Tate, General Richardson, Colonel Allen, Brigadier General Hart) were high-ranking officers, mostly generals. Practical colonial experience and knowledge of the Pacific Islands and their peoples were not called for when Administrators were being selected; all that counted were their military careers and ranks.

The selection of the first "civil" Administrator of mandated New Guinea can be regarded as typical. Of the thirty-two applicants, those with clear administrative experience in the Pacific had no chance. Australian-born Thomas Roberts, former finance minister of Tonga and secretary of the British High Commission for the Western Pacific, was not short-listed. Nor was Seaforth Mackenzie, who had the most experience dating from the days of the military administration and had temporarily filled the position of Acting Administrator. Roberts was "only" a lieutenant, but Mackenzie was a lieutenant colonel. Governor Murray of Papua, who had indicated, after the Australian government's decision to administer Papua and New Guinea separately, that he would prefer to administer New Guinea to Papua, was set aside because under no circumstances did Lucas want him in Rabaul. The shortlist consisted of four brigadier generals (including the three who later became Administrators, Wisdom, Griffiths, and McNicoll), one lieutenant colonel, and a captain. Griffiths, the last Administrator of the military administration, was almost certainly put in second place because the appointments board did not want the smoothness of the transition from a military to a civil administration to be too obvious. As compensation, Griffiths was appointed Administrator of Nauru.[10] Wisdom, who was finally chosen for the mandated territory of New Guinea, had a respectable military career behind him but no experience of colonial administration or of dealing with non-Europeans. In his application, however, Wisdom claimed that he had "a good idea of the true perspective as regards the relations between the European and the native inhabitants." As evidence for this statement, he cited a visit to tea and caoutchouc plantations in Ceylon.[11]

The first civil Administrator was explicitly instructed by the prime minister to give preferential treatment to the officers of the existing military administration when selecting officials for the civil administration, and also to act on Walter Lucas' suggestions concerning personnel. As director of the Expropriation Board, Lucas had filled it with soldiers returning from Europe.[12] Until 1942 the officials who had most contact with the local people, the district and patrol officers, were almost exclusively either officers of the former military administration or Australian soldiers who had returned from Europe. The predominance of the military element among Australian colonial officials continued even after 1945. It is at least an open question whether the training of an officer or soldier was of any advantage for colonial service. In any case, the "soldier-officials" in New Guinea behaved exactly as they had done while on active service, and thus survived: "Once they were entrenched, it was hard to dig them out, however incompetent they proved to be."[13] Soldiers and officers who could not cope with the colonial administration tried themselves out as planters or, most often, as recruiters of indigenous labor. In these undertakings, too, they had the support of the highest authorities. The word went around that Administrator Wisdom had claimed that any soldier who had been in France would be "a successful recruiter" in New Guinea.[14]

Military titles, military language, and military habits permeated life in the

Australian-mandated territory from the start. The same was true of Samoa, where New Zealand had not even bothered to change the Administrator at the beginning of the mandate administration. The last commander of the military administration, Colonel Tate, became the first Administrator of the civil administration, and along with him most of the military officials remained in office. At the start of his career in Apia, Tate had written to a military friend that there were "soft jobs with heavy pay" in Samoa.[15] Tate did a great deal to give comrades who found themselves unemployed at the end of the war a chance in Samoa. The "civil" administration—"nothing more than the old military government under a new name"[16]—employed 134 officials in May 1921. By the end, the German administration had consisted of 46 officials.[17] The authority that the New Zealand administration had lost among Samoans since the influenza epidemic was replaced by authoritarian behavior, and the bureaucratic militarists also increasingly alienated the British settlers, who wistfully remembered the period of German colonial administration: "I was there when Western Samoa was under German control, but the residents did not learn anything about 'Prussianism' until after the war, when they found themselves in British hands," noted an eyewitness.[18]

In a continuously recurring cycle of repression and resistance, the administration felt it was imperative to emphasize military elements as much as possible. "Uniforms and salutes are essential," wrote Administrator Tate, who set great store by always appearing in military uniform.[19] His successor, Richardson, began his period of office by demanding the title "Excellency," which, within the British colonial system, was reserved for the governors-general of Canada, Australia, New Zealand, and South Africa. The authorities in London pandered to these personal vanities by granting the Administrators of New Guinea and Samoa the right to receive fifteen-gun salutes, and the Administrator of Nauru the right to an eleven-gun salute. "This is thought to be a great addition of strength to the Government," rejoiced Brigadier General Wisdom from Rabaul. Wisdom himself placed great value on being addressed as "His Honour the Administrator."[20]

CHARACTERISTICS OF MANDATE POLICY IN THE SOUTH PACIFIC, 1922–1942

The Australian Approach

Militarism was not the only legacy of the war period adopted by the mandate administrations. Certain trends that had emerged between 1914 and 1921 were strengthened rather than weakened. In Australian New Guinea this included the ubiquitous presence of Burns Philp. Burns Philp's plans to take over all the German plantations at once had been unsuccessful,[21] but after the collapse of copra prices, the company was able to keep its monopoly of the far more lucrative transport business until the mid-1920s. The condition, pushed through by Lucas, that the trade of the German plantations and businesses in the process of being liquidated by the Australian government could be carried only by British ships, and that all had to go via Sydney, guaranteed fat profits for Burns Philp. At the end of 1923, the freight rate between Rabaul and Sydney, dictated by Burns Philp, was 50 shillings per ton. Before the war, it had been 20 marks (equal to 20 shillings). Nevertheless, the company's activities in the Pacific Islands were still subsidized by the Australian government to the tune of £55,000 annually. Like others before him, Wisdom discovered that the contracts between Burns Philp and the government had been cooked up behind the back of the Administrator of New Guinea.[22] Only after Hughes' resignation, when Shepherd gradually lost his influence as a gray eminence, did the procedures that had functioned so smoothly between the company and its supporters in the prime minister's office become less effective than they had previously been.

When facing potential trading rivals, Burns Philp had always been quick to demand guarantees that Australia's interests would be placed first. But when its own profits were at stake, wriggling out of such obligations seemed to be the best policy. Circumventing all regulations, the company used the loophole of Bougainville to smuggle the copra it had bought into its own warehouses in the Shortland Islands (British Solomons), whence it was taken directly to San Francisco. Thus Burns Philp avoided the customs and cargo duties that would have been imposed in Sydney and that the Australian government had hoped would bring it direct profit from its takeover of New Guinea.[23]

As long as Lucas enjoyed the prime minister's trust and had the real say in Rabaul, Burns Philp had nothing to fear. Lucas' position was so secure that he did not have to be alert about defending Burns Philp's activities. But it was the German place-names in the territory that kept him awake at night. Most of all, he was worried about Kaiser-Wilhelmsland and the Bismarck Archipelago, for which there were neither British nor indigenous alternatives. When instructing Piesse to put things right, he carefully pointed out that in the selection of new names, the pronunciation of the "thick-lipped (tongued) Melanesians" must be taken into account.[24] Neither King George's Land nor Kitchener Archipelago, proposed by the government geologist of Papua, were ever really accepted; nor was Australnesia, suggested by the Melbourne newspaper *Argus* and favored by Piesse himself. Kaiser-Wilhelmsland became simply North East New Guinea, while the Bismarck Archipelago retained its name, and even Lucas eventually had to come to terms with this. The name New Hanover, given by Captain Carteret in honor of George III, survived, because the government anthropologist, Chinnery, who favored abolishing it, was away on an extended stay in the goldfields of Morobe when the Administrator sought his advice. In some cases the indigenous names adapted by the German administration were given up in favor of the old British colonial names. Thus the Wussi became the Markham River again; Manus went back to being the Admiralty Islands.[25]

For the indigenous population, however, such concerns were secondary for the moment. The military administration had made a number of crucial changes in the everyday life of the Melanesians during the war. For plantation workers, the abolition of corporal punishment was at first a relief; but it was largely a relief on paper only, as illegal punishments were increasingly tolerated and new, brutal punishments (such as Field Punishment No. 1) introduced. As there was no uniform administrative policy, and the central administration did not carry out checks on the site, each district officer decided for himself and his area whether policy was interpreted in a humanitarian or a racist-brutal manner. The lack of central guidelines and of agencies that could have supervised the behavior of colonial officials on the site was the main reason for the growing unrest and agitation among the free Melanesians, those who were not bound to the Europeans by labor contracts. The autonomy of these Melanesians was limited to a hitherto unprecedented extent by widespread recruiting, which the administration did nothing to control. Operations whose cynical brutality is reminiscent of the worst episodes in the history of European contact, and in which some officers of the administration took part, profoundly unsettled the indigenous population and led to numerous violent clashes. In addition, one of the main supports of German colonial policy, the acceptance of the Melanesian principle of internal arbitration of disputes and its implementation by the European-appointed *luluai*, was abandoned. When European and Melanesian views clashed, there was now no middle way left. The German practice of partial acceptance and tolerance of indigenous patterns of behavior and legal notions had been given up quite suddenly and replaced by uncompromisingly western European, Anglo-Saxon norms, which were regarded as absolute. The indigenous people were to be forced to follow this path, with the sanction, if necessary, of the harshest punishments in the European legal repertoire. In addition, it became clearer and clearer that Australian colonial policy was not prepared to make European knowledge available to the Melanesian. The transfer of modernization through education was boycotted by the Australians.

All these aspects of Australian occupation policy were continued under the mandate administration. Although it is understandable that the military administration did not develop a grand framework for its policies, it is astonishing that the mandate administration showed a similar lack of interest in defining principles for implementing the provisions laid down by the League of Nations or for developing a specifically Australian colonial policy in New Guinea. Somehow the impression arises that, after shouting bloody murder and gaining New Guinea at last, the Commonwealth of Australia turned its back on the territory—like a toy in which a child loses interest as soon as he has beaten his rivals. The "basic principle" that New Guinea was to be financially self-supporting without assistance from the Commonwealth, announced by Prime Minister Hughes, certainly contributed to the fact that policy in the Australian mandate of New Guinea was totally dependent on the moods and fluctuations of day-to-day politics.

One month after the beginning of the civil administration, a question was asked in the Australian parliament as to whether the federal government had drawn up a policy for the mandated area. The following reply was given: "The question asked . . . is of so general a character as to make a definite reply difficult."[26] Without further ado, Parliament returned to the agenda. Three months later, when another MP again asked when the House could expect a statement by the prime minister on government policy in the mandated area, the inquisitive parliamentarian was called to order and informed that this sort of question was not permitted.[27]

Piesse wrote one memo after another criticizing Australian procedures in New Guinea. Despite his purely military background, and probably contrary to Hughes' expectations, Piesse was not only concerned with the strategic and economic implications of the mandate, but also took the responsibilities Australia had assumed together with the C class mandate seriously. His first objection was to the unrestrained recruiting of the indigenous population, with all its negative side effects. Like the German colonial administration before him, Piesse was forced to recognize that there was a direct and causal relationship between population decline and the recruitment of workers. Working conditions on the plantations administered by the Expropriation Board were little better than the excesses of the recruiters. By the end of 1921, conditions resembled those during the worst period of the Neuguinea-Kompanie's rule. Lacking all medical attention and forced to work extremely hard without regular food, workers died in great numbers. On expiry of their contracts, laborers were not repatriated but kept in Rabaul, where they had to wait months for their deferred pay. In the meantime, they ran into debt in order to survive. This made it easier to press them into a new labor contract later. At least in the quick repatriation of workers after the expiry of their contracts the German colonial administration had been better, wrote Piesse in an internal memorandum.[28]

The practice of district officers instructing the native police to capture Melanesians and then selling them to the plantations for commission was also continued unchanged by the mandate administration, and was another point criticized by Piesse. Administrator Wisdom even supported recruitment and the forced removal of children from their villages.[29] On the plantations themselves, conditions certainly improved by the time the mandate administration became more settled. But on two decisive points nothing changed: workers were regularly flogged and wages remained at 1914 levels. There is ample evidence that, despite official prohibition, the administration of corporal punishment continued to be a privilege exercised by European employers in New Guinea. The workers were too intimidated by previous negative experiences to complain.[30]

In 1914 the *average* wage of Melanesian plantation workers had been five marks.[31] The equivalent wage of five shillings was the *maximum* wage under the military administration, and it was deliberately kept at this level by the mandate administration. Higher rates of pay "will have the effect of enabling him to avoid work," argued the Administrator, who was at the same time considering expropriating Melanesian land in order to force more Melanesians into working for the Europeans.[32] Early in 1929, when wages were still pegged at five shillings per month, of which less than half was paid out in cash, a strike was held in Rabaul. Led by Police Sergeant Rami and Sumsuma, a local schooner captain, three thousand workers went on strike. There may have been a connection with the announcement of the arrival of the first German steamer since 1914. Both Rami and Sumsuma had started their careers under the German colonial administration and must have been well aware that there had been no fixed maximum wage at that time.[33]

The German colonial administration had attempted to leave free Melanesians as much traditional autonomy as possible. The policy of withdrawing these prerogatives, begun under military rule, was continued under the mandate administration. In 1922 marriage regulations for the indigenous population were promulgated. These gave the Administrator the power to prevent a Melanesian woman from marrying according to traditional customs. It is highly likely that the Sacred Heart Mission was behind this initiative. After the end of the German colonial administration, it saw a good opportunity to press for Christian, Western principles of marriage to be adopted and given priority over indigenous ones, without compromise. An earlier attempt had been unsuccessful, almost ending in disaster for the mission.[34]

Education the Australian Way

Australian attitudes about the transmission of European know-how, however, were quite different. To be sure, it was the mandate administration's explicit policy "to discourage the learning of local dialects," and Tok Pisin was no longer recognized in courts of law. But the mandate administration was more than hesitant when it came to teaching Melanesians English. By 30 June 1922 not more than eleven pounds and eleven shillings had been spent on education in the mandated area.[35] In the same year, the Technical School and the School of Domestic Economy were opened in Rabaul. The Technical School manufactured coal baskets and wastepaper baskets; one of its three classes was made up of students who could neither read nor write, and who were not taught to. In fact, this institution employed underage government laborers, and the name "Technical School" was nothing but a cover. Its mere existence, however, led the League of Nations to believe that the mandate administration was doing something in the field of education. A visitor in October 1925 regarded the whole thing as a bad joke.[36]

According to the Administrator's statement, the School of Domestic Economy had been established "for the purpose of providing wash-boys and cooks."[37] Students had to cook for three days every week and spent the rest of their time washing and ironing. As even Australia's official mandate report admitted, this was nothing but an attempt, financed by Melanesian taxes, "to train natives as domestic servants."[38] To finance the two schools, the mandate administration had introduced a new tax, called the Education Tax. All Melanesians who were not in a contractual relationship with a European had to pay ten shillings education tax in addition to the annual head-tax of ten shillings. The Administrator justified this procedure by pointing to the guidelines, issued by the Australian government, which insisted that the mandate had to be financially self-supporting. Thus it was self-evident that those who derived benefit from the institutions—meaning the indigenous population—should be taxed to pay for them.[39] European employers were also meant to contribute one shilling education tax per Melanesian employee, but it was not collected from them until 1928. In 1933, when it was manifestly clear that the revenue from this tax was not being used to educate the local people, it was renamed Native Labour Tax. In contrast to the local people, Europeans in the mandated area did not have to make a compulsory contribution toward the education of their children: the school for Europeans in Rabaul was free.[40]

In the late 1920s the director of the Queensland Education Authority went to New Guinea to inspect education in the mandated area. He criticized the state schools for what they were: institutions that provided cheap Melanesian labor to Europeans. But even McKenna's modest aim of providing real elementary schooling for Melanesians, not going beyond the level prescribed for ten-year-olds in Australia, was boycotted on all sides and at all levels. The settlers and planters made no secret of the fact that their lack of support for schooling for the indigenous people derived only from the concern that it might enable the Melanesians to question the established system, which was based on the Europeans giving orders and the Melanesians being willing to carry them out. The administration shared these views, but expressed them a little less directly. Immediately before McKenna's arrival in the mandated area, the Ministry for Home and Territories, the authority responsible for issues relating to New Guinea, had put out a memorandum summing up its "policy": "The consensus of opinion in recent years of native educational authorities has been that it is undesirable to stress too much the literary education of natives, which usually makes them something in the nature of an indifferent European, but that education should aim at making a native a better native."[41]

From the early 1920s Australia in New Guinea showed what "making a native a better native" meant in practice. Australian policy clearly demonstrates that the crucial factor in racism is whether the people subject to the colonial administration have the chance to make use of, or to reject, the greater opportunities or imponderables resulting from cultural contact. Forcing a colonized people to accept the hitherto unknown patterns of behavior of its colonial masters is, in essence, as racist in motivation as the notion that the achievements of their colonial masters should be denied to them. The attitudes of the Australians in New Guinea were shaped by the view that, in their behavior to each other, and toward whites, Melanesians had to conform to European legal ideas. On the other hand, Australians did not want Melanesians to copy European

behavior in terms of education and external appearances. Thus Australian poli-
cymakers were not interested in persuading the local people to adopt European dress, as the much and justifiably criticized nineteenth-century
missionaries had tried to do, because they had wanted to force non-Europeans
to adopt European behavior in order to "civilize" them. The objective of Australian policy in the mandated territory of New Guinea, by contrast, was deliberately to maintain a difference between non-Europeans and Europeans.
Therefore Melanesians had to be denied access to European education; and for
the same reason they were also ordered not to wear European clothing. From
their external appearance alone, Melanesians were to be recognizably the
"other," the "primitive." In July 1923 the local people were forbidden to wear
anything but the loincloth. All European clothing owned by Melanesians was
destroyed. Thus the mandated area adopted an ordinance that Murray had
already put into force previously in neighboring Papua.[42] It is doubtful whether
such ordinances, and especially what lay behind them, were ever registered by
the Mandate Commission in Geneva. Nevertheless, the statistics in annual
reports made it clear to the League of Nations that Australian expenditure on
education and schools in New Guinea was steadily decreasing, until by 1937 it
had practically dropped to 1921 levels. To criticism the Australian representative replied that "the natives of New Guinea were most primitive." Right until
the outbreak of the Second World War, it was the mandate administration's
deliberate policy not to have any plans for educating the indigenous people.[43]

Australian Administrative and Legal Policy

A completely different approach was taken to legal policy. Here the German
system of adapting Melanesian legal customs, already undermined by the military administration during the war, was completely abandoned. In 1923 the
Queensland criminal code was adopted, although it was not obvious why this
should have been particularly suitable for New Guinea. Queensland was known
especially for the brutality with which it persecuted the Australian Aborigines.
This clumsy sledgehammer approach to instilling European, Anglo-Saxon values into the criminal justice system is clearly documented in its outcome. At
the end of the first year of the mandate administration, 18 of the 452 indigenous prisoners were serving sentences of more than five years, a length of sentence unknown during German times. The longest sentence was thirteen years;
and ten Melanesians were awaiting execution.[44] The death sentence continued
to be an important factor in Australian "native policy" in New Guinea until the
outbreak of the Pacific War. According to official figures, about 65 Melanesians
were hanged between May 1921 and January 1942. The memoirs of at least
one district officer, who does not suppress the everyday reality of New Guinea
under the Australian mandate administration, however, suggest that the real
figure was much higher.[45]

Similarly, everyday colonial life meant the continuation of the rule of terror of many district officers. It now became clear that the excesses which had been perpetrated in many parts of New Guinea between 1914 and 1921 could not be attributed only to the exceptional circumstances of the war. Rather, the brutal, arbitrary rule of individual officials was the inevitable consequence of a policy that provided no concrete guidelines for relations between the colonial administration and the local population, and left dealings between Europeans and Melanesians largely at the mercy of the mood and personal attitudes of district officials who were rarely accountable to their superiors. It was made clear to independent observers, such as anthropologists, that criticism of the administration's behavior was unwelcome, and in fact would have negative consequences for their own work.[46] Nonetheless, many reports exist of offenses committed by Australian officials against the Melanesian people, and some of the worst crimes left a deep impression on eyewitnesses. It is striking that, again and again, such excesses focused on the sexual humiliation of Melanesians, both women and men. There are reports from all over the mandate area about the native police being misused to procure Melanesian women, who were then sexually abused by Australian officials. In only rare cases were the officials involved disciplined; often their behavior was excused.[47] Women who resisted were flogged; the same applied to anyone who came to their assistance. Under the auspices of the League of Nations, incidents took place that seem almost unbelievable. The worst violations of human rights of which we are informed by local eyewitnesses (of whom a number, including some victims, are still alive) include the instance of an Australian district officer, Edward Taylor, urinating in the face of a victim he had humiliated, and the exhibition of naked men and women who, as "punishment," were tied to cross-shaped structures and, with spread legs, subjected to public humiliation in front of their clan members, who had been ordered to be present.[48] The height of inhumanity was reached in the order, issued by an official, to punish a family that had not built its allotted quota of road by beating two of its children, a brother and sister, in a public place, and in the presence of their parents, until they had sexual intercourse with each other.[49]

How could such incidents take place in a League of Nations mandate? In the interwar period, the world's attention was certainly not fixed on New Guinea. Moreover, under the terms of the C class mandate, foreign observers were rarely able to visit the country. The German missionaries who had stayed in New Guinea had to take an oath of loyalty allowing any statement that could be construed as criticism of the Commonwealth of Australia to be used as a reason for immediate expulsion. A legislative council such as had existed before 1914, in which at least the white section of the population could advise on policy for the colony, and which provided a forum where suggestions could be made and objections expressed, was not reintroduced until the New Guinea Act of 1932. Even then, the number of council members who were not officials was small, and non-Australians were, of course, excluded.[50]

Why was the Australian colonial administration as bad as it was? One reason is that it was apparently not subject to any public scrutiny. In the past, European public opinion had been the best curb on abuses by colonial governments. The most obvious case was the outcry in the German press and parliament when the maltreatment of African people, especially in German South West Africa, had come to light. But the Australian public took little interest in the new territory in the north. This indifference, which continued for years to come, is understandable given the completely new challenges and social disruptions that were the immediate result of the world war and largely questioned the "Australian way of life." Yet this ignorance had long-lasting effects on Australian policy in New Guinea. Nor, as we have seen, was New Guinea of much importance to the Australian government either, once it had succeeded in keeping potential rivals out. Thereafter the government's prime concern was for the territory to pay its own way and not to distract it from its own main task—governing Australia itself—and its main concern—Australia's political and social future.

Anything that could detract from the image Australia liked to project of New Guinea as a quiet and peaceful colony which had been acquired to serve the best interests of the Commonwealth was, from the start, resented and labeled "anti-Australian" smear propaganda. The Australian government simply did not want to accept that, in reality, conditions on the scene were not what they claimed. Australia had won the colony in a kind of moral crusade against its former colonizer. Thus, criticisms of Australia's administration were bound to reflect back on the very justification for Commonwealth colonialism. A vicious circle ensued. To admit the alleged misconduct of Australian officials, let alone to investigate it, would have cast doubt on the moral high ground claimed by Australia. As this was out of the question, the scandalous behavior of district officers and their inhumane treatment of Melanesians not only went unchecked but was more or less condoned, and quite possibly even encouraged. Keeping Australia's image abroad unblemished was considered more important than stopping or reversing increasingly dangerous trends inside its mandate, because this would have meant acknowledging the existence of some dark areas. Moreover, any suggestion that Australia, as a newcomer in the colonial field, could learn from the past experiences (and mistakes) of other European colonial powers was angrily rejected as undue interference in Australia's national affairs, which placed an insulting question mark over its ability to free itself from its own colonial past. The German experience in New Guinea was disregarded primarily for political reasons that had more to do with emotion than with Realpolitik. But even the example of Britain was considered beyond the pale. Precisely because Australia was determined to emancipate itself from its British legacy—all the more so since the war—Britain's wide knowledge of colonial affairs was not considered applicable to Australian New Guinea. In this way, Australia's national emancipation gave rise to an unreflecting, boastful attitude that was directly responsible for the worst abuses in the mandate it had been awarded.

It comes as no surprise, then, that occasional reports by Australian officials openly criticizing abuses were dismissed as German propaganda or electioneering by the Labor Party; the officials themselves were accused of being mentally unstable, if not mad.[51] A report about the mandate administration that the Australian government had commissioned in order to banish negative rumors contained a number of critical comments, despite its general whitewash. The potentially damaging impact of these criticisms was "defused" by the intervention of the British representative of the International Labour Organization (ILO) in Geneva.[52] In the few cases in which members of the Mandate Commission saw through the humbug in the official reports and statistics, Australians blatantly lied. The result was that Australia acquired a reputation that had little to do with the reality of everyday colonial life in the mandated territory of New Guinea.[53]

Nauru

The case of Nauru revealed the full impotence of the Mandate Commission. The president of the commission, the Italian Count Alberto Theodoli, could do nothing but express an empty protest given that, in effect, Britain had passed on the mandate for Nauru to Australia without the agreement of the League of Nations.[54] The original agreement had specified that the Administrators of the island would be appointed by the governments of Australia, Britain, and New Zealand, in turn. In fact, however, this agreement was never implemented. Instead, Australia appointed all the Administrators of Nauru. This also meant that Australia assumed sole responsibility for internal policy there. Paragraphs 2 and 3 of a secret supplementary clause to the Nauru Islands Agreement of 1919, negotiated by the three governments in 1921–1922, explicitly stated that the Executive Administrator was bound to obey the instructions only of the government which had appointed him, and that, conversely, any regulations he issued required the agreement of his government to be valid. An attempt by Churchill, as colonial secretary, to put through a proviso preventing Nauru from being regarded as Australian territory in any respect fell victim to Hughes' determined veto.[55]

In reality, Nauru was an Australian "mandate," while Britain and New Zealand had claims to a share in its commercial exploitation. As in the case of New Guinea and Samoa, all the Administrators were high-ranking military officers (Brigadier General Griffiths, Naval Commander Garsia, Lieutenant Colonel Chalmers) or closely associated with the military (the deputy secretary for defense, Newman). This had been considered necessary, given "the tendency of the Nauruans to create difficulties with the leasing of land necessary for the adequate operations of the British Phosphate Commission."[56] When the Mandate Commission expressed its fears that the Nauruans, and thus the main principles of the League of Nations mandate, might suffer under the economic exploitation of the island, the New Zealand delegate, James Allen (formerly minister for defense) replied that the three governments would not allow Nauru to be exploited. Incidentally, he went on, the mandatories were far from making any profit out of their position. On the contrary, they administered their territories at a loss to themselves. The Australian delegate, Joseph Cook, went one step further in insisting that the three phosphate commissioners were responsible to the Administrator. This was a downright lie, as it had been agreed that the phosphate commissioners were to be directly responsible to their governments, and thus independent of the Administrator.[57]

The Mandate Commission's timid attempts to make it more difficult to exploit the Nauruan people had little effect in reality. According to official figures, phosphate valued at £10,275,632 was exported from Nauru between 1922 and 1941; a sum of £235,993 (2.3 percent) was credited to the Nauruans. This included not only payments to landowners but also the mandate administration's expenditure, which was charged to Nauru as a cost incurred for the benefit of the local population.[58]

The mandatories used all means at their disposal to break Nauruan resistance to the exploitation of their environment and the destruction of their fields and gardens. The case of the Aiwo people, whose land was rich in phosphate and therefore an early target for acquisition, illustrates the promises, tricks, and deceit used in the process. Before Nauru was taken over by the three governments, the Pacific Phosphate Company had already driven the Aiwo from some of their traditional lands, promising that no more would be required in future. Under a new name (British Phosphate Commission), and with the support of the three mandatories, the company now demanded that the Aiwo give up more land for phosphate mining. The Administrator reported that the people "were exceedingly sad and wept bitterly, and that they had absolutely resolved not to leave their houses and land unless forced to do so by the Government, and if the Government forced them many would die."[59] The Aiwo soon accepted their fate. Their own chief even consented to the combined actions of the Australian mandate administration and the British Phosphate Commission: "To put the matter plainly the land owners are most strongly opposed to leasing any more land on the flat, where our houses and our main food supplies are, but the Administrator has explained to us that our phosphates are helping to maintain the food supplies of the world and assisting the poorer people by keeping down food prices, we therefore consider it our duty in this particular instance to help."[60] Pointing the moral finger was an effective tactic even when applied to non-Europeans.

Late in 1930 almost the entire population of Nauru came together to oppose a decision by the Administrator, Newman, to appoint a successor to the late Supreme Chief Daimon. Newman favored a chief whom the phosphate commissioners had recommended as "invaluable" in the distribution of land to the British Phosphate Commission.[61] On Nauru, chiefs were democratically elected by the men and women of each tribe. This traditional practice, which smoothed the way even for women to become chiefs, had been sanctioned by the German administration, with the proviso that the chiefs elect among themselves a head chief, who was to be the administration's main point of contact with the Nauruan people. This procedure was initially adopted unchanged by the Australian military administration.[62] The Administrator's action thus represented a clear violation of a traditional principle, which had so far always been recognized by the Europeans. When the Administrator went on leave, ten of the fourteen chiefs petitioned against the measure he had introduced. Finally, on 17 March 1931, 577 men and women of Nauru over sixteen years of age, representing 41 percent of the indigenous Nauruans and about 80 percent of the adult population, called upon the Australian prime minister to remove Administrator Newman from office and not send him back to Nauru. The chiefs appended a petition listing the main reasons for their request: Newman had consulted neither the chiefs nor the people before making his arbitrary decisions; he had high-handedly canceled land titles that the German administration had recognized and registered; and he neglected education.[63] It is a fact that the Administrator had strongly rejected the idea of providing more than elementary education for the Nauruans. Giving them access to such education would be very unwise, he argued, because disturbances would be the inevitable consequence. The Administrator saw the present situation as confirming his fears, and warned again: "a little learning can become more or less of a danger."[64]

Australia saw no reason to change its Administrator on Nauru. After his return, Newman called together all the chiefs and lectured them like a fire-and-brimstone preacher:

> I feel very sorry for you. . . . You remember the lessons in the Bible . . . you remember they were in the garden of Eden enjoying themselves; Enjoying all the wonderful gifts that God had given them and everything was happy and bright until one day Eve listened to bad advice given by a Serpent and all of us know what happened then.
>
> Now you Chiefs are in the same position. You live on a beautiful Island—I doubt whether the garden of Eden could have been more beautiful—You are surrounded by every comfort that you can wish for. You have the three Great Nations of the World—England, Australia and New Zealand to support you with Australia in executive control; always ready to promote to the utmost your material and moral well being and your social progress; And you have a sympathetic Administration safeguarding your interests and ever watchful over your affairs.[65]

Soon thereafter, the ever watchful administration dismissed the chiefs Dabe and Deigareow. Australia's representative in London was informed that the whole incident concerning the appointment of a new supreme chief and the petitions from the Nauruan people would not be mentioned in the next mandate report, as this would only lead to awkward questions in Geneva.[66]

Having excluded the international public, the three powers got down to business in Nauru. Disregarding the ideas and objections of the Nauruan landowners, the Europeans mined phosphate for all they were worth. The fact that this would irreparably damage the environment, destroy the basis of the people's livelihood in the long term, and, step by step, turn Nauru into a ghostly lunar landscape, was obviously unimportant to them. Now and again, the Nauruans were permitted to vent their bottled-up frustrations on the Chinese coolies.[67] This killed two birds with one stone: the emotions of the local people were redirected toward a useful scapegoat, and rebellious Chinese phosphate workers were kept in check. The system of exploiting the country, its people, and workers brought in from elsewhere functioned extremely well for Australia, Britain, and New Zealand for almost a decade. From the end of 1930, however, this system developed more and more cracks. In 1932, of all people, the head chief imposed by the administration against the wishes of the majority of the population first expressed in public the demand for self-administration for all Nauruans. The shocked phosphate commissioners were at last forced to see that they could not go on as usual forever. Their reaction was to step up phosphate extraction even further.[68]

Japan in Micronesia

At the end of 1921 the administration of Japanese Micronesia passed from the naval ministry to the Ministry of the Interior; in March 1922 the withdrawal of troops began. An imperial decree of 30 March 1922 established a separate South Pacific administration, directly subordinate to the prime minister. The aims of the Japanese mandate administration were no different from those which had been pursued since 1915; if anything, they were intensified. The main objective was to integrate Micronesia into the Japanese empire and to exploit the islands by, and for the benefit of, Japanese settlers. From 1 June 1922 the mandated area was treated as part of Japan in terms of customs and tariff policy. This differed from practice both in the German colonies before the war and in comparable Australian and New Zealand territories after 1921. Japanese policy was directed toward the complete assimilation of local civilizations, even at the cost of the destruction of the Micronesian character of the land and the people. Once the Micronesians had accepted these fundamental features of Japanese policy, or at least given the impression that they had come to terms with them, the existing system allowed them a certain amount of room for maneuver. The extent of this latitude is highly controversial, however. If the Japanese attempt at colonization can be compared with European colonialist enterprises at all, it most resembles French attempts to persuade "their" islanders to abandon their own culture and totally adopt *la civilisation française.* But even this comparison is of only limited validity, because the French were much less consistent in their efforts than the Japanese. Above all, the French, unlike the Japanese, never aimed to wipe out the Pacific Islanders as a separate race; at most, their objectives were limited to making the Pacific peoples give up their traditional cultures. In addition, it is generally accepted that the French system gave the assimilated indigenous population much greater opportunities

Studying the new order. Marshallese girls study a Japanese almanac map, c. 1917. (Photograph by Thomas J. McMahon. Mitchell Library, State Library of New South Wales)

to exert influence, and much more freedom of action, than was ever conceivable under Japanese administration.

There is no doubt that health care and education were considered means of gradually achieving the colonial target. Nevertheless, education and health care in Micronesia were considerably better under the Japanese colonial administration than they had been under the German administration. No comparison with parallel Australian and New Zealand administrations is possible, because there was simply nothing comparable in New Guinea or Samoa.[69]

But even Japanese medical achievements could not alter the fact that the

enormous acceleration of "Western" modernization under the Japanese administration left losers and victims behind. Like the Germans before them, the
Japanese were forced to recognize that the people of Yap rejected just about
everything that both Europeans and Japanese defined as "progress." Even the
fact that Yap was least affected by the influx into Micronesia of Japanese and
Okinawans could not hold up, let alone reverse, the extremely rapid decline in
its population, which had already begun under the German colonial administration (if not under the Spaniards). Before and after 1914 the local population
was subjected to all sorts of medical treatment, yet the causes of the people's
distress was clearly apparent. In their collision with a culture which they
regarded as completely alien, the people of Yap did not react with a mixture of
assimilation and cultural symbiosis—the sort of forward defense practised by
most other South Pacific Islanders. Instead they withdrew into an attitude
described as fatalistic by foreigners for whom the domination of nature was the
ultima ratio of human activity, and who regarded as suspicious any behavior
other than active rebellion against developments over which man has only limited control. Between 1903 and 1911 the indigenous population of Yap fell by
13.5 percent; between 1920 and 1933, by almost 50 percent. In 1933 there
were two hundred deaths annually for every eighty births.[70]

The European delegates at the meetings of the Mandate Commission in
Geneva, however, were much more interested in concealed evidence of military activities possibly undertaken by Japan in its mandated area than in the
decline of the indigenous population of Yap. We know today that, at least until
it left the League of Nations, Japan had no covert military operations and did
not rearm in Micronesia.[71] But Japan, too, had reason to present a distorted
picture of its colonial reality to the world. It was less concerned to put forward
untruths about its native policy than to prevent the loss of face that might
threaten when Japanese customs were revealed to a Europeanized world.[72]

Samoa under the New Zealand Mandate

The undisputed Pacific champions in adapting to European strategies while at
the same time maintaining traditional ways of life were the Samoans. The history of Samoa under the New Zealand mandate administration is full of desperate attempts by the Samoans to find the correct European key to get rid of
their unwanted New Zealand masters. Their determination in pursuing the
goal of self-rule, even after many setbacks, is astounding. New Zealand had
expected that the announcement of the official mandate over Samoa on 26 May
1921[73] would bring to an end the period of instability when the lack of clarity in
the situation had spurred the Samoans on to offer resistance. In order to demonstrate New Zealand's lasting commitment to Samoa, the New Zealand minister for external affairs, Lee, went to Apia one and a half months later. His
courtesy visit to the Samoan house of assembly *(fono)* was quickly transformed
by the Samoan *faipule* assembled there into a demonstration of the indigenous

political will. The spokesperson for the *faipule,* Toelupe, reminded the audience of the first visit by a New Zealand minister for external affairs one year previously, and of his promise that Samoa would be satisfied under New Zealand rule. Nothing had changed, Toelupe pointed out, and then read out another Samoan petition again calling for an end to New Zealand administration.[74] This time, however, the Samoans had gone one step further than in 1919. They asked for the mandate to go directly from New Zealand to Britain; but in addition to a governor appointed from London, local officials were to take care of the day-to-day administration. As well as the usual complaints— such as that New Zealand, unlike Germany, did not consult them—the Samoans, in an appendix to their petition, put forward one of the strongest arguments against the New Zealand mandate in a world dominated by European concepts and ideas. They argued that New Zealand rule over Samoa was illegal, because the war had not invalidated the Berlin Treaty of 1889, which had been agreed to at the time by the Samoan representatives. The point was that, after 1900, Germany had continued to recognize the main terms of the 1889 treaty, granting its rivals, Great Britain and the United States, privileges, and recognizing the Samoan self-administration. The New Zealand Constitution Order, the basis for the current administration of Samoa, by contrast, had been promulgated without taking the terms of the 1889 treaty into account, and without the consent of the Samoans. It was therefore invalid. This document was addressed directly to George V.[75]

A petition to the Prince of Wales, who was known to the Samoans from a visit in 1920, provides more information about the background to the Samoans' ideas and wishes:

> We are much distressed in mind; we are most anxious for our people and the generations of Samoa to come; we fear trouble between the representatives of New Zealand and the Samoans; we wish to avoid trouble and any unfriendly action. . . . This government ignores us. We pay taxes, but have no voice in the legislation or the expenditure. . . . We do not want our right to govern ourselves ignored by the New Zealanders. Help us, and show us how to govern wisely and fairly. . . . Our sons and daughters are educated by the missionaries, and go out to other lands to teach and to preach the Kingdom of God. Similarly our sons can be taught to govern our earthly Kingdom in Samoa; only help and teach us to do this. New Zealanders do not try to help us to govern ourselves, but it seems as if they want everything for themselves.[76]

The strategy pursued by the Samoans in 1919 had failed. At that time, they had appealed indirectly to the Great Powers, in the awareness that they would be making the official decisions about Samoa's future in Paris. It was only logical that the Samoans now appealed directly to the British royal family, because although the mandate had been given to New Zealand, New Zealand was still constitutionally dependent on Britain. The criticisms the Samoans advanced were modeled on the classic European demands for the right to self-determination: they paid taxes but had no influence over legislation, and could not even monitor what happened to their taxes. A special Samoan grievance was that the New Zealand administration had given up the German practice of publishing annual reports on Samoan taxes and expenditure on the Samoan self-administration in the *Savali*.[77] Added to this was the major complaint that the mandate regulations were being ignored. New Zealand was doing nothing to promote the aim, central to the mandate concept, of self-rule for the indigenous people. Finally, the Samoans pointed to the fact that they had already attained a "European" level. Not only were they Christianized and literate, but they were instrumental in passing on these European achievements to other islands in the Pacific. From as early as the end of the nineteenth century, New Zealand subimperialism had been matched by an analogous local imperialism that was Samoan, but European-influenced, in character.

Attempts have been made to discredit these Samoan activities by arguing that they breathe a European spirit.[78] Such reasoning reveals an excessively Eurocentric worldview, because it assumes that non-Europeans are limited, or restrict themselves, to traditional behavior, and that they are incapable of, or resist, accepting European models and applying them to their own situation or transforming them to fit their own needs. The idea of Samoans operating with "European" arguments does not fit into the picture seen by those who refused them political self-determination until 1962. Similarly, it diametrically challenges a European view, still widespread today, according to which non-Europeans should be satisfied with the role of the traditional victim, and which insists that they need European support to help them defend themselves against other Europeans. The fact that as early as 1919 non-Europeans, and especially those who so perfectly embodied Rousseau's noble savage, were able and willing to study European political theories and to make their own selection, according to their own needs and wishes, from what was offered, challenges a number of European preconceptions dating from both before and after the Enlightenment. "We hear it is reported that some white people are persuading us to be discontented. We wish to assure Your Highness that such a report is false. We are quite able to discern the errors of the New Zealand government ourselves, and to act of our own free will," was the Samoan response to any questioning of their ability to operate using "European" political diction.[79] The Administrator warned that the real aim of the Samoans was self-administration, even political independence. Although the European settlers living in Samoa were also dissatisfied with the New Zealand administration, they would not dream of supporting such Samoan objectives.[80]

As in 1919, supreme chief Malietoa Tanumafili wanted to frustrate the *faipule*'s petition at all costs. With the active support of the Administrator, he suggested withdrawing the petition and "reconsidering" it for six months. This time, however, the chiefs were not prepared to allow themselves to be put off so easily. After a stormy meeting, they insisted on sending the petition as it stood to the Colonial Office immediately.[81] The New Zealand government passed the petition on, but as it did so it pressed Britain not to give in to the Samoans on any point. They were "utterly incompetent" to undertake any administrative tasks, it suggested, and the idea of self-administration was absurd. A refusal could be justified in the eyes of the world by pointing out that the *faipule* lacked democratic legitimation. And incidentally, the New Zealand government went on, they must not be allowed to keep appealing directly to the king, thus ignoring the existence of New Zealand, "which Dominion they are inclined to place upon an equal status with Samoa."[82]

When no reply had been received from Whitehall by the beginning of October, the New Zealand government got cold feet. On the instructions of the government, which was openly panicking, the governor-general telegraphed London, pointing out that the Samoans were determined to achieve independence and that a quick reply was absolutely necessary in order definitively to clarify New Zealand's position vis-à-vis Samoa.[83] Behind this lay a letter from Toleafoa Afamasaga to the prime minister of New Zealand, expressing minimum demands: New Zealand was to accept local suggestions for changes in the Samoan constitution, the Samoa Act; the position of the *faipule* was to be legally legitimated; Samoan representatives were to sit in the Legislative Council; Samoans were to be permitted to be assessors; and the head of the Native Affairs Department was to be a Samoan.[84] The reply that finally arrived from London stated that neither Britain nor New Zealand was able to change the mandate they had received from the League of Nations on 17 December 1920.[85] The buck had been passed from Wellington to London, and from London to Geneva. A later attempt by the Samoans to appeal directly to the League of Nations was also unsuccessful, even though this time its democratic character was beyond all doubt.[86]

The *malietoa*, as head of the Samoan oligarchy, could have expected to gain power as a result of greater political autonomy. In European eyes, it remains a mystery why he of all people repeatedly intervened in favor of New Zealand.[87] As far as the New Zealand administration was concerned, he was a useful fool who could be exploited to promote its own interests: "He is a dud—but a very pleasant one—He has no ideas of his own . . . but he is loyal to the core."[88]

But even without the *malietoa*, the number of those who wanted to get rid of the New Zealand mandate administration grew. Every renewed breach of Samoan etiquette increased the size of the group that was dissatisfied with the status quo. What had started as opposition limited to the small circle of *faipule* and a general uneasiness among the majority of the Samoan population turned into a strictly organized mass movement, the *mau*, with a clearly defined objective—political independence.[89] New Zealand was forced to experience for itself a phenomenon that has often been repeated throughout history: once a movement gets off the ground, it cannot be halted by belated concessions. In 1925 New Zealand declared its willingness to grant the Samoan council (*fono a faipule*) statutory recognition, but this was no longer enough to satisfy the

Samoans' desire for more self-administration. It was the same story, a little later, with the "concession" of allowing the two supreme chiefs to become members of the Legislative Council. What would have been welcomed as progress in 1919 or 1921 was too little five years later, when it inspired songs ridiculing Malietoa Tanumafili. Samoan demands were always one step ahead of New Zealand's concessions. More and more Samoans gathered around Tupua Tamasese Lealofi III, the leader of the *mau* movement. The situation was aggravated even more by the fact that he was a member of a noble family that had allegedly been favored by the Germans but had been ousted from the control center of the Samoan oligarchy by the New Zealanders. By 1928, Western Samoa was practically in a state of anarchy, when almost 80 percent of Samoans, following the instructions of the *mau*, stopped paying their head-tax and boycotted the colonial administration at all levels. In a remote corner of the world, and unobserved by the international press, New Zealand soldiers, equipped with seaplanes and tracker dogs, combed the swamps of Samoa, looking for the leaders of the *mau*. Those who were caught were sent to prison in New Zealand. The absolute nadir in New Zealand–Samoan relations was reached on 28 December 1929, when, at a peaceful demonstration, Tupua Tamasese Lealofi III and eight of his closest supporters died in a hail of bullets fired by the New Zealand military police. Lealofi's dying words implored the Samoans not to give up the strategy of passive resistance.[90]

INDIGENOUS INTERPRETATIONS OF COLONIAL RULE AND THE BEWILDERMENT OF EUROPEAN HISTORIOGRAPHY

Given what happened *after* 1918, it is not surprising that the German past seemed increasingly rosy in Samoan eyes. In fact, the period after the outbreak of the First World War was at least as important as the time before 1914 in shaping the image of the Germans in those Pacific societies which had once been under German colonial rule. Twenty years after the German period had come to an end, Samoans already looked back to it as a golden age. Micronesians and Melanesians still have similar associations and use similar expressions. When people in the part of New Guinea that had been German speak of the *"gut taim bipo"* (the "good old times"), they mean, not the period of traditional tribal warfare, but the time after pacification by Germany as a colonial power.[91] After 1914, when relations with the new colonial power grew increasingly acrimonious, a new image of the Germans emerged that could not have existed before, because there were no real grounds for comparison. Added to this was a tendency, which can be observed in almost all human societies and cultures, to idealize the past at the expense of the present. But it would be historically incorrect to dismiss this retrospective, mostly positive, perception of the Germans in the Pacific as pure nostalgia.[92] Two points demand attention.

First, these assessments were based on real historical experience. However, compared with what came before, and especially after it, German colonial rule lost its rough edges, and negative experiences, especially inconsistencies, dissolved in the perceptions of the people. What remained was a purified core of memories consisting predominantly of positive elements. Second, it cannot be stressed enough that European assessments and judgments of European behavior do not necessarily coincide with Melanesian, Micronesian, or Polynesian views and interpretations. Against a completely different historical background, yardsticks for measuring colonial activity may also be completely different. Views of "good" and "bad," "right" and "wrong," and the attributions of blame derived from them, can vary enormously.

The statement that all colonial rule was essentially the same is profoundly Eurocentric and is not true to the experiences of colonized peoples. Any such categorical imperative put forward by European historians of imperialism also raises the objection that, in attempting to smooth out differences, one must consciously accept the fact that generalizations become trivializations, which relativize, play down, and ameliorate the real character of different colonial regimes. If evil is undifferentiated, then everyday experience loses its force, and negative experiences become less real, finally disappearing in a generalized and distant fog. Only a detailed examination of similarities and differences makes it possible to arrive at the sort of historical assessment that is necessary if history is not to be misused simply to confirm preconceived opinions and theories.

Samoan Perceptions

There can be no doubt that the representatives of Wilhelmine Germany and oligarchically structured Samoa shared a number of basic values, which were reversed under New Zealand rule. Both societies placed a high value on ceremonial, ritual forms of salutation and behavior and the exchange of polite addresses, and this facilitated mutual understanding between two cultures that were otherwise extremely different. By contrast, the Samoans perceived the "democratically" undifferentiated behavior of New Zealanders as an insult and open expression of disregard for Samoan mores.[93] It is curious that the colonial representatives of a semiauthoritarian state were more prepared to give the colonized population a certain amount of space than were the emissaries of a democracy, who thought that they could regain lost authority by behaving in an authoritarian and militaristic way. The small, but important, difference between authority and authoritarian behavior plays a significant role in the analysis of indigenous behavior toward European rule. In all of the Pacific societies that Germany colonized, steadfastness, persistence, and willpower were recognized and valued highly, not only among their own people, but equally in the behavior of the other, the enemy—that is, the colonial rulers. In Samoa, this quality was called *mamalu*. Europeans have found it totally incomprehensible that even those who suffered under it admired the power and the success of the stranger.

The automatic disappearance of hitherto accepted boundary posts during the occupation of Samoa seemed, at first, to open the door to greater autonomy. But even short-term satisfaction about the "New Zealand chance" did not change much the Samoan respect for the behavior of the German administration.[94] The greater the pressure on the Germans in Samoa, the more sympathy the Samoans had for them. The influenza epidemic conferred on the German system a semisacrosanct character; the German public health system became a symbol of European efficiency and professionalism as such. The Samoan view of the Germans as irreproachable scholars and scientists who went about their work without offending the local people became almost an obsession. As a rule, Samoans sought medical treatment in American Pago Pago, but if this was not possible, they would, under certain circumstances, go miles farther to be treated by one of the few German priests, just to avoid New Zealand doctors and hospitals.[95]

Samoan contempt for the British-New Zealand system of justice, which took no account of Samoan traditions—"if that is justice what is injustice?" complained the *mau* newspaper[96]—was matched by a growing esteem for the former German system. "Samoa owes Germany nothing except gratitude for the fourteen years during which Germany controlled Western Samoa," wrote a Samoan who was deeply disappointed by developments after 1914, at a time when hardly anyone in Germany still remembered Samoa.[97] Samoans kept in touch with Germans whom they had known in Samoa, and a close affinity existed long after the Germans left there. The wife of the last governor, Erich Schultz, received gifts of dollar notes from Samoa on the first birthday of her child, born in Germany, with the message that the Samoans were aware that times were hard in Germany and that dollars were worth a great deal. After the Second World War, former Samoa-Germans still received CARE packages from Apia, to help them over the worst. And it has long been known that Solf, who had laid the foundations for the special relationship between Germans and Samoans, received telegrams in his new post in Japan, congratulating him on his rescue after the great earthquake of 1923 and expressing the wish of the "Samoan people" that he would return to Samoa as governor.[98]

Since the influenza epidemic, the Samoans' negative experiences under the regime that succeeded the Germans were certainly the strongest influence in shaping their perceptions of the previous German colonial administration. This should not, however, obscure the fact that, even before 1914, a relationship had been achieved in which the Samoans not only respected the German administration but also trusted it in a way that went far beyond the usual reverence expressed by colonial subjects for their colonial masters. This was possible because in Samoa, unlike in Africa, Germany did not put its superior power permanently on display. In certain areas it recognized Samoan prerogatives and priorities, and placed them out of bounds for Europeans. This delicate balance between reciprocal rights and responsibilities worked strikingly well until 1914. But even this deliberate and ingenious cooperation between German officials and the Samoan oligarchy could withstand shocks only so long as those who were responsible for the system enjoyed the support of their respective group. Before the outbreak of the European war, the number of those who saw the prevailing situation as restricting their own aims and interests had grown on both the Samoan and the German sides. As so often happens in history, the status quo could not be preserved forever. Paradoxically, the sudden end New Zealand's military intervention put to the German colonial regime prevented the likely collapse of the system from its own inertia, thus ensuring that the Samoans would see the German past in a positive light.

The View from Micronesia

Something similar applies to the other German territories in the South Pacific. For instance, it is not at all certain whether the German colonial administration in Nauru would have been able to continue steering a narrow course between maintaining indigenous land ownership, honoring the Reich's guarantee to give compensation for damaged land, and allowing the Europeans to exploit the phosphate commercially. Today, however, ecologically ruined Nauru blames the former mandatory powers: Britain, Australia, and New Zealand are accused of having exploited all the rights and privileges of the former German concessions without having observed the duties and protective measures prescribed by the German colonial administration.[99] It is indeed possible that their "German" past may have protected the Nauruans from the worst. Whereas the Banaban people were, in the end, taken away from their home and relocated on a small island in the Fiji archipelago in order to allow phosphate mining to proceed undisturbed over the whole of Ocean Island, the special law that theoretically applied to Nauru at least made it impossible to displace the local people.

Today it is said in Micronesia that the Germans were easier to get along with than the Japanese, who were more overpowering. As in Samoa and Nauru, it is the sharp break in experience before and after 1914 which distinguishes the German from the Japanese administration. It is interesting to observe that many Micronesians are much less critical of the Japanese than are Europeans and Americans. Similarly, the biting criticisms of the mandate administration that one finds in Samoa are not heard in Micronesia—at least, not in western and northern Micronesia. In the mid-1980s it was impossible to deny the feeling that Tokyo's policy of Japanization had been highly successful. Many Micronesians of the generation born between 1920 and 1935 subscribed to and regularly read Japanese newspapers and magazines and spoke Japanese among themselves. Older people who had experienced German rule, looking back, associate the beginning of "modernization"—which they by no means regard as a positive development—with the arrival of the Japanese. Under the Germans little had changed in the traditional way of life; Western clothes were rarely worn. But under Japanese influence traditional life-styles were rapidly given up. The German period is presented as calm. In retrospect, it is seen as a time when Micronesians accepted the minor interventions of the administration all the more readily because they were, on the whole, left in peace. German officials were described as good-natured, affable, not arrogant, and reliable. Unlike the Japanese, they had mercilessly punished any cheating by traders, such as manipulation of copra scales. The small German presence helped to moderate the potential consequences of culture contact and colonial rule, and made the situation less threatening for the Micronesians. The coexistence between Micronesian life-styles and German demands and ideas—now seen as positive—contrasts with the following Japanese period. Because of the large numbers of officials and Asian settlers, Japanese customs permeated almost all areas of life, like an octopus with tentacles reaching into every corner and suffocating indigenous alternatives from the start. What were previously perceived as coherent Micronesian groups and associations dissolved; the "single" Micronesian world broke apart; Micronesian society fragmented. Alcohol abuse became common, and it was possible for Micronesians to possess firearms. Intra-Micronesian disputes not only increased in number, but escalated, assuming new and hitherto unprecedented dimensions. This is the view of the traditional, older generation, a group that is rapidly dying out.[100]

There is evidence that, at the beginning of Japanese rule, many Micronesians were unhappy about the increasing pressure from outside and looked for ways of influencing—or even getting rid of—the Japanese via the Europeans. The last Europeans in Micronesia unanimously report that the intimidated indigenous population was desperately seeking a way out of the dilemma.[101] Japanese administrative officials did not acquire the reputation of being impartial "referees" the Germans had enjoyed, because, as Micronesians saw it, in cases of conflict between settlers and locals the Japanese always decided in favor of the settlers. Even making a complaint was a difficult undertaking for the indigenous people.[102] Relatively few non-Japanese visitors entered the Japanese-mandated territory during the 1920s and 1930s, and those who did come were under constant Japanese surveillance. Their reports suggest that the Japanese policy of education and assimilation was beginning to work, at least among the younger people.[103] Nonetheless, a British secret agent, who in 1926 succeeded in traveling through Micronesia for the War Office in order to reconnoiter Japanese military installations, was asked by Micronesians on three occasions in three different places, when he managed to slip away from his Japanese escort, whether the islands would soon be given back to the Germans.[104] While the Samoans accused the successor regime of having restricted their autonomy, some Micronesians longed for a return of the conditions under which, though they could not prevent foreign rule, it had at least impinged relatively little on the usual rhythm of life.

German "influence" in Micronesia lasted longest in the Mariana Islands. The leaders of the Chamorro and Caroline Island people at the beginning of the 1950s had all attended the German primary school. The German language was still relatively widespread and was used by a number of American officials when dealing with the local people, because it retained the prestigious ring "of somewhat authoritarian efficiency which the islanders are fond of ascribing to the Germans." The handwritten "German" alphabet lasted even longer than the German language, because the Caroline Islanders used it almost exclusively for their own correspondence.[105] A possible reason for this is that the people of the Caroline Islands, who, since the beginning of European contact, had been considered "conservative" compared with the Chamorros, wanted to exclude Japanese influence and control at least from their personal communications.

The Melanesian Outlook

The main feature of the Australian mandate administration in New Guinea continued to be arbitrary rule. The lack of policies, guidelines, and administrative controls meant that relations between Melanesians and Europeans were determined almost exclusively by the personal attitudes of the district officers and patrol officers on the scene. Thus, in some areas all floggings were strictly punished, whereas, in the majority of cases, corporal punishment was not only tolerated, but was administered with increased severity in comparison with what had been permitted under the Germans. There were similar discrepancies in the treatment of "free" Melanesians. It is probably historically correct to state that a number of Australian officials were the first to see Melanesians primarily as human beings with equal rights. This went much further than the common attitude of German officials before 1914, who might have been prepared to protect the Melanesians but nevertheless regarded them essentially as colonial subjects, and thus inferior. But it must be pointed out at the same time, and with equal certainty, that clashes between Australians and Melanesians displayed a degree of brutality and contempt that would have been inconceivable during the German period. In fact, it was probably unique in the Pacific, if we exclude the treatment of the Australian Aborigines. The Australian mandate administration's native policy constantly oscillated between two extremes, but before 1942 it cannot be said that the balance tipped in a more positive direction as time passed.[106]

The local people were completely unsettled by the fact that policies changed with every new official, by the Australian mandate administration's open disregard for Melanesian ideas of law, and, finally, by the seemingly absolutely arbitrary exercise of criminal justice,[107] in which the German system had been abandoned. For Melanesians, Australians were not as predictable as the Germans had been. Predictability in the behavior of strangers is a crucial—if not the most important—factor in any cultural contact. Australian behavior was categorized, and the expressions Melanesians used to describe it speak volumes. "Olsem pikinini bilong King—giaman" (that is what the children of the king [of Britain] are—liars). Or the Australians were simply described as "long-long", which in Tok Pisin expresses something close to "arbitrary."[108]

These experiences of unpredictability in Australian behavior, and of Australian arbitrariness, not only fundamentally influenced the image of Australians in Melanesian eyes, but also encouraged Melanesians to look back at the German regime and retrospectively assess it. The first to speak out were the intellectual élite, those who could read and write. They passed their anger and frustration on to their former teachers whom they now accused of having let them down. "Why do the Germans make no move to free us? Have they forgotten us? Do they not care about us at all? What do they say when you tell them about us? Write to us about it! Our [German] officials should come back again! . . . Our calmness is just a front, in our hearts we have sorrow and grief. Day by day we are waiting for news to arrive that the Germans are coming back, but always in vain. You will never hear that we are happy with the English. Take note of what our heart says: a man had a wife. Another man stole her and she had to stay with him. But her heart was with her first, legal husband, and stayed there. Send our opinion to the paper, so that the English and the Germans read it and comment on it!"

This and similar statements[109] were connected with a growing desire to grasp what had actually happened during the war and with an equally sharpened power of observation directed toward what the new masters were doing: "write and tell us how everything is, what the war was really about, and whether the Germans are coming back, or whether the English are going to stay here? We know nothing for certain, and are grieving for you. Hide nothing from us, but write us the truth, so that we can comfort ourselves and take hope. Just think, in two months' time all the Germans who are still here are to leave the country—some have already left on the Molusia. You know that at Raluana there were canons that were later taken away. Now they have been set up again in Matupit. If you know why, write and tell us!"[110]

No doubt the German missionaries who received such messages from their former students felt flattered. But they did nothing to pass on these complaints and certainly took no action. Rather they were afraid that if such local opinion became public it would jeopardize their already much endangered position.[111] Largely left to themselves, the local people tried using various strategies to deal with the arbitrariness of Australian rule or even manipulate it to their own advantage. "Volunteering" to accompany the colonial administration's punitive expeditions as police-soldiers in order to get the chance to execute paybacks under the guise of official business, a tactic known since before 1914, continued.[112] The *tultul* used his monopoly of the position of interpreter to demand tribute from his fellow villagers who had been charged by the administration. If they refused, he simply translated their statements incorrectly, thus producing a conviction. Everything we know suggests that this was the beginning of corruption in New Guinea. The colonial administration did not notice this development—the first crack in hitherto seemingly closed village social communities, giving way to individualization.[113]

The Anglo-Australian justice system, making no concession to traditional notions, was totally incomprehensible to Melanesians. They tried to come to grips with it in the same way in which they had hitherto approached the supernatural. Since time immemorial Melanesians had believed that they could influence the uncontrollable by means of magic if they had the right charms or spells. Now an old Melanesian made it his special business to develop a recipe, based on betel nuts, for guaranteeing success in Australian trials. The fact that the old man lived on the hill of Namanula, not far from the governor's residence, suggested to Melanesians that his charms would be especially potent.[114]

Until after the turn of the century, violent clashes between Melanesians and European traders, planters, and missionaries were not unusual. Under the Australians, local resistance was directed against officials. A number were attacked and injured or killed. The extent of the hatred that had been stored up, at least among certain segments of the population, became apparent at the beginning of the Pacific War. Unlike the Germans in 1914, the Australians disarmed the Melanesian police because they feared they might make common cause with the Japanese. In the Sepik, where this was no longer possible, local police detachments joined forces and hunted down as many Europeans as they could. Two officials were killed. There are many indications that large numbers of Melanesians saw the arrival of the Japanese as a positive step, which could be described as a "liberation," if this word did not have other connotations.[115]

Just as in Samoa and Micronesia the image of the German administration and of its officials developed as fundamentally different and generally more favorable only in retrospect and in direct comparison with the next regime, so in New Guinea perceptions of the German colonial administration were crucially shaped by contrast with the Australians and the measures they introduced. To start with, judgment was passed on individuals. In people's memories, Albert Hahl grew into an almost superhuman father figure. Even in the 1960s, the Tolais still regarded him as "pren tru bilong mipela," which corresponds pretty exactly to the European notion of "a devoted friend," or "our real friend." An anthropologist working among the Tolai at this time, collecting local interpretations of the past, was asked how Hahl's family was.[116] In a culture where almost everything is built on personal relations, not on institutions, and in which even objects are often given proper names, the German governor's successors lost their identity and became simply "Doctor Hahl Inglis"[117]— Melanesians could hardly have expressed the distance separating them from the Australian governor more clearly.

Evidence of a special emotional relationship between Melanesians and German officials is not limited to Hahl. Early in the 1980s, the last surviving Melanesians who had experienced German colonial rule in Madang insisted that they had had extraordinarily good personal relationships with many Germans. Given the well-known German reactions to the alleged "revolts" of 1904 and 1912, Europeans, who tend to generalize and whose generalized views leave little space for personal relationships, find it difficult to understand such statements. In any case, this indigenous view places a large question mark over

Eurocentric, dogmatic judgments.[118] When the Kai people on the Rai coast south of Madang heard of the death of the German *Bezirksamtmann* Berghausen after the war, they struck up the traditional dirge.[119] Years later, one of his Australian successors was almost hacked to death on the Rai coast. Unusually, this attack was initiated and carried out by women,[120] which strongly suggests that Albert Nurton, too, had abused his position to violate Melanesian women. Another German whose memory has been kept alive in New Guinea to the present day is Franz Boluminski, former *Bezirksamtmann* of Kaewieng. During the 1920s his grave became a shrine for the people, who hoped for a magical transfer of powers through contact with his memorial cross. The Melanesians of his region regarded him as "good, fierce, just, inexorable."[121]

These views of Boluminski take us to the heart of the Melanesian assess-

Boluminski's grave. Kavieng, 1950. (Photograph by W. Brindle. Australian Archives Canberra)

ment of German colonial policy. It is hardly conceivable that a European, at least of the postwar generation, could connect the qualities "inexorable" and "just." For a European, the first adjective has negative connotations; the other is unequivocally positive. The Melanesians, however, saw no contradiction between the two, but almost certainly regarded them as complementary. Everything we know suggests that the local people saw the authoritarian behavior of their German *Bezirksamtmann* as a positive attribute.[122] On the other hand, it is quite possible that the administrative methods used by the East Prussian official would today be presented to the world by Amnesty International as an example of inhumane colonialist practice. The problem of judging Boluminski is supplemented by contemporary Melanesian assessments of the German colonial regime as a whole. Here the description "strict but fair" or "strict but just," which we have often quoted, had established itself.[123] A western European historian of the end of the twentieth century could perhaps accept the attribution "just" if it had originated in Samoa or Micronesia. But this is not the case, for in Samoa this word is hardly used, and though it appears in certain regions of Micronesia, it is by no means as universal as in the former German area of Melanesia. There, however, such judgments are difficult to accept. How can the German colonial system, in which corporal punishment and flogging were the basic means of discipline—and Boluminski was very much in favor of them—be perceived as "just"?

Attempts have been made to explain that German administrative methods closely resembled traditional methods of control practised in Melanesian village society.[124] The argument is that the procedures used by the Germans in dealing with Melanesian cultures (the imposition of the Pax Germanica, if necessary by force, the taking of hostages, punishing the whole community or clan if the real culprit could not be found or evaded punishment) and with individuals (corporal punishment) matched the Melanesians' horizon of experience within their own culture. They were familiar—a crucial factor in encounters with the alien. This does not justify such measures, but it explains why they were widely accepted without much resistance. The only uprising against German rule in the Pacific broke out after the application of corporal punishment by a German official, which would seem to contradict this theory. But it happened in Micronesia, where the German administration had not used corporal punishment before, and it is striking that the one local source we possess does not seem to rate the whipping as particularly significant in the outbreak of unrest, because it does not even mention it. The European editors of the indigenous chronicle found this so remarkable that they appended their own account of this event.[125]

When analyzing reports or stories by Melanesian plantation laborers, especially those working in Samoa, who experienced discriminatory treatment first hand in that they were beaten whereas Samoans were not, it is noticeable that corporal punishment is often made light of and hardly features in their reminiscences. The positive experiences mentioned are: good and regular food; cheap goods; the easy availability of new goods that could be taken home after the expiry of contracts, thus allowing them to pay bride prices and conferring a higher status in the numerous traditional ceremonies of exchange; and, finally, exposure to new ways of behaving in daily contact with the many "others" (that is, Melanesians from other tribes and Europeans). As negative experiences they listed frequent and sometimes bloody clashes with Melanesians from other clans, attempts to harm each other as much as possible, and the monotony and boredom of life on the plantations. Corporal punishment is described as "harsh," but here, too, considered "fair." Others do not mention it at all, or not until they are explicitly asked.[126] This may be an example of psychological repression of unpleasant experiences, but this is not a sufficient explanation, especially as other colonial excesses by Europeans, such as Australian brutality in New Guinea, are still so very much alive in people's memories. Nor were the Melanesian workers in Samoa pleased when the New Zealanders arrived there. On the contrary, on Christmas Day 1914, black workers hoisted the German flag at their quarters as a protest against what they saw as the failure of the New Zealanders to observe the conditions laid down in German contracts. [127]

By 1914, the Germans had the recruiters under control, and the Melanesians knew exactly what to expect on the plantations. This is how a Samoan historian explains the largely positive memories of the black plantation workers.[128] It seems to me that expectations and their fulfillment—or lack of it—are a key that can help late-twentieth-century Europeans understand Pacific interpretations of the German and subsequent colonial regimes. The Pacific categorization of "just" has little to do with European notions of justice. The behavior of the Germans was more predictable than that of the Australians because it was more consistent. The probable reaction of Germans to local actions could be foreseen, and thus they were more susceptible to manipulation, or attempted manipulation, by the local people. Germans supplemented, but did not alter, the Melanesian view of the world. Their appearance on the scene could be explained as a new corollary to a familiar and established system. Coming to terms with German actions and reactions required adjustment but no fundamental change. The existence of the Germans and the methods and measures they used did not fundamentally place the indigenous view of things in question. In retrospect, this clearly distinguished Germans from Australians, whose actions and patterns of behavior appeared erratic, lacking a firm basis, less predictable, and altogether more puzzling. Melanesians were not sure how to behave toward Australians who, at least until 1942, remained a mystery to most of them.

As far as we are aware at present, the universal ethical value system that Asians and Europeans had developed throughout the course of their histories did not exist in any of the precolonial Melanesian societies. The familiar, the known, the related, the personal and close, were antitheses of the alien, the unknown, the dangerous, the life-threatening, and could thus become a substitute for the "good," or even the "just." With the Germans, the Melanesians knew where they stood and could adapt accordingly. Strict discipline, including corporal punishment, was as much an integral part of Pacific cultures as was acceptance of, and respect for, authority and determination—what today would be called leadership qualities.[129] In February 1964 the first parliamentary elections were held in New Guinea, and the Tolai *Bikman,* To Petet Tokaul, informed the candidates that his people would support them if they advocated the reintroduction of "German" methods.[130]

The behavior of the few German colonial officials in situ uniquely shaped Germany's policies in the Pacific. Halfway across the world from home, which meant that communication with their official superiors took weeks, they found personal satisfaction in maintaining close personal contacts with the colonial population under them, and their work provided them with a substitute satisfaction they had never known before. "In relating to the indigenous people, personal qualities are all-important," Hahl had recognized correctly; and he had recommended personal continuity as the crucial factor in creating trust and establishing peaceful relations.[131] But the South Pacific was not a springboard for ambitious careerists, of whom more was expected and who had to provide quick results, and it was certainly not an arena in which fame could be gathered or reputations made. In most cases, attempts to do this amounted to creating a sensation, and they were partly responsible for the worst consequences of colonialism in Africa.

Germany's Pacific colonies were a quiet backwater of Wilhelmine Germany that could develop in its own way so long as the Reich's interest remained minimal, and the most important positions were filled by confident officials who were able to make decisions relatively freely.[132] More than elsewhere, the decisions made by German officials adapted local conditions rather than changed them. In my opinion, the economic aspects of German colonialism, at least in the South Pacific, have been overemphasized at the cost of the psychological factor. It is too easy simply to assume that every decision made by the colonial administration was dictated by economic interests. This was clearly not true. On several occasions Governor Hahl successfully undermined the efforts of economic interest groups who had gained the ear of the German Colonial Office, and who wanted to confiscate phosphate-bearing land belonging to the Marshall Islanders because they thought that the local demands for compensation were too high.[133] Anyone who claims that everyday colonial reality was shaped, not by the people on the site, but by a system of whatever sort in which people were merely bloodless actors,[134] has not grasped the dimensions of past structures and processes.

The potential susceptibility of this noninstitutionalized condition should not be underemphasized. Extreme dependence on the personal qualities of the officials could easily have upset the balanced imbalance between Germans and Pacific Islanders. A few German officials of the sort who went to Africa could very quickly have brought down the whole delicate structure of relations between the colonial administration and the indigenous people. Boeder in

Ponape shows clearly how catastrophic the "master race" mentality could have been in the Pacific.[135]

Conclusions

As we have seen, the former "German" South Pacific experienced a number of colonial systems based on different attitudes toward the indigenous population. This investigation of developments between 1914 and 1921–1922 has not only revealed clear regional differences among the policies of the various colonial powers but has also shown the necessity for a reassessment of Germany's pioneering role. Falling between the extremes of forced assimilation to the extent of ethnic self-denial (Japanese Micronesia) and a general prohibition on the adoption of European life-styles (Australian New Guinea), the original German colonial administration appears to have been surprisingly liberal. On the one hand, it allowed the local people to conserve or adapt traditional life-styles; on the other, it also gave them the chance to participate in the possibilities of European-German ideas of progress rather than blocking their access to modernization altogether. Pressure to do or not to do anything was much weaker under the German colonial administration than it was under the Japanese or Australians, and local societies had greater latitude in which to make their own decisions. The First World War and the handing over of the colonial administrations to Australia, Japan, and New Zealand were by no means nominal changes in the history of New Guinea, Micronesia, and Samoa, respectively. As we have shown, it was clear early on that, deliberately or not, colonial policy underwent basic changes that were perceived by the indigenous peoples as a fundamental break in their relations with Europeans. The fact that there were also continuities is so self-evident that it does not need special emphasis. In the eyes of Melanesians, Micronesians, and Samoans, the new, the different, and the alien were the crucial factors. Finding out that foreign overlords were not all the same, and that their behavior and the order they imposed could be differentiated from each other, was a completely new experience for many Pacific Islanders. For many it was a shock.

The First World War and its consequences represented a turning point in the history of New Guinea, the Micronesian Islands, and Western Samoa. In Micronesia the Japanese administration was largely responsible for the fact that a modern and potentially universal society broke over the population like a spring flood. As enough niches for traditional behavior remained within the Japanese system, however, the indigenous people on the whole came to terms with this event, as they did with natural phenomena such as typhoons. In New Guinea it was the deliberate policy of the Australian mandate administration to prevent the indigenous people from having access to the modern world, and to this end it denied them the material means of learning to handle it. But as the Australian colonial administration, unlike the German administration, was not prepared to alleviate even the worst direct and indirect effects of the impact of introduced modern technologies and ideas, a specifically Australian system of colonial apartheid developed. On the one side was the world of the Europeans, who had growing access to the latest modern conveniences and were increasingly prepared to use them in their everyday lives. On the other side were the indigenous people, mere observers, who were denied the practical advantages of progress. Under these circumstances, it is not surprising that the idea that Europeans were trying to frustrate Melanesian attempts to participate in Western "progress" and its products took root. It also provoked a Melanesian response dominated by a belief centering around the acquisition of these goods. Until the outbreak of the Second World War, a new turning point, the attitude of the Australian administration made it difficult for the Melanesian people under its control gradually to grow into a modern, Western, universal society. Indeed, it delayed this development. Compared with other colonial administrations in the Pacific, Australian rule in New Guinea had possibly the most serious consequences. It is difficult to judge how many of Papua New Guinea's present-day problems can be attributed more or less directly to this historical legacy. In my opinion, however, there is unquestionably a link.

Of all the European colonial systems in the Pacific, the Australian was also probably the most inhumane. Admittedly, it perpetrated none of the sorts of atrocities that took place in Africa, or under National Socialist or Communist regimes. But given a changed world and a changing Zeitgeist, it is more than disconcerting to discover what brutalities were possible during peacetime in the backwaters of world politics. Australian politicians undoubtedly had little experience in developing and implementing a colonial policy. Their extreme nationalism and chauvinism, which elevated racism into a doctrine for political survival, certainly did not make it easier for Australians to deal with an unfamiliar people. Added to this was an exaggerated opinion of themselves that had originated in wartime propaganda, but then took its own course, and subsequently had long-lasting repercussions. It blinded the Australians to their own mistakes, because they saw any criticism of their behavior as automatically casting doubt on their wartime propaganda, and thus on their own political position. To the present day, historical myths whose roots lie in wartime propaganda have hardly been faced up to. Nor have they been discarded by Australian historiography, thus demonstrating the longevity of such ideas.

Something similar can be said of New Zealand's policy in Samoa. This case clearly demonstrates that any historical attempt to interpret colonial reality exclusively on the basis of the colonialists' racist attitudes reflected in the documents will not capture this reality. Indeed, it will distort it, because the question of what consequences it had for the colonized people is more relevant than the search for the roots of European racism. There may be worlds—positive or negative—between (colonial) claims and (colonial) reality. It is obvious that liberal theories and slogans do not, by a long way, constitute a liberal society until they are implemented. By the same token, it is possible for a colonial society that is theoretically built on racist roots to be much more liberal in practice than a society based on theoretically liberal policies.[136] Thus New Zealand's policies in Samoa may appear theoretically more liberal than those of its German predecessor, but in practice they proved to be more authoritarian. What counts in history are not the theories drawn up by politicians or developed by historians. Much more important is the translation of ideas into reality—including all the inconsistencies, chance events, side effects, foreign influences, and peculiarities that comprise everyday, historical reality. How was this past reality experienced and how was it perceived? These alone are fitting subjects for historical analysis and evaluation. Anything else is mere paper history.

Abbreviations

AAC	Australian Archives, Canberra
AAM	Australian Archives, Melbourne
AHM	Archiv der Herz-Jesu-Mission, Hiltrup, Münster
AKM	Archiv der Kapuzinermission, Münster
ANL	Australian National Library, Canberra
ATL	Alexander Turnbull Library, Wellington
AWM	Australian War Memorial, Canberra
BAK	Bundesarchiv, Koblenz
BAP	Bundesarchiv, Potsdam
Bun	Bundle
DKB	*Deutsches Kolonialblatt* (Berlin)
DKG	*Die deutsche Kolonial-Gesetzgebung*
DKZ	*Deutsche Kolonialzeitung* (Berlin)
FRUS	*Papers Relating to the Foreign Relations of the United States*
GPRS	German Provincial Records Samoa, Apia
GStAM	Geheimes Staatsarchiv, Merseburg (now Berlin)
NARA	National Archives of the United States of America, Washington, D.C.
NDM	Archiv der Neuendettelsauer Mission, Neuendettelsau
NML	Nelson Memorial Library, Apia
NZA	National Archives of New Zealand, Wellington
NZDD	New Zealand Department of Defence, Wellington
PAA	Politisches Archiv des Auswärtigen Amtes, Bonn
PMB	Pacific Manuscript Bureau, Canberra
RCSL	Royal Commonwealth Society Library, London
RG	Record Group
RKolA	Reichskolonialamt
RPA	Reichspostamt
UPNG	University of Papua New Guinea, Port Moresby

Notes

PREFACE

1 One of the most recent general histories of the Pacific Islands calls it an epidemic of "measles," Scarr 1990, 263 and 266. For Europeans, it seems, "measles" at least sounds serious, whereas "flu" obviously does not. By far the best account of the epidemic is not by a historian but a journalist. But Field's treatment of sources is so careful and thorough that his criticism of New Zealand historians for having paid "scandalously little attention" to what has happened in Samoa since 1914 is well justified (Field 1984, xvi).

2 Firth 1986, xiv. "It was the old colonial order under new management" (ibid., 2).

3 Boyd 1969, 122, 128, 133, and 140.

4 Salisbury 1970, 40.

5 Griffin, Nelson, and Firth 1979, 54.

6 One characteristic example is the claim that the influence of the companies was always stronger than that of the administration, and that the German governor of New Guinea, Hahl, had to leave because of the pressure of the large companies in the colony (Firth 1989, 201–202, 1986, 5; and the official war history, Mackenzie 1927, 224). Needless to say, the official war history was heavily censored despite the fact that the occupation of the territory involved no real military secrets. Also very revealing are the more general comments on the overall effects of Australian occupation (Mackenzie 1927, 233; and Griffin, Nelson, and Firth 1979, 44). See also May 1989, 121, who rightly points out that in the late 1950s Rowley had already discovered there were significant differences in the way Germans and Australians applied methods that, superficially, seemed to be identical (see Rowley 1958, 192; also 11, 27). It seems that the results of historical research done as early as 1958 were somehow lost by later historians.

7 Registered (sic!) letter from three Tongan Members of Parliament, Nukualofa, 10 November 1919, to the governor of American Samoa, NARA, RG 80, File 3931, Box 33.

8 Gann 1984, 519. See also Griffin, Nelson, and Firth 1979, 8: "Britain was different."

9 Thus the Australian geographer Price 1972, 208; for similar comments, ibid., vi

("enlightened and generous colonialism"), and 219 ("What the Australians brought in was good"). Price 1963, 135: "there are few tropical colonies with so clear a record of humane endeavour."

10   Boyd 1987.

INTRODUCTION: THE GERMAN LEGACY

1   On the Neuguinea-Kompanie debacle, see Firth 1971–1973. On the acquisition of Micronesia, Brown 1977 and Hardach 1988. For German rule in the Marianas, see Hardach 1990*b*; in Ponape, Ehrlich 1978*a*; in the Caroline Islands, Christmann, Hempenstall, and Ballendorf 1991; for the Marshalls, Treue 1976; and for Micronesia as a whole, McKinney 1947. No comprehensive account of German Samoa exists; but see Meleisea 1987, passim. For all of Germany's Pacific possession, see Hiery 1993*b* and Hiery, ed., *Handbuch der "deutschen" Südsee* (Paderborn: Schöningh, 1996).

2   Hardach 1988, 13, refutes the orthodox view (Brown 1977, 151) that the acquisition of the Carolines would have been a logical consequence of the occupation of Kiauchow in 1897 and the naval laws of 1898.

3   The last German government doctor in Yap, Ludwig Kohl-Larsen, 1927, 143. Wächter 1941 had already worked it out that Germany's Pacific colonies were more for prestige than commercial or strategic value.

4   *Stenographische Berichte über die Verhandlungen des Reichstags. X. Legislaturperiode,* 159, sitting of 6 March 1902, vol. 5 (1902), 4637 and 4641.

5   General comments, such as, for example, "as the late-comer in the imperialist division of the world, Germany was anxious to exploit the maximum advantage from those remaining fragments of the earth" (John Moses 1989, 173), are far removed from historical reality. "Inflexible" (ibid., 175).

6   Gann and Duignan 1977, 138–139, and 142–143.

7   The work of Georg Fritz, *Bezirksamtmann* of Saipan, and Erich Schultz (-Ewerth), the last governor of German Samoa, deserves special mention (without wishing to detract from the efforts of others). Schultz continually applied for his contract in Samoa to be extended, "as I intend in any case to conclude the observations, made in the years during which I have been concerned with land and titles in Samoa, as well as during my official and private dealings with Samoans generally" (Schultz to Solf, Apia, 5 February 1907, NML: GPRS I.A. 25). On Fritz, Hardach 1990*b*, 77–78.

8   Interview with Henriette Godinet-Taylor, Apia, 13 January 1989; see also Jacques 1922, 14–15, and Nelson 1979, 64.

9   For Hahl, see Biskup 1968*b* (still the best study), and the English translation of his memoirs, ed. Peter Sack (Hahl 1980). For Solf, see Vietsch 1961. A new biography by Peter Hempenstall will appear soon.

10   Hempenstall 1978, vii.

11   Firth 1986. For an early critique of Firth's views, see Sack 1985; for Firth's defense, Firth 1985.

12   Typical of this one-dimensional view are statements such as the following: "the Germans had the same aims in Melanesia as in Africa. They sought to create a colony for the white man, who should be able to survey his docile black labourers from the comfort of a plantation bungalow. The New Guinean's part in the scheme was to do what he was told, . . . above all to sign a three-year labour contract. Over-

whelming force was to be used against any New Guineans who objected" (Firth, in Griffin, Nelson, and Firth 1979, 39). Similar utilitarian stereotypes can be found in John Moses 1989, 175.

13 See the deliberations of the government council, 4th period, 8th and 10th sessions of 24–28 August and 10 November 1911; *Amtsblatt für das Schutzgebiet Deutsch-Neuguinea* 3 (1911): 207 and 256–257.

14 There is much evidence to support this. For an English source, see, e.g., the statement by J. M. C. Forsayth, British consul to German New Guinea, to an Australian commission late in the war: "As a rule wherever there was land with coconuts on it, they [the European planters] were told that it belonged to the natives, and they [the colonial government] would not allow the natives to sell it." The Parliament of the Commonwealth of Australia, Parliamentary Papers, *British and Australian Trade in the South Pacific*, 1918, 66.

15 The people of the small Witu Islands, for example, made such a large profit from selling their local copra that in 1914 they were able to pay a 50 percent increase in taxes and could still afford to purchase a rowing and sailing cutter for their own use. Report by commander Zuckschwerdt, *Cormoran*, Rabaul, 10 February 1914, BAP: RKolA no. 2656.

16 Hahl, 6 July 1909, to the Secretary for Colonial Affairs, BAP: RKolA no. 5009.

17 Hundreds of local court files document this; see AAC: AA 1963/83, cf. p. 86.

18 Hahl 1980, 13. *Bezirksamtmann* Rudolf Karlowa, manuscript on "Rechtsverhältnisse der Eingeborenen" (law among the indigenous population), Friedrich-Wilhelmshafen, 1 June 1907, to the Government, AAC: AA 1963/83, Bun 212. What we know of indigenous views of German pacification supports this intepretation; see Foster 1987.

19 Frommund 1926, 54–55, and the lefthand illustration on 49.

20 The *Bezirksamtmann* of Rabaul, Stuebel, concluding peace, 16 February 1912, AAC: AA 1963/83 Bun 68.

21 At least nine death sentences were commuted. (See Table 7 in this volume.) On the so-called Madang Revolt, see Hiery 1993c; on end of public executions, UPNG: AL-101; for Fiji. *Annual Colonial Reports of Fiji.* From 1900 to 1902, they give the number of death sentences imposed (twelve in three years); from 1903 to 1910, only the number of actual executions. After 1910 no figures are given for death sentences or executions, but there is evidence that capital punishment continued.

22 See Hiery 1993b, 74–75. Other cases, ibid., passim.

23 Circular issued by Hahl, Rabaul, 9 January 1914, AAC: AA 1963/83, Bun 201.

24 "German New Guinea . . . belonged to that same colonial empire in which the first wars of Wilhelmine Germany were waged: 16,000 out of 70,000 Herero people survived the suppression of their uprising in German South West Africa; another 75,000 Africans died before guerilla resistance in German East Africa collapsed in 1907. The Germans did not go as far as this in New Guinea. . . . But the Germans had the same aims in Melanesia as in Africa" (Griffin, Nelson, and Firth 1979, 39).

25 Ibid.

26 Firth 1986, 34.

27 See the interesting remarks by Ingrid Moses 1977, 308, and Holzknecht 1979, 362.

28 Haber, Rabaul, 2 June 1914, "Verhältnisse im Inselgebiet" (conditions in the island territories), BAP: RKolA no. 2996. For the Sokeh uprising on Ponape, the only event in the "German" Pacific that could be called a colonial war, see Hempenstall

1978, Ehrlich 1978*a* and an indigenous view in *The Book of Luelen.* See also the comment by McKinney 1947, 139: "The Ponape incident was handled in a decisive way which in the long run probably meant more peace, and less oppression, than shilly-shally methods would have."

29   For the government school in Rabaul, see Barschdorff, "Überblick über das Fortbildungswesen im Schutzgebiet Deutsch Neuguinea" (Survey of advanced education in the Protectorate of German New Guinea), *Amtsblatt für das Schutzgebiet Deutsch-Neuguinea* 6 (1914): 110–112. Barschdorff, "Jahresbericht über die Tätigkeit der Regierungsschule in Namanula" (Annual report on the activities of the government school at Namanula), ibid., 134–137. Annual report of the government school in Saipan, ibid., 199–201. Government plan to develop the school system of German New Guinea and Micronesia, including a draft of school regulations: Hahl, Rabaul, 8 January 1914 to the Secretary of Colonial Affairs, BAP: RKolA no. 2756. Official approval by the Colonial Office, 23 June 1914, in ibid.

30   Circular by Governor Solf to all missions, 15 May 1901: from 1 July 1901 "the language of instruction in schools for natives . . . is Samoan," NML: GPRS XV.3. *Samoanisches Gouvernementsblatt* 3 (1900–1910): 29 (no. 9, 15 June 1901). On Europeans urged to attend the government school for Samoans to acquire a knowledge of Samoan, see note by Solf, 15 November 1909, NML: GPRS XV.3.

31   *Bekanntmachung* (official declaration) by the governor, 1 July 1900. *Samoanisches Gouvernementsblatt* 3 (1900–1910): 13 (no. 3, 9 August 1900).

32   *The Parliament of the Commonwealth of Australia. Parliamentary Papers. British and Australian Trade in the South Pacific* (1918), 115. In the courts, English was admissable until December 1912 (ibid.). Zieschank 1918, 58.

33   Meleisea 1987, 48.

34   See my portrait of Mata'afa's role in Hiery 1993*b*, 200–202; "at times abjectly submissive," says Meleisea 1987, 51.

35   "Ansprache des Gouverneurs an die samoanischen Häuptlinge am 14. August 1900 betr. die Selbstverwaltung der Samoaner" (address by the Governor to the Samoan chiefs concerning Samoan autonomous rule, 14 August 1900), *Samoanisches Gouvernementsblatt* 3 (1900–1910): 15–17 (no. 4, 5 September 1900).

36   See Meleisea 1980. On the lot of the Chinese, see John Moses 1973 and Firth 1977. Corporal punishment for the Chinese was abolished in December 1909, not out of any humane considerations, but because the German colonial administration did not want to risk jeopardizing further labor transports from China.

37   Meleisea 1987, passim.

38   Schultz, 10 July 1913, in the Government Council, *Samoanisches Gouvernementsblatt* 4 (1911–1913): 213 (no. 45, 19 July 1913).

39   On the efforts of a group of young, Western-educated Samoans around the government interpreter Taio Tolo, see Hiery 1993*b*, 205–208.

CHAPTER 1: THE FIRST WORLD WAR AS A TURNING POINT

1   Overlack 1992, 47–48.

2   Hiery 1989, 155.

3   Personal file of Erich Schultz in NML: GPRS I. A. 25; *DKZ*, no. 16, 18 April 1914.

4   Braisted 1971, 157, and Rivinius 1987, 132, and 134–135.

5   RCSL: Graeme Cantrell, Notes and Recollections.

6 BAP: RKolA no. 3133; among others: Buri, 12, 17, and 30 November 1903, to Chancellor Bülow.

7 Germany paid a total of 82,000 marks; cf. Treue 1976, 120–122. Thereafter the German colonial administration tried to accommodate the Australian firm in every possible way, because it had an almost panicky fear of further complaints; ibid., 140. There is a large file on the dispute with Burns, Philp & Co., BAP: RKolA nos. 2772–2777.

8 Record of negotiations between Walter Lucas (Burns Philp) and Dr. Hahl, 10 December 1912, and Hahl to Forsyth, 22 February 1913; Burns Philp Archives, Sydney, Box "Mandated Territory." Firth's statement (1986, 167) that it was only 5,000 hectares is incorrect. Australian traders were under the impression that they even received preferential treatment over the Germans. Director of the Buka Plantation & Trading Company Ltd., Constantine George Piggott, to the Australian commission of enquiry on the opportunities for Australian trade in the Pacific; *The Parliament of the Commonwealth of Australia. British and Australian Trade in the South Pacific 1918*, Appendix G, Evidence, 101.

9 German Colonial Secretary, p.p. Conze, Berlin, 8 September 1913, to the Governor in Rabaul, AAC: AA 1963/83, Bun 205.

10 Meaney 1976, 16 and 49.

11 Aldrich 1990, 99 and 223.

12 Ross 1964, 49.

13 Aldrich 1990, 275, and 130–131.

14 AAC: A 2219/1, vol. 3, Memorandum of 31 December 1915, 1.

15 Aldrich 1990, 262. Cf. ibid., 235, 274–275, and Ward 1978, 54.

16 Lissington 1972, 4.

17 Ross 1964, 280–281, Lissington 1972, 4, and McGibbon 1991, 161. In the same year, 1903, the Australian prime minister, Barton, also warned Federal Parliament about the threat posed by Russia's "mighty fleet," and a Labor member, Pearce (later minister for defense), similarly invoked the Russian threat; Meaney 1976, 50.

18 On this, Huttenback 1976, 279–316 ("White Australia"), and O'Connor 1968 ("White New Zealand").

19 Lissington 1972, 6, and Meaney, 1976, 52.

20 Offner 1988, 242.

21 McGibbon 1991, 163–164 and 238; Offner 1988, 242. According to Meaney 1976, 121, this measure was not implemented until the end of 1905.

22 McGibbon 1991, 162.

23 On the visit of the "Great White Fleet," Lissington 1972, 8; Meaney 1976, 163–175; Ward 1978, 63; Offner 1988, 234–235; and McGibbon 1991, 165–166.

24 Lissington 1972, 8.

25 "The Commonwealth Crisis" (as a book, *The Australian Crisis*); Meaney 1976, 159–162 and 188.

26 Meaney 1976, 208.

27 Lissington 1972, 13.

28 Ward 1978, 98. On William Morris Hughes, leader of the influential dock workers' union, cofounder of the New South Wales Labor Party, and member of the Federal Parliament from 1901, see esp. the comprehensive biography by Fitzhardinge 1979.

29 Meaney 1976, 188–189 (quotation, ibid.). Australians who were not of European

descent were a priori exempt from military service (ibid.). Originally, military service was to have been introduced for ten-year-olds (McGibbon 1991, 187). The young recruits were known as "the boy soldiers" (Eddy 1988, 155).

30 On Australia's armament after 1905, Meaney 1976, 261 and 277, and Ward 1978, 84.

31 McGibbon 1991, 234.

32 The *Philomel* was borrowed from the Royal Navy (Lissington 1972, 23; McGibbon 1991, 230). "Statement showing Population and Naval Military Expenditure of the UK, India, and Dominions," NZA: G 2, 21.

33 McGibbon 1991, 189 (cf. 187–188). Here, too, only whites were subject to military service (200).

34 The standard work on Australia's hegemonial ambitions in the Pacific is Thompson 1980; and for New Zealand, Ross 1964. A confidential memorandum from the Australian Prime Minister's Department, dating from late in 1920, sums up the history of Australia's and New Zealand's claims to hegemony in the Pacific and the attitudes of the most prominent politicians toward this in twenty-two pages, "The Spheres of Interest of Australia and New Zealand," AAC: A 2219, vol. 26.

35 Meaney 1976, 22. "The Spheres of Interest of Australia and New Zealand," 1920 9, AAC: A 2219, vol. 26. On the idea of a Monroe Doctrine for the Pacific, Ross 1964, 25; Grattan 1976, 80–82; Thompson 1980, passim; Offner 1988, 232; and Aldrich 1990, 228. On 5 December 1882, at the Intercolonial Convention in Sydney, white representatives of the six Australian colonies (New South Wales, Queensland, South Australia, Tasmania, Victoria, and Western Australia), New Zealand, and Fiji declared that any further acquisition of colonial possessions in the Pacific south of the equator "by any Foreign Power would be highly detrimental to the safety and well being of the British possessions in Australasia, and injurious to the interests of the Empire." "The Spheres of Interest of Australia and New Zealand," 1920, 7, AAC: A 2219, vol. 26. See also Grattan 1976, 82, and Thompson 1980, 84–85.

36 Gordon 1951, 126–127; and Ross 1964, 183–193 (here 190).

37 Ross 1964, 251–252, 261–262, and 266–268. Thirty-seven MPs voted for the annexation; four against.

38 Papua received government grants totaling £ 20,000 annually; Ward 1978, 54 and 53.

39 Overlack 1992, 40. The fear that a foreign power might seize Australia's gold appears frequently in public opinion; cf. Lissington 1972, 14. Australia's wealth was not imaginary. Before 1914 its population enjoyed the highest living standard in the British Empire; Eddy 1988, 156, and Meaney 1976, 188.

40 Figures are taken from, and calculated according to, material in *Annual Reports for Papua,* esp. 1907, 132; 1912, 152; and 1916–1917, 25. In 1906, gold accounted for 72.9 percent by value of all Papuan exports; calculated according to figures in ibid. From this year, considerable quantities of copper were also mined. Between 1888–1889 and 1910–1911 a total of 322,537 ounces of gold, valued at £1,166,947, was mined (*Annual Report for Papua,* 1911, 22). A comparison between these and the official export figures suggests that a considerable amount of gold disappeared via unofficial channels. Australia's aim of maximizing yields in Papua with a minimum of investment is clearly expressed in an internal paper by the responsible official, on the instructions of the minister for external affairs: Memorandum "Pacific Islands" by Atlee Hunt, 1904, 15, AAC: A 1108, 61. On the priority given to strategic interests in New Zealand, Ross 1964, 291–292.

41 *The British Australian* (London), 26 December 1901, 2272. . . . "is but the first step in a policy of expansion that is forced upon Australia by circumstances."

42 On Australia's refusal to accept potential costs, Barclay 1976, 45 (New Hebrides); on Australian–New Zealand rivalry: "The Spheres of Interest of Australia and New Zealand," 1920, esp. 11–12 and 20–21, AAC: A 2219, vol. 26. (Cf. Thompson 1980, 164–165.) On the quarrel about Tonga and the New Hebrides, AAC: A 2219–7 and A 1108, vol. 61 (Memorandum, Earl of Onslow, 11 August 1902). See also Thompson 1980, passim. On Australia's administrative incompetence, "The Spheres of Interest," 1920, 8: Report of the British "Royal Commission to inquire into the working of the Western Pacific Orders-in-Council," 1883: Australia is "quite unfit to be charged with the interests of the indigenous races." Memorandum, Atlee Hunt, 1904, 20, AAC: A 1108, 61. On New Zealand's administrative incompetence, Ross 1964, 283. On New Zealand's administrative problems in the Cook Islands, ibid., 303. The most recent work on the colonial history of the Cook Islands is entitled, characteristically enough, *Years of the Pooh-Bah* (referring to the Lord-High-Everything-Else, a character in the comic operetta *The Mikado* [1885] by Gilbert and Sullivan); see Scott 1991.

43 Offner 1988, 248.

44 "The Spheres of Interest of Australia and New Zealand," 1920, esp. 19, AAC: A 2219, vol. 26. On New Zealand's interest in Polynesia and the New Hebrides, McGibbon 1991, 234–235 (Prime Minister Massey's plans dating from 1913–1914); for Rapa and French Polynesia, Governor Liverpool, Wellington, 4 March 1914, confidential, to Harcourt on conveying New Zealand's wishes: "The Government of New Zealand desires that the Imperial Government should always bear in mind the desire of New Zealand"; NZA: G 26/6; for Rapa, see also NZA: G 48, R 23 (correspondence between the New Zealand government and the Colonial Office, 1912). On Australia's drive westward (Dutch East Indies), Meaney 1976, 205 (Deakin's last major speech in the Federal Parliament, 25 November 1910), and AAC: A 981–Ng 12 (Prime Minister Barton's plans). See also Thompson 1980, 197ff.

45 Late in 1909, in a newspaper interview, a former prime minister of New Zealand, Robert Stout, described Samoa, Tonga, and Fiji as New Zealand's natural heritage; *Samoanische Zeitung,* 1 January 1910, "Deutschland und Neuseeland." (The interview was originally given to William Stead and his *Review of Reviews.*) Three years later, in a speech in Auckland, the incumbent prime minister, Massey, publicly looked forward to the time "when it would be their duty to keep the British flag flying from one end of the Pacific to the other," *New Zealand Times* (Wellington), 27 November 1912.

46 *Brisbane Daily Mail* of 12 November 1903, "Annexing New Guinea": "To make it [German New Guinea] part of the [Australian] Commonwealth might involve even a European war." On the effectiveness of these campaigns, Burry 1909, 8–9.

47 Aldrich 1990, 131 (for its behavior in the New Hebrides). On the influence of Burns Philp on the continuous press campaign against Germany in the Pacific, see reports by the German consul-general in BAP: RKolA no. 3133.

48 Lissington 1972, 12; Meaney 1976, 2, 146–147 and 258; and Offner 1988, 242.

49 Allen had published on both topics; Ross 1964, 290, and Lissington 1972, 9, 11, and 20. On Pearce, Meaney 1976, 154. James Allen came from South Australia, Pearce from Western Australia.

50 McGibbon 1991, 208–209 and 239–243.

51 Allen's notes on his conversation with the Colonial Secretary, Lewis Harcourt, Colonial Office, 12 March 1913, NZA: Personal Papers, Acc. 556 (Allen), 4. Colonial Secretary, confidential, to the Governor of New Zealand, 5 May 1913, NZA: G 48, R 23; Allen, London, 7 April 1913, to Harcourt, ibid.

52 Secret minutes of the meeting between Allen and Churchill on 11 April 1913 and secret memorandum by the British Admiralty of April 1913, "Naval Position of New Zealand," NZA: G 48, box 18: N/17. See also *New Zealand Times,* 29 March 1913, "Colonial Opinion." In London, Allen is reported to have said: "We do not fear a European force. That is the crux of the matter." NZA: Personal Papers, Acc. 556 (Allen), 14.

53 Wagner 1990, 233–251; Peattie 1988, 1–15; and now Frei 1991.

54 Moos 1974, 279–280; Peattie 1988, 23–26 and 31–33; Hardach 1990*a*, 7, 22–25, and 1990*b*, 142–143, 153–157; and Wagner 1990, 248. Figures are from the official annual report, *Jahresberichte über die Entwicklung,* 1912–1913.

55 Diary of Governor Schultz, entries of 20 and 21 August 1914, NZA: G 21/4. The German colonial office marked a telegram received on 4 August 1914 from Apia, asking for news, "no communication." "It can be assumed that the Governor is now informed about the situation." BAP: RKolA no. 2624.

56 Report from the postal agent in Angaur, Shanghai, 22 December 1914, to the Regional Postal Directorate in Bremen, PAA: A. *Der Weltkrieg* no. 13, vol. 12. The head of the neighboring station on Palau did not have a deciphering code either; ibid.

57 Hiery 1989, 155.

58 "The cordiality that exists cannot be too much emphasised. The German is glad to meet us; we are glad to meet him." Statement by the planter S. Garrick in the *Sydney Daily Telegraph,* 23 February 1912 ("German and Briton. Friendly Relations in Samoa"); when New Zealand invaded, British settlers gave Admiral Patey a petition in favor of the Germans in Samoa; Field 1984, 9.

59 On Haber's lack of military training: the Commander of the Australian Expeditionary Force, after negotiating the treaty of surrender with the acting German governor, Rabaul, 26 December 1914, to the German Ministry of Defence, AWM: 33/10. On the condition of German troops: Report by the Acting Governor, Haber, *DKB* 26 (1915), 130–145, esp. 133–135. Klewitz: Report on the activity of the armed power in German New Guinea in the period from 5 August to 21 September 1914, PAA: A. *Der Weltkrieg* no. 13, vol. 14. On the inadequacy of Samoa's military equipment, Hiery 1989, 155.

60 Colonial Secretary Joseph Chamberlain to Prime Minister Salisbury, 18 September 1899. Garvin 1934, 334–335. Boyd's assertion (1968, 148) that the conquest of Samoa had little to do with New Zealand's imperialistic ambitions is completely untenable.

61 McGibbon 1991, 235 and 242–243.

62 Diary of the leader of the Expeditionary Forces, Colonel Holmes, entry of 22 August 1914, AWM: 33/2. Holmes, Rabaul, 19 September (and a postscript of 21 September) 1914 to Chief of General Staff, AWM: 33/10.

63 Colonel Holmes, 27 August 1914, from Townsville, to Colonel Legge, Chief of General Staff, AWM: 33/10. Holmes, 6 September 1914 to the Commander of the Australian squadron, ibid. Report by Holmes, 9 September 1914 to Legge, ibid. Holmes, Rabaul, 14 September 1914 to Chief of General Staff, Melbourne, and 27 October 1914 to the Minister of Defence in Melbourne ("men with rather unfavor-

able reputations, men whom I am informed have Gaol records"), ibid. Holmes, Rabaul, 13 November 1914 to the Minister of Defence ("a leaven of men of evil reputation"), MLS: MSS 15, Box 1. Australia's official war history refers to "those who, drifting without moorings in the ebb and flow of city life" (Mackenzie 1927, 26). According to a report by the New Guinea official Völkl, Rabaul, 20 January 1915, Australian convicts had enlisted as soldiers on the strength of "an official promise that the time spent on the expedition would be set against their sentences," BAP: RKolA no. 2613.

64   Report by William Holmes to Colonel Legge, 9 September 1914, AWM: 33/10. Admiral Patey, 10 September 1914, to the Secretary of the Naval Board, AAM: MP 1049/1–14/0486. Reminiscences of Colonel William Holmes' son, Basil, who took part in the expedition as a lieutenant, AWM: PR 84/304. See also Mackenzie 1927, 31.

65   Holmes, 9 September 1914, to Colonel Legge, AWM: 33/10.

66   According to a note in the papers of Lieutenant Bowen, it could have been as many as 4,010. AWM: 3 DRL 7734; see also Mackenzie 1927.

67   Mackenzie 1927, 38, and esp. Jose 1987, 11–14. German version: Haber, *DKB* 26 (1915), 132.

68   The official Australian versions in Mackenzie 1927, 73–74, and Jose 1987, 81–91. According to German accounts, two Australians were shot dead by their own soldiers in a confused engagement. Reports by participants: von Sigritz, 19 January 1915, on board the *Sonoma,* and Lieutenant in the Reserves E. Kempf, on board the *Sonoma,* 22 January 1915, PAA: A. *Der Weltkrieg* no. 13, vol. 14. Haber, Sydney, 15 December 1914, to the American consul-general, AAC: A 4–NG 7. "Shooting going on all around us. Not knowing whether it was the enemy or our own men. Not knowing the German uniform and not knowing they had natives fighting for them. We were in danger of shooting our own men or being mistaken for the enemy" (an Australian participant, Kabakaul, 11 September 1914, AWM: PR 89/126). Australian losses increased considerably when one of Australia's two submarines, AE 1, disappeared on 14 September 1914 and was never found. The fate of the 3 officers and 32 crew members on board has never been cleared up; see Jose 1987, 97–98. According to statements by the crew of the torpedo boat *Paramatta,* it collided with the submarine and pulled it down. UPNG: AL-101/1, reminiscences of J. R. Fox.

69   The Melanesian soldiers, who had fired from the cover of coconut palms, had caused "a good deal of trouble." Holmes, *Berrima,* 13 September 1914, to the Chief of General Staff, Melbourne, AWM: 33/10. Most of all, Holmes feared a protracted bush war. Holmes, Rabaul, 26 December 1914, to the Ministry of Defence, AWM: 33/10.

70   According to Solf, Haber had displayed "a special skill in gaining important concessions under most difficult circumstances" as early as the Paris negotiations about Morocco. Solf, 8 May 1915, to the acting Chief of the Army General Staff, BAP: RKolA no. 2638. On Haber's view of the negotiations leading to the German surrender, see Haber 1932, 135–136.

71   The treaty of surrender is printed in Mackenzie 1927, 82–85. Haber, together with the majority of the German New Guinea officials, arrived in Berlin on the night of 4 March 1915. From there, many went on to the front. *DKB* 26 (1915), 252–253 (list of the names of those who returned) and 339.

72 Keyßer 1966, 117–120. For Detzner's own account see Detzner 1921. The best historical account of this marginal episode in the war in New Guinea is Biskup 1968a.

73 Secret telegram from the Colonial Secretary to the Australian government, 18 and 19 August 1914, AAC: CP 78/23–14/89/10–11. The colonial secretary urged the Australian government to occupy Nauru, Angaur, and Feys soon. They were important, he explained, because of their rich phospate deposits.

74 Jose 1987, 106, and Field 1984, 14–15. In 1910, Rear Admiral Gühler had enthused that the Samoan culture was superior to that of all nations except Germany, Scandinavia, and "perhaps" England. NML: GPRS XIV.2, vol. 3.

75 From November 1910 at the latest, Japan was regarded as the United States's most likely opponent in the Pacific; a naval plan to be used in the event of war with Japan was ready in 1914. Braisted 1971, 32, 255, and 289.

76 In 1899 Blanco had presented Wilhelm II with his governor's rod; on him, Hardach 1990b, 42–43.

77 Telegram from the German envoy in Stockholm, 2 October 1914, to the German Foreign Office, with the news from Manila (of 28 September 1914) via Washington, and Solf, 2 October 1914 to Zimmermann, PAA: A. *Der Weltkrieg* no. 13, vol. 3; Chief of the German naval staff, 21 October 1914, to the Secretary of State in the German Foreign Office, ibid., vol. 4; Zimmermann, 28 October 1914, via Stockholm and the embassy in Washington, to the German consul in Manila, ibid., vol. 5.

78 Report by the *Stationsleiter* (head of the station), Merz, 7 November 1914, to the German Colonial Office, BAP: RKolA no. 2631.

79 Government Secretary Hans Arbinger, San Francisco, 15 April 1915, to the German Colonial Office, BAP: RKolA no. 2622; see also Kohl-Larsen (government doctor on Yap) 1927, 140.

80 File in AAC: A 981 Marshalls 2, and AWM: 33/10. For the abortive Australian expedition, Fitzhardinge 1970, 254.

81 Sawade in *DKZ* 1916: 126, and the diary of Hanssen, head of the Deutsche Handels- u. Plantagengesellschaft (German Trading and Plantation Company), entry dated 16 February 1915, NZA: G 49/10. On the Japanese squadron's visit to Rabaul at the end of 1914, see Holmes, 29 December 1914, to the Minister of Defence in Melbourne, AWM: 33/10.

82 AAM: MP 1049/1–18/0345.

83 The leaders of the Australian government were informed by a secret cable, in cipher, from the Colonial Secretary, 1 February 1917, AAC: A 981, Marshall 2. For information passed to New Zealand: see Walter Long, secret, 2 March 1917, to Governor General Liverpool, NZA: G 2/35. See also Thompson 1980, 207–208, and Frei 1991, 97–98.

84 See the report by Haber in *DKB* 26 (1915), 139. According to this report, several indigenous people were killed or wounded, but the exact number could not be established.

85 Criminal case brought against Lawetat and Malai, of the Panutibun people, in Megiar-Ragetta, for incitement to insurrection; AAC: AA 1963/83, Bun 221. On the lead-up to the exile, Hempenstall 1978, 187–189, and now Hiery 1993c.

86 Statement by Song from Sarang to *Bezirksamtmann* (district administrator) Dr. Gebhard, 10 September 1914, and statement by the planter Kurt Stiller, Sarang, 10 September 1914; letter from the Rhenish Mission, Bongu, 17 September 1914, AAC: AA 1963/83, Bun 221.

87 Mariana Islands: report by the government doctor, Fritz Salecker, San Francisco, 1 February 1915, BAP: RKolA no. 2622 (summary also printed in *DKB* 26 [1915], 251). On the Marianas, see Hardach 1990*b*; on Samoa, Hiery 1992*a*, 55 and 73.

88 Undated extract from the 1914 plantation report of the Hamburg-Südsee AG, BAP: RKolA no. 2612; report by the District Judge Weber, 17 March 1915, BAP: RKolA no. 2996. Australian sources that claim to be from original German sources have to be examined carefully, though. The diary of the official Behr recounts the beginning of the invasion as "Torpedoboote eingelaufen und wieder ausgelaufen" (torpedo boats entered and left again). The Australian intelligence, unable to decipher the German script, translated it as "native carriers [misreading 'torpedo' for 'träger'] and the cook [misreading 'boote'] who had returned to Rabaul have run away" (MLS:MSS 15, Box 1).

89 Holmes, 26 and 27 December 1914, to the Ministry of Defence in Melbourne, AWM: 33/8 and 33/10; diary entry of 26–29 October 1914, AWM: 33/33–1. In Australian Papua, too, the indigenous population set European plantations afire on news of the outbreak of war in Europe; "Plantations Burned by Natives" and "Bush Fires," *Papuan Times*, 4 and 18 November 1914.

90 Head of Eitape station, Schmaus, 13 November 1914 to the German Colonial Office, BAP: RKolA no. 2612. Schmaus, Hollandia, 14 December 1914, on the occupation of Eitape by Australian troops, BAP: RPA, GA 5091; AKM: C 39, Gayabachronik, 16. The mission plantations were also affected: P. Vormann, St. Anna, 11 October 1914, to the Superior of the Steyl Mission, Noser Library, Madang.

91 Report by Krümling, San Francisco, 24 July 1915, BAP: RKolA no. 2631.

92 The estimates go as high as "about 200 niggers killed," Sergeant Hocking, Rabaul, 3 October 1914, AWM: 3 DRL 2985. The Melanesians who fell into Australian hands during the fight were bayoneted; "the niggers bayoneted," Kenny diary, MLS: MSS 930, 73. Days after the battle, seriously wounded Melanesians were still lying in the bush without any aid. When they were finally picked up and taken to hospitals reserved for the indigenous population, many already had maggots in their wounds; O'Hare diary, MLS: MSS 2935, 12 September 1914 entry.

93 Report by Wuchert, captain in the reserves and owner of a plantation in Pondo, German New Guinea, on the defense of the radio station Bitapaka on 11 September 1914, PAA: A. *Der Weltkrieg* no. 13, vol. 15.

94 AWM: 1 DRL 351, 54; Holmes, Rabaul, 26 December 1914 to the Ministry of Defence, AWM: 33/10; AWM: PR 84/304.

95 Head of Eitape station, Schmaus, Hollandia, 14 December 1914, to the German Colonial Office, BAP: RPA, GA 5091.

96 On unrest among the indigenous population: in Jaluit (on rumors from Nauru, the local people there hastily left the European settlement; report by Dr. Karl Kopp, 20 February 1915, in BAP: RKolA no. 2631); in Solomons (here unrest dissipated quickly, and in Buka the local people even began to build a new road across the island; Station Head Doellinger, Bad Meinberg, 19 April 1915, BAP: RKolA no. 2613). On calmness of the local population, see memorandum by Radlauer in AHM; report by District Commissioner Stuebel, 22 January 1915, on the situation in the district of Käwieng, BAP: RKolA no. 2612.

97 On contact between the Duala in Cameroon and the attacking French, most recently, Digre 1990, 23.

98 AAC: AA 1963/83, Buns 138 and 205. By the outbreak of war, 301,550 marks had been collected for 1914. In the confusion of the Australian occupation, the head-tax from New Hanover (11,000 marks), which had been collected last, could not be properly entered in the books (ibid.). For warnings by the local population: in Morobe: medical assistant and postal agent, Josef Ziegler, Munich, 1 August 1915, to the German Post Office, BAP: RPA, GA 5091; in Yap: report by R. Scholz, Cuxhaven, 21 February 1916, BAP: RKolA no. 2623.

99 Report by the government doctor, Dr. Born, Wilhelmshafen, 19 June 1915, BAP: RKolA no. 2622. See also Brauer 1917, 37.

100 Brewster 1922, 254. The British administration put Sailose into a mental hospital.

101 Baker 1988, 214–222; Barber 1989, 109–110; King 1983, 165–166; and esp. Binney, Chaplin, and Wallace 1979, esp. 82–121. In British Africa, too, a number of peoples hoped for a German victory. Digre 1990, 83–85.

102 Aldrich 1990, 191 and 278.

103 Hubert Murray memorandum, 13 December 1915, ANL: MS 1100, 4/52–366. A memorial to the Papuans killed in the war still stands, totally ignored, in a side street of Port Moresby.

104 Memorandum no. 7/525 from the Military Secretary of Samoa Smith, 28 February 1916, to Administrator Logan, NZA: WA 210/3/10. The whole file is there and in NZA: AD 1/29/120.

105 L. Toleafoa, "Off to the Front," NZA: WA 210/3/2.

106 War diaries of the Rarotongan Detachment in NZA: WA 203/1. Personal files in the Department of Defence, Wellington. Soldiers reporting their experiences in the *Samoa Times*, no. 8, 23 February 1918, and no. 10, 9 March 1918. Samoans of German descent also attempted to take an active part in the war on Germany's side. In American Samoa, the High Court sentenced a man of mixed German-Samoan descent to prison with hard labor for the duration of the war because of "seditious and treasonable language." He is said to have stated that if Germany lost the war he would blow up Pago Pago's power plant. The accused was not given a hearing. American Governor Poyer, 14 July 1917, to the Secretary of the Navy, NARA: RG 80, file 3931, box 33.

107 The Governor of Guam, Roy C. Smith, 27 April 1917, to the Secretary of State for the Navy, NARA: RG 80, box 480 A. One year after China entered the war, the Chinese were sent home to Shantung; Governor William W. Gilmer, 27 February 1919 to Secretary of State for the Navy, Josephus Daniels, ibid., box 483.

108 Judge Advocate General, Department of the Navy, Washington, 21 June 1917, to the Chief of Naval Operations, NARA: RG 80, box 2550: 28573–42:90. Governor Roy C. Smith, Guam, 27 April 1917, to the Secretary of State for the Navy, ibid., 9351–1395: 78.

109 "When these regulations were framed new Guineamen prisoners of war were not in contemplation. Their needs other than subsistence must be few and small." Secretary of the Navy, Washington, 10 October 1917, to the Commandant of the Naval Station, Guam, NARA: RG 80, box 2550: 28573–42:109.

110 *Annual Report of the Governor of Guam* 1917–1918: 32.

111 *Guam News Letter,* January 1919, 2, "New Guinea Prisoners of War Leave," *Annual Report of the Governor of Guam* 1918–1919: 31. Australian Administrator Johnston, Rabaul, 28 January 1919, to the Ministry of Defence, AWM: 33/56.

112 The attacks began with violent polemics in the press. In a memorandum to the

Ministry of Defence, the attorney general, William Morris Hughes (later prime minister), judged that the conditions of surrender were "unduly advantageous to the enemy." Holmes had not possessed the right, he explained, to promise the German officials repatriation to Germany. Accordingly, these arrangements were "void and may be disregarded"; Hughes memorandum, 21 September 1914, AAC: A 4– NG 7. Against the terms of the surrender, the Australian federal government tried to detain the German colonial officials in Australia. British intervention eventually ensured that the agreement was respected; cable from the Colonial Secretary, London, 18 November 1914, ibid. On 3 December 1914, Senator Pearce (soon to become minister of defense) summed up the Australian government's dissatisfaction with the treaty of surrender in the Senate; Hansard 4181. Holmes' letter of justification, 26 December 1914, to the Ministry of Defence, AWM: 33/10; Reminiscences of his son, Basil, AWM: PR 84/304.

113 Holmes, Rabaul, 14 September 1914, to Chief of General Staff, MLS: MSS 15, Box 1. "The British Missionaries are generally invaluable sources for Intelligence;" Intelligence Report Staff Captain Travers, 10 September 1914, ibid., Box 2. Reports by Haber, Sydney, 30 October 1914, *DKB* 26 (1915), 139; Wuchert, captain of the reserves, PAA: A. *Der Weltkrieg* no. 13, vol. 15, and Weber, the District Judge, 17 March 1915, BAP: RKolA no. 2996. Statement by participants in the Cox Affair, plantation owner Hermann Hornung and Otto Paul, 25 and 26 November 1914, AAC: A 1–25/8405. On Samoa, Hiery 1992a, 61. New Zealand troops en route to Samoa stopped in Fiji and took Samoan pupils of British Protestant missions on board as spies.

114 Holmes, Rabaul, 14 September 1914, to Chief of General Staff, Melbourne, AWM: 33/10. Charles S. Manning, Assistant Judge Advocate General, Rabaul, 28 November 1914, to Administrator Holmes, AAC: A 1–25/8405.

115 Holmes, Rabaul, 30 November 1914, to the Australian Minister for Defence, AAC: A 1–25/8405.

116 Holmes order, 28 November 1914, AAC: A 1–25/8405. "The way these Men took it not one squealed"—comment by an eyewitness, J. R. Fox, UPNG: AL-101/1. Further eyewitness accounts by O'Hare, 73–74, MLS: MSS 2935; Principal Medical Officer Maguire, 24 December 1915 to the Minister for Defence, AAC: A 1–25/8405; and Beardsdore, 24 November 1952, Sydney, to Holmes' son-in-law, Travers, AWM: PR 84/202.

117 Holmes order, 4 December 1914, ibid. Holmes, 11 December 1914 to the Ministry of Defence, AWM: 33/10. At the end of the war, the Belgian, like the Germans, was expropriated. The responsible Australian official argued that, given the Belgian's misdemeanors, it would be inappropriate to take his citizenship into consideration; Lucas, 3 July 1924, confidential, to the Australian Minister for Home and Territories McLaren, AAC: A 1–25/8405.

118 Chapter 14, § 450.

119 Charles S. Manning, Assistant Judge Advocate General, Rabaul, 28 November 1914, to the Administrator, AAC: A 1–25/8405.

120 Governor General of Australia, 20 January 1915, confidential, from Melbourne to the Colonial Secretary Harcourt, ANL: MS 696/652.

121 The British consul of Rabaul had withdrawn from the execution of the order in disgust. In reply to international protests, the Australian government produced a report by a retired professor of law at the University of Sydney saying that the pro-

ceedings "conformed to the dictates of justice and humanity"; Cobbett memorandum, 21 January 1916, AAC: A 1–25/8405.

122 Munro Ferguson, 13 May 1915, to Colonial Secretary Harcourt, personally, ANL: MS 696/687–8.

123 Not even British criticism of the Cox Affair prevented Australians from continuing to use corporal punishment. In the South Australian internment camp on Torrens Island, two POWs were tied to trees and whipped in 1915. Another prisoner was bayoneted in the buttocks. Because of strict censorship, these incidents remained largely unknown. Australian Governor General, 25 October 1915, confidential, to the Colonial Secretary, ANL: MS 696/1662. See also Fischer 1989, 196–198.

124 In 1917 the Marist mission received a loan of £1,500 from the Australian Military Administration; AAC: AA 1963/83, Bun 245: "Part 1917 Correspondence."

125 The emotional force of the Germanophobia that erupted in Australia and New Zealand at the beginning of the First World War is astonishing. As yet, no detailed investigation and explanation of this phenomenon exists; but see Fischer 1989, passim.

126 Confidential instruction by Lieutenant Colonel Fred W. Toll, Acting Administrator, 7 March 1915, AWM: 33/12-3. Memorandum by Toll, 30 July 1915, for the Ministry of Defence, AAM: MP 367–404/11/163.

127 Pethebridge, Report no. A 95, Rabaul, 11 August 1915, AAM: MP 367–404/11/163; Pethebridge, Report no. A 99, Rabaul, 28 August 1915, AAC: CP 78/23–14/89/10–1; Report by Lieutenant Preston, 5 November 1915, to Pethebridge, AWM: 33/12-1. Pethebridge, 19 October 1915, to the Australian Governor General: "while I was away an imaginary scare was created. . . . There was absolutely no foundation for the idea that the Germans or Natives had the best idea of rising." AAC: CP 78/34/1–6.

128 Memorandum by Pethebridge, Rabaul, 29 August 1915, to the Commander of the Australian Second Military District, AAM: MP 367, no. 404/11/163. The Germans deported to Australia as POWs by the Administrator included three missionaries from the Neuendettelsauer Missionary Society (Wilhelm Flierl, Hans Raum, and Karl Steck). They had aided the fugitive Captain Detzner, or refused to take the oath of neutrality. The head of the station at Morobe, Hans Klink, was detained because the local administration there, contrary to the conditions of surrender, had opposed the Australian action. The spectacular cases included the temporary detention of the Catholic priests Johann Dicks, Franz Vormann, and Richard Niedurney. Pethebridge could get rid of Dicks, the curate general of Rabaul, only because the (French) bishop secretly supported the Administrator's action. Dicks was considered too "pro-German" (Pethebridge memorandum, 29 August 1915, ibid.). Vormann was interned for ignoring the censorship regulations; Niedurney, because he submitted two indigenous women to corporal punishment; AAC: A 3932 — SC 109. Pethebridge, 17 April 1917, to the Ministry of Defence (Niedurney and Vormann), AWM: 33/4.

129 "Report on Deportations at Nauru" by the Australian Minister for the Navy, Melbourne, 3 December 1917, AAM: MP 367, no. 404/11/24.

130 Report by the postal agent, Angaur, Shanghai, 22 December 1914, BAP: RKolA no. 2622.

131 Marshall Islands: report by the government doctor, Karl Kopp, Meissen, 20 February 1915, BAP: RKolA no. 2631. Truk: Capuchin Mission, Truk, 14 October 1914, to Lorenz, AKM: no number. Ponape: AKM, 59, 124, and BAP: RKolA no. 2622.

132 Station official, Krümling, San Francisco, 24 July 1915, BAP: RKolA no. 2631.

133 Capuchin Mission, Truk, 16 October 1914, to the Superior, AKM: no number. See also Kohl-Larsen 1927, 142. On the courteous behavior of the Japanese toward the Germans, see also Burdick and Moessner 1984, 7–8.

134 Report by the government doctor, Karl Kopp, 20 February 1915, BAP: RKolA no. 2631; F. Scholz (from Yap), Cuxhaven, 21 February 1916, BAP: RKolA no. 2623; copy of the oath signed by Dr. Walter Born, BAP: RKolA no. 2622. Reminiscences of Aloysia Fettig, a Capuchin nun, Catholic Mission, Koror, Palau.

135 Report by Kopp, 20 February 1915, BAP: RKolA no. 2631, and Kohl-Larsen 1927, 156. Some of the Germans spent their relatively short stay in Japan with the geishas, "under Japanese guidance," ibid., 158. The Germans in the Pacific as civilians escaped the fate of the Germans in Tsingtao, who became Japanese POWs. On this, see Burdick and Moessner 1984.

136 Reminiscences of Aloysia Fettig, Catholic Mission, Koror, Palau. Statement by Father Wunibald Fechter to the American Consul General in Yokohama, 11 February 1916, NARA: RG 84, B 162: 1916–711.5, Despatch no. 323. Father Gallus Lehmann (Saipan), Shanghai, 22 June 1916, to the German Consul General, BAP: RKolA no. 2623.

137 On the Liebenzell missionaries, BAP: RKolA no. 2623.

138 Demandt diary, BAK; BAP: RKolA no. 2624.

139 Detailed material on this is in BAP: RKolA no. 2629. Information on conditions in Motuihi: statement, learned by heart, given by the ex-POW Rudolf Kafka (released because he was engaged to a New Zealand woman) to the German Consul in San Francisco, 17 June 1915, BAP: RKolA no. 2625. Undated letter, in cipher, by Fritz Mellert, a cadet from Alsace: he claimed that Dr. Schultz was treated "like a pig" (ibid.).

140 Exactly 296 at the end of May 1918, they included 270 Germans, 3 Russians [*sic!*], 1 Mexican, 1 Dutchman, and 1 Swiss [*sic!*]; report by judge Chapman on the treatment of POWs on Somes Island, 7 June 1918, NZA: G 26/9.

141 Report by judge Chapman, NZA: G 26/9.

142 Demandt diary, BAK; Hanssen diary, 24 December 1914, NZA: G 49/10.

143 Governor General of New Zealand, Wellington, 14 June 1918 to Colonel Logan, NZA: G 21/10. Hanssen diary, 26 January 1915, NZA: G 49/10.

144 Logan, reports no. 10, 11, and 12 (9 August, 2 September, and 2 October 1918), NZA: G 21/10.

CHAPTER 2: THE GERMAN SOUTH PACIFIC UNDER THE SHADOW OF WAR

1 In any conversation, white inhabitants of Papua would immediately start apologizing for the conditions prevailing there; Bassett 1969, 11. Governor Murray, Port Moresby, 15 October 1915 to the Australian Governor General, ANL: MS 696–6960. There are many admiring reports, written by the occupation troops, about the German colony of New Guinea. See among others, the diary of Warrant Officer Lance Balfour Penman, AWM: PR 82/171: "The Germans have evidently spent a lot of money in a wise manner" (ibid., 12).

2 On the behavior of the officers, see eyewitness reports in *Readings in New Guinea History* 1973, 206–207. Provost Marshal Captain L. B. Ravenscroft organized regular

raiding parties inside and outside Rabaul, using soldiers on duty; Administrator Pethebridge, 1 May 1916 and 24 November 1916, to the Ministry of Defence, AWM: 33/55–54. Immediately after the occupation in September 1914, Ravenscroft confiscated all the cash belonging to businesses and authorities and kept much of it for himself. From the post office in Herbertshöhe alone he took 16,000 marks. Captain T. R. Eather, Treasurer, Rabaul, 23 October 1916 to Petherbridge, ibid.

3   Lieutenant E. Carlile, commander of Herbertshöhe, 26 April 1915, to his brother in Australia, AWM: 1 DRL 188.

4   Acting Governor Haber, Berlin, 15 April 1915 to the Secretary of State in the German Colonial Office, BAP: RKolA no. 2613.

5   "There's nothing left to loot—unless we carried away sideboards and chests of drawers, and they are all of solid oak"; Carlile, 6 June 1915, from Rabaul, AWM: 1 DRL 188. There is a great deal of evidence, both Australian and German, from all areas of the protectorate, of looting and lack of discipline among the Australian troops. According to the General Report of the Rabaul Garrison, 137 Australian soldiers were court-martialed between 12 September and 31 December 1914 in Rabaul alone. Their punishments totaled 324 days of "field punishment" and 453 days "forfeited pay" (AWM: 33/36). General Report of Lt. Col. Russel Watson (commander of the expeditionary force after Holmes had been appointed Administrator), undated (early 1915), AWM: 33/6; collector of customs, Sydney, return showing values of goods other than luggage brought or sent to Sydney from Rabaul by or on behalf of Expeditionary Force, AAC: A 2–17/3836. See also Administrator Holmes, 27 October 1914, to the Minister of Defence in Melbourne, AWM: 33/10; report of Basil Holmes to the Administrator, 28 December 1914, about the occupation of Kieta, AWM: 33/3; and AWM: 3 DRL 2943. Diaries written by soldiers Mitchell (entry dated 19 September 1914—even drawers and cupboards were removed from the government building); Read (entry dated 18 September 1914: things that could not be stolen from the government building, such as book shelves, were smashed with rifle butts and bayonets in a fit of vandalism; 1 October 1914: the bell of the mission church in Siar was taken to Sydney); and O'Hare, all in MLS. Report by the captain of the *Manila* (Norddeutscher Lloyd), August Roscher, 13 December 1914 from Amboina (Dutch New Guinea) to the German Colonial Office, BAP: RKolA no. 2612; station leader of Kieta, Doellinger, Bad Meinberg, 19 April 1915, to the German Colonial Office, BAP: RKolA no. 2613.

6   Diary of Private Scheidel, AWM: 3 DRL 2268, esp. entries dated 14 October, 26 October, 1 November, and 14 November 1914. 1914–1915. The Parliament of the Commonwealth of Australia. Rabaul: Alleged misuse of Red Cross Gifts, and Looting by military officers and Privates. Report on, by Hon. W. M. Hughes, Attorney General [Melbourne, 22 July 1915], 7. Administrator Holmes, 27 October 1914, to the Ministry of Defence in Melbourne, AWM: 33/10.

7   On 30 May 1915, ANL: MS 696/23. "A disagreeable scandal," the Governor-General personally, 5 May 1915, to the Colonial Secretary Harcourt, ANL: MS 696/686. 1914–1915. The Parliament of the Commonwealth of Australia. Rabaul: Alleged misuse of Red Cross Gifts, and Looting by military officers and Privates. Report on, by Hon. W. M. Hughes, Attorney General [Melbourne, 22 July 1915]; Prime Minister Hughes, Melbourne, 12 October 1916, to the Governor-General, to be passed on to the Colonial Secretary; AAC: A 2–1917/3836. Debates in the Australian

House of Representatives on 22–23 April, 7, 12, and 27 May 1915, in the Senate on 7 May 1915. Further documents in AAM: MP 367/1/0 – 404/11/298.

8 Report by Administrator Pethebridge, no. A/6, Rabaul, 19 February 1915, to the Ministry of Defence, AWM: 33/12–10.

9 Diary of the Warrant Officer Lance Balfour Penman, left Sydney 20 November 1915, AWM: PR 82/171.

10 But see District Order no. 33, 25 May 1918, in AAC: AA 1963/83, Bun 237. A private in Matupi had told his corporal that if no beer was provided he could look for another guard.

11 Administrator Pethebridge, 15 April and 26 April 1916, from Rabaul to the Ministry of Defence, AWM: 33/54. Lieutenant Carlile, 6 June and 27 June 1915, from Rabaul, AWM: 1 DRL 188.

12 Administrator Pethebridge, 6 November 1915 to the Ministry of Defence in Melbourne, AWM: 33/12-1. One of the "crooks" was Pethebridge's deputy, Lieutenant Mackenzie, author of the official Australian War History of Rabaul. In 1936 he was sentenced to four years' imprisonment for falsification of documents in connection with his attempt to purchase some of the confiscated German plantations; Nelson and Piggott 1987, xxxii.

13 "Enormous quantities of precious metal," report by Haber after traveling through the lower Waria valley, from 22 July to 11 August 1914, to the German Colonial Office, BAP: RKolA no. 2996. Haber found platinum as well as gold. The government of German New Guinea had been aware of the gold deposits for years but had banned mining in the area. Unlike in Papua, the colonial administration had deliberately not granted any privileged mining rights for minerals and oil (which had also been discovered), because it feared an uncontrolled influx of gold miners and prospectors. This, the goverment believed, would have endangered its primary aim of developing the colony's agriculture. Report by Fiebig, junior mining official, Champagne, 25 July 1915, to the German Colonial Office, BAP: RKolA no. 2358.

14 A. L. Joubert, "Gold in New Guinea," *Rabaul Record*, no. 3, 1 May 1916, 6–8.

15 Townsend 1968, 180–182.

16 Letter from Thurnwald, 9 March 1915, from Madang, *DKB* 26 (1915), 304/05; a copy of his diary about the Sepik is in UPNG: AL-125. Holmes, 11 December 1914, to the Ministry of Defence, AWM: 33/10. On Thurnwald, see Melk-Koch 1989.

17 "Needless to say in happy ignorance that the law of the land forbade us doing so," diary of Lt. Commander Gerald Ashby Hill, 111–114, here 110, AWM: 1 DRL 351. See also Thomas J. Denhan: "On the Sepik (Kaiserin Augusta) River. Resources of the River," *Rabaul Record*, no. 9, 1 November 1916, 9. After a heated debate in Germany, birds of paradise, crowned pigeons, and cassowaries were declared protected species on 1 November 1913. Protection was for a limited period (until 15 May 1915), during which time a German ornithologist was to study the behavior of the birds and prepare a scientific report on whether general protection was necessary or not. The white heron was not officially protected, but an export duty of 1,000 marks per kilogram of feathers made the hunt uneconomical. *Amtsblatt für das Schutzgebiet Deutsch-Neuguinea*, 5 (1913): 218 and 275–276. The debate is in BAP: RKolA no. 7789.

18 Hill diary, AWM: 1 DRL 351, 92–93; and MLS: MSS 2935, 30 January 1915 entry.

19 L. Gors, "Bird of Paradise Hunting," *Rabaul Record*, no. 1, 1 March 1916, 10.

20 Kurt Kuhn of the Neuguinea-Kompanie (New Guinea Company), on 11 September 1915 to Administrator Pethebridge, AWM: 33/54.

21 Pethebridge, 12 January 1916 to the Ministry of Defence, ibid., underlinings in original. Pethebridge, 13 September 1915, to the Controller General Trade and Customs, Melbourne, ibid. Information about the smuggling of birds to Dutch New Guinea is in AAC: AA 1963/83, Bun 246, "Akte Pieper." Five years later Administrator Wisdom used similar arguments: "business can be done by us, if we get rid of the sentimental mushiness." Wisdom, Rabaul, 18 November 1921, to the Prime Minister's Office, AAC: A 518/1—A 846/1/77.

22 Birds of Paradise Exportation Ordinance, 27 February 1920, *Government Gazette Rabaul,* vol. 7, no. 2, 28 February 1920; Amendment, 28 January 1921, *Government Gazette Rabaul,* vol. 8, no. 2, 31 January 1921; both in AAC: A 518/1—A 846/1/77.

23 Ordinance, Rabaul, 16 November 1921; *New Guinea Gazette,* no. 17, 17 November 1921, 89. Administrator Wisdom, Rabaul, 18 November 1921, to the Prime Minister's Office, AAC: A 518/1—A 846/1/77. Prime Minister's secretary, 29 April 1922 from Melbourne, to the Secretary of the Wildlife Preservation Society of Australia, AAC: A 518—F 830/1. On the widespread custom of smuggling birds of paradise via Dutch New Guinea, F. M. Cutlack, "Drive for Madang," *Sydney Morning Herald,* 13 September 1921.

24 Memorandum by the Secretary to the Australian Prime Minister, 7 July 1922, to the Administrator of New Guinea; and Administrator Wisdom, Rabaul, 24 August 1922 to the Prime Minister's Secretary, AAC: A 518—F 830/1.

25 "The position at present is that the birds are being shot anyway, and we get nothing out of it." Administrator Wisdom, private, 19 January 1926 from Rabaul to his superior, the Minister for Home and Territories, J. G. McLaren, AAC: A 518—F 830/1. Birds and Animals Protection Ordinance 40/1922 (penalty: £ 100 or six months in prison), AAC: A 518—A 846/1/77. Evidence for the involvement of Australian district officials in the lucrative bird of paradise trade via Dutch New Guinea can be found in Lambert 1942, 84; Townsend 1968, 63–66; and M. H. Ellis, "Rabaul Scandal," *Daily Telegraph* (Sydney), 23 June 1923. The hunting of crowned pigeons, too, was unaffected by the official prohibition. Hunters simply claimed that the birds had attacked them, and that they had shot them "in self-defence" (Townsend 1968, 82).

26 Holmes, 28 November 1914, quoted by the Ministry of Defence, AWM: 33/10.

27 Rowley 1958, 12–33. After Pethebridge's death, Lieutenant-Colonel Mackenzie was Acting Administrator for a short period.

28 District Officer Captain Walters in his office on 18 February 1916 to Fathers Erdweg and Lopinot, AKM: C-39: Gayabachronik, 21.

29 Rejection of an application by the chair of the Australian Methodist Mission, William H. Cox, Rabaul, 8 February 1917 ("it is the wish of the Natives that we purchase") to Administrator Pethebridge, AAC: AA 1963/83, Bun 245: "Part 1917 Correspondence."

30 Intelligence Report Administrator Johnson, no. 10, Rabaul, 15 May 1919, AAC: CP 103/11, New Guinea Reports 2/15. The first Australian troops were paid with German banknotes. Diary of Private Scheidel, Rabaul, 15 October 1914, AWM: 3 DRL 2268. In February 1915, German government revenues to the value of 319,241.66 marks were taken to Sydney in twenty-four chests; report A 13 of Administrator Pethebridge, Rabaul, 10 February 1915, to the Ministry of Defence, AWM: 33/12–10.

31 Administrator Pethebridge, Melbourne, 16 November 1917, AAC: A 3934–SC 30/ 1. Telegram from the Colonial Secretary, 1 March and 22 November 1916. Telegram from the Australian Federal Government, 22 March 1918 to the Colonial Secretary, ibid.

32 Holmes, 4 October 1914 and 26 December 1914, to the Minister of Defence, AWM: 33/10.

33 Memorandum by Administrator Pethebridge, 28 April 1916, to the Ministry of Defence, AAC: A 3934–SC 30/1. The Adminstrator also stated in an interview on a visit to Sydney that New Guinea's trade, shaped by the German colonists, served Australian interests and did not harm them; "Germans in New Guinea," *Samoa Times*, no. 35, 26 August 1916.

34 Table in Intelligence Report no. 27, 20 November 1920, AAM: MP 1049/1–18/ 0587.

35 Statement by Capt. Phibbs, Collector Customs, Rabaul, 5 September 1919, before the Royal Commission, AAC: CP 661/15.

36 Patrol report of the District Officer, Captain Walters, Madang, 15–18 February 1916, AWM: 33/54. In many places, the bush had encroached on the main road from Madang to Alexishafen, and in places it was totally impassable.

37 In Rabaul, Australian officers pulled up the tram tracks and sold them privately. Negotiations of the Court of Enquiry, in *Government Gazette Rabaul* 5, no. 7 (15 July 1918): 62, and no. 8 (15 August 1918): 78. On the deterioration of the trams in Rabaul under military occupation, see also J. J. Cummins, 29 January 1918, to Major N. de H. Rowland, "Report on Tram Lines," AAC: AA 1963/83, Bun 245, and Acting Administrator Mackenzie, 25 February 1918, to the Deputy Judge, ibid., 860/18. At the beginning of the civilian administration, an observer sent to New Guinea by the Australian prime minister to take stock of the situation noted dilapidation everywhere. The collapse of public utilities was especially marked in the outlying stations, but was also clearly visible in the capital. Street lighting had been discontinued. The lamp posts were in a shed belonging to the former Public Works Department which, shortly before the observer's arrival, had been shut down for financial reasons. Lewis F. East, "Interim Report on the Administration of New Guinea. Public works and buildings," confidential, Melbourne, 7 October 1922, AAC: A 981–NG 30, pt. 1.

38 Patrol Leader, Captain Olifent, District Officer of Eitape, 8 March 1919, to the Military Secretary in Melbourne, AAM: MP 367–404/11/245.

39 North of Madang a real battle broke out in July 1915 between 100 "free" locals and 25 Melanesian policemen led by an Australian sergeant; patrol report of Lieutenant W. M. B. Ogilvy, 12 August 1915, AAC: A 457–710/3; statement by Father Kirschbaum to the patrol officer, Olifent, Olifent, 8 March 1919, to the Military Secretary in Melbourne, AAM: MP 367–404/11/245. "The natives are beginning to get out of hand"—thus the Australian governor of neighboring Papua complained about the impact the government's inactivity in occupied German New Guinea was having on his colony (Murray, Port Moresby, 15 October 1915, to the Australian Governor-General, ANL: MS 696–6960). Even in parts of Neu Mecklenburg (now New Ireland), which was administratively relatively well off, having two district officers, there was chaos and disorder. An English planter to the District Officer, Emira, 8 April 1916, AAC: AA 1963/83, Bun 246.

40 Statement by Lieutenant Oliver John Thompson, Government Auditor, Rabaul, 9 October 1919, to the Royal Commission, AAC: CP 661/15/1. One year earlier,

Administrator Johnston had already discovered irregularities in the collection of the head-tax in Bougainville; Johnston, 1 November 1918 to Secretary of Defence, AWM: 33/55. Friends and visitors from Australia were involved in collecting taxes; Bassett 1969, 112. The fact that the patrol or district officer collected head-taxes personally left the door wide open to abuses, even after the introduction of the civilian administration; Townsend 1968, 58–59. See also Overell 1923, 179.

41   In addition to the sergeant responsible, a corporal and a private were also involved. District Court Martial, Rabaul, 16–20 July 1920, AAC: AA 1963/83, Bun 238.

42   The Australian officers regarded collecting the head-tax as a kind of sport, in which the object was to prove that they could collect more than the German administration: "every nigger pays a tax of 10 shillings [according to the official exchange rate, this was the equivalent of 10 marks, the average tax during the German colonial period] per year which they have to be chased for, it seems rather like highway robbery but it is a German custom and of course we are supposed to be administering their laws" (Lieutenant Carlile, Herbertshöhe, 12 September 1915, to his mother, AWM: 1 DRL 188). By the next day, Carlile could report that in Toma district he had collected 5,000 marks more than the German administration (letter of 13 September 1915, ibid.). Abuses ("South African methods") in tax collecting by the officer in charge of native affairs: Report of Administrator Pethebridge, no. A 117, 10 February 1916; AWM: 33/12–9. Double taxation: E. L. Piesse memorandum, 7 and 9 May 1921, for the Secretary in the Prime Minister's Department about talks with the Resident Magistrate of the British Shortland Islands, near Bougainville, and with former Administrator Griffiths, AAC: A 457–710/3.

43   Administration Order no. 20, 23 December 1914, AWM: 33/3.

44   "Acclimatising Native Birds from Australia," *Rabaul Record* 2, no. 7 (1 July 1917): 2.

45   "Rabaul Botanic Reserve Regulations," Rabaul, 15 March 1918, § 14 and 15; *Government Gazette Rabaul* 5, no. 3 (15 March 1918): 23–24. Similar regulations were passed one month later for Käwieng; *Government Gazette Rabaul* 6, no. 10 (25 October 1919): 76–77.

46   In Australia, British colonists regarded tropical trees as "untidy" and "primitive." Whole landscapes fell victim to an "almost maniacal tree-felling" (Butcher and Turnbull 1988, 23). Their appearance thus changed completely. See Butcher and Turnbull 1988, and esp. Bolton 1981.

47   Statement by the Australian Director of the Botanic Gardens Howard Oliver Newport, 6 September 1919, to the Royal Commission, AAC: CP 661/15/1. The German experiments with breeding tropical plants were abandoned, and existing contacts with the Tropical Institutes in Singapore, Ceylon, and Java were broken off (ibid.). The porcelain name-tags were taken home by Australian soldiers as souvenirs; MLS: MSS 930, 149 (26 September 1914). On official orders to cut down trees in Madang, see Captain Skeet, Madang, 1 January 1917, AWM: 33/34; in Rabaul: Intelligence Report Administrator Griffiths, no. 30, 22 February 1921, AAC: CP 103/11, New Guinea Reports 2/15.

48   Radlauer memorandum, AHM. Deer hunting was also permitted with official permission at this stage; decree by the district officer *(Bezirksamtmann)* of Neupommern (New Britain), Toma, 9 August 1914; *Amtsblatt für das Schutzgebiet Deutsch-Neuguinea* 6(1914): 288–289.

49   Memorandum by Administrator Johnson, Rabaul, 9 February 1920, to the Ministry

of Defence, AAC: A 518—A 254/1/1, pt. 1; "Distressing Accident," *Rabaul Record* 3, no. 5 (May 1918): 2.

50   They were known among Pacific Islanders as "bloody pirates"; Scarr 1990, 211 (see also 181) and Buckley and Klugman 1986, 67.

51   Burns, 12 November and 11 December 1907, to Hunt, ANL: MS 52, 32/52–1567, and 32/52–1568.

52   Over lunch, the prime minister, Atlee Hunt, James Burns, and Woodford, a company employee, discussed raising Burns Philp's contract (officially readvertised) for providing postal services between Australia and the New Hebrides; ANL: MS 1100/4: diary entry of 6 January 1904. Burns (Sydney, 11 January 1910) asks Hunt about what behavior is appropriate in order to ensure that the contract is extended; ANL: MS 52, 32—52/1574. Hunt informs Burns about the necessary procedure (Melbourne, 18 January 1910); ibid., 52/1573. Hunt tells Lucas which cabinet ministers opposed extending Burns Philp's postal contract (Melbourne, 19 May 1910); ANL: MS 52, 2—52/124.

53   The Governor-General, 11 January 1915, from Melbourne, to Colonial Secretary Harcourt, personal, ANL: MS 696/645; the Governor-General, Melbourne, 13 April 1915, confidential, to the Colonial Secretary, ibid., 6960; the Governor-General, 15 October 1916, to Stamfordham, personal, ibid., 246; Burns, London, 27 and 29 September 1915, to the Governor-General, ibid., 7234–7241; Grey, Howick, Lesburn, Northumberland, 1 December 1915, to Lord Novar, ibid., 7530.

54   ANL: G 21119 and G 21134.

55   Holmes, 27 October 1914 to the Ministry of Defence in Melbourne, AWM: 33/10 and AAC: A 1—21/11251. The threat Holmes used against the merchants was that the administration would offer no help if there were to be any unrest among the local plantation workers (ibid.). Lieutenant Keith Heritage, Rabaul, 27 October 1914, to the Administrator: "The deportation of the disturbing element allowed negotiations to run smoothly, and . . . the bulk of the goods . . . were taken over by the merchants, much against their will." AWM: 33/36. The company's view in Buckley and Klugman 1983, 10–11. Here, there is no word of the importance of the Administrator for striking Burns Philp's deal. Confidential and personal letter of thanks from Lucas to Holmes (undated, October 1914), MLS: MSS 15, Box 2 ("I see day light now after some anxious moments . . . command me if there is anything I can possibly do for you in Australia").

56   Holmes, Rabaul, 28 November and 11 December 1914, to the Ministry of Defence in Melbourne, AWM: 33/10. On the mixing of military and political motives with the private commercial interests of Burns Philp in Madang, see MLS: MSS 3034, 1 November 1914.

57   Holmes, Rabaul, 29 December 1914, to the Ministry of Defence in Melbourne, AWM: 33/10.

58   Report by Foss, retired American Rear Admiral, NARA: RG 38, K-5-a no. 11331 A (Box 1063). According to this account, Holmes was also a partner in the company; report by Captain August Roscher, Amboina, 13 December 1914; BAP: RKolA no. 2612. Cf. *DKB* 26 (1915), 144. Here Holmes is described as the son-in-law of one of the owners of Burns Philp. The *Australian Dictionary of Biography* is strangely mute on the subject. An indirect hint is found in a private letter of Captain Keith Heritage, Rabaul, 3 November 1914, in which he emphasizes how quickly Burns Philp appeared on the scene in the occupied colony. AWM: 1 DRL 347.

59   S. W. Harris, "Early Recollections of the War," *Rabaul Record* 2, no. 9 (1 September 1917): 8; cf. ibid., no. 2 (1 February 1917): 4.

60   Lieutenant Keith Heritage, Rabaul, 27 October 1914, to the Administrator; Holmes' marginal comment: "since received" (official confirmation), AWM: 33/36. Holmes, 28 October 1914, to the Ministry of Defence: "The commission . . . does not seem excessive," ibid.

61   Memorandum, "Trade between the Commonwealth and the late German Possessions in the Pacific—Burns Philp & Co's participation therein," AAC: A 4—NG 12. Memorandum by Administrator Pethebridge, 17 August 1916, ibid., Burns Philp Archives, Sydney: Box 21, private and confidential report no. 26, 31 March 1916. Only a summary of the events (without the significant details) in Buckley and Klugman 1983, 37.

62   Pethebridge, 3 July 1916, to the Ministry of Defence, AWM: 33/54.

63   Deputy Administrator Mackenzie, 16 February 1918, to the Ministry of Defence. The agreement was allegedly concluded in July 1916 and confirmed by the Ministry of Defence; AWM: 33/55.

64   Agreement between Burns Philp and the Military Administration of New Guinea, December 1916, ibid. The company's view in Buckley and Klugman 1983, 61.

65   Jaluit-Gesellschaft, Hamburg, 21 August 1915 to the German Colonial Office, for the *Germania,* BAP: RKolA no. 2505.

66   Memorandum Chief Law Officer Mackenzie, Melbourne, 2 March 1919, to the Governor-General, AAC: CP 103/11, New Guinea Reports Box 1/13, Sale of Land at Buka; 12,500 acres is the equivalent of just under 5,060 hectares. In February 1918 the Buka Plantations and Trading Company Ltd., which also belonged to Burns Philp, was entered in the land register as the owner of 1,888 hectares on the northeast coast of Bougainville; *Government Gazette Rabaul* 5, no. 2 (15 February 1918): 9-10.

67   Administrator Johnston, 24 February 1919, to the Ministry of Defence, AWM: 33/56.

68   Memorandum of the Secretary to the Australian Governor-General, 18 July 1917, AAC: CP 78/34/1—Bun 9.

69   Administrator Griffiths, 6 November 1920, to the Ministry of Defence, AWM: 33/57.

70   Report by August Roscher, Amboina, 13 December 1914, BAP: RKolA no. 2612.

71   AKM: C-39: Gayabachronik, 40.

72   List of purchase and sale prices, and details of profits made in the period 11 September 1911 to 21 March 1919 in Burns Philp Archives, Sydney, Box 21. The largest profits were made by selling copra in American harbors. Here Australian "patriotism," which was otherwise always appealed to in order to justify privileges, was apparently no obstacle.

73   "The re-occupation [*sic!*] of the Australians of Rabaul, German New Guinea, and Samoa, opened these markets, which accounts to a large extent for the increased turnover." Private and confidential report no. 28/1918; Burns Philp Archives, Sydney, Box 21.

74   "A very substantial amount of inner reserve does not appear . . . it is wise to make a slow and steady annual increase, rather than otherwise. We have also been holding considerable bank deposits in anticipation of the acquirement of the German Pacific Possessions." James Burns, 5 May 1919, to the London Company Director Lord Inchcape; Burns Philp Archives, Sydney, Box "Mandated Territory."

75   ANL: 696/7052, and Burns Philp Archives, Sydney, Box 21: private and confidential report no. 29/1919.

76   Burns Philp Archives, Sydney, Box 21: private and confidential report no. 30/1920.
      It is almost superfluous to mention that the directors of the new company were the
      same as those of the old company (James Burns, James Forsyth, and Lord Inch-
      cape). See also Buckley and Klugman 1983, 108–124.

77   On the notorious "game licences" issued "to disperse the blacks," see Pethebridge's
      memorandum "Notes on the Pacific," 31 December 1915, 9, AAM: MP 367/1–404/
      11/129. The history of relations between British Australians and aborigines has
      recently begun to be written after years of neglect; see, among others, Elder 1988,
      Reynolds 1989, and Markus 1990. Article 127 of the Australian Constitution, 9 July
      1900, deleted in 1967; Sawer 1975, 62.

78   See Healy 1987 and, for one specific case, Inglis 1975.

79   MLS: MSS 2935, 29 September 1914; Father Vormann, Hollandia, 22 November
      1914, to the Superior of the Steyler Missionaries, Noser Library, Madang.

80   AWM: 3 DRL 7734, 5 September 1914 entry. See also Piggott 1984, 50.

81   Diaries of Private Scheidel (9 October 1914 entry) and Colonel A. W. Ralston,
      AWM: 3 DRL 2268 and 2943. Report by Judge Weber, 17 March 1915, BAP:
      RKolA no. 2996; undated extract from Hamburg-Südsee AG's plantation report
      1914, BAP: RKolA no. 2612. See also Piggott 1984, 60.

82   Colonel Holmes, 4 October 1914, to the Ministry of Defence in Melbourne, AWM:
      33/10. In the Sepik district the proportion of police who refused to continue serv-
      ing after the German administration came to an end was especially high. Captain
      Ogilvy, O.C. Native Affairs, Rabaul, 30 December 1915, to the Administrator,
      AAC: AA 1963/83, Bun 245.

83   MLS: MSS 2935, 11 and 28 September 1914; MLS: MSS 3034, 14 September
      1914; AWM: 3 DRL 6061; MLS: MSS 930, 23 September 1914; MLS: MSS 2880,
      2 October 1914; AWM: PR 89/5, 24 October 1914. For other incidents, see Piggott
      1984, 53. The monotony of life as a soldier increased the temptation to let off steam
      at the expense of the local population. This happened repeatedly, even later. In
      mid-July 1915, for example, an Australian soldier went mad, attacked the local peo-
      ple, and emptied the magazine of his gun. Lieutenant Carlile, Commander of Her-
      bertshöhe, 17 May 1915, to his mother, AWM: 1 DRL 188.

84   Holmes, 4 October 1914 and 26 December 1914, to the Ministry of Defence,
      AWM: 33/10.

85   "Nigger": the Governor-General of Australia, Melbourne, 25 December 1918, per-
      sonal and private, to Colonial Secretary Long, ANL: MS 696/1123; undated memo-
      randum by the governor general of Australia "on Administration of Pacific Islands,"
      ibid., 2247; Senator de Largie (Western Australia) in the Senate on 9 August 1917,
      in a debate about the German possessions in the South Pacific, AAC: A 3934—SC
      12/19. Diaries of Colonel A. W. Ralston (AWM: 3 DRL 2943), Lieutenant Com-
      mander G. A. Hill (AWM: 1 DRL 351), Lieutenant Bowen (AWM: 3 DRL 7734),
      Lieutenant Read (MLS: MSS 3034), Naval Medical Officer Dr. Fred Hamilton-
      Kenny (MLS: MSS 930), Private Scheidel (AWM: 3 DRL 2268), A. O'Hare (MLS:
      MSS 2935). Letters from Lieutenant E. K. Carlile, commander of Herbertshöhe,
      later district officer of Morobe, to his mother (AWM: 1 DRL 188), from Lieutenant
      William David Hunter to his wife (AWM: 1 DRL 369). See also the designations
      for the local people used by Lieutenant W. E. McIlwaine, district officer and at the
      same time native magistrate, in the *Rabaul Record* 2, no. 10 (1 October 1917): 10
      ("Lofty and Lorea"), and no. 11 (1 November 1917): 9–10 ("An Interview"). "Kana-
      kas": Colonel Holmes, Rabaul, 26 December 1914, to the Ministry of Defence

(AWM: 33/10); Lance Balfour Penman diary (AWM: PR 82/171). On the "favorite" racist terms used by the Australian troops in New Guinea, see also Piggott 1984, 56–57. The derogatory term "nigger" was by no means used only at the beginning of the military administration. See, for example, the statements made before the Royal Commission on Late German New Guinea at the end of 1919, AAC: CP 661/15/1. Flippant words by the first Australian Administrator of the civil administration, Wisdom: see Wisdom, Rabaul, 22 April 1925, to his superior Minister for Home and Territories, AAC: A 518—D 11215, pt. 1.

86   Firth 1986 completely disregards these basic features of German colonial policy after 1899. But see now my "Das Deutsche Reich in der Südsee. Eine Annäherung an die Erfahrungen verschiedener Kulturen," *Habilitationsschrift,* Freiburg i. Br. 1993.

87   According to Piggott 1984, 57, "a vocabulary of strong but innocent prejudice."

88   Press Officer Jens Lyng, *Rabaul Record* 9 (1 November 1916): 5 ("German New Guinea. Economic and Social Life"). Lyng was one of the Australians who outdid each other in compiling lists of negative qualities allegedly typical of Melanesians. Lyng, "Something about the Natives," *Rabaul Record* 2, no. 3 (1 March 1917): 7–10; no. 9 (1 September 1917): 12–13; see also Piggott 1984, 56. Healy 1987, esp. 216–17, has already emphasized the difference between Australian and German ways of treating the indigenous people of New Guinea. He calls German administrative methods "associationist," and Australian ones "assimilationist."

89   The Melanesian bushman "is always the same, a dirty, smelly, skin-diseased, slobbery, betel-chewing, bleary eyed specimen." Major Ogilvy, Officer-in-Charge of Native Affairs, "Cannibalism and Lost Illusions," *Rabaul Record* 2, no. 6 (1 June 1917): 7. Satirical comments about the peculiarities of Melanesian cultures can be found repeatedly. See, for instance, "Something of the Soothing Sing-Sing," *Rabaul Record,* no. 2 (1 April 1916): 3, or the "jokes" Australian sailors played with the people on the river Sepik, AWM: 1 DRL 351, 125. See also Piggott 1984, 57, and Hiery 1992c, 201.

90   Hiery 1992c, 201.

91   Memorandum by Administrator Johnson, 20 October 1919, to the Royal Commission, AAC: CP 661/15/2. See also H. Thurnwald 1937, 150–151.

92   "The two words 'damn' and 'bloody' . . . sound remarkably funny from the lips of a nigger," MLS: MSS 3034, 12 October 1914. By 1916, the curse "Goodam" had reached as far as the Baining Hills; the *luluai* of the village of Kuruduä, Togogoan, used this expression to spur his people on to work when they no longer reacted to his commands in their mother tongue. Lieutenant H. N. Leach, "The Fringe of the Bainings," *Rabaul Record* 1, no. 7 (1 September 1916): 7.

93   "Something about the Natives," *Rabaul Record* 2, no. 3 (1 March 1917): 8.

94   Lieutenant Gordon Clifton, "Patrol in New Guinea," *Rabaul Record* 1, no. 10 (1 December 1916): 11; Lieutenant McIlwaine, "An Interview," *Rabaul Record* 2, no. 11, 1 November 1917: 10.

95   Johnston, 14 March 1919, to the Ministry of Defence: "corporal punishment for Natives," AWM: 33/56.

96   Captain C. W. Bray, "The Kanaka as a Hospital Patient," *Rabaul Record* 1, no. 5 (1 July 1916): 9; see also Piggott 1984, 54–55.

97   Lambert 1942, 103–105. During his time as director of the native hospital in Rabaul—"an ideal chance to experiment and observe"—Lambert conducted a

series of experiments on Melanesian patients who had been stopped from escaping by a barbed-wire fence. His reaction to the cases of death that obviously occurred was limited to similarly cynical comments; ibid, 99–100.

98 "No native will receive treatment unless the prescribed form is correctly completed and submitted," District Order No. 774, 15 October 1920, AAC: AA 1963/83, Bun 237.

99 Statement by Principal Medical Officer Lt. Col. John Wellesley Flood, Rabaul, 8 September 1919, to the Royal Commission, AAC: CP 661/15/1. In addition to his income from his private practice, the medical officer was paid £650 annually by the government (ibid.).

100 Ibid. and "Dear Hospitals," *Melbourne Herald,* 31 October 1923, AAC: AA 1963/83, Bun 237. With interruptions, Flood had been in Rabaul since December 1914; AAC: CP 661/15/1.

101 Lewis F. East: "Report on the Administration of the Territory of New Guinea," Melbourne, 7 October 1922, AAC: A 981—New Guinea 30, pt. 2. The report disappeared into the prime minister's drawer, and its findings were never published.

102 *Rabaul Record,* no. 7 (1 September 1916): 9. Australian soldiers forced the "nigger police" to catch fish for them using this method. Serious injuries were the logical consequence; MLS: MSS 2935, 23 November 1914.

103 Lieutenant E. Carlile, Commander of Herbertshöhe, 6 June 1915, to his mother, AWM: 1 DRL 188.

104 Lyng 1925, 26.

105 "Education, as far as teaching the Natives to read and write, is a waste of time." Captain Tennent to the Royal Commission, AAC: A 518–A 254/1/1, pt. 1, 34.

106 District Officer McAdam, Rabaul, 10 September 1919, to the Royal Commission, AAC: CP 661/15/1.

107 Speech by Atlee Hunt, 24 January 1920, to a Methodist conference in Queensland, AAC: CP 661/15/2.

108 Circular from Administrator Johnson, no date [c. 1919], to all missions; AAC: CP 661/15/1. Wolfers 1972 provides an excellent survey of the racist legal regulations issued by the Australian administration in New Guinea. He also briefly examines the military administration's "principles," including the ban on Melanesians using public toilets and washrooms, as well as benches in the parks and streets of Rabaul. These offenses incurred a punishment of one month's imprisonment plus "corporal chastisement." See Wolfers 1972 and *Government Gazette Rabaul* 5, no. 3 (15 March 1918): 23–24.

109 AWM: PR 82/171.

110 Vol. 2, no. 6, 1 June 1917, 7; see also Piggott 1984, 57. This contains further examples of disparaging comments made by Australians about Melanesian women.

111 Piggott 1984, 58.

112 Lieutenant W. E. McIlwaine, "Native Law in the Pacific," *Rabaul Record* 2, no. 8 (1 August 1917): 8–9.

113 Troop diary Herbertshöhe, AWM: 33/13, 23 September 1914. On the rape of women hospital patients, see statement by *Heilgehilfe* (Nurse) Müller, report by von Sigriz, on board the *Sonoma,* 19 January 1915, PAA: A. *Der Weltkrieg* no. 13, vol. 14; on female prisoners, Piggott 1984, 58. In Rabaul, Australian officers organized regular hunts for local women "for the purpose of having connection"; documents in AAM: B 543–W 112/4/895.

114 Administrator Thomas Griffiths, 14 July 1920, confidential, to the Minister of Defence; the new District Officer Major McAdam, Manus, 15 July 1920, personal and confidential to the Administrator, AAC: A 457–710/3; See also Piggott 1984, 58.

115 Ibid. Singleton may even have returned. A police master of the same name attracted attention through his illegal recruiting in Kaewieng early in 1921. Former Administrator Griffiths, 7 May 1921 to Piesse, AAC: A 2219, vol. 13.

116 Report by Burrows, Acting Commander of the warship *Una,* 20 April 1917, AAM: MP 367–D 404/11/15. The Administrator had asked Burrows to take a closer look at what was happening in the Solomons after the resident commissioner of the neighboring British Solomons had reported that Melanesians were coming over the border in droves, complaining about Australian rule in Bougainville; AAC: A 457–710/3. Hunter himself had reported that he had shot two indigenous women on a punitive expedition. Report of District Officer Lieutenant A. J. Hunter, Bukuluku, 22 January 1917, ibid.

117 Summary of evidence, Eitape, 15 and 16 October 1921, before District Officer A. J. Thompson. Summary of evidence taken at Wanimo, 20, 21, and 24 October 1921; AAC: A 5–NG 24/1437. While the Melanesian police were away searching the Sepik villages for women for the police master, he assaulted the policemen's wives (ibid.). The official in neighboring Dutch Humboldt Bay complained to a visiting Australian ship that Pole had even sent the police over the border to fetch women for him. (Captain Kenny, Eitape, 23 April 1921, confidential, to the Administrator; ibid.) Pole did not return from leave, took off for England, and from there demanded the discharge money due to him. Deputy Administrator, 3 January 1923, to the Prime Minister's Office, AAC: A 5, NG 24/1437. Morobe: Willis 1974, 67–68, 75–76.

118 Statement by Sergeant Edward Taylor, Police Master of Gasmatta, 9 December 1919. As far as Taylor could find out, the incidents had occurred toward the middle of 1918; AAC: A 457–710/3.

119 AKM: C-39, Gayabachronik, 27.

120 Rowley 1958, 117–118, and Memorandum by Administrator Johnston, Rabaul, 14 June 1918, to the Minister of Defence, AAM: MP 367-C 404/11/109. On the governor's draft regulations, see Hahl, 15 March 1914, to the Secretary of State in the German Colonial Office (copy), AAC: AA 1963/83, Bun 201, and BAP: RKolA no. 2314.

121 Hahl's explanations of the planned labor regulations, esp. Article 52, in ibid. Among the almost revolutionary measures were: a prohibition on recruiting school students, maternity leave for women workers from two months before the confinement, and compulsory smallpox vaccinations for all workers at the employer's expense. The new regulations were intended to be valid for the whole of German New Guinea—that is, including Micronesia. In Micronesia wages had always been paid in cash. The colonial government, too, had always paid its local blue- and white-collar workers in cash, and without deductions (Hahl, ibid.).

122 Missions, settlers, planters, and Pacific companies were up in arms against the government's plans. The government was accused of one-sidedly favoring the indigenous people at the expense of the planters, who were being recklessly harmed; it was claimed that concern for the workers was exaggerated in every respect. Memorandum of the Neuguinea-Kompanie, Berlin, 29 July 1914, BAP: RKolA no. 2314.

123 Rowley 1958, 122.

124 By the end of 1918, the 1917 ordinance had been amended five times. Native Labour Ordinance, 20 January 1919 (with effect from 27 January 1919), *Rabaul Government Gazette,* no. 1, 27 January 1919. Even this was not the end of the experiments and attempts to adapt to the realities of everyday colonial life. By the end of the military administration in April 1921, there had been another twelve revisions, supplementary provisions, and implementing regulations.

125 Statement by Major T. L. McAdam, Officer in Charge of Native Affairs, Rabaul, 10 September 1919, and Wilson Gillan, Treasurer and Paymaster, Rabaul, 5 September 1919, to the Royal Commission, AAC: CP 661/15/1.

126 J. Lyng, *Rabaul Record,* no. 9 (1 November 1916): 5.

127 Lyng, no year [1919], 230, and esp. Rowley 1958, 126–128. According to the Labour Ordinance of May 1915, the recruitment of women without their husbands was officially forbidden (ibid., 127). But even among district officers themselves, this regulation was little known. See, for example, the attitude of the district officer of Kieta, Captain A. R. McGregor, "The Island of Buka", *Rabaul Record,* no. 10 (1 December 1916): 10, who had to have this ban pointed out to him by the local people. In 1917, colonial reality—that is, the existing widespread disregard of this regulation—was again legalized; Rowley 1958, 127. This step was justified by reference to the need to avert homosexuality, which would otherwise arise spontaneously and spread to local village society. Administrator Johnston, memorandum of 20 October 1919 to the Royal Commission, AAC: CP 661/15/2.

128 Memorandum by Administrator Johnston, 20 October 1919, to the Royal Commission, AAC: CP 661/15/2. A recruiting contract that has survived from 1916 estimates the "price" of a male laborer with a three-year contract as 90 marks (four pounds, ten shillings), and that of a single woman as 120 marks (six pounds). Recruiting contract Curt A. Schultze–Adolf Jahn, 2 February 1916, AAC: AA 1963/83, Bun 246.

129 But see the report by the District Officer of Morobe, Carlile, 20 January 1916, to Pethebridge, on the upper Waria people's concern about the activities of the recruiters; AWM: 33/55–54. The brutality of a Chinese recruiter's method in the area of Malala (north of Madang) in 1916 is documented in AAC: AA 1963/83, Bun 245, "Crown Law Office." For an account, partially sanitized, of a recruiter, see S. Hawkes, "Recruiting in the Pacific," *Rabaul Record* 2, no. 2 (1 February 1917): 7–8, and "Illegal Recruiting," ibid., no. 7 (1 July 1917): 4–5.

130 J. Lyng, *Rabaul Record* 1, no. 7 (1 September 1916): 8.

131 Memorandum by Johnston, 20 October 1919, for the Royal Commission, AAC: CP 661/15/2.

132 Report by Komine, 23 January 1918, Intelligence Report Administrator Johnston no. 2, Rabaul, 11 July 1918, AAM: B 539–AIF 112/6/43, and AAC: CP 103/11, New Guinea Reports 2/15; report by Strasberg about his visit to the south coast of Neupommern (New Britain), 27 February –14 April 1918, AAM: MP 367–404/ 11/689.

133 Extract from the logbook of the *Takubar,* Kwoi Bay, 4 March 1918, ibid.

134 Memorandum by the missionary Flierl, "A Treatise on Recruiting and Labour Trade, becoming a most serious problem in this Colony," 15 October 1918, in Flierl, Heldsbach, 17 October 1918, to Administration Headquarters, Rabaul, AAM: MP 367–404/11/689.

135 Radio message from District Officer Dillane, Morobe, 16 January 1919, to the Administrator, AWM: 33/56.

136 In July 1918 a special patrol to Baining in the north of Neupommern (New Britain) had seen, only too clearly, the results of violent recruiting. Administrator Johnston, Rabaul, 16 October 1918 to the Ministry of Defence, AAM: MP 367–404/11/689. The Sepik district was the most affected. In the hinterland of Eitape, the Administrator was shown three hundred recruits—"a wretched looking lot"—who were so unfamiliar with "civilization" that they had to be shown how to wear lavalavas around their hips. None of them knew Pisin nor whom they would be working for. The Administrator himself was convinced that they had been cheated but did not intervene. On the return journey to Madang, a recruiter confessed that "his party had killed 25 to 30 natives." Administrator Johnston, 24 September 1918 to the Ministry of Defence, AWM: 33/55. In late 1918 or early 1919, a recruiter shot seventeen Aseati people on the Sepik. Radio message from Captain Olifent, 22 January 1919, to the Administrator, AWM: 33/56. For recruiting abuses in the Lae area, Willis 1974, 68–72.

137 Marginal comment by George Foster Pearce, 31 December 1918, on a letter from Administrator Johnston, 22 November 1918, AAM: MP 367–404/11/689. Note by the Deputy Chief Censor, 3 January 1919: "Censors instructed accordingly," ibid.

138 Patrol report Lieut. Gl. M. Wilder Neligan, District Officer Talasea, July 1920, AAC: A 2–20/2980.

139 Madang and Namatanai. Intelligence Report Administrator Rabaul, no. 29, 20 January 1921, AAM: MP 1049/1–18/0587.

140 Governor Hahl, Rabaul, 24 May 1913, report no. 368, to the Secretary of State in the German Colonial Office (copy), AAC: AA 1963/83, Bun 205.

141 Table in AAC: A 1–23/18422.

142 Figures for 1919: Major T. L. McAdam, Officer in Charge of Native Affairs, Rabaul, 10 October 1919, to Atlee Hunt, AAC: CP 661/15/1. For figures for 1913, see note 140 above.

143 Secretary to the Prime Minister, Melbourne, 12 February 1923, on the Administrator's report of 3 September 1921 for the drafting of the annual report for the League of Nations, AAC: A 1–23/18422. The table actually specifies 30,849 Melanesian workers, but this was obviously an arithmetical error, as the number for Kokopo (3,421 workers) was added again to the figures for Rabaul (8,260 instead of 4,839).

144 ANL: MS 882/6/686, "Expropriation." Hahl, report no. 368, 24 May 1913, AAC: AA 1963/83, Bun 205.

145 Major Cummins, Director of Census and Statistics for the Military Government, Brisbane, 24 November 1921, to the Australian Prime Minister, AAC: A 518–F 840/1/3, pt. 1. Homosexuality was also known as a consequence of the plantation economy in Papua, the British Solomons, and the New Hebrides. Ibid.; see also Lambert 1942, 22–23, and Reed 1943, 220–221.

146 Piesse, "Return of Indentured Labour New Guinea 9 May 1921," ANL: MS 882/6/144.

147 Hahl, report no. 368, 24 May 1913, AAC: AA 1963/83, Bun 205.

148 Piesse memorandum, "The Native Population and Native Labor," 20 June 1922, AAC: A 1–23/18418. Piesse to East, Melbourne, 14 June 1923, ANL: MS 882/6/464. Piesse, confidential and personal, to Secretary for Home and Territories

J. McLaren, ANL: MS 882/6/490–491. He accused Australian Minister Joseph Cook—who, in 1923 at the Mandate Commission in Geneva, denied any connection between a rise in the number of workers and population decline—of lying; ANL: MS 882/6/538.

149 Appendix to the Administrator's report, Rabaul, 5 October 1922, to the Secretary in the Prime Minister's Department, AAC: A 1–23/18422. Piesse memorandum, "Decline of the Native Population," 11 April 1923, for the Secretary in the Prime Minister's Department, AAC: A 1–23/18418. In it, Piesse criticized the administration and the Administrator in Rabaul for having withheld the statistics from him until he requested them repeatedly. Between 1914 and 1920 the decline in the population of Madang was even more extreme than that in Neu Mecklenburg/New Ireland. Whereas the latter area possessed the best infrastructure in New Guinea, roads in the Madang district had suffered badly from neglect during the war years. It is therefore likely that the result of the 1920 census reflected less a decline in the population than a retreat of the administration. See Rivers 1922, 5, and, for the general problem of population decline in the Pacific, McArthur 1968.

150 Holmes, 27 October 1914, to the Ministry of Defence, AWM: 33/10. Diary of Major Heritage's Kaewieng expedition, 25 October–1 November 1914, AWM: 33/33/1. In three days, Heritage administered a total of 410 blows to twenty-eight people. "All boys and Kanakas between Kapsu and Kaewieng were told that the situation was just the same as before," ibid. See also Nelson 1978, 136. "My arm was aching for about 4 hours"—Sergeant Hocking about his way of making "niggers" work; letter of 16 December 1914, AWM: 3 DRL 2985.

151 Rowley 1958, 137–138. A comparison of the right of employers to punish their employees in the July 1915 ordinance with Hahl's draft of 1914 (BAP: RKolA no. 2314) reveals some improvements and some changes for the worse. Common to both was only the possibility of arrest for a maximum of three days. The Australian ordinance limited corporal punishment to a maximum of ten blows within fourteen days, while Hahl had set the maximum at twenty blows (not ten; Rowley 1958, 137) in the presence of a medical assistant. The former governor of German New Guinea also wanted to allow a fine of up to 30 marks; the Australians regarded 20 marks as the upper limit. The Australians also permitted confinement in chains and in a darkened cell, for which Hahl's draft did not provide.

152 Rowley 1958, 138–139.

153 AKM: 39, Gayabachronik, 19/20.

154 Rowley 1958, 140–142. Even before corporal punishment was reintroduced for offenses other than murder and rape, Ogilvy made frequent use of it. On 18 December 1915 he ordered a house boy to be given twenty strokes with a cane before a group of assembled Melanesian government workers and servants. Ogilvy, O.C. Native Affairs, Rabaul, 6 January 1916 to the Administrator, AWM: 33/54.

155 Report by Administrator Pethebridge, no. A 112, Rabaul, 3 December 1915, to the Minister of Defence; AAM: MP 367–479/27/50 and AWM: 33/12-10. Marginal comment by Minister of Defence Pearce, 7 January 1916, ibid.; see also Rowley 1958, 143. The spectre of white women being threatened by black or brown men was a constant source of concern to European colonial policy in the Pacific. On Papua, see Inglis 1975.

156 Rowley 1958, 144–145.

157 Para. 48, 2. Confinement in a darkened cell had been abolished in March 1918;

Rowley 1958, 145. Sexual offenses were "immorality," attempted rape and rape, attempted homosexuality and adultery, and homosexuality and adultery; labor offenses included "gross insubordination," "defiance of authority," arson—this was intended primarily to prevent the setting fire to plantations—and attempted physical assault and physical assault (to protect supervisors and foremen). Serious criminal offenses were murder (in every case of murder that did not warrant the death penalty, corporal punishment was obligatory), attempted murder, robbery, housebreaking, theft, and "wilful false statements before any court," which, if it were not expressed so vaguely, could be seen as an attempt to introduce something like perjury for the indigenous population. Native Labour Ordinance 1919, § 48, 6.

158 Rowley 1958, 145–146. Effective on 23 May 1919 through the Native Labour Ordinance No. 3A/1919, Rabaul, 22 May 1919; *Government Gazette Rabaul,* 6, no. 5 (23 May 1919): 39.

159 Memorandum by Administrator Johnston and Judge Major N. de H. Rowland, "corporal punishment for Natives," Rabaul, 14 March 1919, to the Minister of Defence, AWM: 33/56.

160 Ibid. and Intelligence Report Administrator Rabaul no. 10, Rabaul, 15 May 1919, AAC: CP 103/11, NG Report, Box 2/15; See also Rowley 1958, 147–148. Leg irons had not been used in German New Guinea, but they were used in Papua. Even there, however, their use had been limited. The ministry of defense therefore sent only the handcuffs but no leg irons; Rowley 1958, 147.

161 "Believe that considerable effect will be obtained by exposing offenders to ridicule. . . . Absolutely no cruelty attached to such imprisonment." Secret telegraphic report from the Administrator, Rabaul, 20 May 1919, to the Ministry of Defence, AAC: A 457–710/3; see also Rowley 1958, 148–149.

162 Statements by Lance Corporal Hector Norman McLean, Police Master, Department of Native Affairs, Rabaul, and Lieutenant Alan Reginald Hanlin, Adjutant Native Police. Proceedings Board of Enquiry, Rabaul, 2–3 December 1919, AAC: A 457–710/3.

163 Statement by Pastor William James Chambers, ibid. Johnston, Rabaul, 19 December 1919 to the Secretary of Defence, AAC: A 457–710/3; see also Rowley 1958, 148, and Thompson 1990, 77. Another eyewitness reported the Administrator, on seeing the "birds," as saying: "Good heavens! I have seen men in agony at the Front, but I have never seen such torture as this." Overell 1923, 172. According to the same source, the missionary did not pass by chance, but was called to help by a soldier who could no longer bear the cries (ibid.).

164 Rowley 1958, 149; cf. ibid., 148. Marginal comment by Minister of Defence, Pearce, 13 December 1920, on a confidential memorandum of the Department of Defence, 28 January 1920, AAC: A 457–710/3. Overell 1923, 171–172, reports that the officer responsible returned to New Guinea shortly thereafter, where his brutal behavior continued. Missionaries prevented his promotion to the rank of major.

165 Trial of planter Hartig, Central Court Rabaul, 9 March 1920, AAC: AA 1963/83, Bun 238. See also Rowley 1958, 149. Field Punishment No. 1 in outlying stations, Willis 1974, 67.

166 Various cases in the court records of the Central Court Rabaul, AAC: AA 1963/83, Bun 239. Cf. *Government Gazette Rabaul,* 6, no. 11 (27 November 1919): 98, judgment of 13 October 1919: "assaulting a native. verdict: guilty. no penalty." See also Rowley 1958, 148.

167 AKM: 39, Gayabachronik, 35.

168 Bassett 1969, 129.

169 Rowley 1958, 150–151. Native Labour Ordinance 1922.

170 Overell 1923, 61; Rowley 1958, 149–150; and Hiery 1992c, 199. During a visit by the Marist bishop of Kieta to Rabaul in 1933, Melanesian plantation workers from Kieta implored him to protect them from flogging by the planters. If they complained to the district officers, the laborers said, they did not intervene, and all that happened was that the planters beat them even more. The bishop noted that "every plantation overseer makes use of a cane" (T. J. Wade, Kieta, 3 November 1933, to Administrator Griffiths, PMB 4). The bishop's plea went unheard and unheeded. In 1935 beating was normal practice in New Guinea and was not punished by the courts. See *Pacific Islands Monthly*, 31 March 1935: "Question of Corporal Punishment in New Guinea."

171 "I am of the considered opinion that the time for their wholesale abolition is not yet"—The Chief Judge, Papua and New Guinea, summing up his position on the question of the abolition of corporal punishment; memorandum, "Corporal Punishment," Supreme Court, Port Moresby, 4 January 1951 [*sic!*] to the Administrator Port Moresby, AAC: A 518-J 840/1/4, pt. 1. The difference between corporal punishment in Papua and New Guinea was that in Papua an individual could be given up to three separate whippings, with a maximum of fifty strokes each time, while in New Guinea, no more than two separate whippings could be administered, with up to twenty-four strokes each time. In Papua, the Administrator had to give his approval, but not in New Guinea. Although New Guinea provisions concerning the actual infliction of a whipping were less severe than the Papuan ones, whipping could be imposed for a larger number of offenses in New Guinea than in Papua; ibid.

172 Pethebridge, Report no. 23A, 10 March 1915, to the Minister of Defence, AAC: CP 78/23–14/89/10/2. Pejorative comments are also found elsewhere: "a collection of old rags," Lieutenant Carlile, Herbertshöhe, 25 March 1915, to his mother, about a meeting between the *luluai* and the Administrator; AWM: 1 DRL 188.

173 Administration Order no. 782, 10 December 1920, no. 9: "Appointment of Native Officials (Luluais and Tultuls)," AAC: 1963/83, Bun 237. Native Administration Ordinance 1921, here § 120 (3); AAC: A 981–NG 30/2.

174 Both Rowley and Firth underestimate the importance of the internal arbitration initiated by the *luluai* with the official approbation and under the protection of the German colonial administration. The reality of Melanesian life under German hegemony, therefore, can hardly be more distorted than it is in Firth's account (1986, 73/74). Rowley (1958, 220–221) is rather more restrained, and he admits that the Australians did not understand the principles on which the system was based. But he also does not see that the confusion during the war was a direct result of the Australians discontinuing former German administrative practices. The fact that the *luluai* imposed fines in shell money both strengthened the position of the Melanesian arbitrator and facilitated the transition toward a society in which, under European pressure, the other model of Melanesian conflict resolution, the blood feud, was supressed. In order not to break too strongly with the earlier tradition, which had never been questioned before, German judges and district officers, to whom Melanesians could appeal against the *luluai*'s decision, also imposed fines in shell money in purely Melanesian affairs. Firth incorrectly states

that the *luluai* were permitted to fine only in marks, not in shell money (1986, 74), but there is a flood of evidence to the contrary (station court records in AAC: AA 1963/83). In general, Firth's account of the significance of shell money under the German colonial administration is completely inaccurate. Governor Bennigsen had forbidden all non-Melanesians (plus Melanesians who were officially recognized as traders) to use shell money, in order to foil the attempt by European and Chinese traders to gain an unfair advantage in the local trade by importing large numbers of shells from outside traditional sites. The use of shell money in indigenous societies was nowhere affected. Firth's argument (1986, 69) that Bennigsen's intention was to ruin the Tolai economy is far-fetched. Verordnung des Gouverneurs von Deutsch-Neuguinea betr. den Handel mit Muschelgeld *(Diwarra)* v. 18 Oktober 1900 u. v. 26. Juli 1901 betr. den Muschelgeldverkehr (Ordinance of the governor of German New Guinea concerning the trade with shell money [*Diwarra*] of 18 October 1900 and of 26 July 1901 concerning trade in shell money); *DKG* 6, no. 171 (1901–1902): 260–261, and no. 244, 362–363. A good contemporary work about shell money on the Gazelle Peninsula is that of the Fijian missionary William Taufa; BAP: RKolA no. 2713.

175 Intelligence Report Administrator, no. 10, Johnston, Rabaul, 15 May 1919, to the Minister of Defence, AAC: CP 103/11, NG Report Box 2/15.

176 Sub-Lieutenant Hext, Manus, 25 January 1915, to the Administrator, AWM: 33/12–10. See also Nelson 1978, 137, and Rowley 1958, 197.

177 Police Patrol, Police Master Sergeant Beckton, 27 April–23 May 1915, AAM: B 543–W 112/7/77. Report Warrant Officer Hill to O.C. Native Affairs, no date, in Report Administrator Pethebridge, no. 80, Rabaul, 8 June 1915, ibid. See also Nelson 1978, 137.

178 Captain H. Balfour Ogilvy, O.C. Native Affairs, Rabaul, 8 October 1915, to Pethebridge, AAC: CP 78/23–14/89/10–1. See also Rowley 1958, 197–198 and Nelson 1978, 137. Nelson mentions only nine dead. But Ogilvy's papers show clearly that in a number of incidents during the punitive expedition at least sixteen Melanesians were shot.

179 Photographic evidence in the Linden-Museum, Stuttgart.

180 Pethebridge's authority to Ogilvy, 15 October 1915, AWM: 33/12–1; Ogilvy, Rabaul, 23 October 1915, to Pethebridge, ibid.; see also Mackenzie 1927, 308–310 and Nelson 1978, 137–138. The figures Nelson gives for Melanesians dead are too low, because he again refers only to one attack instead of to the whole punitive expedition.

181 I. H. Campbell, Choiseul Plantations Ltd., 25 October 1915, to the Administrator, AWM: 33/36. See also Rowley 1958, 198.

182 Pethebridge, Rabaul, 8 February 1917, to Secretary of Defence; AAC: A 457–710/3; report by Commander Burrows, *Una*, 20 April 1917, AAM: MP 367–D 404/11/15; E. L. Piesse's record of a conversation with the British Resident Magistrate of the Shortland Islands, C. B. Nicholson, 7 May 1921, AAC: A 457–710/3; notes on the armed conflicts in Bougainville by Carl Frost, ANL: MSS 3376. See also Mackenzie 1927, 310–312, and Rowley 1958, 199–200.

183 Administrator Johnston, 17 June 1918, to Secretary of Defence, AWM: 33/35; Johnston, 28 February 1919 to Defence, AWM: 33/56, and AAM: MP 367–C 404/11/209. See also Rowley 1958, 201–202.

184 Johnston, 24 September 1918, to the Secretary of Defence, AWM: 33/55; Johnston, 15 March 1919 to Defence, AWM: 33/56. See also Rowley 1958, 202–204.

185 Rowley 1958, 204–205.

186 District Officer Hunter, who was ordered by Johnston to go on a punitive expedition into the Sepik district, warned the Administrator before it began that he would shoot the accused Melanesians rather than take them prisoner: "This will save a lot of unnecessary carrying" (Hunter, Eitape, 17 June 1918, to the Administrator, AAM: MP 367–C 404/11/209). Toward the end of Johnston's period of office, on one of the many punitive expeditions against the Sepik people, a village was set afire and nine of its inhabitants killed on his express orders, because the deputation did not think there was time for an investigation. Johnston, Rabaul, 19 January 1920, to the Ministry of Defence, AAC: CP 103/11, NG Reports, Box 2–556.

187 A positive exception was the temporary district officer of Manus, Captain Foulkes, who used the German method of temporary exile with favorable results. Captain H. S. Foulkes, Lorengau, 17 March and 25 July 1917, to the Administrator, AWM: 33/34. See also Rowley 1958, 200.

188 Rowley 1958, 205.

189 District Officer Charles Wittkopp, Manus, 10 May 1920, to Borchardt, AAC: CP 103/11–New Guinea Reports, Box 2/15. Resumé of File of Papers dealing with Patrols in Drukul, Manus District, 26 June 1920. Father Borchardt to the District Officer Manus, Bundralis, 8 May 1920.

190 See p. 73 above.

191 Reminiscences John Raven Fox, UPNG: AL-101/1.

192 Atlee Hunt, 18 December 1913, to Governor Murray of Papua, ANL: MS 52, 4–52/331.

193 Memorandum of the Supreme Judge, Major Rowland, Rabaul, 12 August 1918, AAC: AA 1963/83, Bun 245.

194 Administrator Pethebridge, Report A4, Rabaul, 30 January 1915, AWM: 33/12–10. See also Nelson 1978, 138–140.

195 Administration Order no. 32, Pethebridge, Rabaul, 1 February 1915, AWM: 33/12–10; Pethebridge, Report A 15, Rabaul, 21 February 1915, ibid.; Captain R. Grant Thorold, Acting Administrator Neu Mecklenburg (New Ireland), Kaewieng, 8 February 1915, to the Administrator, ibid. See also Nelson 1978, 140.

196 Memorandum by Administrator Johnston, Rabaul, 19 September 1919, for the Ministry of Defence, AAC: A 4–NG 6 and AWM: 33/56-3.

197 Instruction issued by the Imperial Commissioner, Rose, Stephansort, 1 August 1891, to Chancellor Schmiele, who had asked for permission for an execution to be carried out on the scene of the crime "as a deterrent." Rose explained that "the proposed manner of executing the native might be provocative and lead to a repetition of the violence," AAC: AA 1963/83, Bun 39: Stationsgericht Herbertshöh (the older name for Herbertshöhe). 1890. File of proceedings for murder against the native Tororuk from Vunabalbal. Application by Schmiele, 15 June 1891, ibid. On Tororuk's offense, Sack 1977, 272.

198 Barely a week after the German government took over the administration, Acting Governor Schnee sharply rejected execution by hanging (calling it "repugnant"); Schnee, Herbertshöhe, 8 April 1899, to the German Colonial Department, BAP: RKolA no. 4949. Formally, the means of executing the death sentence were merely supplemented by shooting; in practice, however, shooting in the future replaced hanging. Gouverneursverordnung betr. die Vollstreckung der Todesstrafe (Governor's order concerning the carrying out of the death sentence), 7 April 1899 (on 1 April 1899, the German government had taken over the administration of the colony from the Neuguinea-Kompanie; the statement by Sack 1977, 277–278 is there-

fore incorrect), *DKG* 4, no. 46 (1898–1899): 56. During the process of introducing the death sentence for the indigenous population, the reasons for its necessity had been progressively narrowed down over a number of drafts; Sack 1977, 266–271.

199 Intelligence Report Administrator Johnston, no. 4 A of 9 October 1918, no. 6 of 9 December 1918, no. 9 of 12 April 1919, no. 18 of 16 February 1920, and many more; AAC: CP 103/11–NG Reports 2/15.

200 Intelligence Report Administrator no. 32, 11 May 1921, Wisdom to the Secretary of the Ministry of Defence, AAM: MP 1049/1–18/0587, and AAC: CP 103/11-NG Reports 2/15. Lieutenant A. W. W. Winstone, Deputy District Officer Rabaul, Natava, 14 April 1921, to the Officer in Charge of Native Affairs, Rabaul, AWM: 33/58.

201 Hempenstall 1978, 150.

202 This account is based on the eyewitness reports in the following court records: Central Court Rabaul, Crown vs. Aluet and Crown vs. Malbrinkkapokman, 4 March 1920, AAC: AA 1963/83, Bun 238. Crown vs. Kaning. Judgment, no date [15 November 1920], Crown vs. Kamninarvet. Judgment, no date [26 January 1921]; AAC: A 457–710/3 (copy).

203 Crown vs. Kaning, AAC: A 457–710/3.

204 Crown vs. Kaminarvet, ibid.

205 Hanlin report, Mandras, 28 September 1919 and idem, Baining Report no. 3, 2 October 1919, in Intelligence Report Administrator Johnston, no. 14, Rabaul, 28 October 1919, AAC: CP 103/11–NG Reports 2/15.

206 Intelligence Report Administrator Johnston, no. 20, Rabaul, 20 April 1920, AAC: CP 103/11–NG Reports 2/15.

207 Crown vs. Kaminarvet, AAC: A 457–710/3.

208 Griffiths, "Training of Native Children by Missions," Rabaul, 25 February 1921, to the Secretary in the Ministry of Defence, AAC: A 457–710/3 (copy).

209 See, for example, the generalizations Fischer noted a few years ago in the northeast of New Guinea, almost by chance. Americans were seen as "friendly, generous, open-handed," Australians as "unfriendly and miserly," and Germans as "friendly, but not exactly open-handed. . . . The 'image' of the teacher is probably the most appropriate." Americans, Australians, and Germans "therefore represent categories, categories of language and thinking, which reflect certain complex values, while on the other hand, individual whites are assigned to one group or the other depending on their behaviour" (Fischer 1987, 154 and 155).

210 Fischer 1987, 160.

211 See Hiery 1992*b*.

212 Fischer 1987, 155.

213 The soldiers taught the Melanesians specifically British songs and airs. Diary O'Hare, entry of 25 December 1914; MLS: MSS 2935. See also Piggott 1984, 45.

214 MLS: MSS 2935, 29 September 1914. It is striking that at first the term "Australians" is not used.

215 Ibid., 13 September 1914 entry.

216 Letter Lieutenant Carlile, Herbertshöhe, 12 February 1915, AWM: 1 DRL 188.

217 Father Fritz Vormann, Hollandia, 22 November 1914, to the Superior of the Divine Word Mission, Noser Library, Madang; Vormann, 14 December 1914, from Wewäk to the Superior, ibid. The term "Kanaka" or "Kanake" can have positive or negative connotations, depending on the speaker, the context, and the intonation used. Here a positive interpretation, with the sense of "they are like us but come

from Sydney" seems most likely to me. Vormann interprets the Melanesian use of the term "Kanaka" for the Australians as a criticism, which is no accident, given his view of the word.

218 Sister Maria Ursula Schütte, Ste.-Foy-les-Lyon, 1 March 1937, to the German consul in Lyon, BAP: RKolA no. 3085.

219 When the Thurnwalds visited Bougainville in September 1933 to undertake field research, they found out that the positive assessment of Döllinger was transferred to them, apparently only because they were Germans. Thurnwald 1937, 162 (with a racist commentary, 163).

220 Lieutenant Carlile, Morobe, 21 December 1915, AWM: 1 DRL 188.

221 Patrol Report Lieutenant W. M. B. Ogilvy, District Officer Madang, 14–16 August 1915, AAC: A 457–710/3 (copy). The village was called Morago. At other places in the colony the population was quick in recognizing the importance of flying the new flag. The occupying party to the Manus islands encountered a "large catamaran with half a dozen natives aboard one of whom was holding up a large Union Jack." The Australians compensated them for "such loyalty" by presenting them with ten sticks of tobacco. Lieutenant Axtens to his father, Rabaul, 1 December 1914, AWM: 2 DRL 308.

222 Native affairs correspondence 1915–1918, AAC: AA 1963/83, Bun 240. On 31 May 1916 the Malays were sentenced to a fine of 15 shillings or seven days in prison for seditious words (ibid.).

223 It is certainly no coincidence that the evidence for this criticism comes from the Sepik district and Neu Mecklenburg. The closure of the government station in Angoram by the Australians smoothed the path for a resumption of tribal fighting and opened the door to abuses by the recruiters. In Neu Mecklenburg, Boluminski's administrative style had created a complicated network of dependencies between the administration and the local people. This collapsed under the impact of war. The Administrator, 7 June 1918 to the Secretary of Defence, passing on a report from the District Officer of Eitape. The district officer had written that he had heard very unflattering comparisons between British and German officials (AWM: 33/55). Letter from a British planter, Emira, 8 April 1916, to the District Officer of New Ireland, conveying the local criticism: "The Kanakers are coming to me complaining but it is not my business to play the 'Kiap' [District Officer]," AAC: AA 1963/83, Bun 246.

224 Lieutenant G. Somerset, District Officer Morobe, Cape Cretin, 28 July 1917, to the Administrator, AWM: 33/12–10. See also Rowley 1958, 145.

225 Board of Proceedings Court of Inquiry, Gasmatta, 9 December 1919, AAC: A 457–710/3.

226 Potsdamhafen: Mackenzie 1927, 311. Sepik: Rowley 1958, 203. The success of Olifent's punitive expeditions in halting the revival of intertribal fighting was only temporary. One year later Angoram had been destroyed again, and a new expedition had to be sent. Administrator Griffiths, 22 June 1920, to Defence, AWM: 33/57; see also Rowley 1958, 205. Karkar: Mackenzie 1927, 311–312, and Rowley 1958, 199.

227 *Government Gazette Rabaul* 5, no. 11 (20 November 1918): 102.

228 Penman diary, AWM: PR 84/171, 33 (cf. also 21). Administrator Johnston, Rabaul, 14 June 1918, to the Ministry of Defence about Melanesian requests for assistance to be given preferential treatment; AWM: 33/12-10.

229 Precis. Crown vs. Rev. Father Schäfer, Eitape, 4 January 1922, AAC: A 457–800/5/
1. For the influential member of the German parliament Matthias Erzberger, and
his impact on German colonial policy, see Gründer 1987 and the biography by
Epstein 1959.

230 Lieutenant W. E. McIlwaine, "Native Law in the Pacific," *Rabaul Record* 2, no. 8
(1 August 1917): 8–9.

231 Captain A. E. Ireland, "A True Narrative of a Cruise to the St. Mathias Group,"
Rabaul Record 1, no. 16 (1 August 1916): 12. In other regions, mothers buried sick
children alive. *Rabaul Record* 2, no. 4 (1 April 1917): 9 ("Superstitions among
Natives," Report by District Officer Captain McAdam, Morobe); *Rabaul Record* 1,
no. 7 (1 September 1916): 8, and no. 10 (1 December 1916): 7.

232 Piesse memorandum, 5 September 1922, ANL: MS 882/6/687; *Rabaul Record* 1,
no. 3 (1 May 1916): 6.

233 The officer responsible for Rabaul statistics, Cummins, Brisbane, 24 November,
1921, to the Australian Prime Minister, AAC: A 518–F 840/1/3, pt. 1.

234 See comments by Thurnwald 1930, 653.

235 Confidential memorandum from Atlee Hunt, Melbourne, 22 October 1914 (draft
19 October), to Governor Murray, AAC: A 518/1—A 800/1/1, pt. 1A (dispatch),
ANL: MS 52, 4-52/346 (draft).

236 Memorandum by Murray, 16 December 1914, AAC: A 518/1–A 800/1/1, pt. 1A.

237 Pethebridge, Rabaul, 30 November 1915, to the Secretary of Defence, AAC: A 1–
1916/5822. Samuel Pethebridge, "Notes on the Pacific," Nauru, 31 December
1915, AAM: MP 367/1–404/11/129.

238 Naval Secretary, 15 December 1914, to the Secretary of Defence, AAM: B 543-
112/4/457.

239 Pethebridge memorandum, 31 December 1915, AAM: MP 367/1–404/11/129.

240 Ibid.

241 New York speech, 31 May 1918, *Argus* (Melbourne) (1 June 1918); London
speech, 12 July 1918, *The Times* (London) (13 July 1918): "Germans in the Pacific."
Documents relating to this are in AAC: A 2219–XR 1, and CP 351–2/7. See also
Thompson 1980, 208.

242 Brigadier General Hubert Foster, 24 May 1917, AAM: B 197–1851/2/81.

243 Pearce, secret, Melbourne, 14 January 1916, to Hughes, AWM: 3 DRL 2222, Bun
1/fo [folder] 3. Hughes, strictly confidential, London, 21 April 1916, to Pearce,
ibid., Bun/fo 3. See also Thompson 1980, 207. For Hughes' distrust of Japan, Frei
1991, 93.

244 The Governor-General of Australia, Melbourne, 6 March 1916, personal, to the
Colonial Secretary, Bonar Law, ANL: MS 696/6904 to 6920.

245 Ibid., and the Governor-General, 12 June 1916, and 14 February 1920 to the King,
ANL: MS 696/48 and 120. The Governor-General, 18 February 1915 to the Colonial Secretary, Harcourt, on 30 November 1915 to Andrew Bonar Law, 24 December 1916 and 5 December 1918 to Long, ANL: MS 696/656–659, 780, 849–850,
and 1103.

246 The Governor-General, Melbourne, 29 May 1919, to Milner, personal, ANL: MS
696/1156–1157.

247 Memorandum by the Governor-General of Australia, 8 August 1919 ("Administration of Pacific Islands"), ANL: MS 696/2241–2253.

248 Bickham Escott, Suva, 31 December 1916, 15 July and 16 September 1917, to

Munro Ferguson, ANL: MS 696/6990, 6999, and 7005. On Liverpool see below, p. 219.

249 William Hervey Phipps, an Australian journalist who was a lieutenant and censor in Rabaul in 1915, wrote: "Properly cultivated, New Guinea as a whole could easily provide Australia with nearly everything," *Triad,* 10 November 1916, 41.

250 Hughes, 14 September 1920, AAC: A 2219–25.

251 AAC: A5–NG 24/273/1 and 2. Instruction dated 14 September 1920, ibid.

252 "Pacific Mandates," *Sydney Morning Herald,* 8 January 1920.

253 AAC: A 2939–SC 367.

254 Report no. 1229 by the American Consul General, Thomas Sammons, Melbourne, 15 September 1922, NARA: RG 59, 862 d.

255 Colonel James Burns: "Australia in the Pacific," 5 November 1914, to Atlee Hunt, personal, ANL: MS 696/6644–6651 and 7159–7166; memorandum by Burns, 19 January 1915, "The future of Australian Interests in the Pacific" (quotation from this), 7173–7176; memorandum by Burns, 18 September 1916, "Pacific Island—Future Administration," 6819–6822. See also Buckley and Klugman 1983, 7.

256 Ibid.; and Burns, Sydney, 8 February 1915, to Atlee Hunt, ANL: MS 52, 32/52–1581 and MS 696/7194.

257 James Burns, Sydney, 5 November 1914, to Atlee Hunt, ANL: MS 696/6642.

258 On Burns' activities in London, see Burns, London, 18 and 19 August 1915, to Adam Forsyth, 27 and 29 September 1915, to Munro Ferguson, ANL: MS 696/7276, 7279, 7234–7239, and 7240–7241; memorandum by Burns, 7 September 1915, to Bonar Law, 6929–6943. On Preparations for the journey, see Munro Ferguson, Melbourne, 11 January 1915, to Harcourt, 645. See also Buckley and Klugman 1983, 26–27.

259 As early as 24 March 1915, Harcourt had informed Munro Ferguson that an exchange with France was conceivable only as a form of cattle trading. Britain could give up all its rights in the New Hebrides; in return, after the war it would pass its part of the Solomon Islands to New Guinea, which would by then be administered by Australia (Harcourt, private and personal, to the Governor-General of Australia, Downing Street, 24 March, and Oxford, 27 March 1915, ANL: MS 696/1324 and 1325). Shortly thereafter, Harcourt left office as colonial secretary, but the plan did not have the support of a majority in the Australian government either. See Thompson 1980, 205.

260 Bonar Law, London, 6 October 1915, secret, to the Australian Governor-General, ANL: MS 696/7251.

261 "There is little doubt that, after the war, the Commonwealth will only have to ask to receive, and anything that residents or officials of the Groups concerned may say or do will not affect the result." Manager Walter H. Lucas, Sydney, 6 December 1915, to E. Carlson Eliot, ANL: MS 696/6923–6926.

262 Ibid.

263 Ibid., and memorandum Walter Lucas, 19 October 1915, to A. Forsyth, a member of the company's board, ANL: MS 696/7280–7281. See also Buckley and Klugman 1983, 27–28.

264 Telegram from Inchcape, 10 December 1918, to Burns Philp, Sydney, BP Archives Sydney: Box "Mandated Territory." Telegram from Inchcape, 3 December 1918, to Burns Philp, Sydney; Burns, 18 November and 25 November 1918, by telegraph, to the company's representative in London; James Burns, Melbourne, 22 Novem-

ber 1918, to Acting Prime Minister Watt; all in ibid. The Governor-General of Australia, Melbourne, 2 December 1918, private and personal, to the Colonial Secretary, ANL: MS 696/2096. Cable from Watt, 2 December 1918, to Hughes, AAC: CP 360/8–1/2.

265 "Our Government are quite in sympathy, and have followed your proposal with much interest. You may rely upon this Government supporting this proposal you have made." Australian government's official reply to Burns Philp's proposal to deport the Germans from New Guinea immediately after the conclusion of peace, and to transfer their property to a new Australian company, undated (late 1918/early 1919); BP Archives, Sydney, Box "Mandated Territories." Only the vaguer interim reply in Buckley and Klugman 1983, 84.

266 James Burns, Sydney, 21 January 1919, to Mackintosh; BP Archives, Box "Mandated Territories."

267 James Burns, Sydney, 10 December 1918, to Lord Inchcape, London, ibid.

268 Burns, 30 December 1918, to Mackintosh, ibid.

269 Burns, 21 January 1919, to Mackintosh, ibid.

270 Watt, Melbourne, 22 January 1919, to O'Connor, personal, ibid.

271 Mackintosh, London, 6 May 1919, to Burns, ibid.

272 Memorandum Burns Philp, London, "Southsea Island Trade," 22 May 1919 to Hughes, ANL: MS 1538, 24/311–314. Minutes of the meeting with Prime Minister Hughes on 23 May 1919, Mackintosh, London, 28 May 1919; Burns Philp Archives, Sydney, Box "Mandated Territory."

273 Ibid. Buckley and Klugman 1983, 91, are remarkably mute here. See in particular their comment in note 17 ibid.

274 Burns, Sydney, 25 June 1919, to Mackintosh; BP Archives, Box "Mandated Territories."

275 Memorandum Shepherd, 28 June 1919, AAC: A 4–NG 12. The firm of Carpenters protested in vain: "interference with the legitimate business of an Australian firm . . . to compel them to ship their copra by steamers of a firm with whom they were in competition, thus disclosing every transaction and putting them entirely in Burns Philp's hands" (ibid.). Memorandum by the Australian Governor-General, 8 August 1919, ANL: MS 696/2252. Communication by the Australian Federal Government about the existing embargo, under whose terms goods could be transported from New Guinea only on British ships, and only to Australia; Melbourne, 10 May 1920, to the Colonial Secretary, AAC: CP 317/7, Bun 4. For the Japanese "danger" to Burns Philp see also Buckley and Klugman 1983, 87–89.

276 Cabinet bill Shepherd, 18 July 1919: "Late German New Guinea," AAC: A 5–NG 24/2028. On 8 July, the cabinet had still favored an independent member from the financial sector. Shepherd succeeded in overturning this recommendation. It was also Shepherd's and Hunt's doing that the military administrator of New Guinea, Johnston, was not called to sit on the commission. A meeting of the secretaries for Home and Territories (Atlee Hunt), Defence (Trumble), and the Prime Minister's Office (Shepherd), had originally placed Johnston in second position, behind Murray but ahead of Hunt and Lucas. Notes by Shepherd, 19 June 1919, ibid.

277 Atlee Hunt, 30 June 1919, to Shepherd, AAC: A 5–NG 24/2028.

278 James Burns, 1 August 1919, to the Governor-General of Australia, personal, ANL: MS 696/7053.

279 The new General Manager, Black, 2 November 1919, by telegraph to Lucas, Burns Philp Archives, Sydney, Box "Mandated Territory."

280 Among others, Lucas, Rabaul, 30 September 1919, private, to Burns, and 18 October 1919, to Black, ibid.

281 Rowley 1958, 296–310.

282 Memorandum by Murray, 14 March 1919, AAC: CP 661/15/1. See also Rowley 1958, 296–310.

283 Memorandum by Administrator Johnston for the Royal Commission, 10 October 1919, AAC: CP 661/15/2. Johnston, Rabaul, 15 October 1919 to the Governor-General, Munro Ferguson, ANL: MS 696/6685–6688. See also Rowley 1958, 309.

284 Murray, 11 February 1920, to the Minister for Home and Territories, ANL: MS 1538/16/205–207.

285 Memorandum of the Officer in charge of Trade & Customs, E. Featherstone Phibbs, Rabaul, 17 July 1920: "Report on Trade for period ending 30th June 1920," AAC: A 1–23/18422. See Table 3 above, p. 53.

286 Johnston, Rabaul, 15 October 1919, to the Governor-General, Munro Ferguson, ANL: MS 696/6685–6688. See also Rowley 1958, 310 and Buckley and Klugman 1983, 94.

287 Memorandum by W. H. Cox for the Australian government: "Some Suggestions as to the Policy in the Mandated Territory of (late) German New Guinea," no date [c. April 1921], AAC: A 2219–19. Memorandum by Bishop Couppé for the Royal Commission, Vunapope, 9 September 1919, AAC: CP 661/15/1.

288 Lucas' annual salary was £21,600. After the civil administration took over in July 1921, the government extended his contract again; AAC: A 518–E 800/1/3, pt. 1. A district officer who, in New Guinea's interests, wanted to send two members of the Expropriation Board headed by Lucas back to Australia was informed by Lucas, not the Administrator, that this matter did not concern him. An Australian judge in Rabaul, who reversed a decision taken by the Expropriation Board, had to pack his bags; Bassett 1969, 19, 37, and 57. Eyewitness Bassett to the members of the Expropriation Board: "the scum of Australia," ibid., 44. See also Thompson 1990, 78. To claim that "B.P. directors were shocked and hurt by Lucas' abandonment" (Buckley and Klugman 1983, 95) is a farce. As general manager and a director of a subsidiary company, the Solomon Islands Development Company, Lucas kept his close links with Burns Philp (ibid., 95 and 254 n. 27).

289 Submission to Cabinet by Lucas, 29 March 1920, ANL: MS 52, 34—52/1627.

290 Interim Report Lewis F. East on the Administration of Papua and New Guinea, AAC: A 981–NG 30, pt. 1.

291 Report on New Guinea Expropriation, no date, AAC: CP 103/11, "New Guinea Mining," 1/5; memorandum by the Chief Surveyor, Major Cummins, Rabaul, 4 January 1919, to the Minister of Defence, AAC: CP 103/11, New Guinea Reports, Box 1/14: "Misc. Papers and returns re Expropriation"; memorandum Deputy Judge, Advoc. General Mackenzie, "Promoting British Interests in German New Guinea," Rabaul, 4 May 1916, AAC: CP 103/11, New Guinea Reports, Box 1/13.

292 Treatment of foreigners and foreign interests in the Territory of New Guinea. A summary to 31st May, 1922, AAC: A 2219/25. See also Rowley 1958, 317–325, and the eyewitnesses Bassett 1969, 38, and Townsend 1968, 27–29.

293 Treatment of foreigners . . . , AAC: A 2219/25.

CHAPTER 3: MICRONESIA AND THE WAR

1   Hambruch 1915, 214–218. Hambruch still provides the best ethnological account of Nauruan life. His book was the result of extensive fieldwork on the island and contains a wealth of information and data. Unfortunately it is available only in German, and this has prevented it from being as widely known as it deserves.

2   See Treue 1976, Williams and Macdonald 1985, and Weeramantry 1992.

3   Memorandum by the Naval Secretary, Melbourne, 3 December 1917, "Report on Deportations at Nauru," AAM: MP 367/1/0–404/11/24.

4   Harold Gaze, 17 September 1914, to the Secretary, Australian Ministry of Defence, cable from the Minister of Defence, Pearce, 19 September 1914, to the Colonial Secretary, and cable from the Colonial Secretary, London, 15 September 1914, to the Governor-General of Australia, ibid. From 12 September 1914 on, Gaze, the Pacific Phosphate Company's representative in Melbourne, continually pestered the Australian secretary for the navy to take steps to have the Germans deported from Nauru and to allow phosphate mining to resume as quickly as possible; AAM: MP 1049/1–14/0454.

5   Holmes, Rabaul, 13 November 1914, to the Minister of Defence in Melbourne, AAM: MP 367/1/0–404/11/163, and AWM: 33/10. Telegraphic instructions from the Australian Minister of Defence, 24 and 27 October 1914, ibid. Secretary of the Navy, 13 October 1914, to British Resident Commissioner, Ocean island and (same date), to the Pacific Phosphate Company, AAM: MP 1049/1–14/0454.

6   *Stationsleiter* (head of station), Wostrack, Tuesküb, 10 June 1917, to the German Colonial Office, BAP: RKolA no. 2631 (an English translation of the same letter can be found in AAC: A 4–NG 38). The Nauruans were strictly forbidden to have any contact with the Germans. Police Chief Peters, Bad Suderode, 4 June 1917, to the German Colonial Office, ibid. According to Wostrack, the Australians feared a Nauruan uprising in favor of the Germans.

7   Cable from the Colonial Secretary, London, 28 December 1914, AAM: MP 1049/1–14/0454.

8   Cable from the Colonial Secretary, 30 November 1915, telegram from the Administrator, 10 December 1915, and reply by the Australian government, 16 December 1915, AAC: A 2219/1.

9   Application by the British High Commissioner for the Western Pacific for a change of name, 12 February 1915, and telegram with the Colonial Secretary's reply, 7 April 1915, ANL: G 21121.

10 Harcourt, 15 April 1914, to the High Commissioner, ANL: G 21123.

11 Telegram from Workman, 4 March 1915, to the Western Pacific High Commission, ANL: G 21120; Workman, 20 April 1915, to the High Commissioner, ANL: G 21123.

12 Undated memorandum [c. 1921], "Ownership of Land in Nauru," AAC: A 518–P 800/1/2.

13 Secret enquiry by the Australian Prime Minister, cable, 5 November 1914 (*sic*: the occupation did not take place until 6 November), to the Colonial Secretary, as to whether Nauru was now open for trade. Negative reply from the Colonial Secretary, 9 November 1914, with instructions to await the arrival of the colonial official. Note in the margin, written by the First Naval Member (Australian): "I fear Nauru has already been opened for trade!" (ibid.).

14   *Financial News,* 28 July 1917, BAP: RKolA no. 2511. Burns Philp had attempted to gain a hold in vain (Buckley and Klugman 1983, 65).

15   The Colonial Secretary, 14 October 1915, to the Pacific Phosphate Company, London, and 21 October 1915 to the British High Commissioner for the Western Pacific, ANL: G 21133. Pacific Phosphate Company, London, 2 March 1920, to the Colonial Secretary, AAC: CP 78/22–20/544. On the transport of the Chinese coolies to Nauru in German times, and on the appalling conditions they suffered, see Firth 1978*a.*

16   Hughes, Paris, 12 March 1919, to the Acting Prime Minister, Watt (secret), AAC: A 518–Q 112/6/1, and CP 360/8, Bun 1/3. Australian government memorandum, undated: "Nauru. Precis," AAC: CP 351/1–Box 6/17.

17   Acting Prime Minister Watt, conveying the cabinet resolution, 1 May 1919, to Hughes (secret), AAC: CP 360/8, Bun 1/4.

18   Hughes, Paris, 7 May 1919, by telegraph to Acting Prime Minister Watt (secret), AAC: CP 360/8, Bun 1/4. "Nauru Precis," AAC: CP 351/1, Box 6/17.

19   Ibid. The term "British Empire" was coined by Lloyd George. On the afternoon of 6 May, during a private conversation with Wilson, the British Prime Minister presented the formula to the American president. Wilson accepted it, stressing that Nauru "would be placed under the regime of the open door" (see Link 1992, 497 and *FRUS, The Paris Peace Conference* 5, 492). The term "empire" never meant that Canada or South Africa were involved in the administration of Nauru (Snelling 1975–1976, 21).

20   Legal report by Robert Garran, 7 May 1919, "re Disposition of Nauru," AAC: CP 351/1–Box 6/17.

21   Telegram, Watt to Hughes, 9 May 1919 (confidential), AAC: CP 360/8, Bun 1/4, and AAC: A 2219–19.

22   "Nauru Precis," AAC: CP 351/1–Box 6/17; Hughes, most secret and confidential, Paris, 4 June 1919, by telegraph to Watt, AAC: A 518–Q 112/6/1, and AAC: CP 360/8, Bun 1/4.

23   Scarr 1967, 270–277; and Williams and Macdonald 1985, 15–16 and 90.

24   Alwin R. Dickinson, Managing Director of the Pacific Phosphate Company, London, 19 June 1919, confidential, to Milner, AAC: CP 351/1–Box 6/17.

25   Milner, 16 July 1919, secret, to the Governors-General of Australia and of New Zealand, AAC: A 518–D 112/6/4, pt. 1 (Australia) and NZA: G 2–51 (New Zealand).

26   John William Salmond, Solicitor General for New Zealand, Memorandum for the Prime Minister, Wellington, 7 October 1919, NZA: G 2–51. See also Weeramantry 1992, 55.

27   Secret telegram in cipher from Milner, 27 September 1919, to the Governor-General of Australia, "private and personal," and Governor-General Ferguson, Melbourne, 30 September 1919, to Prime Minister Hughes, secret and personal; AAC: A 518–D 112/6/4, pt. 1. Milner, 5 December 1919, private and personal telegram to the Governor-General of New Zealand (the delay after informing Australia is typical!), NZA: G 5–97.

28   Secret and confidential telegram from Hughes, 13 October 1919, to the Colonial Secretary, AAC: A 518–D 112/6/4, pt. 1

29   Colonial Secretary, 25 February 1920, confidential, to Governor-General Liverpool, NZA: G 2–51. Milner, confidential, 27 July 1920, to the Governor-General of New Zealand, NZA: G 2–52. "Nauru Island Agreement," AAC: A 6661–391.

30 *The Times* (London), 17 June 1920.

31 Report no. 517 by the American envoy, Arthur Bliss Lane, Berne, 24 August 1922, to the Secretary of State, NARA: RG 59, 862c.

32 Memorandum by the Australian Prime Minister's Department, 13/26 January 1922, "Recruiting of Native Labour for Nauru," AAC: A 518–CA 118/6.

33 Pope, Rabaul, 17 October 1921, to the Administrator of New Guinea, AAC: A 518–CA 118/6. The Administrator of New Guinea, Wisdom, Rabaul, 26 October 1921, to the Prime Minister's Department, ibid. Memorandum Walter Lucas, Technical Adviser, to the Australian Prime Minister, 19 January 1922, ibid. Summary in AAC: A 2219/13.

34 Pope, Melbourne, 4 January 1922, to the Prime Minister's Department, AAC: A 518–CA 118/6. Chambers, British Phosphate Commission, Melbourne, 21 November 1922 to Piesse, ANL: MS 882/3/148.

35 Memorandum by Harold Gaze, Chief Representative of the Australian Phosphate Commission, 18 October 1921, and reply by the Australian Prime Minister, 26 January 1922, to a question from a Labor MP, AAC: A 518–B 118/6, pt. 1.

36 The Administrator of Nauru, Griffiths, 23 April 1923, to the Prime Minister's Department, AAC: A 518–CA 118/6. Administrator Griffiths, 12 May 1924, to the British Phosphate Commission Nauru, ibid.; the Governor-General of Australia, 3 June 1924, by telegraph, to the Colonial Secretary, ibid. The meeting of the Mandate Commission was held on 24 June 1924 in Geneva; Viviani 1970, 56. In general, Viviani's account of Nauruan history is unreliable, because it is riddled with errors and tends to whitewash what happened to the island (see esp. ibid., 38: "They [the Nauruans] were far less affected by the establishment of an industry on their island than most other Pacific islanders"; and similar arguments, 59). On the plight of the New Guineans, she uncritically quotes the New Zealand Phosphate Commissioner's assessment: "they were not a success," ibid.

37 Holmes, Rabaul, 13 November 1914, to the Minister of Defence in Melbourne, AAM: MP 367/1/0–404/11/163, and AWM: 33/10.

38 Diary T. H. Donaldson, entries of 11 and 12 November 1914, PMB: 967. Cf. Viviani 1970, 41.

39 *Rabaul Record* 1, no. 3 (1 May 1916): 8. Administrator Workman, 20 April 1915, to the British High Commissioner, ANL: G 21123. Memorandum James Burns, 12 January 1917: "On the Administration of the British colonies . . . ," 14, AAC: CP 78/34/1–8.

40 Petition from the Nauruans of 18 July 1919 to the King of England, AAC: A 518–P 800/1/2.

41 March 1921. Undated Australian memorandum, "Ownership of Land in Nauru," AAC: A 518–P 800/1/2.

42 The Governor-General of Australia, telegraph of 9 February 1922, to the Colonial Secretary, in his report confirming that instructions had been carried out, AAC: A 6661–392. Report by Administrator Griffiths, no. 2, September 1921, AAC: A 518–H 850/1/2, pt. 2; Administration Order No. 16, 24 September 1921/Compulsory Education Ordinance, 23 September 1921, ibid. Compulsory schooling, introduced on 1 October 1921, applied to Nauruans between the ages of six and sixteen, and Europeans from six to fifteen.

43 Administrator's Annual Report, 31 December 1922, Griffiths, 1 March 1923, AAC: CP 103/11, Nauru Box 1/8.

44   Administration Order No. 21, 29 October 1921/Nauru Lands Ordinance, 24 October 1921, AAC: CP 316/16, and AAC: CP 103/11, Nauru Box 1/5.

45   Administrative Order No. 26, 3 December 1921/Suspension of Sentences Ordinance, 25 November 1921, was typical. It allowed the Administrator to suspend any prison sentence, but also to cancel this suspension without giving any reasons in either case. The person affected had to go straight to prison, without any trial or judgment, to serve out "old" sentences; AAC: CP 316/16.

46   Order relative to the movements of natives between sunrise and sunset, 13 July 1921, AAC: CP 316/16; Administration Order No. 12, 27 August 1921/ Duties of Chiefs of Districts, 26 August 1921, ibid.

47   Administrator Griffiths, Nauru, 23 August 1921, in confidence to the Secretary in the Prime Minister's Department, Melbourne, AAC: A 518–B 118/6, pt. 1.

48   The Nauruans had planned to open their own shop and had already raised £1,000 founding capital; reports no. 3 and no. 6 by Administrator Griffiths, October 1921/ January 1922, AAC: A 518–H 850/1/2, pt. 2. See also Petit-Skinner 1981, 24. The idea of starting a cooperative store had come to Head Chief Detudamo during a visit to the United States (ibid.).

49   Report by Administrator Griffiths, Nauru, 15 September 1921, AAC: CP 103/11, Nauru Box 1/1.

50   Administrator Charles Workman, Pleasant Island, 14 February 1917, confidential, to the British High Commissioner of the Western Pacific, ANL: G 21151.

51   Sawyer diary, MLS: MSS 383, 11 July 1916 entry.

52   Albert Ellis, confidential report, 26 August 1921, AAC: A 518–CA 118/6.

53   Griffiths, Nauru, 14 September 1922, to Piesse; ANL: MS 882/3/127. Lawrence R. Clapp, Government Medical Officer, Health Report Nauru 1922, Nauru, 1 March 1923, AAC: CP 103/11, Nauru Box 1/8. F. G. Morgan, Report on the Investigation of a number of cases of Leprosy at Nauru, Central Pacific, ibid. The doctor on Nauru was monopolized by the European employees of the British Phosphate Commission (although none of the Europeans had contracted leprosy). There was an unpleasant tradition of this sort of behavior. As early as 1917, the government doctor had complained to the Administrator that the Pacific Phosphate Company was putting pressure on him to treat exclusively the employees of the company; ANL: G 21152.

54   Report no. 9, Administrator Griffiths, 1922, AAC: A 518–H 850/1/2, pt. 2.

55   Peattie 1988, 64–68.

56   Missionschronik von Ponape (Mission chronicle of Ponape), 124, AKM: 59.

57   Report by the German government doctor in the Marshall Islands, Dr. Kopp, 20 February 1915, BAP: RKolA no. 2631. See also Purcell 1967, 153.

58   Confidential memo, 18 July 1917, Senior Naval Aide Guam, to the American Commander of Guam, Roy C. Smith (for Saipan), NARA: RG 38, K-5-a: 9217.

59   For example, a series of articles in *Nichi Nichi Shimbun*, 27 July 1915ff. Report No. 259 by the American consul-general in Yokohama, 5 July 1915, NARA: RG 59, 862h. On Yamamoto, see Peattie 1988, 51. Yamamoto also published a popular account of Micronesia's economic potential, *Waga Kokumin no Kaigai Hatten to Nan'yo Shinsen Ryo-chi* (The overseas development of our country and the newly occupied regions in the South Seas; Tokyo, 1917).

60   Peattie 1988, 51. On Japan's plans for a southward advance, see now Frei 1991.

61   For early Japanese trespassing indigenous customs, see Buckley and Klugman 1986, 46.

62   Memo from the War Ministry news service to the German Colonial Office, 28 December 1915, with material from Japanese newspapers, BAP: RKolA no. 2623. See also *DKB* 26 (1915): 148–149; "The Phosphate Deposits of Angaur Island," *Far Eastern Review* 7 (1915): 49–51; and Peattie 1988, 43 and 66–67. On Japanese fortune hunters in Micronesia, see report No. 259 by the American consul-general in Yokohama, 5 July 1915, NARA: RG 59, 862h.

63   Confidential memo from the Senior Naval Aide to the American commander in Guam, Roy C. Smith, 18 July 1917, NARA: RG 38, K-5-a: 9217.

64   "Administration of the South Seas Islands under Japanese Mandate" (1922), appendix, AAC: A 981, Marshalls 1, pt. 2. Report "Administration Japanese Mandate," Geneva, 6 April 1922.

65   Peattie 101–103.

66   Report by A. Robinson, captain of the Burns Philp steamer *Tambo*, 26 June 1918, to the British Resident Commissioner of the Gilbert and Ellice Islands on Ocean Island, AAM: MP 1049/1 — 18/0345. Copra tax: "Administration of the South Seas Islands under Japanese Mandate" (1922), AAC: A 981, Marshalls 1, pt. 2.

67   Undated report [1918] by the Captain of the Australian ship *Pukaki*, which was in the Caroline and Marshall Islands to recruit phosphate workers in 1918, to the British Resident Commissioner of the Gilbert and Ellice Islands, AAM: MP 1049/1 — 189/0345. Confidential Australian navy memo, undated [c. 1920], "Pacific Island Groups in Japanese Occupation," AAM: MP 1049/1 — 1920/090. On 1 August 1922, Matsuda, Japanese representative on the League of Nations' Mandate Commission, confirmed that the Japanese government now regarded unsettled land that had not been planted as the property of the state. "Administration of the South Seas Islands under Japanese Mandate" (1922), AAC: A 981, Marshalls 1, pt. 2.

68   AAM: MP 1049/1 — 1920/090.

69   Telegram from the Japanese Foreign Ministry in Tokyo, 17 February 1915, to the Japanese Consul-General in Australia: "The Imperial Government sanction the continuation by Burns Philp and Co. of shipping and trading relations in the Marshall Islands," AAC: A 1 — 1920/7685. Piesse Memorandum, "Australian Interests in islands north of the equator and Japanese interests in German New Guinea. A review of policy from September, 1914, to July 1920," 10 September 1920, AAC: A 981 — League of Nations 1st Assembly, file 4. Minutes of a meeting of the board of directors of Burns Philp, 8 December 1916, about expanding their operations in the Marshall Islands, ANL: MS 696/7122–7127. Confidential reports by Atkins Kroll & Co. to the American State Department about their trips through Micronesia, NARA: RG 59, 862 l. Letter by the Manager of the Jaluit Company, J. E. Krümling, Yokohama, 2 July 1915, NARA: RG 59, 862 h. The managers of the Jaluit Company's trading stations were expelled in May and June 1915 (whereas the employees were allowed to remain until 1919), ibid. The final remnant of German influence on the Micronesian economy was swept away on 1 March 1916 when the currency based on the silver mark was abolished (German gold continued to be accepted). Confidential memo, Senior Naval Aide, Guam, 18 July 1917, NARA: RG 38, K-5-a: 9217.

70   Private communication of 16 April 1915 from Burns to the Governor-General of Australia, ANL: MS 696/7291.

71   Peattie 1988, 120.

72   Memorandum of the Australian navy's intelligence service, "Pacific Island Groups

in Japanese Occupation" [c. 1920], AAM: MP 1049/1 — 1920/090. Missionschronik von Ponape, 142 (May 1917), AKM: 59. An American historian concludes that the American secret service reports contained "secrets without substance", see Ballendorf 1984.

73 *Asahi* (Tokyo), 28 June 1915, *Fukuoka Nichi Nichi Shinbun*, 23 November 1923; League of Nations, Report on the Administration of the Territory under the Japanese Mandate, Geneva, 6 April 1922, 6–7; Secret Abstracts of Intelligence, General Staff, Straits Settlement 9 (1918), 137, AAC: A 2219/4. "Japanische Ansiedler für die deutsche Südsee," *Vossische Zeitung,* no. 446, 12 September 1915. On the speed of Japanese immigration during the 1920s and 1930s, Peattie 1988, 153–197.

74 Situation report by the naval station in Guam, 4 October 1922, compiled from various sources, esp. communications of 20 May 1921 from the company Atkins Kroll, NARA: RG 38, K-5-a: 9217.

75 Report by R. MacAuslane ("Tambo"), 27 October 1918, to the British Resident Commissioner of Ocean Island, AAC: A 3932–SC 240. Thomas J. McMahon, "The Japanese Occupation of the Marshall Islands," *Stead's Review,* 22 February 1919, 157–160; idem, "Where is Australian Trade?" *Sydney Morning Herald,* 7 December 1918. Conversation with Ngirongor Melimarang, 22 November 1986.

76 Capuchin mission in Truk, 8 and 18 September 1915, to the Superior; AKM: no number. Sawyer diary, 1916, MLS: MSS 383. Purcell 1967, 225, and Peattie 1988, 209, are incorrect.

77 Missionschronik von Ponape, 133 (1916), AKM: 59. The fact that one of the chiefs sent along his own adopted daughter supports this interpretation.

78 Confidential report from Atkins Kroll & Co. to the American Secretary of State, undated [October 1921], NARA: RG 59, 862 l.

79 Conversation with Fumio Ns Rengiil, 23 November 1986. To start with, there were only two houses, each with ten women: conversation with Ngirongor Melimarang, 22 November 1986.

80 Conversations with Ngirongor Melimarang, 22 November 1986 and Fumio Ns Rengiil, 23 November 1986. During the military administration, alcohol could be sold to locals by anyone who had bought a license; chiefs did not need a license. The import of firearms was subject to relatively mild restrictions. Decrees of 26 October 1915 and 17 January 1917: Report on Administration of Japanese Mandate, Geneva, 6 April 1922, Appendix nos. 5 and 6. Purcell's claim (1967, 224) that no alcohol was sold to the local population is based on too uncritical a reading of the mandate reports on the Japanese administration.

81 "People from Yap compelled by force and whisky to work on Angaur," report by Captain Steinhauer of the West-Karolinen Gesellschaft (Western Carolines Company) schooner *Triton,* no date [June 1915], BAP: RKolA no. 2622. Cf. "The Phosphate Deposits of Angaur Island," *Far Eastern Review* 7 (1915): 49–51. F. Scholz (formerly from Yap), Cuxhaven, 21 February 1916, to the German Colonial Office, BAP: RKolA no. 2623. On the Japanese alcohol trade in the Caroline Islands, see report by the Captain of the *Pronto,* Nauru, 6 April 1915, to the Pacific Phosphate Commission, Nauru, ANL: G 21122.

82 Interview with Toshiro Tezuka, head of the island civil administration set up in 1918, "Japan in the South Seas," *Japan Chronicle,* 28 November 1918; League of Nations, Report on the Administration of the Territory under the Japanese Mandate, Geneva, 6 April 1922, 8–9; "De facto compulsory education on Kusaie,"

report by the captain of the Pacific Phosphate Company's recruiting ship, *Pukaki*, no date [1918], to the Resident Commissioner of the Gilbert and Ellice Islands, AAM: MP 1049/1—18/0345.

83   24 September 1916; AKM: C 103.

84   Report by Dönges, missionary from Liebenzell, Truk, 7 December 1915, BAP: RKolA no. 2623.

85   Statement by Maria Sablan Reyes, in Ballendorf, Peck, and Anderson 1986, 46 (see also ibid., 58). The collection edited by Ballendorf contains many informative accounts by islanders of their school days under the Japanese. Accounts by Palau islanders on Japanese education can be found in *Oral Historiography* 1986; also, my own interviews with Pedro Martinez Ada, 14 November 1986, and Fumio Ns Rengiil, 23 November 1986.

86   Where, however, they kept apart from the indigenous children. Statement by Ursula Atalig, in Ballendorf, Peck, and Anderson 1986, 17. Pedro Ada was taken to Japan as a youth during the war to be trained to teach Japanese to the Micronesians. Later he studied a number of subjects, including German and English, at Sophia University in Tokyo (see ibid., 26; also my own conversation with Pedro Martinez Ada, 14 November 1986). The Adas had already been among the most highly privileged Pacific Islanders under the Germans. The indigenous telegraph operators in the German administration were transferred from Yap to Saipan, but were permitted to continue working. Report by the captain of the *Triton* (Western Caroline Company schooner), undated [June 1915], BAP: RKolA no. 2622. Communication from the Deutsch-Niederländische Telegraphengesellschaft (German-Dutch Telegraph Company), Cologne, 12 June 1920, to the German postal ministry, BAP: RKolA no. 2623.

87   Mariana Islands: See the attitudes expressed by indigenous people in Ballendorf, Peck, and Anderson 1986, 28, 44, and 58. Palau: conversation with Fumio Ns Rengiil, 23 November 1986.

88   Missionschronik von Ponape, 127 and 130–131, AKM: 59. Palau: statement by Father Placidus Müller to the American Consul-General in Yokohama. Despatch No. 323 from the Consul-General, 11 February 1916, NARA: RG 84, B 162: 1916/711.5. Truk: letter from the Capuchin mission there to the mission in Lukunor, 30 October 1915; AKM: no number. Truk, Lukunor, and Jaluit: statement by Captain Robert Stobo on Japanese Activities in the Caroline Islands, no date [April 1918], AAC: A 2219/1, vol. 3. Protestant mission: report by Dönges, missionary from Liebenzell, Truk, 7 December 1915, BAP: RKolA no. 2623, also published in *"Chinas Millionen." Monatsschrift der Liebenzeller Mission* 17, no. 3 (March 1916).

89   Missionschronik von Ponape, 133, AKM: 59.

90   Ibid., 143–144.

91   Lehmann, Shanghai, 22 June 1916, BAP: RKolA no. 2623.

92   Aloysia Fettig, "Unsere Erlebnisse auf der Insel Palau-Koror während des Krieges 1914/15" (Our experiences on the island of Palau-Korror during the war, 1914–1915), Archives of the School Sisters of St. Francis, Catholic Mission, Koror, Palau. Statement by Father Wunibald Fechter to the American Consul-General in Yokohama, Despatch from the consul-general No. 323, 11 February 1916, NARA: RG 84, B. 162: 1916/711.5. Conversations with Chuodelechad, 22 November 1986, and Joseph Tellei, 22 November 1986.

93   Missionschronik von Ponape, 126–127, AKM: 59.

94 On the uprising, see Hempenstall 1978.

95 H. Coerper, Liebenzell, 12 June 1918, to the German Colonial Office, BAP: RKolA no. 2623.

96 Missionschronik von Ponape, 141, AKM: 59. League of Nations, Report on the Administration of the Territory under the Japanese Mandate, Geneva, 6 April 1922, 11; See also Shuster 1982, 21. The statement (ibid.) that the first Protestant missionaries from Japan arrived only in 1920 is incorrect.

97 Lopinot, *Karolinenmission*, 36; "Missions in the Pacific," *Sydney Morning Herald*, 18 December 1919; cf. Shuster 1982, 21.

98 A statement made by the head of the civil administration, Tezuka, at the end of November 1918, supports this (*Japan Chronicle*, 28 November 1918).

99 Shuster 1982, 21–22.

100 Report by the American chargé d'affaires, Wheeler, Tokyo, 14 August 1915, NARA: RG 59, 862 h. *Asahi*, 2 August 1915. Communication by the German news agency for the Orient in Tokyo, 16 August 1916, BAP: RKolA no. 2623. Report by Captain Handley of the *Tambo* (a Burns Philp steamer), 30 June 1917, private and confidential to the Resident Commissioner of Ocean Island, C. E. Eliot, ANL: MS 696, 6679. See also Peattie 1988, 109–111.

101 Statement by August Ramarui in *Oral Historiography* (1986). Statements by Ngiraklang and Joseph Tellei about *kanko dan*, ibid. See also Ballendorf, Peck, and Anderson 1986, 25–26. For the impressions of the Chamorros, conversation with Pedro Martinez Ada, 14 November 1986.

102 Catholic Mission Truk, 18 September 1915, to the Superior, AKM: no number. H. Coerper, Liebenzell, 12 June 1918 to the German Colonial Office, BAP: RKolA no. 2326. "Japan and the War," *Japan Weekly Chronicle*, 12 September 1918.

103 Ballendorf, Peck, and Anderson 1986, 25; conversation with Pedro Martinez Ada, 14 November 1986.

104 Report by Krümling, formerly manager of the Jaluit Company in the Marshall Islands, San Francisco, 24 July 1915, BAP: RKolA no. 2631. Missionschronik von Ponape, 126, AKM: 59. Catholic Mission Truk, 30 October 1915 to the missionaries in Lukunor, AKM: no number. Palau: Conversation with Joseph Tellei, 22 November 1986. "We do share the same colour and the same noses, after all" (Loleit, DKZ, 1915: 171). Similar arguments were used to try to win the Melanesians over to the Japanese cause after the occupation of New Guinea in the Second World War. Leadley 1976, 236 B.

105 Statement by Mymelay Bismarck, *Oral Historiography*, 1986.

106 Report by the Captain of the Pacific Phosphate recruiting ship *Pukaki*, undated [1918], to the Resident Commissioner of the Gilbert and Ellice Islands, AAM: MP 1049/1 — 18/0345.

107 Information about the treatment of Korean workers is extremely scanty. We know of a case on Kusaie when Korean plantation laborers, who had run away in 1920 because they were starving, were brutally beaten; at least five died of their injuries. Secret report by Captain B. P. Dickert, no date [1926], AAC: A 981-Marshall/Caroline Islands, 3 old. For Peattie to base his claim (1988, 220) that the Koreans ranked more highly on the single fact that their children, unlike those of the Micronesians, went to *shogakko* schools is inadequate. His statement that the Okinawans were distinguished from the Micronesians in being permitted to drink alcohol (ibid.) does not take into account that, under the conditions of the mandate, the

Japanese were obliged to prohibit the sale of alcohol to the Micronesian population at least for the sake of appearances.

108 Ballendorf, Peck, and Anderson 1986, esp. 36, 40, 48, 49, and 52.

109 Palau: "really scared of the Japanese"—Joseph Tellei, former Palauan police chief in the Japanese colonial administration, in conversation with me, 22 November 1986. According to Tellei, the Japanese used wooden sticks and belts to administer beatings. Ponape, Truk, and Kusaie: "the natives are terribly scared," report by G. A. W. Stevens, *Pronto,* Nauru, 6 April 1915, to the Pacific Phosphate Company Nauru, ANL: G 21122. Kusaie: report by the Captain of the recruiting ship *Pukaki,* undated [1918], to the Resident Commissioner of the Gilbert and Ellice Islands, AAM: MP 1049/1—18/0345. Satowan (Mortlock group): F. W. Thompson reporting on a recruiting expedition to the Caroline and Marshall Islands, Nauru, 21 July 1920, to the Administrator of Nauru, AAC: A 2219, vol. 23. In general: F. Wallin, no date [1915], to James Burns, ANL: MS 696/6950.

110 Nicholas M. Leon Gerrero, a Chamorro from Saipan, in Ballendorf, Peck, and Anderson 1986, 29.

111 Conversation with Joseph Tellei, 22 November 1986; see note 81 above for how people from Yap were compelled to work.

112 In conversation with Captain Robert Stobo from the *Pukaki* in April 1918. Stobo made some (undated) notes "on Japanese Activities in the Caroline Islands," AAC: AA 2219/1, vol. 3. According to a report by the American military attaché in Japan, the Ponapeans were the only Micronesians who did not fear the Japanese and thus earned their respect. Tokyo, 29 April 1920, NARA: RG 38, K-5-a: 13086.

113 Takeo Tezuka, head of the civil administration in the Japanese military government of Micronesia, in an interview with the Tokyo newspaper *Japan Chronicle,* 28 November 1918. On Yap a respected chief visited a radio station employee to say good-bye on the night before the Germans departed (2 November 1914). The German advised the islander to remain calm under the Japanese, as any insurrection would be treated harshly. The islander replied that the people of Yap were no longer capable of organizing military resistance. F. Scholz, Cuxhaven, 21 February 1916, BAP: RKolA no. 2623.

114 Barnett 1960, 83; Shuster 1982, 34; and esp. Tellei 1988, 2–5.

115 Barnett 1960, 83–84, and Tellei 1988, 4.

116 Shuster 1982, 34, and Tellei 1988, 5.

117 Ongesii preached an uncompromising rejection of everything foreign: metal, non-Palauan food, and hospitals. He taught that as the Palauans were of a different skin color from both the Japanese and the whites, they could never share a common path. Consequently, there would also be two heavens, segregated by skin color; Barnett 1960, 84–85, and Shuster 1982, 34–35. Today the Modekngei run a cooperative store and a secondary school in which Palauan traditions are taught. The future of the movement is uncertain; Tellei 1988, 1, 8, and 22–23.

118 Confidential memo, Senior Naval Aide, Guam, 18 July 1917, NARA: RG 38, K-5-a: 9217. Government and mission employees, old people, the sick, and families with a large number of children were exempted from paying tax, as they had been under the Germans. The head-tax was suspended or reduced after typhoon damage, as had been the case before 1915. Criminal and civil court regulations for the South Seas Islands, 11 October 1915, para. 7. Report on Administration of Japanese Mandate, Geneva, 6 April 1922, Appendix no. 4. For the initial attempt to ignore the

headmen, see report by G. A. W. Stevens, Captain of the *Pronto*, Nauru, 6 April 1915, to the Pacific Phosphate Company, ANL: G 21122.

119 Regulations concerning the functions and duties of chiefs in the Marshall Islands, 3 March 1921, AAC: A 518—F 840/1/3, pt. 1. Chiefs could impose punishments of up to twenty days' imprisonment for refusal to obey orders they had given; if official instructions by the Japanese were not followed, they could impose up to thirty days' imprisonment.

120 "Memorandum on the Administration of the Islands in the South Seas under Japanese Mandate," by H. J. Parlett, Counsellor at the British embassy, Tokyo, 1922, AAC: A 981, Marshalls 1, pt. 2; see also Peattie 1988, 86–90.

121 Communication by J. E. Krümling, Manager of the Jaluit Company, Yokohama, 2 July 1915, NARA: RG 59, 862 h. Letter by Krümling from San Francisco, 24 July 1915, BAP: RKolA no. 2631. Report by Captain A. Robinson of the *Tambo* (a Burns Philp steamer), 26 June 1918, to the Resident Commissioner of the Gilbert and Ellice Islands, AAM: MP 1049/1—18/0345. Confidential report by J. R. Handley, Captain of the Burns Philp schooner *Mauno* trading in the Marshall Islands, 15 June 1921, AAC: A 3932—SC 240. See also Peattie 1988, 25 and 119–123.

122 Report by F. W. Thompson after a recruiting expedition to the Caroline Islands for the British Phosphate Commission, Nauru, 21 July 1920, to the Administrator of Nauru, AAC: AA 2219, vol. 23. Similar statements exist for the Mortlock group; see AKM: 51.

123 "Relief of the Starving Inhabitants of Rota," *Guam News Letter* 7 (1915), no. 1: 2–4, no. 3: 6ff., and no. 6: 6. *Annual Report of the Governor of Guam*, 1916, Micronesian Area Research Center. Father Corbinian, Rota, 3 July 1915, to the head of the Capuchin mission in Germany (via Guam), BAP: RKolA no. 2622. Ambassador Bernstorff, Cedarhurst, New York, 18 August 1915, to the German Chancellor (communicated by the Samoan Iiga Pisa, from Guam), ibid.; Protokollarische Erklärung des Stationsleiters Walter Böhme, Saipan, vor Oberregierungsrat Dr. Krauss (Explanation taken down as evidence by the station manager Walter Böhme, Saipan, to the senior executive officer, Dr. Krauss), undated [February 1916], ibid.; Böhme, New York, 8 December 1915, to the German Colonial Office, BAP: RKolA no. 2623.

CHAPTER 4: SAMOA AND THE NEW ZEALAND EXPERIENCE (1914–1921)

1 Marggraff, Tapatapao, 10 and 27 October 1914, to head office in Berlin, BAP: RKolA no. 2624. The firm E. Zuckschwerdt, Nukualofa, 18 December 1914, to Seattle, ibid. Diary of Hanssen, director of the Deutsche Handels- und Plantagengesellschaft Samoa (German Trading and Plantation Company in Samoa), entry of 31 December 1914, NZA: G 49/10.

2 Hanssen diary, 30 November and 14 December 1914, NZA: G 49/10. Riedel, DH & PG, Hamburg, 8 February 1915 to the German Colonial Office, BAP: RKolA no. 2624.

3 Reports by Administrator Logan, no. 51, 14 July 1917, and no. 53, 30 August 1917, NZA: G 21/7. German money could be exchanged until 9 May 1915; from 10 May 1915 only British currency was legal tender. The official exchange rate was one pound for 20.60 marks, or 11 pence per mark. The German money exported from Samoa totaled 1,507,837.45 marks, of which 812,311.45 marks were in silver and

gold coin, and 695,526 marks in notes. Report by Administrator Logan no. 23, 27 September 1915, NZA: G 21/2; Governor of New Zealand, confidential, by telegraph, 12 November 1915, to Administrator Logan, NZA: G 21/3; Report no. 25 by Administrator Logan, 15/22 November 1915, ibid.; Report no. 57A by Administrator Logan, 19 November 1917, NZA: G 21/8. The German money was exchanged for a total of more than £61,474, of which £51,000 was invested in war loans at the end of 1917. Figures from the New Zealand treasury, Wellington, 19 December 1917, ibid.

4   Minister of Defence, Allen, Wellington, 13 and 29 April 1916, to the Commander in Chief of the New Zealand army, General Godley, NZA: WA 252/3. War Diary General Staff, App. I, NZA: WA 210/1. Confidential war diary of the Military Secretary, NZA: WA 211/1.

5   New Zealand's Minister of Defence, Allen, 11 October 1916, to Prime Minister Massey, NZA: Personal Papers, Acc. 556, Box 9.

6   To be precise: £1,975. Bought at "auction" on 16 April 1918; *Samoa Times*, no. 16, 20 April 1918. Burns Philp also acquired the stocks of the German trading firms in neighboring Tonga (Buckley and Klugman 1983, 45).

7   Report Administrator Logan, no. 24, 7 October 1915, NZA: G 21/3.

8   Report Administrator Logan, no. 25, 15–22 November 1915, NZA: G 21/3. The commission's report in NZA: G 26/7. Secret telegram in cipher from Governor-General Liverpool, 1 August 1919, to the Colonial Secretary, personal, NZA: G 5/97.

9   Report Administrator Logan, no. 60, 22 December 1917, NZA: G 21/8. Samoa Kautschuk Cie., 11 January 1919, to Berlin, NZA: G 21/11.

10   Report no. 26A by Administrator Logan, Auckland, 26 January 1916, NZA: G 21/3. Report no. 45 by Administrator Logan, 10 May 1917, NZA: G 21/7.

11   Report Administrator Logan, no. 20, 8 July 1915, NZA: G 21/2.

12   Report Administrator Logan, no. 31, 9 May 1916, NZA: G 21/5.

13   Report Administrator Logan, no. 9/1918, 10 July 1918, NZA: G 21/9.

14   Report Administrator Logan, no. 2/1918, 21 January 1918, NZA: G 21/9. NZDD: no. 15/200, personal file Robert Logan. In addition to Logan, his personal adjutant, the military secretary, and the commander of the military police, among others, were also paid from the Samoan treasury from 1 April 1916; report Administrator Logan, no. 30, 13 April 1916, NZA: G 21/5. Military secretary's confidential war diary, NZA: WA 211/1.

15   Governor-General Liverpool, Wellington, 1 March 1917, confidential, to Logan, NZA: G 21/6. In the meantime, Liverpool instructed Logan to begin investigations "as to commercial value for the forests and the best way to exploit them," ibid.

16   Confidential personal reference by General Godley, 16 June 1913, and 1 September 1914; NZDD: no. 15/200, personal file Robert Logan.

17   Diary of the Head Manager of the German Trading and Plantation Company, Hanssen, entries of 26 and 29 December 1914, NZA: G 49/10; Emil Kleen, Apia, 10 March 1915, to his parents, BAP: RKolA no. 2625; Sawade, *DKZ*, 1916: 104; Malifa Camp, Apia, Samoa, 14 January 1915, NZA: Personal Papers, Acc. 1427, I, 1/4; Moors, Apia, 5 June 1916, to the Chairman of New Zealand's Liberal Party, Ward, NZA: G 21/4. At the end of 1914, New Zealand's army of occupation consisted of 1,351 soldiers, 53 officers, and 6 medical orderlies. War Diary General Staff, App. I, NZA: WA 210/1.

18   Memorandum by Major O. C. Garrison, 16 September 1919, to Administrator Tate,

"Observations and Information respecting last draft," NZA: WA 210/3/5; Major O. C. Garrison, 19 October 1919, to Administrator Tate, ibid. Soldier's letter on "recreation" in Samoa, NZA: WA 210/3/12.

19 *Samoa Times,* no. 28, 13 July 1918, "Shirker Brigade." "Samoa being such a hot place, most out of door games are too strenuous; bowls however is a form of recreation which is very suitable." Captain O. C. Garrison, 18 December 1917, NZA: WA, 210/3/2; War Diary General Staff, NZA: WA 210/1, App. I. Samoa's civilian administration had to pay for the soldiers' billiard tables; Governor Liverpool, confidential to Logan, Wellington, 16 September 1916, NZA: G 21/4.

20 Office of Military Administration, Apia, 2 February 1916, to Resch & Co. Brewers, Maitland, Australia, NZA: WA 210/3/2. In 1915 alcohol to a total value of £12,000 was imported to Samoa, NZA: WA 213/1–2. Resch was a prominent German Australian, which did not, however, save him from being detained as a prisoner of war; Fischer 1989, 121–122, and the photo facing p. 80.

21 Copra exports to the United States were banned from 17 March to 19 October 1916, confidential war diary of the Military Secretary, NZA: WA 211/1; Memorandum by the Minister of Defence, Allen, 27 June 1916, to the Attorney General of New Zealand, NZA: G 21/4; Proclamations by the Military Governor, no. 29, 24 April 1916, and no. 31, 29 May 1916, ibid. From Australia, Atlee Hunt agitated against American trading interests in Samoa; Atlee Hunt, by telegraph, 19 February 1915, to the Prime Minister of New Zealand and the British High Commissioner of the Western Pacific, AAC: A 1108–61.

22 Logan, Apia, 29 January 1917, secret, to Governor-General Liverpool, NZA: G 21/6. On the censorship of the American consul's correspondence, see Administrator Logan's reports no. 19, 8 June 1915, and no. 33, 3 July 1916, NZA: G 21/2 and 4.

23 *Samoa Times,* 21 April 1917, "Sneaking in." As early as 1916 Logan had called the United States' possible entry into the war on the Allied side a hostile act toward Anglo-Saxon commercial interests on Samoa. In this case, he would have been forced to lift the boycott on sending copra to the United States. Report by Administrator Logan, no. 32, 8 June 1916, NZA: G 21/4.

24 Report by Administrator Logan no. 6a, 27 October 1914, NZA: G 21/1. The governor's two Samoan advisers *(fautua)* were each paid 1,000 marks per annum, and the 27 councillors *(faipule)* in the Samoan self-administration, 500 marks annually, ibid.

25 The dog tax was 4 marks per dog. Of this, 3 marks went to *pulenu'us* (government agents in a village) and *leoleos* (village policemen), and one mark to the German administration. The *pulenu'u*'s work was largely financed by the dog tax, as he received only 160 marks annually from the central Samoan administration. Report by Administrator Logan no. 6a, 27 October 1914, NZA: G 21/1.

26 Report by the Administrator no. 6a, 27 October 1914, NZA: G 21/1.

27 Reports by the Administrator, no. 6a, 27 October 1914, no. 8, 25 November 1914, and no. 24, 27 October 1915, NZA: G 21/1 and 3.

28 Reports by the Administrator, no. 6a, 27 October 1914, and no. 8, 25 November 1914, and undated Health Report, ibid., NZA: G 21/1

29 On 1 April 1915, staff costs were £33,177; on 1 April 1916 they amounted to £35,678. Figures put together by the head of the finance administration, Loibl, 8 July 1916, in report by the Administrator, no. 34, 3 August 1916, NZA: G 21/4. Figures for German officials (including the English *Amtmann* or district officer) employed on 1 Jan-

uary 1914 in *DKB* 26 (1915): 202. Abolition of the Education Department: Report by Administrator Logan, no. 3, 10 September 1914, NZA: G 21/1.

30   Report by the Administrator no. 6a, 27 October 1914, NZA: G 21/1.

31   Report by the Administrator, no. 8, 25 November 1914, NZA: G 21/1.

32   Hiery 1989, 165.

33   *Samoa Times,* no. 3, 15 January 1916, and Memorandum by Acting Administrator Patterson, "Business and trade in Samoa," Apia, 16 February 1916, NZA: G 21/4.

34   W. Mulcahy, writing in the *Samoa Times,* 22 January 1916.

35   For Lauati and his movement, see Davidson 1970, Hempenstall 1978, 51–72, and Meleisea 1987, 57 and 82–83 (cf. Hiery 1989, 159–160 and 164). The majority of the exiles (fifty-six) arrived back in Samoa on 18 December 1915, traveling via Sydney. Lauati's family came back one month later, because Lauati himself had died en route. Report no. 26A by Administrator Logan, Auckland, 26 January 1916, NZA: G 21/3; Diary of the Military Secretary, 18 December 1915, and 15 January 1916, NZA: G 21/5; see also Field 1984, 30.

36   Hiery 1989, 162–163. The Administrator's main concern was to introduce the British observance of Sunday as a day of rest. One of his numerous proclamations (no. 50), that of 18 August 1917, prohibited shops from opening on Sundays, as had been the practice hitherto (especially in Apia's Chinese quarter); NZA: G 21/7.

37   Diary of J. R. Graham, entry of 30 August 1914; ATL: MSX 2367; *New Zealand Herald,* 8 September 1914, "Capture of Samoa"; Marggraff, German Samoa Company, Tapatapao, 10 October 1914, to head office in Berlin, BAP: RKolA no. 2624; Administrator Logan, Apia, 2 September 1914, to the Governor-General of New Zealand, NZA: G 21/1; letter from Apia, 5 September 1914, NZA: Personal Papers, Acc. 1427, I 1/4.

38   Report by Administrator Logan no. 6A, 27 October 1914, NZA: G 21/1. This figure relates to 19 September 1918, after the repatriation of Chinese on the *Taiyuan;* NZA: G 21/8. See also Field 1984, 31 (Field gives a figure of 832 Chinese for 1918, without specifying a more precise date).

39   Liverpool, Wellington, 14 June 1915, to Administrator Logan, NZA: G 21/2; Logan, 14 May (report no. 18), 8 July (secret) and 6 August 1915 (report no. 21) to the Governor of New Zealand, ibid.; report by Administrator Logan, no. 22, 2 September 1915, NZA: G 21/3.

40   Report by Administrator Logan, no. 25, 15–22 November 1915, NZA: G 21/3; Proclamation no. 42, 30 January 1917, NZA: G 21/8; see also Field 1984, 31.

41   *Savali,* 12 (1917), no. 8, 1 June 1917, NZA: G 21/8.

42   Logan, 8 October 1917, to the Chinese consul, Apia, NZA: G 21/8; cf. Field 1984, 32.

43   This is the view put forward by Field 1984, 32.

44   Minutes of a meeting of young Samoan public officials, 5 February 1914, BAP: RKolA no. 2760.

45   See Moses 1973, and Firth 1977.

46   Logan, Examination Sina, Native Court Apia, 3 October 1917, NZA: G 21/8; Logan, 8 October 1917, to the Chinese consul in Apia, ibid.

47   Logan, 8 October 1917, to the Chinese consul in Apia; the Chinese consul, Wellington, 10 November 1917, to Governor-General Liverpool, NZA: G 21/8; see also Field 1984, 31–33.

48   *Samoa Times,* no. 16, 20 April 1918. A similar tone is found in various other issues. Report by Administrator Logan, no. 57A, 19 November 1917: "I consider it my duty . . . to keep their race a pure one." See also Field 1984, 33.

49 Memorandum Attorney General A. L. Herdman, Wellington, 27 November 1917, "Treatment of Chinese in Samoa": "necessary, that he [the Administrator] should be armed with despotic power and that his will should be law. . . . the law must be drastic"; NZA: G 21/8. Report by Administrator Logan, no. 59, 15 December 1917, ibid.

50 Governor-General of Australia, Melbourne, 24 January 1916, to the Governor of New Zealand, NZA: G 21/3. Behind Munro Ferguson stood the Australian minister of defense, Pearce. Pearce, Melbourne, 18 January 1916, to Ferguson for the New Zealand government, AAC: CP 78/22–15/22, and A 457–710/3.

51 Acting Administrator of Samoa, Patterson, 16 February 1916, confidential, to Governor Liverpool, NZA: G 21/4.

52 Meleisea 1980, 13, 19 (statements by Melanesian workers in Samoa); "it would not be unfair to say that the Samoan attitude to most foreigners is ethnocentric to some extent. . . . the people of Melanesia were thought of by most Samoans as being a backward people 'in the power of the devil.' Samoans speak disparagingly of the Melanesians skin colour, stressing that they are 'black'" (ibid., 49). Samoans called Melanesians *mea uli* (black beings); ibid., 50, and conversation with Else Rossbach, 11 June 1990.

53 NZA: WA 210/1/1, 24 June 1915; WA 210/1/2, 4 March 1917.

54 Report by Administrator Logan, no. 45, 10 May 1917, NZA: G 21/7.

55 Ibid.; Report by Administrator Logan, no. 24, 27 October 1915, NZA: G 21/3.

56 Logan, Tauranga, 27 August 1919, to Minister of Defence Allen, NZA: IT 17/4; memorandum Commissioner Crown Estates, 4 January 1921, ibid. On repatriation of 198 Melanesians on 3 August 1917, see Diary of the Military Secretary, NZA: WA 211/1; for arrival in Rabaul on 18 August 1917, on the *Solf,* AWM: 33/34. On continuation of corporal punishment by New Zealand, see Diary of the Chief Director of the German Trading and Plantation Company, Hanssen, entry of 22 January 1915, NZA: G 49/10.

57 Logbook *Siar,* Lieutenant Stanley Walker, 3 July 1915: Luluai Narie, village Malung, Jacquenot Bay, AAC: AA 1963/83, Bun 246/64–15. This case demonstrates two further points: first, there was a pretty precise knowledge of when labor contracts expired; and second, the German administration had observed its obligation to repatriate Melanesian workers. Strikes/unrest: Hanssen dairy, 14 and 15 December 1914, NZA: G 49/10; telegram from Administrator Tate, 3 May 1919, to the Governor-General of New Zealand, NZA: G 5/96; Tate, 15 May 1919, to General Robin, ATL: MS 264, no. 6; Report by Administrator Tate no. 4, 26 May 1919, NZA: G 21/11.

58 Memorandum by the Commissioner Crown Estates Samoa, 4 January 1921, NZA: IT 17/4. Notes dating from May 1952, ibid. On the last Melanesians in Samoa and their relations with the Samoans, see Meleisea 1976 and 1980. When the two hundred returnees arrived in Rabaul in late June 1921, the Administrator feared they might pass on to New Guinea ideas about labor relations from Samoa that could give cause for concern. Bassett 1969, 83–84, and Meleisea 1976, 126.

59 Hiery 1989, 164.

60 Walter Behrmann, *DKZ* 32 (1915): 127. Memorandum by Acting Administrator Patterson, "Business and Trade in Samoa," Apia, 16 February 1916, NZA: G 21/4.

61 Report by Administrator Logan, no. 39, 14 December 1916, NZA: G 21/6. *Samoa Times,* no. 49, 2 December 1916. Cutting off and displaying the limbs, and especially the head, of a defeated enemy was a Samoan custom of war.

62 Hiery 1989, 164.

63 Boyd 1968, 160.

64 Meleisea 1987, 110–112.

65 The commander of the military police was, at the same time, the judge for native affairs. A factor in the tolerance of the Samoans may also have been that the Samoan had been convicted of attempted rape (and sexual offenses traditionally attracted severe punishments in Samoa). The Samoan offender received 48 (*sic!*) lashes. There was no legal basis for this form of punishment. *Samoa Times,* no. 52, 23 December 1916.

66 Samoan Epidemic Commission, Minutes of Evidence, NZA: IT 1/8/10. See also Hiery 1993*a*.

67 *Auckland Star,* 10 January 1919, letter from Apia, 26 December 1918.

68 Samoan Epidemic Commission. Minutes of Evidence taken at Savaii, 10–14 June 1919, NZA: IT 1/8/10.

69 Telegram from Logan, 19 November 1918, to the Governor-General of New Zealand; telegram from the Governor-General, 20 November 1918, to Administrator Logan, NZA: G 5–96; Report no. 14 by Administrator Logan, 27 December 1918, NZA: G 21/11.

70 Telegram from Governor-General Liverpool, 5 December 1918, to Administrator Logan, NZA: AD 49/891/3, and G5–96. Telegram from the Governor of Fiji, 6 December 1918, to the Governor-General of New Zealand; the Governor-General of New Zealand, 10 December 1918, by telegraph, to the Governor of Fiji, NZA: G, 5–96. The Governor of Fiji, 24 December 1918 and 25 January 1919, to the Governor-General of New Zealand, NZA: G 13/38.

71 Tate, 29 May 1919, to General Robin, ATL: MS 264, no. 6. For similar assessments: Tate, 5 June 1919, to Robin, ibid., and Tate, 6 April 1919, to Robin, ATL: MS 264, no. 5. Logan's colleagues evidently feared for his mental health when he left (Tate, 3 February 1919, to General Robin, ibid.). "I think the climate must have affected him," Minister of Defence Allen wrote, in confidence, to the Prime Minister of New Zealand on 1 August 1919, NZA: Personal Papers, Acc. 556, Box 9. On the offer of help and the preparations made by the American governor, Poyer, see: report by the American consul in Apia, Mason Mitchell, 29 November 1918, to the State Department; report by the American consul in Apia, no. 325, Mason Mitchell, Apia, 26 June 1919, to the American secretary of state, NARA: RG 84, B 345; Quincy F. Roberts (Mitchell's successor in Apia), *Handbook of Samoa,* 500–501, NARA: RG 59, 862 m; Edwin William Gurr, Pago Pago, 11 March 1919, personal and confidential to the Acting Prime Minister of New Zealand, James Allen, NZA: IT 79/19; Gurr, Pago Pago, 11 March 1919, personal and confidential to acting Administrator Tate, ATL: MS 264, no. 17. A New Zealander, Gurr was one of the Europeans who had lived longest in Samoa. His legal qualifications and his profound knowledge of the Samoans (he was married to a Samoan woman) had secured for him a special position in a number of Samoan colonial administrations (see Field 1984, 44–46). When questioned by the Commission of Enquiry, Logan explained that he had never thought of asking American Samoa for help; if it had been offered, he would have refused. *Samoa Times,* no. 32, 9 August 1919.

72 Statement by Asiato Eliapo, Samoan Epidemic Commission, Minutes of Evidence, NZA: IT 1/8/10.

73 Field 1984, 49. The mortality rate was thought to have been 20. 6 percent (*Samoa*

Times, no. 37, 13 September 1919). A delegation of all Protestant missionaries in Samoa claimed, during a meeting with the acting prime minister of New Zealand, Allen, that there had been at least nine thousand Samoan deaths, giving a mortality rate of 25 percent. Minutes of the meeting on 22 April 1919, NZA: IT acc. 2711–5/12. Further estimates can be found in Field 1984, 47 and 49.

74   NZA: S 1/12/7/8. Marked "Destroy."

75   *Samoa Times*, no. 37, 13 September 1919. On the flu carrying off the more robust members of the population, and for possible explanations, Crosby 1989, 215–222. On the significance of the sudden loss of so many Samoan titleholders, Boyd 1968, 161–162, Field 1984, 34–51, and Meleisea 1987, 121–122.

76   *Amtmann* (District Officer) R. Williams, Fagamalo, Savaii, 9 January 1919, to Logan, NZA: IT 8/10.

77   There had originally been thirty members; see Goodall 1954, 361.

78   See Meleisea 1987, passim.

79   Reports by Administrator Logan, no. 14, 27 December 1918, and no. 1, 20 January 1919 (including a memorandum by N. H. Macdonald, 11 May 1918), NZA: G 21/11. Macdonald's recommendation to the New Zealand Commission was that New Zealand should remove a total of 86,000 acres of land from Samoan control. *Trade between New Zealand and Fiji, Tonga, Western Samoa, and Cook Islands* (Parliamentary Papers of New Zealand, Appendices), 1920, 19.

80   Conversation with Henriette Godinet-Taylor, 13 January 1989.

81   E. Demandt, BAK: Kleine Erwerbungen No. 812 vol. 6, entry of 17 November 1918. On I'iga Pisa, Hiery 1989, 159–160.

82   Report by Administrator Logan, no. 1, 20 January 1919, NZA: G 21/11. Report no. 304 by the American consul, Mason Mitchell, for the State Department, Apia, 30 January 1919, "Dissatisfaction of natives," NARA: RG 38: K-5-a, 2090.

83   Petition, 26 January 1919, NZA: G 21/11. See also Hiery 1992a, 65–66.

84   Tate to the New Zealand Foreign Secretary, Gray, 8 February 1922, ATL: MS 264, no. 2; see Hiery 1992a, 70. On dissemination of the petition, see telegram from Tate, 26 March 1919, to the Governor-General, NZA: G 5/96; Tate, 28 March 1919, to Gurr, ATL: MS 264, no. 17; *Samoa Times*, no. 14, 5 April 1919; see also Hiery 1989, 167–168. On Samoan songs: Gurr, Pago Pago, 20 March and 8 April 1919, to Tate, ATL: MS 264, no. 17. See also Crosby 1989, 240, and Hiery 1992a, 66.

85   Gurr, Pago Pago, 8 April 1919, confidential, to Tate, ATL: MS 264, no. 17.

86   Report of Meeting held at Mulinuu, 28 January 1919, NZA: G 21/11. Letters from Malietoa to Tate, 8 February 1919, ibid. Minutes of talks, 15 February 1919, and report by Administrator Tate, 8 March 1919, "Native Unrest," ibid. See also Hiery 1989, 167.

87   Hiery 1992a, 69–71.

88   Report of Meeting held at Mulinuu, 28 January 1919, NZA: G 21/11.

89   Boyd 1980, 161.

90   "Fortunately he [Allom] heard of this, and in connection with some friends there, they managed to get this declaration altered, and 'Great Britain' was substituted for 'America.'" James Burns, Sydney, 2 April 1919, to the firm's London representative, Mackintosh, Burns Philp Archives, Sydney: Box "Mandated Territory."

91   Burns Philp Archives, Sydney. For its branch's reaction to the outbreak of the war, Buckley and Klugman 1983, 13.

92   Confidential Memorandum by Administrator Tate, 14 February 1922, to the For-
     eign Minister, NZA: IT 82/2. On Toleafoa's brother Afamasaga Maua, Hiery 1989,
     163 and 172 n. 48.

93   Hempenstall 1978, 43–50, and Meleisea 1987, 116–118.

94   Report no. 6 by Administrator Tate, 21 August 1919, NZA: G 21/11.

95   "Under the control of Mr. Toleafoa the proposed Company may prove a success."
     Report of Auditor Arcus, Wellington, 25 August 1919, to the Auditor General, Wel-
     ington, NZA: IT 82/2; undated notes by Tate, "Notes on Company promoted by
     Toeaina Club," ibid; report no. 7 by Administrator Tate, 3 September 1919, NZA:
     G 21/11. The assets of the club members, amounting to £632, were confiscated by
     Tate, who deposited them with the New Zealand Post Office. In March 1931 they
     were transferred to the New Zealand Treasury. Although the *Fono a Faipule*
     repeatedly insisted that the money should be returned to its real owners, nothing
     had happened by May 1939 (after twenty years!), NZA: IT 82/2.

96   Report no. 7 by Administrator Tate, 3 September 1919, NZA: G 21/11; Logan to
     Governor-General Liverpool, Auckland, 14 June 1919, NZA: G 21/12.

97   Memorandum by the Secretary for Native Affairs, Mulinuu, 12 November 1919, to
     the Administrator, NZA: G 21/12. Samoa Constitution Order, 6 November 1919, §
     273, para. 4, ibid. For Samoans' anxiety that their land would be confiscated on the
     basis of the Constitution Order, see Tate, 13 March 1920, to the Foreign Minister,
     NZA: IT 88/3, vol. 1. Unease persisted about this article: memorandum by Admin-
     istrator Tate, "Native Situation. September 1921," Apia, 22 October 1921, NZA: G
     48/S 10.

98   Tate, secret telegram, in cipher, to the Governor-General personally, 28 November
     1919, NZA: G 5–97; Solicitor General Salmond, Wellington, 19 December 1919, to
     the Foreign Minister, NZA: IT 67/12/1; telegrams from the Foreign Minister, Well-
     ington, 14 April and 20 April 1920, to the Administrator of Samoa; telegram from
     the Administrator, 16 April 1920, to the Foreign Ministry, NZA: IT 1/8, no. 1.

99   Telegram from Malietoa and Tuimalealiifano to the Minister of Defence, James
     Allen, Apia, 14 June 1919, "Keep Logan away from Samoa," NZA: IT acc. 2711–5/
     12 (personal file Robert Logan); General Robin, 16 June 1919, to Tate, ATL: MS
     264, no. 6.

100 Dr. Albert Pomare, who had already taken responsibility for the Cook Islands, was
     under consideration as Minister for Samoa. Tate, 23 July 1919, to the New Zealand
     Minister for Defence, Allen, personal and private, ATL: MS 264, no. 18; see also
     Hiery 1989, 172 n. 49. The Administrator's impression that the Samoans would
     offer armed resistance to this appointment may not have been entirely unfounded.
     In any case, this suited Tate very well. In 1918 Logan had granted the Samoans
     permission to own guns so long as a license fee had been paid. Tate, 23 July 1919,
     to General Robin, ATL: MS 264, no. 7; Despatch no. 6/1919 from the Administra-
     tor, 21 August 1919, NZA: G 21/11.

101 Telegram in cipher from Administrator Tate, 27 October 1919, to the Governor-
     General of New Zealand, NZA: G 5–97.

102 Gurr, Pago Pago, 15 March 1919, to Judge Wilson, ATL: MS 264, no. 20. On Gurr,
     see note 71 above; see also Field 1984, 53–54 and 58. Field's suggestion that the
     New Zealand government regarded Tate's attempt to set up a secret police as
     absurd does not reflect the facts.

103 Tate, 22 February 1921, to the Governor of American Samoa, Waldo Evans, personally, NZA: G 26/10 (copy also in AAM: MP 1049/1–20/0276). See also Field 1984, 56.

104 NZA: G 48, Box 33–S 15. The British ambassador in Peking, Clive, 7 July 1920, to the Foreign Office, NZA: G 13–39. "Provisional contract" between the New Zealand Administration on Samoa's emissary to China, Captain Robert J. Carter, and the Chinese, Canton, 7 June 1920, NML: 996. 14 Pap R 17308; confidential report from Carter to the Administrator of Samoa, Hong Kong [July] 1920, ibid.; New Zealand's Foreign Minister, Lee, on the instructions of the Prime Minister, Wellington, 13 December 1921, to the New Zealand High Commissioner in London, James Allen, ibid. See also Field 1984, 56.

105 On the ruthless treatment of the Chinese coolies under the German colonial administration, see Moses 1973, and Firth 1977. In 1921, after the confirmation of its mandate, New Zealand adopted the ban on Chinese marrying Samoan women and made it part of the Samoa Act (which replaced the Samoa Constitution Order); Field 1984, 57. Among the most important articles of criminal law discriminating against the Chinese in Samoa were the reversal of the obligation to furnish proof in the case of a public prosecution (i.e., Chinese had to prove that they had been unjustly accused) and arbitary arrest (a policeman, or someone instructed by a policeman, could arrest a Chinese at any time without a warrant of arrest). (The Chinese Contract Labour Control Ordinance of 2 July 1921, § 6 and 14, NZA: G 48–S/9.) In his last memorandum, Logan implored the Governor-General to prevent by every possible means the "contamination of the Samoans" by the Chinese. (Logan, Auckland, 21 June 1919, to the Private Secretary to the Governor-General, NZA: G 21/12.) Tate recognized that the future commercial exploitation of the copra plantations depended on bringing in Chinese laborers. But to conclude from this that he was more favorably disposed toward the Chinese than Logan had been (Field 1984, 55) is to be blind to Tate's utilitarian motives. We have evidence of a number of extremely racist remarks made by Tate about the Chinese—among others, Tate to Mrs. Gray (wife of the secretary to the New Zealand Foreign Ministry), 4 September 1920, ATL: MS 264, no. 19.

CHAPTER 5: INDIGENOUS REACTIONS TO THE WAR

1 On this, see the interesting comments by the German anthropologist Hans Fischer 1987, 154–155 and 182.

2 Crown Law Officer Captain Brown, Rabaul, 14 January 1918, to the Central Court Judge, AAC: AA 1963/83, Bun 245 ("Part 1917 Correspondence"); Intelligence Report no. 10 by Administrator Johnston, Rabaul, 15 May 1919, AAC: CP 103/11, NG Reports 2/15; see also Mackenzie 1927, 240–241 and 246–249. The relationship between the mark and the pound or shilling had hardly changed for decades in New Guinea. In 1891 one pound was worth 20.50 marks; AAC: G 254–5/129.

3 Census of 1 January 1913: German citizens 80.1 percent, Australians 4.9 percent; *Jahresbericht 1912/13, Statistischer Teil.* The Japanese, who enjoyed legal equality with Europeans, are not included here.

4 Cable from the Australian government, 7 January 1918, in response to the query of

4 January 1918, AAC: A 3932–SC 472/2. On the Colonial Office's action, see Rothwell 1971, 289 and 291.

5   Radio message, Navy Office, Melbourne, 17 April 1918, to the Administrator of New Guinea, AAC: AA 1963/83, Bun 245.

6   Memorandum Administrator Johnston, Rabaul, 14 June 1918, to the Secretary in the Australian Ministry of Defence, AWM: 33/12–10; AAM: MP 367–479/27/50 and C 404/11/109. See also the summary in Spartalis 1983, 209.

7   Memorandum Administration Johnston, Rabaul, 14 June 1918, to the Secretary in the Australian Ministry of Defence, AWM 33/12–10; AAM: MP 367–479/27/50 and C 404/11/109.

8   Ibid.

9   Hudson 1978, 17.

10 Undated statement by J. M. Forsayth (son of "Queen" Emma); "on the whole, reasonable and just," Secretary General of the Methodist Mission, Rev. G. Wheen, Sydney, 14 January 1919, to Commander Banks; "very severe, but the Natives at all times were given justice," Banks, Paddington, 3 January 1919, to the Secretary of Defence, Trumble. Undated Memorandum by Banks [1919], AAM: MP 367–479/27/50.

11 Walter Lucas, "Upon German Control of Natives in the Late German New Guinea Possession," undated [1919], AAM: MP 367–479/27/50; Pethebridge, Melbourne, 28 December 1917, to the Minister of Defence, ibid.

12 In private, an official in the Colonial Office expressed the view that, based on these Melanesian statements, Germany could build a "crushing case" against a continued Australian presence in New Guinea; Rothwell 1971, 290. Milner himself concluded that any humanitarian argument for the transfer of New Guinea would be "eyewash"; Snelling 1975–1976, 21, and Spartalis 1983, 208.

13 Memorandum "On Administration of Pacific Islands," Sydney, 8 August 1919, Governor-General of Australia, secret, to the Colonial Secretary, personal, ANL: 696/2248. See also the opinion expressed in the *Rabaul Record* 1, no. 9 (1 November 1916): 4.

14 Legal report by Robert H. Garran for the Australian government. "The Mandatory System," undated [1919], AAC: CP 351/2/7.

15 He was eventually set free after two years' detention, at the beginning of the mandate administration; Thompson 1992, 273.

16 Report by the Commander of the cruiser *Una*, F. H. Tarrant, Ocean Island, 6 October 1915, AAC: A 4–NG 33. See also Rothwell 1971, 290.

17 Petition of 28 October 1918, in Report no. 53/1918 by Administrator Smith Rewse, Pleasant Island, 29 October 1918, to the British High Commissioner of the Western Pacific, NZA: CO 225, Micro Z 5145–6383. See also: Correspondence relating to the wishes of the Natives of the German Colonies as to their future Government, London, November 1918, 56 (no. 15). The initiative for the petition went back directly to the Colonial Office, which was desperately seeking grounds on which to justify British rule over Nauru; Rothwell 1971, 290.

18 Resident Commissioner of the Gilbert and Ellice Islands, E. C. Eliot, Ocean Island, 9 November 1918, confidential, to the British High Commissioner of the Western Pacific, NZA: CO 225/162.

19 Documents in AAC: 518–D 112/6/1. For the plight of the Banaban people, see Binder 1977, Kituai 1982, and Macdonald 1982, 94–111.

20 Father Corbinian, Rota, 3 July 1915, to the German Colonial Office (via Guam—Washington), BAP: RKolA no. 2622.

21 F. Scholz (former employee at the radio station, Yap), Cuxhaven, 21 February 1916, to the German Colonial Office, BAP: RKolA no. 2623. Scholz was quoting a Yap chief who visited him on the night before the Germans left. Kohl-Larsen 1927, ix, 142–143 and 151–155.

22 Confidential report by Atkins Kroll & Co., undated [October 1917] after a trading trip through the Marshall Islands, NARA: RG 59, 862, l. See also Blakeslee 1921, 188–189.

23 A. Hayes, captain of the *Tambo,* Sydney, 2 May 1916, to Burns Philp, with a confidential copy to Atlee Hunt, AAC: A 3932–SC 240.

24 Ibid.

25 Petition, Jabwor, 15 January 1919. It contains eight signatures and four individual crosses; AAC: A 3932–SC 240. Report of Captain Handley, *Mauno,* to the General Manager of Burns Philp, Wallin, undated [his notes, in diary form, start when the ship left for the Marshall Islands late in November 1918 and end at the beginning of May 1919], ibid.

26 March and June 1918: Captain MacAuslane, *Tambo* (Burns Philp), 22 March and 26 June 1918, to the British Resident Commissioner of Ocean Island, AAC: A 3932–SC 240. April 1918: Statement by Captain Robert Stobo (Pacific Phosphate Company, secret agent) on Japanese Activities in the Caroline Islands, undated [1918, at Kusaie]. May 1918: Captain A. Robinson (Burns Philp), 26 June 1918, to the Resident Commissioner of Ocean Island, AAM: MP 1049/1–18/0345. September 1918: Memorandum by the Australian Naval secret service, "Pacific Island Groups in Japanese Occupation," undated [1919], AAM: MP 1049/1–1920/090. September/October 1918: McMahon (Australian journalist) on the Burns Philp steamer *Tambo* (Captain R. MacAuslane), 27 October 1918, to the Resident Commissioner of Ocean Island, AAC: A 3932–SC 240. Thomas J. McMahon, "The Japanese Occupation of the Marshall Islands," *Stead's Review,* 22 February 1919, 160.

27 Report of Captain Handley, undated [1918/1919], AAC: A 3932–SC 240; *Japan Weekly Chronicle,* 23 January 1919; memorandum by the Australian Naval secret service, "Pacific Island Groups in Japanese Occupation," AAM: MP 1049/1–1920/090. Communication from the Japanese censor about letters from Marshall Islanders to the crew of the *Cormoran* interned in the United States: Report of the American Consul-General in Samoa, 23 November 1918, NARA: RG 38: K 5a: 11266.

28 Letter from the five Supreme Chiefs to the Commander of Ponape, 24 December 1918, AKM: 103.

29 See *The Book of Luelen* 1977, 124.

30 Statement by Captain Robert Stobo on "Japanese Activities in the Caroline Islands," no date [April/May 1918], AAC: AA 2219/1–vol. 3.

31 Report no. 56 by the Administrator, 25 October 1917, NZA: G 21/8. "Abolition of the State Education System," Report no. 3 by the Administrator, 10 September 1914, NZA: G 21/1.

32 Sawade, in *DKZ* 33 (1916), 68. Sawade was physically disabled and was therefore permitted to return to Germany via America during the war.

33 Report by the Administrator, no. 34, 3 August 1916, NZA: G 21/4. "Sheep-breeding," report by the Administrator, no. 8/1918, 17 June 1918, NZA: G 21/9.

34   *Journals of the House of Representatives of New Zealand 1920,* Appendix: "Trade between New Zealand and Fiji, Tonga, Western Samoa, and Cook Islands," 20.

35   Memorandum from the Commissioner for Education, Beaglehole, Apia, 4 July 1919, to the Administrator, NZA: IT 1/12; Moors, Apia, 11 May 1921, to the Secretary in the New Zealand Ministry for External Affairs, Gray, NARA: RG 59, 862 l.

36   Report by Governor-General Liverpool, 4 August 1919, 37, NZA: G 48–Box 4A (original), IT 1/11 (deletions by Minister for External Affairs, Allen). Similarly, the New Zealand government deleted Liverpool's criticism of the still extremely lax health checks on passengers arriving by ship (30/31 in the original), and the New Zealand Governor-General's statement that the Samoans still desired an American administration (28 in the original). Solf's decision: "From the 1st July 1901 on the language of instruction in schools for natives has to be Samoan," circular letter, 15 May 1901, to all missions, NML: GPRS XV.3.

37   Acting Administrator, General Robin, Apia, 27 February 1920, to the New Zealand Minister of External Affairs, NZA: IT 1/3.

38   *Second Report on the Mandate of Samoa (1921/22),* 1922, 30. Memorandum Tate, Apia, 22 October 1921, "Native Situation, September 1921," NZA: G 48/S 10.

39   Field 1984, 66–67.

40   Confidential report by Administrator Tate to the Ministry of Exernal Affairs, "Occurrences of Political Interest" (1921), Apia, 10 February 1922, NZA: G48/S 10.

41   Ibid.; and Tate, 29 March 1919, to General Robin, ATL: MS 264, no. 5.

42   Memorandum by Harry Jay Moors, 2 November 1920, to Tate, NARA: RG 84, B 345 (copy).

43   *New York Times,* 14 April 1919: "Samoans want to join us. New Zealand Rule in former German possession opposed."

44   Gurr, Pago Pago, 11 March 1919, confidential, to the New Zealand Minister of Defence, Allen, personal (with a copy to Administrator Tate), ATL: MS 264, no. 17; Gurr, Pago Pago, 17 and 20 March 1919, to Tate, personal, ibid.; Gurr, Pago Pago, 8 April 1919, confidential, to Tate, ibid.; The American consul, Mason Mitchell, Apia, 5 November 1919, to James D. Moore, Sacramento, NARA: RG 84, B 345.

45   See Olsen 1983, 41–53 and 65.

46   Tate, 6 July 1919, to General Robin, ATL: MS 264, no. 7; see also Hiery 1989, 168–169, and Hiery 1992a, 66–67 and 70.

47   November 1918: a letter from the Australian Commissioner of Trade and Industries, George S. Beeby, from Samoa, intercepted by the American censor in Honolulu: "If the natives had a right to choose, they would vote solidly for German control!" NARA: RG 38, K-5-a: 2090: Official Naval Intelligence; German Samoa, 1902–1918. Letter from Apia, 26 December 1918, in *Auckland Star,* 10 January 1919; *Sydney Morning Herald,* 6 September 1921: "Samoa. A disgruntled people."

48   Geoffrey W. A. Norton, "Samoa. A Visitor's Opinion," *Samoa Times,* no. 43, 25 October 1919 (reprint of an article in the *New Zealand Herald,* 8 October 1919).

49   For example, in a speech to Administrator Tate: Toelupe, Malie, 15 October 1920, NZA: IT 1/20; Aiono Aipovi, 20 October 1920, in Leulomega, ibid.; Vaa-o-Fonoti, 16 December 1920, in Faleapuna, NZA: IT 88/5; Faifai, representing the *alii* and *faipule,* 18 December 1920, in Lufilufi, NZA: IT 1/20.

50   "Statement of wishes and desires of King Malietoa and Samoan Chiefs and others," R. Broadhurst Hill, "Tapu Salaia," Sydney, 9 March 1919, to the Acting Prime Min-

ister of Australia, Watt, AAC: A 3934–SC 12/19. Hill had established contact with Watt via the Speaker of the Australian Parliament, W. E. Elliot Johnston.

51 Tate, 29 May 1919, to General Robin, ATL: MS 264, no. 6.

52 Confidential report by the American consul, Mason Mitchell, no. 342, Apia, 11 March 1920, to the State Department, NARA: RG 84, B 345.

53 Samoa Crown Estates Order 1920, § 11, NZA: G 48–S/9; speech by Minister for External Affairs E. P. Lee, on the second reading of the Samoa Bill on 11 October 1921 in the New Zealand House of Representatives, printed in *The Dominion*, 12 October 1921, AAC: A 2219–27. Lee estimated the value of the Crown Estates as at least one million pounds (ibid.).

54 Order in council, 20 April 1920, to come into force on 1 May 1920, NZA: G 5–96; memorandum from Prime Minister Massey, 19 October 1920, to the Governor-General, NZA: G 13–40; J. D. Gray, Secretary to the Minister for External Affairs, 10 November 1920, to the Minister of External Affairs, Lee, NZA: IT 8/11.

55 English translation of an undated directive [September 1920] from the Samoan chiefs, NZA: IT 88/5. The New Zealand Secretary in charge of the native adminis-tration, Captain Cotton, after talks with six *faipule*, 4 October 1920, to Administra-tor Tate, ibid.

56 Ibid. Governor Solf had encouraged the *faipules* to pass village laws *(Tulafono fa‘a le nu‘u)* which prohibited Samoans from taking up loans from Europeans. This fol-lowed a unanimous request by the *faipule* at a *fono* in August 1907 that tried to find ways of preventing Samoans from falling into debt to Europeans. Issued by the Samoan self-government, these statutes became binding in September and Octo-ber 1907. A further ordinance by the governor declared all fiscal transactions between Europeans and Samoans (which included giving credit to the latter) null and void. Samoan debts had to be written off the books of European traders. "Ver-ordnung des Gouverneurs vom 10.01.1908 betr. das Verbot des Schuldenmachens für die Samoaner," *Samoanisches Gouvernementsblatt* 3 (1900–1910): 208–209 (no. 65, 18 January 1908).

57 Memorandum Administrator Tate, Apia, 6 October 1920, to the Ministry for Exter-nal Affairs, "Native Unrest," NZA: IT 88/5; Tate, Apia, 30 December 1920, to the Minister for External Affairs, ibid.; memorandum by Tate, 3 January 1921, for the Minister for External Affairs, "Native Unrest—The Sa," ibid.; report by the Ameri-can consul Quincy F. Roberts, Apia, 17 December 1920, NARA: RG 84, B 345; Dr. J. Allen Thomson, Director of the Dominion Museum, 15 January 1921 to the Min-ister for Internal Affairs after travelling to Samoa, NZA: IT 67/12/1; *New Zealand Times* (Wellington), 26 January 1921, "Unrest in Samoa." On developments in American Samoa and Terhune's suicide, see Olsen 1983, 41–51.

58 Memorandum Tate, Apia, 3 January 1921, for the New Zealand Minister of External Affairs, "Native Unrest—The Sa," NZA: IT 88/5; speech by Vaa-o-Fonoti, 16 December 1920 to Administrator Tate in Faleapuna, ibid. See also Eteuati 1982, 47.

59 Tate, 3 January 1921, to the Minister for External Affairs, "Native Unrest," NZA: IT 88/5.

60 Tate, memorandum "Native Sa," Apia, 31 January 1921, to the Minister of External Affairs, NZA: IT 88/5.

61 Minutes *Fono a Faipule*, Mulinuu, 2 February 1921, NZA: IT 88/3, vol. 1; "Law of Vacant Titles," *Savali*, 15 March 1921, NZA: G 48/S 10; Annual Report 1920/21 by

Norman H. Macdonald, Secretary Native Affairs, Apia, 31 March 1921, NZA: G 48/S 8; Samoa Native Land and Title Commission Order Amendment, 20 December 1920, § 13, NZA: G 48/S 9.

62   Report by the American Consul, Quincy F. Roberts, Apia, 17 December 1920, NARA: RG 84, B 345; Tate, Apia, 30 December 1920, to the Ministry of External Affairs, NZA: IT 88/5; Secretary to the New Zealand Ministry of External Affairs, Gray, Wellington, 10 January 1921, to the Navy Ministry, ibid. See also Goodall 1954, 361.

63   C-class mandate for Samoa, issued on 17 December 1920, sent with accompanying letter from Monnet, Geneva, 11 February 1921, NZA: IT 62/12/1.

CHAPTER 6: PARIS, THE VERSAILLES TREATY, AND THE FATE OF GERMANY'S SOUTH PACIFIC COLONIES

1   Peace Congress Paris. Secret. I.C. 120. Reg. No. 795. Minutes of the meeting at the Quai d'Orsay, Paris, 24 January 1919, AAC: CP 351/1–Box 4; *FRUS, The Paris Peace Conference* 3, 718.

2   Ibid.; Peace Congress Paris. Secret. I.C. 120. Reg. No. 795. Minutes of the meeting at the Quai d'Orsay, Paris, 24 January 1919, AAC: CP 351/1–Box 4.

3   *FRUS, The Paris Peace Conference* 3, 719–722. On Hughes' trick with the map, see the American Consul-General in Australia, Melbourne, 2 February 1921, strictly confidential, to the Secretary of State, NARA: RG 59, 862 c. See also Hudson 1978, 20.

4   Minutes of the meeting of 24 January 1919, AAC: CP 351/1–Box 4; *FRUS, The Paris Peace Conference* 3, 724–727. Massey was so nervous during his presentation, that he even claimed Solf had been governor of Fiji, ibid. For the general attitude of the Australian and New Zealand representatives at the Peace Conference, see Snelling 1975–1976.

5   Peace Congress Paris. Secret. I.C. 122. Reg. No. 942. Minutes of the meeting at the Quai d'Orsay, 27 January 1919, AAC: CP 351/1–Box 4; *FRUS, The Paris Peace Conference* 3, 738–740. See also Peattie 1988, 53. Makino's point about the Micronesian right to self-determination was based on the position put forward by Yoshino Sakuzo. A professor at the Imperial University of Tokyo, Yoshino supported the right of self-determination in principle but thought the Micronesians were still too uncivilized; *Japan Advertiser*, 28 December 1918. For Yoshino's views, see Peattie 1988, 52–53.

6   Peace Congress Paris. Secret. I.C. 122. Reg. No. 942. Minutes of the meeting at the Quai d'Orsay, 27 January 1919, AAC: CP 351/1–Box 4; *FRUS, The Paris Peace Conference* 3, 740–743. On Hughes' visit to Wilson and their mutual dislike for each other, see Hughes 1950, 229, and Walworth 1986, 72 n. 37.

7   Peace Congress Paris. Secret. I.C. 122. Reg. No. 942. Minutes of the meeting at the Quai d'Orsay, 27 January 1919, AAC: CP 351/1–Box 4; *FRUS, The Paris Peace Conference* 3, 745–747.

8   British Empire Delegation 4 (fourth meeting), secret. Minutes of the meeting in the Villa Majestic, Paris, 27 January 1919, from 6.30 P.M.; AAC: CP 351/1–Box 4.

9   British Empire Delegation 5 (fifth meeting), secret. Minutes of the meeting in the Villa Majestic, Paris, 28 January 1919, at 3.00 P.M. Report by Lloyd George of his conversation with Wilson on the same morning, ibid.; Memorandum, "The

Mandatory System and the Disposal of the German Pacific Colonies," AAC: CP 351/1–X 2/7.

10   Peace Congress Paris. Secret. I.C. 123. Reg. No. 943. Minutes of the meeting at the Quai d'Orsay, 28 January 1919, at 11.00 A.M., AAC: CP 351/1–Box 4; *FRUS, The Paris Peace Conference* 3, 749–751. Nine British, seven American, six Japanese, five French, four Italian, and three Chinese delegates were present. Of the secret agreements concluded during the war, the only one which is relevant here is that between London and Tokyo concerning mutual recognition of each other's sphere of influence in the Pacific, with the equator as the dividing line. The texts of the Japanese initiatives and the Foreign Office note of 13 February 1917 are reproduced in Kajima 1980, 190–195. The entry into this agreement of Russia (5 March 1917), France (1 March 1917), and Italy (28 March 1917) are documented in ibid., 196–202.

11   Peace Congress Paris. Secret. I.C. 123. Reg. No. 943. Minutes of the meeting at the Quai d'Orsay, 28 January 1919, at 11.00 A.M., AAC: CP 351/1–Box 4. See also *FRUS, The Paris Peace Conference* 3, 751–753 (the wording of the printed version of the minutes is slightly different).

12   On 28 January 1919; because of the time difference, 28 January in Samoa was 29 January in Paris.

13   Massey, confidential, to Minister for Defence, Allen, personal, Paris, 26 April 1919, NZA: Personal Papers, Acc. 556, Box 9; see also Hiery 1992*a*, 79 n. 70.

14   Peace Congress Paris. Secret. I.C. 123. Reg. No. 943. Minutes of the meeting at the Quai d'Orsay, 28 January 1919, at 11.00 A.M., AAC: CP 351/1–Box 4. *FRUS, The Paris Peace Conference* 3, 753–754; See also Link 1992, 497.

15   New Zealand Prime Minister Massey, Paris, 26 April 1919, to Allen, NZA: Personal Papers Acc. 556, Box 9; see also Snelling 1975–1976, 20.

16   Minutes of the plenary session of 14 February 1919, 15, AAC: CP 351/1, no. 14: Preliminary Peace Conference; *FRUS, The Paris Peace Conference* 3, 229. For Rustum Haidar, the Emir's secretary, see Tibawi 1978, 339.

17   Peace Congress Paris. Secret. I.C. 124. Reg. No. 1147. Minutes of the meeting at the Quai d'Orsay, 28 January 1919, at 4 P.M., AAC: CP 351/1–Box 4. See also *FRUS, The Paris Peace Conference* 3, 771 (here again, the wording of the protocol is slightly different).

18   British Empire Delegation 6 (sixth meeting). Minutes of the meeting in 23, rue Nitôt, Paris, 29 January 1919, at 11.30 A.M., and annex (Draft Resolution on Mandates, eight points), AAC: CP 351/1–Box 4.

19   Peace Congress Paris. Secret. I.C. 127. Reg. No. 1148. Minutes of the meeting at the Quai d'Orsay, 30 January 1919, at 11.00 A.M., and Annex A: British "Draft Resolution in reference to Mandatories," 29 January 1919, AAC: CP 351/1–Box 4; *FRUS, The Paris Peace Conference* 3, 785–796.

20   Peace Congress Paris. Secret. I.C. 128. Reg. No. 1149. Minutes of the meeting at the Quai d'Orsay, 30 January 1919, at 3.30 P.M., AAC: CP 351/1–Box 4; *FRUS, The Paris Peace Conference* 3, 797–817. There are again some differences between the two versions which are altogether not unimportant. On Hughes' press campaign, see Fitzhardinge 1967, 136; Hudson 1978, 25; Spartalis 1983, 136; and Walworth 1986, 78.

21   Hughes 1950, 242–243; Hughes, telegram no. 124, Paris, 31 January 1919, to Acting Prime Minister Watt, AAC: CP 360/8, Bundle 1/3. Earlier authors have por-

trayed a diametrically opposed picture. According to this view, Hughes was the loser, because he eventually acceded to the mandatory principle as such (Hudson 1978, 25–26). But what Hughes really wanted was Australian control over New Guinea. And in this aim he finally succeeded, precisely because he put Australia's stakes as high as he could. British views of Wilson became increasingly extreme as time passed. Late in 1920, the British ambassador to Washington, A. Geddes, called Wilson "an abnormal individual": telegram no. 811 from the British ambassador, Washington, 30 November 1920, quoted in a secret communication from the Colonial Secretary, Milner, 20 December 1920, to the Governors-General of the British Dominions (Dominions no. 509), NZA: G 2–53.

22 Appendix to the minutes of the afternoon session of 30 January 1919, AAC: CP 351/1–Box 4. Not in *FRUS*. There, only the draft is given (*FRUS, The Paris Peace Conference* 3, 795–796).

23 For a similar assessment of Lloyd George's success at the conference, see Link 1992, xxix.

24 Hughes 1950, 239. Memorandum by the legal adviser to the Australian delegation, J. G. Latham, Paris, 21 February 1919, and Robert Garran, "The Ex-German Colonies," no date [1919], AAC: A 2219–vol. 9, and CP 351/1, no. 16. Secret minutes of the 9th meeting of the British Empire Delegation, Villa Majestic, Paris, 20 February 1919, and the meeting of 8 March 1919, AAC: CP 251/1–Box 4. The New Zealanders saw, before the Australians, that C class mandates differed from colonies only in name: "After all once in possession and applying your own laws it does not seem to make much difference what your power is called": New Zealand General Godley from Paris to Minister for External Affairs, Allen, 7 February 1919, NZA: WA 252/5.

25 The C class mandate certificates were sent out from Geneva by the Secretary-General of the League of Nations on 11 February 1921; New Zealand was the last to receive its certificate, which arrived on 30 April 1921 (Note by the New Zealand Minister for External Affairs, NZA: G 2/54). For Japanese resistance, see Colonial Secretary Winston Churchill, 23 February 1921, secret, to Jellicoe, ibid.; for Australia, AAC: A 981, League of Nations 1st Assembly, pt. 1, and A4-NG 23.

26 Telegram Hughes, London, 22 July 1921, to Acting Prime Minister Joseph Cook, AAC: A 981, League of Nations 2nd Assembly, pt. 1.

27 NZA: G 2–55. U.S. Government Memorandum, 24 August 1921, "Position of the Government of the United States concerning Mandates," ibid.; see also Blakeslee 1922–1923, 100, and Wilson's original protest in *FRUS, The Paris Peace Conference* 5, 492; Link 1992, 497.

28 A great deal has been written on the American–Japanese controversy about Yap. See, among others, Blakeslee 1922–1923, 103–104; Braisted 1971, 527–534; and Rattan 1972. On Wilson's reservation, see Link 1992, 250 and 275; *FRUS, The Paris Peace Conference* 4, 486 and 5, 109. On Lansing's plea for internationalization, ibid., 4, 653–654. As the radio-telephone and cable station on Yap was maintained by a German-Dutch company, the Netherlands also showed a passing interest in a League of Nations mandate for the island. Memorandum of talks between a Counsillor from the Netherlands Embassy in the United States with the 3rd Assistant Secretary of the American State Department, 31 March 1920, NARA: RG 59, 862 i.

29 Oberhochstadt, 28 November 1914, to Solf, BAK: Nachlaß No. 53 (Solf papers), no. 109.

30   Hayashima 1982, esp. 106–108.

31   Hardach 1990*a*, 9.

32   Irmer 1915, 60; see also ibid., 75 and 76: "We have no more time to go after tiny, insignificant colonies."

33   Submission by the Provincial of the Marist Mission, Father A. Steffen, Meppen, 21 February 1918, to the German Colonial Office, BAP: RKolA no. 2641.

34   Solf, Berlin, 25 March 1918, to Riedel, BAK: Nachlaß No. 53 (Solf papers), no. 125. As early as June 1917, speaking to the Deutsche Kolonialgesellschaft (German Colonial Society) in Leipzig, Solf had hinted at the possibility of Germany giving up its Pacific colonies; Fischer 1971, 472. How, after all this, Fischer could claim that the German colonial secretary included Germany's colonies in the South Pacific among "Germany's vital objectives" remains a mystery. (See Fischer 1971, 792.) For Paasche's statement, see Neuguinea-Kompanie, strictly confidential, Berlin 7 and 11 May 1915 to Neuen-dettelsauer Mission, NDM: AZ 53/41–42.

35   Memorandum, 25 November 1916, BAK: Nachlaß No. 53 (Solf papers), no. 48 (not in Fischer). On Solf's ideas for a German "central Africa," Fischer 1971, 415–416, and 792–796. Fischer's sweeping statement that late in 1916, and again in May 1917, the German Naval Staff called for the acquisition of Tahiti or New Caledonia in addition to the retention of Germany's South Pacific possessions needs to be specified and located within the context of the priorities of the Naval Staff and the German Colonial Office. It seems highly doubtful that the admiralty placed as much value on keeping the Pacific colonies as Fischer suggests. It is more likely that after the experience of military engagements in the Pacific a German presence would make sense only if it were to be strategically protected (by Tahiti or New Caledonia, for example). This, however, is not to say that the navy regarded retaining Germany's South Pacific colonies as an important war aim. In fact, it is fairly certain that the opposite was the case. A simple list of supposed war aims has little historical meaning without some discussion of the rating, significance, and wider place of these "aims"; see Fischer 1971, 417 and 471.

36   Irmer 1915, 59.

37   Grapow 1916, 60 (italics printed bold in the original), and ibid., 53. One year later, Solf appointed Grapow to work on the central Africa project; Fischer 1971, 796.

38   Solf, Berlin, 4 July 1916, BAK: Nachlaß No. 53 (Solf papers), no. 156.

39   Deputy Chancellor of Germany, Delbrück, Berlin, 28 April 1915, to Wilhelm II, GStAM: 2.2.1, no. 32469; conversation with Berta Anspach, 28 March 1992. Quotation: Solf to Ludendorff, in reply to his telegraphed query of 23 December 1917, PAA: *Südsee Nr. 14. Deutsch-Neu-Guinea,* vol. 4. Speculations by Firth (1978*b*, 44–45) and Sack (1990) miss the point. Firth's statement that Hahl "was almost certainly forced to resign" (1978*b*, 44) is untenable. It is, in essence, based on a rumor that circulated among the Australians in New Guinea during the war; see Lyng, no date [1919], 235. On the beginning of the dissolution of the Colonial Office's administration of New Guinea, see note by Kalkmann, 28 August 1917, BAP: RKolA no. 2511.

40   Valentini, 18 November 1917, to Hertling, conveying Wilhelm II's message, GStAM: 2.2.1, no. 32474. On Ludendorff's negative attitude toward German colonies in the Pacific, Fischer 1971, 792. According to Fischer, the German supreme military command in the Pacific wanted to retain only Samoa, "because of its phosphate deposits"; ibid. There was no phosphate on Samoa.

41   Documents in BAP: RKolA nos. 7057, 7058, and 7059.

42   Minutes of a meeting between Hahl and Johannes Bell (Minister for Colonial Affairs), 8 May 1919, BAP: 7058. Haber, Versailles, 24 May 1919, to Bell, ibid.

43   For the British attitude in general, see Louis 1967, 57–62, 65–68, 70–71, and esp. 82–83, on the African colonies in particular, see Digre 1990, 68–75, 85–91, and esp. 90–91. According to the colonial secretary, Walter Long, the notion that German colonies should be returned because their occupation broke Britain's wartime promise not to acquire foreign territories was "a ridiculous idea" (11 October 1917, confidential and personal, to the Governor-General of Australia, ANL: 696/1455). Long gave an assurance that the British government had avoided taking an official position in favor of annexing the colonies only out of respect for diplomatic sensitivities. Any such declaration, he pointed out, would be counterproductive at the moment, as there were strong feelings against annexation in both America and Russia. The British government's position in favor of annexing the German colonies, however, was unaffected, and had never changed. (Long, Downing Street, 28 December 1917, private and personal, to the Governor-General of Australia, ANL: 696/1470.) "I regard it as essential to the Empire that the Colonies should be retained under our own control. Their return to Germany is unthinkable"; Long, personal and confidential to the Governor-General of Australia, Downing Street, 8 February 1918, ANL: 696/1474. "Whatever happens, these Colonies can never be returned to Germany, and it follows as an almost inevitable corollary that...they should remain with us"; Long, Downing Street, 7 November 1918, private and personal, to the Governor-General of Australia, ANL 696/1527. On Long's attitude, Rothwell 1971, 69. A general failing of Rothwell's account is that he uncritically accepts British memoirs, especially of the war and the peace conference written essentially as justifications shortly before the beginning of the Second World War. In a number of cases pertaining directly to our topic, Rothwell makes statements that are simply incorrect (e.g., Rothwell 1971, 71–72, where he claims that before 1914 New Zealand was not very worried by the Japanese threat). Lloyd George's apparent offer to give up German East Africa was only a rhetorical one, as it was connected with a French withdrawal from the Cameroons, which he knew would never materialize. *FRUS, The Paris Peace Conference* 6, 144.

44   British "Memorandum on German War Aims," by Long, sent to the Dominions on 13 September 1917, NZA: G 2–40; confidential memorandum by the Political Intelligence Department, Foreign Office, 15 November 1918; "German Colonies and popular feeling in Germany," AAC: A 3934–SC 12/19.

45   Fischer 1989, 1–7.

46   Thereupon Hughes founded the National Labor Party, soon renamed the Nationalist Party, after the liberals joined. Crowley 1974, 333–336, and Macintyre 1986, 163–168.

47   On 9 August 1917, see AAC: A 3934–SC 12/19. On the issue of a Labor Party divided over the future of New Guinea, see Thompson 1980, 213–214, and esp. Thompson 1972.

48   "Those captured islands," *Australian Worker,* 6 June 1918; resolution of the Interstate Conference of the Australian Labor Party, 24 June 1918, printed in *Argus* (Melbourne), 25 June 1918. On the attitudes of Australian newspapers, Thompson 1980, 216–217. As a whole, the Australian press showed less interest in New

Guinea in 1918–1919 than it had in 1883, when Queensland had tried to annex the island; ibid., 216.

49 Holman, 14 November 1918, to Charles Wade, AAC: A 3934–SC 12/19.

50 Ibid. Originally the Legislative Council in Sydney had passed a motion that favored placing German New Guinea under British or international control; Thompson 1980, 218.

51 Commonwealth of Australia. Parliamentary Debates vol. 86, 7784–7801 (Senate, 14 November 1918), 7833–7844, 7858–7889, and 7929–7947 (House of Representatives, 14/15 November 1918). The member for Melbourne Ports, Mathews (Labor), pointed out that, after all, it was better to have the Germans in New Guinea than the Japanese. He feared that Australia and New Zealand would go to war with each other over Germany's Pacific colonies (ibid.).

52 Watt, 19 November and 2 December 1918, to the Premier of New South Wales, AAC: A 3934–SC 12/19. On 30 November 1918, the cabinet expressed its formal support for Australian, not international, control of New Guinea. Telegram no. 228 from Acting Prime Minister Watt, 30 November 1918, to Hughes, AAC: CP 360/8, Bun 1/2.

53 Australian Labor Party election manifesto for the federal elections of 1919, in the *Daily Telegraph* (Sydney), 5 November 1919.

54 Rowley 1958, 317. Lynch was convinced by the argument that if Australia refused the mandate for New Guinea, it would fall not to the United States of America, because it was not a member of the League of Nations, but to Japan. Ibid.

55 The Governor-General of Australia, Sydney, 25 December 1918, private and confidential, to the Colonial Secretary, Long, ANL: 696/1122. On wartime plans for the annexation of New Caledonia and the New Hebrides, see the Governor-General, 25 January, 17 March, 13 May, and 19 May 1915, Melbourne, to Colonial Secretary Harcourt, ANL: 696/6957, 669, 689–691, and 692. Pointing to Fisher's reservations about a financial involvement in pursuing such political ambitions, Thompson, in my opinion, plays down the significance of Australia's imperialist designs too much; see Thompson 1980, 205–206. Certainly the general mood in Australia during the war was not one of restraint. (Timor: memorandum by the Australian Secretary for External Affairs, 25 May 1915, AAC: A 2219–7.) The raising of the Australian flag in the interior of East Timor: secret naval report, R. Hockings, China Station, Singapore, 28–30 December 1915, AAC: CP 78/23–14/89/112. Christmas and Ocean Islands: the Governor-General of Australia, 28 December 1917, to the Colonial Secretary, conveying the wishes of the Australian Cabinet, AAC: A 2219–7.

56 Watt, 20 March 1919, by telegraph, to Hughes, AAC: CP 360/8, Bun 1/3; secret telegram from Watt, no. 56, 28 April 1919, to Hughes, AAC: CP 360/8, Bun 1/4. Involved in the initiative were the Anglican archbishop of Melbourne, the Presbyterians, the London Missionary Society, the Methodists, and the Baptists, ibid. See also Thompson 1980, 208–209 and 215.

57 *Melbourne Herald*, 14 July 1919. Solomons: Secretary to the Prime Minister, Starling, 19 September 1919, by telegraph—"secret, personal"—to the Governor-General, to be conveyed to London, ANL: 696/6627.

58 On 13 May 1915, to Harcourt, personal, ANL: 696/687–688. See also Thompson 1980, 205.

59 The Governor-General of Australia, 6 April 1915, to Harcourt, personal, ANL: 696/677; See also Fitzhardinge 1970, 255–256. "The Line" refers to the equator, which

as early as the end of 1914 the colonial secretary had suggested as the line of demarcation between the Japanese and the British spheres of interest. The Governor-General of Australia, Melbourne, 20 January 1915, to Harcourt, personal (concerning his conversations with some of Australia's "leading men" whom, on Harcourt's instructions, he was to prepare carefully for this idea), ANL: 696/650. See also Louis 1966, 409–410; Fitzhardinge 1970, 255; and Frei 1991, 97–98.

60 This was Lloyd George's constant fear; Martin 1982, 173.

61 Walter Lucas, 15 December 1920, to Piesse about Rupert Hornabrook, AAC: A 4–NG 1. Dr. Rupert Hornabrook, a South Australian, was one of the lone fighters who, publishing articles in provincial newspapers, took a constant stand against Australian nationalism, chauvinism, and racism. He believed that their own colonial history made white Australians incapable of dealing with blacks without lapsing into racism and exploitation: "The Australian is not the class of man to govern tropical Pacific Islands inhabited by colored races—there is far too much of the 'White Australia' twaddle in his veins . . . " (Rupert Hornabrook, 28 November 1921, to his brother Charlie in Adelaide, AAC: A 518–E 800/1/3, pt. 1). In letters to Lloyd George and Milner, Hornabrook advocated a British mandate over New Guinea and an Imperial Pacific Federation of Britain's Pacific islands (ibid.; cf. his article, "Is Australia wise? The Pacific Island Question," in *The Mail* (Adelaide), 12 July 1919, and the summary of a lecture he gave in Adelaide, in the *South Australian Advertiser* (Adelaide), 24 November 1921). On Hornabrook, Frei 1991, 106–107. Apart from Hornabrook, the sharpest criticism of Australia's presence and policy in the Pacific Islands was expressed by Stead's *Review of Reviews* (Melbourne) and the Sydney *Daily Telegraph* (see, among others, the following articles: 26 March 1919, "Island of Nauru"; 21 July 1919, "The New Empire in the Pacific. Our Responsiblities. To administer, not to exploit"; and 21 December 1920, "Australia's Mandate." For details of Munro Ferguson's ideas, see pp. 105–106 above). For British fears that the Empire would disintegrate, Rothwell 1971, 264.

62 Liverpool, 28 January 1916, private, to Bonar Law, NZA: G 48–32–R23. Liverpool, Wellington, 4 December 1918, confidential, to Long, NZA: G 26/9.

63 Petition, 18 December 1915, NZA: G 21/3. The objective was a Crown Colony under a civil governor; 27 of the 37 signatories were British citizens.

64 The *Truth* (Auckland), editorial, 25 October 1919: "A white New Zealand."

65 Ibid., 3 April 1920: "Politician back from Samoa." On McCombs, see *The Oxford History of New Zealand*, 1992, 216 and 220.

66 Gray, Wellington, 11 October 1922, to Tate, personal, ATL: MS 264, no. 3; Tate, 28 October 1922, to Gray, ibid.

67 See for example, the criticism in the *Japan Advertiser*, 26 February 1919, AAC: A 2219–4.

68 Representative of this opinion are, among others, commentaries in the dailies *Hochi* (editorial, 2 November 1917: "The retention of the German Colonies and the future of Tsingtao"), and *Chugai Shogyo* (12 May 1919), and in the magazine *Nanyo* (among others, by Yasui Seitaro in the September issue of 1917). One of the leading members of the "strategic school" was Ichikawa Hanzan, editor of the journal *Yorodzu Choho*. (See his views in *The Japan Chronicle*, 3 February 1918, "Japan's Peace Conditions"; see also Frei 1991, 100.) On the need for a Japanese presence for reasons of prestige, see explanation by the leader of the Japanese peace delegation, Baron Makino, early February 1919 in New York, en route to

Paris, in *Japan Advertiser,* 11 February 1919. For the whole discussion, Peattie 1988, 50–52.

69 This position was held in particular by the MP Hayashi Kiroku, a university professor. Hayashi's views are in *Taiyo,* 18 November 1917.

70 Intelligence Report by Captain Gould, *Jubilee* (Pacific Phosphate Company recruiting ship) to the Administrator of Nauru, 2 October 1917, AAC: A 2219–1. On stepping-stones to the southern regions: Peattie 1988, 51. On Dutch East India: "When the old woman [the Netherlands] dies, poverty stricken Japan should have a voice in the distribution of her effects," *Nanyo Oyobi Nipponjin,* 10 December 1917, AAC: A 2219–1 (English translation, ibid.). On India as an objective, see Takekoshi in *Yuben,* January 1916, "Expansion to the South," AAC: A 2219–2. On Japan's most aggressive wartime dreams for the Pacific, Frei 1991, 95 (conquest of Australia and New Zealand); ibid., 70, on the split in the concept of *nan'yo* (Pacific expansion) into an inner *(uchi)* and an outer *(soto)* direction after the conquest of Micronesia. The latter included Southeast Asia and India.

71 Thompson 1980, 211, and Frei 1991, 100–101.

72 Confidential Memorandum from Atlee Hunt to the Lieutenant Governor of Papua, Murray, Melbourne, 22 October 1914, AAC: A 518/1–A 800/1/1, pt. 1A; see also Frei 1991, 96–97.

73 Thompson 1980, 211, and Frei 1991, 96–99.

74 Frei 1991, 100.

75 Pomeroy 1951, 63, and Walworth 1986, 70 n. 28. Whether only Lansing knew of the Anglo-Japanese agreement or whether Wilson had also been informed is a matter of dispute. After the war Balfour claimed that the American president had been aware of the secret arrangement, but Wilson denied this. Spartalis 1983, 52. See also *FRUS, The Paris Peace Conference* 5, 126–127, 134 and 11, 79.

76 Precisely this chain of thought was suggested by Martin as early as 1982 (102–105, and 151–153). According to this view, the mandate system was "an excellent solution for the American dilemma in the region [the Pacific]"; ibid., 152.

77 Pomeroy 1951, 65–66, Braisted 1971, 447, and original memorandum by the Third Assistant Secretary of State (Breckinridge Long), 14 December 1918, *FRUS, The Paris Peace Conference* 2, 512–515.

78 "German rule was a great improvement over the Spanish, and, upon the whole, was reasonably successful in a material sense; and, in general, not unduly harsh" (Blakeslee 1921, 183). Blakeslee, a professor of Clark University, was the historical adviser to the American peace delegation. On him, Gelfand 1963, 63–65, and 270–271.

79 They included, among other things, giving the League of Nations mandate to a small nation (the Netherlands?); Braisted 1971, 448.

80 The justification used was that the French warship *Montcalm* had helped to conquer Germany's Pacific colonies; Aldrich 1990, 279.

CHAPTER 7: "NEW" COLONIAL POLICY AND INDIGENOUS INTERPRETATIONS OF COLONIAL RULE IN THE LIGHT OF THE FIRST WORLD WAR

1 Hahl, *DKZ,* no. 12, 20 December 1918, 179. Henry Stead: "Japan and the Pacific," *The Mid-Pacific* 9 (1918): 255–258. In May 1921, the German foreign office

handed over the secret survey maps of Germany's former colonies in the Pacific, which the navy had prepared, to the U.S. Navy. The Americans did not take up further German offers; Braisted 1971, 543–544.

2   F. W. Thompson's report of a recruiting trip through the Caroline and Marshall Islands for the Pacific Phosphate Company, Nauru, 21 July 1920, to the Administrator, AAC: A 2219–vol. 23. Thompson conscientiously noted one machine gun at the Japanese headquarters in Ponape (the mandate regulations had not yet come into force).

3   Memorandum by the Prime Minister's Department, "'Madras Maru' Incident at Rabaul," 12 July 1920, AAC: A 3932-SC 397. Documents relating to Japanese agitation in AAM: MP 1049/1–18/0491.

4   *The Times* (London), 2 February 1921.

5   Memorandum Director of Military Intelligence, Major Piesse, 24 March 1919, to the Chief of the General Staff, AAM: MP 1049/1–18/0491. On Piesse, Fitzhardinge 1970, 251; Fischer 1989, 80, and 103 (during the war Piesse's duties included shadowing the Germans in Australia); Thompson 1990, 70; and Edwards 1983, 52–58.

6   Peattie 1988, 71.

7   Report Naval Station Guam, 4 October 1922, NARA: RG 38, K-5-a: 9217. Memorandum Piesse, 10 September 1920: "Australian interests in islands north of the equator and Japanese interests in German New Guinea. A review of policy from September, 1914, to July, 1920," AAC: A 981-League of Nations 1st Assembly, file 4.

8   Peattie 1988, 68.

9   The Australian military administration had set up a cannon emplacement in Raluana, near Rabaul, in June–July 1918. The two six-inch cannons were dismantled at the beginning of the civil administration and put into storage, enabling them to be set up again in a few days' time. The gun emplacements remained; ammunition for the cannons was sent to northern Australia. The Australian attorney-general declared that these procedures fulfilled the requirements of the C class mandate. Intelligence Report Administrator Johnston, no. 2, Rabaul, 11 July 1918, AAC: CP 103/11, NG Reports 2/15 (setting up the cannons); memorandum Piesse, "Armaments in the New Guinea Territory," 7 April 1921, AAC: CP 360/13/4; the Prime Minister's Secretary, Deane, Melbourne, 5 May 1922, to the Attorney-General of Australia, AAC: A 432–29/4495; report by Attorney-General Garran, 23 May 1922, AAC: A 518-C 810/1. A telegraphic query, 29 August 1921, Administrator Wisdom to the Prime Minister, asking whether the two cannons should be sent to Australia, received a negative reply (ibid.).

10   List of recommendations by the Prime Minister's Secretary, Shepherd, 10 December 1920; undated marginal comment on Murray's application by Lucas, ibid., AAC: A 518-G 800/1/3; Murray's query, ibid. See also the memorandum by Murray, 24 February 1919, 3: "If German New Guinea is administered separately from Papua I should be offered my choice of the two. . . . I am the only Australian with any experience of the civil government of native races." AAC: CP 661/15/1. Three days later Murray claimed a governorship over both, Papua and the Northern Territory. Murray, 27 February 1919, to the Prime Minister, AAC: A 2–19/1308. Additional documents concerning the filling of the post in AAC: A 457, 650/1; See also Thompson 1990, 71. Griffiths' personal file in AAC: A 518–852/1/451.

11   Wisdom's application, addressed to the Secretary of the Prime Minister's Department, no date [late November 1920], AAC: A 518–852/1/186.

12   Wisdom, Rabaul, 12 April 1921, to the Prime Minister's Secretary about the implementation of the prime minister's instructions, "Establishment of civil government in the late German New Guinea Possession," 16 August 1920, AAC: A 518-E 800/1/ 3, pt. 1. The relative power and influence of Wisdom and Lucas in the early days of the mandate is also reflected in their respective salaries. The director of the Expropriation Board was paid £2,000 annually; the Administrator, only £1,800.

13   The MP for Capricornia (Queensland), F. M. Forde (Labor), after visiting the mandated territory, writing in the *Melbourne Herald,* 17 October 1923; cf. also F. M. Forde, "Riot of Coconuts," ibid., 24 October 1923.

14   "New Guinea Affairs," the *Age* (Melbourne), 4 June 1921.

15   Tate, 22 May 1919, to Major C. E. Andrews, Wellington, ATL: MS 264, no. 17.

16   Chair of the Apia Chamber of Commerce, Croudacre, writing in the *Argus* (Melbourne), 2 October 1920: "Mandate over Samoa."

17   On 1 January 1914; *DKB* 26 (1915): 202. On the number of officials under the New Zealand administration, see *The Age* (Melbourne), 31 May 1921: "The South Seas" (letter from the Samoa correspondent), NZA: G 5–96. A detailed report by the American consul in Apia mentions 127 European officials in Samoa in August 1921. The Department for Native Affairs in Apia, which under the Germans had been conducted autonomously by 149 Samoans (in 1914), now employed 6 European officials and 293 Samoan subaltern officials. (Confidential report by Quincy F. Roberts, Apia, 5 August 1921, to the Secretary of State, NARA: RG 59, 862 m). The first "real" Administrator of the civil administration, General Richardson, like Wisdom in New Guinea, was selected solely on the basis of his military achievements; Field 1984, 61.

18   Henry Stead, *Review of Reviews,* 28 May 1921. On the impression that military "civil" officials made on the Samoans, see *Sydney Morning Herald,* 8 September 1921, "Disaffected Natives."

19   Tate, Apia, 14 February 1922, to the Minister for External Affairs, NZA: IT 1/2. The "militaristic impression" did not impress the Samoans; it was more of a provocation to them; Peter Rasmussen, Apia, 13 January 1989.

20   Piesse, 12 September 1923, Melbourne, to Administrator Griffiths of Nauru, ANL: MS 882, 3/3, 882/3/217; quotation by Wisdom, ibid. On the Administrator of Samoa's desire for a title, see Richardson, Apia, 14 June 1923, to the Minister for External Affairs, NZA: IT 1/2; confidential communication of the decision taken in London, 29 June 1923, ibid.

21   Thompson 1990, 81–82. But see Buckley and Klugman 1983, 96.

22   Wisdom, Rabaul, 22 April 1925, to the Secretary of the Ministry for Home and Territories, AAC: A 518-D 112/5, pt. 1. Contracts between Burns Philp and the Commonwealth government in AAC: A 518-D 112/2, and E 112/2. See also *The Herald* (Melbourne), 1 November 1923, "High Freight Rates to New Guinea," and the report by Canning in AAC: A 518-C-800/1/3, pt 1.

23   Confidential report by the American Consul-General, Melbourne, 6 October 1921, NARA: RG 59, 862 d.

24   "Very restless about the continuance of German names," Lucas, Melbourne, 26 October 1922, to Piesse, AAC: A 518-B 836/2.

25   Circular memorandum no. 374 by the Administrator, 9 June 1924, to all District Officers, AAC: A 518-B 836/2. This circular laid down the official spelling for place-names, which has remained valid to the present day: Kaewieng became Kavi-

eng; Eitape became Aitape; and Wanimo was changed to Vanimo. See: *Argus* (Melbourne), 6 April 1920, "Pacific Possessions. Name for New Territory"; Piesse, 27 April 1920, to Charles Hedley, Director of the Australian Museum, ANL: MS 882, 6/1, 882/6/5; Evan Stanley, Port Moresby, 8 December 1922, to Piesse, ibid., 882/6/3; memorandum by Lucas for the Prime Minister, 17 August 1920, "Name for late German New Guinea Possessions," AAC: CP 103/11, NG Reports 22; Deputy Administrator Wanliss, 16 February 1923, to the Prime Minister's Secretary, AAC: A 518-B 836/2. Under Administrator Griffiths, some German names were reintroduced in 1933–1934, for example, Seeadler (instead of Sea Eagle) Harbour. Even names such as Stubbenkammer and Ko[ö]nigstuhl (places that resembled the original locations on Germany's largest island, Rügen) were retained; AAC: A 518-B 836/2. Some of the remaining German names found in Papua New Guinea today are listed in Mühlhäusler 1980, 187.

26   *Commonwealth of Australia. Parliamentary Papers,* vol. 95, 9100, session of 16 June 1921, question by Gibson, reply by Joseph Cook (Acting Prime Minister).

27   Ibid., vol. 97, 11581, session of 29 September 1921, MP Cameron, query and reprimand.

28   On 22 October 1920, to the Prime Minister's Secretary, AAC: A 457–710/3. Report by the American Consul of Soerabaya, Java, 5 September 1922, to the State Department, NARA: RG 59, 862 d; E. Mansfield-Hardy, 6 April 1922, MLS: B 956.

29   "We must have power to recruit children at an early stage . . . and make a contract binding them to us." Wisdom, 3 August 1921, to the Secretary in the Prime Minister's Department, ANL: MS 882, 6/2, 882/6/177.

30   "The indentured labour are frightened to a degree of their masters; the latter gives them a hell of a hiding and then says, 'Now suppose you talk along kiap along me, me fightem you; you look out you bastard; behind he go finish me fight you planety too much; now you savee you black bastard.' ('If you talk to the district officer about me, I'll beat you up; watch out, when he is gone, I'll beat you black and blue, savvy?')." H. E. A. Cameron, Longan General Hospital, Bahmatt Island, Ninigo Group, 12 February 1924, confidential, to Cardew, Commissioner of Native Affairs, Rabaul, AAC: A 1–25/4670. Cameron had six years of experience in New Guinea; four in the administration and two on the Expropriation Board.

31   Lyng, no date [1919], 58.

32   Wisdom, 3 August 1921, to the Secretary in the Prime Minister's Department, ANL: MS 882, 6/2, 882/6/176.

33   Documents in AAC: A 518-A 254/1/1, pt. 1. Gammage 1975, the only attempt to analyze the strike so far, does not mention this possible connection.

34   Administrator Wisdom, 28 December 1921, to the Sacred Heart Mission, AAC: A 457–800/5/1; Marriage and Divorce of Natives Regulation 1922, § 3b, ibid. For the mission's attempt before 1914, see now Hiery 1994.

35   *Daily Telegraph* (Sydney), 3 July 1923, "New Guinea Law"; *The Parliament of the Commonwealth of Australia. Parliamentary Papers. Report to the League of Nations for 1922/23,* 1421.

36   Thompson 1990, 83; "Ulpean" in AAC: A 518-C 818/1/3, pt. 1. "Orders have been fulfilled for coal baskets, waste-paper baskets, etc.," Administrator Wisdom, summing up school activities in his original annual report for 1922–1923, 105, AAC: A 518-C 849/1/3. The Australian authorities deleted this passage, without replacement, in the mandate report sent to Geneva.

37 Wisdom, in his original annual report for 1922–1923, 105, AAC: A 518-C 849/1/3.

38 *Report to the League of Nations for 1922/1923,* 1421.

39 Memorandum Wisdom, Rabaul, 3 August 1921, to the Secretary in the Prime Minister's office, AAC: A 518-F 840/1/3, pt. 1.

40 Natives Taxes Ordinance, 28 October 1921, retrospectively effective from 1 July 1921, AAC: A 518-A 846/1/60. The punishment for nonpayment of head and education taxes was six months' imprisonment with hard labor. Fathers of families with more than three children "by one wife" were exempt from taxation (ibid.). The education tax raised considerable amounts of money from the "free" Melanesians—£5,092 in 1924–1925 alone. AAC: A 518-C 818/1/3, pt. 1.

41 Memorandum Captain J. A. Carrodus, 23 April 1928, AAC: A 518-C 818/1/3, pt. 1. On Carrodus, Thompson 1990, 80. A typical example of the prejudices and racist attitudes of the Europeans in the mandated area toward schooling for Melanesians is to be found in the *Rabaul Times,* 13 November 1936, "Our uneducated natives." On resistance to McKenna's education plans, see B. J. McKenna, "Report on Native Education in the Mandated Territory of New Guinea," Brisbane, 20 August 1929, AAC: A 518-C 818/1/3, pt. 1; extract from the Legislative Council Debate, 22–24 July 1929, on McKenna's ideas, ibid. Even the fact that he did not, in principle, want to change the existing discriminatory situation did not help McKenna's cause: "we must ensure that . . . we do not allow him to habour the impression that, once having been initiated into those elementary secrets, he is mentally equal to the White race" (ibid.). The conclusion drawn by the Administrator from McKenna's report was that one priority of a new education policy for the Australian mandate of New Guinea must be to encourage the natives systematically to produce souvenirs for tourists. Wisdom, Rabaul, 14 May 1931, to the Secretary in the prime minister's office, AAC: A 518-C 818/1/3, pt. 1.

42 Police Force Ordinance no. 114 1922/23, *Government Gazette,* no. 62, AAC: A 1–23/24782. Radio message from the Acting Administrator to Australia, Rabaul, 16 August 1923, ibid. On sentences for the wearing of European dress, see Lawrence 1974.

43 "No good purpose can be served in laying down any hard and fast plan in regard to education." Memorandum "Native Education," Acting Administrator H. Page, Rabaul, 21 October 1938, to the Secretary in the Prime Minister's Department, AAC: A 518-C 818/1/3, pt. 2; League of Nations. Permanent Mandates Commission. Minutes of 34th Session, 17th meeting, 20 June 1938, AAC: A 981-NG 30/3.

44 "Return showing number of natives in the gaols of the Territory on 30th June 1922 with the duration of sentences they are serving," AAC: A 1–23/18422.

45 Townsend 1968, 153–154, reports that, in three cases in all, he single-handedly hanged Melanesians. In one of these three case alone, five Melanesian men were executed. If we assume that Townsend executed only one Melanesian in each of the two remaining cases (he himself is silent on this), then he alone would have been responsible for 11 percent of all Australian executions, which is unlikely. In 1946 Townsend became a United Nations official and served the organization for ten years (ibid., 9). On official figures for executions, Nelson 1978, 144. The manner in which executions were carried out was the cause of heated debates. In July 1923, libel charges were pending in Rabaul because the hangman regarded the comment "he had not conducted his last hanging properly" as a slur on his personal honor. *Daily Telegraph* (Sydney), 7 July 1923, M. H. Ellis, "Forced Labour."

46 Thompson 1990, 83. During the Pacific War the Australian administration issued an official directive instructing officials "not [to] record matters of contentious nature in patrol reports, matters which are likely to embarrass ANGAU [Australian New Guinea Administrative Unit]. . . . Officers will also desist from the practice of oblique advertising by direct or veiled reference to the incompetence, blundering or even illegal action of other officers in reports" (Kituai 1988, 164–165).

47 "Wilkins was a rough sort of chap, but an excellent patrol officer except for drink and women. He . . . had the respect of the natives except in one important particular, namely women. . . . He undoubtedly had marys [indigenous women] wherever he went and there is more than a suspicion of 'pulling' [Tok Pisin: rape] in one case." (Administrator Wisdom, Rabaul, 23 June 1924, to the Secretary in the Ministry for Home and Territories, Melbourne, AAC: A 1–25/4670; statements by local eyewitnesses on the rapes committed by the patrol officer, and on his victims, ibid.). Among the Australian public, the administration managed to discredit reports of Wilkins' crimes as the fantasies of a sick ex-official; Thompson 1990, 79. For similar cases of rape: see Administrator Wisdom, 30 December 1922, to the Secretary in the Prime Minister's Office, AAC: A 518/1-N 840/1/3 (concerning Arthur Walter Windus Winstone, chief clerk to the Military Administration in Rabaul, thereafter inspecting district officer of the Mandate Administration responsible to the Chief Court, Rabaul); Secretary of the Mandate Administration, Page, 24 April 1924, to Administrator Wisdom (about the deputy district officer of Aitape, G. K. Freeman), AAC: A1–25/4670. In his final report, the official investigating the cases of Freeman and Wilkins had recommended "that a public investigation of these matters will aggravate the position and give feeders of the press opportunities to write distorted and exaggerated accounts. It is improper to suggest that the present 'mess' be cleaned up and those responsible replaced by saner officials." Acting District Officer of Aitape, E. W. Oakley (who had himself been accused), 8 February 1924, to the Government Secretary in Rabaul, ibid. On 17 January 1922, Bishop Couppé passed on to the Administrator the missions' concern over the supervision of native women by officials; AAC: A 457–800/5/1. See also Böhm 1975, 111; NDM: Bergmann 6, 23–24 (women and girls in fear of being abused by the district officer), and ibid., 7, 169–171 (women forced to take part in orgies). Indigenous statements: Manasupe, June 1922, NDM: MS 322, 141; Sai and Limu in Griffin, Nelson, and Firth 1979, 66.

48 Kituai 1988, 222, 227, and 245.

49 Amean 1973, 24. One of the victims committed suicide on the same night (ibid.).

50 Legislative Council, AAC: A 518–846/1/130. Its first meeting took place on 9 May 1933. An advisory council had been set up in 1926. After vigorous protests by the Administrator, it consisted only of the Administrator himself and five of his subordinates; ibid. Before 1914 the government council had also included representatives of the non-German community, Hiery 1993b.

51 Thompson 1990, 75 and 79. A typical response by Prime Minister Hughes to a question in the House concerning the continuation of the practice of flogging: "I suppose it is a lie, as usual." *Commonwealth of Australia. Parliamentary Papers*, vol. 97, 12395 (session of 3 November 1921).

52 Thompson 1990, 79–81. I cannot fully agree with Thompson's statement that the author of the report, Ainsworth "was a critical and independently-minded observer" (ibid., 79). A more precise reading of the report shows clearly that, on

crucial issues (such as the uninterrupted continuation of corporal punishment), Ainsworth relied fully on emollient statements by officials, making no independent attempt to get to the bottom of obviously contradictory reports, or even to investigate them more closely. Some of his "recommendations" to the Australian federal government (which paid him £500) reveal his general ignorance of Melanesian conditions. Thus, for a culture in which prosperity and economic and social relations are essentially defined in terms of pig ownership, he recommended that "the last thing on earth in the way of animals that should be owned by natives is the pig." Ainsworth Report, recommendations, 8, no. 88, AAC: A 518-M 850/1/3.

53 Thompson 1990, 84. On 3 August 1922, the Australian delegate, Joseph Cook, replied to a question put by the Swedish delegate Bugge-Wicksell in the Mandate Commission that Field Punishment No. 1 was used only in cases of military discipline in New Guinea (although the need for this in a demilitarized territory remained unclear). Société des Nations. Commission permanente des Mandats. Procés-verbaux de la deuxiéme session tenue à Genève du 1er au 11 aôut 1922, Geneva, 19 August 1922, 33 (6th session, 3 August 1922), AAC: A 2219–24.

54 Ibid., 40 (7th session, 4 August 1922). See also Weeramantry 1992, 379.

55 Churchill, 21 September 1921, to the Governor-General of Australia, and Dean, Prime Minister's Secretary, 14 February 1922, to the Governor-General, for transmission to London. Carrying out: Governor-General, 23 February 1922, to the Colonial Secretary, AAC: A 6661–391.

56 Prime Minister of New Zealand, 28 February 1925, to the Prime Minister of Australia, approving Australia's procedures, AAC: A 518/1-AR 118/12.

57 Full text of the discussions in the minutes of the meeting: Société des Nations. Commission permanente des Mandats. Procès-verbaux de la deuxième session tenue à Genève du 1er au 11 aôut 1922, Geneva, 19 August 1922, 58 (11th session, 7 August 1922), AAC: A 2219–24. Official (published) positions are in Weeramantry 1992, 381 and 383.

58 Weeramantry 1992, 365–367. Figures are calculated according to table 16.1, ibid.

59 Griffiths, Nauru, 28 August 1924, to the Island Manager, Matthew Thom, AAC: 518-D 112/6/1.

60 English translation of a letter from Chief Dabe, Nauru, 9 September 1924, to Island Manager Thom, AAC: A 518-D 112/6/1. For the treatment of the Aiwo after 1945, see Weeramantry 1992, 384–390.

61 Harold Gaze, British Phosphate Commission, Melbourne, 9 December 1930, personal and confidential, to the Australian Prime Minister's Secretary, AAC: A 518–O 800/1/2.

62 See Hahl 1942, 39, and *Report on the Administration of Nauru, 17 December 1920–31 December 1921,* 1922, 6. A photograph of the chiefs of "German" Nauru, including two women (the chiefs Eiginoba and Bodane), is reproduced in Williams and Macdonald 1985, after p. 54.

63 Petition from the chiefs Bop, Gaunibur, Dabe, Deireragea, Buraman, Amwano, Deigareow, Tsiminita, Evaeo, and Denca, Nauru, 29 November 1930, to the Prime Minister of Australia, AAC: A 518–O 800/1/2; petition from Nauruans over sixteen years of age to the Prime Minister of Australia, Nauru, 17 March 1931, ibid. In 1930, Nauru had a total indigenous population of 1,411; Pacific Islands Year Book 1944, 142. The list contains 495 signatures (85.8 percent), and 82 names followed by a cross (14.2 percent). The latter figure is possibly somewhat high, as many

names have obviously had marks added to them later. This suggests that the marks are not the X's of illiterate Nauruans, but that they may have been made later by the Australian administration, which wanted particularly to emphasize the names of some of the petitioners when presenting and analyzing the petition. List of complaints by Deireragea, Evaio, Bop, Deigareow, Amwano, Gaunibur, Tsiminita, Dave, Denca, and Buraman, to the Prime Minister of Australia, Nauru, 20 March 1931, AAC: A 518–O 800/1/2. See also Thompson 1992, 274–275.

64   Newman, Canberra, 30 March 1931, to the Secretary in the Prime Minister's Department, AAC: A 518–O 800/1/2; memorandum by Administrator Newman, Nauru, 25 May 1931, on the education of Nauruans, AAC: A 518-C 818/1/2; see also Weeramantry 1992, 112–113.

65   Minutes of the meeting between Administrator Newman and the chiefs of Nauru, Court House, Nauru, 25 May 1931, AAC: A 518-O 800/1/2.

66   Communication from the Australian Prime Minister, 14 April 1932, to the Australian High Commissioner in London, AAC: A 518, O 800/1/2. Neither Williams and Macdonald 1985 nor Weeramantry 1992 mentions the conflict. On the dismissal of the two chiefs, see Dabe, Nauru, 24 September 1931, to the Prime Minister of Australia, AAC: A 518, O 800/1/2. See also Thompson 1992, 275, who states that the Nauruan chiefs tried unsuccessfully to contact Geneva directly, via the Australian delegate to the League of Nations.

67   Williams and Macdonald 1985, 206–207.

68   Williams and Macdonald 1985, 282. Average annual exports of phosphate from Nauru: 1921–1932, 262 tons; 1933–1940, 633 tons; calculated from statistics in Weeramantry 1992, 369 (table 16.2).

69   The Australian prime minister's commissioner for New Guinea came to the same conclusion: "A comparison with the Japanese Administration, therefore, must leave us open to the criticism that the Japanese administration is more liberal [*sic!*], and is doing more for the natives." Memorandum Piesse, 2 November 1922, AAC: A 981 Marshall Islands 1, pt. 2. Similarly, a memorandum by Piesse, 30 August 1922, ibid.

70   Dr. Buse, "Die Gesundheitsverhältnisse auf Jap" (Health conditions on Yap), *Amtsblatt für das Schutzgebiet Deutsch-Neuguinea* 5, no. 8 (15 April 1913): 73–75; AAC: A 981 Marshall and Caroline Islands 1, pt. 3. In 1933, the indigenous population of Yap was 4,000; the Japanese census of 1 November 1920 had recorded 8,340; the German censuses of 1 April 1903, 7,155, and of 1 January 1911, 6,187. *Jahresberichte* for 1903–1904 and 1910–1911, and *Report on the Administration of the Territory under Japanese Mandate,* Geneva, 6 April 1922, 6 and 7, in AAC: A 981 Marshall and Caroline Islands, 2.

71   See Ballendorf 1984.

72   "Prostitution is practically unknown in the Islands": *Mandate report* 1921/22, 24, AAC: A 981 Marshall and Caroline islands 1, pt. 2.

73   *New Zealand Gazette,* no. 51 (1921), NZA: G 5–99.

74   Minutes of the meeting between Minister for External Affairs Lee, his Secretary, the Administrator, 27 *faiuple,* and the two *fautua,* Malietoa and Tuimaleali'ifano, Mulinuu, 16 July 1921, NZA: G 48-S/8.

75   Samoan petition of 16 July 1921, ibid. It was signed by 28 *faipule,* their spokesperson, Toelupe, and the bearer of the title of *mata'afa* who, although he was a member of the inner core of the Samoan oligarchy, was not a council delegate. The

other three *faipule* could not sign because they were prevented from leaving their island, Savai'i, in time for the minister for external affairs' visit. The American Consul in Samoa, Quincy F. Roberts, 5 August 1921, from Apia, to the Secretary of State, "Unrest in Western Samoa under New Zealand as a Mandatory Power," NARA: RG 59, 862 m; "it represents the unanimous native opinion," ibid. On the petition, see the summary in Field 1984, 57–58. Davidson, the "authority" on Samoan history, dismisses the petition in half a sentence (Davidson 1967, 101). Boyd (1969, 142) follows the same practice. It is not mentioned at all by Meleisea (1987).

76   The basic outline of the petition most likely dates from August 1920 and was intended to be handed over to the prince at that time. But according to the text, this would have contravened Samoan etiquette. No date, same signatures as on the petition to George V, NZA: G 48/S 8.

77   "I fear that anything done in this direction would not be understood, and would produce endless useless and absurd discussion, and probably hostile criticism": Administrator Tate, on his refusal to comply with the Samoan request for a continuation of the German practice of publishing an annual report accounting for how Samoan taxes were spent, Apia, 11 February 1921, to the Minister for External Affairs, NZA: IT 88/3, vol. 1.

78   See, for example, Boyd 1980, 174.

79   Samoan petition to the Prince of Wales, NZA: G 48/S 8.

80   Memorandum from Tate, 27 August 1921, to the Minister for External Affairs, and Memorandum from the Acting Prime Minister, Bell, Wellington, 31 August 1921, for the Governor-General (to be conveyed to London), NZA: G 48/S 8.

81   Minutes of the meeting, Mulinuu, 16 July 1921 (Malietoa's speech, ibid.), NZA: G 48/S 8. "I wish to assure you that the Fautuas will loyally support the present Administration": Malietoa Tanumafili, Matautu, 28 July 1921, to Administrator Tate, ibid. Memorandum Tate, 29 July 1921 to the Minister for External Affairs, "Native Petition, 1921," NML: 996. 14 Pap R 17308; memorandum Acting Prime Minister F. Bell, Wellington, 24 August 1921, with the petition to be conveyed via the Governor-General to London, NZA: G 48/S 8; *The Samoan and His Story* [1929], 516, by the American consul in Apia, Quincy F. Roberts, NARA: RG 59, 862 m; confidential report by Quincy F. Roberts, Apia, 5 August 1921, to the American Secetary of State, ibid.

82   Memorandum Tate, 29 July 1921, "Native Petition, 1921," NML: 996. 14 Pap R 17308; memorandum by Acting Prime Minister Bell, Wellington, 24 August 1921, to the Governor-General and Colonial Office, NZA: G 48/S 8. Bell added the standard accusation to Tate's arguments: "not the outcome of . . . the Samoan people, but is the result of white influence that is hostile to New Zealand's control of the Mandated Territory" (ibid.).

83   Cipher telegram, secret, "p" (personal), from Governor-General Jellicoe, 10 October 1921, NZA: G 5–99.

84   Confidential memorandum by Administrator Tate, 14 February 1921, to the Minister for External Affairs, containing information about Toleafoa Afamasaga's activities, NZA: IT 82/2.

85   Telegram in code from the Colonial Secretary, 5 November 1921, to the Governor-General of New Zealand, to be passed on to the Samoans, NZA: G 5–99.

86   On 1 September 1928, the League of Nations Mandate Commission rejected a

petition that 7,982 of the 9,325 Samoan taxpayers (85.6 percent) had signed, calling for New Zealand to be replaced as the mandatory power and demanding greater political autonomy. Expressing its position on this appeal, the New Zealand government suggested that the large number of signatures was insignificant, because the supreme chief, Malietoa Tanumafili, was the only really legitimate representative of Samoa, and he supported New Zealand (Prime Minister J. G. Coates, Wellington, 24 April 1928, to the Secretary-General of the League of Nations, NZA: IT 1/1/61; petition, ibid.; see also Field 1984, 126–127). The doubts expressed by Davidson (1967, 133) about the authenticity of the signatures are unfounded. They are merely another expression of New Zealand's wishful thinking, an attempt to play down Samoan resistance to the colonial administration.

87 Hiery 1992a, 71.

88 Administrator Richardson, Vailima, 13 December 1926, to the New Zealand government, NZA: G48-S/17.

89 See Gifford 1964, Wendt 1965, and Field 1984.

90 Field 1984, 147–159, esp. 157.

91 Reed 1943, 153–154 (apologetic of Australian policies); Willey 1965, 78–81, Biskup 1968b, 356, and Holzknecht 1979, 217. On Samoa, Keesing 1934, 75: "toi toi isi" ("go easy time"), conversation with Henriette Godinet-Taylor, 13 January 1989; "Samoa was happy," conversation with Lemau, 19 January 1989; similar statements were heard in Amaile, 18 January 1989.

92 Hardach 1990b, 208 (for Micronesia).

93 ". . . boorish behaviour towards the Princes and Chiefs of Samoa. Probably it is because New Zealand is not a country of Chiefs. Therefore they hate to see the chiefly attitude of the Samoans"; *New Zealand Samoa Guardian,* the *mau* newspaper, 11 December 1930, "Conduct of the Government."

94 Observations by the New Zealander Gurr, whose long experience of Samoan habits was used by the Americans in Tutuila, are the most interesting and informative source for the attitude of the Samoans toward the German administration: E. W. Gurr, Pago Pago, 10 April 1918, to N. H. Macdonald, in Administrator's report no. 6 (1918), 18 April 1918, NZA: G 21/9; Gurr, 11 March and 16 June 1919, personal and confidential, to Minister of Defence James Allen, NZA: IT 79/19.

95 Report by Administrator Tate, 22 October 1921, NZA: G 48/S 10; Tate, 5 March 1919, to General Robin, ATL: MS 264, no. 5; R. W. Makgill, District Health Office, Apia, 14 December 1920, to Director of General Health, Wellington, "Report on Medical Services of Samoa," 6, NML: 996. 14 Pap R 17308; speech by the President of the *faipule,* Toelupe, 15 October 1920, in Malie, NZA: IT 1/20; *New Zealand Samoa Guardian,* 25 September 1930, "The care of health," Amoa, 24 January 1989.

96 *New Zealand Samoa Guardian,* 25 September 1930. "I think the natives regard British justice as rather a joke in many aspects . . . British justice . . . has been regarded in some quarters as an oppression," wrote Administrator Tate as early as 22 October 1921; NZA: G 48/S 10.

97 "Sulimoni," writing in the *New Zealand Samoa Guardian,* no. 3/64, 24 July 1930, 2.

98 Vietsch 1961, 99 and 259, and Hempenstall 1978, 68. *Der Kolonialdeutsche* 2 (1922): 108; interviews with Brenner, Goemann, and Schwab, 29 May 1991.

99 Weeramantry 1992, 190 and 193–194.

100 Interview with Ngirongor Melimarang, 22 November 1986 and Joseph Tellei, 22

November 1986. *Oral Historiography* 1986 (Joseph Tellei); *The Book of Luelen* 1977, 124. See also Joseph and Murray 1951, 43; Ballendorf 1988, 142; and Hardach 1990*b*, 208.

101 German-Dutch Telegraph Company in Cologne, 12 June 1920, to the German Postmaster General, reporting the observations of their last representative on Yap, the Dutchman van ter Horst, BAP: RKolA no. 2623 (copy). Extract from a confidential report by Captain Handley, captain of the Burns Philp schooner *Mauno*, 15 June 1921, on a journey through the Marshall Islands, AAC: A 3932-SC 240.

102 Report by an unnamed European visitor about local advances and complaints in the Truk Archipelago, Yokohama, 11 August 1924, to the Consul-General of the United States, NARA: RG 59, 862 i.

103 See the numerous reports by Price 1936*a*, 1936*b*, 1937, and 1944.

104 Undated [1926] secret report by Captain B. P. Dicker, 15th Punjab Regiment, Indian Army, on his journey through Micronesia, AAC: A 981 Marshall and Caroline Islands, 3 old. The three locations were Truk, Kusaie, and Jaluit. The question about the return of the Germans is especially interesting in the last two cases, because even after 1922 they remained centers of the American Board Mission.

105 Mühlhäusler 1980, 165.

106 Careful observers early noted this trend; confidential report by the American Consul-General in Melbourne, 6 October 1921 to the Secretary of State, with a detailed memorandum by the Acting Vice Consul Ray Fox, "The Administration of the Australian Mandated Territory of New Guinea," NARA: RG 59, 862 d.

107 Thompson 1990, 79–80.

108 Marjorie Masson, "Under the Mandate. Will the Native make good?" *Sydney Daily Telegraph*, 19 September 1921; see also Bassett 1969, 24. Campbell Brown, "Interim Report Commonwealth New Guinea Expedition, 9 December 1920–14 November 1921, Sydney, 26 May 1922," 25, AAC: A 2219–25. The literal meaning of *long-long* is "crazy, abnormal."

109 Hefâcnuc early in February 1922 to Keyßer, NDM: Nachlaß Keyßer Bd. 41 Heft A, 22. Similar statements, ibid., 16 (Geyguec, 15 September 1921); Heft B, 3–4 (Yezicnuc, April 1922), 10–11 (Desiang, 29 March 1922), and 18–19 (Sai, 11 June 1922).

110 Mocjuc 10 February 1921 to Keyßer, NDM: Nachlaß Keyßer Bd. 41 Heft A, 11. For the Australian battery, see p. 336 n. 9.

111 See the comments appended to reports about atrocities committed by Australian government officials: "for the files of the mission house only, do not make public"; "very strictly confidential"; "not for the press!" NDM: Az 53/43–44. In 1922 the German missions still lived under the threat of being closed down and having its staff deported.

112 Townsend 1968, 86–87, and 154.

113 Leadley 1976, 21.

114 UPNG: AL-264/2: Lulu Miller Reminiscences.

115 "It was unfortunate that they [the Japanese] lost the war to Australians and Americans," writes Aigili naively, but typically; UPNG: AL-284/1. Statements by local people in favor of the Japanese and against the Australians can also be found in Leadley 1976, 236B and 236C/1. See also Townsend 1968, 223 and 227–228; Kituai 1988, 174, 244, and 253.

116 Biskup 1968*b*, 347; see also Salisbury 1970, 34.

117 M. H. Ellis, "Peter Pan of New Guinea," *Daily Telegraph* (Sydney), 30 June 1923. This practice could still be observed as late as 1936; Perkins 1989, 63.

118 Douglas 1981, 27. "The Madangs hated the Germans" claims Firth 1986, 6.

119 *Der Kolonialdeutsche* 1 (1921): 139.

120 Townsend 1968, 84.

121 F. M. Cutlack, "Rabaul. Boluminskihs Road. A great Colonist," *Sydney Morning Herald,* 12 September 1921; see also Bassett 1969, 132. The cult of Boluminski's grave, and the attribution of supernatural powers to him, was still in full swing in the 1930s; Hempenstall 1987, 99, and Perkins 1989, 63 n. 28. The best description of Boluminski is in the travel notes by the Luxemburg writer Jacques (Jacques 1922, 51–53).

122 "A just man, and those natives respected him for both his justice and his assertion of authority," Cutlack, writing in the *Sydney Morning Herald,* 12 September 1921; see n. 121 above.

123 Hempenstall 1987, 93, Perkins 1989, 62, and the reminiscences of Lulu Miller, UPNG: AL-264/2. "Just and progressive," Rev. J. W. Burton, Melbourne Town Hall, 21 July 1921, ANL: MS 882/6/570. By way of contrast the Australians were perceived as "unjust, therefore we are fed up with them." A Melanesian called Hungto, 11 August 1932, NDM: MS 322, 152. Hungto also inquired whether "Kaiser Wilhelm still stays in Holland or whether he returned to Germany recently?" ibid.

124 I. Moses 1977, 308, and Holzknecht 1979, 362.

125 See *The Book of Luelen* 1977, 144 and 145 n. 1.

126 Meleisea 1976, 129–130, and 1980, 15, 17, 25, 27, 29, 36, and 41; Aigili, UPNG: AL-284/1.

127 Hanssen diary, entry of 8 January 1915, NZA: G 49/10.

128 Meleisea 1976, 131–132, and 1980, 41.

129 Latukefu 1978, 101 and 106.

130 Willey 1965, 81.

131 Hahl 1942, 79. See now also Hempenstall (1987, 98 and 100), who emphasizes the significance of personal qualities in the development of colonial rule particularly in New Guinea.

132 Firth (1986, 69) states that in making decisions the German governor was always dependent on the German colonial office. There could not be a more inaccurate description of the colonial reality experienced by Pacific Islanders under German influence. Hempenstall (1987, 98) has already cautiously pointed to this misrepresentation. For Samoa, where the German foreign office gave Solf carte blanche for "native policy" when he took up office (see Hempenstall 1977, 214), Firth's statement is not correct even in a formal legal sense.

133 Weeramantry 1992, 192, and Firth 1992, 256–258.

134 Thus Firth 1978*b*, 47.

135 On Boeder's responsibility for the Sokeh uprising, see Hempenstall 1978, 98–106 and 207.

136 On this, and on Micronesia in particular, see the interesting observations in Firth 1992.

Bibliography

MANUSCRIPT SOURCES

AAC Australian Archives. Canberra.

German Records
AA 1963/83 Station and District Court Files, German New Guinea.
G 254   Court Files, German New Guinea.

Australian Records. CRS (Commonwealth Records Series).
A 1   Department of Home and Territories. Correspondence Files, 1903–1938.
A 2   Prime Minister. Correspondence, 1904–1920.
A 4   Department of Home and Territories. Correspondence, 1911–1923. 1 box.
            - NG 1–57: New Guinea, Miscellaneous Documents.
A 5   Department of Home and Territories. Correspondence, 1924.
A 457   Prime Minister. Correspondence.
A 518   Prime Minister's Department. Territories Branch, 1918–1960.
A 981   External Affairs. General Correspondence.
A 1108   Prime Minister. Pacific Branch, 1901–1921. 66 vols.
A 2218   Prime Minister. Pacific Branch. Volumes of Papers concerning Austra-
            lian Relations with Pacific Islands 1862–1923. Compiled by E. L. Piesse.
            25 vols.
A 2219   Volumes of Papers concerning Australian External Relations 1900–1923.
            Compiled by E. L. Piesse. 27 vols.
A 2939   Prime Minister. Secret and Confidential Correspondence.
A 3932   Prime Minister. Secret and Confidential Correspondence.
A 3934   Prime Minister's Correspondence. Secret and Confidential, 1906–1931.
A 6661   Governor General's Correspondence, 1888–1936.
CP 78/22   Governor General. General Correspondence, 1912–1927.
CP 78/23   Correspondence relating to the War of 1914–1918.
CP 78/34   Miscellaneous Unregistered Correspondence, 1912–1927. 14 vols.
CP 103/11   Prime Minister's Department.
CP 316/16   Nauru. Administration Orders 1921–1923. 1 bundle.

CP 317/7   Prime Minister's Secretary. Copies of Cablegrams.

CP 351/1   Imperial Conferences. British War Cabinet. Delegation at Paris.

CP 360/8   Cables Exchanged between Prime Minister Hughes and Acting Prime Minister Watt, 1918–1919. 1 bundle.

CP 360/13   Prime Minister's Department. Outwords Correspondence.

CP 368/6   Papers relating to Disputes between the British Phosphate Commissioners, 1920–1926. 3 bundles.

CP 661/15   Royal Commission on Late German New Guinea. Final Report. 2 boxes.

AAM Australian Archives. Melbourne.

B 197   Defence. Secret and Confidential Correspondence, 1906–1939.

B 539   Australian Imperial Forces.

B 543   Defence Correspondence, 1914–1917.

MP 367   Defence Correspondence, 1917–1929.

MP 1049/1   Navy Correspondence, 1911–1921. Secret and Confidential Files.

AHM Archiv der Herz-Jesu-Mission [Sacred Heart Mission]. Hiltrup, Münster.

C 2 Südsee   (South Seas).

AKM Archiv der Kapuzinermission [Capuchin Mission]. Münster.

C	***Die Einzelnen Missionen [Mission Fields].***
39	Gayabachronik.
40–50	Jap [Yap].
51	Mortlock.
52–55	Palau.
56–103	Ponape.
104–106	Rota.
107–111	Saipan.
112–122	Truk.
D	***Die Vertreibung [Expulsion].***
123	Während des Krieges [During the War].
124	In der Verbannung [In Exile].

ANL Australian National Library. Canberra.

MS 52   Atlee Hunt Papers.

MS 696   Lord Novar (Ronald Munro Ferguson) Papers.

MS 882   Piesse Papers.

MS 1100   Atlee Hunt Papers (Diaries).

MS 1538   Hughes Papers.

MS 3376   Carl Frost. Manuscripts and Original Proclamations relating to German New Guinea and the German Solomon Islands and the Great War.

MS 4653   Glynn Papers.

G 21117–   Microfilms of the Western Pacific High Commission.
21152

Archives Arch-Diocese of Samoa. Apia.

D   *Mgr. Pierre Broyer, 1846–1918.*
11.1   British Military Occupation of Samoa 1914–1918.

ATL Alexander Turnbull Library. Wellington.

MS 264   Robert Ward Tate Papers.
MSX 2367   Diary. J. R. Graham.

AWM Australian War Memorial. Canberra.

33   *New Guinea Campaign Records 1914–1918.*
1 DRL 188   Letters. Lieutenant E. K. Carlile.
1 DRL 347   Letters. Captain Keith Heritage.
1 DRL 351   Diary. Lieutenant Commander G. A. Hill.
1 DRL 369   Letters. Lieutenant William David Hunter.
2 DRL 308   Papers. Lieutenant J. W. Axtens.
3 DRL 2222   Papers. Minister of Defence G. F. Pearce.
3 DRL 2268   Diary. Private N. D. Scheidel.
3 DRL 2943   Diary. Colonol A. W. Ralston.
3 DRL 2985   Letters. Sergeant Frank A. W. Hocking.
3 DRL 6061   Diary. A. R. Bollard.
3 DRL 7734   Papers. Lieutenant Bowen.
PR 82/171   Diary. Warrant Officer Lance Balfour Penman.
PR 84/304   Basil Homes. Reminiscences.
PR 89/5   Diary. Lieutenant F. A. Graham.
PR 89/126   Diary. William John Lane.

BAK Bundesarchiv. Koblenz.

Kleine Erwerbungen No. 812 E. Demandt, "Aus Samoas schweren Tagen während des Europäischen Krieges." Tagebücher [Diaries], 1914–1919. 6 vols.
Nachlaß No. 53 Wilhelm Solf Papers.

BAP Bundesarchiv. Potsdam.

RKolA   Reichskolonialamt [Records of the German Colonial Office]. A good, though incomplete, survey can be found in *Journal of Pacific History* 6 (1971): 151–161, and 12 (1977): 86–92.
RPA   Reichspostamt [Records of the German Office for Postal Affairs].

Burns Philp Archives. Fisher Library. Sydney. These records have now been transferred and can be consulted in the A.N.U. Archives of Business and Labour, Canberra.

Catholic Mission. Koror. Palau. Archives of the School Sisters of St. Francis.

Aloysia Fettig, "Unsere Erlebnisse auf der Insel Palau-Korror während des Krieges 1914/15." Unpublished recollections.

GStAM Geheimes Staatsarchiv Preußischer Kulturbesitz. Merseburg. As a result of German reunification, these records have now been returned to their origin, the Geheimes Staatsarchiv at Berlin.

2.2.1   Zivilkabinett.

MLS Mitchell Library. Sydney.

B 695   T. J. Denham. New Guinea Notebook.
B 758   E. Riddell. Western Samoa.
B 956   K.A.O.S. "Territory of New Guinea—The Reasons."
MSS 15   Papers. William Holmes.
MSS 383   Diary. Arthur John Sawyer.
MSS 930   Diary. Naval Medical Officer Dr. Fred Hamilton-Kenny.
MSS 2880   Diary. Jack W. Martin.
MSS 2935   Diary. Private A. O'Hare.
MSS 3034   Diary. Lieutenant Clarence H. Read.

NARA National Archives of the United States of America. Washington, D.C.
Record Groups (RG)

RG No. 38   Naval Attaché Reports, 1887–1939.
RG No. 59   Correspondence of the Department of State, Decimal File 1910–1929.
RG No. 80   General Records of the Navy. Secretariat of the Navy. General Correspondence 1916–1926.
RG No. 84   Records of Foreign Service Posts.
  B 162   Correspondence. American Embassy, Tokyo 1914–1921.
  B 345   Apia, 1914–1921.
RG No. 256 Records of the American Commission to Negotiate Peace.

NDM Archiv der Neuendettelsauer Mission. Neuendettelsau.

Az 53/41–42 Akte Neuguinea. Regierungsstellen (Neuguinea-Kompanie und "Fall Detzner").
Az 53/43–44 Akte Neuguinea. Regierungsstellen (Deutsche Regierung und australische Mandatsregierung).
Keyßer Nachlaß Bd. 41 Heft A und B (Sattelberger Gemeindebriefe).
MS 322/323 Briefe von Eingeborenen.
W. Bergmann, "Vierzig Jahre in Neuguinea." Unpublished MS, 10 vols.

NML Nelson Memorial Library. Apia, Samoa i Sisifo.

996. 14 Pap R 17308. E. Nixon-Westwood. Papers and Letters on Samoan History.

GPRS   *German Provincial Records, Samoa.* No order; the files still bear the old German numbers.

Noser Library. Madang.

Missionaries of the Divine Word. Reports and Correspondence.

NZA National Archives of New Zealand. Wellington.

AD   *Army Department.*

EA   *External Affairs. Department of External Affairs/Ministry of Foreign Affairs (AAEG).*
Series 311: Western Samoa

G   *Governor-General of New Zealand.*
 G 2   Confidential Inwards Despatches from the Secretary of State.
 G 5   Telegrams to and from the Secretary of State.
 G 13 Miscellaneous Inwards Letters and Copies of Outwards Letters.
 G 21 Inwards Despatches to and from the Governor relating to Samoa. General Files.
 G 26 Confidential Outwards Despatches to the Secretary of State.
 G 48 Classified Office Files.
 G 49 Miscellaneous Office Papers.

IT   *Island Territories Department.*

N   *Navy Department.*

BMO *Samoan Archives of the British Military Occupation 1914–1920.*

S   *Statistics Department.*

WA *War Archives.*
Series 210–215: Samoan Expeditionary Force.
Series 252: Sir Alexander Godley's Correspondence.

Personal Papers, Acc. 556: The Ministerial Papers of Hon. James Allen (1912–1919).

Personal Papers, Acc. 1427: Puttick Papers.

CO 225 Microfilms of the Colonial Office, Original Correspondence, Western Pacific.

NZDD New Zealand Department of Defence. Wellington.

Personal files.

PAA Politisches Archiv des Auswärtigen Amtes. Bonn.

Abteilung A. Akten betreffend den Krieg 1914. Rückwirkung auf Ost-Asien und die Kolonien. *Der Weltkrieg* no. 13. 23 vols.
Südsee Nr. 14. Deutsch-Neu-Guinea. 4 vols.

PMB Pacific Manuscript Bureau. Canberra.

4   Papers of the Catholic Mission, Bougainville.
967 T. H. Donaldson. Nauru Diary.

RCSL Royal Commonwealth Society Library. London.

Graeme Cantrell. Notes and Recollections.

UPNG University of Papua New Guinea. Port Moresby.

New Guinea Collection of the Michael Somare Library. Manuscript Section.

AL-90   Bertram Calcutt, "'Stone Age and Steel': New Guinea in 1921–1933." Manuscript.

AL-101   Fox Brothers Collection.

AL-125   Diary of Richard Thurnwald, 7 December 1913–11 November 1915.

AL-264   Papers of Mrs. Louisa (Lulu) Miller.

AL-284/1   Rudolph Aigili, "My Father's Experience and Life during the German Government and Second World War." Manuscript.

ORAL AND PUBLISHED SOURCES

Ada, Pedro Martinez (b. 1903). Interview by author, 14 November 1986. Tape recording. Guam.

The Age (Melbourne). Various issues.

Aldrich, Robert. 1990. *The French Presence in the South Pacific, 1842–1940.* Honolulu: Macmillan.

Amaile: Antelea Tipasa Tui Lua'ai (b. ca. 1908) and Tekelo Makisi (b. 1900). Interview by author with the help of Père Joseph Allais, 18 January 1989. Tape recording. Amaile, Western Samoa.

Amean, A. 1973. "Early Methods of Punishment in the Highlands 1936–1960." *Oral History* (Port Moresby), no. 7 (October): 23–26.

Amoa, former speaker of the *fono a faipule.* Interview by author, 24 January 1989. Apia.

Amtsblatt für das Schutzgebiet Deutsch-Neuguinea (Rabaul). Vols. 1 (1909)–6 (1914).

Annual Colonial Reports. Fiji (London). Various issues.

Annual Colonial Reports. Papua (London). Various issues.

Annual Reports of the Governor of Guam. Various issues. Guam: Micronesian Area Research Center.

Anspach (-Hahl), Berta. Interview by author, 28 March 1992. Tape recording. Munich.

Argus (Melbourne). Various issues.

Asahi (Tokyo). Various issues.

Auckland Star. 1919.

The Australian Worker (Brisbane). 1918.

Baker, Paul. 1988. *King and Country Call: New Zealanders, Conscription, and the Great War.* Auckland: Auckland University Press.

Ballendorf, Dirk Anthony. 1984. "Secrets without Substance: U.S. Intelligence in the Japanese Mandates, 1915–1935." *Journal of Pacific History* 19:83–99.

————. 1988. "The Japanese and the Americans: Contrasting Historical Periods of Economic and Social Development in Palau." *Journal of the Pacific Society* 10, no. 3 (October): 140–146.

Ballendorf, Dirk Anthony, William M. Peck, and G. G. Anderson. 1986. *An Oral History of the Japanese Schooling Experience of Chamorros at Saipan and in the Commonwealth of the Northern Mariana Islands.* Guam: Micronesian Area Research Center.

Barber, Laurie. 1989. *New Zealand. A Short History.* London/Sydney/Auckland/Johannesburg: Hutchinson.

Barclay, Glen St. J. 1976. *The Empire Is Marching: A Study of the Military Effort of the British Empire 1800–1945.* London: Weidenfeld and Nicholson.

Barnett, H. G. 1961. *Being a Palauan.* New York: Holt, Rinehart & Winston.

Bassett, Marnie. 1969. *Letters from New Guinea 1921.* Melbourne: The Hawthorn Press.

Binder, Pearl. 1977. *Treasure Islands: The Trials of the Ocean Islanders.* London: Blond & Briggs.

Binney, Judith, Gillian Chaplin, and Craig Wallace. 1979. *Mihaia: The Prophet Rua Kenana and His Community at Maungapohatu.* Wellington: Oxford University Press.

Biskup, Peter. 1968*a*. "Hermann Detzner: New Guinea's First Coast Watcher." *The Journal of the Papua and New Guinea Society* 2. 1: 5–21.

———. 1968*b*. "Dr. Albert Hahl: Sketch of a German Colonial Official." *The Australian Journal of Politics and History* 14: 342–357.

Blakeslee, George H. 1921. "Japan's New Island Possessions in the Pacific: History and Present Status." *The Journal of International Relations* 12.2:173–191.

———. 1922/23. "The Mandates of the Pacific." *Foreign Affairs* 1:98–115.

Böhm, Karl. 1975. *Das Leben einiger Inselvölker Neuguineas. Beobachtungen eines Missionars auf den Vulkaninseln Manam, Boesa, Biem und Ubrub.* Collectanea Instituti Anthropos 6. St. Augustin: Anthropos-Institut.

Bolton, Geoffrey. 1981. *Spoils and Spoilers. Australians Make Their Environment 1788–1980.* Sydney, London, and Boston: Allen & Unwin.

Book of Luelen, The. 1977. Edited by John L. Fischer, Saul H. Riesenberg, and Marjorie G. Whiting. Pacific History Series 9. Canberra: Australian National University Press.

Boyd, Mary. 1968. "The Military Administration of Western Samoa, 1914–1919." *The New Zealand Journal of History* 2:148–164.

———. 1969. "The Record in Western Samoa to 1945." In *New Zealand's Record in the Pacific Islands in the Twentieth Century,* edited by Angus Ross, 115–188. Auckland/London/New York: Longman Paul for the New Zealand Institute of International Affairs.

———. 1980. "Coping with Samoan Resistance after the 1918 Influenza Epidemic: Colonel Tate's Problems and Perplexities." *Journal of Pacific History* 15:155–174.

———. 1987. "Racial Attitudes of New Zealand Officials in Western Samoa." *The New Zealand Journal of History* 21:139–155.

Braisted, William Reynolds. 1971. *The United States Navy in the Pacific, 1909–1922.* Austin/London: University of Texas Press.

Brauer, Otto. 1917. *Die Kreuzerfahrten des 'Prinz Eitel Friedrich.'* Berlin: August Scherl.

Brenner, Karl, Mathilde Goemann, and Adelheid Schwab. Interview by author, 29 May 1991. Tape recording. Esslingen, Germany.

Brewster, A. B. 1922. *The Hill Tribes of Fiji. A Record of Forty Years' Intimate connection with the Tribes of the Mountainous Interior of Fiji with a Description of their Habits in War and Peace, Methods of Living, Characteristics Mental and Physical, from the Days of Cannibalism to the Present Time.* London: Seeley, Service & Co.

The British Australian 1901. (London).

Brown, Richard G. 1977. "The German Acquisition of the Caroline Islands, 1898–99." In *Germany in the Pacific and Far East, 1870–1914,* edited by John A. Moses and Paul M. Kennedy, 137–155. St. Lucia: University of Queensland Press.

Buckley, K., and K. Klugman. 1983. *"The Australian Presence in the Pacific": Burns Philp 1914–1946.* Sydney/London/Boston: Allen & Unwin.

———. 1986. *South Pacific Focus: A Record in Words and Photographs of Burns Philp at Work.* Sydney/London/Boston: Allen & Unwin.

Burdick, Charles, and Ursula Moessner. 1984. *The German Prisoners-of-War in Japan, 1914–1920.* Lanham/New York/London: University Press of America.

Burry, B[essie] Pullen. 1909. *In a German Colony; or Four Weeks in New Britain.* London: Methuen.

Butcher, Barry, and David Turnbull. 1988. "Aborigines, Europeans and the Environment." In *A Most Valuable Acquisition. A People's History of Australia since 1788,* edited by Verity Burgmann and Jenny Lee, 13–28. Fitzroy/Ringwood/Harmondsworth/New York/Ontario/Auckland: McPhee Gribble in association with Penguin Books Australia.

Chinas Millionen. Monatsschrift der Liebenzeller Mission (Bad Liebenzell). Various issues.

Christmann, Helmut, Peter Hempenstall, and Dirk Anthony Ballendorf. 1991. *Die Karolinen-Inseln in deutscher Zeit. Eine kolonialgeschichtliche Fallstudie.* Munich/Hamburg: LIT.

Chugai Shogyo (Tokyo). 1919.

Chuodelechad (b. 1904) Interview by author with the help of Francesca Remengesau, 22 November 1986. Tape recording. Koror, Belau.

Crosby, Alfred W. 1989. *America's Forgotten Pandemic: The Influenza of 1918.* Cambridge: Cambridge University Press.

Crowley, Frank, ed. 1974. *A New History of Australia.* Melbourne: Heinemann.

Daily Telegraph (Sydney). Various issues.

Davidson, J[ames] W[ightman]. 1967. *Samoa mo Samoa. The Emergence of the Independent State of Western Samoa.* Melbourne: Oxford University Press.

———. 1970. "Lauaki Namulau'ulu Mamoe. A Traditionalist in Samoan Politics." In *Pacific Islands Portraits,* edited by J. W. Davidson and Deryck Scarr, 267–299 and 331–334. Canberra: Australian National University Press.

Detzner, Hermann. 1921. *Vier Jahre unter Kannibalen. Von 1914 bis zum Waffenstillstand unter deutscher Flagge im unerforschten Innern von Neuguinea.* Berlin: August Scherl.

Digre, Brian. 1990. *Imperialism's New Clothes. The Repartition of Tropical Africa, 1914–1919.* American University Studies, ser. 9, vol. 79. New York/Bern/Frankfurt a. M./Paris: Peter Lang.

DKB Deutsches Kolonialblatt. Amtsblatt für die Schutzgebiete des Deutschen Reichs (Berlin). Vols. 1 (1890)–32 (1921).

DKG Die deutsche Kolonial-Gesetzgebung. Sammlung der auf die deutschen Schutzgebiete bezüglichen Gesetze, Verordnungen, Erlasse und internationalen Vereinbarungen, mit Anmerkungen und Sachregister. Auf Grund amtlicher Quellen und zum dienstlichen Gebrauch, vols. 1 (1893)–12 (1908). Berlin: Ernst Siegfried Mittler und Sohn, 1893–1909.

DKZ Deutsche Kolonialzeitung (Berlin). Various issues.

The Dominion (Wellington). 1921.

Douglas, Janetta. 1981. "Taim Bilong Ol Jeman." *Paradise: In-Flight with Air Niugini,* no. 30 (July): 25–27.

Eddy, John. 1988. "Australia. Nationalism and Nation-Making from Federation to Gallipoli." In *The Rise of Colonial Nationalism. Australia, New Zealand, Can-*

ada and South Africa First Assert Their Nationalities, edited by John Eddy and Deryck Schreuder, 131–159. Sydney/Wellington/London/Boston: Unwin Hyman.

Edwards, P. G. 1983. *Prime Ministers and Diplomats. The Making of Australian Foreign Policy 1901–1949.* Melbourne: Oxford University Press.

Ehrlich, Paul. 1978a. " 'The Clothes of Men': Ponape Island and German Colonial Rule 1899–1914." Ph.D. diss., State University of New York at Stony Brook.

———. 1978b. "Henry Nanpei. Pre-eminently a Ponapean." In *More Pacific Islands Portraits,* edited by Deryck Scarr, 131–154. Canberra: Australian National University Press.

Elder, Bruce. 1988. *Blood on the Wattle: Massacres and Maltreatment of Australian Aborigines since 1788.* Frenchs Forest: Child & Associates.

Epstein, Klaus. 1959. *Matthias Erzberger and the Dilemma of German Democracy.* Princeton, New Jersey: Princeton University Press.

Eteuati, Kilifoti Sisilia. 1982. "Evaevaga Samoa. Assertion of Samoan Autonomy 1920–1936." Ph.D. diss., Australian National University, Canberra.

Field, Michael J. 1984. *Mau: Samoa's Struggle against New Zealand Oppression.* Wellington/Auckland/Christchurch: Reed.

Firth, Stewart G. 1971–1973. "The New Guinea Company, 1885–1899. A Case of Unprofitable Imperialism." *Historical Studies* 15:361–377.

———. 1977. "Governors versus Settlers: The Dispute over Chinese Labour in German Samoa." *New Zealand Journal of History* 11:155–179.

———. 1978a. "German Labour Policy in Nauru and Angaur, 1906–1914." *Journal of Pacific History* 13:36–52.

———. 1978b. "Albert Hahl: Governor of German New Guinea." In *Papua New Guinea Portraits. The Expatriate Experience,* edited by James Griffin, 28–47. Canberra: Australian National University Press.

———. 1985. "German New Guinea: The Archival Perspective." *Journal of Pacific History* 20:94–103.

———. 1986. *New Guinea under the Germans.* 2d ed. Port Moresby: WEB Books.

———. 1989. "Labour in German New Guinea." In *Papua New Guinea: A Century of Colonial Impact 1884–1984,* edited by Sione Latukefu, 179–202. Port Moresby: The National Research Institute and the University of Papua New Guinea.

———. 1992. "Racism and Forms of Colonial Domination: The Case of the Radiation Atolls in the Marshall Islands, 1912–1990." In *Rassendiskriminierung, Kolonialpolitik und ethnisch-nationale Identität. Referate des 2. Internationalen Kolonialgeschichtlichen Symposiums 1991,* edited by Wilfried Wagner. Bremer Asien-Pazifik Studien, 2: 252–265. Münster/Hamburg: LIT.

Fischer, Fritz. 1971. *Griff nach der Weltmacht. Die Kriegszielpolitik des kaiserlichen Deutschland 1914/18.* 4th ed. Düsseldorf: Droste.

Fischer, Gerhard. 1989. *Enemy Aliens: Internment and the Homefront Experience in Australia 1914–1920.* St. Lucia: Queensland University Press.

Fischer, Hans. 1987. *Heilserwartung: Geister, Medien und Träumer in Neuguinea.* Frankfurt a. M./New York: Campus.

Fitzhardinge, L. F. 1967. "W. M. Hughes at the Paris Peace Conference, 1919." *Journal of Commonwealth Political Studies* 5:130–142.

———. 1970. "Australia, Japan and Great Britain, 1914–18: A Study in Triangular Diplomacy." *Historical Studies* 14:250–259.

————. 1979. *The Little Digger 1914–1952. William Morris Hughes. A Political Biogra-phy.* Vol. 2. London/Sydney/Melbourne/Singapore/Manila: Angus & Rob-ertson.

Foster, Robert J. 1987. "Komine and Tanga: A Note on Writing the History of German New Guinea." *Journal of Pacific History* 22: 56–64.

Frei, Henry P. 1991. *Japan's Southward Advance and Australia. From the Sixteenth Century to World War II.* Carlton: Melbourne University Press.

Frommund, Bernhard. 1926. *Deutsch-Neuguinea eine Perle der Südsee. Erlebnisse und Eindrücke eines Deutschen auf Deutsch-Neuguinea 1905–1908.* Hamburg: Volkmar-Verlag Dr. Hartmann und Brandt.

FRUS: *Papers Relating to the Foreign Relations of the United States.* 1919. *The Paris Peace Conference,* 13 vols. Washington D.C.: United States Government Printing Office, 1942–1947.

Gammage, Bill. 1975. "The Rabaul Strike, 1929." *Journal of Pacific History* 10. 3–4:3–29.

Gann, Lewis H. 1984. "Western and Japanese Colonialism: Some Preliminary Compari-sons." In *The Japanese Colonial Empire, 1895–1945,* edited by Ramon H. Myers and Mark R. Peattie, 497–525. Princeton, N.J.: Princeton Univer-sity Press.

Gann, L. H., and Peter Duignan. 1977. *The Rulers of German Africa 1884–1914.* Stan-ford, Calif.: Stanford University Press.

Garvin, J. L. 1934. *Empire and World Policy. The Life of Joseph Chamberlain.* Vol. 3. London: Macmillan.

Gash, Noel, and June Whittaker. 1975. *A Pictorial History of New Guinea.* Milton/Gladesville/Elwood/Adelaide/Auckland: The Jacaranda Press.

Gelfand, Lawrence E. 1963. *The Inquiry: American Preparations for Peace, 1917–1919.* New Haven, Conn.: Yale University Press.

Gifford, M. C. 1964. "The Nature and Origins of the Mau Movement in Western Sa-moa, 1926–1936." M.A. thesis, University of Auckland.

Godinet-Taylor, Henriette (b. 1898). Interview by author, 13 January 1989. Tape record-ing. Apia.

Goodall, Norman. 1954. *A History of the London Misionary Society 1895–1945.* Lon-don/New York/Toronto: Oxford University Press.

Gordon, Donald Craigie. 1951. *The Australian Frontier in New Guinea 1870–1885.* New York: Columbia University Press.

Government Gazette Rabaul. Vols. 1 (1914)–8 (1921). Rabaul: British Administration of German New Guinea.

Grapow, [Max] von. 1916. *Die Deutsche Flagge im Stillen Ozean.* Berlin. Dietrich Reimer (Ernst Vohsen).

Grattan, C. Hartley. 1976. "Australia and New Zealand and Pacific-Asia." In *Oceania and Beyond. Essays on the Pacific since 1945,* edited by F. P. King, 79–116. Westport/London: Greenwood Press.

Griffin, James, Hank Nelson, and Stewart Firth. 1979. *Papua New Guinea: A Political History.* Richmond/Victoria: Heinemann Educational.

Gründer, Horst. 1987. "Kulturkampf in Übersee. Katholische Mission und deutscher Kolonialstaat in Togo und Samoa." *Archiv für Kulturgeschichte* 69: 453–472.

Guam News Letter. Vols. 6 (1914–1915)–13 (1921–1922).

Haber, Eduard. 1932. "Deutsch-Neuguinea im Weltkriege." In *Festschrift für Carl*

Uhlig zum sechzigsten Geburtstag von seinen Freunden und Schülern dargebracht, 131–140. Öhringen: Verlag der Hohenloheschen Buchhandlung F. Rau.

Hahl, Albert. 1942. *Deutsch-Neuguinea.* 2d ed. Berlin: Reimer.

———. 1980. *Governor in New Guinea.* Edited and translated by Peter G. Sack and Dymphna Clark. Canberra: Australian National University Press.

Hambruch, Paul. 1915. *Nauru.* Vol. 2: *Ergebnisse der Südsee-Expedition 1908–1910,* edited by G. Thilenius, II B, 1,2. Hamburg: L. Friederichsen & Co.

Hanlon, David. 1988. "Another Side of Henry Nanpei." *Journal of Pacific History* 23:36–51.

Hardach, Gerd. 1988. "Bausteine für ein größeres Deutschland. Die Annexion der Karolinen und Marianen 1898–1899." *Zeitschrift für Unternehmensgeschichte* 33:1–20.

———. 1990a. "Südsee und Nanyo: Deutsch-japanische Rivalität in Mikronesien, 1885–1920." In *Deutschland-Japan in der Zwischenkriegszeit,* edited by Josef Kreiner and Regine Mathias, 1–26. Bonn: Bouvier.

———. 1990b. *König Kopra. Die Marianen unter deutscher Herrschaft 1899–1914.* Beiträge zur Kolonial- und Überseegeschichte 49. Stuttgart: Franz Steiner.

Hayashima, Akira. 1982. *Die Illusion des Sonderfriedens. Deutsche Verständigungspolitik mit Japan im ersten Weltkrieg.* Studien zur Geschichte des Neunzehnten Jahrhunderts 11. Munich/Vienna: Oldenbourg.

Healy, Allan M. 1987. "Monocultural Administration in a Multicultural Environment: The Australians in Papua New Guinea." In *From Colony to Coloniser: Studies in Australian Administrative History,* edited by J. J. Eddy and J. R. Nethercote, 207–224. Sydney: Hale and Iremonger in association with the Royal Australian Institute of Public Administration.

Hempenstall, Peter J. 1977. "Native Resistance and German Control Policy in the Pacific: The Case of Samoa and Ponape." In *Germany in the Pacific and Far East, 1870–1914,* edited by John A. Moses and Paul M. Kennedy, 209–233. St. Lucia: University of Queensland Press.

———. 1978. *Pacific Islanders under German Rule: A Study in the Meaning of Colonial Resistance.* Canberra: Australian National University Press.

———. 1987. "The Neglected Empire: The Superstructure of the German Colonial State in German Melanesia." In *Germans in the Tropics: Essays in German Colonial History,* edited by Arthur J. Knoll and Lewis H. Gann, 93–117. New York/Westport/London: Greenwood Press.

The Herald (Melbourne). Various issues.

Hiery, Hermann. 1989. "Samoaner zwischen Deutschland und Neuseeland (1914–1920)." In *Kolonisation und Dekolonisation. Referate des Internationalen Kolonialgeschichtlichen Symposiums '89 an der Pädagogischen Hochschule Schwäbisch Gmünd,* edited by Helmut Christmann. Gmünder Hochschulreihe 8: 155–178. Schwäbisch Gmünd: Pädagogische Hochschule.

———. 1992a. "West Samoans between Germany and New Zealand 1914–1921." *War & Society* 10:53–80.

———. 1992b. "'Stori bilong waitman tru.' Erstkontakt in melanesischer Sicht." *Geschichte und Kulturen* 4:63–75.

———. 1992*c*. "Praktizierter Rassismus. Das Fallbeispiel Australien in Neuguinea (1914–1921)." In *Rassendiskriminierung, Kolonialpolitik und ethnischnationale Identität. Referate des 2. Internationalen Kolonialgeschichtlichen Symposiums 1991 in Berlin,* edited by Wilfried Wagner. Bremer Asien-Pazifik Studien Vol. 2: 197–205. Münster/Hamburg: LIT.

———. 1993*a.* "Die Grippeepidemie auf Samoa 1918." *Geschichte Lernen* 31:25–30.

———. 1993*b.* "Das Deutsche Reich in der Südsee (1900–1921). Eine Annäherung an die Erfahrungen verschiedener Kulturen." Freiburg i.Br.: Habilitationsschrift.

———. 1993*c.* "The Madang Revolt: A Chimera." *Small Wars and Insurgencies,* no. 4, 165–180.

———. 1994. "Melanesische Sexualität, europäische Mission und deutsche Kolonialverwaltung: Die Ehegesetzgebung in Deutsch-Neuguinea 1904 und ihre Folgen." In *Kolonien und Missionen. Referate des 3. Internationalen Kolonialgeschichtlichen Symposiums 1993 in Bremen,* edited by Wilfried Wagner. Bremer Asien-Pazifik Studien, 12: 535–547. Münster/Hamburg: LIT.

A History of Palau. Edited by Palau Community Action Agency. 1978. Vol. 3: *Japanese Administration.* Koror: U.S. Naval Military Government.

Holzknecht, Philip-Walter. 1979. "Bômbôm—Bingsu—Ngamalac (Strangers—Missionaries—Village People). German Exploration and Contact in the Morobe Province of Papua New Guinea: 1884–1930." M.A. thesis, University of Papua New Guinea, Port Moresby.

Hudson, W. J. 1978. *Billy Hughes in Paris. The Birth of Australian Diplomacy.* Melbourne: Nelson.

Hughes, William Morris. 1950. *Policies and Potentates.* Sydney/London: Angus & Robertson.

Huttenback, Robert A. 1972–1973. "No Strangers within the Gates: Attitudes and Policies towards the Non-White Residents of the British Empire of Settlement." *The Journal of Imperial and Commonwealth History* 1:271–302.

———. 1976. *Racism and Empire: White Settlers and Colored Immigrants in the British Self-Governing Colonies 1830–1910.* Ithaca/London: Cornell University Press.

Inglis, Amirah. 1975. *The White Women's Protection Ordinance. Sexual Anxiety and Politics in Papua.* London/Toronto: Sussex University Press.

Irmer, Georg. 1915. *Völkerdämmerung im Stillen Ozean.* Leipzig: S. Hirzel.

Jacques, Norbert. 1922. *Südsee. Ein Reisebuch.* Munich: Drei Masken Verlag.

Jahresberichte über die Entwicklung der deutschen Schutzgebiete. 1900–1913. Berlin: Ernst Siegfried Mittler und Sohn.

Japan Advertiser (Tokyo). Various issues.

Japan Chronicle (Tokyo). Various issues.

Japan Weekly Chronicle (Tokyo). Various issues.

Jose, Arthur W. 1987. *The Royal Australian Navy 1914–1918.* Sydney, 1928. Reprint, St. Lucia: University of Queensland Press. Vol. 9 of *The Official History of Australia in the War of 1914–1918.*

Joseph, Alice, and Veronica F. Murray. 1951. *Chamorros and Carolinians of Saipan: Personality Studies.* Cambridge, Mass.: Harvard University Press.

Journals of the House of Representatives of New Zealand (and *Appendices*). Wellington. Various issues.

Kajima, Morinosuke. 1980. *The Diplomacy of Japan, 1894–1992.*Vol. 3: *First World War, Paris Peace Conference, Washington Conference.* Tokyo: Kajima Institute of International Peace.

Keesing, Felix M. 1934. *Modern Samoa. Its Government and Changing Life.* London: Allen & Unwin.

Keyßer, Christian. 1966. *Das bin bloß ich. Lebenserinnerungen.* Aus dem Nachlaß herausgegeben von W. Fugmann. Neuendettelsau: Freimund.

King, Michael. 1983. *Maori. A Photographic and Social History.* Auckland: Heinemann.

Kituai, August Ibrum Kumaniari. 1982. "An Example of Pacific Micro-Nationalism. The Banaban Case." *Bikmaus. A Journal of Papua New Guinea Affairs, Ideas and the Arts* 3.4: 3–48.

––––––. 1988. *My Gun, My Brother: Experiences of Papua New Guinea Policemen 1920–1960.* Canberra: Australian National University.

Kohl [Larsen], Ludwig. 1927. *Leben, Liebe, Träume in einem Südseeparadies. Ein Erinnerungsbuch.* Stuttgart: Strecker & Schröder.

Der Kolonialdeutsche. Vols. 1–2, 1921–1922.

Lambert, S. M. 1942. *A Doctor in Paradise.* London: J. M. Dent & Sons.

Lane-Poole, C. E. n.d. [1925]. *The Forest Resources of the Territories of Papua and New Guinea. Report presented to the Parliament of the Commonwealth of Australia.*

Latukefu, Sione. 1978. "The Impact of South Sea Islands Missionaries on Melanesia." In *Mission, Church, and Sect in Oceania,* edited by James A. Boutilier, Daniel T. Hughes, and Sharon W. Tiffany. Association for Social Anthropology in Oceania Monograph 6:91–108. Lanham/London: University Press of America.

Lawrence, Willie. 1974. "Dispensing Justice in the Mandated Territory of New Guinea, 1921–1940." *Yagl-Ambu. Papua New Guinea Journal of the Social Sciences and Humanities* 1:140–142.

Leadley, A. J. 1976. "A History of the Japanese Occupation of the New Guinea Islands, and Its Effects, with Special Reference to the Tolai People of the Gazelle Peninsula." M.A. thesis,University of Papua New Guinea, Port Moresby.

Leary, L. P. 1918. *New Zealanders in Samoa.* London: William Heinemann.

Lemau (b. ca. 1900). Interview by author with the help of Père Joseph Allais. 19 January 1989. Tape recording. Mutiatele, Western Samoa.

Link, Arthur, ed. 1992. *The Deliberations of the Council of Four (March 24–June 28, 1919). Notes of the Official Interpreter Paul Mantoux.* Vol. 1. Princeton, N.J.: Princeton University Press.

Lissington, M. P. 1972. *New Zealand and Japan 1900–1941.* Wellington: Department of Internal Affairs, Historical Publications Branch.

Lopinot, Callistus. 1964. *Die Karolinenmission der spanischen und deutschen Kapuziner 1886–1919.* Rome: hectographed typescript.

Louis, William Roger. 1966. "Australia and the German Colonies in the Pacific, 1914–1919." *Journal of Modern History* 38:407–421.

––––––. 1967. *Great Britain and Germany's Lost Colonies 1914–1919.* Oxford: Clarendon Press.

Lowe, Peter. 1969*a*. "The British Empire and the Anglo-Japanese Alliance 1911–1915." *History* 54:212–225.

———. 1969*b*. *Great Britain and Japan 1911–15. A Study of British Far Eastern Policy.* London: Macmillan, New York: St. Martin's Press.

Lyng, J[ames]. n.d. [1919]. *Our New Possession (Late German New Guinea).* Melbourne: Melbourne Publishing Company.

———. 1925. *Island Films. Reminiscences of "German New Guinea."* Sydney: Eagle Press.

Macdonald, Barrie. 1982. *Cinderellas of the Empire. Towards a History of Kiribati and Tuvalu.* Canberra/London/Miami: Australian National University Press.

Macintyre, Stuart. 1986. *The Oxford History of Australia.* Vol. 4, *1901–1942 The Succeeding Age.* Melbourne: Oxford University Press.

Mackenzie, S. S. 1927. *The Australians at Rabaul. The Capture and Administration of the German Possessions in the Southern Pacific.* Vol. 10 of *The Official History of Australia in the War of 1914–1918.* Melbourne: Angus and Robertson.

Maguire, F. A., and R. W. Cilento. 1930. "The Occupation of German New Guinea." In *The Official History of Australian Army Medical Services in the War of 1914–1918,* edited by A. G. Butler, 1:781–810. Melbourne: Australian War Memorial.

The Mail (Adelaide). 1919.

Markus, Andrew. 1990. *Governing Savages.* Sydney/Wellington/London/Boston: Allen & Unwin.

Martin, William S., Jr. 1982. "The Colonial-Mandate Question at the Paris Peace Conference of 1919: The United States and the Disposition of the German Colonies in Africa and the Pacific." Ph.D. diss., University of Southern Mississippi, Hattiesburg. Ann Arbor: University Microfilms International, 1985.

May, Ron J. 1989. "The Impact of Early Contact in the Sepik." In *Papua New Guinea: A Century of Colonial Impact 1884–1984,* edited by Sione Latukefu, 109–132. Port Moresby: The National Research Institute and the University of Papua New Guinea.

McArthur, Norma. 1968. *Island Populations of the Pacific.* Canberra: Australian National University Press.

McGibbon, Ian. 1991. *The Path to Gallipoli. Defending New Zealand 1840–1915.* N.p. [Wellington]: Department of Internal Affairs, Historical Branch.

McKinney, Robert Quentin. 1947. "Micronesia under German Rule 1885–1914." M.A. thesis, Leland Stanford Junior University.

Meaney, Neville. 1976. *The Search for Security in the Pacific, 1901–14.* Sydney: Sydney University Press.

Meleisea, Malama. 1976. "The Last Days of the Melanesian Labour Trade in Western Samoa." *Journal of Pacific History* 11:126–132.

———. 1980. *O Tama Uli. Melanesians in Samoa.* Suva: University of the South Pacific, Institute of Pacific Studies.

———. 1987. *The Making of Modern Samoa. Traditional Authority and Colonial Administration in the History of Western Samoa.* Suva: University of the South Pacific, Institute of Pacific Studies.

Melimarang, Ngirongor (b. 1898), alias Gabriel McNamara. Interview by author with the help of Francesca Remengesau, 22 November 1986. Tape recording. Koror, Belau.

Melk-Koch, Marion. 1989. *Auf der Suche nach der menschlichen Gesellschaft: Richard Thurnwald.* Berlin: Dietrich Reimer.

The Mid-Pacific, September, 1918.

Moses, Ingrid. 1977. "The Extension of Colonial Rule in Kaiser Wilhelmsland." In *Germany in the Pacific and Far East, 1870–1914,* edited by John A. Moses and Paul M. Kennedy, 288–312. St. Lucia: University of Queensland Press.

Moses, John A. 1973. "The Coolie Labour Question and German Colonial Policy in Samoa, 1900–14." *Journal of Pacific History* 8:101–124. Reprinted in *Germany in the Pacific and Far East, 1870–1914,* edited by John A. Moses and Paul M. Kennedy, 234–261. St. Lucia: University of Queensland Press, 1977.

———. 1989. "Imperial German Priorities in New Guinea 1885–1914." In *Papua New Guinea: A Century of Colonial Impact 1884–1984,* edited by Sione Latukefu. 163–177. Port Moresby: The National Research Institute and the University of Papua New Guinea.

Mühlhäusler, Peter. 1980. "German as a Contact Language in the Pacific." *Michigan Germanic Studies* 6.2:163–189.

Namanula Times (Rabaul-Namanula) 1915–1916.

Nelson, Hank. 1978. "The Swinging Index: Capital Punishment and British and Australian Administrations in Papua and New Guinea, 1888–1945." *Journal of Pacific History* 13:130–152.

———. 1982. *Taim Bilong Masta. The Australian Involvement with Papua New Guinea.* Sydney: Australian Broadcasting Commission.

Nelson, H[ank], and M[ichael] Piggott. 1987. Introduction to the University of Queensland Press edition of the *Official History of Australia in the War of 1914–1918,* 10: xiii–xxxiii. St. Lucia: University of Queensland Press.

Newbury, Colin. 1987–1988. "Spoils of War: Sub-Imperial Collaboration in South West Africa and New Guinea, 1914–20." *The Journal of Imperial and Commonwealth History* 16.3:86–106.

New York Times. 1919.

The New Zealand Gazette (Wellington). Various issues.

New Zealand Herald (Auckland). Various issues.

New Zealand Official Year-Book. 1923. Wellington: Government Printer.

The New Zealand Samoa Guardian. (Auckland). 1930.

New Zealand Times (Wellington). Various issues.

Nichi Nichi Shimbun (Tokyo). 1915.

Nish, Ian H. 1972. *Alliance in Decline. A Study in Anglo-Japanese Relations 1908–23.* University of London Historical Studies 33. London: Athlone Press.

O'Connor, P. S. 1968. "Keeping New Zealand White, 1908–1920." *The New Zealand Journal of History* 2:41–65.

Offner, Avner. 1988. " 'Pacific Rim' Societies: Asian Labour and White Nationalism." In *The Rise of Colonial Nationalism. Australia, New Zealand, Canada and South Africa First Assert Their Nationalities,* edited by John Eddy and Deryck Schreuder, 227–247. Sydney/Wellington/London/Boston: Unwin Hyman.

Olsen, Frederick Harris. 1976. "The Navy and the White Man's Burden. Naval Administration of Samoa." Ph.D. diss., Washington University, St. Louis, Mo. Ann Arbor: University Microfilms International, 1983.

"An Oral Historiography of the Japanese Administration in Palau." 1986. Final Report. Guam: Micronesian Area Research Center.

Overell, Lilian. 1923. *A Woman's Impressions of German New Guinea.* London: John Lane.

Overlack, Peter. 1992. "Australian Defence Awareness and German Naval Planning in the Pacific, 1900–14." *War & Society* 10:37–51.

The Oxford History of New Zealand. 1992. 2d ed. Edited by Geoffrey W. Rice. Auckland/Melbourne/Oxford/New York: Oxford University Press.

Pacific Islands Year Book. 1944. 5th ed. Suva: Pacific Publications.

Pacific Islands Monthly (Sydney). Various issues.

The Papuan Times (Port Moresby). 1914–1916.

The Parliament of the Commonwealth of Australia. Parliamentary Papers. Canberra. Various issues.

Peattie, Mark R. 1988. *Nan'yo: The Rise and Fall of the Japanese in Micronesia, 1885–1945.* Pacific Islands Monography Series 4. Honolulu: University of Hawai'i Press.

Perkins, John. 1989. " 'Sharing the White Man's Burden.' Nazi Colonial Revisionism and Australia's New Guinea Mandate." *Journal of Pacific History* 24:54–69.

Petit-Skinner, Solange. 1981. *The Nauruans.* San Francisco: Macduff.

Piggott, Michael. 1984. "The Coconut Lancers: A Study of the Men of the Australian Naval and Military Expeditionary Force in New Guinea, 1914–1921." B.A. thesis, Australian National University, Canberra.

Plimmer, William Neil. 1966. "The Military Occupation of Western Samoa, 1914–1920." M.A. thesis, Victoria University, Wellington.

Pomeroy, Earl S. 1951. *Pacific Outpost: American Strategy in Guam and Micronesia.* Stanford, Calif.: Stanford University Press.

Price, A[rchibald] Grenfell. 1963. *The Western Invasions of the Pacific and Its Continents: A Study of Moving Frontiers and Changing Landscapes 1513–1958.* Oxford: Clarendon Press.

———. 1972. *Island Continent: Aspects of the Historical Geography of Australia and Its Territories.* Sydney/London/Melbourne/Brisbane/Singapore: Angus & Robertson.

Price, Willard. 1936a. *Rip Tide in the South Seas.* London/Toronto: William Heinemann.

———. 1936b. "Mysterious Micronesia: Yap, Map, and Other Islands under Japanese Mandate Are Museums of Primitive Man." *The National Geographic Magazine* 69: 481–510.

———. 1937. "Fahrt ins japanische Mikronesien." *Atlantis. Länder/Völker/Reisen* 9: 577–587.

———. 1944. *Japan's Islands of Mystery.* London/Toronto: William Heinemann.

Purcell, David Campbell, Jr. 1967. "Japanese Expansion in the South Pacific, 1890–1935." Ph.D. diss., University of Pennsylvania.

———. 1976. "The Economics of Exploitation: The Japanese in the Mariana, Caroline and Marshall Islands, 1915–1940." *Journal of Pacific History* 11:189–211.

Pyenson, Lewis. 1985. *Cultural Imperialism and Exact Sciences: German Expansion Overseas 1900–1930.* Studies in History and Culture 1. New York/Bern/Frankfurt: Peter Lang.

Rabaul Record. Vols. 1 (1916)–3 (1918).

Rasmussen, Peter. Interview by author, 13 January 1989. Tape recording. Apia.

Rabaul Times. 1936.

Rattan, Sumitra. 1972. "The Yap Controversy and Its Significance." *Journal of Pacific History* 7:124–136.

Readings in New Guinea History. 1973. Edited by B. Jinks, P. Biskup, and H. Nelson. Sydney/London: Angus and Robertson.

Reed, Stephen Windsor. 1943. *The Making of Modern New Guinea: With Special Reference to Culture Contact in the Mandated Territory*. Memoirs of the American Philosophical Society 18 (1942). Philadelphia: The American Philosophical Society.

Reeves, L. C. 1915. *Australians in Action*. Sydney: Australian News Co.

Rengiil, Fumio Ns. Interview by author, 23 November 1986. Tape recording. Koror, Belau.

Reynolds, Henry. 1989. *Dispossession: Black Australians and White Invaders*. Sydney/Wellington/London/Boston: Allen & Unwin.

Rittlinger, Herbert. 1936. *Südseefahrt*. Berlin/Leipzig/Vienna: Goldmann.

Rivers, W. H. R. 1922. *Essays in the Depopulation of Melanesia*. London: Cambridge University Press.

Rivinius, Karl Josef. 1987. *Weltlicher Schutz und Mission. Das deutsche Protektorat über die katholische Mission von Süd-Shantung*. Bonner Beiträge zur Kirchengeschichte 14. Cologne/Vienna: Böhlan.

Ross, Angus. 1964. *New Zealand Aspirations in the Pacific in the Nineteenth Century*. Oxford: Clarendon Press.

Ross, Colin. 1933. *Haha Whenua—das Land, das ich gesucht. Mit Kind und Kegel durch die Südsee*. Leipzig: F. A. Brockhaus.

Rossbach, Else (b. 1904). Interview by author, 11 June 1990. Tape recording. Berlin.

Rothwell, V. H. 1971. *British War Aims and Peace Diplomacy 1914–18*. Oxford: Clarendon Press.

Rowe, N. A. 1930. *Samoa under the Sailing Gods*. London/New York: Putnam.

Rowley, C. D. 1954. "Native Officials and Magistrates of German New Guinea, 1897–1921," *South Pacific*, January–February, 772–781.

———. 1958. *The Australians in German New Guinea 1914–1921*. Carlton: Melbourne University Press.

———. 1971. "The Occupation of German New Guinea 1914–1921." In *Australia and Papua New Guinea*, edited by W. J. Hudson, 57–73. Sydney: Sydney University Press.

Sack, Peter G. 1977. "Law, Politics and Native 'Crimes' in German New Guinea." In *Germany in the Pacific and Far East, 1870–1914*, edited by John A. Moses and Paul M. Kennedy, 262–287. St. Lucia: University of Queensland Press.

———. 1985. "A History of German New Guinea: A Debate about Evidence and Judgement." *Journal of Pacific History* 20:84–94.

———. 1990. "The End of the Hahl Era in German New Guinea: Voluntary Career Change or Removal from Office?" *Journal of Pacific History* 25:227–232.

Salisbury, Richard F. 1970. *Vunamami. Economic Transformation in Traditional Society*. Berkeley/Los Angeles/London: University of California Press.

Samoanisches Gouvernementsblatt (Apia). Vols. 3 (1900–1910)–5 (1914).

Samoa Times (Apia). 1914–1922.

Sawer, Geoffrey. 1975. *The Australian Constitution.* Canberra: Australian Government Publishing Service.

Scarr, Deryck. 1967. *Fragments of Empire: A History of the Western Pacific High Commission 1877–1914.* Canberra/London: Australian National University Press/C. Hurst.

———. 1990. *History of the Pacific Islands: Kingdom of the Reefs.* Melbourne: Macmillan.

Scharpenberg, Anneliese. 1977. "Die Deutsche Südseephosphat-Aktiengesellschaft Bremen." *Bremisches Jahrbuch* 55:127–219.

Scott, Dick. 1991. *Years of the Pooh-Bah: A Cook Islands History.* Rarotonga/Auckland: CITC/Hodder and Stoughton.

Shuster, Donald R. 1982. "State Shinto in Micronesia during Japanese Rule, 1914–1945." *Pacific Studies* 5.2:20–43.

Smith, S. J. 1923. "The Seizure and Occupation of Samoa." In *The Official History of New Zealand's Effort in the Great War.* Vol. 4, *The War Effort of New Zealand,* edited by H. T. B. Drew, 23–41. Auckland: Whitcombe and Tombs.

Snelling, R. C. 1975–1976. "Peacemaking, 1919: Australia, New Zealand and the British Empire Delegation at Versailles." *The Journal of Imperial and Commonwealth History* 4:15–28.

South Australian Advertiser (Adelaide). 1921.

Spartalis, Peter. 1983. *The Diplomatic Battles of Billy Hughes.* Sydney: Hale & Iremonger.

Stead's Review of Reviews. Various issues.

Stenographische Berichte über die Verhandlungen des Reichstags. (Berlin). Various issues.

Sydney Morning Herald. Various issues.

Tellei, Joseph (b. 1901). Interview by author, 22 November 1986. Tape recording. Koror, Belau.

Tellei, Patrick. 1988. "Modekngei: What is it, can it survive? View of a non-Modekngei Palauan." Graduate term paper, University of Hawai'i, Manoa.

Thomas, Gordon. 1946. "The Story of Rabaul." In *Where the Trade-Winds Blow: Stories and Sketches of the South Pacific Islands,* edited by R. W. Robson and Judy Tudor, 134–142. Sydney: Pacific Publications.

Thompson, Roger C. 1972. "The Labor Party and Australian Imperialism in the Pacific, 1901–1919." *Labour History* 23:27–37.

———. 1980. *Australian Imperialism in the Pacific. The Expansionist Era 1820–1920.* Carlton: Melbourne University Press.

———. 1990. "Making a Mandate. The Formation of Australia's New Guinea Policies 1919–1925." *Journal of Pacific History* 25:68–84.

———. 1992. "Edge of Empire: Australian Colonization in Nauru, 1919–1939." In *Pacific History: Papers from the 8th Pacific History Association Conference,* edited by Donald H. Rubinstein, 273–280. Mangilao: University of Guam Press & Micronesian Area Research Center.

Thurnwald, Hilde. 1937. *Menschen der Südsee. Charaktere und Schicksale in Buin auf Bougainville, Salomo-Archipel.* Stuttgart: Enke.

Thurnwald, Richard. 1930. "Papuanisches und melanesisches Gebiet südlich des Äquators einschließlich Neuguinea." In *Das Eingeborenenrecht. Sitten und Gewohnheitsrechte der Eingeborenen der ehemaligen deutschen Kolonien in Afrika und in der Südsee,* edited by Erich Schultz-Ewerth and Leonhard Adam, 2:545–656. Stuttgart; Strecker & Schröder.

———. 1936. "The Price of the White Man's Peace." *Pacific Affairs* 9:347–357.

Tibawi, A. L. 1978. *Anglo-Arab Relations and the Questions of Palestine 1914–1921.* London: Luzac.

The Times (London). Various issues.

Townsend, George Wilfred L. 1968. *District Officer. From Untamed New Guinea to Lake Success, 1921–1946.* Sydney: Pacific Publications.

Townsend, Mary Evelyn. 1930. *The Rise and Fall of Germany's Colonial Empire 1884–1918.* New York: Macmillan.

Treue, Wolfgang. 1976. *Die Jaluit-Gesellschaft auf den Marshall-Inseln 1887–1914. Ein Beitrag zur Kolonial- und Verwaltungsgeschichte in der Epoche des deutschen Kaiserreichs.* Schriften zur Sozial- und Wirtschaftsgeschichte 26. Berlin: Duncker & Humblot.

Triad. 1916.

The Truth (Auckland). Various issues.

Vietsch, Eberhard von. 1961. *Wilhelm Solf. Botschafter zwischen den Zeiten.* Tübingen: Wunderlich.

Viviani, Nancy. 1970. *Nauru. Phosphate und Political Progress.* Canberra: Australian National University Press.

Wächter, Emil. 1941. *Der Prestigegedanke in der deutschen Politik von 1890 bis 1914.* Berner Untersuchungen zur Allgemeinen Geschichte 11. Aarau: H. R. Sauerländer & Co.

Wagner, Wieland. 1990. *Japans Außenpolitk in der frühen Meiji-Zeit (1869–1894). Die ideologische und politische Grundlegung des japanischen Führungsanspruchs in Süd-ostasien.* Ph.D. diss., University of Freiburg i. Br., 1989. Beiträge zur Kolonial- und Überseegeschichte 48. Stuttgart: Steiner.

Walworth, Arthur. 1986. *Wilson and His Peacemakers: American Diplomacy at the Paris Peace Conference, 1919.* New York/London: W. W. Norton.

Ward, Herbert T. 1970. *Flight of the Cormoran.* New York/Washington/Hollywood: Vantage Press.

Ward, Russel. 1978. *The History of Australia. The Twentieth Century 1901–1975.* London: Heinemann Educational.

Weeramantry, Christopher. 1992. *Nauru. Environmental Damage under International Trusteeship.* Melbourne/Oxford/Auckland/New York: Oxford University Press.

Wendt, Albert. 1965. "Guardians and Wards. A Study of the Origins, Causes and the First Two Years of the Mau in Western Samoa." M.A. thesis, Victoria University, Wellington.

West, Francis, ed. 1970. *Selected Letters of Hubert Murray.* Melbourne/London/Wellington/New York: Oxford University Press.

Willey, Keith. 1965. *Assignment New Guinea.* Milton/Ryde/Melbourne: Jacaranda Press.

Williams, Francis Edgar. 1976. *'The Vailala Madness' and Other Essays.* Edited by Erik Schwimmer. London: C. Hurst.

Williams, Maslyn, and Barrie Macdonald. 1985. *The Phosphateers. A History of The British Phosphate Commissioners and the Christmas Island Phosphate Commission.* Carlton: Melbourne University Press.

Willis, Ian. 1974. *Lae. Village and City.* Carlton: Melbourne University Press.

Wolfers, Edward P. 1972. "Trusteeship without Trust: A Short History of Interracial Relations and the Law in Papua and New Guinea." In *Racism: The Australian Experience. A Study of Race Prejudice in Australia,* edited by F. S. Stevens, 61–147. Vol. 3: *Colonialism.* Sydney: Australia and New Zealand Book Company, New York: Taplinger, and Ontario: Burns & MacEachern.

Wu, David Y. H. 1982. *The Chinese in Papua New Guinea: 1880–1980.* Hong Kong: The Chinese University Press.

Zieschank, Frieda. 1918. *Ein Jahrzehnt in Samoa (1906–1916).* Leipzig: E. Haberland.

Index

ABOUT THE AUTHOR

HERMANN JOSEPH HIERY received his Ph.D. from Freiburg University. He spent three years in Papua New Guinea as Lecturer for Social Science at the Divine Word Institute in Madang, and as Research Affiliate to the history department of the University of Papua New Guinea. He presently lives in London, where he is Permanent Research Fellow at the German Historical Institute. He also serves as *Privatdozent* for modern history at the University of Freiburg, Germany.